Best wishes x

Good Knitting

Susan Crawford

A Stitch In Time

Volume 2

A Stitch In Time

Vintage Knitting Patterns 1930 – 1959 : Vol. 2

Susan Crawford & Jane Waller

Arbour House Publishing

www.arbourhousepublishing.com

Text Copyright © 2011 Susan Crawford & Jane Waller
Technical Information Copyright © 2011 Susan Crawford
Pattern Adaptions Copyright © 2011 Susan Crawford
Photographs Copyright © 2011 Susan Crawford

Credits
Editor: Susan Crawford
Creative Director: Susan Crawford
Photography: Susan Crawford
Additional Photography: Charlie Moon
Hair & Make Up: Susan Crawford, Catherine-Elizabeth, Lola Valentine
Styling: Susan Crawford
Book Design: Gavin Crawford
Artwork, Graphic Design & Pattern Restoration: Gavin Crawford
Pattern Writing: Susan Crawford
Technical Editing: Jen Arnall-Culliford
Chart Design: Jen Arnall-Culliford
Models: Theodora Burrow, Lola Valentine, Charlie Moon, Julia Templeton,
Lucy Baines, Vicky Laverty, Dayna Austin, Jess Wilson, Hayley Green

Published in 2011 by Arbour House Publishing Ltd, Southport, UK
www.arbourhousepublishing.com

Photographed on a Canon EOS 400D in various locations in Southport and Liverpool, UK
This book was produced on RISC OS using Ovation Pro, together with Photodesk, ArtWorks, DPscan, plus other custom written software.

British Library Cataloguing-in-Publication Data
A catalogue record fro this book is available from the British Library

ISBN 978-0-955-6206-5-2

First edition: July, 2011

Printed and bound in the UK on FSC paper and using vegetable based inks

The original patterns in this book are up to 80 years of age and therefore any lack of quality in their reproduction is due to the condition of the original pattern. The publishers cannot guarantee that these original patterns do not contain errors and can take no responsibility for this.

Contents

This book is dedicated to Dorothy Crawford, who has worked tirelessly for two years knitting garment after garment without complaint and always asking for more! It is highly likely that without her this book would not have been completed. Thank you Dorothy.

ACKNOWLEDGEMENTS

A book of this size is a huge project and could not have been achieved without the help of an amazing band of people who all contributed so much:

Thank you, first of all to a willing band of knitters who volunteered their help with this book: Dorothy Crawford, Louise Harries, Tom Van Deijnen, Torya Winters, Irene Jackson, Angela Spink, Vanessa Hubbard, Sarah Moore, Caroline Stead, Linda Laidlaw, Janet Baker, Susan Crowe, Sophia Gfroerer, Jo Bodley, Ingrid Murnane, Grace Murnane, Lorna Erlam, Kathleen Farrington, Theodora Burrow, Daisy Perkins, Jill Hohenstein, Sue Rossiter and Jo Gay.

To Catherine Wilson for many, many hours of sewing up, tea making and unceasing support.

To Ingrid Murnane for all her invaluable assistance.

To my beautiful models, Lola Valentine, Charlie Moon, Julia Templeton, Lucy Baines, Dayna Austin, Vicky Laverty, Hayley Green and Jess Wilson, who gave up so much of their time to help create this book and particularly to Theodora Burrow, my muse and good friend.

To Scott Willis for shooting our fabulous photoshoot video.

To Jen Arnall-Culliford who not only ensured all the patterns are correct, but made sense of my words and numbers and kept me going each time I ran out of steam.

To the lovely Daisy Perkins, who typed every single pattern in this book without a word of complaint, for making us smile and for being such a great intern.

A huge thank you to the yarn companies who so willingly supplied yarns – to Biggan Design, Fyberspates, Knitshop, Jamieson's of Shetland, Jamieson & Smith, Skein Queen, Posh Yarns, Texere and most of all to John & Juliet Arbon of Fibre Harvest, who made a dream come true, by creating Excelana.

Finally thanks are due to the Magazine Editors, Designers and Yarn Companies who created so many wonderful patterns for us to still enjoy today.

Introduction

We began work on this second volume of A Stitch in Time over two and a half years ago, sitting on the floor with several hundred patterns and magazines in piles in front of us. These were sifted and reduced to around 200 patterns divided into three decades. We then began to look at each decade individually, determining whether there was a good balance of patterns in each era – cardigans, jumpers, hats, gloves, scarves, long sleeve, short sleeve, lace, cable, texture, stocking stitch, ribbing, colour work etc. As this fine tuning took shape the list slowly reduced to around 120 patterns. From previous experience we knew that some of these patterns would not work out successfully, so it made sense to begin with more than we needed.

As time progressed, there were more failures than expected and some missing pieces of the jigsaw still to be found. Visits to textile fairs and charity shops and many hours searching ebay found those missing pieces, and many other finds besides, so over the next year or so, the selection changed and evolved until a new set of 120 patterns established itself.

We knew the time would come when the number of patterns would have to be reduced still further – actually right up to the last possible moment patterns still had to be swapped or removed. Convincing everyone involved that 80 patterns in one book was not an act of madness was not easy, but it is a collection and to take any one pattern away would impact on the story as a whole. So – this book does indeed have 80 patterns. Of these, many have presented a real challenge to Susan as the pattern writer. We wanted to give you, the knitter, multi-sized versions of designs that would never normally be considered suitable – large pattern repeats, varying row counts, unusual garment construction; bringing to life some incredible designs and stitch patterns which may otherwise only ever have been knitted in the future by one or two people. We have been able to cover a much greater range of sizes for most of the patterns, hopefully providing everyone who buys the book with the opportunity to knit these beautiful designs for themselves.

Opening up this volume to a far wider pattern search has provided us with a treasure trove of fabulous designs, some from quite unexpected sources – such as a pull-out supplement from a 1930s magazine giving us 'The Sunday Pictorial Beret'. Single pattern leaflets written for department stores also make an appearance alongside our favourite – Woman's Weekly. We have also introduced designs from yarn companies of the day, such as Copleys, Golden Eagle, Bestway and Weldons. All of these patterns reveal a staggering wealth of creativity that went un-sung and un-credited at the time and we hope that by celebrating them in this book, we give them a new lease of life and an acknowledgement of just how amazing the creators of these designs were.

The production of this book has not been easy, completely taking over our lives. The scale and logistics of the project has made it almost inevitable that there would be complications – ten separate photo shoots alone are enough to drive anyone mad! But we hope that the finished result is something that will be treasured, loved and used for many years to come by every one of you and that it has been worth the wait!

Susan & Jane

About This Book

This volume is arranged simply, in decades. We chose to present the book this way as on this occasion we have used many more single patterns than we did in Volume One. As these are not dated in the same way as a magazine, it seemed inappropriate to try and 'guess' exact years of publication. In a number of the re-written patterns we have replaced lengthy long hand instructions with charts so that the chosen pattern could actually be included. Some of these long hand patterns are 8 pages long or more, for only one size, and it would have been impossible to use them in this format. The original patterns have been reproduced alongside the new multi sized versions, but it has proved necessary to reduce them in size to use them in the book – they were just too big or over too many pages to leave in their original form.

The shaping and fit of the updated patterns, whilst expanded to fit the modern body, retain the original proportions of these designs; so if a garment was designed to be worn fitted to the waist, that is where the 'new' pattern is designed to fit also. Therefore, regardless of size worked, you should still achieve a garment with the correct vintage fit, but proportional to your body size. The 'Fit and Finish' chapter expands on this greatly, explaining how to ensure that any garment you knit will fit you perfectly.

Most of the yarns used in the book are standard yarn weights and can be substituted by using the standard yarn tension given in the patterns along with the meterage per 50/100g. However, I have chosen the yarns carefully to work successfully with the stitch pattern and fabric required. Some designs require the yarn to drape and fall, others for the yarn to be firm and crisp and others for the yarn to retain its shape and have great stretch. Please ensure when substituting yarns that you look at the photos carefully to see how the garment works on the model and also consider the yarn composition of the specified yarn before making your substitution. The majority of the yarns used are 4 ply (fingering) weight. Some are finer and some are thicker but the majority are 4 ply. If you have not knitted a 4 ply garment before, it may at first seem slow as you get used to the small needles and fine yarn, but over time you can build up great speed as the hand moves far less to make each individual stitch than with larger needles and thicker yarn. I particularly enjoy working with natural fibres and wool most of all. I believe wool contains all the properties needed for a perfect vintage garment – stretch, recovery, warmth – and I would recommend it above any alternative.

The majority of designs in the book are knitted in pieces as they were in the original patterns. I have changed only one or two to be knitted in the round where the pattern did not make sense knitted as it was. The 'Fair Isle is Fashionable' beret for instance was knitted in 5 separate panels sewn together! Vintage patterns were generally seamed, partly for ease of pattern writing, but mainly because they were based on dressmaking principles and the seams were included to add strength and structure to a garment, to prevent stretch and distortion and help ensure a garment's long life.

Since Volume One was first published, I have been asked on a regular basis for guidance on the finishing techniques I use, so this volume also includes a whole section devoted to this and also on how best to achieve the perfect vintage fit. The 'Knitting Know How' pages also explain how to get the best from the book and what techniques have been used. Please do take time to read these pages and also the 'Fit and Finish' chapter which will help you achieve a professional looking garment. Also, please do read through your chosen pattern before embarking on knitting. Pattern notes are provided at the beginning and throughout patterns where necessary, to assist, particularly for the more complicated of instructions. There are also instances when more than one instruction needs to be followed at the same time – reading ahead prepares you for this.

Finally, I am frequently asked about the clothing and styling in my photos: All clothing, jewellery and accessories used in the photo shoots belong to myself or to our 'house' model, Theo. All of the items used are vintage other than two or three new pieces which have a great retro look. Various brands of make-up have been used on the photo shoots but we mainly used Bourjois foundations – shades 51 and 52 and Mac eye shadows and lipsticks, usually Ruby Woo and Party Line. I have also used a vintage Chanel lipstick – No 1 Velvet, which is a beautiful pure red, but unfortunately no longer available.

I love to see photos of completed knitted treasures, particularly when styled in a retro way, so please do join me on facebook, ravelry, twitter and on my blog *(details can be found on my website at www.susancrawfordvintage.com)* to share your finished creations.

Susan

Knitting Know How

This book is not a learn to knit book. There are excellent books available and groups to join, which will help any beginner knitter get started. However, this section looks at the particular skills and techniques used throughout the pages of this book in a little more detail but is by no means exhaustive. If you have a preferred buttonhole or cast on for example please use the method you are happy with.

THE IMPORTANCE OF TENSION SQUARES

It is always important that you knit a tension square before beginning to knit from a pattern. However when using vintage knitting patterns it is, if possible, even more important, as being even slightly out with the finished dimensions can completely alter the fit of a garment from 'vintage' to not so vintage. There are a small number of patterns in the book which rely on slight changes in tension to obtain different sizes and it is essential with these to obtain the correct tension.

The tension needed for each pattern is the tension established by one person – me, so you are trying to match the tension I obtained when I worked my own tension square for each pattern. So it really doesn't matter if you have 'standard' tension as I very well may not! Just one stitch out in a 10cm (4in) square can result in a garment that should be 100cm (40in) in circumference measuring 106cm (42in) and falling off at the shoulders.

Other good reasons for tension squares
- You get to know the pattern and make your mistakes over a small number of stitches.
- You can test wash the swatch to see how it behaves.
- You have a permanent record of your project.
- If for any reason your garment develops a hole, you can undo your square and use the yarn for darning.
- You can save up your squares and make a blanket.

CAST ON METHODS

Unless otherwise stated I usually use a cable cast on for all the projects in the book – worked by placing the right needle behind the last stitch cast on, working another stitch and placing it on the left needle. If you prefer to use a long tail cast on you may prefer to knit into the back of the stitch on the first row. This is not necessary with a cable cast on and is not taken into account in the patterns.

Alternate cable cast on
Where a significant amount of stretch is required at the cast on edge and a 1×1 rib is to be knitted, the alternate cable cast on can be used (See Fair Isle is Fashionable). Worked as for the cable cast on, but sts are cast on alternately as knit then purl. The first stitch on your needle is worked as a purl st. An excellent tutorial is available to download and print off from www.woollywormhead.com/knit-and-crochet-1

W&T (WRAP AND TURN)

Used in conjunction with short rows, wrap and turns are performed on the first un-worked stitch to prevent steps appearing in your work. The method used most frequently in the book is worked as follows:

Work the number of stitches specified in the pattern, then slip the next stitch on to the right hand needle, then bring the yarn to the opposite side of the work to where it is sitting. Pass the slipped stitch back onto the left needle then turn the work round. The yarn will be at the wrong side of the work to work your next stitch, so again take it to the opposite side of the work from where it is sitting behind the un-worked stitch, then work the following stitch, on the LH needle. On the next or a subsequent row, you will work across the wrapped sts and it is essential you knit or purl the wrap together with the stitch it is wrapped around to avoid an ugly stitch.

On a knit row: Put right needle through wrap at front of work as though to knit, then put needle through wrapped stitch also knitwise, now knit the wrap and the stitch together.

On a purl row: Put right needle through wrap from back of work as though to purl, then put needle through wrapped st also from back of work, purlwise, then purl the wrap and the stitch together.

Yarn over method
This method is used in the Springtime Bolero pattern, and is a very simple way of working a w&t.

Row 1: Pattern required number of stitches, turn, YO, then work back to end of row.
Row 2: Pattern to YO, work YO and foll st tog, patt additional no of required sts, turn, YO, then work back to end of row.
Continue in this manner, always remembering to work previous YO worked together with st following it and working a subsequent YO after the work has been turned each time.

THREE NEEDLE CAST OFF (OR THREE NEEDLE BIND OFF)

The majority of vintage patterns have sewn shoulder seams for added stability and strength, but occasionally three needle cast off is used. To do this, hold both needles in the left hand with work RS together. Insert a third needle into the first stitch of each needle and knit these two sts together. Repeat this process then cast the first stitch off over the second. Continue in this way until all sts have been cast off.

FAIR ISLE/INTARSIA COMBINATION COLOUR WORK

A number of the designs in the book feature colour work which is knitted using a combination of Fair Isle and intarsia techniques, carrying colours across single motifs but not from one motif to the next, using separate small balls of yarn for each motif. This is so that large areas where only one colour is used does not need to have a second colour carried behind it. This can be seen on the Trimmed With Roses Twin Set. Ensure when moving on to the next motif that yarns are crossed over each other at the back to prevent holes occurring. Within each motif yarns can be carried across the back of work as in Fair Isle.

UK AND US CROCHET TERMINOLOGY

On any pattern that includes crochet terminology, the UK abbreviation is used first then is followed by the US abbreviation in brackets. For a full list of abbreviations used throughout the book see page 13. You can also read more about the crochet techniques used in the 'Fit and Finish' chapter.

SIZING CHARTS

Thorough sizing charts are included at the beginning of each pattern. Please read these carefully to make your choice of size to knit. The Finished Measurements are the measurements the garment needs to be to fit the 'to fit' size correctly to achieve the appropriate vintage fit. Ensure you choose the correct 'to fit' size according to your personal measurements and make adjustments to this where necessary (see 'Fit and Finish' chapter). The required amount of ease and adjustments to length have already been made to the finished measurements to create the correct overall vintage fit.

NEGATIVE EASE

Many of the patterns in this book are written with negative ease. Using negative ease means that the garment is intended to be smaller than the wearer, and that it will stretch significantly when worn. This means the finished width of the garment during knitting may be significantly smaller than the intended wearer. This is deliberate and it is important that you use the 'to fit' measurement when choosing your size.

STANDARD YARN TENSION

Where ever possible, standard yarn tension is provided on each pattern when the stitch pattern used has a different tension. This should help with yarn substitution and also helps you understand more clearly what yarn is being used in the pattern.

LOOKING AFTER YOUR KNITWEAR

Some of the yarns used in the book are machine washable. I use my hand wash cycle set at 30 degrees and with the spin switched off for almost all my knitwear. However, before you ever put a finished garment in the washing machine, I would recommend washing your tension square first to see how it behaves. If there is any sign of felting, pilling or shrinkage always hand wash. In fact, if in doubt always hand wash. Keep left over yarn and a spare button if used together with a label stating which garment it is from for repairs. If you need to darn your garment make sure you do this whilst any holes are still small. Don't wait for them to grow before dealing with the problem.

Some of the yarns used in the book, such as Shetland wool or mercerised cotton, are very robust yarns and can take plenty of heat and/or steam whereas other yarns such as silk, silk blends and merinos are more delicate and care must be taken to keep them protected from direct heat or contact with an iron. Again if in doubt, use your tension square to test the yarn's response before subjecting your garment pieces to heat.

Blocking

When a pattern instruction requires your knitting to be blocked, the individual pieces should be pinned out to the finished sizes stated in the sizing chart. Knitting can be wet blocked where the pieces are first washed before pinning or alternatively you can spray the knitted pieces with water. I usually place a damp tea towel or muslin over the work to further protect it and then move a steam iron over the work from just above the surface. There are a number of designs in the book which should not be blocked or pressed and this is stated in the Making Up section of the pattern. Ribbing is also not usually pressed or blocked.

Abbreviations

K	Knit
P	Purl
st(s)	stitch(es)
st st	stocking stitch
m	metres
yds	yards
cm	centimetres
in	inches
mm	millimetres
g	gram
DPNs	double pointed needles
CN	cable needle
MC	main colour
CC	contrast colour
LH	left hand
RH	right hand
RS	right side
WS	wrong side
Patt	pattern
Alt	alternate
Beg	beginning
Rep	repeat
Cont	continue
foll	following
folls	follows
rem	remaining
tog	together
rev st st	reverse stocking stitch
PM	place marker
SM	slip marker
Sl1	slip one st (purlwise unless directed otherwise)
Sl2	slip two sts (purlwise unless directed otherwise)
Sl3	slip three sts (purlwise unless directed otherwise)

psso	pass slipped stitch over
YO	yarn over (also known as yarn forward or yarn round needle)
inc	increase (if used during an instruction ie. Inc 1 st, work either as Kfb or Pfb depending on how sts presented on needle)
dec	decrease, usually by knitting or purling two together
Kfb	Knit into front and back of next stitch
Pfb	Purl into front and back of next stitch
K2tog	Knit two together
K3tog	Knit three together
P2tog	Purl two together
P3tog	Purl three together
P5tog	Purl five together
tbl	through back of loop
K1tbl	Knit one through back of loop
K3tbl	Knit three through back of loops
P1tbl	Purl one through back of loop
K2togtbl	Knit two together through back of loop
P2togtbl	Purl two together through back of loop
M1	make one, by knitting into loop lying between stitches
M1P	make one, by purling into loop lying between stitches
SKPO	slip one, knit one, pass slip stitch over
w&t	wrap and turn (see knitting know how)
MB	make bobble (see specific abbreviations on pattern for details)
ch (ch)	chain
sp (sp)	space
sl st (sl st)	slip stitch
DC (SC)	double crochet (single crochet)

Fit and Finish

The Vintage Fit

To enable us to understand how to create a garment with the perfect vintage fit we obviously need to know what the fit is that we are looking for. There is actually more than one vintage fit so we have looked at each of the decades to understand further what fit we are trying to achieve. Some people also feel that they can't wear 'vintage' and we hope that by reading this information, it will help you choose a look and a shape that you can wear.

1930s

The basic shape of a sweater changed dramatically from the long line tubular shapes seen in the 1920s, with sweaters ending at the waist, usually emphasised with a deep, ribbed waist band.

Shaping was minimal and often worked on a single row immediately above the waist band. Additional shaping was introduced at the armhole, narrowing the shoulder line, with the armhole seam sitting on the shoulder ball itself. The lack of shaping and deep waistband also created a slightly blousoned effect around the wearer's middle.

Necklines were often draped or 'softened' in one of a number of inventive ways, discreetly creating additional bust room and drawing the eye to the décolletage and away from the chest. In addition to this, the front of the garment would often have a greater number of stitches than the back up to the underarm, when increased shaping would be worked over the same number of rows as the back, ingeniously 'scooping' out the excess fabric often found at the front seam area between the arm and the breast.

Sleeves, if short, were mainly full, and if long were often very long with detail at the cuff, drawing the eye downwards and creating an illusion of length. Belts were often shown worn over the ribbing to emphasise the waist even more.

Garments were mainly knitted in fine yarns – 4, 3 and 2 ply wools – but surprisingly, thicker yarns also made an impact during this time reflecting the amazing creativity and commercial growth in the yarn industry at this time.

Underwear was soft and relatively unformed with the bust-line much lower than is the norm today.

1940s

In some ways there are a lot of similarities in the jumper shapes of the 1930s and 1940s. However, after the deep rib band, shaping was often increased more gradually at regular intervals up to the armhole. (Garment length had grown a couple of inches by this point usually – with 28cm (11in) to the armhole now extending to 33cm (13in).

Armhole depth deepened slightly at this time too, now offering 16½ to 18cm (6½ to 7in) depth on an 81cm (32in) bust garment. (In the 1930s this could be as little as 14cm (5½in)). This extra depth allowed for increased shaping to be worked at the armhole, narrowing the shoulder line further and for the armhole seam to sit high on the arm socket joint.

Necklines were often cut high and square to emphasise this straight line across the shoulders. This was exaggerated even further with the puffed, gathered and box head sleeves sitting high on the ball and socket joint, helped along by knitted shoulder or sleeve pads.

Sleeve length extended to just above the elbow but with less fullness than in the 1930s.

Cardigans were cut in a similar way but with a deep V neck, sometimes starting just above the welt itself. This shaping significantly reduced the number of buttons needed.

Negative ease became extremely popular and was used extensively in the 1940s to create garments with incredible stretch.

Patterns were written for fine yarns on the whole with designs for every aspect of clothing offered, including underwear and dresses. With a shortage of yarns throughout most of the 1940s, fair Isle patterns became increasingly popular allowing oddments of yarns to be used.

1950s

The line of sweaters altered more significantly in the 1950s, with an increasing availability of yarns allowing garments to be worn to the hip, teamed with rounder, softer shoulders and deeper armholes, providing a 'batwing' effect.

The longer body length meant that waist shaping could be incorporated into designs creating an hour glass shape and drawing attention to the hips for the first time. Sleeves were sometimes worked in one piece along with the body, streamlining the overall look. Suddenly cardigans had 9, 10 even 11 buttons as though celebrating the availability of a previously restricted commodity.

Necklines were either cut low into scoops – V's, squares, and Sweetheart necklines being particularly popular – or were cut very high around the neck.

Negative ease was again used around the bust to create the Sweater Girl effect. To accompany this longer line sweater came boleros, worn high above the waist and generally curved at the front.

This shift to longer line garments, meant that looser, long straight sweaters and cardigans also began to appear, softening the silhouette still further.

A much wider variety of yarns and weights became available in the 1950s, with angora in particular, increasingly popular.

Alongside very fine yarns, thicker yarns became more and more popular with DK and Aran weight yarns as they are known in the UK, or Sports and Worsted weights, appearing more and more in 1950s patterns.

By far the most popular look of 1950s knitwear was undoubtedly the twin set, with neat high neck jumpers worn underneath matching round or V-neck cardigans.

A change in the type of bra being worn, emphasised and lifted the bust-line much more than in the last two decades. This coupled with waist hugging girdles altered the female form under the jumper dramatically.

Perfecting the Vintage Fit

Now we can see how the garments from each period are supposed to fit us, how do we make sure that they do? In this Volume, comprehensive sizing charts have been produced to enable you to compare your own measurements to that of the pattern so that you can make adjustments if necessary.

On most garments, but most significantly on vintage garments, the placement of the shoulder seam is of paramount importance. Shoulder to shoulder measurements have been given whenever possible on the sizing charts so that you can be certain your garment is going to fit correctly.

To make the appropriate comparisons you will first need to measure yourself. Its not easy to do this by yourself so enlist the help of a friend. Try and use a reasonably new tape measure too as over time they stretch and are not always accurate. So that you can keep a record of your measurements I have included a personal measurement chart which can be found on page 397. Please feel free to take photocopies of the chart, to update on a regular basis.

It is best to record measurements in both inches and centimetres as patterns can require either. It is also best to date your chart so you don't keep using a chart from a short while ago that turns out to be five years old! Also do bear in mind that there may be times when additional measurements may also be needed, such as round arm immediately above the elbow, but these are very specific so I have not included them here.

So now we have to compare our own measurements to that of the chosen pattern so that we can see where the little tweeks may need to be made. To do this easily I suggest drawing a simple schematic. Write in the dimensions of the garment based on the given pattern in one colour pen, and then write your own required dimensions around it in a different coloured pen and from there start to make notes on adjusting the pattern.

So, what changes may you need to make and how do you make them? Below I have listed a number of common problems and how to deal with them.

Shoulders narrower than the finished pattern
Increase the number of decreases worked at the armhole to remove the extra shoulder stitches. Ensure the adjustment is balanced on all four shoulder cast offs.

You need the extra width at the front but it will make the back gape
(1)   Knit the back to the size you require, then knit the front to the larger size needed, but at the armhole work extra decreases to remove the extra stitches so that the shoulders match. Also a great way to prevent gaping on cardigan fronts.

(2)   Work front and back in smaller of sizes needed but shortly below your bust line, change to a slightly larger needle on the front only and use until armhole decreases completed. Change back to smaller needles.

(3)   If a lower neckline with a straight front edge, work front in larger size as required, then alter the front neckline rather than the shoulder to include the extra stitches. K2tog before each cast off stitch on centre front to create a softly gathered neckline.

(4)   The stretch in many 1940s garments is great for larger busts, just remember to add extra length to accommodate the added horizontal stretch. Lower cut 1950s garments are also fabulous for showing off what nature gave us! To wear the 30s styles add a bit of length below the armhole to provide some extra fabric for blousing. Combine this with method 2 if a lot more fabric is needed at the front.

You may need the extra bust room but you have a narrow waist

(1) Cast on the required size for your back for both front and back pieces but on front increase the number of increases worked either on single increase row or if incremental increases work more until front has required number of stitches, for the size needed. Work extra decreases at armholes on front only, until shoulder sts match.

(2) Work front and back in smaller of sizes needed but shortly below your bust line change to a slightly larger needle on the front only and use until armhole decreases completed. Change back to smaller needles.

(3) If a longer line garment, work as required in pattern until waist area, now change to smaller needles and work approx 9cm (3in) in tighter gauge, then change back to larger needles.

Small all over but with proportionally bigger cup size

Negative ease of 1940s garments is fabulous for you. Work to the size you need for the back and just let the garment do the rest of the work. Alternatively use techniques (1) or (2) from the previous section.

Broad back but flatter chest

(1) Work back to larger size and front to smaller but work fewer decreases at armhole on front so that shoulders match.

(2) If lower neckline with straight edge front, work both front and back to larger size. Work armholes as specified but k2tog along centre front as casting off to close front up. Using gathers in this way on a smaller chest gives the illusion of more shape.

Longer body

Work extra length between the ribbing if there is one and the armhole shaping. If there are increases to be worked extra rows should be divided evenly between the increases. Avoid altering the length of the armhole if at all possible.

Sloping Shoulders

1940s shoulder shaping with small knitted sleeve pads work great for creating a straight shoulder line. 1930s styles positively celebrate slim, sloping shoulders so no problems there!

Broad Shoulders

You can either celebrate your shoulders and go for the 40s look and as long as you get the shoulder seam position right you can go without shoulder pads or the 50s styles with their longer softer shoulder lines are great to de-emphasise them for you.

Spare Tyre

The 1930s method of working increases on the first row after ribbing is great for hiding a spare tyre, as you have as many stitches on the needle as you will at the fullest part of the bust. By adding a bit of extra length below the armhole you'll also give yourself plenty of fabric to blouse the sweater over the welt to disguise it further. Be careful not to add too much length as you could completely change the shape of your garment. In these instances it may be better to commence at cast on edge with more stitches than the resulting number of stitches at bust, working decreases from the natural waist upwards.

Broad Hips and/or rounded tummy

The 1930s and 1940s styles tend to finish above or only just touching the hip, but if you want to give yourself extra width, work rib bands or first 3 to 4 inches of garment on larger needles than stated then change down to the required needles. This is a simple way of avoiding negative ease pulling across hips and tummy.

If knitting a longer line 1950 style garment cast on for the size needed to accommodate your hip measurement. If your waist is proportionately smaller work additional decreases until required waist measurement reached for the smaller size or if there are no decreases being worked to the waist, work waist area on smaller needles as suggested above.

There are many other ways to create extra shaping including darts, short row shaping etc. Some of these techniques are covered at length in other titles so I have restricted my suggestions to popular vintage methods.

Perfecting the Vintage Finish

Most British vintage patterns between the 1930s and 1950s tend to be designed as separate flat pieces so therefore do require sewing up, with patterns often giving little or no explanation as to how to go about it. The basic skills you will need to sew up most of these garments are back stitch, mattress stitch, flat slip stitch, and darning in ends. To do this you will need:

- Darning or Sewing Up Needles
- Pins
- Scissors

I also find it particularly useful to use a basic mannequin or tailor's dummy to pin my garment to whilst 'finishing' is in progress.

ORDER OF SEWING UP

Although this order may differ from time to time, the 'usual' order of construction if not explained on a pattern is as follows:

(1) Press pieces
(2) Join shoulder seams
(3) Work any picked up edgings
(4) Join side seams
(5) Sew up sleeve seams
(6) Set in sleeves
(7) Attach any collar or bands
(8) Darn in all ends
(9) Sew in shoulder pads if applicable
(10) Sew on buttons or other fastenings

There are always exceptions to this order but far more garments are sewn up in this order than not, so if you are unsure follow this order and you shouldn't go far wrong.

SEAMING
Mattress Stitch

Mattress stitch is preferable to back stitch when sewing vertical seams together. One of the main reasons for this is the direction the inside of the seam lies. With back stitch the seam tries to stand up creating a noticeable ridge, however mattress stitch lies flat against the body of the garment, making it a perfect stitch for side seams.

To commence mattress stitch place the two pieces of work flat in front of you, right sides up. Starting at the bottom of the right hand piece, take a darning needle threaded with the same yarn, under the cross thread of one or two stitches. Repeat on the left hand piece. Do not draw up tightly and leave a long end. Repeat this process several times. Hold the end of the yarn in one hand and gently but firmly draw the yarn up. It is important that you have not gone through any of the stitches as it will not be easy to draw the work together. Continue up the seam.

Mattress stitch is very easily removed if a mistake is made by just drawing the thread through.

Back Stitch

I use back stitch when sewing in sleeves as I haven't found a stronger stitch to use. Also when working so many sleeves with gathers and puffs I find that back stitch is by far the best stitch to use to work through a number of layers. I use the yarn that I have knitted with as a general rule.

Back stitch is worked with the WS of the work uppermost, and with RS together.

Bring the yarn through from the underside of the work, avoiding breaking stitches if possible. Take the needle backwards about a stitch length through to the underside of the fabric and bring it back through to the uppermost side approximately one stitch further forward than where you initially started. Now take the needle back to the underside of the work inserting the needle at the point where it first came through and bringing it out a stitch further forward again. Repeat this process until complete.

BUTTONHOLES

As a general rule, buttonholes in this book are worked over two rows. If you would prefer to use an alternative method please do, bearing in mind that the instructions are worded to incorporate the two rows of buttonhole instruction.

SLEEVE PADS

Several different sleeve pads are used in the book. Do experiment with them and see which style suits the garment you are knitting best. All the patterns below are using 4 ply yarn.

Half Moon Sleeve Pads
(from Golden Eagle Lady's Jumper)
Using 3.25 mm needles cast on 30 sts.
Row 1: Knit.
Row 2: Purl.

Row 3: Knit to last 2 sts, turn.
Row 4: Purl to last 2 sts, turn.
Cont working 2 sts less each side till 10 sts rem in centre, turn. Now working from centre work 2 sts extra each side till all sts have been worked one more. Knit 1 row. Cast off. With RS tog, sew up side edges. Turn to RS and stuff with waste yarn. Sew up remaining seam.

These pads sit inside the top of the sleeve head supporting the gathered sleeve. Stitch into position after trying on garment with sleeve pads pinned in position to check correct fit.

Triangular Shoulder Pad
Using the same yarn as your garment is knitted in and 2.75mm needles, cast on 50 sts. Commencing with a K row, work in stocking stitch until you have a square. Cast off. Fold the square diagonally in half with WS together. Now fold in half again across the first fold. You will now have a triangle formed of several layers of knitting. Slip stitch through all layers around the edges creating a solid triangle. Attach to the garment on the underside with the straight edge extending into the sleeve head and the pointed end attached to the shoulder seam. Before sewing in position, try on with pad pinned in position to check correct fit.

Sleeve Roll
Work as for the Triangular shoulder pad above, but rather than folding into a triangle, roll the square into a tight sausage and stitch all round making a roll. Insert the roll into top of a gathered or puffed sleeve to emphasize and hold its shape. Stitch into place after trying on the garment with the roll in position.

KNITTED BUTTONS
There are a number of different knitted buttons you can make, but the following method is by far my favourite as it is simplicity itself. You can see how effective the buttons look on the 'Ripple Jumper'.

Using 4 ply yarn and 3mm needles cast on 6 sts, leaving a tail about 10cm (4in) long. Commencing with a K row, work in stocking stitch for 6 rows. Cast off, leaving a tail about approx 20cm (8in) long. Thread the tail through a sewing up needle and work running stitches around the edges of the knitted square. Once you have gone right round the square, draw up the sts. Before closing up completely, take the tail from the cast on sts and push it into the button as stuffing. Draw the sts up completely and sew up the button. Use the remaining length of yarn still attached to sew the button in place.

This method can be used with all different weights of yarn, although the size of the button will vary depending on what yarn is used.

CROCHET

Double Crochet (Single Crochet)
Shown as DC (SC), you will find that in the patterns of the period double crochet was used as a trim frequently. It is also used to tidy or firm up an otherwise imperfect edging of a garment. If you are not familiar with crochet this stitch is very simple to master.

To start your work, insert your crochet hook under the top loops of your knitted stitch, draw yarn through with the hook. You now have a stitch. * Insert hook under next stitch, repeat as before, you now have two stitches on hook. Grab yarn with hook again and draw it through both stitches. One double crochet has now been worked. With each subsequent stitch you already have the first stitch waiting on your hook, so it is only necessary to work from *. At the end of the work slip stitch the last stitch to the first stitch worked.

Crocheted Button Loops
A crochet button loop is actually just a short series of chain stitches worked independently of the double crochet border and then re-attached usually one chain along.

To make a button loop, insert hook through work from front to back. Draw yarn through onto hook. Grab yarn with hook and draw through stitch on hook. Repeat until chain is long enough to go round button. Attach by inserting hook through knitting, yarn round hook, draw through, now slip stitch to work.

Crocheted Buttons

There are many different types of crochet buttons. This is an example of a very simple version which is used frequently in vintage patterns:

Using an appropriate size crochet hook for the yarn being used, make 5 chain, make into a ring with a slip stitch, then work 9 DC (SC) around the ring. Work a further 3 rounds the same. The work will begin to roll in on itself as the circumference of the circle fails to get bigger as increases are not worked. Draw the yarn through the last chain on your hook, and leave a long end. Stuff the button with oddments of wool left over from darning in ends and sew up at the back using the long end left. Do not cut off the end, use it to sew the button in place.

PERFECT FITTING GLOVES

A very simple way to get the perfect fitting glove is to place your hand on a piece of paper with fingers slightly apart and to draw round it. Repeat this process for the other hand. This becomes your template for your gloves and in particular, finger and thumb length. Work your gloves to fit this template at all times to ensure your gloves are a perfect fit.

INSERTING A SLEEVE

Through much experimentation I have not found anything that works as well as back stitch for inserting a sleeve head. To begin place a pin at the armhole seam of the sleeve, fold the sleeve head in half and mark the centre top with a second pin. Insert the sleeve into the armhole and match the first pin to side seam and second pin to shoulder seam. (Remember, body inside out, sleeve right side out, with RS together). Place pins on either side of the first pin, working your way up on each side from armhole seam. Any excess fabric should be eased into position around the top third of the sleeve, evenly on either side of the second pin. Once sleeve is positioned correctly, join using back stitch starting at underarm and working round the sleeve.

BOX HEAD SLEEVES

The formation of a box head sleeve head creates a permanent three dimensional shape at the top of the sleeve. The top of the sleeve is somewhat like an inverted 'T' as you can see from the image below.

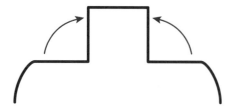

To create the shape required, join the cast off sts at the bottom of the inverted T to the side edges of the centre column of stitches (See arrows) by sewing together on WS of work using a neat back stitch. Turn to RS and place a pin at the centre of the cast off sts of the centre column to mark the centre of your sleeve head. Match this to the corresponding shoulder seam. Also match sleeve and side seams. The sleeve head should fit neatly.

There should not be any easing or gathering needed. If the garment is sitting on the wearer correctly, the shoulder joint will support the box head to some extent. The shape can be further emphasized by knitting sleeve pads to fit inside the box head.

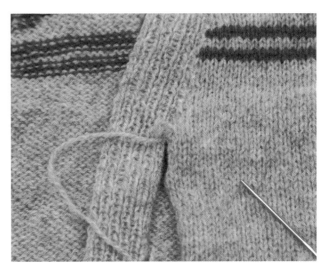

All gathering on a gathered sleeve head is usually done around the top section of the sleeve head with gathers starting and ending at the same distance from the centre of the sleeve head. Using the same yarn as the garment is knitted in run a line of running stitches along the edge of the sleeve between the specified points. Ensure you place a pin or a marker at the centre of the sleeve head. Knot the end and then pull the yarn up gathering the sleeve as you do. Ease the sleeve into position matching the centre of the sleeve head to the shoulder seam and insert as before.

SEWING ON A BUTTON BAND

With work laid out on a flat surface with RS facing, commence at bottom edge of garment and at cast on edge of band, stretching band slightly up edge at all times. Use the same yarn as knitting and a fine sewing up needle if possible. Sew up using a flat slip stitch as shown, catching the edge stitch of both the body and band with each stitch made, taking care not to break through knitted stitches.

Draw stitches up firmly but do not pull too tightly as the garment, band or both may pucker.

Once the band is attached for almost the entire length of garment, adjust the length of the band to fit and cast off all stitches. Finish sewing on band and darn in any ends along join on the WS of work. This method means there is not a seam on either side of the band and that the band will lie flat. It is best worked from the RS of the work.

If you find that the band is undulating instead of lying flat you have not stretched it enough and there is too much fabric in the band. If the band is pulling the edges of the garment up, the band is too short. By working steadily from one edge to another on a flat surface, the garment can be checked as you proceed.

PICKING UP STITCHES

Divide required number of stitches to pick up evenly along edge (for example if 160 stitches to pick up, divide up into 40 or 20 stitch groups). Fold work in half and mark with a pin, then keep dividing and pinning until required number of sections are present. Work with RS facing and start at very first stitch. If you work into second stitch rather than first the picked up stitches will appear to pull up. Using one needle only, take needle under first stitch taking care not to break stitch and to pick up both loops. Knit a stitch as normal. Continue in this way, picking up required number of stitches evenly within each section. If necessary the odd stitch can be moved from one section to another but not from one side of the work to the other as the picked up section will become unbalanced. If picking up a long band around a garment it is better to use a circular needle than a straight needle so the stitches can spread out. Once all the stitches have been picked up, the first row you work will be on the WS. When casting off ensure cast off edge is not tight. If necessary change to a larger needle to prevent this.

SEWING ON A COLLAR

Collars are best attached using a flat slip stitch as on button bands. If possible place garment on a mannequin or tailor's dummy and pin collar into position, matching centre back of both the collar and the garment. Also ensure collar ends meet the garment at the correct point at both front edges.

Work from the RS of the garment, using a flat slip stitch through an edge stitch on each of the pieces.

Draw stitches up firmly but not too tightly so as not to pucker work. To prevent movement I tend to sew from the centre back to one front edge and then from the second front edge to the centre back.

Darn in all ends along join. Joining the collar in this way ensures there is no visible seam on either side of the work and that the collar will lie correctly.

INSERTING A ZIP

Pin the closed zip to WS of work ensuring closures at top of zip do not extend beyond the knitting. Keep knitted edges as close together as possible without inhibiting the opening and closing of the zip. Turn raw edges at top of zip to inside and pin in place. Check zip will open, then using matching sewing thread and a sharp sewing needle sew zip into place from RS of work, using a neat back stitch.

Work as close to the teeth of the zip as possible without preventing the zip from opening. Re-inforce bottom edge of zip several times.

Pin co-ordinating ribbon over outer edge of zip as shown and pin into place. Slip stitch into place down inner edges to zip and on outer edges to garment. Ensure the ribbon covers raw edges at top and bottom of zip for comfort when wearing and remember to fold raw edges of ribbon to inside also.

Catch top and bottom of each piece of ribbon to garment. Check zip opens throughout process so that it is not necessary to unpick a lot of work!

DARNING IN ENDS ON MOTIFS
Always darn in ends around outer edges of motif. Do not take ends across the main background colour or across centre of motif. Always leave a short end of about 2–3mm after cutting off waste yarn to allow for shrinkage or movement when the garment is washed.

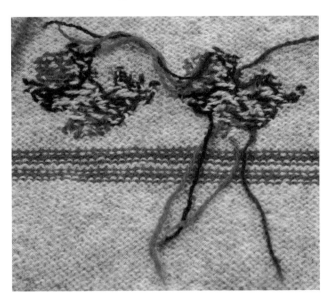

EMBROIDERY
Simple embroidery was often used in vintage knitwear, particularly during the 1940s and 1950s. A basic grasp of a few stitches is all any knitter needs to tackle most of these projects. The Tyrolean Jumper Cardigan from the 1950s uses several of these basic stitches as we can see.

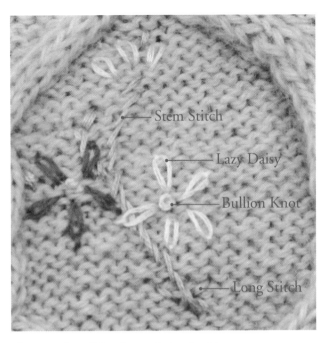

I have used traditional stranded embroidery cottons, available from most haberdashers which come in an array of colours. Stranded embroidery cottons are constructed from 6 strands plied together. I have used 3 strands throughout. Cut a length of thread, then open up the strands at one end, dividing the strands into 2 sections of 3 strands each. Gradually split the length by pulling apart and separating the 2 sections. As only 3 strands are being used this means that each length provides 2 lengths of thread. If you don't have an embroidery needle, a fine sewing up needle will suffice. Always tie a knot at the end of your thread when commencing to work, and do not worry about breaking the knitted stitches as the embroidery stitches need something to anchor to. There are a number of excellent embroidery stitch technique books available. The book I usually refer to is The Embroidery Stitch Bible by Betty Barnden, published in the UK by Search Press. An excellent online resource can be found on the Embroider's Guild website at www.embroiderersguild.com/stitch/stitches

RIBBON TRIMS
Adding ribbon trims is not just pretty, it is also a really useful method of preventing seams from stretching. It is particularly helpful where areas of a garment are heavy and subject to stress, such as the seams of a coat or jacket. Ribbon trims also help support button bands – attaching the buttons to the ribbon not just to the knitted fabric, protects the band from distortion. Ribbon is best attached using a whip stitch worked in sewing thread to match the ribbon, with the stitches only catching the WS of the knitted stitches.

Choosing the Right Buttons

Without doubt, one of the guaranteed ways to make or break a garment is picking the right or the wrong buttons. For vintage inspired knitting try and find buttons that reflect the period the garment is from. If you wish to buy genuine vintage buttons, they are very easily found these days at textile fairs, charity shops and online. Bear in mind however, that numbers of any one type of button are limited so sometimes you can be lucky and other times not so. If I see large numbers of one button I usually try to buy them. Here are some tips on what to look out for when buying vintage buttons:

1930s

Lots of small buttons were used on garments, sometimes 10 or even 12 was not uncommon. If the garment requires medium sized buttons, between 6 and 10 should suffice. Large single decorative buttons can come in handy for coats and jackets. Look out for unusually shaped buttons, sometimes two colour, also buttons made of tortoise shell, bone, plastic, glass and bakelite.

1940s

Far fewer buttons were usually used. Cardigans and jackets were restricted to 3 buttons during war time Britain. Neckbands on high necked sweaters often need a single small button for closure. Back neck opening usually require 3 or 4 matching small buttons. Metal buttons were scarce as metals had to be handed in for the war effort. Buttons tended to be circular for ease of manufacture, some were made of wood but many were plastic or bakelite. Look out for hand painted buttons which pop up now and again.

1950s

Buttons became a prominent feature on garments again as supplies became more plentiful. It was not unusual for cardigans to need 12 buttons. An abundance of sweater cardigans also mean buttons were needed for decoration on these too. Circular, flower shaped, ovals, square, glass, plastic, enamel, small and huge buttons were in abundance in this period.

1930s

Hand knitting came of age in the 1930s with an enormous variety of designs, shapes, patterns and colours being used to knit beautiful patterns. These were usually designed in lightweight yarns, including natural and artificial silks, wool or silk boucles, as well as cottons and wools, from an ever growing number of yarn manufacturers such as Copley's, Weldons, Patons & Baldwins and many more.

These garments were designed to flatter womanly curves. Short in the body, they gave an appearance of longer legs and a high waist line. To emphasise slim waists, garments often had puffed sleeves sometimes with additional padding to make shoulders seem wider. New or rediscovered stitch patterns were used extensively, offering the knitter a myriad of designs to choose from in lace, basket stitches, ribs, arrowheads, twisted cables, drop stitches, wave patterns and more. Unusual necklines were created offering collars, jabots, tucks, pleats, asymmetrical openings, buttons, plackets, folds and drapes. Add to this a kaleidoscope of colours available from every wool shop and it is no surprise that knitting became such a popular past time, with patterns now appearing on a weekly basis in "Woman's Weekly" and "The Lady".

Charming Neckline

MATERIALS
Fyberspates Scrumptious 4 ply 45% silk/55% merino (365m/399yds per 100g skein)
5 (5, 6, 7, 8, 8) skeins shade 309 (midnight) – MC
1 skein (all sizes) shade 310 (natural) – CC
1 pair 2.75mm (US #2) needles
1 pair 3.25mm (US #3) needles

TENSION
27½ sts & 35 rows = 10cm (4in) using 3.25mm needles over stocking stitch

Standard Yarn Tension
28 sts & 37 rows = 10cm (4in) using 3.5mm needles over stocking stitch

ABBREVIATIONS
See page 13 for standard abbreviations

SIZING
Measurements given in centimetres followed by inches in parentheses

To Fit	76–81 (30–32)	86–92 (34–36)	97–102 (38–40)	107–112 (42–44)	117–122 (46–48)	127–132 (50–52)
Finished Measurements						
Actual Bust Size	89 (35)	99 (39)	109 (43)	119 (47)	129½ (51)	139½ (55)
Length to underarm	30½ (12)	32 (12½)	33 (13)	34 (13½)	35½ (14)	37 (14½)
Armhole Depth	20 (8)	22 (8¾)	24½ (9½)	25 (9¾)	26¾ (10½)	28 (11)
Finished Length	50½ (20)	54 (21½)	57½ (22½)	59 (23)	62¼ (24½)	65 (25½)
Sleeve Length	46 (18)	46 (18)	47 (18½)	48 (19)	49½ (19½)	49½ (19½)

Garment shown in photographs is for first size 76–81 (30–32)

BACK
Using 2.75mm needles and MC, cast on 122 (136, 150, 164, 178, 192) sts.
Next row (RS): * K1, P1, rep from * to end of row.
Rep this row until rib measures 8cm (3in).
Change to 3.25mm needles and commencing with a K row work in stocking stitch, until work measures 30½ (32, 33, 34, 35½, 37) cm (12, 12½, 13, 13½, 14, 14½ in) from beginning, ending with a WS row.

Shape Raglan
K2tog at each end of next and every foll RS row until 72 (78, 88, 114, 128, 142) sts rem, then K2tog at each end of every row until 32 (38, 40, 38, 40, 46) sts rem.
Cast off loosely.

FRONT
Work as given for the back until work measures 30½ (32, 33, 34, 35½, 37) cm (12, 12½, 13, 13½, 14, 14½ in) from beginning, ending with a WS row.

Shape Raglan
K2tog at each end of the next row and every foll RS row until 100 (112, 130, 142, 154, 172) sts rem. Continue without further shaping until 31 (35, 35, 39, 43, 47) rows have been worked from beg of armhole shaping (10, 12, 16, 18, 20, 28 rows without shaping).

Next row (WS): * P2, P4tog, repeat from * to last 4 sts, P4 (52, 58, 67, 73, 79, 88 sts).

First, 1st and 6th sizes only
Change to 2.75mm needles and using CC, K 1 row.

3rd, 4th and 5th sizes only
Change to 2.75mm needles and using CC, K2tog, K to end of row (66, 72, 78 sts).

All sizes
Work in pattern for neck as folls:
Row 1 (WS): Using CC, * K1, P1, repeat from * to end.
Row 2: Using MC, K to end.
Row 3: Using MC, * K1, Sl1, repeat from * to end.
Row 4: Using CC, K to end.
Repeat these 4 rows a further 3 times, (there will be 4 stripes in MC at this point). Work rows 1 and 2 only once more but in CC, then cast off (52, 58, 66, 72, 78, 88) sts loosely still using CC.

SLEEVES
Using 2.75mm needles and CC, cast on 50 (56, 64, 70, 76, 82) sts and work in pattern as for front neck as folls:
Row 1 (WS): Using CC, * K1, P1, repeat from * to end.
Row 2: Using MC, K to end.
Row 3: Using MC, * K1, Sl1, repeat from * to end.

Row 4: Using CC, K to end.

Rep these 3 rows a further 3 times (there will be 4 stripes of MC), then work rows 1 and 2 only but using CC, once more. Change to 3.25mm needles and MC.

Next row (WS): Pfb across row (100, 112, 128, 140, 152, 164 sts).

Commencing with a K row, work in stocking stitch without further shaping until sleeve measures 46 (46, 47, 48, 49½, 49½) cm (18, 18, 18½, 19, 19½, 19½ in) from cast on edge, ending with a WS row.

Shape Sleeve Head

K2tog at each end of next row and every alt row until 54 (62, 78, 88, 96, 104) sts rem. Place a marker or waste yarn at each end of the last row worked, then K2tog at each end of every row until 2 sts rem. K2tog, draw yarn through and fasten off.

MAKING UP

Press all pieces through a damp cloth on WS of work. Sew sleeves into Raglan armholes, noting that the back raglan extends to the top of the sleeve head raglan. The front raglan including the neck border will extend to the marker on each sleeve. The upper front slope of the sleeve is part of the neck. Sew up side and sleeve seams. Darn in all ends.

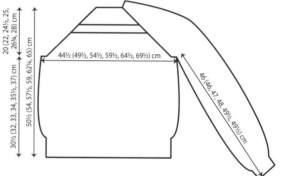

M OST original is this design, yet so easy that a beginner can make it. The main part is in stocking-stitch in green, the neck and wristbands in a fancy stitch in green and white.

MATERIALS.—7 oz. of Paton's Super, or Beehive Scotch Fingering, 4-ply in green, and 1 oz. of the same wool in white, 1 pair each of No. 9 and No. 13 knitting needles and a medium size crochet hook.

TENSION.—Worked at a tension of 13 sts. to 2 inches in width, this jumper will measure 38 inches all round under arms, but as it is meant to be loose and bloused, it should be worn by a 34-36-inch bust size. Length from lower edge to under arms, is 10 inches. Length from lower edge to back of neck is 17½ inches, whilst the sleeve measures 27 inches from cast-on, to cast-off edge.

ABBREVIATIONS.—On page 3.

The Back

With No. 13 needles and green wool cast on 122 sts. and work in ribbing of k. 1, p. 1 for 3 inches. Change to No. 9 needles and work in st.st. (1 row k., 1 row p. alternately) until work measures 10 inches from beginning, finishing with a p. row. Then shape the Raglan armholes by knitting 2 tog. at each end of the next row and every alternate row after until 72 sts. remain, then k. 2 tog. at each end of every row until 32 sts. remain. Cast off loosely.

The Front

Work as given for the back until knitting measures 10 inches from beginning, ending with a p. row; then k. 2 tog. at each end of the next row and every alternate row until 100 sts. remain. Then continue without further shaping until 31 rows in all have been worked from the beginning of the armhole shaping. On next row, which is a p. row work thus :—

Next row—* P. 2, p. 4 tog., repeat from * till 4 remain, p. 4.

Change to No. 13 needles and white wool and k. 1 row. Then work in pattern for neck as follows :—

1st row—With white wool, * k. 1, p. 1. Repeat from * to end. *2nd row*—With green wool, k.

3rd row—With green wool, * k. 1, slip 1. Repeat from * to end of row. *4th row*—With white wool, k.

Repeat the last 4 rows until 4 green stripes in all have been worked. Then work 2 more rows in pattern with white wool, and cast off.

Sleeves (both alike)

With No. 13 needles and white wool cast on 50 sts. and work in pattern as given for front neck until 4 green stripes have been worked. Work 2 more rows in pattern with white wool, then change to No. 9 needles and green wool only, and continue in st.st., knitting twice into every st. on the first row only, then work without shaping until sleeve measures 18 inches from the beginning, finishing with a p. row. Then shape the top by knitting 2 tog. at each end of the next row and every alternate row after, until 54 sts. remain and then k. 2 tog. at each end of every row until 4 sts. remain. Cast off.

To Make Up

Sew sleeves into Raglan armholes. Press all but the ribbing with a warm iron over a damp cloth. Join side and sleeve seams. With green wool work 1 row of d.c. around the back and sides of the neck edge, but omit working crochet over front neck edge.

SUCH pretty sleeves and neckline has this apple-green jumper—they are "gathered" into narrow bands of green and white.

Charming Neckline

This Attractive Affair

MATERIALS
Knitshop Mercerised 4ply Cotton 100% cotton (125m per 50g ball)
8 (9, 10, 11, 13) balls shade Beige – MC
3 (3, 4, 4, 5) balls shade Bordeaux – CC
1 pair 3.25mm (US #3) needles
2mm crochet hook
4 buttons

TENSION
26 sts & 35 rows = 10cm (4in) using 3.25mm needles over 8 row stripe pattern

ABBREVIATIONS
See page 13 for standard abbreviations

SIZING
Measurements given in centimetres followed by inches in parentheses

To Fit	81–86 (32–34)	92–97 (36–38)	102–106 (40–42)	106–112 (42–44)	117–122 (46–48)
Finished Measurements					
Actual Bust Size	95 (37½)	104 (41)	113 (44½)	122 (48)	131 (51½)
Length to underarm	41 (16)	43½ (17)	46 (18)	49 (19)	51 (20)
Armhole Depth	18 (7)	19 (7½)	20 (8)	21½ (8½)	23 (9)
Finished Length	59 (23)	62½ (24½)	66 (26)	70½ (28)	74 (29)
Shoulder to Shoulder	34 (13½)	38 (15)	41 (16)	44½ (17½)	48 (19)

Garment shown in photographs is for first size 81–86 (32–34)

PATTERN NOTES
This garment features an interesting construction. The main body is knitted in four pieces, with the main back and front panels knitted from side to side. Additional side panels are worked which are worked vertically and which fit from the front main panel round to the back panel. The petal collar is worked in four separate pieces and the cuffs are also worked separately to the sleeves which in turn are very unusually, knitted from side seam to side seam.

STRIPE PATTERN
Row 1 (RS): Using MC, K.
Row 2: Using MC, P.
Row 3: As row 1.
Row 4: As row 2.
Row 5: As row 1.
Row 6: As row 2.
Row 7: Using CC, K.
Row 8: Using CC, K.
These 8 rows form stripe pattern with garter stitch ridge.
Work this stripe pattern throughout.

BACK
(Worked from side to side commencing at left side seam)
Using 3.25mm needles and MC, cast on 34 (40, 46, 54, 60) sts.
Commencing with row 1 of stripe pattern, work 7 (9, 11, 13, 15) rows.

Armhole & Shoulder Shaping
On next and foll 7 alt rows (all of which will be WS rows) inc 1 st at end of row (42, 48, 54, 62, 68 sts). Work 1 row without shaping, thus ending on a RS row.
Next row (WS): Patt to end, then cast on 38 (42, 44, 48, 52) sts for armhole (80, 90, 98, 110, 120 sts).
Work 8 rows without further shaping.
*Inc 1 st at beg of next row (81, 91, 99, 111, 121 sts), then work a further 7 (9, 11, 13, 15) rows without shaping. Rep these 8 (10, 12, 14, 16) rows twice more (83, 93, 101, 113, 123 sts).

Shape Lower Body
** **Next row** (RS): K to end of row, then cast on 73 sts for lower body (156, 166, 174, 186, 196 sts).
Work without further shaping for 54 rows ending with a RS row.
Next row (WS): Cast off 73 sts, P to end of row (83, 93, 101, 113, 123 sts).

Next row (RS): Cast off 30 sts at beg of next row for front opening, patt to end of row.

Next row: Patt to end of row, then cast on 30 sts. On next and foll 6 alt rows, inc 1 st at neck edge (146, 156, 164, 176, 186 sts), ending with a RS row.

Next row (WS): Cast off 73 sts at beg of next row, patt to end (73, 83, 91, 103, 113 sts), then cast on 10 sts for neck shaping (83, 93, 101, 113, 123 sts). Work as for back from *** to end.

SIDE PANELS (Make two)
Using 3.25mm needles and MC, cast on 84 (94, 106, 118, 130) sts. Commencing with row 1, work in stripe patt for 120 rows. Cast off.

SLEEVES (Worked from side seam to side seam)
Using 3.25mm needles and MC, cast on 44 sts. Commencing with row 1 of stripe pattern, work in patt for 8 (10, 12, 14, 16) rows, then inc 1 st at end of next (RS) and every foll alt row until 64 (66, 68, 70, 72) sts (this creates sleeve head shaping), then inc 1 st at same end of every row 0 (2, 4, 6, 8) times. Work 4 rows without shaping ending with a RS row. Dec 1 st at same end of every row 0 (2, 4, 6, 8) times, then dec 1 st at beg of next (WS) and every foll alt row until 44 sts. Work 8 (10, 12, 14, 16) rows without further shaping. Cast off.

CUFFS
Using 3.25mm needles and MC, cast on 86 (94, 102, 110, 118) sts. Commencing with row 1 of stripe pattern, work without shaping for 24 rows. Using MC, work 8 rows in garter stitch. Cast off fairly loosely.

*** Work 7 (9, 11, 13, 15) rows without further shaping, then dec 1 st at shoulder edge (end) of next row. Rep these 8 (10, 12, 14, 16) rows twice more, then work 8 rows without further shaping ending with a WS row (80, 90, 98, 110, 120 sts).

Next row (RS): Cast off 38 (42, 44, 48, 52) sts, K to end (42, 48, 54, 62, 68 sts).

On next and foll 7 alt rows dec 1 st at armhole edge (34, 40, 46, 54, 60 sts)

Work 6 (8, 10, 12, 14) more rows without further shaping. Cast off.

FRONT
Work as for back as far as **, taking note that work commences from the right side seam.

Shape Neck and Lower Body
Next row (RS): Cast off 10 sts for neck (73, 83, 91, 103, 113 sts), patt to end of row, then cast on 73 sts for lower body (146, 156, 164, 176, 186 sts).

Next row: Patt to end.

Next and foll 6 alt rows: Dec 1 st at neck edge (139, 149, 157, 169, 179 sts) ending with a WS row.

Work 10 rows without further shaping.

PETAL COLLAR (Worked in 4 separate pieces)

Using 3.25mm needles and MC, cast on 36 sts. Working in garter stitch but maintaining colour stripe patt, dec 1st at end of every WS row until 22 sts rem. Work 2 rows without shaping, then inc 1 st at same edge on every alt row until 36 sts on needles. Cast off fairly loosely. Make three more pieces.

MAKING UP

Firmly press all pieces with a damp cloth and warm iron on WS of work. Sew up shoulder and upper side seams. Pin side panels into position, joining side edges of panel to 73 cast on/off stitches on main body pieces. Join cast off edge of panel to straight edge of lower body pieces, taking panels from front to back as shown. Turn over hem along bottom edge at first purl ridge on side panels. Slip stitch into place.
Sew WS of cuff to RS of sleeve at straight side edge. Fold cuff over sleeve, then fold sleeve in half with RS together and sew up side seam through all layers. Set in sleeve matching centre of sleeve head with shoulder seam. Commencing at centre back pin collar pieces into place, matching the stripes with the main body pieces. The four collar pieces will overlap. Ensure front two collar pieces are overlapping back pieces.

Using a crochet hook and MC, work a row of DC (SC) down one side of neck opening and up second side. Darn in all ends. Again using crochet hook

and MC, work 24 chains and join into circle with a slip stitch. Draw through yarn leaving a long end. Make a second chain in the same way but with 18 chain sts. Sew four buttons in place as shown on photograph. Using long end attach longer crochet loop to one one side of front opening immediately behind the button closest to top of work on left hand side. Repeat the process with the shorter crochet loop on the lower button. To fasten, twist loop in an '8' and wrap around corresponding button. Press once more.

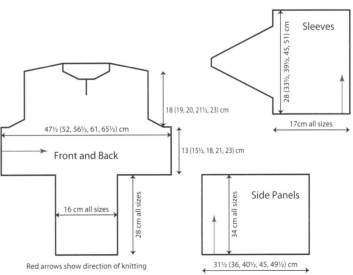

Red arrows show direction of knitting

MATERIALS: 9 ozs. of "Beehive" Botany Wool String (original uses 7 ozs. blue, No. 1244; 2 ozs. black). A pair No. 10 "Beehive" knitting needles. 6 buttons.
MEASUREMENTS: To fit bust 33 to 34 inches; length, 20 inches; sleeve seam, 6½ inches.
TENSION: 7 stitches to the inch.

BACK

With blue wool, cast on 34 stitches. 1ST ROW: Knit. 2ND ROW: Purl. Repeat these two rows twice more. Change to black wool; knit next 2 rows.

Change to blue wool again. 9TH ROW: Knit. 10TH ROW: Purl to last stitch, increase in last stitch. Repeat last 2 rows twice more. Change to black wool. 15TH ROW: Knit. 16TH ROW: Knit to last stitch, inc. in last stitch. Repeat last 8 rows once.

With blue wool cast on 38 stitches for armhole. Work 6 rows stocking-stitch in blue, then knit 2 rows black. * NEXT ROW: Blue. Increase at beginning of row. Work 5 more rows in blue, then knit 2 rows in black. Repeat from * three times. ¶

NEXT ROW: Blue. Knit to end, then cast on 72 stitches. Work in pattern, 6 rows blue in stocking-stitch and 2 rows black in garter-stitch until there are 6 black stripes, then work 5 rows in blue. Cast off 72 stitches at beginning of next row. Purl to end of row.

¶¶ Work 2 rows black, 6 rows blue, decreasing at end of the last blue row. Repeat from * 3 times, then work 2 rows black, 6 rows blue. NEXT ROW: Cast off 38 in blue, join in black. Knit to end. NEXT ROW: Black. Knit to last 2 stitches, knit 2 together. NEXT ROW: Blue, knit. NEXT ROW: Purl to last 2 stitches, p. 2 tog.

Repeat last 2 rows twice more, then repeat last 8 rows once. (34 stitches). Now work 2 rows black and 6 blue, without shaping. Cast off.

FRONT

Work as for back as far as ¶.
NEXT ROW: Blue, cast off 10, knit to end, then cast on 72 stitches. NEXT ROW: Purl to end. NEXT ROW: k. 2 tog, knit to end. NEXT ROW: Purl.
Repeat last 2 rows in blue, then work 2 rows in black, decreasing at beginning of the 1st row, then work 6 rows in blue, decreasing at beginning of the knit rows. Work 2 rows black, decreasing at beginning of the 1st of them, then work 6 rows blue and 2 rows black without shaping.

Work 2 rows blue, then cast off 30 stitches for neck opening, knit to end. NEXT ROW: Purl, then cast on 30 stitches. NEXT ROW: Knit. NEXT ROW: Purl. Work 2 rows black and 6 rows blue. Now increasing at neck edge in alternate rows (commencing with 2nd row), work 2 black, 6 blue, 2 black, 5 blue. Cast off 72 stitches at beginning of next row. Purl to end, then cast on 10 stitches at top edge. Now work as from ¶¶ in back.

SIDE PANELS.

With blue wool, cast on 94 stitches. Work 2 rows in blue, then work 2 black and 6 blue, twelve times. Cast off. Make a similar piece for other side.

SLEEVES.

Cast on 44 stitches. Work in pattern as for body, 6 rows blue and 2 black, then keeping in the striped pattern, increase at top edge in every alternate row until there are 64 stitches. Work on these for 32 rows, then decrease at top edge in alternate rows until there are 44 stitches. Work 2 rows black and 6 blue without shaping. Cast off.

CUFFS.

Cast on 86 stitches. Work 6 rows blue and 2 black until there are 3 black stripes, then work 8 rows in garter-stitch. Cast off.

COLLAR.

This is worked in 4 pieces, all in garter-stitch. Cast on 36 stitches. Work 8 rows blue and 2 black, decreasing at end of 2nd and every alternate row until 22 stitches remain. Work the next 2 rows in black without shaping, then increase at same edge in every alternate row until there are 36 stitches on needle. Cast off.

Make 3 more pieces to match.

TO MAKE UP.

Press all pieces with a damp cloth and hot iron. Sew up shoulder and under-arm seams. Pin side panels into position, the cast-on stitches to the top. Sew in panels, then turn up the lower edge into a half-inch hem to prevent curling up. Sew cast-on edge of cuffs to sleeve and turn back. Sew in sleeves. Sew the sections of collar to neck, overlapping them about 1 inch. Crochet a row of D.C. round front opening. Sew buttons each side; fasten with loops.

THIS attractive affair, making strategic use of pin-stripes running both ways, can be copied in either knitting or crochet. The knitted version, seen above, is carried out mainly in stocking-stitch, the side panels being made separately and neatly stitched into position.

The Jan Sweater

MATERIALS
Excelana 4 Ply Luxury Wool 100% pure new British wool (159m/174yds per 50g ball)
5 (6, 6, 7, 8) balls shade Powdered Egg
1 pair 2.75mm (US #2) needles
1 pair 3.25mm (US #3) needles

TENSION
26 sts & 36 rows = 10cm (4in) using 3.25mm needles over stitch pattern

Standard Yarn Tension
28 sts & 36 rows = 10cm (4in) using 3mm needles over stocking stitch

ABBREVIATIONS
See page 13 for standard abbreviations

SIZING
Measurements given in centimetres followed by inches in parentheses

To Fit	76–81 (30–32)	86–92 (34–36)	97–102 (38–40)	107–112 (42–44)	117–122 (46–48)
Finished Measurements					
Actual Bust Size	86 (34)	97 (38)	107 (42)	119 (47)	129 (51)
Length to underarm	30 (12)	30 (12)	33 (13)	35½ (14)	38 (15)
Finished Length	48 (19)	48 (19)	52 (20½)	54½ (21½)	58½ (23)
Shoulder to shoulder	32 (12½)	37½ (15)	37½ (15)	40½ (16)	43 (17)

Garment shown in photographs is for first size 76–81 (30–32)

PATTERN NOTES
This garment is constructed in 4 separate pieces. It is designed with some wearing ease to allow the body to 'blouse' slightly over the ribbed welt. The boat neck neckline is not joined together except for where the sleeve head meets the body. If the wearer has narrow shoulders, the neck can be sewn together for approximately an inch to prevent the garment slipping off the shoulders. The simple eyelet pattern is worked with a centre eyelet and the pattern mirroring itself on either side of this centre pattern repeat. The pattern is easy to lengthen just by working more repeats of the pattern, below the armhole shaping.

Back
Using 2.75mm needles cast on 86 (100, 114, 128, 142) sts.
Next row: * K1, P1, rep from * to end.
Repeat this row until work measures 8½cm (3½in) ending with a WS row.
Next row (Inc): Rib 5 (0, 5, 0, 6) * rib 2 (3, 3, 4, 4), Kfb, rep from * to last 6 (0, 9, 3, 11) sts, rib to end (111, 125, 139, 153, 167 sts).
Change to 3.25mm needles and work in stitch pattern as folls: (also shown on chart)
Row 1 (WS): P.
Row 2: K.
Row 3: P.
Row 4: K6, * YO, K2tog, K5, repeat from * to end.
Row 5: P.
Row 6: K.
Row 7: P.
Row 8: K5, [YO, K2tog, K5] 7 (8, 9, 10, 11) times, YO, K2tog, K1, [YO, K5, K2tog] 7 (8, 9, 10, 11) times, YO, K5 (112, 126, 140, 154, 168 sts).

Row 9: P.
Row 10: K.
Row 11: P.
Row 12: K4, [YO, K2tog, K5] 7 (8, 9, 10, 11) times, YO, K2tog, K2, K2tog, [YO, K5, K2tog] 7 (8, 9, 10, 11) times, YO, K4.
Row 13: P.
Row 14: K.
Row 15: P.
Row 16: K3, [YO, K2tog, K5] 7 (8, 9, 10, 11) times, YO, K2tog, K4, K2tog, [YO, K5, K2tog] 7 (8, 9, 10, 11) times, YO, K3.
Row 17: P.
Row 18: K.
Row 19: P.
Row 20: K2, [YO, K2tog, K5] 7 (8, 9, 10, 11) times, YO, K2tog, K6, K2tog, [YO, K5, K2tog] 7 (8, 9, 10, 11) times, YO, K2.
Row 21: P.
Row 22: K.

Row 23: P.

Row 24: K1, [YO, K2tog, K5] 7 (8, 9, 10, 11) times, YO, K2tog, K8, K2tog, [YO, K5, K2tog] 7 (8, 9, 10, 11) times, YO, K1.

Row 25: P.

Row 26: K.

Row 27: P.

Row 28: K7, [YO, K2tog, K5] 6 (7, 8, 9, 10) times, YO, K2tog, K10, K2tog, [YO, K5, K2tog] 6 (7, 8, 9, 10) times, YO, K7.

Row 29: P.

Row 30: K.

Row 31: P.

Row 32: K6, [YO, K2tog, K5] 7 (8, 9, 10, 11) times, [K2tog, YO, K5] 8 (9, 10, 11, 12) times, K1.

Row 33: P.

Row 34: K.

Row 35: P.

Row 36: K5, [YO, K2tog, K5] 7 (8, 9, 10, 11) times, YO, K2tog, K2tog, [YO, K5, K2tog] 7 (8, 9, 10, 11) times, YO, K5.

Repeat from row 9 until work measures 30 (30, 33, 35½, 38) cm (12, 12, 13, 14, 15 in), or desired length to underarm, ending with a WS row.

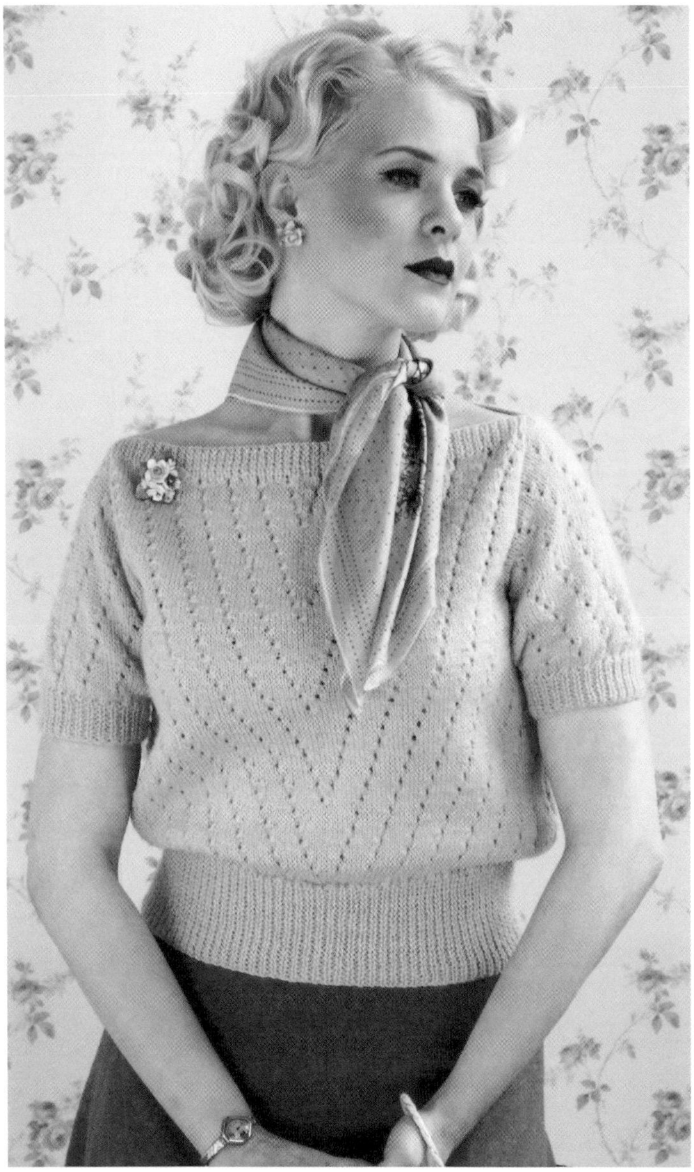

Next row (Inc): Rib 0 (0, 8, 5, 2), * Kfb, rib 2 (2, 2, 3, 4), rep from * to last 2 (2, 8, 5, 2) sts, Kfb, rib to end (83, 83, 97, 111, 125 sts).
Change to 3.25mm needles and commencing with row 1, work in pattern as for back until sleeve measures 13 (13, 14, 15, 15) cm (5, 5, 5½, 5½, 6 in) (84, 84, 98, 112, 126 sts). On rows 8, 12, 16, 20, 24 and 36, the eyelet motif is repeated 5 (5, 6, 7, 8) times on each side. On row 28 it is repeated 4 (4, 5, 6, 7) times. On row 32 it is repeated 5 (5, 6, 7, 8) times at the start of the row, and 6 (6, 7, 8, 9) times at the end of the row.

Sleeve shaping

Cast off 3 sts at the beginning of every row until 18 (18, 20, 28, 30) sts rem.
Cast off rem sts.

MAKING UP

Steam pieces on wrong side with a warm iron and a damp cloth. Join underarm seams. Sew up sleeve seams and sew sleeves in place. (Work a tacking stitch across front and back shoulders to hold in place whilst attaching sleeves). Darn in all ends.

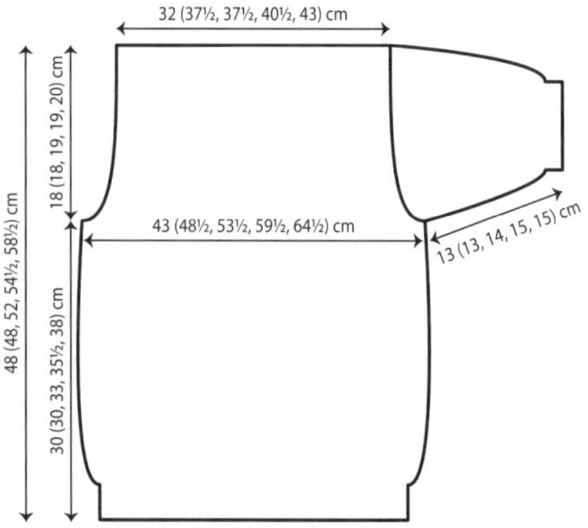

Armhole shaping

Keeping pattern correct, cast off 7 sts at beginning of the next 2 (2, 2, 4, 4) rows, then decrease 1 st at each end of every alt row 7 (7, 14, 11, 14) times (84, 98, 98, 104, 112 sts). Continue working in pattern until armhole measures 18 (18, 19, 19, 20) cm (7, 7, 7½, 7½, 8 in) from cast off, ending with a WS row.
Next row (RS): * K1, P1, rep from * to end.
Repeat this row until rib measures 2½cm (1in).
Cast off fairly loosely in rib.

FRONT

Work exactly as for back.

SLEEVES

Using 2.75mm needles cast on 62 (62, 76, 90, 104) sts.
Next row: * K1, P1, rep from * to end.
Repeat this row until work measures 4cm (1½in) ending with a WS row.

Key
- ☐ Knit on RS, Purl on WS
- ⧄ K2tog on RS
- ⊡ Yarnover
- ▩ No stitch, ignore these squares and move straight to next knitting instruction
- ☐ Pattern repeat

Chart (Shows only RS rows)

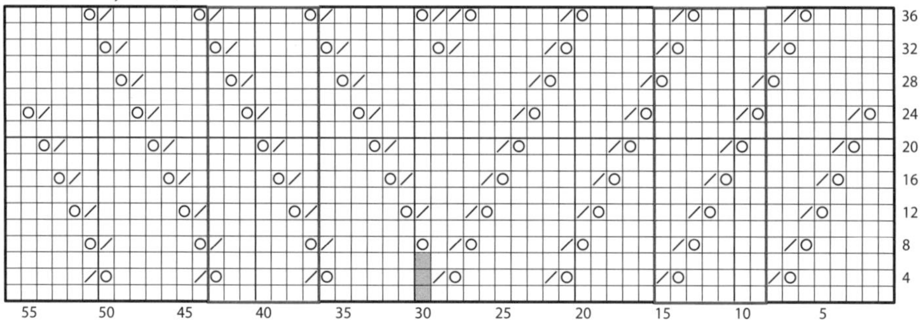

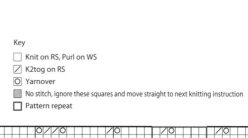

A Charmingly Fanciful Blouse for that Well Dressed Look

JAN

Saxony Blouse No. 2703

Size 14
1 Pr. Standard No. 2 Needles—14 in.
1 Pr. Standard No. 3 Needles—14 in.
Scale: 8 sts. to 1 in.
Jack Frost Saxony—3 Fold—6 1-oz. Balls

BACK—With No. 2 Needles cast on 100 sts. K. 1, P. 1, for 4 in. Change to No. 3 Needles, increasing to 125 sts. at even intervals across the row. Work in Pat. as follows:

PATTERN:

Row 1—Purl.

Row 2—Knit.

Row 3—Purl.

Row 4—K. 6, * Y. O., K. 2 tog., K. 5, repeat from * across row.

Rows 5, 6, 7—Repeat rows 1, 2, 3.

Row 8—K. 5, * Y. O., K. 2 tog., K. 5, repeat from * 7 times, Y. O., K. 2 tog., K. 1, ** Y. O., K. 5, K. 2 tog., repeat from ** to end of row, ending Y. O., K. 5.

Rows 9, 10, 11—Repeat rows 1, 2, 3.

Row 12—K. 4, * Y. O., K. 2 tog., K. 5, repeat from * 7 times, Y. O., K. 2 tog., K. 2, K. 2 tog., ** Y. O., K. 5, K. 2 tog., repeat from ** to end of row, ending Y. O., K. 4.

Rows 13, 14, 15—Repeat rows 1, 2, 3.

Row 16—K. 3 * Y. O., K. 2 tog., K. 5, repeat from * 7 times, Y. O., K. 2 tog., K. 4, K. 2 tog. ** Y. O., K. 5, K. 2 tog., repeat from ** to end of row, ending Y. O., K. 3.

Rows 17, 18, 19—Repeat rows 1, 2, 3.

Row 20—K. 2, * Y. O., K. 2 tog., K. 5, ** Y. O., K. 5, K. 2 tog., repeat from ** K. 2 tog., K. 6, K. 2 tog., ** Y. O., K. 2. to end of row, ending Y. O., K. 2.

Rows 21, 22, 23—Repeat rows 1, 2, 3.

Row 24—K. 1, * Y. O., K. 2 tog., K. 5, repeat from * 7 times, Y. O., K. 2 tog., K. 8, K. 2 tog., ** Y. O., K. 5, K. 2 tog., repeat from ** to end of row, ending Y. O., K. 1.

Rows 25, 26, 27—Repeat rows 1, 2, 3.

Row 28—K. 7 * Y. O., K. 2 tog., K. 5, repeat from * 7 times, * * K. 2 tog., K. 10, K. 2 tog., ** Y. O., K. 5, K. 2 tog., repeat from ** to end of row, ending Y. O., K. 7.

Rows 29, 30, 31—Repeat rows 1, 2, 3.

Row 32—K. 6, * Y. O., K. 2 tog., K. 5, repeat from * 7 times, ** K. 2 tog., Y. O., K. 5, repeat from ** across row, ending K. 6.

Rows 33, 34, 35—Repeat rows 1, 2, 3.

Row 36—K. 5, * Y. O., K. 2 tog., K. 5, repeat from * 7 times, Y. O., K. 2 tog., ** Y. O., K. 5, K. 2 tog., repeat from ** across row, ending Y. O., K. 5.

Repeat from Row 9 until piece measures 7½ in. from ribbing, or desired length to underarm. Bind off 7 sts. at the beginning of the next 2 rows, then decrease 1 st. at each end every other row 7 times. Continue working even in Pat. until piece measures 6½ in. from 1st bound off sts. at underarm. Discontinue Pat. and work in a rib of K. 1, P. 1, for 1 in. Bind off.

FRONT—Work to correspond with back.

Sew shoulder and underarm seams.

SLEEVES—With No. 2 Needles cast on 62 sts. K. 1, P. 1, for 1½ in. Change to No. 3 Needles, increasing to 125 sts. at even intervals across the row. Work in Pat. for 5 in. Bind off 7 sts. at the beginning of every row until 28 sts. are left on the needle. Bind off remaining sts.

Sew sleeve seams and sew sleeves in place.

Helen

MATERIALS
Excelana 4 Ply Luxury Wool 100% pure new British wool (159m/174yds per 50g ball)
4 (5) balls shade Alabaster
1 pair 2.75mm (US #2) needles
1 pair 8mm (US #11) needles

TENSION
1 pattern repeat (14 sts) = 9cm (3¾in) using 8mm needles over stitch pattern

Standard Yarn Tension
28 sts & 36 rows = 10cm (4in) using 3mm needles over stocking stitch

ABBREVIATIONS
See page 13 for standard abbreviations

SIZING
Measurements given in centimetres followed by inches in parentheses

To Fit	76–112	117–152
	(30–44)	(46–60)
Finished Measurements (after pressing)		
Length	167½ (66)	172½ (68in)
Width (at centre)	45½ (18)	54½ (21½)

Garment shown in photographs is for first size 76–112 (30–44)

PATTERN NOTES
This very simple two-row lace pattern is worked in one piece from cuff to cuff. The pattern is work using 4 ply yarn and large needles. The wrap must be pressed after knitting to reveal the pattern properly.

STITCH PATTERN (worked over 14 sts)
Row 1 (RS): * K2, K2tog, K3, YO, K2, YO, K3, K2tog, rep from * to end.
Row 2: P.

Start at Cuff
Using 2.75mm needles cast on 64 (72) sts.
Next row: * K2, P2, repeat from * to end.
Repeat this row for approx 10cm (4in) ending with a RS row.

1st size only
Next row: Continuing in rib, work 2 sts tog at each end of row (62 sts).

2nd size only
Next row: Continuing in rib, inc 4 sts evenly across row (76 sts).

Both sizes
Change to 8mm needles.
Row 1 (RS): K10, * K2, K2tog, K3, YO, K2, YO, K3, K2tog, repeat from * to last 10 sts, K10.
Row 2: K10, P to last 10 sts, K10.
Repeat these 2 rows until the work measures 157½ (162½) cm (62, 64 in) from cast on, ending with row 2.
Change to 2.75mm needles, and work cuff as folls:

1st size only
Next row: Working in rib, inc 1 st at each end of row (64 sts).

2nd size only
Next row: Working in rib, dec 4 sts evenly across row (72 sts).

Both sizes
Continue in rib as for first cuff.

MAKING UP
Press work well on reverse of work, through a damp cloth, pinning out to size. Sew up the cuff seams and a further 10cm (4in) up the sleeve seams. Darn in all ends.

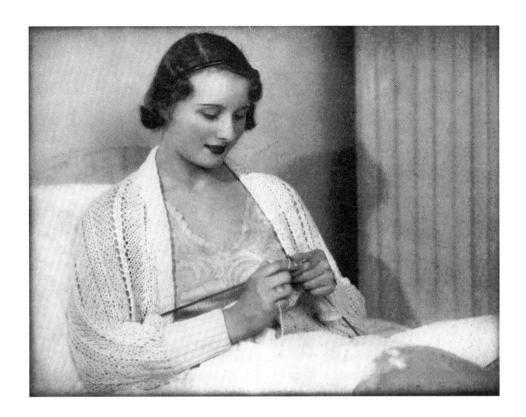

"HELEN"

For the convalescent or for breakfast in bed, this bed wrap is ideal for comfort and it is quite attractive too. It makes a welcome gift for young and old.

MEASUREMENTS.   Length, including cuff, 60 inches.

MATERIALS.
5 ozs. BAIRNS-WEAR Gossamer Lustre Wool, 4-ply.
2 size 000 wooden needles and 2 No. 12 BAIRNS-WEAR knitting needles.

ABBREVIATIONS. k.=knit. p.=purl. tog.=together. st.=stitch.

Cast 64 sts. on the No. 12 needles.

1st row. Slip 1, k. 1 *. K. 2, p. 2, repeat from * to the last 2 sts., k. 2.

Repeat this row for 4 inches, decreasing two stitches on the last row. Change to the big needles.

1st row. Slip 1, k .9, * k. 2, knit 2 tog., k. 3, pick up and knit into the loop, between stitches of previous row. K. 2, pick up and knit into loop, k. 3, k. 2 tog., repeat from * to the last 10 stitches, k. 10.

2nd row. Slip 1, k. 9, purl to the last 10 stitches, k. 10. Repeat these two rows until the work measures 62 inches from the commencement, ending with the 2nd row. Change to the fine needles, and work the cuff as given for the first, increasing two stitches on the first row.

TO MAKE UP. Press under damp cloth with a hot iron. Sew up the cuff seam and four inches beyond.

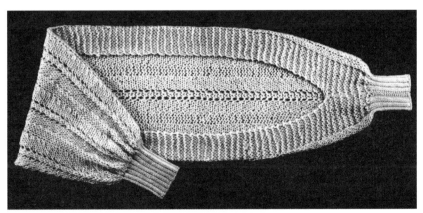

Just a long straight piece — so easy to knit — with a tight ribbing at each end for the cuffs   The original model was made up in a pretty shell pink.

Striped Sun Top

MATERIALS

Knitshop 4 Ply Mercerised Cotton 100% cotton (125m per 50g ball)
2 (2, 2, 2, 2, 3) balls shade green – MC
2 (2, 2, 2, 2, 3) balls shade white – A
2 (2, 2, 2, 2, 3) balls shade fushia pink – B
1 2.5mm (US #1–2) circular needle
1 pair 2.5mm (US #1–2) needles
3 buttons

TENSION

40 sts & 38 rows = 10cm (4in) using 2.5mm needles over rib pattern
25 sts = 10cm when rib stretched out on needle

ABBREVIATIONS

See page 13 for standard abbreviations

SIZING

Measurements given in centimetres followed by inches in parentheses

To Fit	81 (32)	86 (34)	92 (36)	97 (38)	102 (40)	106 (42)
Finished Measurements						
Actual Bust Size	52½ (20½)	57 (22½)	62 (24½)	67 (26½)	72 (28½)	78 (30½)
Length of Back	13 (5)	14 (5½)	15 (6)	16 (6¼)	17 (6¾)	18 (7)
Finished Length	36½ (14½)	39 (15½)	41½ (16½)	44 (17½)	47½ (19)	49½ (19½)

Garment in photograph is for first size 81 (32)

PATTERN NOTES

Garment is worked in the round up to back shaping. Stitches are then cast off and upper body is worked in rows for the remainder of the garment. After yarn colour changes, a K row is always worked.

BODICE

Using 2.5mm needles and B, cast on 210 (230, 250, 270, 290, 310) sts using alternate cable cast on (see 'Knitting Know How'). Join into round, taking care not to twist cast on edge.

Round 1: * P1, K1, rep from * to end.
Rep this round until 24 (26, 28, 30, 32, 34) rounds worked.
Change to MC, K 1 round, then work in rib as set previously for a further 24 (26, 28, 30, 32, 34) rows.

Shape Centre Back

Next round: Still working in MC, cast off 40 (48, 56, 64, 72, 80) sts in rib patt. Change to A and straight needles and working in rows from this point, K to end (170, 182, 194, 206, 218, 230 sts).
Continue in rib, dec 1 st at each end of 3rd (5th, 9th, 3rd, 7th, 9th) row and then on 8 foll 3rd (3rd, 3rd, 4th, 4th, 4th) rows (152, 164, 176, 188, 200, 212 sts).
Work 1 row.
Change to B and K one row. Continue in rib, dec 1 st at each end of 10 foll 3rd rows (132, 144, 156, 168, 180, 192 sts), ending with a WS row.

Divide for Neck

Next row: Rib 50 (55, 60, 65, 70, 75) sts, K2tog twice, then * pass first of these over second (to cast off), K2tog and repeat from * until 32 (34, 36, 38, 40, 42) sts from the centre have been cast off, rib to end, turn and leave first 50 (55, 60, 65, 70, 75) sts on holder or spare needle and work on rem 50 (55, 60, 65, 70, 75) sts only. ** Dec 1 st at neck edge of every row and 1 st at side edge on every alt row until 1 st rem. Draw through yarn and fasten off.
With RS facing rejoin B to rem sts and work as for first side from **

COLLAR

Using 2.5mm needles and MC, cast on 188 (192, 196, 200, 204, 208) sts using alternate cable cast on method.
Next row: * P1, K1, rep from * to end.
Rep this row a further 3 times.
Next row: Rib 4 sts, cast off 2 sts, rib to end.
Next row: Rib to cast off sts, cast on 2, rib to end.
Rib a further 4 rows, then rep 2 buttonhole rows once more.
Rib 4 more rows (16 rows in MC in total)
Change to A, K 1 row.

Rib one row, then rep 2
buttonhole rows once, then rib
a further 2 rows.

Next row: [Rib 20 (15, 15, 12, 12, 10), rib3tog] 3 (4, 4, 5,
5, 6) times, rib 10 (9, 11, 10, 11, 10), rib3tog, rib 9 (9, 9, 9,
10, 10), [rib3tog] twice, rib 9 (9, 9, 9, 10, 10), rib3tog, rib
10 (9, 11, 10, 11, 10), [rib3tog, rib 20 (15, 15, 12, 12, 10)]
3 (4, 4, 5, 5, 6) times (168, 168, 172, 172, 176, 176 sts).
Cast off fairly tightly.

MAKING UP

Do not press. Sew collar in place, matching centre front of
neck to centre of neckband. Darn in all ends. Sew on
buttons to correspond with buttonholes.

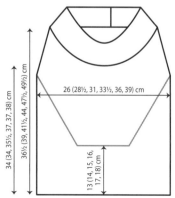

Materials: 5 ozs. Diana Non-Shrink Knitting, 4-ply. Original uses 1 oz. white; 2 ozs. each of red, No. 5634, and green, No. 86. A set of four No. 13 and four No. 12 "Nimble" needles, pointed both ends. A No. 9 "Inox" crochet hook. Three buttons.

MEASUREMENTS: To fit 32–34-inch bust; length from top of red point, 12 inches.

TENSION: 11 stitches to an inch on No. 13 needles, 10 to an inch on No. 12 needles.

BODICE

With No. 13 needles and red wool, cast on 210 stitches and divide equally on to 3 needles. Work 3 inches in rounds of k. 1, p. 1 rib, then change to No. 12 needles and green wool, knit one row and then work 2½ inches in k. 1, p. 1 rib.

NEXT ROW: Cast off 40 stitches in green, then join in white wool, and work on 2 needles on remaining stitches in rib (but knit the 1st row), decreasing at each end of every 3rd row until 132 stitches remain, changing to red wool when white stripe is 3 inches deep.

Divide work for neck shaping :—Rib 50, cast off 32, taking 2 stitches together each time, rib to end. Now decrease at front edge on every row and at side edge on every alternate row until all stitches are gone.

Join wool to remaining stitches and work to correspond.

COLLAR

On two No. 12 needles, cast on 188 stitches loosely in green wool and rib for 16 rows.

a striped, backless sun-top to wear with shorts

Change to white wool and No. 13 needles, knit 1 row, then rib 5 rows. NEXT ROW: (Rib 20, rib 3 tog.,) 3 times, rib 10, rib 3 tog., rib 9, (rib 3 tog.) twice, rib 9, rib 3 tog., rib 10, (rib 3 tog., rib 20) 3 times. Cast off fairly tightly.

TO MAKE UP

Do not press. Work a row of d.c. up sloped edges and top of bodice and round neck edge, using appropriate wools. Sew collar to neck edge, placing it over top of bodice and stitching with green wool. Make 3 button-loops to fasten collar, and sew on buttons to correspond.

Summery – And A New Pattern!

MATERIALS
Baby Rooster 100% superwash merino wool (125m/137yds per 50g ball)
10 (12, 14) balls shade 407
1 pair 2.25mm (US #1) needles
1 pair 3.75mm (US #5) needles
2 safety pins
Stitch holders

TENSION
1 patt rep = 7½cm (3in) & height = 3cm (1¼in) using 3.75mm needles
24 sts & 39 rows = 10cm (4in) using 3.75mm needles over moss st

Standard Yarn Tension
25 sts & 34 rows = 10cm (4in) using 3.25mm needles over stocking stitch

ABBREVIATIONS
See page 13 for standard abbreviations

SIZING
Measurements given in centimetres followed by inches in parentheses

To Fit	81–92 (32–36)	97–106 (38–42)	112–122 (44–48)
Finished Measurements			
Actual Bust Size	90 (35½)	105 (41½)	120 (47)
Length to underarm	28 (11)	31 (12¼)	34 (13½)
Finished Length	48½ (19)	52½ (20¾)	57 (22½)
Armhole Depth	20½ (8)	21½ (8½)	23 (9)
Shoulder to shoulder	38 (15)	42 (16½)	46 (18)
Sleeve Length	12 (4¾)	12 (4¾)	12 (4¾)

Garment shown in photographs is for first size 81–92 (32–36)

PATTERN NOTES
Please note that the left and right upper fronts of this garment are worked over a different number of stitches to each other – 1 stitch difference. This means that there is 1 more neck decrease worked on the left front than on the right front.

BACK
Using 2.25mm needles, cast on 100 (118, 136) sts and commence work as folls:

Next row: * K1, P1, rep from * to end of row.
Rep this row until rib measures 10cm (4in).

Inc Row: * Rib 8 (9, 11), Kfb, rep from * a further 10 times, rib to end. (111, 129, 147 sts).

Change to 3.75mm needles and work pattern as folls (also shown on chart):

Row 1: K2, * YO, K1, [P3, K1] 4 times, YO, K1, repeat from * until 1 st rems, K1 (123, 143, 163 sts).

Row 2: K1, P3, * [K3, P1] 3 times, K3, P5, repeat from * ending the last repeat with P4 instead of P5.

Row 3: K3, * YO, K1, [P3, K1] 4 times, YO, K3, repeat from * to end (135, 157, 179 sts).

Row 4: K1, P4, * [K3, P1] 3 times, K3, P7, repeat from * ending the last repeat with P5 instead of P7.

Row 5: K4, * YO, K1, [P3, K1] 4 times, YO, K5 repeat from * ending the last repeat with K4 instead of K5 (147, 171, 195 sts).

Row 6: K1, P5, * [K3, P1] 3 times, K3, P9, repeat from * ending the last repeat with P6 instead of P9.

Row 7: K5, * YO, K1, [P2tog, P1, K1] 4 times, YO, K7, repeat from * ending the last repeat with K5 instead of K7 (135, 157, 179 sts).

Row 8: K1, P6, * [K2, P1] 3 times, K2, P11, repeat from * ending the last repeat with P7 instead of P11.

Row 9: K6, * YO, K1, [P2tog, K1] 4 times, YO, K9, repeat from * ending the last repeat with K6 instead of K9 (123, 143, 163 sts).

Row 10: K1, P7, * [K1, P1] 3 times, K1, P13, repeat from * ending the last repeat with P8 instead of P13.

Row 11: K7, * YO, [K2tog, K1] 3 times, YO, K11, repeat from * ending the last repeat with K7 instead of K11 (117, 136, 155 sts).

Row 12: K1, P9, * P2tog, P17, repeat from * ending the last repeat with P10 instead of P17 (111, 129, 147 sts).

These 12 rows comprise 1 shell pattern. Work 5 (6, 7) more complete shell patterns. †

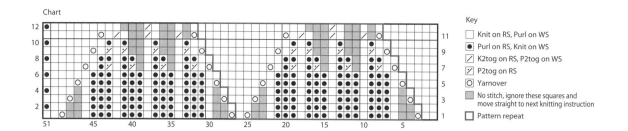

Chart

Key

☐ Knit on RS, Purl on WS
● Purl on RS, Knit on WS
⧄ K2tog on RS, P2tog on WS
⧅ P2tog on RS
○ Yarnover
▨ No stitch, ignore these squares and move straight to next knitting instruction
☐ Pattern repeat

Shape Armholes

Next row (RS): Cast off 2 sts (1 st rem on RH needle), * P1, K1, repeat from * to end.

Next row (WS): Cast off 2 sts (1 st rem on RH needle), * P1, K1, repeat from * to end.

Cont to work in moss stitch as set, cast off 2 sts at beg of next 4 (6, 8) rows (99, 113, 127) then work 2 sts tog at the beg of foll 8 (12, 16) rows (91, 101, 111 sts).

Maintaining moss stitch pattern, work without further shaping until armhole measures 20½ (21½, 23) cm (8, 8½, 9 in). Cast off all sts.

FRONT

Work as for the back to †.

Shape Neck and Armholes

Next row (RS): Cast off 2 sts (1 st rem on RH needle), [P1, K1] 26 (31, 35) times, P1, turn and leave rem 55 (64, 73) sts on a spare needle. Continue on these 54 (63, 72) sts only.

LEFT FRONT

Next row (WS): [K1, P1] 4 times, (P1, K1) to last 0 (1, 0) st, P 0 (1, 0).

Next row: Cast off 2 sts, work in moss st as set to last 8 sts, [K1, P1] 4 times (52, 61, 70 sts). Repeat these 2 rows 1 (2, 3) times more (50, 57, 64 sts).

** Continue in pattern as now set, working 2 sts tog at beg of alt rows 4 (6, 8) times and at the same time shape the neck edge by working 2 sts tog immediately before the rib border sts on next and every foll 4th row until 31 (35, 40) sts rem.

Work in moss stitch without further shaping until front measures same as back to shoulder, ending with a WS row.

Next row: Cast off 23 (27, 32) sts, then continue to work in K1, P1 rib as set on the rem 8 sts for 11½ (12, 12½) cm (4½, 4¾, 5 in) for the back neckband.

Place sts on stitch holder or safety pin.

RIGHT FRONT

With RS facing, rejoin yarn to neck edge of rem 55 (64, 73) sts.

Next row (RS): [K1, P1] 4 times, (P1, K1) to last 1 (0, 1) st, P 1 (0, 1).

Next row: Cast off 2 sts (1 st rem on RH needle), work in moss st to last 8 sts, [K1, P1] 4 times (53, 62, 71 sts). Repeat these 2 rows 2 (3, 4) times more (49, 56, 63 sts).

Continue as from ** on Left Front Shoulder until 31 (35, 40) sts rem. Continue without further shaping until right front measures same as left front to cast off sts at shoulder, ending with a RS row. Cast off 23 (27, 32) sts and place rem 8 sts on to a stitch holder or safety pin.

SLEEVES

Using 3.75mm needles, cast on 93 (111, 129) sts and work 4 complete shell patterns as for back.

Shape Sleeve Head

Working in moss stitch from this point, work 2 sts tog at each end of every row until 17 sts rem. Cast off rem sts. Work a second sleeve in the same manner.

JABOT

Using 3.75mm needles, cast on 26 sts.
Row 1 (RS): * K1, P1, repeat from * to end.
Row 2: * P1, K1, repeat from * to end.
Last 2 rows set moss stitch. Inc 1 st at each end of next and 13 following RS rows (54 sts).
Then work 4 rows in single rib and cast off.
Work a second piece in the same manner.

MAKING UP

Block using damp cloth and iron on WS of work. Join shoulder seams. Check back neck edging is correct length to reach across back neck when slightly stretched. Adjust to fit if necessary, then on WS of work, use three needle cast off to join edging ends together, then using a flat slip st attach to back neck. Sew up sleeve and side seams then set sleeves into armholes, matching centre top of sleeve with shoulder. Gather the ribbed ends of the two jabot pieces and attach them to the front of the neck as shown in the photographs. If to be worn on garment permanently sew jabot in place through jabot and garment front.

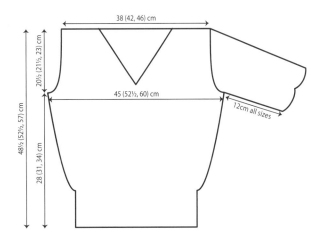

Summery—And A New Pattern!

This Shell Pattern Knitting Is Completely Out-of-the-ordinary!

MATERIALS

SEVEN ounces of Greenock crochet wool (obtainable only at any of the branches of the Scotch Wool & Hosiery Stores), a pair of No. 9 and No. 13 Stratnoid knitting pins.

TENSION AND MEASUREMENTS

WORKED at a tension of 6 sts. to the inch in width on No. 9 pins, the following measurements are attained after light pressing: Round the bust, 34 inches; front length from shoulder to lower edge, 18½ inches; back length, 18 inches; side seam, 13 inches; sleeve seam, 6 inches.

ABBREVIATIONS

K., KNIT; p., purl; st., stitch; tog., together; inc., increase (by working into the back and front of the same stitch); m., make (by bringing the wool to the front of the needle); dec., decrease. Directions in brackets are worked the number of times stated immediately after the brackets. M.s., moss-stitch (k. 1 and p. 1 alternately, and on subsequent rows the sts. are reversed). Single rib is k. 1 and p. 1 alternately.

TO WORK THE BACK

WITH No. 13 pins cast on 100 sts. and work 36 rows in single rib.

INCREASE Row: * Rib 9, inc.; repeat from * to end (110 sts.).

NEXT Row: All purl, increasing 1 st. in the last st. (111 sts.)

Change to No. 9 pins and work in pattern as follows:

1ST Row: K. 2, * m. 1, k. 1, (p. 3, k. 1) 4 times, m. 1, k. 1; repeat from * until 1 remains, k. 1.

2ND Row: K. 1, p. 3, * (k. 3, p. 1) 3 times, k. 3, p. 5; repeat from *, ending the last repeat with p. 4 instead of p. 5.

3RD Row: k. 3, * m. 1, k. 1, (p. 3, k. 1) 4 times, m. 1, k. 3; repeat from * to end.

4TH Row: K. 1, p. 4, * (k. 3, p. 1) 3 times, k. 3, p. 7; repeat from *, ending the last repeat with p. 5 instead of p. 7.

5TH Row: K. 4, * m. 1, k. 1, (p. 3, k. 1) 4 times, m. 1, k. 5; repeat from *, ending the last repeat with k. 4 instead of k. 5.

6TH Row: K. 1, p. 5, * (k. 3, p. 1) 3 times, k. 3, p. 9; repeat from *, ending the last repeat with p. 6 instead of p. 9.

7TH Row: K. 5, * m. 1, k. 1, (p. 2 tog., p. 1, k.1) 4 times, m. 1, k. 7; repeat from *, ending the last repeat with k. 5 instead of k. 7.

8TH Row: K. 1, p. 6, * (k. 2, p. 1) 3 times, k. 2, p. 11; repeat from *, ending the last repeat with p. 7 instead of p. 11.

9TH Row: K. 6, * m. 1, k. 1, p. 2 tog., k. 1) 4 times, m. 1,

k. 9; repeat from *, ending the last repeat with k. 6 instead of k. 9.

10TH Row: K. 1, p. 7, * (k. 1, p. 1) 3 times, k. 1, p. 13; repeat from *, ending the last repeat with p. 8 instead of p. 13.

11TH Row: K. 7, * m. 1, (k. 2 tog., k. 1) 3 times, m. 1, k. 11; repeat from *, ending the last repeat with k. 7 instead of k. 11.

12TH Row: K. 1, p. 9, * p. 2 tog., p. 17; repeat from *, ending the last repeat with p. 10, instead of p. 17.

These 12 rows comprise one shell pattern.

Work 5 complete patterns more to armholes.

TO SHAPE THE ARMHOLES.—Begin to work in m.s. and cast off 2 sts. at the beginning of each of the next 6 rows, then take 2 sts. tog. at the beginning of each of the following 8 rows, when 91 sts. will remain.

Work 46 rows straight in m.s. to shoulders.

Cast off straight across.

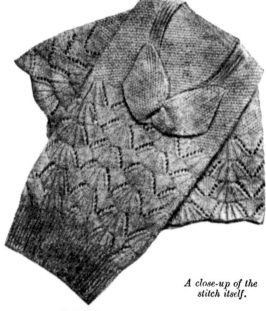

A close-up of the stitch itself.

THE FRONT

WORK exactly as for the back until 6 complete patterns have been worked.

TO SHAPE THE NECK AND ARMHOLES.—Cast off 2 sts. (1 st. on pin) and work in m.s. for 53 sts. more. Leave the remaining 55 sts. on a spare pin until needed for the Right-Half Front, and work the Left-Half Front thus:

NEXT Row: (K. 1, p. 1) 4 times, m.s. to end.

NEXT Row: Cast off 2 sts., m.s. until 8 remain, rib 8.

Repeat these last 2 rows once more.

** Continue in pattern as now set, taking 2 sts. tog. at the beginning of every alternate row (armhole end) 4 times. At the same time shape the neck edge by taking 2 sts. tog. just inside the 8 border sts. on the next and every following 4th row until 31 sts. remain.

Work 6 rows in m.s.

NEXT Row: Cast off 23, continue to work in single rib on the remaining 8 sts. for 4½ inches for the back neck-band. Cast off.

THE RIGHT-FRONT SHOULDER

JOIN the wool to neck end of spare-pin sts. and work as follows: (k. 1, p. 1) 4 times, m.s. to end.

NEXT Row: Cast off 2, m.s. until 8 remain, rib 8.

Repeat these 2 rows once.

Continue as from ** on Left. Front Shoulder until 31 sts. remain. Work 6 rows straight on these sts.

Cast off straight across.

THE SLEEVES

WITH No. 9 pins cast on 93 sts. and work 4 complete patterns as on the back. Continue in

Fun to work—and becoming to wear.

The measurements of the jumper.

FRONT 17" 18½"

BACK 17" 13" 18"

SLEEVE 6"

m.s., taking 2 sts. tog. at each end of every row until 17 sts. remain. Cast off. Work a second sleeve in the same manner.

THE JABOT

WITH No. 9 pins cast on 26 sts. and work in m.s. for **2** rows.

NEXT Row : K. 2 tog., m.s. until **1** st. remains, inc.
NEXT Row : All m.s.
Repeat these 2 rows 13 times more,
then work 4 rows in single rib and cast off.
Work a second piece in the same manner.

TO MAKE UP THE JUMPER

FIRST press all pieces with a hot iron and a damp cloth over the wrong side of the work. Join the shoulder seams, beginning at the armhole end, and, taking 1 st. from each side at a time, stitch the loose ribbed band across the back of the neck.

Set the sleeves into the armholes, and press all pieces while the work is open. Join the sleeve and side seams in one long line and press. Gather the ribbed ends of the two jabot pieces, and stitch them to the front of the neck, as shown in the illustration.

A Pretty Frilled Jumper

MATERIALS
Jamieson & Smith 2 ply jumper yarn 100% Shetland wool (118m/129yds per 25g ball)
13 (14, 16, 18) balls shade FC24
1 pair 3mm (US #2–3) needles
1 pair 3.25mm (US #3) needles
2 buttons
Small press stud

TENSION
24 sts & 34 rows = 10cm (4in) using 3.25mm needles over 2 row pattern and after blocking

Standard Yarn Tension
30 sts & 32 rows = 10cm (4in) using 3.25mm needles over stocking stitch

ABBREVIATIONS
See page 13 for standard abbreviations

SIZING
Measurements given in centimetres followed by inches in parentheses

To Fit	81–86 (32–34)	92–97 (36–38)	102–106 (40–42)	112–117 (44–46)
Finished Measurements				
Actual Bust Size	94½ (37)	104½ (41)	114½ (45)	124½ (49)
Length to underarm	35½ (14)	37½ (14¾)	39 (15½)	40½ (16)
Armhole Depth	17 (6½)	19 (7½)	20 (7¾)	21 (8¼)
Finished Length	52½ (20½)	56½ (22¼)	59 (23¼)	61½ (24¼)
Shoulder to Shoulder	43½ (17)	48½ (19)	53½ (21)	58 (23)
Sleeve Length	47 (18½)	47 (18½)	48 (19)	49½ (19½)

Garment shown in photographs is for first size 81–86 (32–34)

PATTERN NOTES
The lower part of the main body of this garment is worked from side to side in two pieces.
The ribbed welt stitches are picked up along the bottom edge of the work and worked downwards, then the upper yoke stitches are then picked up from the top of the work and worked vertically upwards. Please see the schematic to see how the pieces fit together.

LOWER FRONT
Using 3.25mm needles, cast on 64 (68, 72, 76) sts and work in patt as folls:
Row 1 (RS): * K2, P2, rep from * to end of row.
Row 2: P.

At same time, commence shaping of left armhole by inc 1 st at beg of every P row 10 times, taking increased sts into pattern (74, 78, 82, 86 sts). Place a marker or waste yarn at the beg of the last inc row.

Continue on these sts for a further 35½ (40½, 45½, 50½) cm (14, 16, 18, 20 in), ending with a RS row. Place a marker at the end of the last row worked.
Commence shaping of right armhole by dec 1 st at the beg of the foll 10 purl rows (64 sts).
Cast off on WS.

With RS of work facing, and using 3mm needles, pick up 128 (144, 160, 180) sts along the unshaped lower edge of lower front (marked A on the diagram) and work in rib as folls:
Next row: * K2, P2, rep from * to end of row.
Rep this row until rib measures 9cm (3½in). Cast off loosely in rib.

LOWER BACK
Work exactly as for lower front.

BACK YOKE
Using 3.25mm needles and with RS facing, pick up and K 104 (116, 128, 140) sts along the uppermost edge of lower back between markers.
First row (WS): P.
Work in pattern as for lower back until work measures 13 (15, 16, 17) cm (5, 5½, 6, 6½ in) ending with a WS row.

Shape Shoulders

Cast off 8 (9, 10, 11) sts at beg of foll 8 rows (40, 44, 48, 52 sts).

Cast off rem sts.

RIGHT FRONT YOKE

Taking front lower body, measure 25 (27, 30, 32½) cm (10, 10½, 12, 13 in) along upper edge starting at right armhole edge (at marker) and place pin to mark this point. Using 3.25mm needles, pick up and K 60 (64, 72, 78) sts along RS upper edge of lower front, starting at pin and working to armhole edge.

Next row (WS): P.

Next row: * P2, K2, rep from * to end of row.

Work a further 7 (9, 11, 13) rows in patt ending with a WS row.

Next row (Buttonhole): Patt 8 sts, cast off 4, patt to end.

Next row: P to cast off sts, turn, cast on 4, turn, P8.

Work 14 (16, 16, 20) more rows, then on two following rows make another buttonhole.

Work 4 (4, 6, 6) more rows ending with a WS row.

Neck Shaping

Cast off 10 (10, 12, 13) sts at beg of next (RS) row and foll alt row (40, 44, 48, 52 sts) then dec 1 st at neck edge on foll 8 rows (32, 36, 40, 44 sts).

Shape Shoulder

Cast off 8 (9, 10, 11) sts at beg of next WS and foll 3 alt rows.

LEFT FRONT YOKE

With RS of lower front facing, and using 3.25mm needles pick up and K 54 (60, 68, 72) sts evenly across upper edge of lower front. The picked up stitches will extend past the centre front and approx 8 stitches will need to be picked up from BEHIND the right front yoke.

Next row (WS): P.

Next row: * K2, P2, rep from * to end of row.

Continue working these 2 rows as set until work measures same as right front to beginning of neck shaping ending with a RS row.

Shape Neck

Cast off 7 (8, 10, 10) sts at beg of next 2 foll WS rows (40, 44, 48, 52 sts), then dec 1 st at neck edge on foll 8 rows (32, 36, 40, 44 sts).

Shape Shoulder

Cast off 8 (9, 10, 11) sts at beg of next and foll 3 RS rows.

SLEEVES

Using 3.25mm needles, cast on 48 (52, 56, 60) sts.

Row 1 (RS): * K2, P2, rep from * to end.

Row 2: P.

Rep patt as set above, inc 1 st at each end of 6th and every foll 8th row until 88 (92, 96, 100) sts. Continue without further shaping until work measures 47 (47, 48, 49½) cm (18½, 18,5, 19, 19½ in).

MAKING UP

Press work lightly on wrong side, using a warm iron over a damp cloth, but do not press frills.

Sew up shoulder seams, join side and sleeve seams then set in sleeves, matching centre top of sleeve head to shoulder seam and ensuring side seams line up.

Sew the neck frill round neck, commencing at bottom of right front opening and ending at top of opening on left side, using a flat slip stitch (see 'Fit and Finish' chapter). Take care to match centre point of frill to centre back of neck. Adjust length of frill as required and cast off.

Sew sleeve frills in place commencing at centre of cast on, attaching around cast on edge and then up centre of sleeve for approx 10cm (4in). Sew buttons in place and attach press stud to underside of right front frill at top of neck opening to hold frill in place. Darn in all ends.

Shape Sleeve Head

Dec 1 st at each end of every row until 36 (40, 44, 48) sts rem, then dec 1 st at beg of every row until 16 sts rem. Cast off.

NECK FRILL

Using 3.25mm needles, cast on 12 sts.
Row 1: K.
Row 2: P.
Row 3: K8, turn.
Row 4: P8.
Row 5: P.
Row 6: K.
Row 7: P8, turn.
Row 8: K8.

Rep these 8 rows until shorter side of work measures 61 (62½, 64, 66) cm (24, 24½, 25, 26 in). Leave sts on spare needle.

SLEEVE FRILLS (Make two)

Work exactly as for neck frill until shorter side of work measures 21½ (23, 25, 27½) cm (8½, 9, 10, 10¾ in). Cast off.

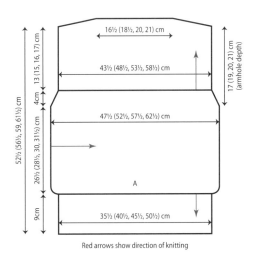

16½ (18½, 20, 21) cm

13 (15, 16, 17) cm

17 (19, 20, 21) cm (armhole depth)

43½ (48½, 53½, 58½) cm

4cm

47½ (52½, 57½, 62½) cm

52½ (56½, 59, 61½) cm

26½ (28½, 30, 31½) cm

A

9cm

35½ (40½, 45½, 50½) cm

Red arrows show direction of knitting

A Pretty Frilled Jumper

MATERIALS

Nine ounces of Sirdar Super Shetland Wool, 3-ply; a pair each of Nos. 10 and 11 "Aero" knitting pins; 2 buttons.

MEASUREMENTS

To fit a 34-inch bust; length from shoulder to lower edge, 18½ ins.; sleeve seam, 18½ ins.

TENSION

Eight sts. and 10 rows to 1 in.
NOTE.—*The main part of the jumper is worked from side to side.*

THE LOWER FRONT.—With No. 10 pins cast on 64 sts. and work 20 rows in the following pattern, increasing at the beginning of every p. row only:

1st row : K. 2, p. 2 alternately to end of row.
2nd row : P.
Continue without alteration for 13 ins., then dec. at the beginning only of the following 10 p. rows. Cast off.
With right side of work towards you, and using No. 11 pins, pick up 126 sts. along the lower (unshaped) edge and work in k. 2, p. 2 rib for 3½ ins. Cast off.
Work the lower back in the same way.

THE BACK YOKE.—With No. 10 pins cast on 104 sts. and work 5 ins. in pattern. Shape shoulders by casting off 8 sts. at the beginning of following 8 rows. Cast off.

RIGHT FRONT YOKE.—With No. 10 pins cast on 60 sts. and work 10 rows in pattern, then work a buttonhole as follows :
Next row : Work 8, cast off 4, work to end.
Next row : P. back, casting on 4 sts. over cast-off sts.
Work 20 more rows, then on two following rows make another buttonhole. Work 6 more rows, then cast off 10 sts. at beginning of next 2 alternate rows, commencing at neck edge. Dec. at neck edge of following 8 rows.
Shape shoulder by casting off 8 sts. at beginning of next 4 p. rows. Fasten off.

LEFT FRONT YOKE.—With No. 10 pins. cast on 54 sts. and work 4 ins. in pattern, then cast off 7 sts. at beginning of next 2 alternate rows, commencing at neck edge. Now dec. at neck edge of following 8 rows. Work shoulder to match right yoke, with shapings reversed.

THE SLEEVES.—With No. 10 pins cast on 48 sts. and work in pattern, increasing at each end of every 8th row until there are 88 sts. Work 20 more rows.

Dec. at both ends of every row until 36 sts. remain, then dec. at beginning only of every row until 16 sts. remain. Cast off. Make another sleeve to match.

THE FRILLS.—With No. 10 pins cast on 12 sts.
1st row : K. all sts. *2nd row :* P. all sts. *3rd row :* K. 8, turn. *4th row :* P. 8. *5th row :* P. all sts. *6th row :* K. all sts. *7th row :* P. 8, turn. *8th row :* K. 8.
For neck frill repeat these 8 rows until shorter side of work measures 18½ ins. For sleeves work two pieces, each 10 ins. along shorter edge.

TO MAKE UP

Press work lightly on wrong side, using a hot iron over a damp cloth, but do not press frills. Join the yoke pieces to main parts of back and front, overlapping the front edges of yoke. Sew up shoulder seams, sew in sleeves, then join side and sleeve seams. Sew the neck frilling round neck, commencing at bottom of front opening and leaving about 1 in. of neck edge free at other side. The sleeve frills are arranged to continue up the sleeve on the side opposite to the seam.

Quick Work in Thick Wool

MATERIALS

Fyberspates Scrumptious Aran 45% silk/55% merino wool (165m/180yds per 100g skein)
4 (4, 5, 5, 6, 6) skeins shade 401 (Cherry)
1 pair 6mm (US #10) needles
1 pair 4mm (US #6) needles
1 6mm (US #10) circular needle
4 stitch holders
6 buttons (optional)

TENSION

20 sts & 23 rows = 10cm (4in) using 6mm needles over twisted rib pattern (unstretched)

Standard Yarn Tension

18 sts & 24 rows using 5mm needles over stocking stitch

ABBREVIATIONS

See page 13 for standard abbreviations

SIZING

Measurements given in centimetres followed by inches in parentheses

To Fit	81–86 (32–34)	92–97 (36–38)	102–107 (40–42)	112–117 (44–46)	122–127 (48–50)	132–137 (52–54)
Finished Measurements						
Actual Bust Size	73 (23¾)	81 (32)	89 (35)	97 (38)	105 (41¼)	113 (44½)
Length to underarm	34 (13½)	34 (13½)	35½ (14)	37 (14½)	37 (14½)	38 (15)
Armhole Depth	17½ (6¾)	18 (7)	19 (7½)	20 (8)	21 (8½)	22 (9)
Finished Length	51½ (20¼)	52 (20½)	54½ (21½)	57 (22½)	58 (23)	60 (24)
Round Arm	30½ (12)	30½ (12)	30½ (12)	34½ (13½)	34½ (13½)	38½ (15)

Garment shown in photographs is for first size 81–86 (32–34)

PATTERN NOTES

This is a very simple pattern using a basic twisted rib pattern. However the raglan decreases are unusually worked on the wrong side of the work, and it is essential that these decreases are worked as specified.

TWISTED RIB PATTERN (4 st repeat)
Row 1 (RS): K3tbl, P1.
Row 2: P to end.
These 2 rows form pattern.

BACK AND FRONT ALIKE
Using 4mm needles, cast on 72 (80, 88, 96, 104, 112) sts and work in rib as folls:
Next row (RS): * K1, P1, rep from * to end.
Repeat until work measures 7½cm (3in) ending with a RS row.
Next row (WS): * K1, P1, rep from * to last 2 sts, K1, patt into front and back of last st (73, 81, 89, 97, 105, 113 sts).
Change to 6mm needles and work in Twisted Rib pattern with edging sts as folls:
Row 1 (RS): K1, * K3tbl, P1, repeat from * to end.
Row 2: K1, P to end.
Repeat these 2 rows until work measures 34 (34, 35½, 37, 37, 38) cm (13½, 13½, 14, 14½, 14½, 15 in) from commencement, ending with a RS row.

Shape Armholes
With WS facing proceed as folls:
Cast off 6 sts at beginning of the next 2 rows (61, 69, 77, 85, 93, 101 sts) then dec one st at beg of next 4 rows (57, 65, 73, 81, 89, 97 sts). Work without further shaping for 10 (12, 14, 16, 18, 20) more rows, ending with a RS row.

Shape Yoke and Neck
Row 1 (WS): K1, * P2tog, P2, repeat from * to end of row (43, 49, 55, 61, 67, 73 sts).
Row 2: K1, * K2tbl, P1, repeat from * to end of row.
Row 3: K1, P to end of row.
Repeat the last 2 rows 3 more times.
Row 10: As row 2.
Row 11: K1, * P2tog, P1, repeat from * to end of row (29, 33, 37, 41, 45, 49 sts).
Row 12: K1, * K1tbl, P1, repeat from * to end of row.
Row 13: As row 3.

Repeat these last 2 rows 3 more times, then row 12 once more. Place rem (29, 33, 37, 41, 45, 49) sts on a stitch holder.

SLEEVES

Using 4mm needles cast on 61 (61, 61, 69, 69, 77) sts and work 6 rows in garter st.

Change to 6mm needles and work in Twisted Rib pattern as set for back until sleeve measures 10 (10, 11, 11, 12, 12) cm (4, 4, 4½, 4½, 4¾, 4¾ in) from cast on edge ending with a RS row.

Shape Sleeve Head

With WS facing proceed as folls:

Cast off 6 sts at beginning of the next 2 rows (49, 49, 49, 57, 57, 65 sts) then dec 1 st at beg of next 4 rows (45, 45, 45, 53, 53, 61 sts). Work without further shaping for 10 (12, 14, 16, 18, 20) more rows, ending with a RS row.

Continue shaping as folls:

Row 1 (WS): K1, * P2tog, P2, repeat from * to end of row (34, 34, 34, 40, 40, 46 sts).

Row 2: K1, * K2tbl, P1, repeat from * to end of row.

Row 3: K1, P to end of row.

Repeat the last 2 rows 3 more times.

Row 10: As row 2.

Row 11: K1, * P2tog, P1, repeat from * to end of row (23, 23, 23, 27, 27, 31 sts).

Row 12: K1, * K1tbl, P1, repeat from * to end of row.

Row 13: As row 3.

Repeat these last 2 rows 3 more times, then row 12 once more. Place rem 23 (23, 23, 27, 27, 31) sts on a stitch holder.

MAKING UP

Join raglan seams.

Neckband

(instructions given for working in the round or flat)

In the round

Commencing at right back raglan, with RS facing and using 6mm circular needles, K across 29 (33, 37, 41, 45, 49) sts from back, K across 23 (23, 23, 27, 27, 31) sts on left sleeve holder, 29 (33, 37, 41, 45, 49) sts across front and 23 (23, 23, 27, 27, 31) sts across right sleeve (104, 112, 120, 136, 144, 160 sts). Work in rounds as follows:

Round 1: P.

Round 2: K.

Round 3: P.

Cast off knitwise.

Flat

If you would prefer to knit neckband on straight needles, leave right front raglan seam unsewn, knit across sts on long 6mm straight needle, then knit three rows. Cast off knitwise. Sew up remaining raglan seam.

Sew up side and sleeve seams. Darn in all ends. Sew on decorative buttons as in photo if desired.

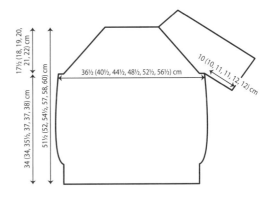

2 rows and decrease once at beginning of next 4 rows. Continue straight in pattern for 10 more rows.

IST ROW: Slip 1, * p. 2 tog., p. 2. Repeat from * to end of row. 2ND ROW: Slip 1, * k. 2 (knit into backs of stitches), p. 1. Repeat from * to end of row. 3RD ROW: Slip 1, p. to end of row. Repeat these last 2 rows 3 times more.

10TH ROW: As 2nd. 11TH ROW: Slip 1, * p. 2 tog., p. 1. Repeat from * to end of row. 12TH ROW: Slip 1, * k. 1 (into back of stitch), p. 1. Repeat from * to end of row. 13TH ROW: As 2nd. Repeat last 2 rows 3 times more.

20TH ROW: As 12th row. Work 4 rows in garter-stitch. Cast off.

SLEEVES

Using No. 8 needles, cast on 61 stitches and work 6 rows in garter-stitch. Change to No. 6 needles and work in pattern until sleeve measures 4 inches from commencement.

To shape top of sleeve work from ** in instructions for back and front.

TO MAKE UP

Pin out pieces to measurement and press lightly on wrong side under a damp cloth. Sew up side seams and insert sleeves carefully, so that the ribs fit together neatly. Stitch buttons into position as shown in the photograph.

QUICK WORK IN THICK WOOL.

MATERIALS: 9 ozs. "Totem" wool (original uses mist blue, No. 1908). A pair No. 6, and a pair No. 8 "Beehive" needles. Six buttons.

MEASUREMENTS: To fit 33-35 inch bust; length from shoulder, 20 inches; sleeve seam, 4 inches.

TENSION: 4½ stitches to the inch measured over the ribbed pattern.

BACK AND FRONT ALIKE

Using No. 8 needles, cast on 72 stitches, and work 3 inches in k. 1, p. 1, rib, increasing in last stitch.

Change to No. 6 needles and work in pattern.

IST ROW: Slip 1, * k. 3, (knit into backs of k. stitches), p. 1, Repeat from * to end. 2ND ROW: Slip 1, p. to end. Repeat these 2 rows until work measures 12½ inches from commencement. Here shape armholes.

**Now with wrong side of work facing, proceed as follows:—

Cast off 6 stitches at beginning of the next

● Very simple to knit, this attractive affair in thick wool, with boat-shaped neckline nicely fitted by a narrowing of the ribbed pattern.

The Sunday Pictorial Beret

MATERIALS
Excelana 4 Ply Luxury Wool, 100% pure new British wool (159m/174yds per 50g ball)
2 balls shade Saharan Sand
1 pair 2.75mm (US #2) needles
1 pair 3.25mm (US #3) needles

TENSION
26 sts & 44 rows = 10cm (4in) using 3.25mm needles over garter stitch

Standard Yarn Tension
28 sts & 36 rows = 10cm (4in) using 3.25mm needles over stocking stitch

ABBREVIATIONS
See page 13 for standard abbreviations

SIZING
One Size

Finished Measurements
To fit head circumference approx 58cm (23in)
Depth 22cm (8¾in)

PATTERN NOTES
This charming beret is worked entirely in garter stitch (knit every row). It is knitted flat on two needles from the bottom up and then sewn together at the back seam. Increases are worked over three rows to create fullness, then the majority of the hat is worked straight, allowing extra or less depth to be worked very easily. The bow is knitted in two pieces and attached afterwards. It is therefore optional and the beret can be customised to suit your outfit.

Using 2.75mm needles, cast on 108 sts. Knit the next 4 rows. Change to 3.25mm needles. Knit 2 rows.
Row 7 (Inc): [K4, Kfb, K4] 4 times, [K1, Kfb, K1] 12 times, [K4, Kfb, K4] 4 times (128 sts).
K 3 rows.
Row 11 (Inc): [K4, Kfb, K5] 4 times, [K1, Kfb, K1] 16 times, [K4, Kfb, K5] 4 times (152 sts).
K 5 rows.
Row 17 (Inc): K52, [K3, Kfb, K2] 8 times, K52 (160 sts).
K 45 rows, or number of rows required.

CROWN SHAPING
Row 63: * K14, K2tog, rep from * to end of row (150 sts).
K 3 rows.
Row 67: * K13, K2tog, rep from * to end of row (140 sts).
K 1 row.
Row 69: * K12, K2tog, rep from * to end of row (130 sts).
K 1 row.
Row 71: * K11, K2tog, rep from * to end of row (120 sts).
K 1 row.
Continue working decreases in this way reducing number of stitches between decreases on every alternate row until 20 sts remain.
Next row: *K1, K2tog, rep from * to last 2 sts, K2tog.
Break yarn, leaving a long length; and using sewing up needle, draw yarn through remaining stitches. Using same yarn and needle, sew up back seam.

BOW ONE
Using 3.25mm needles, cast on 16 sts.
Row 1: K.
Row 2: K1, K2tog, K to last 2 sts, Kfb, K1.
Repeat these 2 rows a further 24 times then cast off. Put to one side.

BOW TWO
Using 3.25mm needles, cast on 20 sts.
Row 1: K.
Row 2: K1, K2tog, K to last 2 sts, Kfb, K1.
Repeat these 2 rows a further 24 times then cast off. Put to one side.

BOW CENTRE
Using 3.25mm needles cast on 6 sts, leaving a long end.
K 10 rows, then cast off, also leaving a long end.

MAKING UP
Press bows on reverse of work, with a damp cloth. Place larger bow over smaller bow and tease into position. Run a few stitches across centre of the two bows and draw up, gathering middle of bows. Wrap bow centre around the middle, hiding all stitching. Position on hat over back seam and at an angle, as shown in photos and pin in place. Stitch from underside of hat, using yarn still attached to bow centre after casting on and casting off. Darn in all ends.

BERET

MATERIALS.
3 oz. W. B. Becnit Wool. 1 pair No. 11 and 1 pair No. 10 knitting needles.

MEASUREMENTS.
10 in. in diameter.

TENSION.
13 sts. to 2 in. in width, 7 rows to 1 in. in depth.

With No. 11 needles, cast on 108 stitches. Work in garter st. K. 4 rows. Change to No. 10 needles. K. 2 rows.

7th Row: (K. 4, K. twice into next st., K. 4) 4 times. (K. 1, K twice into next st., K. 1) 12 times. (K. 4, K. twice into next st., K. 4) 4 times. (128 sts.). K. 3 rows.

11th Row: (K. 4, K. twice into next st. K. 5) 4 times. (K. 1 K. twice into next st. K. 1) 16 times. (K. 4 K. twice into next st. K. 5) 4 times. (152 sts.) K. 5 rows.

17th Row: K. 52. (K 3, K. twice into next st. K. 2) 8 times. K. 52 (160sts.). K. 45 rows.

Shape Top: 1st row: * K.14, K.2 tog. Rep. from * to end. K. 3 rows.

5th row: * K. 13, K. 2 tog. Rep. from * to end. K. 1 row.

7th Row: *K. 12 K 2 tog. Rep. from * to end. K. 1 row.

9th row: * K. 11 K. 2 tog. Rep. from * to end. K. 1 row. Continue dec. in this way every alternate row until 20 sts. remain.

Last Row: * K. 1, K. 2 tog. Rep. from * to last 2 sts. K. 2 tog. Draw up. Sew back seam.

Bow Ends: No. 11 needles. Cast on 16 sts.

1st Row: K.

2nd row: K. 1 K. 2 tog. K. to last 2 sts. K. twice into next st., K. 1. Repeat these 2 rows 24 times more. Cast off. Cast on 20 sts. Work as for first bow end.

Slot: Cast on 6 sts. Work as for bow end for 8 rows. Cast off.

To make up: Press with warm iron and damp cloth. Fix "slot" into position and pass "bow" through. Fix this into position.

Dinah's Lacy Jumper

MATERIALS
Baby Rooster 100% superwash merino wool (125m/137yds per 50g ball)
7 (8, 9, 10, 12, 13, 16) balls shade 405 (Iced Gem)
1 pair 2.75mm (US #2) needles
1 pair 3.25mm (US #3) needles
1 pair 3.75mm (US #5) needles
3mm crochet hook
Stitch holder
1 button

TENSION
32 sts & 36 rows = 10cm (4in) using 3.25mm needles over 4-row twisted stitch pattern
34 sts & 32 rows = 10cm (4in) using 3.25mm needles over rib pattern

Standard Yarn Tension
25 sts & 34 rows = 10cm (4in) using 3.25mm needles over stocking stitch

ABBREVIATIONS
See page 13 for standard abbreviations

SIZING
Measurements given in centimetres followed by inches in parentheses

To Fit	71–76 (28–30)	81–86 (32–34)	86–92 (34–36)	97–102 (38–40)	107–112 (42–44)	117–122 (46–48)	127–132 (50–52)
Finished Measurements							
Actual Bust Size	60 (23½)	71 (28)	76 (30)	86 (34)	96 (38)	106 (41½)	121 (47½)
Length to underarm	29 (11½)	30 (12)	32 (12½)	33 (13)	34½ (13½)	37 (14½)	40 (15½)
Armhole Depth	18 (7)	21 (8)	21 (8)	22 (8½)	23 (9)	23 (9)	24 (9½)
Finished Length	47 (18½)	51 (20)	53 (21)	55 (21½)	57½ (22½)	60 (23½)	64 (25)
Shoulder to Shoulder	26 (10)	28 (11)	29½ (11½)	30½ (12)	33 (13)	35 (13¾)	37½ (14¾)

Garment shown in photograph is for second size for 81–86 (32–34)

BACK
Using 2.75mm needles, cast on 80 (96, 104, 120, 136, 152, 176) sts.
Row 1 (RS): K1, * K2, P2, repeat from * to the last 3 sts, K3.
Row 2: K1, * P2, K2 repeat from * to last 3 sts, P2, K1.
Repeat these 2 rows for 9cm (3½in) ending with row 2.
Change to 3.25mm needles and work in twisted stitch pattern as folls:
Row 1 (RS): K1, K2tog, YO, * P2, YO, Sl1, K1, psso, P2, K2tog, YO, repeat from * to last 5 sts, P2, YO, Sl1, K1, psso, K1.
Row 2: K1, * P2, K2, repeat from * to last 3 sts, P2, K1.
Row 3: K1, * YO, Sl1, K1, psso, P2, K2tog, YO, P2, repeat from * to last 7 sts, YO, Sl1, K1, psso, P2, K2tog, YO, K1.
Row 4: As row 2.
These 4 rows form pattern. Continue in pattern, inc 1 st at each end of next and 8 foll 8th rows (98, 114, 122, 138, 154, 170, 194 sts), taking new sts into pattern as they are made, but retaining a knit st at each end of row as an edging st.
Work without further shaping until piece measures 29 (30, 32, 33, 34½, 37, 40) cm (11½, 12, 12½, 13½, 13½, 14½, 15½ in) ending with a WS row.

Shape Armholes
Cast off 4 (4, 5, 5, 6, 6, 6) sts at beg of next 2 (4, 4, 6, 6, 8, 10) rows (90, 98, 102, 108, 118, 122, 134 sts).
Dec 1 at each end of every foll alt row 1 (1, 1, 2, 3, 1, 3) times (88, 96, 100, 104, 112, 120, 128 sts).
Continue in pattern until work measures 34 (38, 38, 42, 44½, 47, 51) cm (13½, 15, 15, 16½, 17½, 18½, 20 in), ending with a pattern row 4. † Work in rib from this point as folls:
Row 1 (RS): K1, P0 (0, 2, 0, 0, 0, 0), * K2, P2, repeat from * to last 3 (3, 5, 3, 3, 3, 3) sts, P0 (0, 2, 0, 0, 0, 0), K3.
Row 2: K1 (1, 3, 1, 1, 1, 1), * P2, K2 repeat from * to last 3 (3, 5, 3, 3, 3, 3) sts, P2, K1 (1, 3, 1, 1, 1, 1).

Continue in rib patt until work measures 47 (51, 53, 55, 57½, 60, 64) cm (18½, 20, 21, 21½, 22½, 23½, 25 in), ending with a WS row.

Shape Shoulders
Cast off 9 (10, 10, 10, 11, 12, 13) sts at beginning of next 6 rows.
Cast off rem 34 (36, 40, 44, 46, 48, 50) sts.

FRONT

Work as for back to † (work measures 34 (38, 38, 40, 43, 45½, 49½) cm (13½, 15, 15, 16, 17, 18, 19½ in) ending with row 4).

Divide for Front Neck

Next row (RS): K1, P0 (0, 2, 0, 0, 0, 0), * K2, P2, repeat from * 6 (7, 7, 8, 9, 10, 11) more times, patt 15, turn, and work on these sts only, placing rem sts on stitch holder (44, 48, 50, 52, 56, 60, 64 sts). Continue as set above, maintaining stitch patt on centre 15 sts until front measures 7 (7, 7, 11, 11, 13, 13) rows less to start of shoulder shaping than back, ending with a RS row.
Cast off 10 (14, 14, 14, 14, 14, 14) sts at beg of next row (30, 34, 34, 38, 42, 46, 50 sts).
Dec 1 st at neck edge on 3 (4, 4, 8, 9, 10, 11) foll rows (27, 30, 30, 30, 33, 36, 39 sts). Work 3 (2, 2, 2, 1, 2, 1) rows without further shaping, ending with a WS row.

Shape Shoulders

Cast off 9 (10, 10, 10, 11, 12, 13) sts at beg of next and foll 2 alt rows.

Rejoin yarn to 44 (48, 50, 52, 56, 60, 64) right shoulder stitches and work to match left shoulder, reversing shapings.

SLEEVES

Using 2.75mm needles cast on 64 (72, 80, 88, 96, 104, 112) sts, work in rib, as for back until work measures 2½cm (1in) ending with a RS row.
Next row (WS): Working in rib, inc 16 sts evenly across row (80, 88, 96, 104, 112, 120, 128 sts).
Change to 3.25mm needles, and commencing with row 1, work in twisted stitch pattern until sleeve measures 10cm (4in) from cast on edge, ending with a WS row.

Shape Sleeve Head

Dec 1 st at beg of every row until 20 (24, 32, 36, 40, 44, 48) sts rem. Cast off rem sts.

COLLAR

Using 2.75mm needles, cast on 86 (86, 90, 94, 94, 98, 98) sts.
Row 1 (RS): K2, * P2, K2, rep from * to end of row.
Row 2 (WS): P2, * K2, P2, rep from * to end of row.
These 2 rows set 2 by 2 rib, cont to work in rib until piece measures 2½cm (1in), ending with a RS row.
Next row (WS): Inc 2 (2, 6, 2, 2, 6, 6) sts evenly across row (88, 88, 96, 96, 96, 104, 104 sts).
Change to 3.25mm needles and work in twisted stitch pattern for 12 rows. Change to 3.75mm needles and work in twisted stitch pattern for 9 rows, ending with Row 1.
Cast off loosely.

MAKING UP

Do not press. Sew together side, shoulder and sleeve seams, insert sleeves, gathering in any excess at sleeve head to fit. Stitch collar to neck edge using flat slip stitch as shown in 'Fit and Finish' chapter. Using 3mm crochet hook make button loop on right side of front opening (See 'Fit and Finish'). Sew button to left side. Darn in all ends.

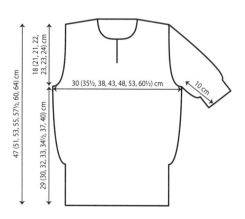

18 (21, 22, 22, 23, 23, 24) cm
30 (35½, 38, 43, 48, 53, 60½) cm
10 cm
47 (51, 53, 55, 57½, 60, 64) cm
29 (30, 32, 33, 34½, 37, 40) cm

In a delicate shade of blue is Dinah's lacy jumper. Although it looks so airy-fairy, it is made from a firm, silky texture wool which stands up to endless washing without the garment losing its shape. The pattern is particularly suitable for a beginner to try her hand on.

Materials: 5 ozs. Halcyon Non-Shrink Knitting, 3-ply. Original uses blue, No. 5462. A pair each of No. 12, No. 10 and No. 9 "Beehive" needles. One button.

MEASUREMENTS: To fit 31–33-inch bust; length from top of shoulder, 18 inches; sleeve seam, 4 inches.

TENSION: 8 stitches to an inch, measured over the pattern.

BACK

With No. 12 needles, cast on 96 stitches. 1ST ROW (wrong side of work): k. 1, * p. 2, k. 2; repeat from * to last 3 stitches, p. 2, k. 1. 2ND ROW: k. 1, * k. 2, p. 2; repeat from * to the last 3 stitches, k. 2, k. 1. Repeat these 2 rows for 3½ inches.

(With right side of work facing.) Change to No. 10 needles and pattern:—1ST ROW: k. 1, k. 2 tog., k. 1, wool round needle, * p. 2, wool forward, slip 1, k. 1, pass slipped stitch over, p. 2, k. 2 tog., w.r.n., repeat from * to last 5 stitches, p. 2, wl. fwd., sl. 1, k. 1, p.s.s.o., k. 1. 2ND ROW: k. 1, * p. 2, k. 2; repeat from * to last 3 stitches, p. 2, k. 1. 3RD ROW: k. 1, * wl. fwd., sl. 1, k. 1, p.s.s.o., p. 2, k. 2 tog., w.r.n., p. 2; repeat from * to last 7 stitches, wl. fwd., sl. 1, k. 1, p.s.s.o., p. 2, k. 2 tog., wl. fwd., k. 1. 4TH ROW: As 2nd.

These 4 rows form pattern. Continue in pattern, increasing at each end of next and every following 8th row until there are 114 stitches on the needle, taking new stitches into pattern as they are made, always keeping your border stitch in plain knitting at edge.

Work straight until side edge measures 11½ inches, then shape armhole thus:—Cast off 4 stitches at beginning of next 4 rows, then k. 2 tog. at beginning of every row until 96 remain. NEXT ROW (right side of work): k. 1, * slip 1, k. 1, p.s.s.o., p. 2, k. 2 tog., w.r.n., p. 2, wl. fwd., repeat from * to last 3 stitches, k. 2 tog., k. 1. 2ND ROW: k. 1, p. 1, * k. 2, p. 2, repeat from * to last 2 stitches, p. 1, k. 1. 3RD ROW: k. 2, * w.r.n., p. 2, wl. fwd., sl. 1, k. 1, p.s.s.o., p. 2, k. 2 tog., repeat from * to last 6 stitches, k. 2 tog., w.r.n., p. 2, wl. fwd., k. 2. 4TH ROW: k. 1, * p. 2, k. 2, repeat from * to last 3 stitches, p. 2, k. 1. Repeat these 4 rows until back measures 14 inches, ending with the 4th row.

Change to rib, as for 2nd row of welt, and work straight until back measures 17½ inches. Shape shoulders by casting off 10 stitches at beginning of next 6 rows; cast off.

FRONT

Work exactly as for back until 14 inches have been done. Now work on first 48 stitches only, leaving remainder on a spare needle. With front of work facing, work 33 in rib and 15 in lace pattern, and continue until front measures 17 inches, ending at centre edge. NEXT ROW: Cast off 14, then decrease at this edge on every row until 30 remain. Work straight (one or two rows only) until work

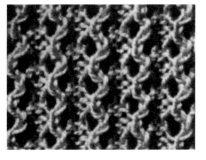

measures 17½ inches, then shape shoulder by casting off 10 stitches at beginning of next 3 alternate rows, armhole edge.

Join wool to remaining stitches and work to correspond.

SLEEVES

With No. 12 needles, cast on 72 stitches and work in rib, as for welt, for 1 inch. NEXT ROW: (with wrong side facing) In rib, increasing in 5th and every following 4th stitch until 7 remain, rib 7 (88 stitches).

Now change to No. 10 needles, and work 3 inches in pattern. Shape top by casting off 4 at beginning of next 2 rows, then k. 2 tog. at each end of every alternate row until 24 remain; cast off.

COLLAR

With No. 12 needles, cast on 86 stitches and work 1 inch in k. 2, p. 2 rib. Change to No. 10 needles and pattern:—1ST ROW: k. 2, * w.r.n., p. 2, wl. fwd., s. 1, k. 1, p.s.s.o., p. 2, k. 2 tog.; repeat from * to last 4 stitches, w.r.n., p. 2, wl. fwd., k. 2 (88 stitches). 2ND ROW: k. 1, * p. 2, k. 2; repeat from * to last 3 stitches, p. 2, k. 1. 3RD ROW: k. 1, * wl. fwd., s. 1, k. 1, p.s.s.o., p. 2, k. 2 tog., w.r.n., p. 2; repeat from * to last 7 stitches, wl. fwd., s. 1, k. 1, p.s.s.o., p. 2, k. 2 tog., wl. fwd., k. 1. 4TH ROW: As 2nd.

Now change to No. 9 needles and repeat pattern twice more. NEXT ROW: k. 2, * wl. fwd., s. 1, k. 1, p.s.s.o., k. 2 tog., wl. fwd., k. 1, w.r.n., p. 2, wl. fwd., k. 1; repeat from * to last 4 stitches, k. 2 tog., wl. fwd., k. 2. Cast off loosely.

TO MAKE UP

Do not press. Sew together side, shoulder and sleeve seams; insert sleeves. Stitch collar to neck edge. Make a buttonloop on right side of front opening and sew on button to left side.

Tri-Cable Stitch Jumper

MATERIALS
Shilasdair Luxury 4ply 20% cashmere/40% angora/40% lambswool (185m/230yds per 50g skein)
7 (8, 9, 9, 10, 11) skeins, shade T
1 pair 3mm (US #2–3) needles
1 pair 3.75mm (US #5) needles
7 buttons

TENSION
1 patt rep (16 sts) = 5¾cm (2¼in) using 3.75mm needles.
28 sts and 36 rows = 10cm (4in) using 3.75mm needles over stitch pattern.

ABBREVIATIONS
See page 13 for standard abbreviations

Specific abbreviations for this pattern
C6B: Slip next 3 sts to cable needle and hold at back of work, K3, K3 from cable needle
C6F: Slip next 3 sts to cable needle and hold at front of work, K3, K3 from cable needle

SIZING
Measurements given in centimetres followed by inches in parentheses

To Fit	81–86 (32–34)	92–97 (36–38)	102–107 (40–42)	107–112 (42–44)	112–117 (44–46)	117–122 (46–48)
Finished Measurements						
Actual Bust Size	92 (36)	100 (39)	104 (41)	108½ (43)	116 (45½)	123 (48½)
Length to underarm	33 (13)	34 (13½)	35½ (14)	35½ (14)	37 (14½)	38 (15)
Armhole Depth	16½ (6½)	18 (7)	19 (7½)	20 (8)	21½ (8½)	23 (9)
Finished Length	49½ (19½)	52 (20½)	54½ (21½)	55½ (22)	58½ (23)	61 (24)
Shoulder to shoulder	35½ (14)	37 (14½)	38½ (15)	40 (15½)	40½ (16½)	43 (17)

Garment shown in photographs for is first size 81–86 (32–34)

PATTERN NOTES
Please make a note of last row worked before each set of shaping instructions to ensure a perfect match on back and fronts.

BACK
Using 3mm needles, cast on 128 (138, 144, 150, 160, 170) sts.
Next row (RS): * K1, P1, rep from * to end.
Continue in rib as set until work measures 7½cm (3in) from cast on ending with a RS row.
Next row (WS): Rib to last st, then inc 1 into last st (129, 139, 145, 151, 161, 171 sts).

1st, 3rd and 5th Sizes only
(Please ensure you use the correct chart for the size you are knitting).
Change to 3.75mm needles, and work in pattern as foll:
Row 1 (RS): Following row 1 of chart A, work st 4 once, then repeat the marked section 8 (9, 10) times.
Row 2 (WS): Following row 2 of chart A, repeat the marked section 8 (9, 10) times, then work st 4 once.
Cont to work in patt as set until work measures 33 (35½, 38) cm (13, 14, 15 in) ending with a WS row.

4th Size only
(Please ensure you use the correct chart for the size you are knitting).
Change to 3.75mm needles, and work in pattern as foll:
Row 1 (RS): Following row 1 of Chart A, work sts 1–4 once, repeat the marked section 9 times, then work sts 21–23 once.
Row 2 (WS): Following row 2 of Chart A, work sts 23–21 once, repeat the marked section 9 times, then work sts 4–1 once.
Cont to work in patt as set until work measures 37cm 14½in ending with a WS row.

2nd and 6th Sizes only
(Please ensure you use the correct chart for the size you are knitting).
Change to 3.75mm needles and work in pattern as foll:
Row 1 (RS): Following row 1 of Chart B, repeat marked sts 1–16, 4 (5) times in total, work sts 17–27 once, then repeat the marked sts 28–33, 4 (5) times in total.

Row 2 (WS): Following row 2 of Chart B, repeat marked sts 33–28, 4 (5) times in total, work sts 27–17 once, then repeat marked sts 16–1, 4 (5) times in total.

Continue to work in pattern as set until work measures 34½ (39½) cm (13½, 15½ in) ending with a WS row.

Shape Armholes

Whilst continuing to maintain pattern, shape armhole as folls:

Cast off 4 (5, 5, 5, 6, 7) sts at beg of next 6 (6, 6, 8, 6, 6) rows, then 3 (3, 4, 0, 5, 5) sts at beg of next 2 rows (99, 103, 107, 111, 115, 119 sts).

Continue in pattern without further shaping until work measures 49½ (52, 54½, 55½, 58½, 61) cm (19½, 20½, 21½, 22, 23, 24 in) ending with a WS row.

Shape Shoulders

Whilst continuing to maintain pattern, cast off 8 sts at the beg of the next 6 rows, then 10 (10, 12, 12, 14, 16) sts at the beg of the next 2 rows (31, 35, 35, 39, 39, 39 sts).

Cast off rem sts.

LEFT FRONT

Using 3mm needles, cast on 70 (74, 76, 80, 86, 92) sts.

Next row (RS): * K1, P1, rep from * to last 10 sts, K10.

Next row: K9 * P1, K1, rep from * to last st, P1.

Continue in rib as set until work measures 7½cm (3in) from cast on ending with a WS row. Dec 0 (1, 0, 1, 0, 0) st at the end of this last row (70, 73, 76, 79, 86, 92 sts).

Change to 3.75mm needles and with RS facing (side edge) work as folls:

Next row (RS): Following row 1 of chart C, start and end as indicated, and repeat the marked section 3 (3, 3, 3, 4, 4) times, K9.

Next row (WS): K9, work row 2 of chart starting and ending as indicated.

Continue working from chart with 9 sts in garter st for button band at front edge, until front measures 33 (34½, 35½, 37, 38, 39½) cm 13 (13½, 14, 14½, 15, 15½ in) ending with a WS row.

Shape Armhole

Whilst continuing to maintain pattern, shape armhole as folls:

Cast off 4 (5, 5, 5, 6, 7) sts at beg of next and foll 2 (2, 2, 3, 2, 2) RS rows, then cast off 3 (3, 4, 0, 5, 5) sts at beg of foll RS row (55, 55, 57, 59, 63, 66 sts).

Continue in pattern without further shaping until work measures 39½ (42, 44½, 45½, 49½, 52) cm (15½, 16½, 17½, 18, 19½, 20½ in) ending with a WS row.

Key

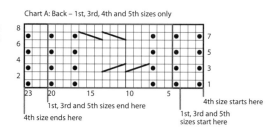

☐ Knit on RS, Purl on WS
⊡ Purl on RS, Knit on WS
▱ C6B
▱ C6F
☐ Pattern repeat

Chart A: Back – 1st, 3rd, 4th and 5th sizes only

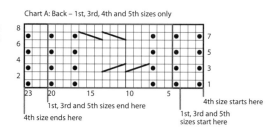

1st, 3rd and 5th sizes end here
4th size ends here
4th size starts here
1st, 3rd and 5th sizes start here

Chart B: Back – 2nd and 6th sizes only

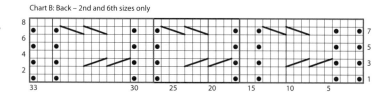

Chart C: Left Front – All sizes

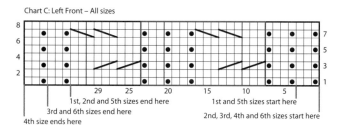

1st, 2nd and 5th sizes end here
3rd and 6th sizes end here
4th size ends here
1st and 5th sizes start here
2nd, 3rd, 4th and 6th sizes start here

Chart D: Right Front – All sizes

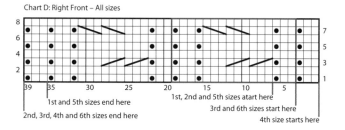

1st and 5th sizes end here
2nd, 3rd, and 4th and 6th sizes end here
1st, 2nd and 5th sizes start here
3rd and 6th sizes start here
4th size starts here

Chart E: Sleeves – All sizes

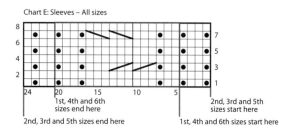

1st, 4th and 6th sizes end here
2nd, 3rd and 5th sizes end here
2nd, 3rd and 5th sizes start here
1st, 4th and 6th sizes start here

*** Shape neck

Whilst maintaining pattern, shape neck as folls:

Next row (WS): Cast off 15 sts, P to end (40, 40, 42, 44, 48, 51 sts).

Dec 1 st at neck edge on every foll row until 34 (34, 36, 36, 38, 40) sts rem. Continue on these sts without further shaping until work measures 49½ (52, 54½, 55½, 58½, 61) cm (19½, 20½, 21½, 22, 23, 24 in) ending with a WS row.

Shape Shoulder

Next row: Cast off 8 sts, patt to end.

Next row: P.

Repeat these 2 rows twice more, then cast off rem 10 (10, 12, 12, 14, 16) sts.

RIGHT FRONT

Using 3mm needles, cast on 70 (74, 76, 80, 86, 92) sts.

Row 1: K9, * P1, K1 repeat from * to last st, P1.

Row 2: * K1, P1, rep from * to last 10 sts, K10.

Repeat these 2 rows three times more.

Next row: K3, cast off 3 sts to make buttonhole, K3 (includes st remaining after cast off), * P1, K1, repeat from * to last st, P1.

Next row: (K1, P1) to garter st band, knit to end, casting on 3 sts over those cast off on previous row.

Continue as set by rows 1 and 2 until rib measures 2 rows less than left front ribbing.

Next row: K3, cast off 3 to make button hole, K3 (includes st remaining after cast off), * P1, K1, repeat from * to last st, P1.

Next row: Dec 0 (1, 0, 1, 0, 0) st then work in rib to garter st band, knit to end, casting on 3 sts over those cast off on previous row (70, 73, 76, 79, 86, 92 sts).

Change to 3.75mm needles.

Next row (RS): K9, following row 1 of chart D, start and end as indicated, and repeat the marked section 3 (3, 3, 3, 4, 4) times.

Next row (WS): Work from row 2 of chart D, starting and ending as indicated, to last 9 sts, K9.

Buttonhole Placement

Work a buttonhole on every 20th (24th, 26th, 26th, 24th, 26th) row, 5 (5, 5, 5, 6, 6) times from last buttonhole worked.

At the same time, continue in pattern as set, reversing garter st band as set above, until front measures 39½ (42, 44½, 45½, 49½, 52) cm (15½, 16½, 17½, 18, 19½, 20½ in) ending with a RS row.

Shape Armhole

Remembering to work buttonholes as set, and whilst continuing to maintain pattern, shape armhole as folls: Cast off 4 (5, 5, 5, 6, 7) sts at beg of next and foll 2 (2, 2, 3, 2, 2) WS rows, then cast off 3 (3, 4, 0, 5, 5) sts at beg of foll WS row (55, 55, 57, 59, 63, 66 sts).

Continue in pattern without further shaping until work measures 39½ (42, 44½, 45½, 49½, 52) cm (15½, 16½, 17½, 18, 19½, 20½ in) ending with a RS row.

Continue as for left front from *** reversing all shapings.

SLEEVES

Using 3mm needles, cast on 48 (48, 56, 64, 64, 72) sts.

Next row (RS): * K1, P1, rep from * to end.

Continue in rib as set until work measures 7½cm (3in) from cast on ending with a RS row.

Next row (WS): Working in rib, inc 0 (8, 0, 0, 8, 8) sts evenly across row (48, 56, 56, 64, 72, 80 sts).

Change to 3.75mm needles and commencing with row 1, work from sleeve chart as foll:

Row 1 (RS): Starting and ending as indicated on the chart, work row 1 of chart E, repeating the marked section 3 (3, 3, 4, 4, 5) times.

Continue in pattern as set, inc one st at each end of every 4th row 4 (4, 12, 12, 12, 12) times, and then at each end of every 6th row, working additional stitches into pattern until 96 (104, 112, 120, 128, 136) sts.

Continue in pattern without further shaping until sleeve measures 47 (48½, 48½, 48½, 49½, 49½) cm (18½, 19, 19, 19, 19½, 19½ in).

Shape Sleeve Head

Whilst continuing to maintain pattern, work 2 sts tog at each end of every row until 20 (20, 20, 24, 24, 28) sts rem. Cast off rem sts.

COLLAR

Using 3.75mm needles, cast on 9 sts and knit in garter stitch for 86cm (34in). If you would prefer tie to be longer than shown in photograph, work extra length before casting off. Cast off.

MAKING UP

Sew shoulder seams. Attach garter stitch tie to neck, matching centre back neck to centre of tie, pinning first and stretching slightly to fit. DO NOT attach tie to button bands. Sew up side and sleeve seams. Insert sleeves and sew in place, taking care to match centre of sleeve head to shoulder seam and matching side seams. Sew buttons down left front to correspond with buttonholes. Darn in all ends.

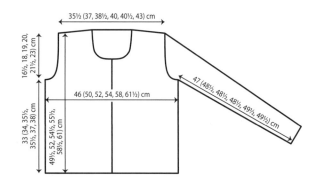

MATERIALS REQUIRED.

11 ozs. Lister's "Lavenda," 4-ply.
1 pair Needles, No. 11. 1 pair Needles, No. 9.
7 Buttons.

ABBREVIATIONS.

K. = Knit ; P. = Purl ; Tog. = Together ;
Sts. = Stitches ; Ins. = Inches.

MEASUREMENTS.

To fit 34 to 36 inch Bust.

Length	17½ ins.
Sleeve Seam (under-arm)	18½ ins.

TENSION.

1 pattern (16 stitches) equals 2½ inches in width.
10 rows equal 1 inch in length.

BACK.

With No. 11 needles, cast on 128 sts. and knit in
k. 1, p. 1 rib for 3 ins.

Next row.—K. 1, p. 1 to end of row, k. 2 into
last stitch.

Change to No. 9 needles and following pattern :—

1st row.—P. 1, k. 2, *, p. 1, k. 9, p. 1, k. 2, p. 1,
k. 2. Repeat from * to end of row, ending p. 1.

2nd row.—Purl.

3rd row.—P. 1, k. 2, *, p. 1, slip next 3 sts. on to
wool needle *behind work*, knit next 3 sts., k. 3 sts.
from * to end of row, ending p. 1. **Repeat**
from * to end of row, ending p. 1.

4th row.—Purl.

5th row.—As 1st row.

6th row.—Purl.

7th row.—P. 1, k. 2, *, p. 1, k. 3, slip next 3 sts. on
to wool needle *in front of work*, knit next 3 sts.,
knit 3 sts. from wool needle, p. 1, k. 2, p. 1, k. 2.
Repeat from * to end of row, ending p. 1.

8th row.—Purl.

Continue in this pattern until work measures 10½ ins.
With right side of work facing, shape for armhole as
follows (twisting cable where necessary) :—

Next row.—Cast off 4, k. 8, *, p. 1, k. 2, p. 1, k. 2,
p. 1, k. 9. Repeat from * to end of row.

Next row.—Cast off 4, purl to end of row.

Next row.—Cast off 4, k. 4, *, p. 1, k. 2, p. 1, k. 2,
p. 1, k. 9. Repeat from * to end of row.

Next row.—Cast off 4, purl to end of row.

Next row.—Cast off 4, *, p. 1, k. 2, p. 1, k. 2,
p. 1, k. 9. Repeat from * to end of row.

Next row.—Cast off 4, purl to end of row.

Next row.—Cast off 3, *, p. 1, k. 2, p. 1, k. 2,
p. 1, k. 2. Repeat from * to end of row.

Next row.—Cast off 3, purl to end of row.

Next row.—K. 1, p. 1, *, k. 2, p. 1, k. 9, p. 1,
k. 2, p. 1. Repeat from * to end of row, ending k. 1.

Next row.—Cast off 8, knit to end of row in pattern.
Repeat this row seven more times. Cast off
remaining stitches.

LEFT FRONT.

With No. 11 needles, cast on 70 sts.

1st row.—K. 1, p. 1 for first 61 sts. Knit last 9 sts.

2nd row.—K. 9, *, p. 1, k. 1. Repeat from * to end
of row, ending p. 1.

Repeat these 2 rows until work measures 3 ins. Change
to No. 9 needles, starting at k. 1, p. 1 rib edge.

Next row.—P. 1, k. 2, p. 1, *, k. 9, p. 1, k. 2, p. 1,
k. 2, p. 1. Repeat from * to within 18 sts. of end of
row, knit last 18 sts.

Next row.—K. 9, purl to end of row.

LEFT FRONT.

With No. 11 needles, cast on 70 sts.

1st row.—K. 1, p. 1 for first 61 sts. Knit last 9 sts.

2nd row.—K. 9, *, p. 1, k. 1. Repeat from * to end
of row, ending p. 1.

Repeat these 2 rows until work measures 3 ins. Change
to No. 9 needles, starting at k. 1, p. 1 rib edge.

Next row.—P. 1, k. 2, p. 1, *, k. 9, p. 1, k. 2, p. 1,
k. 2, p. 1. Repeat from * to within 18 sts. of end of
row, knit last 18 sts.

Next row.—K. 9, purl to end of row.

Continue in this manner, in cable pattern with
garter stitch border, until work measures 10½ ins.
Starting at cable pattern edge, shape for armhole as
follows (twisting cable where necessary) :—

Next row.—Cast off 4, k. 8, *, p. 1, k. 2, p. 1,
k. 2, p. 1, k. 9. Repeat from * to within 9 sts. of
end of row, knit last 9 sts.

Next row.—K. 9, purl to end of row.

Next row.—Cast off 4, k. 4, *, p. 1, k. 2, p. 1,
k. 2, p. 1, k. 9. Repeat from * to within 9 sts. of
end of row, knit last 9 sts.

Next row.—K. 9, purl to end of row.

Next row.—Cast off 4, *, p. 1, k. 2, p. 1, k. 2,
p. 1, k. 9. Repeat from * to within 9 sts. of end of
row, knit last 9 sts.

Next row.—K. 9, purl to end of row.

Next row.—Cast off 3, *, p. 1, k. 2, p. 1, k. 2,
p. 1, k. 9. Repeat from * to within 9 sts. of end of
row, knit last 9 sts.

Next row.—K. 9, purl to end of row.

Next row.—K. 1, p. 1, k. 2, p. 1, k. 9, *, p. 1,
k. 2, p. 1, k. 2, p. 1, k. 9. Repeat from * to within
9 sts. of end of row, knit last 9 sts.

Repeat last 2 rows (twisting cable where necessary)
until work measures 15 ins. Starting at garter stitch
edge, shape for neck as follows :—

Next row.—Cast off 15, purl to end of row.

Next row.—Knit to end in pattern, knit last 2 tog.

Next row.—K. 2 tog., purl to end of row.

Repeat last 2 rows until 32 sts. remain. Continue on
these sts., without decreasing, until work measures
17 ins. Starting at armhole edge, shape for shoulders
as follows :—

Next row.—Cast off 8, knit to end in pattern.

Next row.—Purl.

Repeat these 2 rows twice, cast off remaining 8 sts.

RIGHT FRONT.

With No. 11 needles, cast on 70 sts.

1st row.—K. 9, *, p. 1, k. 1. Repeat from * on last
61 sts.

2nd row.—K. 1, p. 1 for 60 sts, knit last 10 sts.
Repeat these 2 rows four times.

Next row.—K. 3, *, p. 1, k. 1. Repeat from * to end of row,
ending p. 1.

Next row.—K. 1, p. 1 to within 9 sts. of end of row,
k. 3, cast on 3 in place of cast off ones, k. 3.

Continue as 1st and 2nd rows, in rib with garter stitch
border, for 2 rows less than Left Front ribbing.
Make another buttonhole as before. Change to
No. 9 needles.

Next row.—K. 9, *, k. 9, p. 1, k. 2, p. 1, k. 2, p. 1.
Repeat from * to within 13 sts. of end of row, ending
k. 9, p. 1, k. 2, p. 1.

Next row.—P. 61, k. 9.

Repeat these 2 rows, twisting cable as before, and
making a buttonhole in the garter stitch border every
2 ins. as before, until work measures 10½ ins.
Continuing in pattern, with border and buttonholes,
Shape for armhole as follows :—

Next purl row.—Cast off 4, purl to end of row.

Next purl row.—Cast off 4, purl to end of row.

Next purl row.—Cast off 4, purl to end of row.

Next purl row.—Cast off 3, purl to end of row.

Continue in pattern as before, with border and
buttonholes, until work measures 15 ins. Starting at
garter stitch edge, shape for neck as follows :—

Cast off 15, knit to end in pattern.

Next row.—Purl to end, k. last 2 tog.

Next row.—K. 2 tog., knit to end in pattern.

Repeat last 2 rows until 32 sts. remain. Continue on
these sts. until work measures 17 ins. Starting at
armhole edge, shape for shoulders as follows :—

Next row.—Cast off 8, purl to end of row.

Next row.—Knit in pattern.

Repeat these 2 rows twice. Cast off remaining 8 sts.

SLEEVES.

With No. 11 needles, cast on 48 sts. and knit in
k. 1, p. 1 rib for 3 ins. Change to No. 9 needles
and work thus :—

Next row.—*, K. 2, p. 1, k. 9, p. 1, k. 2, p. 1.
Repeat from * to end of row.

Next row.—Purl.

Continue in pattern, twisting cables as before, and
increasing once at each end of every 6th row, until
there are 96 sts. on needle. Continue in pattern
without shaping until work measures 18½ ins.
Keeping pattern unbroken, shape for armhole by
knitting 2 tog. at each end of each row until 20 sts.
remain. Cast off.

COLLAR.

With No. 9 needles, cast on 9 sts. and knit in garter
stitch for 32 ins. Cast off.

TO MAKE UP.

Press lightly under damp cloth all parts except
k. 1, p. 1 rib. Sew up shoulder seams. Sew sleeves
into armholes and garter stitch tie in position,
stretching to draw in Jumper neck. Sew up side
and sleeve seams. Sew buttons down left front to
correspond with buttonholes.

Fez and Scarf

MATERIALS
Shilasdair Luxury 4ply 20% cashmere/40% angora/40% lambswool (185m/230yds per 50g skein)
2 skeins shade 188
1 pair 3.25mm (US #3) needles

TENSION
25 sts & 38 rows = 10cm (4in) using 3.25mm needles over bobble pattern before pressing
23 sts & 31 rows = 10cm (4in) using 3.25mm needles over unstretched rib

ABBREVIATIONS
See page 13 for standard abbreviations

Specific abbreviations for this pattern
MB (Make bobble): K5 into next st, slip 1st loop over foll 4 loops on needle. Slip 2nd loop over foll 3 loops on needle. Continue until only 1 loop left on needle

FINISHED SIZE
Scarf (75g of yarn used) – Length 81cm (32in) Width at widest part 28cm (11in)
Fez (25g of yarn used) – Circumference 48cm (19in)

PATTERN NOTES
The fez is designed to be worn far back on the head and is shaped so that the front of the hat is longer than the back to allow for this style. If you wish to make the fez deeper work extra stocking stitch rows before commencement of crown shaping. Bear in mind that extra yarn will be needed for this.

Scarf

Using 3.25mm needles, cast on 64 sts. Commencing with a K row work 2 rows in stocking stitch. Work in Bobble patt as folls:

Row 1 (RS): * K3, MB, rep from * to end.
Row 2 & every foll WS row: P.
Row 3: K.
Row 5: K2, * MB, K3, rep from * to last 2 sts, MB, K1.
Row 7: K.
Row 9: K1, * MB, K3, rep from * to last 3 sts, MB, K2.
Row 11: K.
Row 13: * MB, K3, rep from * to end of row.
Row 15: K.
Row 16: P

These 16 rows form pattern. Continue in pattern until work measures 12cm (4¾in) from cast on, ending with a RS row.
Next row (WS): P2tog, P to last 2 sts, P2tog (62 sts), placing marker or waste yarn at end of row.

Work in ribbing as folls:
Row 1 (RS): * P2, K1, rep from * to last 2 sts, P2.
Row 2: * K2, P1, rep from * until 2 sts rem, K2.
Rep these 2 rows until work measures 56cm (22in) from marker, ending with a RS row.

Next row: Kfb, K1, * P1, K2, rep to last 3 sts, P1, K1, Kfb (64 sts).
Commencing with row 1, work in Bobble patt for 12cm (4¾in) ending with a WS row. Cast off. Darn in all ends.

Fez

Using 3.25mm needles, cast on 48 sts. Commencing with row 1, work in Bobble patt and at same time cast on 6 sts at beg of every row, working additional sts into pattern, until 108 sts. Place marker or waste yarn at the end of this last row. Continue without further shaping until work measures 8cm (3in) from marker, ending with a WS row. Commencing with a K row, work in stocking stitch for 3cm (1¼in), ending with a P row.

Shape Crown
Row 1: * K10, K2tog, rep from * to end of row (99 sts).
Next & every foll alt row: P.
Row 3: * K9, K2tog, rep from * to end of row (90 sts).
Row 5: * K8, K2tog, rep from * to end of row (81 sts).

Continue in this manner decreasing 9 sts on every K row, working 1 st less between decs on each subsequent decrease row, until 18 sts rem. P 1 row, then break off yarn, leaving a long end, and draw yarn through rem sts, drawing up sts and fastening off end. Sew up back seam. Darn in all ends.

FEZ and SCARF

SUCH an interesting knobby pattern is used for the fez and ends of the scarf.

MATERIALS.—3 oz. Paton's Super, or Beehive, Scotch Fingering, 3-ply, 1 pair of No. 9 knitting needles and a medium sized crochet hook.

TENSION.—7 sts. to 1 inch in width over the stocking stitch and knob pattern sections. The fez will fit an average head size. Scarf will measure 31 ½ inches in length.

The Scarf

With No. 9 needles cast on 64 sts. and work 2 rows in st.-st. (one row k., one row p.). Then work in knobby pattern as follows :—

1st row : * K. 3, make a knob (i.e., knit 5 times into the next st., so that you have 5 loops on right needle all worked from this one st.; then slip the 1st loop over the other four, to drop off the needle; then slip off the 2nd loop, then the 3rd, then the 4th; now only the 5th st. of the group remains); rep. from * to end of row.

2nd and every alternate row—P.

3rd row : K.

5th row : K. 2, * make a knob, k. 3; rep. from * till 2 remain, make a knob, k. 1.

7th row : K.

9th row : K. 1, * make a knob, k. 3; rep. from * till 3 remain, make a knob, k. 2.

11th row : K.

13th row : * Make a knob, k. 3; rep. from * to end of row.

15th row : K.

16th row : P.

These 16 rows form the knobby pattern.

Continue to rep. them till scarf measures 4¾ inches, but k. 2 tog. at both ends of the last row only. Then work in ribbing as follows :

1st row : (With right side of work facing you) * p. 2, k. 1; rep. from * till 2 remain, p. 2.

2nd row : * K. 2, p. 1; rep. from * till 2 remain, k. 2.

Rep. these 2 rows for 22 inches, knitting twice into the first and last st. on the last row only. Then work in knobby pattern (being sure to start with the right side of the work facing you) for 4¾ inches. Cast off. Press lightly.

The Fez

With No. 9 needles cast on 48 sts. and working in nobby pattern, cast on 6 sts. at the beginning of every row until there are 108 sts. on needle. Then continue in knobby pattern till the short ends (short parts of strip) measure 2¾ inches. Then beginning with the right side of work facing you, work in st.-st. for 1 ½ inches, finishing with a p. row.

Next row : * K. 10, k. 2 tog.; rep. from * to end of row (99 sts.).

Next row : P.

Next row : * K. 9, k. 2 tog.; rep. from * to end of row (90 sts.).

Next row : P.

Next row : * K. 8, k. 2 tog.; rep. from * to end of row (81 sts.).

Next row : P.

Now continue like this, decreasing 9 sts. every k. row, always working 1 st. less between the decs. every dec. row until 18 sts. remain. P. 1 row. Break off wool, leaving a length hanging. Thread this in a darning needle and slip it through the remaining sts. Draw up and fasten off end. Press hat with a hot iron over a damp cloth. Join the side seam. Make a tuck about ¼ inch wide all round hat just where the st.-st. part starts run-stitching it with the wool.

With right side of work towards you, work 1 row of d.c. all round lower edge of hat.

Lady Georgina Curzon's Jumper

MATERIALS
Excelana Luxury DK wool 100% pure new British wool (119m/130yds per 50g ball)
7 (8, 8, 9, 10, 11) balls shade Nile Green
1 pair 3.75mm (US #5) needles
1 pair 5.5mm (US #9) needles
2 buttons

TENSION
18 sts & 24 rows = 10cm (4in) using 5.5mm needles over textured pattern
27 sts & 24 rows = 10cm (4in) using 5.5mm needles over ribbing

Standard Yarn Tension
23 sts & 28 rows = 10cm (4in) using 3.75mm needles over stocking stitch

ABBREVIATIONS
See page 13 for standard abbreviations

SIZING
Measurements given in centimetres followed by inches in parentheses

To Fit	81–86 (32–34)	86–92 (34–36)	92–97 (36–38)	102–106 (40–42)	106–112 (42–44)	112–117 (44–46)
Finished Measurements						
Actual Bust Size	80½ (31½)	83½ (33)	89½ (35)	95½ (37½)	101½ (40)	104½ (41)
Length to underarm	30½ (12)	32 (12½)	33 (13)	34½ (13½)	35½ (14)	37 (14½)
Armhole Depth	17½ (7)	19 (7½)	20 (8)	21½ (8½)	23 (9)	24 (9½)
Finished Length	48 (19)	51 (20)	53 (21)	56 (22)	58½ (23)	61 (24)
Shoulder to Shoulder	24½ (9½)	26½ (10½)	29 (11½)	31 (12¼)	33½ (13)	35½ (14)
Sleeve Length	46 (18)	47 (18½)	48 (19)	48 (19)	48 (19)	49½ (19½)

Garment shown in photographs is for first size 81–86 (32–34)

FRONT
Using 3.75mm needles cast on 79 (83, 91, 99, 107, 111) sts.
Row 1 (RS): * P1, K1, repeat from * to last st, P1.
Row 2: * K1, P1, repeat from * to last st, K1.
Row 3: * P1, K1, repeat from * to last st, P1.
Repeat rows 2–3 until 10cm (4in) of ribbing have been worked, finishing on row 3.

Next row: K1, * (P1, K1, P1, into next st), rib 5, repeat from * twice more, (P1, K1, P1, into next st), rib 4, P29 (33, 41, 49, 57, 61), P2tog, rib 4, ** (P1, K1, P1, into next st), rib 5, repeat from ** twice more, (P1, K1, P1, into next st), K1 (94, 98, 106, 114, 122, 126 sts).

Change to 5.5mm needles, and proceed as folls:
Row 1 (RS): [P1, K1] 16 (17, 19, 21, 23, 24) times, [YO, Sl1, K2tog, psso, YO, K3] 5 times, [K1, P1] 16 (17, 19, 21, 23, 24) times.
Row 2: [K1, P1] 16 (17, 19, 21, 23, 24) times, P30, [P1, K1] 16 (17, 19, 21, 23, 24) times.
Row 3: [P1, K1] 16 (17, 19, 21, 23, 24) times, [K3, YO, Sl1, K2tog, psso, YO] 5 times, [K1, P1] 16 (17, 19, 21, 23, 24) times.
Row 4: As row 2.

Repeat last 4 rows until work measures 30½ (32, 33, 34½, 35½, 37) cm (12, 12½, 13, 13½, 14, 14½ in) from commencement, ending with row 4.

Shape Armholes
Whilst maintaining pattern, cast off 8 sts at beg of next 2 rows 78 (82, 90, 98, 106, 110) sts, then work 2 sts tog at each end of next and every following row until 66 (72, 78, 84, 90, 96) sts rem.
Patt one row.

Next row (RS): Patt 33 (36, 39, 42, 45, 48) sts, turn and work on these sts for right half of front as folls:

1st, 3rd and 5th sizes only
Row 1 (WS): * P1, K1, rep from * to last st, P1.
Row 2: * K1, P1, rep from * to last K1.

2nd, 4th and 6th sizes only
Row 1 (WS): * P1, K1, rep from * to end.
Row 2: As row 1.

All sizes
Rep the last 2 rows until 9 (10, 11½, 13, 14, 15) cm (3½, 4, 4½, 5, 5½, 6 in) of ribbing has been worked above the patt panel, ending with row 2.

Shape Neck
Row 1 (WS): Cast off 8 (9, 10, 11, 12, 13) sts purlwise, rib to end (25, 27, 29, 31, 33, 35 sts).
Row 2: Rib to last 2 sts, work 2tog (24, 26, 28, 30, 32, 34 sts).
Cont in rib on rem sts until work measures 17½ (19, 20, 21½, 23, 24) cm (7, 7½, 8, 8½, 9, 9½ in) from commencement of armhole shaping, ending with a WS row.

Shape Shoulders
Cast off 8 (8, 9, 10, 10, 11) sts at beg of next and foll alt row.
Cast off rem 8 (10, 10, 10, 12, 12) sts.
With RS facing rejoin yarn to rem 33 (36, 39, 42, 45, 48) sts at centre front, and work in patt to end. Then set rib as folls:

1st, 3rd and 5th sizes only
Row 1 (WS): * K1, P1, rep from * to last st, K1.
Row 2: * P1, K1, rep from * to last P1.

2nd, 4th and 6th sizes only
Row 1 (WS): * K1, P1, rep from * to end.
Row 2: As row 1.

All sizes
Continue as set until work measures same as right front at commencement of neck shaping ending with row 1.

Shape Neck
Next row (RS): Cast off 8 (9, 10, 11, 12, 13) sts knitwise, rib to end (25, 27, 29, 31, 33, 35 sts).
Next row: Rib to last 2 sts, work 2tog (24, 26, 28, 30, 32, 34 sts).
Continue in patt until left front measures same as right, to start of shoulder shaping, ending with a RS row.

Shape Shoulders
Cast off 8 (8, 9, 10, 10, 11) sts at beg of next and foll alt row.
Cast off rem 8 (10, 10, 10, 12, 12) sts.

BACK
Using 3.75mm needles cast on 79 (83, 91, 99, 107, 111) sts.
Continue as for front until armhole shaping has been completed and 66 (72, 78, 84, 90, 96) sts rem. Continue in rib only until armhole measures same as front to start of shoulder shaping, ending with a WS row.

Shape Shoulders
Cast off 8 (8, 9, 10, 10, 11) sts at beg of next and foll 3 rows, then cast off 8 (10, 10, 10, 12, 12) sts at beg of foll 2 rows. Cast off rem 18 (20, 22, 24, 26, 28) sts.

SLEEVES
Using 3.75mm needles, cast on 44 (48, 52, 56, 60, 64) sts. Work in rib as for back until work measures 10cm (4in), and inc 0 (2, 4, 0, 2, 4) sts evenly across last WS row (44, 50, 56, 56, 62, 68 sts).
Using 5.5mm needles proceed in pattern as folls:
Row 1 (RS): K1 * YO, Sl1, K2tog, psso, YO, K3, repeat from * to last st, K1.
Row 2: P.
Row 3: K1, * K3, YO, Sl1, K2tog, psso, YO, repeat from * to last st, K1.
Row 4: P.
Repeat these 4 rows 6 (5, 4, 6, 5, 4) times more, then inc at each end of next and every foll 8th row until 56 (60, 64, 68, 72, 76) sts, taking additional sts into pattern.
Work in patt without further shaping until work measures 46 (47, 48, 48, 48, 49½) cm (18, 18½, 19, 19, 19, 19½ in).
Next row: * K1, P1, repeat from * to end.
Repeat last row 3 times.

Shape Sleeve Head
Continuing in rib patt, dec 1 st at each end of next and every foll row until 18 sts rem.
Cast off in rib.

COLLAR

Using 3.75mm needles, cast on 69 (71, 73, 75, 77, 79) sts.
Work as folls:

Row 1: * K1, P1, repeat from * to last st, K1.

Row 2: * P1, K1, repeat from * to last st, P1.

Row 3: As row 1.

Next row: Rib 20 (21, 22, 23, 24, 25), (P1, K1, P1) all into next st, [rib 3, (P1, K1, P1 into next st)] 7 times, rib 20 (21, 22, 23, 24, 25) (85, 87, 89, 91, 93, 95 sts).

Cont in rib until work measures 9 (9, 9, 10, 10, 10) cm (3½, 3½, 3½, 4, 4, 4 in).

Cast off loosely in rib.

MAKING UP

Press lightly on WS of work using a damp cloth. Join shoulder seams. Sew up side and sleeve seams. Slip stitch collar in place, matching centre back and corners to end of cast off sts on front. Fold back cast off sts as shown on photographs and sew button through both layers to hold in place. Darn in all ends.

Lady's Jumper

MATERIALS: Long Sleeve Model: 12 ozs. "Speedinit" Wool.
Short Sleeve Model: 9 ozs. "Speedinit" Wool.
1 pair No. 9 "Coploid" Knitting Needles.
1 pair No. 5 "Coploid" Knitting Needles.
3 Buttons.
1 Belt.

MEASUREMENTS: Length from top of shoulder to lower edge, 19 inches.
Width all round at underarm, to fit a 34-36 inch bust.
Length of sleeve seam, long, 19 inches; short, 3 inches.

TENSION: Using No. 5 needles, work to produce 4½ sts. and 6 rows to 1 square inch in smooth fabric (1 row K., 1 row P.), so that this piece of knitting would fit exactly the cut out Knitting Tension Measure on the opposite page.

ABBREVIATIONS: K.—knit. P.—purl. St.—stitch. Tog.—together. Wl.fwd.—wool forward. Sl.—slip. p.s.s.o.—pass the slipped st. over.

THE FRONT.

Using No. 9 needles, cast on 79 sts.

1st Row.—Working into the back of the sts., * P.1, K.1. Repeat from * to the last st., P.1.

2nd Row.—* K.1, P.1. Repeat from * to the last st., K.1.

3rd Row.—* P.1, K.1. Repeat from * to the last st., P.1.

Repeat the 2nd and 3rd rows until 4 inches of ribbing have been worked, finishing at the end of a 3rd row.

Next Row.—K.1, * (P.1, K.1, P.1 into the next st. to increase), rib 5 sts. Repeat from * twice more, (P.1, K.1, P.1 into the next st.), rib 4 sts., P.29, P.2 tog., rib 4 sts., ** (P.1, K.1, P.1 into the next st.), rib 5 sts. Repeat from ** twice more, (P.1, K.1, P.1 into the next st.), K.1.

There are now 94 sts. on the needle.

Using No. 5 needles, proceed as follows:—

1st Row.—(P.1, K.1) 16 times,* wl fwd., sl.1, K.2 tog., p.s.s.o., wl.fwd., K.3. Repeat from * to the last 32 sts., (K.1, P.1) 16 times.

2nd Row.—(K.1, P.1) 16 times, P. to the last 32 sts., (P.1, K.1) 16 times.

3rd Row.—(P.1, K.1) 16 times, * K.3, wl.fwd., sl.1, K.2 tog., p.s.s.o., wl.fwd. Repeat from * to the last 32 sts., (K.1, P.1) 16 times.

4th Row.—As the 2nd row.

Repeat the last 4 rows until the work measures 12 inches from the commencement, finishing at the end of a 4th row.

Shape the Armholes as follows:—

Keeping the continuity of the pattern and ribs correct, cast off 8 sts. at the beginning of the next 2 rows, then decrease by working 2 sts. together at both ends of the next row and every following row until 6 decreases in all have been worked and there are 66 sts. left on the needle.

Next Row.—(P.1, K.1) 9 times, * wl.fwd., sl.1, K.2 tog., p.s.s.o., wl.fwd., K.3. Repeat from * to the last 18 sts., (K.1, P.1) 9 times.

Next Row.—(K.1, P.1) 16 times, K.1, **turn** and work on these 33 sts. for the **Right Half of the Front** as follows:—

1st Row.—* P.1, K.1 Repeat from * to the last st., P.1.

2nd Row.—* K.1, P.1. Repeat from * to the last st., K.1.

Repeat the last 2 rows until 3½ inches of ribbing above the pattern panel have been worked, finishing at the front edge i.e. the end of a 2nd row.

Shape the Neck as follows:—

1st Row.—Cast off 8 sts. purlwise, rib to the end.

2nd Row.—Rib to the last 2 sts., P.2 tog.

Continue in rib on the remaining 24 sts. until the work measures 6½ inches from the commencement of the armhole, finishing at the neck edge.

Shape the Shoulder as follows:—

1st Row.—Rib to the last 8 sts., turn.

2nd Row.—Rib to the neck.

3rd Row.—Rib to the last 16 sts., turn.

4th Row.—Rib to the neck. Cast off.

Rejoining the wool to the remaining sts., cast on 2 sts. and proceed for the **Left Half of the Front** as follows:—

Working into the back of the cast on sts. on the first row only, proceed in rib to match the side just worked, casting off 10 sts. knitwise for the neck instead of 8 sts., the neck and shoulder shapings being worked at opposite edges.

THE BACK.

Work exactly as the instructions for the Front up to the completion of the armhole shaping, when 66 sts. remain on the needle.

Next Row.—(P.1, K.1) 8 times, (P.1, K.1 into the next st.), * P.1, K.1. Repeat from * to the last st., P.1. (67 sts. now on the needle.)

Now proceed in rib until the armhole measures the same as on the Front.

Shape the Shoulders as follows:—

1st and 2nd Row.—Rib to the last 8 sts., turn.

3rd and 4th Rows.—Rib to the last 16 sts., turn. Break off wool. Slip all the sts. on to one needle, rejoin the wool and cast off all across.

THE LONG SLEEVE.

Using No. 9 needles, cast on 44 sts.

Working into the back of the sts. on the first row only as at the commencement of the work, proceed in K.1, P.1 rib for 4 inches.

Using No. 5 needles, proceed in pattern as follows:—

1st Row.—K.1, * wl.fwd., sl.1, K.2 tog., p.s.s.o., wl.fwd., K.3. Repeat from * to the last st., K.1.

2nd Row.—Purl.

3rd Row.—K.1, * K.3, wl.fwd., sl.1, K.2 tog., p.s.s.o., wl.fwd. Repeat from * to the last st., K.1.

4th Row.—Purl.

Repeat these 4 rows 6 times more.

Now increase as follows:—

1st Row.—Increase by working into the front and back of the first st., * wl.fwd., sl.1, K.2 tog., p.s.s.o., wl.fwd., K.3. Repeat from * to the last st., wl.fwd., K.1.

2nd and every alternate row:—Purl.

3rd Row.—K.2 tog., wl.fwd., * K.3, wl.fwd., sl.1, K.2 tog., p.s.s.o., wl.fwd. Repeat from * to the last 2 sts., K.2.

5th Row.—K.2. Work as the 1st pattern row from * to the last 2 sts., wl.fwd., K.2 tog.

7th Row.—As the 3rd row.

9th Row.—Increase in the first st., K.1. Work as a 1st pattern row from * to the last 2 sts., wl.fwd., K.2.

11th Row.—K.1, sl.1, K.1, p.s.s.o., wl.fwd. Work as a 3rd pattern row from * to the last 3 sts., K.3.

13th Row.—K.3. Work as a 1st pattern row from * to the last 3 sts., wl.fwd., K.2 tog., K.1.

15th Row.—As the 11th row.

17th Row.—Increase in the first st., K.2. Work as a 1st pattern row from * to the last 2 sts., wl.fwd., K.2.

19th Row.—K.1, * wl.fwd., sl.1, K.2 tog., p.s.s.o., wl.fwd., K.3. Repeat from * to the last st., K.1.

21st Row.—K.1, * K.3, wl.fwd., sl.1, K.2 tog., p.s.s.o., wl.fwd. Repeat from * to the last st., K.1.

23rd Row.—As the 19th row.

25th Row.—K.1, wl.fwd. Work as a 3rd pattern row from * to the last st., increase in the last st.

27th Row.—K.2. Work as a 1st pattern row from * to the last 2 sts., wl.fwd., K.2 tog.

29th Row.—K.2 tog., wl.fwd. Work as a 3rd pattern row from * to the last 2 sts., K.2.

31st Row.—As the 27th row.

33rd Row.—K.2, wl.fwd. Work as a 3rd pattern row from * to the last 2 sts., increase in the next st., K.1.

35th Row.—K.3. Work as a 1st pattern row from * to the last 3 sts., wl.fwd., sl.1, K.1, p.s.s.o., K.1.

37th Row.—K.1, sl.1, K.1, p.s.s.o., wl.fwd. Work as a 3rd pattern row from * to the last 3 sts., K.3.

39th Row.—As the 35th row.

41st Row.—K.1, wl.fwd., K.2 tog., wl.fwd. Work as a 3rd pattern row from * to the last 3 sts., K.1, increase in the next st., K.1.

43rd Row.—K.1, * K.3, wl.fwd., sl.1, K.2 tog., p.s.s.o., wl.fwd. Repeat from * to the last st., K.1.

44th Row.—Purl.

There are now 56 sts. on the needle.

Continue without further increase, repeating the 4 pattern rows until the work measures 18 inches.

Next Row.—* K.1, P.1. Repeat from * to the end.

Repeat the last row 3 times more.

Shape the Top as follows:—

Working in K.1, P.1 rib, decrease at both ends of every following row until 18 sts. remain. Cast off.

Work another sleeve in the same manner.

THE SHORT SLEEVE.

Using No. 9 needles, cast on 56 sts.

Working into the back of the sts. on the first row only, proceed in K.1, P.1 rib for one inch.

Change to No. 5 needles and continue in rib until the work measures 3 inches.

Shape the top and complete as the instruction for the long sleeve.

Work another sleeve in the same manner.

THE COLLAR.

Using No. 9 needles, cast on 69 sts.

Working into the back of the sts. on the first row only, proceed as follows:—

1st Row.—* K.1, P.1. Repeat from * to the last st., K.1.

2nd Row.—* P.1, K.1. Repeat from * to the last st., P.1.

3rd Row.—As the 1st row.

Next Row.—(P.1, K.1) 10 times, (P.1, K.1, P.1 into the next st.), * rib 3 sts., (P.1, K.1, P.1 into the next st.). Repeat from * to the last 20 sts., (K.1, P.1) 10 times.

There are now 85 sts. on the needle.

Continue in rib on these sts. until the work measures 3½ inches. Cast off in rib **loosely.**

MAKE UP.

Omitting all ribbing with the exception of the top of the sleeves, press the work on the wrong side with a damp cloth and a hot iron.

Stitch the shoulders of the Back and Front together.

Stitch the 2 cast on sts. at the base of the front opening neatly on to the wrong side.

Stitch the side and sleeve seams and stitch the sleeves into position.

Mark the centre of the collar and place the cast on edge of this to the centre of the back of the neck.

Stitch round the neck leaving free the cast off sts. at each side of the front opening.

Work 3 loops on to the Right half of the front opening at equal distances apart.

Attach 3 buttons on to the Left side to correspond.

Work a loop on each side seam in the required position through which to pass the belt.

Dainty and Useful

MATERIALS
Excelana 4 Ply Luxury Wool 100% pure new British wool (159m/174yds per 50g ball)
9 balls shade Ruby Red
1 pair 5mm (US #8) needles
Crochet hook
Cardboard

TENSION
19 sts & 30 rows using 5mm needles over 12 row stitch pattern

Standard Yarn Tension
28 sts & 36 rows = 10cm (4in) using 3mm needles over stocking stitch

ABBREVIATIONS
See page 13 for standard abbreviations

MEASUREMENTS
101cm × 100cm (40in × 39in) before blocking

Using 5mm needles cast on 192 sts (or any number divisible by 12 if a bigger or smaller square is required) and work in pattern as folls:

Row 1 (RS): * K2tog, YO, K10 repeat from * to end.
Row 2: K9, YO, K2tog, * K10, YO, K2tog, repeat from * to last st, K1.
Row 3: K2, K2tog, YO, * K10, K2tog, YO, repeat from * to last 8 sts, K8.
Row 4: K7, YO, K2tog, * K10, YO, K2tog, repeat from * to last 3 sts, K3.
Row 5: K4, K2tog, YO, * K10, K2tog, YO, repeat from * to last 6 sts, K6.
Row 6: K5, YO, K2tog, * K10, YO, K2tog, repeat from * to last 5 sts, K5.
Row 7: K6, K2tog, YO, * K10, K2tog, YO, repeat from * to last 4 sts, K4.
Row 8: K3, YO, K2tog, * K10, YO, K2tog, repeat from * to last 7 sts, K7.
Row 9: K8, K2tog, YO, * K10, K2tog, YO, repeat from * to last 2 sts, K2.
Row 10: K1, YO, K2tog, * K10, YO, K2tog, repeat from * to last 9 sts, K9.
Row 11: * K10, K2tog, YO, repeat from * to last 12 sts, K12.
Row 12: K11, * YO, K2tog, K10, repeat from * to last 13 sts, YO, K2tog, K11.
Repeat these 12 rows of pattern until the shawl measures approx 100cm (39in) ending with row 12. Cast off.

MAKING UP
Dampen shawl and pin out to size on a blanket or frame. Steam gently with a warm iron without touching surface. Leave to thoroughly dry before removing pins.

FRINGE
Using a piece of cardboard about 5cm (2in) wide, wind the wool around the card and cut along one edge making strands of wool 10cm (4in) long. Using a crochet hook take two lengths of the wool and double into two, place the crochet hook through a stitch of the knitting along one side, pull the loop through then pull the ends of wool through the loop, thus forming a knot. Repeat all round the outer edges of shawl, or as preferred.

DAINTY AND USEFUL

This Shawl is Easy to Knit and the Pattern is Reversible

an attractive pattern which is easy to knit. To make it you will require :—

150z. Baldwin and Walker's Ladyship Ripple-sheen.

1 pair knitting needles, No. 6.

Measurement : 45in. square, not including the fringe.

Tension before pressing : 5½ st. to 1in. in width ; 4½ ridges to 1in. in depth.

Note.—If the needles stated do not produce this tension, try different sizes until you get it correct.

Alteration in Size.—For a larger shawl, use thicker needles. or a size which produces fewer stitches to the inch. For a smaller shawl, use finer needles, or a size which produces a larger number of stitches to the inch.

Abbreviations.—K., knit; st., stitches; m. 1, make a stitch by bringing the wool forward ; tog., together; rep., repeat.

Begin by casting on 192 st. (or any number divisible by 12 if a bigger or smaller square is required) and work in the pattern as follows :

1st row.—* K. 2 tog., m. 1, k. 10. Rep. from * to end of row.

2nd row.—K. 9. m. 1, k. 2 tog., * k. 10, m. 1, k. 2 tog. Rep. from * to the last st., k. 1.

3rd row.—K. 2, k. 2 tog., m. 1, * k. 10, k. 2 tog., m. 1. Rep. from * to the last 8 st., k. 8.

4th row.—K. 7, m. 1, k. 2 tog., * k. 10, m. 1, k. 2 tog. Rep. from * to the last 3 st., k. 3.

5th row.—K. 4, k. 2 tog., m. 1, * k. 10, k. 2 tog., m. 1. Rep. from * to the last 6 st., k. 6.

6th row.—K. 5, m. 1, k. 2 tog., * k. 10, m. 1, k. 2 tog. Rep. from * to the last 5 st., k. 5.

7th row.—K. 6, k. 2 tog., m. 1, * k. 10, k. 2 tog., m. 1. Rep. from * to the last 4 st., k. 4.

8th row.—K. 3, m. 1, k. 2 tog., * k. 10, m. 1, k. 2 tog. Rep. from * to the last 7 st., k. 7.

9th row.—K. 8, k. 2 tog., m. 1, * k. 10, k. 2 tog., m. 1. Rep. from * to the last 2 st., k. 2.

10th row.—K. 1, m. 1, k. 2 tog., * k. 10, m. 1, k. 2 tog. Rep. from * to the last 9 st., k. 9.

11th row.—* K. 10, k. 2 tog., m. 1. Rep. from * to the last 12 st., k. 12.

12th row.—* K. 11, * m. 1, k. 2 tog., k. 10. Rep. from * to the last 11 st., k. 11.

Repeat these 12 rows of pattern until the shawl measures 45in. square. Cast off.

THE FRINGE

Using a piece of cardboard about 2in. wide, wind the wool around the cardboard, and cut along one edge, making the strands of wool 4in. long. Using a crochet hook, take two of the lengths of wool and double into two, place the crochet hook through a stitch of the knitting along one side, pull the loop through, then pull the ends of wool through the loop, thus forming a knot.

Repeat all round the outer edges of shawl.

I N spite of the variety of bed-jackets and wraps one sees in the shops nowadays, the hand-knitted shawl still holds its own on account of its comfort and convenience.

Elderly folk appreciate the extra warmth across the shoulders which a shawl affords ; being more easily slipped on it may be preferable to a sleeved wrap for the invalid who can only sit up for short periods ; and in the outfit of the young baby, of course, the shawl is an important item.

Illustrated here is a reversible shawl of

A Swagger Coat

MATERIALS
Fyberspates Scrumptious Aran 45% silk/55% merino (165m per 100g skein)
8 (9, 11, 12, 13, 14) skeins shade 403 (Water)
1 pair 5.5mm (US #9) needles
2 buttons

TENSION
16 sts & 23 rows = 10cm (4in) using 5.5mm needles over 2 row pattern

Standard Yarn Tension
18½ sts & 24 rows = 10cm (4in) using 5mm needles over stocking stitch

ABBREVIATIONS
See page 13 for standard abbreviations

SIZING
Measurements given in centimetres followed by inches in parentheses

To Fit	76–81 (30–32)	86–92 (34–36)	97–102 (38–40)	107–112 (42–44)	117–122 (46–48)	127–132 (50–52)
Finished Measurements						
Actual Bust Size	95½ (37½)	107 (42)	118 (46½)	129½ (51)	140½ (55)	152 (60)
Length to underarm	81 (32)	81 (32)	81 (32)	81 (32)	81 (32)	81 (32)
Armhole Depth	20½ (8)	21½ (8½)	23 (9)	24 (9½)	25½ (10)	26½ (10½)
Finished Length	101½ (40)	102½ (40½)	104 (41)	105 (41½)	106½ (42)	107½ (42½)
Shoulder to shoulder	34½ (13½)	35½ (14)	37 (14½)	38 (15)	39½ (15½)	40½ (16)
Sleeve Length	47 (18½)	47 (18½)	47 (18½)	48 (19)	48 (19)	48 (19)

Garment shown in photographs for first size 76–81 (30–32)

PATTERN NOTES
Please note that this coat is designed to be open at the front and for the front sections not to meet. The back of the coat is also narrower than the combined front pieces which means the side seams of the coat sit slightly further back under the arm than usual. This allows for a neat fit to the back of the coat without excess fabric to flare out and change the line of the coat. The extra stitches in the fronts allow for the bust and for movement when wearing the coat.

BACK
Using 5.5mm needles, cast 65 (73, 81, 89, 97, 105) sts.
K 11 rows for border. Commence working in patt as folls:
Row 1 (RS): K.
Row 2: K1, * P7 (8, 9, 10, 11, 12), K1, repeat from * to end.
These 2 rows form patt, rep until work measures 81cm (32in) or required length, ending with a WS row.

Shape Armholes
Dec 1 (2, 2, 3, 3, 3) sts at beg of next 10 (4, 6, 6, 6, 8) rows then 0 (1, 1, 1, 1, 1) sts at beg of foll 0 (8, 10, 10, 16, 16) rows (55, 57, 59, 61, 63, 65 sts). Work in patt without further shaping until work measures 20½ (21½, 23, 24, 25½, 26½) cm (8, 8½, 9, 9½, 10, 10½ in) ending with a WS row.

Shape Shoulders
Cast off 5 sts at beg of next 8 (8, 8, 6, 6, 6) rows then 0 (0, 0, 6, 7, 7) sts at beg of foll 0 (0, 0, 2, 2, 2) rows (15, 17, 19, 19, 19, 21 sts). Cast off rem sts.

LEFT FRONT
Using 5.5mm needles, cast on 44 (49, 54, 59, 64, 69) sts.
K 11 rows for border. Commence working in patt as folls:
Row 1 (RS): K.
Row 2: K4 for front border * P7 (8, 9, 10, 11, 12), K1, repeat from * to end.
Rep these 2 rows until work measures same as back to armhole ending with a WS row.

Shape Armhole

Whilst maintaining patt, cast off 2 (3, 3, 3, 3, 3) sts at beg of next row and every foll alt row 3 (3, 5, 7, 7, 7) times more (36, 37, 36, 35, 40, 45 sts), then cast off 1 st at beg of 5 (6, 5, 3, 7, 12) foll alt rows (31, 31, 31, 32, 33, 33 sts). Work without shaping until front is 12 rows shorter than back to start of shoulder shaping, ending with a RS row.

Shape Neck

Cast off 3 sts at beg of next row (28, 28, 28, 29, 30, 30 sts) and every foll alt row twice more (22, 22, 22, 23, 24, 24 sts), then dec 1 st at beg of every foll alt row twice more (20, 20, 20, 21, 22, 22 sts).

Work without further shaping until armhole measures same as back to start of shoulder shaping, ending with a WS row.

Shape Shoulder

Cast off 5 sts at beg of next and 3 (3, 3, 4, 4, 4) foll alt rows then cast off rem 0 (0, 0, 6, 7, 7) sts on foll alt row.

RIGHT FRONT

Using 5.5mm needles, cast on 44 (49, 54, 59, 64, 69) sts
K 11 rows for border.
Commence working in patt as folls:
Row 1 (RS): K.
Row 2: * K1, P7 (8, 9, 10, 11, 12), repeat from, * until 4 sts rem, K4 for front border.
Rep these 2 rows until work measures same as back to armhole ending with a RS row.

Shape Armhole

Cast off 2 (3, 3, 3, 3, 3) sts at beg of next row and every foll alt row 3 (3, 5, 7, 7, 7) times more (36, 37, 36, 35, 40, 45 sts), then cast off 1 st at beg of 5 (6, 5, 3, 7, 12) foll alt rows (31, 31, 31, 32, 33, 33 sts). Work without shaping until front is 11 rows shorter than back to start of shoulder shaping, ending with a WS row.

Shape Neck

Cast off 3 sts at beg of next row (28, 28, 28, 29, 30, 30 sts) and every foll alt row twice more (22, 22, 22, 23, 24, 24 sts) then dec 1 st at beg of every foll alt row twice more (20, 20, 20, 21, 22, 22 sts).

Work without further shaping until armhole measures same as back to start of shoulder shaping, ending with a RS row.

Shape Shoulder

Cast off 5 sts at beg of next and 3 (3, 3, 4, 4, 4) foll alt rows then cast off rem 0 (0, 0, 6, 7, 7) sts on foll alt row.

SLEEVES

Working from the top of sleeve, cast on 15 (17, 19, 21, 23, 25) sts using 5.5mm needles.
Set-up row (WS): P7 (8, 9, 10, 11, 12), K1, P7 (8, 9, 10, 11, 12).

Now work inc pattern to shape sleeve head.
Inc 1 st at each end of next 16 (18, 20, 22, 24, 26) rows, and take increased sts into 7 (8, 9, 10, 11, 12) by 1 rib as worked on back and fronts.
Work without shaping for a further 14 rows.
Cast on 3 sts at beg of next 2 rows (53, 59, 65, 71, 77, 83 sts). Work 6 rows without shaping.

Sleeve Shaping

Dec 1 st at each end of next and every foll 8th (8th, 8th, 6th, 6th, 6th) row until 43 (49, 53, 55, 57, 59) sts rem.
Work without further shaping until sleeve measures 44½ (44½, 44½, 46, 46, 46) cm (17½, 17½, 17½, 18, 18, 18 in), ending with a RS row.
K 11 rows. Cast off all rem sts.

POCKET (Make two)

Using 5.5mm needles, cast on 28 (31, 34, 37, 40, 43) sts and work in patt as folls:
Row 1 (RS): K.
Row 2: K4, * P7 (8, 9, 10, 11, 12), K1, repeat from * to end.
These 2 rows form patt. Rep until 34 (38, 42, 46, 50, 54) rows have been worked. Cast off.

TIE COLLAR

Using 5.5mm needles, cast on 20 sts.
K 9 rows, with row 9 being treated as WS row.
Work vertical buttonhole as folls:
Next row (RS): K9, Sl1 knitwise, turn and work on these 10 sts only leaving rem 10 sts on holder.
Row 1: P1, K9.
Row 2: Sl1 knitwise, K9.
These 2 rows form patt, rep these rows a further 3 times, then work row 1 once more. Leave sts on spare needle or holder – don't break yarn.
Using a second ball of yarn, rejoin yarn to rem 10 sts at centre leaving a long end for reinforcing the buttonhole.
Next row (RS): Sl1 knitwise, K9.
Next row: K9, P1.
Rep these 2 rows a further 3 times. Break off yarn leaving a long end once again. Place both sets of sts on to one needle with first st having yarn length attached. Knit across all sts (20 sts).
Continuing to work in garter st, dec 1 st at each end of next and every foll 6th row until 10 sts rem. Work a further 131 (133, 135, 135, 135, 137) rows without shaping.
Inc at each end of next and every foll 6th until 20 sts ending with a WS row.
Work buttonhole as before.
K 9 rows. Cast off.

MAKING UP

Press work firmly with a damp cloth with WS of work facing. Join shoulder seams. Sew side and sleeve seams. Insert sleeve taking care to match centre of sleeve head with shoulder seam and matching side seams.

Position pockets at desired distance from underarm, matching pocket edge to first garter st ridge at centre front. (see garment photos for further guidance). Sew pockets in place, from RS of work.

Using lengths of yarn left on buttonholes, overstitch ends of buttonholes to strengthen.

Pin centre of tie to centre back of coat. Starting at this point slip stitch one end of the band into place, stopping 5cm (2in) short of beginning of garter st border. Leave a gap of 3cm (1½in) then continue to sew in place for a further 2cm. Repeat with other end of band.

Position one button approx 14cm (5½in) down from shoulder seam on 2nd full stocking stitch stripe from armhole edge on each front piece.
Darn in all ends.

To Fasten Tie

Draw left end of tie through the right neck slot from the inside and fasten to the right button then draw the right end of tie through the left front slot from outside to inside then bring back over the top of the tie and fasten to the left button.

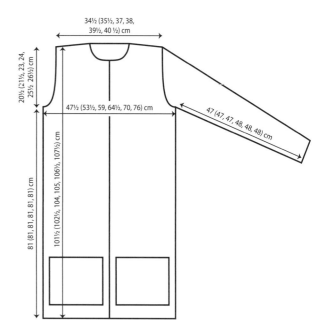

A SWAGGER COAT

Designed for an Extra-Thick Wool it is Very Quickly Made.

HERE is the coat ideal for the country tramp, as it combines cosiness without weight and is just the right length. The broad stripes give a smart and slim effect, which suits all figures.

MATERIALS: 1½ lb. of W.B. "Kwiknit" wool in blue, a pair of knitting needles No. 3 and No. 5, and two large buttons. (The nearest equivalent to the size of this wool is Double Knitting wool.)

TENSION AND MEASUREMENTS: Worked at a tension of 4 sts. to the inch in width with the No. 3 needles, the following measurements are attained after pressing: across each front at the underarm, 12 inches; across the back at the same place, 17 inches; front and back length from shoulder to hem, 38 inches; side seam, 30 inches; sleeve seam, 17 inches.

ABBREVIATIONS: K., knit plain; P., purl; tog., together; inc., increase (by working into the back and front of the same st.); st., stitch; dec., decrease (by taking 2 sts. tog. according to the pattern).

To Work the Back

BEGIN at the lower edge and, using No. 3 needles, cast on 65 sts. K. 11 rows for border.
Now work the pattern as follows:
1st row: With the right side facing, all knit.
2nd row: K. 1, * p. 7, k. 1, repeat from * to end.
Repeat these 2 rows 72 times more to armholes.
To Shape the Armholes: Cast off 1 st. at the beginning of the next 10 rows, which leaves 55 sts. Work 26 rows straight up to the shoulder-line.
To Slope the Shoulders: Cast off 5 sts. at the beginning of the next 8 rows. Cast off the remaining sts.

THE LEFT FRONT.—Begin at the lower edge and cast on 44 sts. with the No. 3 needles. K. 11 rows for the border.
Now work in pattern as follows:
1st row: With right side facing, all knit.
2nd row: (for left front only): k. 4 for front border, * p. 7, k. 1, repeat from * to end.
(On the right front the 2nd row is reversed and worked as follows: * k. 1, p. 7, repeat from * until 4 sts. remain, k. 4 front border.)
Repeat these 2 rows until there are as many rows up to the armhole as on the back. (On the right front work one row more.)
To Shape the Front Armhole: Cast off 2 sts. at the beginning of the next row, and every alternate row (arm end) 4 times, then cast off 1 st. at the beginning of alternate rows (arm end) 5 times, which leaves 31 sts. Work 12 rows in pattern with k. 4 border at the front end to the neck.
To shape the neck cast off 3 sts. from the beginning of the next row and following alternate rows (neck end) 3 times, after which cast off 1 st. from the beginning of alternate row (neck end) 3 times, which leaves 19 sts.
Work 2 rows up to the shoulder line.
To slope the shoulder, cast off 5 sts. from the beginning of the next row and two following alternate rows (arm end) then cast off the 4 remaining sts.
THE RIGHT FRONT.—Work as given for the left front, with alterations as stated.
THE SLEEVE.—Begin at the top and using No. 3 needles, cast on 15 sts. Work one row thus: P. 7, k. 1, p. 7.
Now work the following increase pattern:
1st row (and every odd row): With right side facing, inc. in the first st., k. until 1 st. remains, inc. in the last st.
2nd row: P. 1 and k. 1 in the 1st st., p. 7, * k. 1, p. 7, in following patterns repeat from *, inc. in the last st.
4th row: K. 1 and p. 1 in the first st., p. 1, k. 1, * p. 7, k. 1, repeat from * until 2 remain, p. 1, inc. in the last st.
6th row: K. 1 and p. 1 in the 1st st., p. 3, k. 1, * p. 7, k. 1, repeat from * until 4 remain, p. 3, inc. in the last st.
8th row: K. 1 and p. 1 in the 1st st., p. 5, k. 1, * p. 7, k. 1, repeat from * until 6 remain, p. 5, inc. in the last st.
Repeat these 8 rows until there are 47 sts. on the needle. Cast on 3 sts. at the beginning of each of the next 2 rows, making 53 sts. altogether for the full width of the sleeve. Work 6 rows straight. To slope the sleeve seam take 2 sts. tog. at each end of the next row, and every following 8th row, until the sts. are reduced to 43. Work 43 rows, then k. 11 rows and cast off.
Work the second sleeve in the same manner.

THE POCKETS.—With No. 3 needles cast on 27 sts. and work the two pattern rows as given on the left front 17 times (34 rows).
Cast off and work the second pocket in the same manner.

THE TIE COLLAR.—With No. 5 needles cast on 20 sts. and k. 9 rows. For the buttonhole k. 7 rows on the first 10 sts., then sl.-st. down the end of this row (by bringing the wool through each st. with a crochet hook to avoid cutting the wool), then on the second set of 10 sts. k. 7 rows.
Now work on all the sts. and dec. on the next row (by taking tog. the 3rd and 4th st. from each end) and every following 6th row until only 10 sts. remain. K. 131 rows.
Now inc. in the third st. from each end of the next row and every following 6th row until the 5th inc. row is worked with 20 sts. Work the buttonhole as before, then on all the sts. k. 9 rows and cast off.

To Make Up the Coat

FIRST press all with a damp cloth over the wrong side of the work.
Sew the shoulder seams, taking only 1 st. from each side at a time, then sew the top of the sleeves into the armholes and press these seams while the work is open. Join the side and sleeve seams, putting the sleeve to the side seam in one continuous line and press. Sew the pockets to the right side of the coat, placing them so that the k. 4 border forms the top edge.
Sew the edge of the collar to the wrong side of the neck, beginning at the first inc. row of the collar, for half an inch only, then leave a gap of 1½ inches to form a slot, and continue sewing round the neck edge to within 2 inches of the opposite end of the collar; leave a similar gap for the second slot and sew the collar to the last half inch of the neck, leaving this end of the tie long enough to pass round the other end. Press all seams and sew one button on each front, 5½ inches down from the shoulder at the second broad stripe, in position to meet the tie buttonholes.
To fasten the tie collar in wear, draw the left end through the right neck slot from the inside, and fasten to the right-front button. Draw the right tie end through the left neck slot from underneath, and over the opposite part of the collar which is buttoned down, then underneath in a tying motion, and fasten this end to the left front button.

The broad stripes give the coat a very slimming effect—which is most becoming.

The cravat collar is very neat and cosy and gives a charming finish to the coat.

A Fez is so Piquant!

MATERIALS
Baby Rooster 100% superwash merino wool (125m/137yds per 50g ball)
2 balls shade 405 (Ice Gem)
1 pair 4.5mm (US #7) needles
1 pair 3.5mm (US #5) needles

TENSION
20 sts & 24 rows = 10cm (4in) using 4.5mm needles over stocking stitch
18 garter stitch ridges = 10cm (4in) using 4.5mm needles

Standard Yarn Tension
25 sts & 34 rows = 10cm (4in) using 3.25mm needles over stocking stitch

ABBREVIATIONS
See page 13 for standard abbreviations

SIZING
Circumference = 58cm (23in)

BRIM (Worked sideways)
Using 3.5mm needles, cast on 16 sts. Work in garter st
(knit every row) for 181 rows. Cast off, leaving one stitch
on the needle.

CROWN
Using the needle with one stitch on it, pick up and knit 1 st
on every garter st ridge around long edge of brim (90 sts).
Commencing with a P row, work 4 rows in stocking stitch.
Next row (WS): [P4, Pfb] 18 times (108 sts).
Change to 4.5mm needles and commencing with a knit row,
work 30 rows in stocking stitch.

Row 1 (Dec): [K7, K2tog] 12 times (96 sts).
P next and every foll alt row.
Row 3 (Dec): [K6, K2tog] 12 times (84 sts).
Row 5 (Dec): [K5, K2tog] 12 times (72 sts).
Continue in this way, dec on every alt row, working 1 st less
between decs on each alt row, until 7th dec you have [K1,
K2tog] 12 times and 24 sts rem.
Row 15: K2tog 12 times (12 sts).
Row 17: K2tog 6 times (6 sts).
Work 9 rows in stocking stitch, on these 6 sts, then break
yarn leaving a length approx 46cm (18in) long attached.
Draw yarn through sts and fasten off.

MAKING UP
Turn work to WS and
commencing at top, sew edges
to together as far as garter
stitch brim. Work seam on RS
of brim. Darn in all ends. Fold
up brim and catch into place.

Made in camel hair wool, this Fez looks like an extravagance!

A Fez is so Piquant!

Perhaps You Like To Look Sophisticated ? Then The Fez Is For You !

THE CROWN

WITH the No. 11 needle pick up and k. 1 st. at the end of each ridge on the long side of the brim. Work 4 rows of s.s.

NEXT ROW : (p. 7, p. in the front and back of the next st. to increase one) 12 times, 108 sts. on.

Change to No. 7 needles and work 16 rows in s.s., which finishes the straight part of the hat, so if a deeper crown is desired before shaping the top, more rows may be worked here.

YOU can make this smart Fez so easily in a day ! And it is quite the newest " pull-on " you can wear.

MATERIALS : Two ounces of Greenock Camel Hair and Wool (4-ply) in fawn (obtainable only at one of the branches of the Scotch Wool & Hosiery Stores), a pair of No. 7 and No. 11 bone knitting needles.

ABBREVIATIONS : K., knit plain ; p., purl ; tog., together ; s.s., stocking-stitch (k. on the right side of the work and p. back) ; st., stitch. Directions in brackets are worked the number of times stated immediately after the brackets.

TO WORK

BEGIN with the brim and cast on 16 sts. with the No. 7 needles, and k. plain 191 rows (96 ridges) for all round the brim. Cast off, leaving 1 st. on the needle which pass on to a No. 11 needle.

1ST DECREASE ROW : (k. 7, k. 2 tog.) 12 times.

Purl 1 row and every alternate row.

2ND DECREASE ROW : (K. 6, k. 2 tog.) 12 times.

3RD DECREASE ROW : (K. 5, k. 2 tog.) 12 times.

Continue in this way decreasing on every alternate row, and getting 1 st. less between the decreases on each subsequent row, until in the 7th decrease row you have (k. 1, k. 2 tog.) 12 times.

On the 8th decrease row k. 2 tog. 12 times.

9TH DECREASE ROW : K. 2 tog. 6 times.

On the remaining 6 sts. work 9 rows in s.s., then cut the wool leaving about half a yard, and darn through these sts. Leave the wool hanging for the present, while the cap is being pressed on the wrong side with a damp cloth over the knitting. Do not press the ridged brim. Now continue sewing the back seam of the crown and brim, and press this lightly.

Cryscelle

MATERIALS

Knitshop Mulberry Silk 100% mulberry silk (250m per 100g skein)
4 (5, 5, 6) skeins shade Black – MC
3 (3, 4, 4) skeins shade Silver White – CC
1 pair 2.75mm (US #2) needles
1 pair 3mm (US #2–3) needles
1 pair 10mm (US #15) needles
Crochet hook
5 buttons
Stitch holders

TENSION

27 sts & 34 rows = 10cm (4in) using 3mm needles over stocking stitch
Drop stitch pattern on sleeve depth of one rep = 4cm (1½in)

Standard Yarn Tension

25–30 sts = 10cm (4in) using 2.5–3.5mm needles

ABBREVIATIONS

See page 13 for standard abbreviations

SIZING

Measurements given in centimetres followed by inches in parentheses

To Fit	76–81 (30–32)	86–92 (34–36)	97–102 (38–40)	107–112 (42–44)
Finished Measurements				
Actual Bust Size	89 (35)	101 (40)	112½ (44½)	124½ (49)
Length to underarm	28 (11)	29 (11½)	32 (12½)	33 (13)
Armhole Depth	15½ (6)	16½ (6½)	19 (7½)	20 (8)
Finished Length	43½ (17)	45½ (18)	51 (20)	53 (21)
Shoulder to Shoulder	31 (12)	37 (14½)	43 (17)	49 (19½)
Sleeve Length	44 (17½)	47 (18½)	47 (18½)	51 (20)

Garment shown in photographs is for second size 86–92 (34–36)

FRONT

Using 2.75mm needles and MC, cast on 106 (122, 138, 154) sts.

Row 1 (RS): * K1, P1, repeat from * to end.

Rep this row until rib measures 6½cm (2½in).

Change to 3mm needles and commencing with a K row, work 4 rows in stocking stitch. Inc 1 st at each end of next and every foll 6th (6th, 8th, 8th) row 10 times (128, 144, 160, 176 sts). Continue without further shaping until work measures 28 (29, 32, 33) cm (11, 11½, 12½, 13 in) ending with a WS row.

Shape Armholes

Cast off 12 sts at beg of next 2 rows (104, 120, 136, 152 sts), then cast off 2 sts at beg of foll 2 rows (100, 116, 132, 148 sts).

Work 2 sts tog at each end of foll 8 rows (84, 100, 116, 132 sts).

Continue without further shaping, until armhole measures 15½ (16½, 19, 20) cm (6, 6½, 7½, 8 in) ending with a WS row.

Shape Shoulders

Cast off 6 (8, 10, 12) sts at beg of next 6 rows. Cast off rem 48 (52, 56, 60) sts.

BACK

Using 2.75mm needles and MC, cast on 90 (106, 122, 138) sts.

Row 1: * K1, P1, rep from * to end.

Repeat this row until rib measures 6½cm (2½in).

Change to 3mm needles.

Commencing with a K row, work 4 rows in stocking stitch. Inc 1 st at each end of next and every foll 6th (6th, 8th, 8th) row until 112 (128, 144, 160) sts. Continue without further shaping until work measures 28 (29, 32, 33) cm (11, 11½, 12½, 13 in) ending with a WS row.

Shape Armholes

Cast off 7 sts at beg of next 2 rows (98, 114, 130, 146 sts). Work 2 sts tog at each end of foll 7 rows (84, 100, 116, 132 sts).

Continue without further shaping, until armhole measures 5½ (6½, 9, 10) cm (2, 2½, 3½, 4 in) ending with a WS row.

Divide for Back Opening
Next row (RS): K41 (49, 57, 65) cast off foll 2 sts, K to end.
Next row: P41 (49, 57, 65), then slip rem 41 (49, 57, 65) sts onto a holder or waste yarn.
Work on rem sts for left back as folls:
Continue in stocking stitch until armhole measures 15½ (16½, 19, 20) cm (6, 6½, 7½, 8 in) ending with a RS row.

Shape Shoulder
Cast off 6 (8, 10, 12) sts at beg of next and foll 2 alt rows (23, 25, 27, 29 sts). Cast off rem 23 (25, 27, 29) sts.
With WS facing rejoin yarn to rem 41 (49, 57, 65) sts.
Next row: P.
Continue in stocking stitch until armhole measures 15½ (16½, 19, 20) cm (6, 6½, 7½, 8 in) ending with a WS row.

Shape Shoulder
Cast off 6 (8, 10, 12) sts at beg of next and foll 2 alt rows (23, 25, 27, 29 sts). Cast off rem 23 (25, 27, 29) sts.

SLEEVES
Using 3mm needles and MC, cast on 44 (48, 52, 56) sts.
Next row (RS): K.
Rep this row for 3cm (1½in) ending with a RS row.
Next row (Inc): * Kfb, M1 (2 sts made), rep from * to last st, Kfb (131, 143, 155, 167 sts).
Next row: K.
Proceed in stripes as folls, for which 2 balls of yarn will be required, carrying the ball not in use up the side of the work to avoid many ends:
Row 1: Using A and 10mm needle, * K1 wrapping yarn round needle twice, rep from * to last st, K1.
Row 2: Change to 3mm needles, * P1 dropping the extra wrapped yarn off needle, rep from * to last st, P1.
Rows 3, 4 & 5: Using 3mm needles and MC, K.
Row 6: K3, * Kfb, K3, rep from * to end (163, 178, 193, 208 sts).
Row 7: Change to 10mm needles and A, * K1 wrapping yarn round needle twice, rep from * to last st, K1.
Row 8: Change to 3mm needles, * P1 dropping the extra wrapped yarn off needle, rep from * to last st, P1.
Rows 9 to 12: Using 3mm needles and MC, K.

Rows 7 to 12 inclusive completes one pattern. Repeat rows 7 to 12 inclusive, until work measures approx 44 (47, 47, 51) cm (17½, 18½, 18½, 20 in) from cast on, then rep rows 7 & 8 only once more.

Shape Sleeve Head
Using 3mm needles and MC, cast off 10 sts at beg of next 2 rows (K both rows) (143, 158, 173, 188 sts).
Using 3mm needles and MC, K2tog at both ends of next 2 rows (K both rows) (139, 154, 169, 184 sts).
Row 5: Change to 10mm needle and A, * K1 wrapping yarn round needle twice, rep from * to last st, K1.
Row 6: Change to 3mm needles, * P1 dropping the extra wrapped yarn off needle, rep from * to last st, P1.
Rows 7 to 10: Using 3mm needles and MC, K2tog, K to last 2 sts, K2tog (131, 146, 161, 176 sts).

Neckband (Crochet edging)
Using 2.75mm crochet hook, MC and with RS facing, start at bottom of left neck opening and work a row of DC (SC) up opening, work 2 DC (SC) into corner st, then continue in DC (SC) along left back neck, across front neck, and along right back neck. At corner work 2 DC (SC) into corner st, then work a row of DC (SC) down right neck opening. Work a 2nd row of DC (SC) across all DC (SC), working 5 button loops on left neck opening (with first loop within 2 DC (SC) of bottom and last loop at top of neck opening) at same time. Fasten off.

Sew up side seams. Sew up sleeve seams using A for main sleeve, leaving long stitch between each garter stitch section. Sew up cuff using MC. Pin sleeve into position starting at side seam. Pin to within 5cm (2in) of shoulder seam and then commencing pinning up other side of sleeve to same point. Gather up remaining excess fabric in sleeve head and pin in position, creating puff sleeve. Sew sleeve in place using MC. Sew 5 buttons in place. Darn in all ends.

If required, knit 2 sleeve pads using A, as described in 'Fit and Finish' chapter, and sew into place, extending the sleeve pad very slightly into sleeve head to enhance 'puff' of sleeve.

Repeat rows 5 to 10 inclusive, 3 more times (107, 122, 137, 152 sts) then still using 3mm needles and MC, cast off all rem sts, knitting 2 sts tog whilst casting off.

MAKING UP
Press work on WS using a damp cloth to protect work. Join shoulder seams.

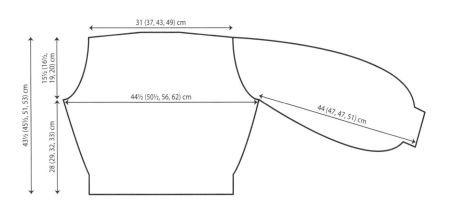

31 (37, 43, 49) cm

15½ (16½, 19, 20) cm

44½ (50½, 56, 62) cm

44 (47, 47, 51) cm

43½ (45½, 51, 53) cm

28 (29, 32, 33) cm

LADY'S EVENING JUMPER

Long bishop sleeves set off by deep shirring, allied to a plain-fabric tailored looking bodice, will make this Evening Jumper an outstanding success. Choose an exotic looking necklace or clip. Black with Black and White, or Black and Turquoise sleeves. Royal Blue with Blue and White or Blue and Guardsman Red.

MATERIALS :

"CRYSCELLE"

To ensure even winding, care should be taken to keep the hank perfectly taut on the hands, otherwise the yarn is apt to tangle.

8 ozs. "Cryscelle," Black No. 60.
4 ozs. "Cryscelle," Turquoise No. 206.
1 pair No. 12 "Coploid" Knitting Needles.
1 pair No. 10 "Coploid" Knitting Needles.
1 pair No. 000 "Coploid" Knitting Needles.
1 "Lightning" Zipp Fastener, 5 inches long.
2 Shoulder Pads.
6 Press Fasteners.

MEASUREMENTS : Length from top of shoulder to lower edge, 18½ inches. Width all round at underarm, to fit a 34 inch bust. Length of sleeve seam, 18½ inches.

TENSION : Using No. 10 Needles, work to produce 8 sts. and 10 rows to one square inch in smooth fabric (1 row K., 1 row P.), so that this piece of knitting would fit exactly the cut-out Knitting Tension Measure on the opposite page.

TO ENSURE SATISFACTION, "CRYSCELLE" AS SPECIFIED IN THIS LEAFLET MUST BE USED AND THE KNITTING INSTRUCTIONS MUST BE FOLLOWED EXACTLY, OTHERWISE THE GARMENT WILL NOT WORK OUT TO MEASUREMENTS.

ABBREVIATIONS : K.—knit.   P.—purl.   St.—stitch.   Tog.—together.
Yrn. fwd.—yarn forward.

THE FRONT.

Using No. 12 needles and Black yarn, cast on 122 sts.

1st Row.—Working into the back of the sts., * K.1, P.1. Repeat from * to the end.

2nd Row.—* K.1, P.1. Repeat from * to the end.

Repeat the 2nd row, until 2½ inches of ribbing have been worked.

Change to No. 10 needles and proceed in smooth fabric as follows :—

1st Row.—Knit.

2nd Row.—K.1, P. to the last st., K.1.

3rd and 4th Rows.—As the 1st and 2nd rows.

5th Row.—K.1, increase by picking up the thread which lies between the st. just worked and the following st. and placing this on the left-hand needle K. into the back of it, K. to the last st., pick up the thread which lies between the st. just worked and the last st. and placing this on the left-hand needle K. into the back of it, K.1.

" CRYSCELLE "

6th Row.—K.1, P. to the last st., K.1.
7th-10th Rows.—Repeat the 1st and 2nd rows twice.

Repeat rows 5-10 inclusive 9 times more, then repeat the 5th row, when there will be 144 sts. on the needle.

Proceed without further increase, until the work measures 11½ inches from the commencement, finishing at the end of a P. row.

Shape the Armholes as follows :—
Continuing in smooth fabric, cast off 12 sts. at the beginning of the next 2 rows, then cast off 2 sts. at the beginning of the following 2 rows.

Now decrease 1 st. by working 2 sts. together at both ends of the following 8 rows, when 100 sts. will remain.

Proceed without further shaping, until the work measures 6½ inches from the commencement of the armhole, finishing at the end of a P. row.

Shape the Shoulders as follows :—
1st Row.—K. to the last 6 sts., turn.
2nd Row.—P. to the last 6 sts., turn.
3rd Row.—K. to the last 12 sts., turn.
4th Row.—P. to the last 12 sts., turn.
5th Row.—K. to the last 18 sts., turn.
6th Row.—P. to the last 18 sts., turn.
7th Row.—K. to the last 23 sts., turn.
8th Row.—P. to the last 23 sts., turn.
9th Row.—K. to the last 28 sts., turn.
10th Row.—P. to the last 28 sts. Break off the yarn.

Slip all the sts. on to one needle, turn, and with the right side of the work facing, rejoin the yarn and cast off knitwise all across.

THE BACK.
Using No. 12 needles and Black yarn, cast on 106 sts.

Working into the back of the sts. on the first row only, proceed in K.1, P.1 rib for 2½ inches, as worked on the lower edge of the Front.

Change to No. 10 needles and work 4 rows in smooth fabric.

Continuing in smooth fabric, increase as on the Front at both ends of the next row and every following 6th row, until there are 128 sts. on the needle.

Proceed without further increase, until the work measures 11½ inches from the commencement, finishing at the end of a P. row.

Shape the Armholes as follows :—
Continuing in smooth fabric, cast off 7 sts. at the beginning of the next 2 rows, then decrease 1 st. at both ends of the following 7 rows, when 100 sts. will remain.

Proceed without further shaping, until the work measures 2½ inches from the commencement of the armhole, finishing at the end of a P. row.

Divide for the Back Opening as follows :—
Next Row.—K.49, cast off the following 2 sts., K. to the end.
Next Row.—K.1, P.47, K.1. Slip the remaining 49 sts. on to a safety pin and leave for the present, **turn.**

Proceed in smooth fabric on the former set of sts. for the Left side of the Back, until the work measures 6½ inches from the commencement of the armhole, finishing at the centre edge.

Shape the Shoulder as follows :—
1st Row.—K. to the last 6 sts., turn.
2nd and every alternate Row.—P. to the last st., K.1.
3rd Row.—K. to the last 12 sts., turn.
5th Row.—K. to the last 18 sts., turn.
7th Row.—K. to the last 23 sts., turn.
9th Row.—K. to the last 28 sts., turn.
10th Row.—P. to the last st., K.1.
Cast off knitwise.

Slip the sts. from the safety pin on to a No. 10 needle, join the yarn and proceed to work the Right side of the Back to match the Left side.

THE SLEEVE.
Using No. 10 needles and Black yarn, cast on 48 sts.

Working into the back of the sts. on the first row only, proceed in garter st. (every row K.), for 1½ inches.

Next Row.—* K. into the front and back of the first st., pick up the thread which lies between the st. just worked and the following st. and placing this on the left-hand needle K. it in the ordinary way. Repeat from * to the last st., K. into the front and back of the last st. (143 sts. now on the needle.)

Proceed in stripes as follows, for which 2 balls of yarn will be required, 1 ball of Turquoise and 1 ball of Black, carrying the colour not in use up the side of the work to avoid many ends :—

1st Row.—Using a No. 000 needle and Blue yarn, * K.1, yrn. fwd. Repeat from * to the last st., K.1.
2nd Row.—Using a No. 10 needle, * P.1, let the yrn. fwd. of the previous row slip off the needle. Repeat from * to the last st., P.1.
3rd Row.—Using No. 10 needles and Black yarn, knit.
4th and 5th Rows.—Repeat the 3rd row twice.
6th Row.—Using No. 10 needles and Black yarn, K.3, * K. into the front and back of the next st., K.3. Repeat from * to the end. (178 sts. now on the needle.)
7th Row.—Using a No. 000 needle and Blue yarn, * K.1, yrn. fwd. Repeat from * to the last st., K.1.
8th Row.—Using a No. 10.needle, * P.1, let the yrn. fwd. of the previous row slip off the needle. Repeat from * to the last st., P.1.
9th-12th Rows.—Using No. 10 needles and Black yarn, knit.
Rows 7-12 inclusive complete one pattern.
Repeat rows 7-12 inclusive 13 times more, then repeat the 7th and 8th rows.
Break of the Blue yarn.

Shape the Top as follows, rejoining the Blue yarn when required :—
1st and 2nd Rows.—Using No. 10 needles and Black yarn, cast off 10 sts., K. to the end.
3rd and 4th Rows.—Using No. 10 needles and Black yarn, K.2 tog., K. to the last 2 sts., K.2 tog.
5th Row.—Using a No. 000 needle and Blue yarn, * K.1, yrn. fwd. Repeat from * to the last st., K.1.
6th Row.—Using a No. 10 needle, * P.1, let the yrn. fwd. of the previous row slip off the needle. Repeat from * to the last st., P.1.
7th-10th Rows.—Using No. 10 needles and Black yarn, K.2 tog., K. to the last 2 sts., K.2 tog.
11th-28th Rows.—Repeat rows 5-10 inclusive 3 times. (122 sts. remain.)
Using No. 10 needles and Black yarn, cast off, knitting 2 sts. tog. whilst casting off.
Work another sleeve in the same manner.

MAKE-UP.
Join the shoulders of the Back to the same number of sts. as on the shoulders of the Front, leaving the remainder of the Back free for the neck.

Omitting the ribbing and garter st. on the lower edge of the sleeves, press the work on the wrong side, using a hot iron over a **dry** cloth. On no account press the work on the right side, nor without a cloth between the iron and the fabric.

Join the side seams.

Join the sleeve seams, leaving the garter st. at the lower edge free.

Stitch the sleeves into the armholes, placing the sleeve seam ½-inch to the front of the side seam and forming the cast-off edge of the top into small tucks on the wrong side of the work at the top of the armhole.

Neatly stitch the tapes of the Zipp fastener to the wrong side of the Back opening, leaving sufficient space for the "runner" to move easily.

Attach 3 press-fasteners to the garter st. cuff of each sleeve, to close.

Stitch the shoulder pads to the top of the sleeves at the shoulder line.

One Never Tires of Ribbing

MATERIALS
Excelana Luxury 4 ply wool 100% pure new British wool (159m/174yds per 50g ball)
7 (8, 9) balls shade Saharan Sand
1 pair 3.25mm (US #3) needles
10 buttons

TENSION
44 sts & 34 rows = 10cm (4in) using 3.25mm needles over rib pattern
26 sts & 32 rows = 10cm (4in) using 3.25mm needles over stocking stitch

Standard Yarn Tension
28 sts & 36 rows = 10cm (4in) using 3mm needles over stocking stitch

ABBREVIATIONS
See page 13 for standard abbreviations

SIZING
Measurements given in centimetres followed by inches in parentheses

To Fit	81–86 (32–34)	86–92 (34–36)	97–102 (38–40)
Finished Measurements			
Actual Bust Size	88 (34½)	92 (36)	102 (40)
Length to underarm	29 (11½)	30½ (12)	33½ (13)
Armhole Depth	15½ (6)	18 (7)	20 (8)
Finished Length	44½ (17½)	48½ (19)	53½ (21)
Shoulder to Shoulder	32½ (12¾)	35 (13¾)	39 (15½)

Garment shown in photographs is for first size 81–86 (32–34)

PATTERN NOTES
The front is divided at the armhole into three sections with a centre panel that is worked separately once the sides have been completed. This is worn buttoned over the side panels.

BACK
Using 3.25mm needles, cast on 108 (116, 124) sts and work as folls:
Row 1 (RS): K1, P2, * K2, P2, repeat from * to last st, K1.
Row 2 (WS): P1, K2, * P2, K2, repeat from * to last st, P1.
Repeat these 2 rows until work measures 10cm (4in) from cast on edge, ending on a WS row. Continue in patt but at same time inc 1 st at each end of next then every foll 6th row until 128 (134, 146) sts. Work 1 (13, 11) rows without shaping (lengthen body at this point if required), then continue as folls:
Next row (RS): K47 (50, 56), P2, [K2, P2] 8 times, K47 (50, 56).
Keep 34 sts at centre in rib patt and sts at each side in stocking stitch from this point. Work 7 rows.

Shape Armholes
Cast off 4 sts at beg of next 4 rows (112, 118, 130 sts), then dec 1 st at end end of next and foll 6 alt rows (98, 104, 116 sts). Continue without further shaping until armhole measures 15½ (18, 20) cm (6, 7, 8 in) ending with a WS row.

Neck and Shoulder Shaping
Whilst maintaining patt, cast off 8 (9, 10) sts at beg of next 4 rows (66, 68, 76 sts).
Next row (RS): Patt 24 (25, 29), cast off centre 18 sts, patt to end (48, 50, 58 sts).
Working on last 24 (25, 29) sts only, cast off 8 (9, 10) sts at beg of row, patt to neck, turn, cast off 8 sts at neck edge and patt to end, turn, cast off rem 8 (8, 11) sts.

With WS facing rejoin yarn to rem 24 (25, 29) sts.
Next row (WS): Cast off 8 sts at neck edge, patt to end, turn, cast off 8 (9, 10) sts at shoulder, turn and cast off rem 8 (8, 11) sts.

FRONT
Using 3.25mm needles, cast on 108 (116, 124) sts and work as folls:
Row 1 (RS): K1, P2, * K2, P2, repeat from * to last st, K1.
Row 2 (WS): P1, K2, * P2, K2, repeat from * to last st, P1.
Repeat these 2 rows until work measures 10cm (4in) from cast on edge, ending on a WS row. Continue in patt and at same time inc 1 st at each end of next then every foll 6th

row until 128 (134, 146) sts. Work 1 (13, 11) rows without inc (lengthen body at this point if required), then continue as folls:

Divide for Front Neck
Next row (RS): K19 (22, 28), turn and place rem 109 (112, 118) sts on a holder and work on first 19 (22, 28) sts only.
Next row (WS): Cast on 28 sts, P across all sts (47, 50, 56 sts).
Commencing with a K row, work 6 rows in stocking stitch ending with a WS row.

Shape Armhole
Continuing in stocking stitch, cast off 4 sts at beg of next and foll alt row (39, 42, 48 sts) then dec 1 st on foll 7 alt rows (32, 35, 41 sts) ending with a RS row.
Work 2 rows without further shaping, ending with a RS row.

Shape Front Band
Next row (WS): Cast on 9 sts, [K1, P1] 4 times, K1, P to end (41, 44, 50 sts).
Row 1: K32 (35, 41), [P1, K1] 4 times, P1.
Row 2: [K1, P1] 4 times, K1, P32 (35, 41).
These 2 rows set patt, continue in this manner without further shaping until armhole measures same as back to start of shoulder shaping ending with a WS row.

Shape Shoulder
Whilst maintaining stocking stitch patt, and continuing to work ribbed front band, cast off 8 (9, 10) sts at beg of next and and foll 3 (2, 2) RS rows, then 0 (8, 11) sts on foll RS row (9 sts). Continue working in ribbing on rem 9 sts for a further 6cm (2¼in), leave sts on safety pin or waste yarn.

With RS facing, leave centre 90 sts on a holder and rejoin yarn to rem 19 (22, 28) sts.
Next row: Cast on 28, K across all sts (47, 50, 56 sts).
Commencing with a P row work 8 rows in stocking stitch, ending with a RS row.

Shape Armhole
Cast off 4 sts at beg of next and foll alt row (39, 42, 48 sts), then dec 1 st on next and foll 6 alt rows (32, 35, 41 sts), ending with a RS row. Work 3 rows without further shaping, ending on a WS row.

Shape Front Band
Next row (RS): Cast on 9 sts, [P1, K1] 4 times, P1, K32 (35, 41) (41, 44, 50 sts).
Row 1 (WS): P32 (35, 41), [K1, P1] 4 times, K1.
Row 2: [P1, K1] 4 times, P1, K32 (35, 41).
These 2 rows form patt, continue without further shaping until front measures same as back to start of shoulder shaping ending with a RS row.

Shape Shoulder

Whilst maintaining stocking stitch patt, and continuing to work ribbed front band, cast off 8 (9, 10) sts at beg of next and and foll 3 (2, 2) RS rows, then 0 (8, 11) sts on foll RS row (9 sts). Continue working in ribbing on rem 9 sts for a further 6cm (2¼in), leave sts on safety pin or waste yarn.

Centre Front Panel

With RS facing rejoin yarn to rem 90 sts, and work in rib as folls:

Next row (RS): P2, * K2, P2, rep from * to end.
Next row: K2, * P2, K2, rep from * to end.
These 2 rows set patt. Continue in patt until 28 rows have been worked, ending with a WS row.

Next row: Cast off 28 sts, rib until you have 34 sts on right hand needle, cast off rem 28 sts. With WS facing, rejoin yarn to rem 34 sts and maintaining patt, work 9 more rows in ribbing, ending with a WS row.

Next row (Buttonhole): Rib 4, cast off 2, rib until 6 sts rem, cast off 2, rib to end.
Next row: Work in rib, casting on 2 sts over those cast off on previous row.
Work 8 rows without shaping.
Rep 2 buttonhole rows once more. Work 2 rows without shaping, then cast off in rib.

SLEEVES (Worked from the top down)

Using 3.25mm needles, cast on 34 sts. Commencing with a K row work in stocking stitch, and at same time, inc 1 st at each end of every row until 98 (106, 110) sts, ending with a WS row. Work 6 (10, 16) rows without shaping, then dec 1 st at each end of next and every foll 8th row until 68 (72, 76) sts rem ending with a RS row.
Work 3 rows without shaping. Change to rib pattern as folls:
Next row (RS): K1, P2 * K2, P2, repeat from * to last st, K1.
Next row: P1, *K2, P2, rep from * to last 3 sts, K2, P1.
These 2 rows set rib patt. Work in rib and at same time continue dec 1 st at each end of 3rd (8th row since last dec) and every foll 8th row until 60 (64, 68) sts rem. Continue to maintain rib patt, and dec 1 st at each end of every row until 1 st rems. Draw yarn through and fasten off.

MAKING UP

Press work lightly on WS using a damp cloth. With work on a flat surface carefully pin centre panel in place over underlaps, ensuring ribbing at centre is not distorted. Mark button positions. Turn work over and slip stitch under lap loosely into place along cast on edge. Sew on buttons. On RS of work turn back corner of each upper ribbed section to create triangle as shown. Sew on a button to hold in place. Ensure there are no gaps between the sections. Join shoulder seams. Adjust back neck band to fit – using three needle cast off method to join ends together. Slip stitch back neck band into place. Sew side and sleeve seams, joining ribbed section of sleeves with a flat slip stitch. Set in sleeves taking care to match centre of sleeve head to shoulder seam and matching side seams. On RS fold back pointed end of sleeve, adjust length to fit then sew in place with a button as shown. Darn in all ends.

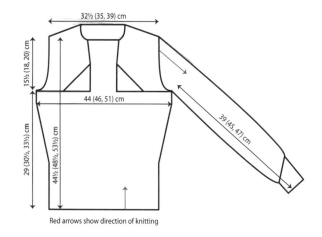

32½ (35, 39) cm

15½ (18, 20) cm

44 (46, 51) cm

29 (30½, 33½) cm

44½ (48½, 53½) cm

39 (45, 47) cm

Red arrows show direction of knitting

ONE NEVER TIRES OF RIBBING

CARRIED out in " Rosedale" fingering, in which there's a wide range of fashionable colours, and trimmed with chromium buttons.

MATERIALS.

8 ozs. of W.B. 3-ply " Rosedale " fingering, one pair of No. 9 knitting needles, ten chromium buttons about the size of a threepenny piece, and a belt.

MEASUREMENTS.

Length from shoulder, at neck edge, 19½ inches ; width all round under arms, with ribbing stretched out, 34 inches ; length of sleeve seam, to edge of turned-back cuff, 18 inches.

TENSION.

15 sts. to 2 inches in width and 8 rows to 1 inch in depth in the ribbing, when stretched out.

ABBREVIATIONS.

K. = knit ; p. = purl ; sts. = stitches ; st.st. = stocking-stitch ; dec. = decrease or decreasing ; inc. = increase or increasing ; rep. = repeat ; tog. = together.

IF you cast on with two needles always work into the back of all cast-on sts. to produce firm edges, but if you use the thumb method this is not necessary.

THE BACK.

BEGIN at lower edge. Cast on 108 sts. and work in following pattern :—

1st row.—K. 1, p. 2, * k. 2, p. 2. Rep. from * to end, finishing k. 1. **2nd row.**—P. 1, k. 2, * p. 2, k. 2. Rep. from * to end, finishing p. 1.

Rep. these two rows until work measures 4 inches from beginning, finishing after a 2nd row, then continue in ribbing, *but at same time* inc. 1 st. at both ends of next row, then at both ends of every 6th row following until there are 128 sts. Work one row without inc., then continue as follows :—

Next row.—K. 47, then p. 2 and k. 2 alternately over next 34 sts., k. 47. Now keep 34 sts. in centre in ribbing and sts. at each side in st.st. throughout back. When seven more rows have been worked in this way, shape armholes.

The Armhole Shaping.

Cast off 4 sts. at beginning of each of next four rows, then dec. 1 st. at both ends of needle on each of next seven k.

rows, leaving 98 sts. Continue without dec. until armholes measure 6 inches in depth on the straight, finishing after a p. row, then shape neck and shoulders.

The Neck and Shoulder Shaping.

1st row.—Work until 8 sts. remain, turn. **2nd row.**—Work until 8 sts. remain, turn. **3rd row.**—Work until 16 sts. remain, turn. **4th row.**—Work until 16 sts. remain, turn. **5th row.**—Work 24 sts., cast off the next 18 sts., then work until 24 sts. remain, turn. **6th row.**—Work to neck. **7th row.**—Cast off 8, then work across all sts. **8th row.**—Cast off the 32 shoulder sts.

Join wool at neck edge of other side. **6th row.**—Work until 24 sts. remain, turn. **7th row.**—Work to neck. **8th row.**—Cast off 8, then work across all sts. **9th row.**—Cast off the 32 shoulder sts.

THE FRONT.

Work this in exactly same way as back until there are 128 sts., then work one row without inc., finishing after a row on wrong side, then divide for front neck and shape armholes as follows :—

Next row.—K. 19, turn, place remaining 109 sts. on a st.-holder for the present, and continue on first 19 only. **Next row.**—Cast on 28 sts., p. into back threads of these 28, then p. 19 (47).

Work six rows st.st. on these 47 sts. (finishing after a p. row), then continue in st.st., and shape armhole by casting off 4 sts. at beginning of next two k. rows, then dec. 1 st. on same edge on next seven k. rows (32). Work two rows without dec., finishing at front edge after a k. row.

Next row.—Cast on 9, then k. 1 and p. 1 into back threads of these 9, p. to end (41). Continue in st.st. without dec. (keeping 9 sts. at front edge in ribbing), until armhole edge is six rows deeper than that of back, finishing after a k. row ; then shape shoulder.

It's essential that you should knit at same tension as the original.

The Shoulder Shaping.

1st row.—Rib 9, p. until 8 sts. remain, turn. **2nd row.**—Work back to neck. **3rd row.**—Rib 9, p. until 16 sts. remain, turn. **4th row.**—Work back to neck. **5th row.**—Rib 9, p. until 24 sts. remain, turn. **6th row.**—Work back to neck. **7th row.**—Rib 9, p. to end. **8th row.**—Cast off 32 shoulder sts., then continue in ribbing on 9 sts. at the front edge for 2¼ inches. Cast off in rib.

Go back to remaining 109 sts., pass first 90 on to a spare piece of wool, then place remaining 19 sts. on a k. needle with point at front, and continue on these 19 as follows :—

Next row.—Cast on 28, k. into back threads, then k. remaining 19 sts. (47). Work eight rows st.st. on these 47 sts., finishing after a k. row.

Continue in st.st. and shape armhole by casting off 4 sts. at beginning of next two p. rows, then dec. 1 st. on same edge on each of next seven k. rows (32). Work three rows without dec., finishing at front edge after a p. row.

Next row.—Cast on 9, then p. 1 and k. 1 into back threads, k. to end (41). Now finish this side to match the other, remembering to leave shoulder sts. unworked at end of k. rows.

Go back to 90 sts. in centre and place these on a k. needle. Work 28 rows in ribbing, finishing after a 2nd row.

Next row.—Cast off 28 sts., rib 33 more, cast off remaining 28 sts. Rejoin wool to last st. of 34 in centre and work nine more rows in ribbing, finishing after a row on wrong side, then make first two buttonholes as follows :—

Next row.—Rib 4, cast off 2, rib until 6 remain, cast off 2, rib 3. In next row cast on two sets of 2 sts. in place of those cast off. Work eight more rows, then make two buttonholes on next two rows as before, then work two more rows and cast off in rib.

Sew up shoulders by backstitching edges tog. with ⅛-inch turnings on wrong side, then sew cast-off edges of ribbing tog. at the back and sew one edge to back neck.

THE SLEEVES.

Begin at shoulder line. Cast on 34 sts. and k. into back threads. Continue in st.st., beginning with a p. row, and inc. 1 st. at both ends of needle on every row until there are 98 sts. Work six rows without inc., then dec. 1 st. at both ends of next row, then at both ends of every 8th row following, until 68 sts. remain. Work three rows without dec. (finishing after a p. row), then change to rib pattern as follows :—

Next row.—K. 1, p. 2, * k. 2, p. 2. Rep. from * to end, finishing k. 1.

Continue in rib pattern (still dec. at both ends of every 8th row following from last dec. until 60 sts. remain), then, *still working in rib pattern*, dec. 1 st. at both ends of needle on every row until all sts. are taken off.

THE MAKING UP.

Sew sleeves into armholes by overcasting edge loops tog. on wrong side. Press work lightly on wrong side with a warm iron and damp cloth. Press the st.st. parts again in same way on right side.

Sew up side and sleeve seams in same way as sleeves were sewn in and press them. Fold up ribbing points of cuff, so that the points come over one inch of the st.st.

DESIGNED to fit a figure with from 32 to 34-inch bust measurement.

part, and catch down with a button 1 inch below the point.

Sew 28 cast-on sts. of each front at sides, under ribbing, then sew down side edges of each front as far as cast-on 9 sts. at each side and sew down these 9 also. Turn 34 cast-off sts. on each side of front over, as illustrated, and catch down with a button.

Sew two buttons on front edge borders to match buttonholes on the loose piece of ribbing, then sew the two remaining buttons under these on the front piece, at equal distances apart. Make a buttonhole loop on each side seam at waist, and pass belt through.

REMEMBER to use the materials prescribed and knit at the same tension, or you can't expect the garment to turn out the same size as the model.

Pay careful attention to pressing and making up.

Simple – But So Attractive!

MATERIALS
Excelana 4 Ply Luxury Wool 100% pure new British wool (159m/174yds per 50g ball)
8 (9, 10, 11, 12, 14) balls shade Cornflower Blue
1 pair 2.25mm (US #1) needles
1 pair 3.75mm (US #5) needles

TENSION
36 sts & 35 rows = 10cm (4in) using 3.75mm needles over rib pattern (before blocking)

Standard Yarn Tension
28 sts & 36 rows = 10cm (4in) using 3mm needles over stocking stitch

ABBREVIATIONS
See page 13 for standard abbreviations

SIZING
Measurements given in centimetres followed by inches in parentheses

To Fit	76–81 (30–32)	86–92 (34–36)	97–102 (38–40)	107–112 (42–44)	117–122 (46–48)	127–132 (50–52)
Finished Measurements						
Actual Bust Size	66 (26)	76 (30)	86 (34)	96 (38)	104 (41)	116 (45½)
Length to underarm	36 (14)	37 (14½)	38 (15)	39 (15½)	41 (16)	42 (16½)
Armhole Depth	16 (6½)	18 (7)	19 (7½)	20 (8)	21½ (8½)	23 (9)
Finished Length	52 (20½)	55 (21½)	57 (22½)	59 (23)	62½ (24½)	65 (25½)
Shoulder to Shoulder	25½ (10)	26½ (10½)	28 (11)	30 (11¾)	33½ (13)	36½ (14½)
Sleeve Length	48 (19)	48 (19)	48 (19)	48 (19)	49½ (19½)	49½ (19½)

Garment shown in photographs for first size 76–81 (30–32)

PATTERN NOTES
Block Rib Pattern
Row 1 (RS): * K2, P2, repeat from * to end.
Repeat this row 10 more times.
Row 12: P.
Row 13: K.
Row 14: * P2, K2, repeat from * to end.
Repeat this row 10 more times.
Row 25: K.
Row 26: P.
These 26 rows form pattern.

BACK
Using 2.25mm needles, cast on 100 (116, 136, 152, 168, 188) sts.
Next row: * K1, P1, rep from * to end.
Rep this row until rib measures 8cm (3in) from cast on edge ending with a RS row.
Inc Row (WS): Rib 2 (10, 11, 9, 8, 8), M1, * rib 5 (5, 6, 7, 8, 9), M1, repeat from * to last 3 (11, 11, 10, 8, 9) sts, rib 3 (11, 11, 10, 8, 9) (120, 136, 156, 172, 188, 208 sts).
Change to 3.75mm needles and commencing with row 1, work in Block Rib patt without shaping until work measures 36 (37, 38, 39, 41, 42) cm (14, 14½, 15, 15½, 16, 16½ in), ending with a WS row.

Shape Armholes
Whilst maintaining pattern, cast off 3 (3, 5, 5, 6, 7) sts at beg of next 6 (8, 8, 8, 8, 8) rows (102, 112, 116, 132, 140, 152 sts).
Dec 1 st at each end of 5 (8, 8, 12, 10, 10) foll rows (92, 96, 100, 108, 120, 132 sts). **
Continue without further shaping until armhole measures 16 (18, 19, 20, 21½, 23) cm (6½, 7, 7½, 8, 8½, 9 in).
Cast off.

FRONT
Work as for back until ** reached. Continue without further shaping until front measures 26 rows less than back to cast off edge, ending with a WS row.

Shape Neck
Next row: Pattern 42 (44, 46, 50, 56, 62) sts and slip these on to stitch holder, cast off next 8 sts, pattern to end.
Continue on rem 42 (44, 46, 50, 56, 62) sts.

Shape Right Front
Continue in pattern as set, dec 1 st at neck edge of next 14 rows (28, 30, 32, 36, 42, 48 sts). Work without further shaping until front measures same as back. Cast off.

Shape Left Front
With RS facing, rejoin yarn to rem 42 (44, 46, 50, 56, 62) sts. Dec 1 st at neck edge of next 14 rows (28, 30, 32, 36, 42, 48 sts). Work without further shaping until front measures same as back. Cast off.

Left Shoulder

Work without further shaping on these 22 (24, 26, 30, 36, 42) sts, remembering to work 8 st knit border at all times, for 25 rows, then maintaining patt, inc 1 st at neck edge of every row until 36 (38, 40, 44, 50, 56) sts ending with a WS row. Slip these sts onto a spare needle. Break off yarn.

With RS facing, rejoin yarn to rem sts and work as for left shoulder until 36 (38, 40, 44, 50, 56) sts ending with a WS row. Cast on 8 sts, then work across 36 (38, 40, 44, 50, 56) sts on spare needle (80, 84, 88, 96, 108, 120 sts).
Rep 4 row pattern 7 (9, 10, 11, 13, 15) times then work rows 1 and 2 only once more.
Work 10 rows in garter st.
Cast off loosely.

MAKING UP

Carefully block all pieces on WS of work. Join shoulder seams, then sew on collar using flat slip stitch as shown in 'Fit and Finish' chapter. Sew up side and sleeve seams, matching the pattern, then set in sleeve matching centre of sleeve head to shoulder seam and side seams together. Ease any excess fabric into top of sleeve head. Darn in all ends.

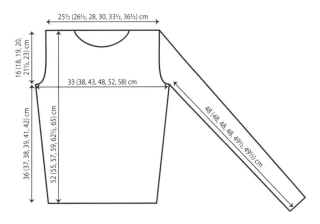

SLEEVES

Using 2.25mm needles cast on 56 (64, 68, 72, 76, 80) sts.
Next row (RS): * K1, P1, rep from * to end.
Rep this row until rib measures 8cm (3in) from cast on edge ending with a WS row.
Change to 3.75mm needles, and commencing with row 1, work 9 rows in Block Rib pattern.
Whilst continuing to maintain pattern, inc 1 st at each end of next and 9 foll 10th (11th, 11th, 11th, 12th, 12th) rows, working inc sts into rib pattern (76, 84, 88, 92, 96, 100 sts).
Work without further shaping until sleeve measures 48 (48, 48, 48, 49½, 49½) cm (19, 19, 19, 19, 19½, 19½ in).

Shape Sleeve Head

Dec 1 st at each end of every row until 8 sts rem. Cast off rem sts.

COLLAR (worked in one piece from back)

Using 3.75mm needles, cast on 80 (84, 88, 96 108, 120) sts and work 10 rows in garter st.
Work in patt as folls:
Row 1 (RS): K.
Row 2: K8, P until 8 sts rem, K8.
Row 3: As row 2.
Row 4: As row 1.
Rep these 4 rows a further 9 (11, 12, 13, 15, 17) times, then rep rows 1 and 2 only once more.

Shape Neck

Work 22 (24, 26, 30, 36, 42) sts in pattern and place on stitch holder, cast off 36 sts for back neck and work in pattern to end.

SIMPLE—BUT SO ATTRACTIVE!

And It Is Easy Enough For Beginners

MATERIALS

*N*INE ounces of " Sirdar " 3-ply Super Shetland Wool ; a pair each of " Aero " knitting pins No. 9 and No. 13.

TENSION AND MEASUREMENTS

*W*ORKED at a tension of 7 sts. to the inch in width on No. 9 pins, the following measurements are attained after light pressing : Round the bust, 35 inches ; front length from shoulder seam to lower edge, 20 inches ; back length, 19 inches ; side seam, 13 inches ; sleeve seam, 19 inches.

ABBREVIATIONS

K., KNIT ; p., purl ; st., stitch ; tog., together ; inc., increase (by working into the back and front of the same stitch) ; dec., decrease. Single rib is k. 1 and p. 1 alternately ; directions in brackets are worked the number of times stated immediately after the brackets.

THE BACK

*W*ITH No. 13 pins cast on 100 sts. and work 33 rows in single rib.

INCREASE ROW : * Rib 4, inc. ; repeat from * to end (120 sts.).

Change to No. 9 pins and continue in pattern as follows :

1ST ROW : * K. 2, p. 2 ; repeat from * to end.

Repeat this row 10 times more.

12TH ROW : All purl.

13TH ROW : All knit.

14TH ROW : * P. 2, k. 2 ; repeat from * to end.

Repeat this row 10 times more.

25TH ROW : All knit.

26TH ROW : All purl.

These 26 rows complete 1 pattern.

Repeat the 26 pattern rows twice more, then 10 rows of the next pattern to armholes.

TO SHAPE THE ARMHOLES : Continue in pattern, casting off 3 sts. at the beginning of each of the next 6 rows, then work 2 sts. tog. at the beginning of each of the following 10 rows, when 92 sts. will remain.

Continue straight in pattern on these sts. for 40 rows more.

Cast off straight across.

THE FRONT

*W*ORK exactly the same as the back until the armhole shaping is finished and 92 sts. remain.

Work 16 rows straight on these sts. to neck.

TO SHAPE THE NECK

*N*EXT ROW : Pattern 42 sts. and slip these on to a stitch-holder until needed for the Left Front Shoulder, cast off 8, pattern to end (42 sts. for Right Front Shoulder).

THE RIGHT FRONT SHOULDER.—Continue in pattern as now set, taking 2 sts. tog. at the neck end of every row until 28 sts. remain. Work 19 rows straight on these sts. Cast off straight across.

THE LEFT FRONT SHOULDER.—Slip a No. 9 pin through the 42 Left Front Shoulder sts. with point towards the neck end. Work exactly the same as the Right Front Shoulder.

THE LONG SLEEVES

*W*ITH No. 13 pins cast on 56 sts. and work 34 rows in single rib.

Change to No. 9 pins and work 9 rows in pattern, as on back.

Continue in pattern, increasing 1 st. at both ends of the next row and every following 10th row, working the increase sts. in the rib pattern as they are added, until there are 76 sts on the pins.

Work 36 rows straight on these sts., or for length of sleeve seam desired.

TO SHAPE THE SLEEVE TOP.—Continue in pattern, taking 2 sts. tog. at both ends of every row until 8 sts. remain. Cast off.

Work a second sleeve in the same manner.

FOR SHORT SLEEVES.—With the No. 13 pins cast on 76 sts. and work 1 inch in single rib. Change to No. 9 pins and work 1 pattern of 26 sts. as at the beginning of the back, then shape the top of the sleeve as on the long sleeves.

THE COLLAR

*B*EGIN at the back and with No. 9 pins cast on 80 sts. and work 10 rows plain.

Continue in pattern as follows :

1ST ROW : All knit.

2ND ROW : K. 8, p. until 8 remain, k. 8.

3RD ROW : As 2nd row.

4TH ROW. : As 1st row.

Repeat the 4 pattern rows 9 times more, then 2 rows of next pattern to neck.

TO SHAPE THE NECK.—Work 22 sts. in pattern and slip these on a stitch-holder until needed for the Right Shoulder, cast off 36 sts. for the back of the neck and work in pattern to end (22 sts. for Left Shoulder).

THE LEFT SHOULDER.—Work straight on these 22 sts. for 25 rows, then continue in pattern, increasing 1 st. at the neck end of every row until there are 36 sts. on the pins. Slip these sts. on to a spare pin for the moment.

Pass the Right Shoulder sts. on a No. 9 pin (point towards the neck end) and work exactly the same as the Left Shoulder until there are 36 sts. on the row. Cast on 8 sts., and then on to the same pin work the 36 Left Shoulder sts. (80 sts. now on).

Work 30 rows in pattern, then knit 10 rows plain and cast off.

Isn't the square collar becoming ? It is worked in stripes of plain and purl.

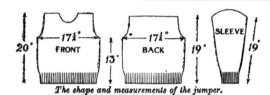

The shape and measurements of the jumper.

TO MAKE UP THE JUMPER

*F*IRST press all pieces lightly on the wrong side with a hot iron over a damp cloth. Join the shoulder seams, beginning at the armhole end and taking 1 st. from each side at a time. Stitch the collar to neck, matching the shaped edges. Set the sleeves into armholes and press these seams while the work is open. Join the sleeve and side seams in one long line and press.

As Pink As A Rosebud

MATERIALS
Fyberspates Scrumptious 4 ply 45% silk/55% superwash merino (365m/399yds per 100g skein)
3 (3, 4, 4, 4, 5, 5) skeins shade 306 (Baby Pink)
1 pair 4mm (US #6) needles
2 metres of 5cm wide satin ribbon

TENSION
21 sts & 44 rows = 10cm (4in) using 4mm needles over garter stitch

Standard Yarn Tension
28 sts & 37 rows = 10cm (4in) using 3.5mm needles over stocking stitch

ABBREVIATIONS
See page 13 for standard abbreviations

SIZING
Measurements given in centimetres followed by inches in parentheses

To Fit	81–86 (32–34)	86–92 (34–36)	97–102 (38–40)	102–106 (40–42)	106–112 (42–44)	112–117 (44–46)	117–122 (46–48)
Finished Measurements							
Actual Bust Size [1]	94½ (37¼)	100½ (39½)	107½ (42½)	112½ (44½)	119½ (47½)	124 (49)	131 (51½)
Length to underarm [2]	11 (4½)	13 (5)	14 (5½)	15½ (6)	16½ (6½)	18 (7)	19 (7½)
Armhole Depth	19 (7½)	19 (7½)	20 (8)	20 (8)	21½ (8½)	21½ (8½)	23 (9)
Frill Depth	14 (5½)	14 (5½)	14 (5½)	14 (5½)	14 (5½)	14 (5½)	14 (5½)
Finished Length	44 (17½)	46 (18)	48 (19)	49½ (19½)	52 (20½)	53½ (21)	56 (22)
Shoulder to Shoulder	37 (14½)	38 (15)	39 (15½)	41 (16)	43 (17)	46 (18)	47½ (18¾)

[1] Front measurement taken at widest point and overlap not taken into consideration
[2] Length to underarm does not include 14cm depth of frill, but this is added to finished length

Garment shown in photographs is for first size 81–86 (32–34)

PATTERN NOTES
This jacket is knitted in separate pieces with a frill knitted to travel round the entire outer edge of the body. The frill is worked using short rows, turning the work after 15 sts. Please note, to create the holes as shown in the original photos it is necessary to turn the work WITHOUT working wraps. The work should just be turned. The sleeves are worked from side seam to side seam.

BACK
Using 4mm needles, cast on 98 (104, 110, 116, 122, 128, 134) sts. Work in garter stitch (knit every row) until work measures 11 (13, 14, 15½, 16½, 18, 19) cm (4½, 5, 5½, 6, 6½, 7, 7½ in).

Shape Armholes
Cast off 8 (10, 12, 13, 12, 12, 13) sts at beg of next 2 rows (82, 84, 86, 90, 98, 104, 108 sts), then dec 1 st at beg of next 4 (4, 4, 4, 8, 8, 8) rows (78, 80, 82, 86, 90, 96, 100 sts). Continue without further shaping until armhole measures approx 19 (19, 20, 20, 21½, 21½, 23) cm (7½, 7½, 8, 8, 8½, 8½, 9 in).

Shape Shoulders
Cast off 12 (12, 12, 13, 14, 15, 16) sts at beg of next 4 rows (30, 32, 34, 34, 34, 36, 36 sts). Cast off rem 30 (32, 34, 34, 34, 36, 36) sts.

LEFT FRONT
Using 4mm needles, cast on 30 (34, 38, 40, 44, 46, 50) sts. Working in garter st, inc 1 st at end of next row and at beg of foll row (32, 36, 40, 42, 46, 48, 52 sts).
Rep these 2 rows 5 times more (42, 46, 50, 52, 56, 58, 62 sts).
Continue in garter st, inc 1 st at end of next row and foll 7 alt rows (50, 54, 58, 60, 64, 66, 70 sts).
Work without further shaping until side edge measures same as back to commencement of armhole shaping, ending with a WS row.

Shape Armhole
Cast off 8 (10, 12, 13, 12, 12, 13) sts at beg of next row (42, 44, 46, 47, 52, 54, 57 sts).
Work without further shaping for 19 more rows, then dec 1 st at neck edge of next and 17 (19, 21, 20, 23, 23, 24) foll

alt rows (24, 24, 24, 26, 28, 30, 32 sts).
Work without further shaping until front armhole measures same as back to start of shoulder shaping, ending with a WS row.

Shape Shoulder
Cast off 12 (12, 12, 13, 14, 15, 16) sts at beg of next and foll alt row.

RIGHT FRONT
Using 4mm needles, cast on 30 (34, 38, 40, 44, 46, 50) sts.
Working in garter st, inc 1 st at beg of next row and at end of foll row (32, 36, 40, 42, 46, 48, 52 sts).
Rep these 2 rows 5 times more (42, 46, 50, 52, 56, 58, 62 sts).
Continue in garter st, inc 1 st at beg of next row and foll 7 alt rows (50, 54, 58, 60, 64, 66, 70 sts).
Work without further shaping until side edge measures same as back to commencement of armhole shaping, ending with a RS row.

Shape Armhole
Cast off 8 (10, 12, 13, 12, 12, 13) sts at beg of next row (42, 44, 46, 47, 52, 54, 57 sts).
Work without further shaping for 19 more rows, then dec 1 st at neck edge of next and 17 (19, 21, 20, 23, 23, 24) foll alt rows (24, 24, 24, 26, 28, 30, 32 sts).
Work without further shaping until front armhole measures same as back to start of shoulder shaping, ending with a RS row.

Shape Shoulder
Cast off 12 (12, 12, 13, 14, 15, 16) sts at beg of next and foll alt row.

FRILL
Using 4mm needles, cast on 30 sts. Work patt as folls:
Rows 1 & 2: K15, turn and K15 (first short row worked).
Row 3: K30.
Row 4: K30.
Repeat these 4 rows until the straight edge of the frill is long enough to go round the entire jacket, joining at the centre back of neck. There are 528 rows on the straight edge of this frill on the original jacket. Leave sts on holder so length can be adjusted to fit.

SLEEVES (Worked side to side)
Using 4mm needles, cast on 16 sts.
** **Row 1**: K1, Kfb, K to end (17 sts).
Rows 2 & 3: K15, turn and K15.
Row 4: K.
Rep from ** until 43 (43, 45, 45, 47, 47, 49) sts.
Continue as set but without working any further increases until a further 16 reps have been worked, ending with row 4.
** **Row 1**: K2tog, K to end (42, 42, 44, 44, 46, 46, 48 sts).
Rows 2 & 3: K15, turn and K15.
Row 4: K.
Rep from ** until 16 sts rem.
Cast off.

MAKING UP
Press pieces lightly through a damp cloth. Join shoulder and side seams. Commencing at centre back neck and cast on end of frill, pin frill down right front and across front cast on, across back and left front cast ons, then up left front and across second part of back neck. Adjust length to fit. Cast off sts and sew two ends of frill together. Attach frill to garment using flat slip stitch as for a collar (See 'Fit and Finishing' chapter). Sew sleeve seams and set sleeves into armholes matching centre of sleeve head with shoulder seam and matching side seams.

Cut ribbon into 4 equal lengths and sew one piece to widest point of right front on wrong side of work. Attach second piece of ribbon to appropriate point on left front, adjusting to fit before securing. Repeat the process on the widest point of the left front but attach to right side of work and attach corresponding ribbon on right front to underside of work. Darn in all ends. Fold collar back.

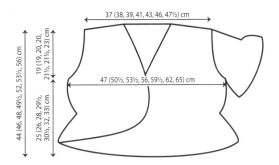

As Pink As A Rosebud!

A Delightful Frilly Bedjacket That You Can Make For Christmas

The frill forms a little turn-down collar at the back!

MATERIALS

FIVE ounces of "Greenock" 3-ply Super Fingering (obtainable only from branches of Scotch Wool & Hosiery Stores); a pair of "Stratnoid" knitting pins No. 8.

TENSION AND MEASUREMENTS

WORKED at a tension of 6 sts. to the inch in width the following measurements are attained after tight pressing: Across the back at the underarms, 16½ inches; across each front at the same place, excluding frill, 8½ inches; front and back length from shoulder seam to lower edge of frill, 16 inches; side seam from underarm to lower edge of frill, 9 inches. The frill measures 5 inches from the straight edge to the fluted edge.

ABBREVIATIONS

K., KNIT; inc., increase (by working into the back and front of the same stitch. The jacket is worked in plain knitting throughout.

THE BACK

CAST on 98 sts. and work 50 rows plain, working into the back of the sts. on the first row to give a firm edge.

To Shape the Armholes.—Cast off 8 sts. at the beginning of each of the next 2 rows, then work 2 sts. tog. at the beginning of each of the next four rows (78 sts.).

Continue straight on these sts. for 70 rows more to shoulders.

To Slope the Shoulders.—Cast off 12 sts. at the beginning of each of the next 4 rows. Cast off the remaining sts.

THE FRONT.

BEGIN at the lower edge and cast on 30 sts. Work 1 row into the back of these sts. to give a firm edge. Continue in plain knitting, increasing at the end of the next row and beginning of following row for the shaped edge, to which the frill is afterwards sewn. Repeat these 2 rows 5 times more (42 sts.).

Continue in plain knitting, increasing at the shaped end of next row and seven following alternate rows, when there will be 50 sts. on the pins.

Work 22 rows straight on these sts. to armhole.

To Shape the Armhole.—Continue in plain knitting, casting off 8 sts. at the beginning of next row (armhole end), when 42 sts. will remain.

Continue straight on these sts. for 19 rows more, then continue in plain knitting, working 2 sts. tog. at the front end of every alternate row for 15 decreases (27 sts.).

Work 24 rows straight on these sts. to shoulder.

To Slope the Shoulder.—Cast off 12 sts. at the beginning of next and following alternate row (armhole end), then cast off the 3 remaining sts.

Work a second piece in the same manner.

Join the shoulder seams, beginning at the armhole end and taking 1 st. from each side at a time. Then join side seams. Press the seams lightly with the edge of the iron.

THE FRILL.

CAST on 30 sts. Continue in pattern as follows:

** 1st Row: K. 15, turn and k. 15 (this makes a little gore to form the frilly edge).

3rd Row: K. 30. 4th Row: K. 30.

Repeat these 4 rows from ** until the straight edge of the frill is long enough to go round the entire jacket, joining at the centre back of neck. There are 528 rows on the straight edge of this frill on the original jacket.

THE SLEEVES

CAST on 16 sts. and work 1 row into the back of these sts.

**Next Row: K. 1, inc. in the next st., k. to end (17 sts.).

Next Row: K. 15, turn and k. 15.

Next Row: K. 1, inc. in the next st., k. to end (17 sts.).

Next Row: K. 15, turn and k. 15.

Next Row: Knit across all the sts.

Repeat from **, increasing in the 2nd st. at the beginning of every 4th row, that is, every alternate long row, counting the gore of 15 sts. as 2 rows, until there are 43 sts. on the pins.

Continue these rows *without* increasing, until there are 30 long rows more (still working the gores), counting the rows at the armhole end.

Continue in pattern decreasing by taking 2 sts. tog. at the armhole edge of every 4th row until 16 sts. remain. Cast off.

Work a second sleeve in the same manner.

Set the sleeves into armholes, and stitch ribbons to each front for fastening.

Softly feminine—and very cosy!

Lady's Jumper-Cardigan

MATERIALS
Excelana Luxury 4 ply wool 100% pure new British wool (159m/174yds per 50g ball)
8 (10, 10, 13, 13) shade Persian Grey
1 pair 3.25mm (US #3) needles
1 pair 3.75mm (US #5) needles
– or –
1 pair 2.75mm (US #2) needles
1 pair 3.25mm (US #3) needles
1 cable needle
10 buttons

TENSION
1st, 3rd and 5th sizes only
18 st patt rep = 5cm using 3.25mm needles
30 rows = 10cm (4in) using 3.25mm needles over 20 row patt

2nd and 4th sizes only
18 st patt rep = 5½cm using 3.75mm needles
25 rows = 10cm (4in) using 3.75mm needles over 20 row patt

Standard Yarn Tension
28 sts & 36 rows = 10cm (4in) using 3mm needles over stocking stitch

ABBREVIATIONS
See page 13 for standard abbreviations

Specific abbreviations for this pattern
C9F: Slip next 4 sts to cable needle and hold at front, K5 then K4 from cable needle

SIZING
Measurements given in centimetres followed by inches in parentheses

To Fit	76–81 (30–32)	86–92 (34–36)	97–102 (38–40)	107–112 (42–44)	117–122 (46–48)
Finished Measurements					
Actual Bust Size	85½ (33½)	95 (37½)	105½ (41½)	117 (46)	125½ (49½)
Length to underarm	35 (13¾)	35 (13¾)	38 (15)	39 (15½)	41½ (16½)
Armhole Depth	17 (6½)	17¼ (6¾)	20¼ (8)	20½ (8¼)	23¾ (9¼)
Finished Length	52 (20½)	52¼ (20½)	58¼ (23)	59½ (23½)	60¾ (24)
Shoulder to Shoulder	29 (11½)	32 (12½)	38 (15)	41½ (16¼)	46½ (18¼)

Garment shown in photographs is for first size 76–81 (30–32)

PATTERN NOTES
To provide more sizes on a pattern with such a large pattern repeat, the 2nd and 4th sizes are knitted on different needle sizes to the other sizes. It is imperative that the right tension is achieved for this pattern to obtain the size required. The front armholes are longer than the back so the shoulder seam sits at the back of the garment. Buttonholes are worked on every 19th and 20th rows of the 20 row patt reps and on the ribbed welt and yoke. These instructions are not referred to throughout the pattern so it is important to remember to work these buttonholes. The yoke is worked around the neck opening created by the front and back, the sleeves are sew in after the yoke is worked. The garment therefore has a slightly dropped shoulder effect. The stitch pattern has a variable stitch count (16 or 18 sts in the repeat section). Where stitch counts are given in the pattern they are specific to the intended row. If you change the number of rows worked, then the stitch counts may no longer work correctly.

RIGHT FRONT
Using 2.75 (3.25, 2.75, 3.25, 2.75) mm needles cast on 64 (64, 82, 82, 100) sts.
Row 1: K2, * P1, K1, repeat from * to end.
Repeat row 1 again.
Row 3: K2, P1, cast off 2, K1, * P1, K1, repeat from * to end.
Row 4: K2, P1, * K1, P1, repeat from * to last 3 sts, cast on 2, K1, P1, K1.

Repeat row 1, 12 times, and rows 3–4 once, row 1, 12 times, then row 3 only once more.
Using 3.25 (3.75, 3.25, 3.75, 3.25) mm needles proceed as folls:
Row 1 (WS): K1, [P1 (1, 2, 2, 2), Pfb] 10 times, [P1, (1, 2, 2, 3), Pfb] 13 times, P8 (8, 3, 3, 8), [K1, P1] twice, cast on 2, K1, P1, K1 (87, 87, 105, 105, 123 sts).

Row 2: K2, [P1, K1] 3 times, P1, * taking a cable needle slip 4 sts on to it, letting needle fall in front of work, K5, bring 4 sts back and slip onto needle again, knit these 4 (referred to on chart as C9F), P9, repeat from * to last 6 sts, K4, P1, K1.

Row 3: K2, * P4, K9, P4, K1, repeat from * to last 13 sts, P4, K1, (P1, K1) 4 times.

Now work from chart as folls:

** Row 1 (RS): K2, [P1, K1] 3 times, P1, working from right to left of chart row 1, repeating marked section 4 (4, 5, 5, 6) times, P1, K1.

Row 2 (WS): K2, working from left to right of chart row 2, repeating marked section 4 (4, 5, 5, 6) times, K1, (P1, K1) 4 times.

Last 2 rows set edge sts and chart. Make buttonholes at front edge on rows 19 and 20 of each repeat throughout.

Work as set, until row 19 (19, 9, 9, 19) of chart has been worked for the 4th (3rd, 5th, 4th, 5th) time (85, 85, 105, 105, 121 sts).

Shape Armhole

Next row (WS): Maintaining patt, cast off 18 sts, patt to end (1st, 2nd and 5th sizes casting on for button hole) (69, 69, 87, 87, 105 sts).

Continuing to maintain patt as set (now repeating marked section 3 (3, 4, 4, 5) times) and working buttonholes as required, work 26 (16, 36, 36, 36) rows in patt thus ending on chart row 6 (16, 16, 16, 16) (63, 63, 79, 79, 95 sts). Divide for neck as folls:

Next row (RS): K2, [P1, K1] 3 times, slip these 8 sts on to a holder or waste yarn, cast off the next 32 (32, 39, 39, 46) sts, then patt to end (23, 23, 32, 32, 41 sts).

Work a further 34 (34, 34, 34, 34, 44) rows in pattern as set.

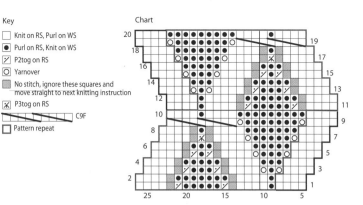

Key

☐ Knit on RS, Purl on WS
⬛ Purl on RS, Knit on WS
▱ P2tog on RS
◯ Yarnover
▨ No stitch, ignore these squares and move straight to next knitting instruction
⊠ P3tog on RS
⎯⎯ C9F
☐ Pattern repeat

Chart

Shape Shoulder

Cast off 12 (12, 16, 16, 21) sts at beg of next row, patt to end. Patt one row, then cast off rem sts.

LEFT FRONT

Using 2.75 (3.25, 2.75, 3.25, 2.75) mm needles cast on 64 (64, 82, 82, 100) sts.

Row 1: * K1, P1, repeat from * to last 2 sts, K2.

Repeat this row 30 times.

Using 3.25 (3.75, 3.25, 3.75, 3.25) mm needles proceed as folls:

Row 1 (WS): [K1, P1] 4 times, K1, P8 (8, 3, 3, 8), [Pfb, P1 (1, 2, 2, 3)] 13 times, [Pfb, P1, (1, 2, 2, 2)] 10 times,, K1 (87, 87, 105, 105, 123 sts).

Row 2: K1, P1, K4, * P9, C9F, repeat from * to last 9 sts, P1, [K1, P1] 3 times, K2.

Row 3: [K1, P1] 4 times, K1, * P4, K1, P4, K9, repeat from * to last 6 sts, P4, K2.

Set chart as folls:

** Row 1 (RS): K1, P1, work from right to left of chart row 11 (by starting in the middle of the chart, the stitch pattern mirrors the pattern on the right front), repeating marked section 4 (4, 5, 5, 6) times, P1, [K1, P1] 3 times, K2.

Row 2: (K1, P1) 4 times, K1, work from left to right of chart row 12, repeating marked section 4 (4, 5, 5, 6) times, K2.

Last 2 rows set edge sts and chart. Work as set until row 8 (8, 18, 18, 8) of chart has been worked for the 4th (3rd, 5th, 4th, 5th) time (79, 79, 95, 95, 111 sts).

Shape Armhole

Next row (RS): Whilst maintaining patt, cast off 16 sts, patt to end (69, 69, 87, 87, 105 sts).

Continuing to maintain patt as set (now repeating marked section 3 (3, 4, 4, 5) times), work 26 (16, 36, 36, 36) rows in patt thus ending on chart row 5 (15, 15, 15, 15) (63, 63, 79, 79, 95 sts). Divide for neck as folls:

Next row (WS): [K1, P1] 4 times, slip these 8 sts on to a holder, cast off the next 32 (32, 39, 39, 46) sts, then patt to end (23, 23, 32, 32, 41 sts). Work a further 35 (35, 35, 35, 35, 45) rows in pattern as set.

Shape Shoulder

With RS facing, cast off 12 (12, 16, 16, 21) sts at beg of next row, patt to end. Patt one row, then cast off rem sts.

BACK

Using 2.75 (3.25, 2.75, 3.25, 2.75) mm needles cast on 102 (102, 126, 126, 150) sts.

Row 1: K2, * P1, K1, repeat from * to end.

Repeat this row 30 times.

Using 3.25 (3.75, 3.25, 3.75, 3.25) mm needles proceed as folls:

Row 1 (WS): K1, * P1, Pfb, repeat from * to last st, K1 (152, 152, 188, 188, 224 sts).

Row 2: K1, P1, * C9F, P9, repeat from * to last 6 sts, K4, P1, K1.

Row 3: K2, * P4, K9, P4, K1, repeat from * to last 6 sts, P4, K2.

Work from chart as folls:

** **Row 1**: K1, P1, work from chart row 1, repeating marked section 8 (8, 10, 10, 12) times, P1, K1.

Row 2: K2, work from chart row 2, repeating marked section 8 (8, 10, 10, 12) times, K2.

Last 2 rows set edge sts and chart. Work as set until row 18 (18, 8, 8, 18) of chart has been worked for the 4th (3rd, 5th, 4th, 5th) time (136, 136, 168, 168, 200 sts).

Shape Armholes

Next row (RS): Cast off 17 sts in patt, P1, YO, * C9F, YO, P7, YO, repeat from * to last 6 sts, K4, P1, K1 (134, 134, 170, 170, 206 sts).

Next row: Cast off 18 sts in patt, K2, P4, * K9, P4, K1, P4, repeat from * to last 2 sts, K2 (116, 116, 152, 152, 188 sts).

Whilst maintaining patt and edge sts as set (now working marked section 6 (6, 8, 8, 10) times), work 25 (15, 35, 35, 35) rows in patt thus ending on chart row 5 (15, 5, 5, 15) (104, 104, 136, 136, 168 sts). Divide for back neck as folls:

Next row (WS): Patt 23 (23, 32, 32, 41) sts, cast off centre 58 (58, 72, 72, 86) sts, patt to end.

Working on last 23 (23, 32, 32, 41) sts only, work in patt for a further 15 (19, 15, 15, 25) rows, thus ending on chart row 1 (15, 1, 1, 1).

Shape Shoulder

Cast off 12 (12, 16, 16, 21) sts at beg of next row, turn and patt to neck edge. Cast off rem sts.

With RS facing, rejoin yarn at neck edge and work on rem 23 (23, 32, 32, 41) sts in patt for a further 16 (20, 16, 16, 26) rows thus ending on chart row 2 (16, 2, 2, 2).

Shape Shoulder

With RS facing, cast off 12 (12, 16, 16, 21) sts at beg of next row, turn and patt to neck edge. Cast off rem sts.

Sew up shoulder seams.

YOKE

Using 2.75 (3.25, 2.75, 3.25, 2.75) mm needles with RS facing, and commencing with sts of right front, work in rib across 8 sts on holder, pick up and knit 32 (32, 40, 40, 46) sts from the right front, 43 (43, 43, 43, 53) sts up right side of neck, 59 (59, 73, 73, 87) sts across back neck, 43 (43, 43, 43, 53) sts down left side of neck, 32 (32, 40, 40, 46) across left front and work in rib across 8 sts on 2nd holder (225, 225, 255, 255, 301 sts).

Row 1: [K1, P1] 20 (20, 24, 24, 27) times, P2, [K1, P1] 20 (20, 20, 20, 25) times, P2, [K1, P1] 29 (29, 36, 36, 43) times, P2, [K1, P1] 20 (20, 20, 20, 25) times, P1, [P1, K1] 20 (20, 24, 24, 27) times.

Row 2: K2, [P1, K1] 18 (18, 22, 22, 25) times, P2tog, K1, P2tog, [K1, P1] 18 (18, 18, 18, 23) times, [K1, P2tog] twice, [K1, P1] 27 (27, 34, 34, 41) times, [K1, P2tog] twice, [K1, P1] 18 (18, 18, 18, 23) times, [K1, P2tog] twice, [K1, P1] 18 (18, 22, 22, 25) times, K2 (217, 217, 247, 247, 293 sts).

Row 3: * K1, P1, repeat from * to last st, K1.

Row 4: K2, [P1, K1] 17 (17, 21, 21, 24) times, P1, P2tog, K1, P2tog, [P1, K1] 17 (17, 17, 17, 22) times, P1, P2tog, K1, P2tog, [P1, K1] 26 (26, 33, 33, 40) times, P1, P2tog, K1, P2tog, [P1, K1] 17 (17, 17, 17, 22) times, P1, P2tog, K1, P2tog, [P1, K1] 18 (18, 22, 22, 25) times, K1 (209, 209, 239, 239, 285 sts).

Row 5: [K1, P1] 18 (18, 22, 22, 25) times, K2, P1, K1, [K1, P1] 17 (17, 17, 17, 22) times, K2, P1, K1, [K1, P1] 26 (26, 33, 33, 40) times, K2, P1, K1, [K1, P1] 17 (17, 17, 17, 22) times, K2, P1, K1, [K1, P1] 18 (18, 22, 22, 25) times, K1.

Row 6: K2, P1, cast off 2 sts, [K1, P1] 15 (15, 19, 19, 22) times, [K1, P2tog] twice, [K1, P1] 16 (16, 16, 16, 21) times, [K1, P2tog] twice, [K1, P1] 25 (25, 32, 32, 39) times, [K1, P2tog] twice, [K1, P1] 16 (16, 16, 16, 21) times, [K1, P2tog] twice, [K1, P1] 17 (17, 21, 21, 24) times, K2 (199, 199, 229, 229, 275 sts).

Row 7: * K1, P1, repeat from * to last 3 sts, cast on 2, K1, P1, K1 (201, 201, 231, 231, 277 sts).

Keeping continuity of of rib, decrease once at each corner st in the next and every foll alt row until 161 (161, 191, 191, 237) sts rem, ending with a RS row.

Next row (WS): K2, P1, cast off 2 sts, [K1, P1] 12 (12, 16, 16, 19) times, [K1, P2tog] twice, [K1, P1] 10 (10, 10, 10, 15) times, [K1, P2tog] twice, [K1, P1] 19 (19, 26, 26, 33) times, [K1, P2tog] twice, [K1, P1] 10 (10, 10, 10, 15) times, [K1, P2tog] twice, [K1, P1] 14 (14, 18, 18, 21) times, K2 (151, 151, 181, 181, 227 sts).

Next row: * K1, P1 repeat from * to last 3 sts, cast on 2 sts, K1, P1, K1 (153, 153, 183, 183, 229 sts). Cast off.

SLEEVES

Using 2.75 (3.25, 2.75, 3.25, 2.75) mm needles, cast on 54 (54, 72, 72, 90) sts.

Row 1: K2, * P1, K1, repeat from * to end.

Repeat this row 30 times.

Next row: K1, P0 (0, 9, 9, 18) * P1, Pfb, repeat from * to last 1 (1, 10, 10, 19) sts, purl to last st, K1 (80, 80, 98, 98, 116 sts).

Change to 4mm needles and work chart and edge sts as set for back, repeating marked section 4 (4, 5, 5, 6) times, until row 12 has been worked for the first time (72, 72, 88, 88, 104, 104 sts).

Row 1: Inc in first st, P1, work from chart row 13, repeating marked section 4 (4, 5, 5, 6) times, inc in next st purlways, K1.

Row 2: K1, P1, K1, work from chart row 14, repeating marked section 4 (4, 5, 5, 6) times, K1, P1, K1.

Cont to work as set, and taking increased sts into patt, inc 1 st at each end of chart row 19 and on 13 foll 6th rows. Then work 3 rows without shaping (last row should be chart row 20) (128, 128, 146, 146, 164) sts at the end of final chart row 20).

Work 40 (12, 40, 12, 40) more rows in pattern as set. Cast off.

MAKING UP

Using damp cloth press lightly on WS of work. Sew up side seams. Sew up sleeve seams, leaving 6½cm (2½in) open at the top, to sew to armhole. Sew in the sleeves, carefully matching side seams. Sew on buttons to correspond with buttonholes. Darn in all ends.

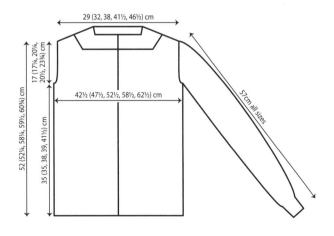

JUMPER-CARDIGAN
FROM BEEHIVE, OR PATON'S SUPER, FINGERING

N° 3814

PATONS & BALDWINS

LADY'S JUMPER-CARDIGAN—"Yvette" design

MATERIALS:—8 ozs. BEEHIVE, or PATON'S SUPER, Scotch Fingering Wool, 3-ply. Two No. 8 and two No. 10 "BEEHIVE" Knitting Needles (or "INOX," if Metal preferred), measured by the Beehive gauge. Ten Buttons.

MEASUREMENTS:—Length from top of shoulder, 18½ ins. Width all round at under-arm, 35 ins. Length of sleeve from under-arm, 17 ins.

ABBREVIATIONS :—K.=Knit plain; P.= Purl; tog.=together; w.r.n.=wool round needle; w.o.n=wool over needle.

❡ Work at a tension to produce one pattern to 2 inches, measured flat—the correct size will only be obtained by exactly following this instruction!

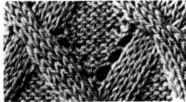

Important!—This illustration shows a piece of fabric knitted to the correct tension.

THE RIGHT FRONT.—Using the No. 10 Needles, cast on 64 stitches.

1st row.—K. 2, * P. 1, K. 1, repeat from * to the end of the row. Repeat this row once.

3rd row.—K. 2, P. 1, cast off 2 stitches, K. 1, * P. 1, K. 1, repeat from * to the end of the row.

4th row.—K. 2, P. 1, * K. 1, P. 1, repeat from * to the last 3 stitches, cast on 2 stitches, K. 1, P. 1, K. 1.

Repeat the 1st row twelve times, the 3rd and 4th rows once, the 1st row twelve times, then the 3rd row once.

Using the No. 8 Needles, proceed as follows:—

1st row.—K. 1, * P. 1, increase once in the next stitch purlways, repeat from * to the last 15 stitches, P. 8, (K. 1, P. 1) twice, cast on 2 stitches, K. 1, P. 1, K. 1 (there should now be 87 stitches on the needle).

2nd row.—K. 2, (P. 1, K. 1) three times, P. 1, * taking a spare needle, slip the next 4 stitches on to it, letting this needle fall to the front of the work, knit the next 5 stitches, bring the 4 stitches back

and slip them on to the needle again, knit these 4 stitches (the crossing of these 9 stitches will now be termed "twist" throughout), P. 9, repeat from * to the last 6 stitches, K. 4, P. 1, K. 1.

3rd row.—K. 2, * P. 4, K. 9, P. 4, K. 1, repeat from * to the last 13 stitches, P. 4, K. 1, (P. 1, K. 1) four times.

Proceed as follows:—

**1st row.—K. 2, (P. 1, K. 1) three times, P. 1, * K. 4, P. 1, K. 4, P. 2 tog., P. 5, P. 2 tog., repeat from * to the last 6 stitches, K. 4, P. 1, K. 1.

2nd row.—K. 2, * P. 4, K. 7, P. 4, K. 1, repeat from * to the last 13 stitches, P. 4, K. 1, (P. 1, K. 1) four times.

3rd row.—K. 2, (P. 1, K. 1) three times, P. 1, * K. 4, w.r.n., P. 1, w.o.n., K. 4, P. 2 tog., P. 3, P. 2 tog., repeat from * to the last 6 stitches, K. 4, P. 1, K. 1.

4th row.—K. 2, * P. 4, K. 5, P. 4, K. 3, repeat from * to the last 13 stitches, P. 4, K. 1, (P. 1, K. 1) four times.

5th row.—K. 2, (P. 1, K. 1) three times, P. 1, * K. 4, w.r.n., P. 3, w.o.n., K. 4, P. 2 tog., P. 1, P. 2 tog., repeat from * to the last 6 stitches, K. 4, P. 1, K. 1.

6th row.—K. 2, * P. 4, K. 3, P. 4, K. 5, repeat from * to the last 13 stitches, P. 4, K. 1, (P. 1, K. 1) four times.

7th row.—K. 2, (P. 1, K. 1) three times, P. 1, * K. 4, w.r.n., P. 5, w.o.n., K. 4, P. 3 tog., repeat from * to the last 6 stitches, K. 4, P. 1, K. 1.

8th row.—K. 2, * P. 4, K. 1, P. 4, K. 7, repeat from * to the last 13 stitches, P. 4, K. 1, (P. 1, K. 1) four times.

9th row.—K. 2, (P. 1, K. 1) three times, P. 1, K. 4, * w.r.n., P. 7, w.o.n., twist, repeat from * to the last 2 stitches, P. 1, K. 1.

10th row.—K. 2, * P. 4, K. 1, P. 4, K. 9, repeat from * to the last 13 stitches, P. 4, K. 1, (P. 1, K. 1) four times.

11th row.—K. 2, (P. 1, K. 1) three times, P. 1, * K. 4, P. 2 tog., P. 5, P. 2 tog., K. 4, P. 1, repeat from * to the last 6 stitches, K. 4, P. 1, K. 1.

12th row.—K. 2, * P. 4, K. 1, P. 4, K. 7, repeat from * to the last 13 stitches, P. 4, K. 1, (P. 1, K. 1) four times.

13th row.—K. 2, (P. 1, K. 1) three times, P. 1, * K. 4, P. 2 tog., P. 3, P. 2 tog., K. 4, w.o.n., repeat from * to the last 6 stitches, K. 4, P. 1, K. 1.

14th row.—K. 2, * P. 4, K. 3, P. 4, K. 5, repeat

from * to the last 13 stitches, P. 4, K. 1, (P. 1, K. 1) four times.

15th row.—K. 2, (P. 1, K. 1) three times, P. 1, * K. 4, P. 2 tog., P. 1, P. 2 tog., K. 4, w.r.n., P. 3, w.o.n., repeat from * to the last 6 stitches, K. 4, P. 1, K. 1.

16th row.—K. 2, * P. 4, K. 5, P. 4, K. 3, repeat from * to the last 13 stitches, P. 4, K. 1, (P. 1, K. 1) four times.

17th row.—K. 2, (P. 1, K. 1) three times, P. 1, * K. 4, P. 3 tog., K. 4, w.r.n., P. 5, w.o.n., repeat from * to the last 6 stitches, K. 4, P. 1, K. 1.

18th row.—K. 2, * P. 4, K. 7, P. 4, K. 1, repeat from * to the last 13 stitches, P. 4, K. 1, (P. 1, K. 1) four times.

19th row.—K. 2, P. 1, cast off 2 stitches, (K. 1, P. 1) twice, * twist, w.r.n., P. 7, w.o.n., repeat from * to the last 6 stitches, K. 4, P. 1, K. 1.

20th row.—K. 2, * P. 4, K. 9, P. 4, K. 1, repeat from * to the last 11 stitches, P. 4, (K. 1, P. 1) twice, cast on 2 stitches, K. 1, P. 1, K. 1 **.

Repeat from ** to ** twice, then from the 1st to the 19th row once.

In the next row cast off 18 stitches in pattern, K. 2, *P. 4, K. 9, P. 4, K. 1, repeat from * to the last 11 stitches, P. 4, (K. 1, P. 1) twice, cast on 2 stitches, K. 1, P. 1, K. 1.

Repeat from ** to ** once, then from the 1st to the 6th row once.

In the next row K. 2, (P. 1, K. 1) three times, slip these 8 stitches on to a piece of wool, cast off 32 stitches in pattern, K. 5, w.r.n., P. 5, w.o.n., K. 4, P. 3 tog., K. 4, P. 1, K. 1.

Work on these 23 stitches as follows:—

1st row.—K. 2, P. 4, K. 1, P. 4, K. 7, P. 4, K. 1.

2nd row.—K. 5, w.r.n., P. 7, w.o.n., twist, P. 1, K. 1.

3rd row.—K. 2, P. 4, K. 1, P. 4, K. 9, P. 4, K. 1.

4th row.—K. 5, P. 2 tog., P. 5, P. 2 tog., (K. 4, P. 1) twice, K. 1.

5th row.—K. 2, P. 4, K. 1, P. 4, K. 7, P. 4, K. 1.

6th row.—K. 5, P. 2 tog., P. 3, P. 2 tog., K. 4, w.r.n., P. 1, w.o.n., K. 4, P. 1, K. 1.

7th row.—K. 2, P. 4, K. 3, P. 4, K. 5, P. 4, K. 1.

8th row.—K. 5, P. 2 tog., P. 1, P. 2 tog., K. 4, w.r.n., P. 3, w.o.n., K. 4, P. 1, K. 1.

9th row.—K. 2, P. 4, K. 5, P. 4, K. 3, P. 4, K. 1.

10th row.—K. 5, P. 3 tog., K. 4, w.r.n., P. 5, w.o.n., K. 4, P. 1, K. 1.

11th row.—K. 2, P. 4, K. 7, (P. 4, K. 1) twice.

12th row.—K. 1, twist, w.r.n., P. 7, w.o.n., K. 4, P. 1, K. 1.

13th row.—K. 2, P. 4, K. 9, (P. 4, K. 1) twice.

14th row.—K. 5, P. 1, K. 4, P. 2 tog., P. 5, P. 2 tog., K. 4, P. 1, K. 1.

15th row.—K. 2, P. 4, K. 7, (P. 4, K. 1) twice.

16th row.—K. 5, w.r.n., P. 1, w.o.n., K. 4, P. 2 tog., P. 3, P. 2 tog., K. 4, P. 1, K. 1.

17th row.—K. 2, P. 4, K. 5, P. 4, K. 3, P. 4, K. 1.

18th row.—K. 5, w.r.n., P. 3, w.o.n., K. 4, P. 2 tog., P. 1, P. 2 tog., K. 4, P. 1, K. 1.

19th row.—K. 2, P. 4, K. 3, P. 4, K. 5, P. 4, K. 1.

20th row.—K. 5, w.r.n., P. 5, w.o.n., K. 4, P. 3 tog., K. 4, P. 1, K. 1.

Repeat from the 1st to the 13th row once.

Shape for the shoulder as follows:—

1st row.—K. 5, P. 1, K. 4, P. 2 tog., P. 1, turn.

2nd row.—K. 2, (P. 4, K. 1) twice.

3rd row.—K. 5, P. 1, K. 4, P. 6, P. 2 tog., K. 4, P. 1, K. 1.

Cast off in pattern.

THE LEFT FRONT.—Using the No. 10 Needles, cast on 64 stitches.

1st row.—* K. 1, P. 1, repeat from * to the last 2 stitches, K. 2.

Repeat this row thirty times.

Using the No. 8 Needles, proceed as follows:—

1st row.—(K. 1, P. 1) four times, K. 1, P. 8, * increase once in the next stitch purlways, P. 1, repeat from * to the last stitch, K. 1 (there should now be 87 stitches on the needle).

2nd row.—K. 1, P. 1, K. 4, * P. 9, twist, repeat from * to the last 9 stitches, P. 1, (K. 1, P. 1) three times, K. 2.

3rd row.—(K. 1, P. 1) four times, K. 1, * P. 4, K. 1, P. 4, K. 9, repeat from * to the last 6 stitches, P. 4, K. 2.

Proceed as follows:—

**1st row.—K. 1, P. 1, K. 4, * P. 2 tog., P. 5, P. 2 tog., K. 4, P. 1, K. 4, repeat from * to the last 9 stitches, P. 1, (K. 1, P. 1) three times, K. 2.

2nd row.—(K. 1, P. 1) four times, K. 1, * P. 4, K. 1, P. 4, K. 7, repeat from * to the last 6 stitches, P. 4, K. 2.

3rd row.—K. 1, P. 1, K. 4, * P. 2 tog., P. 3, P. 2 tog., K. 4, w.r.n., P. 1, w.o.n., K. 4, repeat from * to the last 9 stitches, P. 1, (K. 1, P. 1) three times, K. 2.

4th row.—(K. 1, P. 1) four times, K. 1, * P. 4, K. 3, P. 4, K. 5, repeat from * to the last 6 stitches, P. 4, K. 2.

5th row.—K. 1, P. 1, K. 4, * P. 2 tog., P. 1, P. 2 tog., K. 4, w.r.n., P. 3, w.o.n., K. 4, repeat from * to the last 9 stitches, P. 1, (K. 1, P. 1) three times, K. 2.

6th row.—(K. 1, P. 1) four times, K. 1, * P. 4,

K. 5, P. 4, K. 3, repeat from * to the last 6 stitches, P. 4, K. 2.
7th row.—K. 1, P. 1, K. 4, * P. 3 tog., K. 4, w.r.n., P. 5, w.o.n., K. 4, repeat from * to the last 9 stitches, P. 1, (K. 1, P. 1) three times, K. 2.
8th row.—(K. 1, P. 1) four times, K. 1, * P. 4, K. 7, P. 4, K. 1, repeat from * to the last 6 stitches, P. 4, K. 2.
9th row.—K. 1, P. 1, * twist, w.r.n., P. 7, w.o.n., repeat from * to the last 13 stitches, K. 4, P. 1, (K. 1, P. 1) three times, K. 2.
10th row.—(K. 1, P. 1) four times, K. 1, * P. 4, K. 9, P. 4, K. 1, repeat from * to the last 6 stitches, P. 4, K. 2.
11th row.—K. 1, P. 1, K. 4, * P. 1, K. 4, P. 2 tog., P. 5, P. 2 tog., K. 4, repeat from * to the last 9 stitches, P. 1, (K. 1, P. 1) three times, K. 2.
12th row.—(K. 1, P. 1) four times, K. 1, * P. 4, K. 7, P. 4, K. 1, repeat from * to the last 6 stitches, P. 4, K. 2.
13th row.—K. 1, P. 1, K. 4, * w.r.n., P. 1, w.o.n., K. 4, P. 2 tog., P. 3, P. 2 tog., K. 4, repeat from * to the last 9 stitches, P. 1, (K. 1, P. 1) three times, K. 2.
14th row.—(K. 1, P. 1) four times, K. 1, * P. 4, K. 5, P. 4, K. 3, repeat from * to the last 6 stitches, P. 4, K. 2.
15th row.—K. 1, P. 1, K. 4, * w.r.n., P. 3, w.o.n., K. 4, P. 2 tog., P. 1, P. 2 tog., K. 4, repeat from * to the last 9 stitches, P. 1, (K. 1, P. 1) three times, K. 2.
16th row.—(K. 1, P. 1) four times, K. 1, * P. 4, K. 3, P. 4, K. 5, repeat from * to the last 6 stitches, P. 4, K. 2.
17th row.—K. 1, P. 1, K. 4, * w.r.n., P. 5, w.o.n., K. 4, P. 3 tog., K. 4, repeat from * to the last 9 stitches, P. 1, (K. 1, P. 1) three times, K. 2.
18th row.—(K. 1, P. 1) four times, K. 1, * P. 4, K. 1, P. 4, K. 7, repeat from * to the last 6 stitches, P. 4, K. 2.
19th row.—K. 1, P. 1, K. 4, * w.r.n., P. 7, w.o.n., twist, repeat from * to the last 9 stitches, P. 1, (K. 1, P. 1) three times, K. 2.
20th row.—(K. 1, P. 1) four times, K. 1, * P. 4, K. 1, P. 4, K. 9, repeat from * to the last 6 stitches, P. 4, K. 2 **.
Repeat from ** to ** twice, then from the 1st to the 18th row once.
In the next row cast off 16 stitches in pattern, K. 1, P. 1, K. 4, * w.r.n., P. 7, w.o.n., twist, repeat from * to the last 9 stitches, P. 1, (K. 1, P. 1) three times, K. 2.
In the following row (K. 1, P. 1) four times, K. 1, * P. 4, K. 1, P. 4, K. 9, repeat from * to the last 6 stitches, P. 4, K. 2.
Repeat from ** to ** once, then from the 1st to the 5th row once.
In the next row (K. 1, P. 1) four times, slip these 8 stitches on to a piece of wool, cast off 32 stitches in pattern, K. 1, P. 4, K. 5, P. 4, K. 3, P. 4, K. 2. Work on these 23 stitches as follows:—
1st row.—K. 1, P. 1, K. 4, P. 3 tog., K. 4, w.r.n., P. 5, w.o.n., K. 5.
2nd row.—K. 1, P. 4, K. 7, P. 4, K. 1, P. 4, K. 2.
3rd row.—K. 1, P. 1, twist, w.r.n., P. 7, w.o.n., K. 5.
4th row.—K. 1, P. 4, K. 9, P. 4, K. 1, P. 4, K. 2.
5th row.—K. 1, (P. 1, K. 4) twice, P. 2 tog., P. 5, P. 2 tog., K. 5.
6th row.—K. 1, P. 4, K. 7, P. 4, K. 1, P. 4, K. 2.
7th row.—K. 1, P. 1, K. 4, w.r.n., P. 1, w.o.n., K. 4, P. 2 tog., P. 3, P. 2 tog., K. 5.
8th row.—K. 1, P. 4, K. 5, P. 4, K. 3, P. 4, K. 2.
9th row.—K. 1, P. 1, K. 4, w.r.n., P. 3, w.o.n., K. 4, P. 2 tog., P. 1, P. 2 tog., K. 5.
10th row.—K. 1, P. 4, K. 3, P. 4, K. 5, P. 4, K. 2.
11th row.—K. 1, P. 1, K. 4, w.r.n., P. 5, w.o.n., K. 4, P. 3 tog., K. 5.
12th row.—(K. 1, P. 4) twice, K. 7, P. 4, K. 2.
13th row.—K. 1, P. 1, K. 4, w.r.n., P. 7, w.o.n., twist, K. 1.
14th row.—(K. 1, P. 4) twice, K. 9, P. 4, K. 2.
15th row.—K. 1, P. 1, K. 4, P. 2 tog., P. 5, P. 2 tog., K. 4, P. 1, K. 5.
16th row.—(K. 1, P. 4) twice, K. 7, P. 4, K. 2.
17th row.—K. 1, P. 1, K. 4, P. 2 tog., P. 3, P. 2 tog., K. 4, w.r.n., P. 1, w.o.n., K. 5.
18th row.—K. 1, P. 4, K. 3, P. 4, K. 5, P. 4, K. 2.
19th row.—K. 1, P. 1, K. 4, P. 2 tog., P. 1, P. 2 tog., K. 4, w.r.n., P. 3, w.o.n., K. 5.
20th row.—K. 1, P. 4, K. 5, P. 4, K. 3, P. 4, K. 2.
Repeat from the 1st to the 15th row once.
Shape for the shoulder as follows:—
1st row.—(K. 1, P. 4) twice, K. 2, turn.
2nd row.—P. 2, K. 4, P. 1, K. 5.
Cast off in pattern.
THE BACK.—Using the No. 10 Needles, cast on 102 stitches.
1st row.—K. 2, * P. 1, K. 1, repeat from * to the end of the row.
Repeat this row thirty times.
Using the No. 8 Needles, proceed as follows:—
1st row.—K. 1, * P. 1, increase once in the next stitch purlways, repeat from * to the last stitch, K. 1 (there should now be 152 stitches on the needle).
2nd row.—K. 1, P. 1, * twist, P. 9, repeat from * to the last 6 stitches, K. 4, P. 1, K. 1.
3rd row.—K. 2, * P. 4, K. 9, P. 4, K. 1, repeat from * to the last 6 stitches, P. 4, K. 2.
Proceed as follows:—
****1st row.**—K. 1, P. 1, * K. 4, P. 1, K. 4, P. 2 tog., P. 5, P. 2 tog., repeat from * to the last 6 stitches, K. 4, P. 1, K. 1.
2nd row.—K. 2, * P. 4, K. 7, P. 4, K. 1, repeat from * to the last 6 stitches, P. 4, K. 2.
3rd row.—K. 1, P. 1, * K. 4, w.r.n., P. 1, w.o.n., K. 4, P. 2 tog., P. 3, P. 2 tog., repeat from * to the last 6 stitches, K. 4, P. 1, K. 1.
4th row.—K. 2, * P. 4, K. 5, P. 4, K. 3, repeat from * to the last 6 stitches, P. 4, K. 2.
5th row.—K. 1, P. 1, * K. 4, w.r.n., P. 3, w.o.n., K. 4, P. 2 tog., P. 1, P. 2 tog., repeat from * to the last 6 stitches, K. 4, P. 1, K. 1.
6th row.—K. 2, * P. 4, K. 3, P. 4, K. 5, repeat from * to the last 6 stitches, P. 4, K. 2.
7th row.—K. 1, P. 1, * K. 4, w.r.n., P. 5, w.o.n., K. 4, P. 3 tog., repeat from * to the last 6 stitches, K. 4, P. 1, K. 1.
8th row.—K. 2, * P. 4, K. 1, P. 4, K. 7, repeat from * to the last 6 stitches, P. 4, K. 2.
9th row.—K. 1, P. 1, K. 4, * w.r.n., P. 7, w.o.n., twist, repeat from * to the last 2 stitches, P. 1, K. 1.
10th row.—K. 2, P. 4, * K. 1, P. 4, K. 9, P. 4, repeat from * to the last 2 stitches, K. 2.
11th row.—K. 1, P. 1, * K. 4, P. 2 tog., P. 5, P. 2 tog., K. 4, P. 1, repeat from * to the last 6 stitches, K. 4, P. 1, K. 1.
12th row.—K. 2, P. 4, * K. 1, P. 4, K. 7, P. 4, repeat from * to the last 2 stitches, K. 2.
13th row.—K. 1, P. 1, * K. 4, P. 2 tog., P. 3, P. 2 tog., K. 4, w.r.n., P. 1, w.o.n., repeat from * to the last 6 stitches, K. 4, P. 1, K. 1.
14th row.—K. 2, P. 4, * K. 3, P. 4, K. 5, P. 4, repeat from * to the last 2 stitches, K. 2.
15th row.—K. 1, P. 1, * K. 4, P. 2 tog., P. 1, P. 2 tog., K. 4, w.r.n., P. 3, w.o.n., repeat from * to the last 6 stitches, K. 4, P. 1, K. 1.
16th row.—K. 2, P. 4, * K. 5, P. 4, K. 3, P. 4, repeat from * to the last 2 stitches, K. 2.
17th row.—K. 1, P. 1, * K. 4, P. 3 tog., K. 4, w.r.n., P. 5, w.o.n., repeat from * to the last 6 stitches, K. 4, P. 1, K. 1.
18th row.—K. 2, P. 4, * K. 7, P. 4, K. 1, P. 4, repeat from * to the last 2 stitches, K. 2.
19th row.—K. 1, P. 1, * twist, w.r.n., P. 7, w.o.n., repeat from * to the last 6 stitches, K. 4, P. 1, K. 1.
20th row.—K. 2, P. 4, * K. 9, P. 4, K. 1, P. 4, repeat from * to the last 2 stitches, K. 2 **.
Repeat from ** to ** twice, then from the 1st to the 18th row once.
In the next row cast off 17 stitches in pattern, P. 1, w.o.n., * twist, w.r.n., P. 7, w.o.n., repeat from * to the last 6 stitches, K. 4, P. 1, K. 1.
In the following row cast off 18 stitches in pattern, K. 2, P. 4, * K. 9, P. 4, K. 1, P. 4, repeat from * to the last 2 stitches, K. 2.
Repeat from ** to ** twice, then from the 1st to the 5th row once.
In the next row K. 2, P. 4, K. 3, P. 4, K. 5, P. 4, K. 1, cast off 58 stitches in pattern, K. 1, P. 4, K. 3, P. 4, K. 5, P. 4, K. 2.
Work on the last 23 stitches as follows:—
1st row.—K. 1, P. 1, K. 4, w.r.n., P. 5, w.o.n., K. 4, P. 3 tog., K. 5.
2nd row.—(K. 1, P. 4) twice, K. 7, P. 4, K. 2.
3rd row.—K. 1, P. 1, K. 4, w.r.n., P. 7, w.o.n., twist, K. 1.
4th row.—(K. 1, P. 4) twice, K. 9, P. 4, K. 2.
5th row.—K. 1, P. 1, K. 4, P. 2 tog., P. 5, P. 2 tog., K. 4, P. 1, K. 5.
6th row.—(K. 1, P. 4) twice, K. 7, P. 4, K. 2.
7th row.—K. 1, P. 1, K. 4, P. 2 tog., P. 3, P. 2 tog., K. 4, w.r.n., P. 1, w.o.n., K. 5.
8th row.—K. 1, P. 4, K. 3, P. 4, K. 5, P. 4, K. 2.
9th row.—K. 1, P. 1, K. 4, P. 2 tog., P. 1, P. 2 tog., K. 4, w.r.n., P. 3, w.o.n., K. 5.
10th row.—K. 1, P. 4, K. 5, P. 4, K. 3, P. 4, K. 2.
11th row.—K. 1, P. 1, K. 4, P. 3 tog., K. 4, w.r.n., P. 5, w.o.n., K. 5.
12th row.—K. 1, P. 4, K. 7, P. 4, K. 1, P. 4, K. 2.
13th row.—K. 1, P. 1, twist, w.r.n., P. 7, w.o.n., K. 5.
14th row.—K. 1, P. 4, K. 9, (P. 4, K. 1) twice, K. 1.
15th row.—K. 1, P. 1, K. 4, P. 1, K. 4, P. 2 tog., P. 5, P. 2 tog., K. 5.
Shape for the shoulder as follows:—
1st row.—K. 1, P. 4, K. 7, turn.
2nd row.—P. 7, K. 5.
Cast off in pattern.
Join in the wool at the neck edge and work on the remaining 23 stitches as follows:—
1st row.—K. 5, w.r.n., P. 5, w.o.n., K. 4, P. 3 tog., K. 4, P. 1, K. 1.
2nd row.—K. 2, P. 4, K. 1, P. 4, K. 7, P. 4, K. 1.
3rd row.—K. 5, w.r.n., P. 7, w.o.n., twist, P. 1, K. 1.
4th row.—K. 2, P. 4, K. 1, P. 4, K. 9, P. 4, K. 1.
5th row.—K. 5, P. 2 tog., P. 5, P. 2 tog., (K. 4, P. 1) twice, K. 1.
6th row.—K. 2, P. 4, K. 1, P. 4, K. 7, P. 4, K. 1.
7th row.—K. 5, P. 2 tog., P. 3, P. 2 tog., K. 4, w.r.n., P. 1, w.o.n., K. 4, P. 1, K. 1.
8th row.—K. 2, P. 4, K. 3, P. 4, K. 5, P. 4, K. 1.
9th row.—K. 5, P. 2 tog., P. 1, P. 2 tog., K. 4, w.r.n., P. 3, w.o.n., K. 4, P. 1, K. 1.
10th row.—K. 2, P. 4, K. 5, P. 4, K. 3, P. 4, K. 1.
11th row.—K. 5, P. 3 tog., K. 4, w.r.n., P. 5, w.o.n., K. 4, P. 1, K. 1.
12th row.—K. 2, P. 4, K. 7, (P. 4, K. 1) twice.
13th row.—K. 1, twist, w.r.n., P. 7, w.o.n., K. 4, P. 1, K. 1.
14th row.—K. 2, P. 4, K. 9, (P. 4, K. 1) twice.
Shape for the shoulder as follows:—
1st row.—K. 5, P. 1, K. 4, P. 2 tog., P. 1, turn.
2nd row.—K. 2, (P. 4, K. 1) twice.
3rd row.—K. 5, P. 1, K. 4, P. 6, P. 2 tog., K. 4, P. 1, K. 1.
Cast off in pattern.
Sew up the shoulder seams.
THE YOKE.—Using the No. 10 Needles, with the right side of the work facing, commence on the stitches of the Right Front and work in rib across the 8 stitches which were left, knit up 32 stitches from the Right Front, 43 down the side of the neck, 59 along the back, 43 down the other side, 32 along the Left Front and work in rib across the 8 stitches which were left (there should now be 225 stitches on the needle).
1st row.—(K. 1, P. 1) twenty times, P. 2, (K. 1, P. 1) twenty times, P. 2, (K. 1, P. 1) twenty-nine times, P. 2, (K. 1, P. 1) twenty times, P. 1, (P. 1, K. 1) twenty times.
2nd row.—K. 2, (P. 1, K. 1) eighteen times, P. 2 tog., K. 1, P. 2 tog., (K. 1, P. 1) eighteen times, (K. 1, P. 2 tog.) twice, (K. 1, P. 1) twenty-seven times, (K. 1, P. 2 tog.) twice, (K. 1, P. 1) eighteen times, (K. 1, P. 2 tog.) twice, (K. 1, P. 1) eighteen times, K. 2.
3rd row.—* K. 1, P. 1, repeat from * to the last stitch, K. 1.
4th row.—K. 2, (P. 1, K. 1) seventeen times, P. 1, P. 2 tog., K. 1, P. 2 tog., (P. 1, K. 1) seventeen times, P. 1, P. 2 tog., K. 1, P. 2 tog., (P. 1, K. 1) twenty-six times, P. 1, P. 2 tog., K. 1, P. 2 tog., (P. 1, K. 1) seventeen times, P. 1, P. 2 tog., K. 1, P. 2 tog., (P. 1, K. 1) eighteen times, K. 1.
5th row.—(K. 1, P. 1) eighteen times, K. 2, P. 1, K. 1, (K. 1, P. 1) seventeen times, K. 2, P. 1, K. 1, (K. 1, P. 1) twenty-six times, K. 2, P. 1, K. 1, (K. 1, P. 1) seventeen times, K. 2, P. 1, K. 1, (K. 1, P. 1) eighteen times, K. 1.
6th row.—K. 2, P. 1, cast off 2 stitches, (K. 1, P. 1) fifteen times, (K. 1, P. 2 tog.) twice, (K. 1, P. 1) sixteen times, (K. 1, P. 2 tog.) twice, (K. 1, P. 1) twenty-five times, (K. 1, P. 2 tog.) twice, (K. 1, P. 1) sixteen times, (K. 1, P. 2 tog.) twice, (K. 1, P. 1) seventeen times, K. 2.
7th row.—* K. 1, P. 1, repeat from * to the last 3 stitches, cast on 2 stitches, K. 1, P. 1, K. 1.
Keeping the continuity of the rib, decrease once at each side of each corner stitch in the next and every alternate row until 161 stitches remain, ending with the wrong side of the work facing.
In the next row K. 2, P. 1, cast off 2 stitches, (K. 1, P. 1) twelve times, (K. 1, P. 2 tog.) twice, (K. 1, P. 1) ten times, (K. 1, P. 2 tog.) twice, (K. 1, P. 1) nineteen times, (K. 1, P. 2 tog.) twice, (K. 1, P. 1) ten times, (K. 1, P. 2 tog.) twice, (K. 1, P. 1) fourteen times, K. 2.
In the following row * K. 1, P. 1, repeat from * to the last 3 stitches, cast on 2 stitches, K. 1, P. 1, K. 1.
Cast off firmly.
THE SLEEVES.—Using the No. 10 Needles, cast on 54 stitches.
1st row.—K. 2, * P. 1, K. 1, repeat from * to the end of the row. Repeat this row thirty times.
Using the No. 8 Needles, proceed as follows:—
1st row.—K. 1, * P. 1, increase once in the next stitch purlways, repeat from * to the last stitch, K. 1 (there should now be 80 stitches on the needle).
Continue as given for the Back until the 12th row of the pattern has been worked.
Proceed as follows:—
1st row.—Increase once in the first stitch, P. 1, * K. 4, P. 2 tog., P. 3, P. 2 tog., K. 4, w.r.n., P. 1, w.o.n., repeat from * to the last 6 stitches, K. 4, increase once in the next stitch purlways, K. 1.
2nd row.—K. 1, P. 1, K. 1, P. 4, * K. 3, P. 4, K. 5, P. 4, repeat from * to the last 3 stitches, K. 1, P. 1, K. 1.
3rd row.—K. 2, P. 1, * K. 4, P. 2 tog., P. 1, P. 2 tog., K. 4, w.r.n., P. 3, w.o.n., repeat from * to the last 7 stitches, K. 4, P. 1, K. 2.
4th row.—K. 1, P. 1, K. 1, P. 4, * K. 5, P. 4, K. 3, P. 4, repeat from * to the last 3 stitches, K. 1, P. 1, K. 1.
5th row.—K. 2, P. 1, * K. 4, P. 3 tog., K. 4, w.r.n., P. 5, w.o.n., repeat from * to the last 7 stitches, K. 4, P. 1, K. 2.
6th row.—K. 1, P. 1, K. 1, P. 4, * K. 7, P. 4, K. 1, P. 4, repeat from * to last 3 stitches, K. 1, P. 1, K. 1.
7th row.—K. 1, increase once in the next stitch, P. 1, * twist, w.r.n., P. 7, w.o.n., repeat from * to the last 7 stitches, K. 4, increase once in the next stitch purlways, K. 2.
8th row.—K. 1, P. 2, K. 1, P. 4, * K. 9, P. 4, K. 1,

P. 4, repeat from * to the last 4 stitches, K. 1, P. 2, K. 1.

9th row.—K. 3, P. 1, * K. 4, P. 1, K. 4, P. 2 tog., P. 5, P. 2 tog., repeat from * to the last 8 stitches, K. 4, P. 1, K. 3.

10th row.—K. 1, P. 2, K. 1, * P. 4, K. 7, P. 4, K. 1, repeat from * to last 8 stitches, P. 4, K. 1, P. 2, K. 1.

11th row.—K. 3, P. 1, * K. 4, w.r.n., P. 1, w.o.n., K. 4, P. 2 tog., P. 3, P. 2 tog., repeat from * to the last 8 stitches, K. 4, P. 1, K. 3.

12th row.—K. 1, P. 2, K. 1, * P. 4, K. 5, P. 4, K. 3, repeat from * to the last 8 stitches, P. 4, K. 1, P. 2, K. 1.

13th row.—K. 1, increase once in the next stitch, K. 1, P. 1, * K. 4, w.r.n., P. 3, w.o.n., K. 4, P. 2 tog., P. 1, P. 2 tog., repeat from * to last 8 stitches, K. 4, P. 1, increase once in next stitch, K. 2.

14th row.—K. 1, P. 3, K. 1, * P. 4, K. 3, P. 4, K. 5, repeat from * to the last 9 stitches, P. 4, K. 1, P. 3, K. 1.

15th row.—K. 4, P. 1, * K. 4, w.r.n., P. 5, w.o.n., K. 4, P. 3 tog., repeat from * to the last 9 stitches, K. 4, P. 1, K. 4.

16th row.—K. 1, P. 3, K. 1, * P. 4, K. 1, P. 4, K. 7, repeat from * to last 9 stitches, P. 4, K. 1, P. 3, K. 1.

17th row.—Twist, * w.r.n., P. 7, w.o.n., twist, repeat from * to the last 5 stitches, P. 1, K. 4.

18th row.—K. 1, P. 3, K. 1, P. 4, * K. 1, P. 4, K. 9, P. 4, repeat from * to the last 5 stitches, K. 1, P. 3, K. 1.

19th row.—K. 1, increase once in the next stitch, K. 2, P. 1, * K. 4, P. 2 tog., P. 5, P. 2 tog., K. 4, P. 1, repeat from * to the last 9 stitches, K. 4, P. 1, K. 1, increase once in the next stitch, K. 2.

20th row.—(K. 1, P. 4) three times, * K. 7, P. 4, K. 1, P. 4, repeat from * to the last stitch, K. 1.

21st row.—K. 5, P. 1, * K. 4, P. 2 tog., P. 3, P. 2 tog., K. 4, w.r.n., P. 1, w.o.n., repeat from * to the last 10 stitches, K. 4, P. 1, K. 5.

22nd row.—(K. 1, P. 4) twice, * K. 3, P. 4, K. 5, P. 4, repeat from * to last 6 stitches, K. 1, P. 4, K. 1.

23rd row.—K. 5, P. 1, * K. 4, P. 2 tog., P. 1, P. 2 tog., K. 4, w.r.n., P. 3, w.o.n., repeat from * to the last 10 stitches, K. 4, P. 1, K. 5.

24th row.—(K. 1, P. 4) twice, * K. 5, P. 4, K. 3, P. 4, repeat from * to the last 6 stitches, K. 1, P. 4, K. 1.

25th row.—Increase once in the first stitch, K. 4, P. 1, * K. 4, P. 3 tog., K. 4, w.r.n., P. 5, w.o.n., repeat from * to the last 10 stitches, K. 4, P. 1, K. 3, increase once in next stitch, K. 1.

26th row.—K. 2, P. 4, K. 1, P. 4, * K. 7, P. 4, K. 1, P. 4, repeat from * to last 7 stitches, K. 1, P. 4, K. 2.

27th row.—K. 1, P. 1, K. 4, P. 1, * twist, w.r.n., P. 7, w.o.n., repeat from * to the last 11 stitches, twist, P. 1, K. 1.

28th row.—K. 2, P. 4, K. 1, P. 4, * K. 9, P. 4, K. 1, P. 4, repeat from * to the last 7 stitches, K. 1, P. 4, K. 2.

29th row.—K. 1, P. 1, K. 4, P. 1, * K. 4, P. 1, K. 4, P. 2 tog., P. 5, P. 2 tog., repeat from * to the last 11 stitches, (K. 4, P. 1) twice, K. 1.

30th row.—K. 2, P. 4, K. 1, * P. 4, K. 7, P. 4, K. 1, repeat from * to the last 11 stitches, P. 4, K. 1, P. 4, K. 2.

31st row.—Increase once in the first stitch, P. 1, K. 4, P. 1, * K. 4, w.r.n., P. 1, w.o.n., K. 4, P. 2 tog., P. 3, P. 2 tog., repeat from * to the last 11 stitches, K. 4, w.r.n., P. 1, w.o.n., K. 4, increase once in the next stitch purlways, K. 1.

32nd row.—K. 1, P. 1, K. 4, P. 4, K. 3, * P. 4, K. 5, P. 4, K. 3, repeat from * to the last 12 stitches, (P. 4, K. 1) twice, P. 1, K. 1.

33rd row.—K. 2, P. 1, K. 4, P. 1, * K. 4, w.r.n., P. 3, w.o.n., K. 4, P. 2 tog., P. 1, P. 2 tog., repeat from * to the last 14 stitches, K. 4, w.r.n., P. 3, w.o.n., K. 4, P. 1, K. 2.

34th row.—K. 1, P. 1, K. 1, P. 4, K. 5, * P. 4, K. 3, P. 4, K. 5, repeat from * to the last 12 stitches, (P. 4, K. 1) twice, P. 1, K. 1.

35th row.—K. 2, P. 1, K. 4, P. 1, * K. 4, w.r.n., P. 5, w.o.n., K. 4, P. 3 tog., repeat from * to the last 16 stitches, K. 4, w.r.n., P. 5, w.o.n., K. 4, P. 1, K. 2.

36th row.—K. 1, P. 1, K. 1, P. 4, K. 7, * P. 4, K. 1, P. 4, K. 7, repeat from * to the last 12 stitches, (P. 4, K. 1) twice, P. 1, K. 1.

Repeat from the 7th to the 36th row once, then from the 7th to the 28th row once.

Proceed as follows:—

**1st row.—K. 1, (P. 1, K. 4) three times, * P. 2 tog., P. 5, P. 2 tog., K. 4, P. 1, K. 4, repeat from * to the last 2 stitches, P. 1, K. 1.

2nd row.—K. 2, * P. 4, K. 1, P. 4, K. 7, repeat from * to the last 16 stitches, (P. 4, K. 1) three times, K. 1.

3rd row.—K. 1, P. 1, K. 4, P. 1, * K. 4, w.r.n., P. 1, w.o.n., K. 4, P. 2 tog., P. 3, P. 2 tog., repeat from * to the last 11 stitches, (K. 4, P. 1) twice, K. 1.

4th row.—K. 2, P. 4, K. 1, * P. 4, K. 5, P. 4, K. 3, repeat from * to the last 11 stitches, (P. 4, K. 1) twice, K. 1.

5th row.—K. 1, P. 1, K. 4, P. 1, * K. 4, w.r.n., P. 3, w.o.n., K. 4, P. 2 tog., P. 1, P. 2 tog., repeat from * to the last 11 stitches, (K. 4, P. 1) twice, K. 1.

6th row.—K. 2, P. 4, K. 1, * P. 4, K. 3, P. 4, K. 5, repeat from * to the last 11 stitches, (P. 4, K. 1) twice, K. 1.

7th row.—K. 1, P. 1, K. 4, P. 1, * K. 4, w.r.n., P. 5, w.o.n., K. 4, P. 3 tog., repeat from * to the last 11 stitches, (K. 4, P. 1) twice, K. 1.

8th row.—K. 2, P. 4, K. 1, * P. 4, K. 1, P. 4, K. 7, repeat from * to the last 11 stitches, (P. 4, K. 1) twice, K. 1.

9th row.—K. 1, P. 1, * twist, w.r.n., P. 7, w.o.n., repeat from * to the last 16 stitches, twist, P. 1, K. 4, P. 1, K. 1.

10th row.—K. 2, P. 4, K. 1, * P. 4, K. 1, P. 4, K. 9, repeat from * to the last 11 stitches, (P. 4, K. 1) twice, K. 1.

11th row.—K. 1, P. 1, * K. 4, P. 1, K. 4, P. 2 tog., P. 5, P. 2 tog., repeat from * to the last 16 stitches, (K. 4, P. 1) three times, K. 1.

12th row.—K. 2, P. 4, K. 1, * P. 4, K. 1, P. 4, K. 7, repeat from * to the last 11 stitches, (P. 4, K. 1) twice, K. 1.

13th row.—K. 1, (P. 1, K. 4) twice, * P. 2 tog., P. 3, P. 2 tog., K. 4, w.r.n., P. 1, w.o.n., K. 4, repeat from * to the last 7 stitches, P. 1, K. 4, P. 1, K. 1.

14th row.—K. 2, P. 4, K. 1, * P. 4, K. 3, P. 4, K. 5, repeat from * to the last 11 stitches, (P. 4, K. 1) twice, K. 1.

15th row.—K. 1, (P. 1, K. 4) twice, * P. 2 tog., P. 1, P. 2 tog., K. 4, w.r.n., P. 3, w.o.n., K. 4, repeat from * to the last 7 stitches, P. 1, K. 4, P. 1, K. 1.

16th row.—K. 2, P. 4, K. 1, * P. 4, K. 5, P. 4, K. 3, repeat from * to the last 11 stitches, (P. 4, K. 1) twice, K. 1.

17th row.—K. 1, (P. 1, K. 4) twice, * P. 3 tog., K. 4, w.r.n., P. 5, w.o.n., K. 4, repeat from * to the last 7 stitches, P. 1, K. 4, P. 1, K. 1.

18th row.—K. 2, P. 4, K. 1, * P. 4, K. 7, P. 4, K. 1, repeat from * to the last 11 stitches, (P. 4, K. 1) twice, K. 1.

19th row.—K. 1, P. 1, K. 4, P. 1, * twist, w.r.n., P. 7, w.o.n., repeat from * to the last 11 stitches, twist, P. 1, K. 1.

20th row.—K. 2, * P. 4, K. 1, P. 4, K. 9, repeat from * to the last 16 stitches, (P. 4, K. 1) three times, K. 1 **.

Repeat from ** to ** once. Cast off in pattern.
Work another Sleeve in the same manner.

TO MAKE UP THE JUMPER-CARDIGAN.
With a damp cloth and hot iron press lightly. Sew up the side seams. Sew up the sleeve seams, leaving 2½ inches open at the top. Sew in the sleeves, placing seam to seam. Sew on buttons to correspond with the button-holes.

1940s

The outbreak of war in 1939, created yarn and dye shortages throughout Europe, with women being advised to use what supplies there were, to knit for the troops rather than for themselves. As time passed women, men and children were all encouraged to knit as much clothing for themselves as possible, as supplies of other materials became more and more scarce.

Thriftiness was encouraged with designs offered employing yarn saving techniques such as elbow length sleeves and cardigans cut with deep V necks and only two or three buttons for fastenings. Fair Isle also became popular, allowing for small oddments of yarn to be used up. The introduction of the 'Make Do and Mend' philosophy in Britain brought out great ingenuity in knitters, unravelling one garment to make another, knitting buttons, stuffing shoulder pads with torn stockings, knitting sleeves from the top down, two at a time, so the knitter could stop when the wool ran out!

Unfortunately it took years after war ended for the prosperity seen in America to begin to reach Britain, but gradually things did improve and with this, styles became more flamboyant, coinciding with the launch of the 'New Look' in 1947. Designs became rounder and softer, using more yarn, as women rediscovered their femininity.

Pretty For Every Day

MATERIALS
Rowan Cashsoft 4ply 57% merino/33% microfibre/10% cashmere (180m/197yds per 50g ball)
8 (9, 10, 12, 13) balls shade 437 (Thunder)
– or –
Excelana 4ply Luxury Wool 100% pure new British wool (159m/174yds per 50g ball)
8 (10, 12, 13, 14) balls shade Persian Grey
1 pair 3mm (US #2–3) needles

TENSION
Main rib pattern – 37 sts & 40 rows = 10cm (4in) using 3mm needles
Rev st st – 28 sts = 10cm (4in) using 3mm needles

Bobble section measures 12cm (individual bobble section of K2, P8 measures 4cm)
6 row bobble section measures 1½cm (½in) in height

Standard Yarn Tension
Cashsoft 4ply & Excelana – 28 sts & 36 rows using 3.25/3mm needles over stocking stitch

ABBREVIATIONS
See page 13 for standard abbreviations

Specific abbreviations for this pattern
MB (Make bobble): (K1, P1, K1, P1, K1) into same st. The bobbles are completed 3 rows later by purling 5 together on a WS row

SIZING
Measurements given in centimetres followed by inches in parentheses

To Fit	76–81 (30–32)	86–92 (34–36)	97–102 (38–40)	107–112 (42–44)	117–122 (46–48)
Finished Measurements					
Actual Bust Size	74½ (29½)	85½ (33½)	94 (37)	105 (41½)	113½ (44½)
Length to underarm	31 (12)	34 (13½)	35½ (14)	37 (14½)	38 (15)
Armhole Depth	16½ (6½)	20 (8)	21½ (8½)	23 (9)	24 (9½)
Finished Length	47½ (18½)	54 (21½)	57 (22½)	60 (23½)	62 (24½)
Shoulder to Shoulder	30 (12)	33 (13)	35½ (14)	38 (15)	40 (16)
Sleeve Length	46 (18)	48 (19)	48 (19)	49½ (19½)	49½ (19½)

Garment shown in photographs is for first size to fit 76–81 (30–32)

FRONT AND BACK ALIKE
Using 3mm needles, cast on 124 (144, 160, 180, 196) sts.
Row 1 (RS): P1, [K2, P8] 3 (4, 4, 4, 4) times, K2, P4, [K2, P2] 12 (12, 16, 21, 25) times, K2, P4, [K2, P8] 3 (4, 4, 4, 4) times, K2, P1.
Row 2: K1, [P2, K8] 3 (4, 4, 4, 4) times, P2, K4, [P2, K2] 12 (12, 16, 21, 25) times, P2, K4, [P2, K8] 3 (4, 4, 4, 4) times, P2, K1.
Row 3: P1, [MB twice, P8] 3 (4, 4, 4, 4) times, MB twice, P4, [K2, P2] 12 (12, 16, 21, 25) times, K2 P4, [MB twice, P8] 3 (4, 4, 4, 4) times, MB twice, P1 (188, 224, 240, 264, 288 sts).
Row 4: K69 (87, 87, 87, 87), [P2, K2] 12 (12, 16, 21, 25) times, P2, K69 (87, 87, 87, 87).
Row 5: P69 (87, 87, 87, 87), [K2, P2] 12 (12, 16, 21, 25) times, K2, P69 (87, 87, 87, 87).

Row 6: K1, * [P5tog] twice, K8, rep from * 2 (3, 3, 3, 3) more times, [P5tog] twice, K4 [P2, K2] 12 (12, 16, 21, 25) times, P2, K4, ** [P5tog] twice, K8, rep from ** 2 (3, 3, 3, 3) more times, [P5tog] twice, K1 (124, 144, 160, 180, 196 sts). These 6 rows form the pattern.

Continue in pattern as set, inc 1 st at each end of 13th and every foll 14th (15th, 15th, 16th, 17th) row, 6 times, working inc sts in rev st st (138, 158, 174, 194, 210 sts counted after rows 1, 2 or 6).

Continue without further shaping until work measures approx 30 (33, 34½, 36, 37) cm (11¾, 13, 13½, 14, 14½ in), ending with 6th row of pattern (approx 20, 22, 23, 24, 25 patt reps worked respectively).

Shape Sleeve Head

Dec 1 st at each end of every row until 40 (36, 34, 34, 34) sts rem. Cast off in rib.

MAKING UP

Sew shoulder seams together for approx 7½cm (3in) from each side edge (or further if preferred).

Sew up sleeve and side seams, then set in sleeve, matching centre top of sleeve head to shoulder seam and side seams together. Darn in all ends. Do not press.

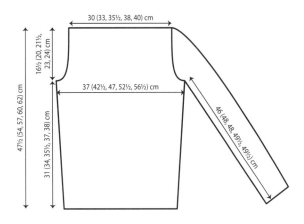

Next row (RS): P0 (2, 2, 2, 2), (K2, P2) to last 2 (4, 4, 4, 4) sts, K2, P0 (2, 2, 2, 2).

Next row (WS): K0 (2, 2, 2, 2), (P2, K2) to last 2 (4, 4, 4, 4) sts, P2, K0 (2, 2, 2, 2).

Continue in pattern as set by last 2 rows, until work measures 31 (34, 35½, 37, 38) cm (12, 13½, 14, 14½, 15 in), ending with a WS row.

Shape Armholes

Cast off 8 (8, 10, 10, 10) sts at beg of next 2 rows (122, 142, 154, 174, 190 sts). Cast off 0 (0, 0, 4, 5) sts at beg of next 0 (0, 0, 4, 4) rows (122, 142, 154, 158, 170 sts). Dec 1 st at each end of next 6 (6, 11, 9, 11) rows (110, 122, 132, 140, 148 sts).

Continue without further shaping until armhole measures 16½ (20, 21½, 23, 24) cm (6½, 8, 8½, 9, 9½ in), ending with a WS row. Cast off in rib.

SLEEVES

Using 3mm needles, cast on 60 (68, 72, 76, 80) sts and work in rib as folls:

Next row (RS): * K2, P2, rep from * to end.

Inc 1 st at each end of every foll 6th row, 19 times (98, 106, 110, 114, 118 sts).

Continue without further shaping until work measures 46 (48, 48, 49½, 49½) cm (18, 19, 19, 19½, 19½ in), ending with a WS row.

BESTWAY
LEAFLET **3**d·
No. 608

PRETTY FOR EVERY DAY
In 3-ply Wool (8 ozs.)

PRETTY FOR EVERY DAY

● **Designed by Sarah Redwood, Fashion Editress of "Woman's Illustrated"**

THIS jumper has something almost classical in its simplicity, and this means that it is just as becoming for you to wear as it is for our model. The slim lines of ribbing are clear cut and graceful, the decorative side panels break the line and make it interesting. It is very simple to knit because the back is exactly the same as the front and the sleeves are quite plain.

MATERIALS : *8 ozs. of Sirdar Super Shetland wool, 3-ply (7 ozs. for alternative short - sleeved version), and 1 pair of No. 11 knitting needles,*

TENSION : *8 sts. to 1 inch in width and 11 rows to 1 inch in depth with ribbing contracted.*

MEASUREMENTS : *Bust, 33-35 inches ; length from neck to lower edge, 18 inches ; long sleeve down underarm, 18 inches ; short sleeve down under-arm, 4½ inches.*

ABBREVIATIONS

K., knit ; p., purl ; st.(s)., stitch(es) ; tog., together ; rep., repeat ; inc., increase (by knitting twice into same st.).

Note : *The sts. in brackets must be worked the number of times stated immediately after the second bracket.*

SPECIAL points to notice are the patterned side panels and the new straight neck.

THE FRONT

Cast on 124 sts. and work thus :

1st pattern row (right side of work) : P. 1, (k. 2, p. 8) 3 times, k. 2, p. 4, (k. 2, p. 2) 12 times, k. 2, p. 4, (k. 2, p. 8) 3 times, k. 2, p. 1.

2nd pattern row : K. 1, (p. 2, k. 8) 3 times, p. 2, k. 4, (p. 2, k. 2) 12 times, p. 2, k. 4, (p. 2, k. 8) 3 times, p. 2, k. 1.

3rd pattern row : P. 1, (k. 1, p. 1, k. 1, p. 1, k. 1 all into each of the next 2 sts., p. 8) 3 times, k. 1, p. 1, k. 1, p. 1, k. 1 all into each of the next 2 sts., p. 4, (k. 2, p. 2) 12 times, k. 2, p. 4, (k. 1, p. 1, k. 1, p. 1, k. 1 all into each of the next 2 sts., p. 8) 3 times, k. 1, p. 1, k. 1, p. 1, k. 1 all into each of the next 2 sts., p. 1.

4th pattern row : K. 69, (p. 2, k. 2) 12 times, p. 2, k. 69.

5th pattern row : P. 69, (k. 2, p. 2) 12 times, k. 2, p. 69.

6th pattern row : K. 1, * (p. 5 tog.) twice, k. 8 ; rep. from * twice, (p. 5 tog.) twice, k. 4, (p. 2, k. 2) 12 times, p. 2, k. 4, ** (p. 5 tog.) twice, k. 8 ; rep. from ** twice, (p. 5 tog.) twice, k. 1.

These 6 rows form the pattern. Proceed in pattern and, taking care to keep its continuity, inc. 1 st. at both ends of needle on the 13th row and every 10th row after until sts. are increased to 138. Continue without further shaping until the 20th pattern has been completed, then work all sts. in double rib thus :

Next row : K. 2, * p. 2, k. 2 ; rep. from * to end of row.

Proceed in double rib until work measures 11½ inches from cast-on edge.

Shape the armholes by casting off 8 sts. at start of next 2 rows, then take 2 tog. at both ends of needle until sts. are reduced to 110. Continue without further shaping until work measures 18 inches from cast-on edge. Cast off fairly loosely in rib.

THE BACK

Work exactly as given for front.

THE LONG SLEEVES (both alike)

Cast on 60 sts. and work in ribs of k. 2, p. 2, but inc. 1 st. at both ends of needle on every

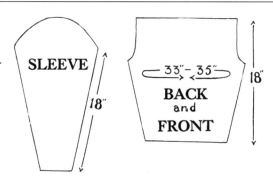

8th row until sts. are increased to 98. Proceed without further shaping until work measures 18 inches.

Shape the top by taking 2 tog. at both ends of needle on every row until sts. are reduced to 40. Cast off in rib.

THE ALTERNATIVE SHORT SLEEVES (both alike)

Cast on 80 sts. and work in ribs of k. 2, p. 2, but inc. 1 st. at both ends of needle on every 4th row until sts. number 98. Proceed without any further shaping until work measures 4½ inches.

Shape the top exactly as given for long sleeve.

TO MAKE UP

Join shoulder edges to a depth of 3 inches, starting at armhole edge. Set sleeves into armholes, then join sleeve and side seams. Lightly press work with a warm iron over a damp cloth, taking care to avoid stretching the ribbing.

'Fair Isle is Fashionable' Beret and Mitts

MATERIALS
Beret
Excelana 4 Ply Luxury Wool 100% pure new British wool (159m/174yds per 50g ball)
1 ball shade Alabaster – MC
1 ball shade Nile Green – A
1 ball shade Ruby Red – B
1 ball shade French Rose – C
1 2.75mm (US #2) circular needle (length 40cm)
1 3.25mm (US #3) circular needle (length 40cm)
1 set of 3.25mm (US #3) Double Pointed Needles (DPNs)
Stitch marker

Mitts
Excelana 4 Ply Luxury Wool 100% pure new British wool (159m/174yds per 50g ball)
1 ball shade Alabaster – MC
1 ball shade Nile Green – A
1 ball shade Ruby Red – B
1 ball shade French Rose – C
1 set of 2.75mm (US #2) Double Pointed Needles (DPNs)
1 set of 3.25mm (US #3) Double Pointed Needles (DPNs)

TENSION
26 sts & 30 rows = 10cm (4in) using 3.25mm needles over Fair Isle pattern

Standard Yarn Tension
28 sts & 36 rows = 10cm (4in) using 3mm needles over stocking stitch

ABBREVIATIONS
See page 13 for standard abbreviations

SIZING
One Size

Finished Measurements
Beret: To fit head circumference approx 58cm (23in)
Mitts: To fit medium adult female hand

PATTERN NOTES

If knitting both beret and mitts from same yarn only one ball of each contrast colour will be needed and 2 balls of the Main Colour.

This beret is knitted in the round on a short circular needle, however over the last few rounds it will be necessary to change to DPNs to complete the beret. The alternate cable cast on method used creates a ribbed cast on providing additional stretch for the brim. To work mitts in the round, yarns not in use for thumb should be woven behind thumb stitches and likewise MC should be stranded behind hand stitches, in those rounds where it wouldn't otherwise be used.

Beret (worked from bottom up)

Using 2.75mm circular needles and A, cast on 150 sts, using alternate cable cast on method (See 'Knitting Know How'). Join into round, taking care not to twist cast on edge.
Round 1: * P1, K1, rep from * to end of round, PM.
Rep this round a further 9 times.
Change to 3.25mm circular needle and commencing with round 1, work from chart, repeating each row 5 times across round. Continue in this manner, working each round of chart as set 5 times across all sts, changing to DPNs when necessary, until 30 sts rem.

MAKING UP

Break yarn leaving a long end, thread onto sewing up needle and draw yarn through rem sts and fasten off. Darn in all ends.
Place beret over an appropriate sized dinner plate. Place damp cloth over beret and steam. Leave to dry.

Chart (Beret)

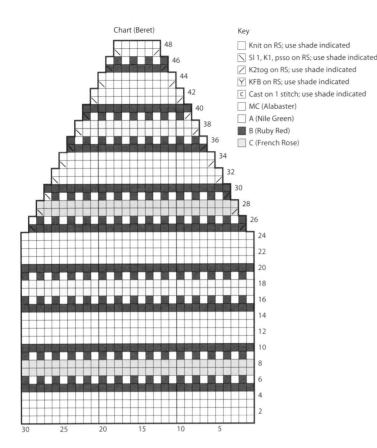

Key

- ☐ Knit on RS; use shade indicated
- ◩ Sl 1, K1, psso on RS; use shade indicated
- ◪ K2tog on RS; use shade indicated
- Y KFB on RS; use shade indicated
- C Cast on 1 stitch; use shade indicated
- ☐ MC (Alabaster)
- ☐ A (Nile Green)
- ■ B (Ruby Red)
- ▨ C (French Rose)

Mitts (Both mitts worked alike)

Using 2.75mm DPNs and MC, cast on 52 sts. Join into round, taking care not to twist cast on edge.

Rounds 1 & 2: Using MC, * K1, P1, rep from * to end of round, PM.
Rounds 3 & 4: Using B, * K1, P1, rep from * to end of round.
Rounds 5 & 6: As rounds 1 & 2.
Rounds 7 & 8: Using C, * K1, P1, rep from * to end of round.
Rounds 9 & 10: As rounds 1 & 2.
Rounds 11 & 12: Using B, * K1, P1, rep from * to end of round.
Rounds 13 & 14: As rounds 1 & 2.
Rounds 15 & 16: Using A, * K1, P1, rep from * to end of round.
Rounds 17 & 18: As rounds 1 & 2.
Rounds 19 & 20: Using B, * K1, P1, rep from * to end of round.

Change to 3.25mm DPNs and using MC, K 4 rounds.

Increasing for Thumb

Working from rnd 1 of chart, K25, PM, Kfb, Kfb, PM, K25 (54 sts). Continue as set by chart, working all stitches from right to left on first half of round, and then working all sts from left to right on second half of round. Work incs as indicated on chart, on every other round for thumb until round 14 is complete, and there are 16 sts between markers.

Next round (round 15 of chart): Using B, K25, remove marker, place 16 thumb sts on waste yarn, cast on 2 sts, remove 2nd marker, K25 (52 sts).
Cont to work from chart on these 52 sts, now working from right to left on both halves of the round. Work decs as shown, until 20 sts rem.

Divide 10 sts from front and back onto 2 DPNs and graft sts together. (Alternately, turn mitts inside out and cast off using three needle cast off method). See 'Knitting Know How'.

Thumb

Using DPNs and MC, knit across 16 sts on waste yarn, then pick up 2 sts across gusset (18 sts).
Next round: K2tog, K to last 4 sts, Sl1, K1, psso, K2 (16 sts).
Continue in stocking stitch without further shaping, until thumb is required length.
Next round: K1, (K2tog) to last st, K1 (9 sts).
Next round: K.
Next round: K1, K2tog to end (5 sts). Break off yarn, draw through rem sts, and fasten off.

Making Up
Darn in all ends and block lightly.

Chart (Mittens)

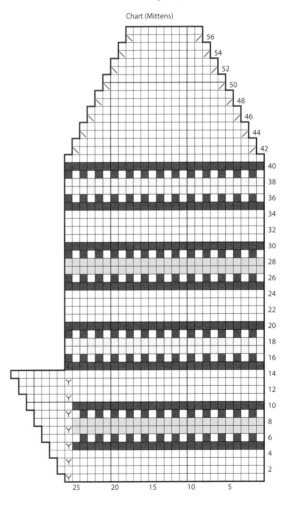

Fair Isle Mitts

Materials Required: For the Cap: 1 oz. Newhill and Earnshaw's "Pastorelle" 3-ply Fingering in Natural, and about ¼ oz. of Brown, Rust and Azure. One pair knitting needles, size 8. Similar amounts of wool for the Mittens.

Measurements: Cap: 20 ins. Mitts: 6 ins.×3½ ins. For size smaller use No. 9 or 10 needles. Keep cap on size 8 needles.

Tension: 6 sts. and 8 rows=1 in.

Abbreviations for Colours: N= natural; B=brown; A=azure blue; R=rust.

Note: When knitting the row in brown, take natural wool across the back, catching it in with every other st. by holding Nat. wool in left hand and knitting below the natural thread for 1st st. then above it for the 2nd st. as for Fair Isle weaving.

To make the Cap: Cast on in N 32 sts. Work 10 rows in Double Knitting as follows:

1st row: K.1, bring wool forward as for purling, sl.1 purlways and rep. to end.

2nd row: As 1st.

Rep. these 2 rows 4 times.

Refer to Chart A, working as for st. st., commence with the 4 rows of N. and continue exactly as chart until the 8 sts. remain. Break off wool and run through the sts.

Work 5 pieces likewise.

To Make up: Run a thread right round the top through the 40 rows and draw together tightly, leaving just the small hole as illustration. Darn in ends at sides, and place together on the wrong side. Run closely along near the edges, taking care that pattern matches.

Press seams under a damp cloth and warm iron.

Fair Isle Mitts

There's an easy-to-follow Chart for the Mitts, too

To Make the Mitts: Using the No. 8 needles, cast on 52 sts. in N. Rib 2 rows as follows: K.1, p.1 to end.

Keeping to the rib, work next 2 rows in B. 2 rows in N. 2 rows in R. 2 rows in N. 2 rows in B. 2 rows in N. 2 rows in A. 2 rows in N. 2 rows in B.

Increasings for Thumb: Following 1st row of Chart B pat. 25 sts., inc. by knitting into the back of the loop before the next st., k.2, inc. as before, pat. 25. Next row: P. in N.

Continuing as in Chart B., inc. over previous inc.'s. on every row right side facing as instructed and keep all thumb sts. in N., until 7 inc's completed (=16 sts. in all for thumb on needle).

15th row: Work as chart to thumb sts., leave needle hanging. Now with an extra needle, k. the 16 thumb sts. in st. st. for 12 rows.

Shape Top of Thumb: K.1, k.2 tog., to ending k.1.

Next row: P.

Next row: K.2 tog., to end. Break off wool and run through sts. Sew down seam.

Pick up first needle, and continue as in Chart B only working rows 16, 19, 26 and 29 in 1B. 1N. to end. (So that you do not get 2B. sts. tog.).

Shape Top: 31st row: K.2 tog., k.21, sl.1, k.1, p.s.s.o., k.2 tog, k.21, sl.1, k.1, p.s.s.o.

Next row: P.

Now continue in N. and st. st. and dec. over each dec. on every row, *right side facing* until 22 sts. in all on needle.

Put 11 sts. on each of 2 needles and holding tog. to shape, graft tog. the sts. along top, and sew down seam.

Work another likewise.

CHART B

X = BROWN
□ = NATURAL
O = RUST
• = AZURE

THUMB STS

11 STS.

26 STS. = ½ OF MITT.

FAIR ISLE IS FASHIONABLE:
Even the Novice can make this
Cap and Mitts Set with the aid of the "Dorette" Charts

Gay Bolero

MATERIALS
Jamieson's Spindrift 100% Shetland wool (105m per 25g ball)
3 (4, 5, 5, 6) balls shade 343 (Ivory) – MC
3 (4, 5, 5, 6) balls shade 526 (Spice) – CC
1 pair 3.25mm (US #3) needles
Stitch marker

TENSION
28 sts & 60 rows over ridge pattern using 3.25mm needles (unstretched)
28 sts & 40 rows over ridge pattern using 3.25mm needles (stretched)

Standard Yarn Tension
30 sts & 32 rows = 10cm (4in) using 3.25mm needles over stocking stitch

ABBREVIATIONS
See page 13 for standard abbreviations

SIZING
Measurements given in centimetres followed by inches in parentheses

To Fit	71–76 (28–30)	81–86 (32–34)	92–97 (36–38)	102–106 (40–42)	112–117 (44–46)
Finished Measurements					
Actual Bust Size	78½ (31)	88½ (35)	98½ (39)	108½ (42½)	118½ (46½)
Length to underarm	15 (6)	16 (6½)	17 (6¾)	18 (7)	19 (7½)
Armhole Depth	16½ (6½)	18 (7)	19½ (7½)	21½ (8½)	22½ (8¾)
Finished Length	31½ (12½)	34 (13½)	36½ (14½)	39½ (15½)	41½ (16½)
Shoulder to Shoulder	32 (12½)	35 (14)	38½ (15)	42 (16½)	45 (17½)

Garment shown in photographs for first size 71–76 (28–30)

PATTERN NOTES
Garment fronts commence at centre front bottom edge and work progresses both across and upwards with the introduction of a mitred centre point (see images). The back is worked from cast on point at lower edge upwards.

The sleeves are each worked in two pieces commencing at side seam and worked side to side to centre front. Each sleeve consists of two main pieces which mirror each other. There is a centre strip worked vertically down the centre of each sleeve which is knitted separately to the main pieces.

STRIPE PATTERN
Row 1 (RS): Using MC, K.
Row 2 (WS): K.
Row 3: P.
Row 4: K.
Row 5: P.
Row 6: K.
Change to CC.
Row 7: K.
Row 8: P.
Row 9: K.
Row 10: P.
These 10 rows form pattern.

RIGHT FRONT
Worked from centre front of bottom edge – greater number of stitches before marker are for centre front edge.

Using 3.25mm needles and MC, cast on 160 (174, 188, 202, 214) sts.
Row 1 (WS): K.
Row 2: P107 (117, 127, 137, 145), P3tog and mark this stitch, P50 (54, 58, 62, 66) (158, 172, 186, 200, 212 sts).
Row 3: K.
Row 4: P to last st before marked st, P3tog (this is new marked stitch), P49 (53, 57, 61, 65) (156, 170, 184, 198, 210 sts).
Row 5: K.
Row 6: Cast off 10 (12, 14, 16, 16) sts loosely. Slip rem st on RH needle back to LH needle and join in CC: K to 1 st before marked st, K3tog (and mark this st), K48 (52, 56, 60, 64) (144, 156, 168, 180, 192 sts).
Row 7: P (purling last st with MC and CC together – continue working last st of each alt row with both colours).
Row 8: K to 1 st before marked st, K3tog (and mark this st),

K to end (142, 154, 166, 178, 190 sts).
Row 9: P.
Change to MC.
Row 10: As row 8 (140, 152, 164, 176, 188 sts).
Row 11: K.
Row 12: P to 1 st before marked st, P3tog (and mark this st), P to end (138, 150, 162, 174, 186 sts).
Row 13: K.
Row 14: As row 12 (136, 148, 160, 172, 184 sts).
Row 15: K.
Change to CC.
Row 16: As row 8 (134, 146, 158, 170, 182 sts).
Row 17: P.
Row 18: As row 8 (132, 144, 156, 168, 180 sts).
Row 19: P.
Change to MC.
Continue to work in stripe pattern as established, and working 3 sts together around marked stitch on every RS row, work a further 36 (40, 44, 48, 52) rows in pattern (96, 104, 112, 120, 128 sts).

Shape Armhole
Maintaining stripe and dec patt as set, cast off 36 (40, 44, 48, 52) sts at start of next row (58, 62, 66, 70, 74 sts), then dec 1 st at end of next and 10 foll alt rows, remembering to also work centre decs on RS rows (27, 31, 35, 39, 43 sts).

** You should now have 13 (15, 17, 19, 21) sts each side of the marked st. Now work in stripe and dec patt as set but with no further armhole shaping until 1 st rem. Break yarn and draw through stitch to fasten off.

LEFT FRONT
Using MC, cast on 160 (174, 188, 202, 214) sts.
Row 1: K.
Row 2: P50 (54, 58, 62, 66), P3tog and mark this stitch, P107 (117, 127, 137, 145) (158, 172, 186, 200, 212 sts).
Row 3: K.
Row 4: P to last st before marked st, P3tog (this is new marked stitch), P to end (156, 170, 184, 198, 210 sts).
Row 5: Cast off 10 (12, 14, 16, 16) sts loosely. K to end. Join in CC.
Row 6: K to 1 st before marked st, K3tog (and mark this st), K to end (144, 156, 168, 180, 192 sts).
Row 7: P.
Row 8: As row 6 (142, 154, 166, 178, 190 sts).
Row 9: P.
Change to MC.
Row 10: As row 6 (140, 152, 164, 176, 188 sts).
Row 11: K.
Row 12: Purl to 1 st before marked st, P3tog (and mark this st), P to end (138, 150, 162, 174, 186 sts).
Row 13: K.
Row 14: As row 12 (136, 148, 160, 172, 184 sts).
Row 15: K.
Change to CC.
Row 16: As row 6 (134, 146, 158, 170, 182 sts).
Row 17: P.

Row 18: As row 6 (132, 144, 156, 168, 180 sts).
Row 19: P.
Change to MC.
Continue to work in stripe pattern as established, and working 3 sts together around marked stitch on every RS row, work a further 35 (39, 43, 47, 51) rows in pattern (96, 104, 112, 120, 128 sts).

Shape Armhole
Maintaining stripe and dec patt as set, cast off 36 (40, 44, 48, 52) sts at start of next row (60, 64, 68, 72, 76 sts), work a RS row (remembering to work centre dec), then dec 1 st at end of next and 10 foll alt rows (27, 31, 35, 39, 43 sts).

Complete as for right front from **.

BACK
Using MC and 3.25mm needles, cast on 110 (124, 138, 152, 166) sts.
Row 1: K.
Row 2: P.
Row 3: K.
Row 4: P.
Row 5: K.
Change to CC.
Row 6: K.
Row 7: P.
Row 8: K.
Row 9: P.
Change to MC.
Row 10: K.
Work in patt as set by these 10 rows until back matches front to start of armhole shaping, ending with a WS row (approx 90, 96, 102, 108, 114 rows in total).

Shape Armhole
Whilst maintaining stripe pattern, cast off 3 (5, 6, 7, 9) sts at beginning of next 2 rows (104, 114, 126, 138, 148 sts), then decrease one st at each end of following 7 (8, 9, 10, 11) rows (90, 98, 108, 118, 126 sts).
Cont on these sts until work measures 16½ (18, 19½, 20½, 21½) cm (6½, 7, 7½, 8, 8½ in) from where armhole shaping commenced.

Shape Shoulders
Cast off 9 (9, 10, 11, 11) sts at beg of next 4 rows (54, 62, 68, 74, 82 sts).
Cast off 9 (10, 10, 11, 12) sts at beg of next 2 rows (36, 42, 48, 52, 58 sts).
Cast off 9 (10, 11, 11, 12) sts at beg of next 2 rows.
Cast off rem 18 (22, 26, 30, 34) sts.

SLEEVES
Right Half (Make two alike)
Using MC and 3.25mm needles, cast on 96 (108, 120, 133, 145) sts.
Row 1 (WS): K.
Row 2 (RS): P58 (64, 70, 77, 83), P3tog and mark this st, P35 (41, 47, 53, 59) (94, 106, 118, 131, 143 sts).

*** **Row 3**: K.

Row 4: P to 1 st before marked st, P3tog (this is new marked st), P to end (92, 104, 116, 129, 141 sts).

Row 5: K.

Change to CC.

Row 6: K to 1 st before marked st, K3tog (this is new marked st), K to end (90, 102, 114, 127, 139 sts).

Row 7: P.

Row 8: As row 6 (88, 100, 112, 125, 137 sts).

Row 9: P.

Change to MC.

Row 10: As row 6 (86, 98, 110, 123, 135 sts).***

Cont decreasing at marked st on each alt row until 54 (58, 62, 67, 71) sts rem, ending with a WS row. Cast off 20 (22, 24, 27, 29) sts at beg of next row, working dec as normal (32, 34, 36, 38, 40 sts), maintaining stripes and normal decreases work 1 row, then dec 1 st at same edge as cast off sts on 11 foll rows. Cast off rem 9 (11, 13, 15, 17) sts.

Left Half (Make two alike)

Using MC and 3.25mm needles, cast on 96 (108, 120, 133, 145) sts.

Row 1: K.

Row 2: P35 (41, 47, 53, 59), P3tog (mark this stitch), P58 (64, 70, 77, 83).

Work as for right half from *** to ***.

Cont decreasing at marker on each alt row until 52 (56, 60, 65, 69) sts rem, ending with a RS row. Cast off 20 (22, 24, 27, 29) sts at beg of next row (32, 34, 36, 38, 40 sts), then whilst maintaining stripe and decrease pattern, dec 1 st at same edge on 11 foll rows. Cast off rem 9 (11, 13, 15, 17) sts.

CENTRE SLEEVE STRIPS

Using CC and 3.25mm needles, cast on 58 (64, 70, 77, 83) sts.

Next row: K.

Next row: P.

Cast off loosely.

Work another strip.

MAKING UP

Press all pieces, taking care to match pieces where necessary. Join shoulders, slip stitching back neck border pieces together and sewing in place along back neck. Join side seams taking great care to match stripes.

With RS together, join narrow strip to long cast on edge of one half of a sleeve, using a neat back stitch. Now join other long edge of strip to other half of sleeve in same way. Repeat with second sleeve. Join side seams taking care to match stripes. Measure 4½cm from shoulder seam on both fronts and on back, placing a pin to mark place. Insert sleeves, stretching stripes up to meet pin marker, easing in

armhole excess where necessary. Match centre of narrow strip to shoulder seam and gather remaining sleeve head into position between centre and pins. Tack sleeve in place, turn to RS and check that a vertical stripe is running length of sleeve as far as pin. Turn back to inside and back stitch in place. Darn in all ends and lightly press.

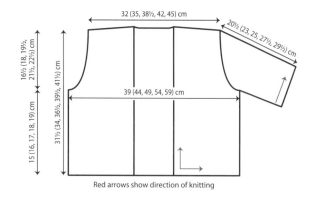

Red arrows show direction of knitting

Gay bolero

Measurements.
To fit 34-36 inch Bust measurement.
Length : 15 ins.
Length of underside seam : 5 ins.

Materials required.
7 ozs. Lister's Lavenda 3 ply : (4 ozs. Ground shade, 3 ozs. Contrasting shade, or 1 oz. of each of 3 Contrasting shades to be used alternately). Pair needles No. 10.

Abbreviations.
k = Knit.
p = Purl.
sts. = Stitches.
ins. = Inches.
tog. = Together.
G. = Ground wool.
C. = Contrasting wool.

Tension.
7½ sts. and 10 rows equal one inch.
N.B. The tension of the knitting controls the size of the finished garment. Before commencing, cast on 15 sts. and work in one row knit, one row purl, for 20 rows. If your sample has less sts. per inch than our tension, try again on smaller needles, and *vice versa*, then work the garment on the needles which produce our tension.

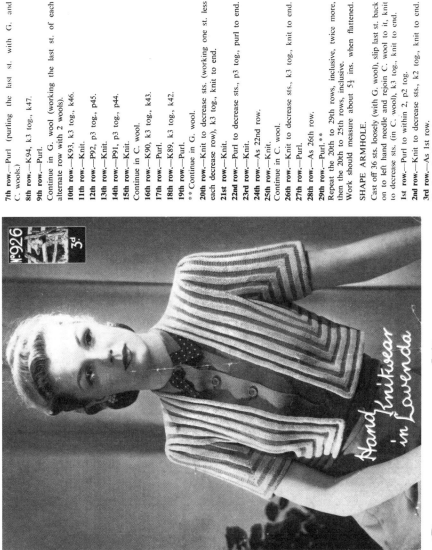

RIGHT FRONT.

Using Ground wool, cast on 160 sts. *by thumb method.*
1st row.—Knit.
2nd row.—P107, p3 tog., p50.
3rd row.—Knit.
4th row.—P106, p3 tog., p49.
5th row.—Knit.
6th row.—Cast off 10 sts. loosely (this piece goes round the neck). Slip 11th st. from right hand needle back to left and join C. wool.
Continue in C. wool :—K95, k3 tog., k48.

7th row.—Purl (purling the last st. with G. and C. wools.)
8th row.—K94, k3 tog., k47.
9th row.—Purl.
Continue in G. wool (working the last st. of each alternate row with 2 wools).
10th row.—K93, k3 tog., k46.
11th row.—Knit.
12th row.—P92, p3 tog., p45.
13th row.—Knit.
14th row.—P91, p3 tog., p44.
15th row.—Knit.
Continue in C. wool.
16th row.—K90, k3 tog., k43.
17th row.—Purl.
18th row.—K89, k3 tog., k42.
19th row.—Purl.
** Continue in G. wool.
20th row.—Knit to decrease sts. (working one st. less each decrease row), k3 tog., knit to end.
21st row.—Knit.
22nd row.—Purl to decrease sts., p3 tog., purl to end.
23rd row.—As 22nd row.
24th row.—Knit.
25th row.—Knit.
Continue in C. wool.
26th row.—Knit to decrease sts., k3 tog., knit to end.
27th row.—Purl.
28th row.—As 26th row.
29th row.—Purl.**
Repeat the 20th to 29th rows, inclusive, twice more, then the 20th to 25th rows, inclusive.
Work should measure about 5¼ ins. when flattened.

SHAPE ARMHOLE.
Cast off 36 sts. loosely (with G. wool), slip last st. back on to left hand needle and rejoin C. wool to it, knit to decrease sts. (in C. wool), k3 tog., knit to end.
1st row.—Purl to within 2, p2 tog.
2nd row.—Knit to decrease sts., k2 tog., knit to end.
3rd row.—As 1st row.
Continue in G. wool.
4th row.—As 2nd row.
5th row.—Knit to within 2, k2 tog.
6th row.—Purl to decrease sts., p3 tog., purl to end.
7th row.—As 5th row.
Repeat 6th and 7th rows.
Continue in C. wool.
10th row.—As 2nd row.

*** Repeat these 10 rows until there are 27 sts. on needle (there should be an *equal* number of sts. on each side of the decrease st.), then continue in pattern, decreasing at the centre only each alternate row until no more sts. remain.

LEFT FRONT.

Using Ground wool, cast on 160 sts. *by thumb method.*
1st row.—Knit.
2nd row.—P50, p3 tog., p107.
3rd row.—Knit.
4th row.—P49, p3 tog., p106.
5th row.—Cast off 10 sts. loosely. Knit to end. Join C. wool.
6th row.—K48, k3 tog., k95.
7th row.—Purl.
8th row.—K47, k3 tog., k94.
9th row.—Purl.
Continue in G. wool.
10th row.—K46, k3 tog., k93.
11th row.—Knit.
12th row.—P45, p3 tog., p92.
13th row.—Knit.
14th row.—P44, p3 tog., p91.
15th row.—Knit.
Continue in C. wool.
16th row.—K43, k3 tog., k90.
17th row.—Purl.
18th row.—K42, k3 tog., k89.
19th row.—Purl.
Continue as Right Front from ** to ** until the same number of stripes have been worked but finishing after a 24th row.

SHAPE ARMHOLE.
Next row.—Cast off 36 sts. loosely. Knit to end.
Continue in C. wool.
Next row.—As 26th row.
Continue as follows :—
1st row.—P2 tog., purl to end.
2nd row.—Knit to decrease sts., k3 tog., knit to end.
3rd row.—As 1st row.
Continue in G. wool.
4th row.—As 2nd row.
5th row.—K2 tog., knit to end.
6th row.—Purl to decrease sts., p3 tog., purl to end.
7th row.—As 5th row.
Repeat 6th and 7th rows.
10th row.—As 2nd row.
Continue as Right Front from *** to end.

BACK.

Using Ground wool, cast on 110 sts.
1st row.—Knit.
2nd row.—Purl.
3rd row.—Knit.
4th row.—Purl.
5th row.—Knit.
Join C. wool.
6th row.—Knit.
7th row.—Purl.
8th row.—Knit.
9th row.—Purl.
Continue in G. wool.
10th row.—Knit.
Repeat these 10 rows until the same number of stripes as Fronts to armholes have been worked.

SHAPE ARMHOLES. (Keeping stripes unbroken) :—
Cast off 3 sts. at beginning of next 2 rows, then decrease one st. at each end of following 7 rows (90 sts.).
Continue on these sts. until work measures 6¼ ins. from where armhole shaping commenced.

SHAPE SHOULDERS.
Cast off 9 sts. at beginning of next 8 rows.
Cast off remaining sts.

SLEEVES.

Right Half :
Using Ground wool, cast on 96 sts.
1st row.—Knit.
2nd row.—P58, p3 tog., p35.
3rd row.—Knit.
4th row.—P57, p3 tog., p34.
5th row.—Knit.
Change to C. wool.
6th row.—K56, k3 tog., k33.
7th row.—Purl.
8th row.—K55, k3 tog., k32.
9th row.—Purl.
Continue in G. wool.
10th row.—K54, k3 tog., k31.
** Continue thus, decreasing one st. on each side of centre st. each alternate row until work measures 4 ins., then, commencing with right side facing, cast off 20 sts. at beginning of next row then, still decreasing at centre, commence decreasing one st. at cast off edge every row until the centre st. is reached. Cast off remaining sts.

Left Half :
Using Ground wool, cast on 96 sts.
1st row.—Knit.
2nd row.—P35, p3 tog., p58.
3rd row.—Knit.
4th row.—P34, p3 tog., p57.
5th row.—Knit.
Change to C. wool.
6th row.—K33, k3 tog., k56.
7th row.—Purl.
8th row.—K32, k3 tog., k55.
9th row.—Purl.
Continue in G. wool.
10th row.—K31, k3 tog., k54.
Continue as Right Half Sleeve from ** to end.
Work 2 more Halves.

Centre Sleeve Strips :
Using C. wool, cast on 58 sts.
Next row.—Knit.
Next row.—Purl.
Cast off loosely.
Work another Strip.

TO MAKE UP.

Before pressing, neatly join side seams, then take a left and right half sleeve and join the longer cast on edges one to each side of a centre strip. The smooth side of the strip is the right side and it should reach all down longer cast on edge to corner. Pin out and *very lightly* press each piece on wrong side under damp cloth, taking care not to flatten the *outside* stripe too much, as this should curl under as far as the next stripe. Join shoulder seams and neatly stitch the 2 strips on fronts round neck to join at centre back. Join side seams of sleeve and fit into armhole with side seam of sleeve about 3 stripes to front of Bolero side seam. Slightly ease the next 4 front stripes of Bolero into sleeve, then pleat surplus sleeve fullness in 2 pleats on either side of shoulder seam. Press seams.

Lavenda Leaflet No. 926

Kasha

MATERIALS
First Size 76–86cm (30–34in)
Skein Queen Blush 80% merino/20% cashmere (400m/437yds approx per 100g skein)
3 skeins shade Vintage Gold
1 pair 2.75mm (US #2) needles

Tension
One diamond measured across widest part (see pattern notes) = 7cm (2¾in) using 2.75mm needles.
1 Patt rep of rows = 10cm (4¼in) using 2.75mm needles.

Second Size 86–97cm (34–38in)
Skein Queen Blush 80% merino/20% cashmere (400m/437 yds approx per 100g skein)
3 skeins shade Vintage Gold
1 pair 3.25mm (US #3) needles

Tension
One diamond measured across widest part (see pattern notes) = 8cm (3in) using 3.25mm needles.
1 Patt rep of rows = 11cm (4½in) using 3.25mm needles.

Third Size 102–112cm (40–44in)
Skein Queen Lotus Cashmere DK 100% cashmere (183m/200yds per 55g skein)
8 skeins shade Petrol Blue
1 pair 3.25mm (US #3) needles
1 pair 3.75mm (US #5) needles

Tension
One diamond measured across widest part (see pattern notes) = 9cm (3½in) using 3.75mm needles.
1 Patt rep of rows = 12cm (4¾in) using 3.75mm needles.

ABBREVIATIONS
See page 13 for standard abbreviations

Specific abbreviations for this pattern
5 out of 1: (K1, P1, K1, P1, K1) all into next stitch

SIZING
Measurements given in centimetres followed by inches in parentheses

To Fit	76–86 (30–34)	86–97 (34–38)	102–112 (40–44)
Fished Measurements			
Actual Bust Size	84 (33)	96 (38)	108 (42½)
Length to underarm	31½ (12½)	34 (13½)	36½ (14½)
Armhole Depth	20 (8)	22 (8½)	24 (9½)
Finished Length	51½ (20½)	56 (22)	60½ (24)
Sleeve Length	13 (5)	14 (5½)	15 (6)

Garment shown in photographs is for second size 86–97 (34–38)

PATTERN NOTES
To work tension square cast on 29 sts and work one repeat of chart A using recommended needles. To calculate tension, dampen swatch, dry flat and measure half way across sample at widest point for stitch count. The full length of the swatch is required for the row count. It is very important to achieve tension as specified for the appropriate sizes. The sides of the garment are shaped as illustrated in chart A.

BACK
Using 2.75 (3.25, 3.25) mm needles, cast on 108 sts.
Row 1: Sl1, K1, * P1, K1, rep from * to end.
Repeat this row until rib measures 6½cm (2½in) ending with a WS row.

Next row (RS): Sl1, K1, P1 * inc in next st, P1, [K1, P1] 5 times, rep from * to the last 7 sts, inc in next st, [P1, K1] 3 times (117 sts).

3rd size only
Change to 3.75mm needles.

Row 3: K2tog, P2, * [K1, P2] twice, K2, YO, P1, K5, P1, YO, K2, [P2, K1] twice, Sl1, K2tog, psso, YO, K2tog, rep from * to last 27 sts, [K1, P2] twice, K2, YO, P1, K5, P1, YO, K2, [P2, K1] twice, P2, K2tog.

Row 4: K2tog, K1, [P1, K2] twice, * P2, K2, P5, K2, P2, K2, P1, K2, P5, K2, P1, K2, rep from * to last 22 sts, P2, K2, P5, K2, P2, [K2, P1] twice, K1, K2tog (141 sts).

Row 5: K2tog, [K1, P2] twice, * K2, YO, P2, K5, P2, YO, K2, P2, K1, P2, Sl1, K2tog, psso, YO, K2tog, P2, K1, P2, rep from * to last 21 sts, K2, YO, P2, K5, P2, YO, K2, [P2, K1] twice, K2tog.

Row 6: K2tog, * K2, P1, K2, P2, 5 out of 1, K2, P5tog, K2, 5 out of 1, P2, K2, P1, K2, P3, rep from * to last 27 sts, K2, P1, K2, P2, 5 out of 1, K2, P5tog, K2, 5 out of 1, P2, K2, P1, K2, K2tog (159 sts).

Row 7: K2tog, * P1, K1, P2, K2, YO, K5, P2, K1, P2, K5, YO, K2, P2, K1, P1, Sl1, K2tog, psso, YO, K2tog, rep from * to last 29 sts, P1, K1, P2, K2, YO, K5, P2, K1, P2, K5, YO, K2, P2, K1, P1, K2tog.

Row 8: K2tog, * P1, K2, P2, K1, P5, K2, P1, K2, P5, K1, P2, K2, P1, K1, P3, K1, rep from * to last 29 sts, P1, K2, P2, K1, P5, K2, P1, K2, P5, K1, P2, K2, P1, K2tog (157 sts).

All sizes

Now work from chart A as folls:

Work set-up row (WS) once, repeating marked section 5 times (141 sts).
Now work rows 1 to 36 from chart twice, and then work rows 1 to 18 once more, in each row the marked section is repeated 5 times.
The stitch count in this pattern changes frequently, as folls:

Row 1: 153 sts.	**Row 19**: 163 sts.
Row 3: 155 sts.	**Row 21**: 161 sts.
Row 5: 157 sts.	**Row 23**: 159 sts.
Row 6: 181 sts.	**Row 24**: 179 sts.
Row 7: 183 sts.	**Row 25**: 177 sts.
Row 9: 185 sts.	**Row 27**: 175 sts.
Row 11: 187 sts.	**Row 29**: 173 sts.
Row 12: 211 sts.	**Row 30**: 193 sts.
Row 13: 213 sts.	**Row 31**: 191 sts.
Row 15: 215 sts.	**Row 33**: 189 sts.
Row 17: 205 sts.	**Row 35**: 177 sts.
Row 18: 153 sts.	**Row 36**: 141 sts.

Shape Armholes

Row 1 (RS): Cast off 10 sts, K1 (making 2 sts on RH needle), [P2, K1] twice, * P2, K2, YO, K5, YO, K2, [P2, K1] 5 times, rep from * to last 5 sts, P2, K3 (153 sts).

Row 2: Cast off 10 sts, P1 (making 2 sts on RH needle), * [K2, P1] twice, K2, P2, K1, P5, K1, P2, [K2, P1] 3 times, rep from * to last st, K1 (143 sts).

Key

☐ Knit on RS, Purl on WS
⬤ Purl on RS, Knit on WS
╱ K2tog on RS
⋏ Sl1, K2tog, psso
○ Yarnover
⋀ P5tog
Ⅴ 5 out of 1 (K1, P1, K1, P1, K1 all into next stitch)
Ⅴ Sl1
5 K5 on RS, P5 on WS
▢ No stitch: ignore these squares and move straight to next knitting instruction
☐ Omit these stitches when working sleeves
☐ Pattern repeat

Chart A: Back

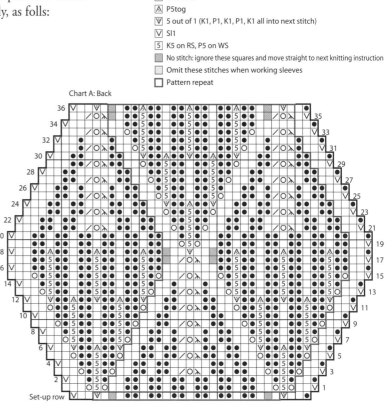

Set-up row

Row 9: K2tog, * P2, K2, YO, P1, K5, P2, K1, P2, K5, P1, YO, K2, P2, K1, Sl1, K2tog, psso, YO, K2tog, K1, rep from * to last 27 sts, P2, K2, YO, P1, K5, P2, K1, P2, K5, P1, YO, K2, P2, K2tog.

Row 10: K2tog, K1, * P2, K2, P5, K2, P1, K2, P5, K2, P2, K2, P5, K2, rep from * to last 26 sts, P2, K2, P5, K2, P1, K2, P5, K2, P2, K1, K2tog (155 sts).

Row 11: K2tog, * K2, YO, P2, K5, P2, K1, P2, K5, P2, YO, K2, P2, Sl1, K2tog, psso, YO, K2tog, P2, rep from * to last 25 sts, K2, YO, P2, K5, P2, K1, P2, K5, P2, YO, K2, K2tog.

Now work from chart A rows 12–36, then repeat 1–35 once more, this time the marked section is worked 4 times in each row (143 sts).

Next row (WS): Sl1, P5, * [K2, P5tog, K2, P1] 3 times, P4, rep from * to last st, K1 (95 sts).

Leave sts on a holder to cast off with fronts.

RIGHT FRONT

Using 2.75 (3.25, 3.25) mm needles, cast on 72 sts.

Row 1: Sl1, K1, * P1, K1, rep from * to end.

Row 2: As row 1.

Row 3 (buttonhole): Sl1, K1, P1, K1, cast off 3 sts, rib to end.

Row 4 (buttonhole): Work in rib as set, casting on 3 sts over those cast off on previous row.

Continue in rib as set, until work measures 6½cm (2½in) ending with a WS row, and at the same time work a further buttonhole as above after 20 rows of ribbing have been worked.

Next row (RS): Sl1, [K1, P1] 4 times, * inc in next st, P1, [K1, P1] 5 times, rep from * to last 3 sts, inc in next st, P1, K1 (78 sts).

3rd size only

Change to 3.75mm needles.

All sizes

Now work from chart B as folls:

Work set-up row (WS) once, repeating marked section 3 times (90 sts).

Now work rows 1 to 36 from chart once, making a buttonhole as before on rows 15–16, in each row the marked section is repeated 3 times.

Work rows 1–36 from chart once more (marked section repeated 3 times in each row), this time working buttonholes on rows 1–2 and rows 23–24. Finally, work rows 1 to 17 once more this time working a buttonhole on rows 9–10.

As before, the stitch counts change frequently as folls (not including changes for buttonholes):

Row 1: 96 sts.	**Row 19**: 96 sts.
Row 6: 108 sts.	**Row 24**: 108 sts.
Row 12: 120 sts.	**Row 30**: 120 sts.
Row 17: 114 sts.	**Row 35**: 114 sts.
Row 18: 90 sts.	**Row 36**: 90 sts.

Next row (WS): Sl1, P5, [K2, P5tog, K2, P1] 3 times, P1, * 5 out of 1, P2, [K2, P5tog, K2, P1] 3 times, P1, rep from * to last 9 sts, K1, [P1, K1] 4 times (86 sts).

Next row (RS): Sl1, [K1, P1] 4 times, K2, * [P2, K1] 5 times, P2, K2, YO, K5, YO, K2, rep from * to the last 23 sts, [P2, K1] 5 times, P2, K6 (90 sts).

Shape Armholes

Row 1 (WS): Cast off 10 sts, P1 (making 2 sts on right hand needle), [K2, P1] 3 times, K2, P2, * K1, P5, K1, P2, [K2, P1] 5 times, K2, P2, rep from * once, K1, [P1, K1] 4 times (80 sts).

Row 2: Sl1, [K1, P1] 4 times, K2, * [P2, K1] twice, Sl1, K2tog, psso, YO, K2tog, [K1, P1] twice, K2, YO, P1, K5, P1, YO, K2, rep from * once, [P2, K1] 3 times, P2, K2tog (79 sts).

Row 3: K2tog, K1, [P1, K2] 3 times, P2, * K2, P5, K2, P2, K2, P1, K2, P5, K2, P1, K2, P2, rep from * once, K1, [P1, K1] 4 times (78 sts).

Row 4: Sl1, [K1, P1] 4 times, K2, * P2, K1, P2, Sl1, K2tog, psso, YO, K2tog, P2, K1, P2, K2, YO, P2, K5, P2, YO, K2, rep from * once, [P2, K1] 3 times, K2tog (77 sts).

Row 5: K2tog, [K2, P1] 3 times, P1, * 5 out of 1, K2, P5tog, K2, 5 out of 1, P2, K2, P1, K2, P3, K2, P1, K2, P2, rep from * once, K1 [P1, K1] 4 times (84 sts).

Row 6: Sl1, [K1, P1] 4 times, K2, * P2, K1, P1, Sl1, K2tog, psso, YO, K2tog, P1, K1 P2, K2, YO, K5, P2, K1, P2, K5, YO, K2, rep from * once, [P2, K1] twice, P1, K2tog (83 sts).

Row 7: K2tog, [P1, K2] twice, P2, * K1, P5, K2, P1, K2, P5, K1, P2, K2, P1, K1, P3, K1, P1, K2, P2, rep from * once, K1, [P1, K1] 4 times (82 sts).

Row 8: Sl1, [K1, P1] 4 times, K2, * P2, K1, Sl1, K2tog, psso, YO, K2tog, K1, P2, K2, YO, P1, K5, P2, K1, P2, K5, P1, YO, K2, rep from * once, P2, K1, P2, K2tog (81 sts).

Row 9: K2tog, K1, P1, K2, P2, * K2, P5, K2, P1, [K2, P5, K2, P2] twice, rep from * once, K1, [P1, K1] 4 times (80 sts).

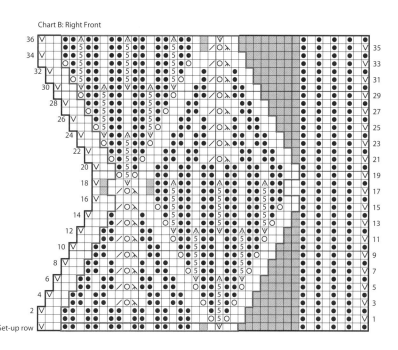

Chart B: Right Front

Row 10: Sl1, [K1, P1] 4 times, K2, * P2, Sl1, K2tog, psso, YO, K2tog, P2, K2, YO, P2, K5, P2, K1, P2, K5, P2, YO, K2, rep from * once, P2, K1, K2tog (79 sts).

Row 11: K2tog, K2, P2, * 5 out of 1, [K2, P5tog, K2, 5 out of 1] twice, P2, K2, P3, K2, P2, rep from * once, K1 [P1, K1] 4 times (86 sts).

Row 12: Sl1, K1, P1, K1, cast off 3, P1 (making 2 sts on needle after cast off sts), K2 * P1, Sl1, K2tog, psso, YO, K2tog, P1, K2, YO, K5, [P2, K1, P2, K5] twice, YO, K2, rep from * once, P1, K2tog (82 sts).

Row 13: K2tog, P2, * K1, P5, [K2, P1, K2, P5] twice, K1, P2, K1, P3, K1, P2, rep from * once, K1 P1, cast on 3, [P1, K1] twice (84 sts).

Repeat from row 33–36 of chart B once (marked section is repeated twice in each row), then from row 1–18 once, work another buttonhole (as before) in row 17–18 of patt (64 sts).

Shape Neck

Row 1 (RS): Cast off 9 sts, K1 (making 2 sts on right needle) * [P2, K1] 5 times, P2, K2, YO, K5, YO, K2, rep from * once, K1 (59 sts).

Row 2: Sl1, * P2, K1, P5, K1, P2, [K2, P1] 5 times, K2, rep from * once, K2tog (58 sts).

Row 3: K2tog, P1, K1, * P2, K1, Sl1, K2tog, psso, YO, K2tog, [K1, P2] twice, K2 YO, P1, K5, P1, YO, K2, * P2, K1, rep from * to * once, K1 (57 sts).

Row 4: Sl1, P2, * K2, P5, K2, P2, K2, P1, K2, P5, K2, P1, * K2, P2, rep from * to * once, K2tog (56 sts).

Row 5: K2tog, * P2, Sl1, K2tog, psso, YO, K2tog, P2, K1, P2, K2, YO, P2, K5, P2, YO, K2, * P2, K1, rep from * to * once, K1 (55 sts).

Row 6: Sl1, P2, * 5 out of 1, K2, P5tog, K2, 5 out of 1, P2,

K2, P1, K2, P3, * K2, P1, K2, P2, rep from * to * once, K1, K2tog (62 sts).

Row 7: K2tog, K2, * YO, K2tog, P1, K1, P2, K2, YO, K5, P2, K1, P2, K5, YO, K2 * P2, K1, P1, Sl1, K2tog, psso, rep from * to * once, K1 (63 sts).

Row 8: Sl1, P2, * K1, P5, K2, P1, K2, P5, K1, P2, K2, P1, K1, P3, * K1, P1, K2, P2, rep from * to * once, K2tog (62 sts).

Row 9: K2tog, K2, P1, * K1, P2, K2, YO, P1, K5, P2, K1, P2, K5, P1, YO, K2, * P2, K1, Sl1, K2tog, psso, YO, K2tog, rep from * to * once, K1 (63 sts).

Row 10: Sl1, P2, K2, P5, K2, P1, [K2, P5, K2, P2] twice, [K2, P5, K2, P1] twice, P1, K2, P1, K1, P1, K2tog (62 sts).

Row 11: K2tog, P1, K1, * P2, K2, YO, P2, K5, P2, K1, P2, K5, P2, YO, K2, * P2, Sl1, K2tog, psso, YO, K2tog, rep from * to * once, K1 (63 sts).

Row 12: Sl1, P2, * 5 out of 1, [K2, P5tog, K2, 5 out of 1] twice, P2, K2, * P3, K2, P2, rep from * to * once, P1, K2tog (70 sts).

Row 13: K2tog, P2, * K2, YO, K5, [P2, K1, P2, K5] twice, YO, K2 * P1, Sl1, K2tog, psso, YO, K2tog, P1, rep from * to * once, K1 (71 sts).

Row 14: Sl1, P2, * K1, P5, [K2, P1, K2, P5] twice, K1, P2, K1, * P3, K1, P2, rep from * to * once, K2tog (70 sts).

Row 15: K2tog, K2, * YO, P1, K5, [P2, K1, P2, K5] twice, P1, YO, K2, * Sl1, K2tog, psso, YO, K2tog, K2 rep from * to * once, K1 (71 sts).

Repeat from row 16–35 of chart A (as given for back) once, working marked section once only in each row (41 sts).

Next row: Sl1, P5, [K2, P5tog, K2, P1] 3 times, P4, K1 (29 sts).

Leave stitches on a holder to cast off with back.

LEFT FRONT

Using 2.75 (3.25, 3.25) mm needles, cast on 72 sts.

Row 1: Sl1, P1, * K1, P1, rep from * to last 2 sts, K2.

Rep row until ribbing measures 6½cm (2½in) from cast-on edge, ending with a WS row.

Next row (RS): Sl1, P1,* inc in next st, P1, [K1, P1] 5 times, rep from * to last 10 sts, inc in next st, [P1, K1] 4 times, K1 (78 sts).

3rd size only

Change to 3.75mm needles.

All sizes

Now work from chart C as folls:

Work set-up row (WS) once, repeating marked section 3 times (90 sts).

Work rows 1 to 36 from chart C twice, in each row the marked section is repeated 3 times.

Then work rows 1 to 17 once more (114 sts).

As before, the stitch counts change frequently and will be the same as for the right front.

Next row (WS): Sl1, [P1, K1] 4 times, * P2, [K2, P5tog, K2, P1] 3 times, P1, 5 out of 1, rep from * once, P2, [K2, P5tog, K2, P1] 3 times, P4, K1 (86 sts).

Shape Armhole

Row 1 (RS): Cast off 10 sts, K1 (making 2 sts on right hand needle), [P2, K1] 3 times, P2, K2 * YO, K5, YO, K2, [P2, K1] 5 times, P2, K2, rep from * once [P1, K1] 4 times, K1 (80 sts).

Row 2: Sl1, [P1, K1] 4 times, * P2, [K2, P1] 5 times, K2, P2, K1, P5, K1, rep from * once, P2, [K2, P1] 3 times, K2, K2tog (79 sts).

Row 3: K2tog, P1, [K1, P2] 3 times, K2, * YO, P1, K5, P1, YO, K2, [P2, K1] twice, Sl1, K2tog, psso, YO, K2tog, [K1, P2] twice, K2, rep from * once, [P1, K1] 4 times, K1 (78 sts).

Row 4: Sl1, [P1, K1] 4 times, * P2, K2, P1, K2, P5, K2, P1, K2, P2, K2, P5, K2, rep from * once, P2, [K2, P1] 3 times, K2tog (77 sts).

Row 5: K2tog, [P2, K1] twice, P2, K2, * YO, P2, K5, P2, YO, K2, P2, K1, P2, Sl1, K2tog, psso, YO, K2tog, P2, K1, P2, K2, rep from * once, [P1, K1] 4 times, K1 (76 sts).

Row 6: Sl1, [P1, K1] 4 times, * P2, K2, P1, K2, P3, K2, P1, K2, P2, 5 out of 1, K2, P5tog, K2, 5 out of 1, rep from * once, P2, K2, P1, K2, P1, K1, K2tog (83 sts).

Row 7: K2tog, [K1, P2] twice, K2, * YO, K5, P2, K1, P2, K5, YO, K2, P2, K1, P1, Sl1, K2tog, psso, YO, K2tog, P1, K1, P2, K2, rep from * once [P1, K1] 4 times, K1 (82 sts).

Row 8: Sl1, [P1, K1] 4 times, * P2, K2, P1, K1, P3, K1, P1, K2, P2, K1, P5, K2, P1, K2, P5, K1, rep from * once, P2, K2, P1, K2, K2tog (81 sts).

Row 9: K2tog, P1, K1, P2, K2, * YO, P1, K5, P2, K1, P2, K5, P1, YO, K2, P2, K1, Sl1, K2tog, psso, YO, K2tog, K1, P2, K2, rep from * once, [P1, K1] 4 times, K1 (80 sts).

Row 10: Sl1, [P1, K1] 4 times, * [P2, K2, P5, K2] twice, P1, K2, P5, K2, rep from * once, P2, K2, P1, K2tog (79 sts).

Row 11: K2tog, P2, K2, * YO, P2, K5, P2, K1, P2, K5, P2, YO, K2, P2, Sl1, K2tog, psso, YO, K2tog, P2, K2, rep from * once, [P1, K1] 4 times, K1 (78 sts).

Row 12: Sl1, [P1, K1] 4 times, * P2, K2, P3, K2, P2, [5 out of 1, K2, P5tog, K2] twice, 5 out of 1, rep from * once, P2, K1, K2tog (85 sts).

Row 13: K2tog, K2, * YO, K5, [P2, K1, P2, K5] twice, YO, K2, P1, Sl1, K2tog, psso, YO, K2tog, P1, K2, rep from * once [P1, K1] 4 times, K1 (84 sts).

Repeat from chart C row 32–36 once, then from row 1–17 once, working marked section twice in each row (80 sts).

Shape Neck

Row 1 (WS): Cast off 9 sts, P1 (making 2 sts on

right needle), * [K2, P5tog, K2, P1] 3 times, P1, 5 out of 1, P2, rep from * once, K1 (55 sts).

Row 2: Sl1, * K2, YO, K5, YO, K2, [P2, K1] 5 times, P2, rep from * once, K2tog (58 sts).

Row 3: K2tog, K1, * [P1, K2] 5 times, P2, K1, P5, K1, P2, * K2, rep from * to * once, K1 (57 sts).

Row 4: Sl1, * K2, YO, P1, K5, P1, YO, K2, P2, K1, P2, K1, Sl1, K2tog, psso, YO, K2tog, * [K1, P2] twice, rep from * to * once, K1, P2, K1, K2tog (56 sts).

Row 5: K2tog, * K2, P5, K2, P1, K2, P2, K2, P5, K2, P2, * K2, P1, rep from * to * once, K1 (55 sts).

Row 6: Sl1, * K2, YO, P2, K5, P2, YO, K2, P2, K1, P2, Sl1, K2tog, psso, YO, K2tog, * P2, K1, P2, rep from * to * once, P1, K2tog (54 sts).

Row 7: K2tog, * P3, K2, P1, K2, P2, 5 out of 1, K2, P5tog, K2, 5 out of 1, P2, * K2, P1, K2, rep from * to * once, K1 (61 sts).

Row 8: Sl1, * K2, YO, K5, P2, K1, P2, K5, YO, K2, P2, K1, P1, Sl1, K2tog, psso, * YO, K2tog, P1, K1, P2, rep from * to * K2tog (60 sts).

Row 9: K2tog, * K1, P1, K2, P2, K1, P5, K2, P1, K2, P5, K1, P2 * K2, P1, K1, P3, rep from * to * once, K1 (59 sts).

Row 10: Sl1, * K2, YO, P1, K5, P2, K1, P2, K5, P1, YO, K2, P2, K1, * Sl1, K2tog, psso, YO, K2tog, K1, P2, rep from * to * once, K2tog (60 sts).

Row 11: K2tog, * K2, P1, [P1, K2, P5, K2] twice, P2, * K2, P5, rep from * to * once, K1 (59 sts).

Row 12: Sl1, * K2, YO, P2, K5, P2, K1, P2, K5, P2, YO, K2, * P2, Sl1, K2tog, psso, YO, K2tog, P2, rep from * to * once, P1, K2tog (60 sts).

Row 13: K2tog, * P2, [5 out of 1, K2, P5tog, K2] twice, 5 out of 1, P2, * K2, P3, K2, rep from * to * once, K1 (67 sts).

Work rows 13–35 from chart A (as given for back) once, working marked section once in each row (41 sts).

Next row (WS): Sl1, P5, [K2, P5tog, K2, P1] 3 times, P4, K1 (29 sts).

Leave stitches on a holder to cast off with back.

Chart C: Left Front and Sleeves

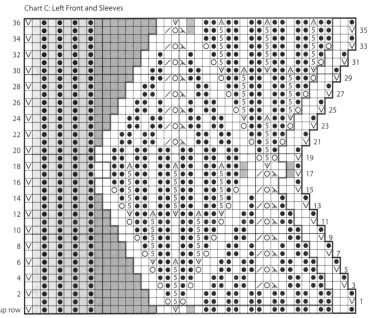

SLEEVES

Using 2.75 (3.25, 3.25) mm needles, cast on 74 sts.
Row 1: Sl1, K1, * P1, K1, rep from * to end.
Rep this row until ribbing measures 3cm (1¼in) ending with a WS row.

Next row: Sl1, K1, P1, *inc in next st, P1, K1, P1, rep from * to last 3 sts, inc in next st, P1, K1, (92 sts).
Next row: Sl1, * P2, 5 out of 1, P2, K2, [P1, K2] 5 times, rep from * to last 3 sts, P2, K1 (108 sts).

3rd size only
Change to 3.75mm needles.

All sizes
Work from chart C rows 1–35, omitting the ribbed sts of border as shown on the chart, the marked section is repeated 4 times on each row (140 sts).
Next row (WS): Sl1, P4, [P1, K2, P5tog, K2] 3 times, * P2, 5 out of 1, P1, [P1, K2, P5tog, K2] 3 times, rep from * to last 3 sts, P2, K1 (104 sts).

Shape Top
After each start of row cast off in the following section, 1 st will remain on right needle.
Row 1 (RS): Cast off 5 sts, [P2, K1] 4 times, * P2, K2, YO, K5, YO, K2, [P2, K1] 5 times, rep from * to last 8 sts, P2, K6 (105 sts).

Row 2: Cast off 5 sts, * K2, [P1, K2] 5 times, P2, K1, P5, K1, P2, rep from * to last 15 sts [K2, P1] 5 times (100 sts).
Row 3: Cast off 1 st, P1, K1, *Sl1, K2tog, psso, YO, K2tog, [K1, P2] twice, K2, YO, P1, K5, P1, YO, K2, [P2, K1] twice, rep from * to last 12 sts, Sl1, K2tog, psso, YO, K2tog, [K1, P2] twice, K1 (97 sts).
Row 4: Cast off 1 st, K1, * P1, K2, P5, K2, P1, K2, P2, K2, P5, K2, P2, K2, rep from * to last 10 sts, P1, K2, P5, K2 (96 sts).
Row 5: Cast off 1 st, * Sl1, K2tog, psso, YO, K2tog, P2, K1, P2, K2, YO, P2, K5, P2, YO, K2, P2, K1, P2, rep from * to last 10 sts, Sl1, K2tog, psso, YO, K2tog, P2, K1, P2 (93 sts).
Row 6: Cast off 1 st, * P1, K2, P3, K2, P1, K2, P2, 5 out of 1, K2, P5tog, K2, 5 out of 1, P2, K2, rep from * to last 7 sts, P1, K2, P3, K1 (104 sts).
Row 7: * Sl1, K2tog, psso, YO, K2tog, P1, K1, P2, K2, YO, K5, P2, K1, P2, K5, YO, K2, P2, K1, P1, rep from * to last 8 sts, Sl1, K2tog, psso, YO, K2tog, P1, K1, P1 (102 sts).
Row 8: Cast off 1 st, * K1, P3, K1, P1, K2, P2, K1, P5, K2, P1, K2, P5, K1, P2, K2, P1, rep from * to last 4 sts, K1, P3 (101 sts).
Row 9: Cast off 1 st, YO, K2tog, * K1, P2, K2, YO, P1, K5, P2, K1, P2, K5, P1, YO, K2, P2, K1, Sl1, K2tog, psso,

YO, K2tog, rep from * to last st, K1 (100 sts).
Row 10: Cast off 1 st, * P3, K2, P2, K2, P5, K2, P1, K2, P5, [K2, P2] twice, rep from * to last 2 sts, P1, K1 (99 sts).
Row 11: Cast off 1 sts, * YO, K2tog, P2, K2, YO, P2, K5, P2, K1, P2, K5, P2, YO, K2, P2, Sl1, K2tog, psso, rep from * to last st, K1 (98 sts).
Row 12: Cast off 1 st, * K2, P2, [5 out of 1, K2, P5tog, K2] twice, 5 out of 1, P2, K2, P3, rep from * to end (109 sts).
Row 13: Cast off 1 st, * YO, K2tog, P1, K2, YO, K5, [P2, K1, P2, K5] twice, YO, K2, P1, Sl1, K2tog, psso, rep from * once, YO, K2tog, P1, K2, YO, K5, [P2 K1, P2, K5] twice, YO, K2, P2, K1 (110 sts).
Row 14: Cast off 1 st, K1, * P2, K1, P5, [K2, P1, K2, P5] twice, K1, P2, K1, P3, K1, rep from * once, P2, K1, P5, [K2, P1, K2, P5] twice, K1, P2, K1, P3 (109 sts).
Row 15: Cast off 1 st, * YO, K2tog, K2, YO, P1, [K5, P2, K1, P2] twice, K5, P1, YO, K2, Sl1, K2tog, psso, rep from * once, YO, K2tog, K2, YO, P1, [K5, P2, K1, P2] twice, K5, P1, YO, K2, P2 (110 sts).
Row 16: Cast off 1 st, * P2, K2, P5, K2, [P1, K2, P5, K2] twice, P5, rep from * to end (109 sts).
Row 17: Cast off 1 st, * YO, K2tog, [K1, P2, K5, P2] 3 times, K1, Sl1, K2tog, psso, rep from * once, YO, K2tog, [K1, P2, K5, P2] 3 times, K3 (104 sts).
Row 18: Cast off 1 st, P1, * [K2, P5tog, K2, P1] 3 times, P1, 5 out of 1, P2, rep from * once, [K2, P5tog, K2, P1] 3 times, P3 (75 sts).
Row 19: Cast off 1 st, * K2, [P2, K1] 5 times, P2, K2, YO, K5, YO, rep from * once, K2 [P2, K1] 5 times, P2, K2 (78 sts).
Row 20: Cast off 1 st, * [K2, P1] 5 times, K2, P2, K1, P5, K1, P2, rep from * once, [K2, P1] 5 times, K2, P2, K1 (77 sts).
Row 21: Cast off 1 st, K1, * [P2, K1] twice, Sl1, K2tog, psso, YO, K2tog, [K1, P2] twice, K2, YO, P1, K5, P1, YO, K2, rep from * once, [P2, K1] twice, Sl1, K2tog, psso, YO, K2tog, [K1, P2] twice, K1 (74 sts).
Row 22: Cast off 1 st, K1, * P1, K2, P5, K2, P1, K2, P2, K2, P5, K2, P2, K2, rep from * once, P1, K2, P5, K2, P1, K2, P2 (73 sts).
Row 23: Cast off 1 st, * P2, K1, P2, Sl1, K2tog, psso, YO, K2tog, P2, K1, P2, K2, YO, P2, K5, P2, YO, K2, rep from * once, P2, K1, P2, Sl1, K2tog, psso, YO, K2tog, P2, K1, P2 (70 sts).
Row 24: Cast off 1 st, * P1, K2, P3, K2, P1, K2, P2, 5 out of 1, K2, P5tog, K2, 5 out of 1, P2, K2, rep from * once, P1, K2, P3, K2, P1, K2, P1 (77 sts).
Row 25: Cast off 1 st, P1, * K1, P1, Sl1, K2tog, psso, YO, K2tog, P1, K1, P2, K2, YO, K5, P2, K1, P2, K5, YO, K2, P2, rep from * once, K1, P1, Sl1, K2tog, psso, YO, K2tog, P1, K1, P1 (74 sts).
Row 26: Cast off 1 st, * K1, P3, K1, P1, K2, P2, K1, P5, K2, P1, K2, P5, K1, P2, K2, P1, rep from * once, K1, P3, K1, P1, K2 (73 sts).
Row 27: Cast off 1 st, * K1, Sl1, K2tog, psso, YO, K2tog, K1, P2, K2, YO, P1, K5, P2, K1, P2, K5, P1, YO, K2, P2, rep from * once, K1, Sl1, K2tog, psso, YO, K2tog, K1 (70 sts).
Row 28: Cast off 1 st, P3, * K2, P2, K2, P5, K2, P1, K2,

P5, K2, P2, K2, P5, rep from * once, K1 (69 sts).
Row 29: Cast off 1 st, K2tog, * YO, K2tog, P2, K2, YO, P2, K5, P2, K1, P2, K5, P2, YO, K2, P2, Sl1, K2tog, psso, rep from * once, YO, K1 (68 sts).
Row 30: Cast off 1 st, P1, * K2, P2, [5 out of 1, K2, P5tog, K2] twice, 5 out of 1, P2, K2, P3, rep from * once, K1 (75 sts).
Row 31: * Sl1, K2tog, psso, YO, K2tog, P1, K2, YO, K5, [P2, K1, P2, K5] twice, YO, K2, P1, rep from * once, Sl1, K2tog, psso (73 sts).
Row 32: Cast off 1 st, * P2, K1, P5, [K2, P1, K2, P5] twice, K1, P2, K1, P3, * K1, rep from * to * once (72 sts).
Row 33: Cast off 1 st, * YO, K2tog, K2, YO, P1, K5, [P2, K1, P2, K5] twice, P1, YO, K2, * Sl1, K2tog, psso, rep from * to * once, K1 (73 sts).
Row 34: Cast off 1 st, P1, * [K2, P5, K2, P1] twice, K2, P5, K2, * P7, rep from * to * once, P5 (72 sts).
Row 35: Cast off 1 st, * YO, K2tog, K1, [P2, K5, P2, K1] 3 times, * Sl1, K2tog, psso, rep from * to * once, K1 (69 sts).
Row 36: Cast off 1 st, * [K2, P5tog, K2, P1] twice, K2, P5tog, K2, * P5, rep from * to * once, P4 (44 sts). Cast off.

COLLAR
Using 2.75 (3.25, 3.25) mm needles, cast on 129 sts.
Row 1: Sl1, K2tog, * P1, K1, rep from * to last 4 sts, P1, K2togtbl, K1 (127 sts).
Row 2: Sl1, * P1, K1, rep from * to end.
Row 3: Sl1, P2tog, * K1, P1, rep from * to last 4 sts, K1, P2togtbl, K1 (125 sts).
Row 4: Sl1, * K1, P1, rep from * to last 2 sts, K2.
Repeat rows 1-4 6 times (101 sts). Cast off.

SLEEVE PADS (Make two)
See 'Fit and Finish' chapter.

MAKING UP
Press each piece separately on WS under damp cloth with a warm iron.

Return stitches on back and fronts to needles and cast off fronts with back using the 3-needle cast off method. Sew up the side and sleeve seams following the shape of the pieces created by the lace pattern. Sew in the sleeves, matching seams and centre of sleeve head with shoulder seam. Sew collar in position as shown in 'Fit and Finish' chapter. Sew on buttons to correspond with buttonholes. Sew sleeve pads in place, beginning just before sleeve seam, extending into sleeve head. See 'Fit and Finish' chapter for further instructions. Darn in all ends.

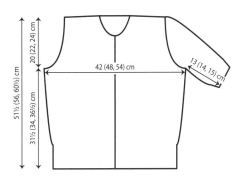

Design No. 1035 - Price 4ᴰ

KNITTED IN

Sirdar

SUPER SHETLAND WOOL 3-PLY
OR SIRDAR 'KASHA' WOOL 3-PLY

Sirdar Leaflet No. 1035

LADY'S CARDIGAN JUMPER

MATERIALS.

8 ozs. Sirdar Super Shetland Wool, 3-ply, or Sirdar Kasha Wool, 3-ply.
1 pair Knitting Needles, No. 10.
8 Buttons.

MEASUREMENTS.

Width all round at underarm, 34 inches.
Length from top of shoulder, 18½ inches.
Length of sleeve seam, 5 inches.

TENSION.

One pattern equals 3 inches in width.

NOTE.—It is very important that the garment is worked at this tension, in order to produce the given measurements. If the needles stated do not produce this tension, try other sizes until it is obtained.

ABBREVIATIONS.

K. knit; p. purl; sts. stitches; tog. together; sl.1, slip one stitch knitways; wl. fwd. wool forward; w.r.n. wool round needle; w.o.n. wool over needle; p.s.s.o. pass the slipped stitch over; t.b.l. through back of loops.

Always knit into the back of the first row of stitches unless the thumb method of casting on is used when it is not necessary.

THE BACK.

Cast on 108 sts.

1st ROW Sl.1, k.1, * p.1, k.1, repeat from * to end of row.

Repeat the 1st row 29 times.

31st ROW. Sl.1, (k.1, p.1) twice, * increase once in the next st., p.1, (k.1, p.1) 5 times, repeat from * to the last 7 sts., increase once in the next st., (p.1, k.1) 3 times (117 sts.).

NEXT ROW Sl.1, p.2, * (k.1, p.1, k.1, p.1, k.1) all into the next st., making 5 sts. from the one st. (this will now be termed 5 out of 1), p.2, k.2, (p.1, k.2) 5 times, p.2, repeat from * to the last 4 sts., 5 out of 1, p.2, k.1.

Proceed as follows :—

1st ROW Sl.1, k.2, * wl. fwd., k.5, wl. fwd., k.2, (p.2, k.1) 5 times, p.2, k.2, repeat from * to the last 8 sts., wl. fwd., k.5, wl. fwd., k.3.

2nd ROW Sl.1, p.2, * k.1, p.5, k.1, p.2, (k.2, p.1) 5 times, k.2, p.2, repeat from * to the last 10 sts., k.1, p.5, k.1, p.2, k.1.

3rd ROW Sl.1, k.2, * w.r.n., p.1, k.5, p.1, w.o.n., k.2, p.2, k.1, p.2, k.1. sl.1, k.2 tog., p.s.s.o., wl. fwd., k.2 tog., (k.1, p.2) twice, k.2, repeat from * to the last 10 sts., w.r.n., p.1, k.5, p.1, w.o.n., k.3.

4th ROW Sl.1, p.2, * k.2, p.5, k.2, p.2, k.2, p.1, k.2, p.5, k.2, p.1, k.2, p.2, repeat from * to the last 12 sts., k.2, p.5, k.2, p.2, k.1.

5th ROW Sl.1, k.2, * w.r.n., p.2, k.5, p.2, w.o.n., k.2, p.2, k.1, p.2, sl.1, k.2 tog., p.s.s.o., wl. fwd., k.2 tog., p.2, k.1, p.2, k.2, repeat from * to the last 12 sts., w.r.n., p.2, k.5, p.2, w.o.n., k.3.

6th ROW Sl.1, p.2, * 5 out of 1, k.2, p.5 tog., k.2, 5 out of 1, p.2, k.2, p.1, k.2, p.3, k.2, p.1, k.2, p.2, repeat from * to the last 14 sts., 5 out of 1, k.2, p.5 tog., k.2, 5 out of 1, p.2, k.1.

7th ROW Sl.1, k.2, * wl. fwd., k.5, p.2, k.1, p.2, k.5, wl. fwd., k.2, p.2, k.1, p.1, sl.1, k.2 tog., p.s.s.o., wl. fwd., k.2 tog., p.1, k.1, p.2, k.2, repeat from * to the last 18 sts., wl. fwd., k.5, p.2, k.1, p.2, k.5, wl. fwd., k.3.

8th ROW Sl.1, p.2, * k.1, p.5, k.2, p.1, k.2, p.5, k.1, p.2, k.2, p.1, k.1, p.3, k.1, p.1, k.2, p.2, repeat from * to the last 20 sts., k.1, p.5, k.2, p.1, k.2, p.5, k.1, p.2, k.1.

9th ROW Sl.1, k.2, * w.r.n., p.1, k.5, p.2, k.1, p.2, k.5, p.1, w.o.n., k.2, p.2, k.1, sl. 1, k.2, tog., p.s.s.o., wl. fwd., k.2 tog., k.1, p.2, k.2, repeat from * to the last 20 sts., w.r.n., p.1, k.5, p.2, k.1, p.2, k.5, p.1, w.o.n., k.3.

10th ROW Sl.1, p.2, * k.2, p.5, k.2, p.1, (k.2, p.5, k.2, p.2) twice, repeat from * to the last 22 sts., k.2, p.5, k.2, p.1, k.2, p.5, k.2, p.2, k.1.

11th ROW. Sl.1, k.2, * w.r.n., p.2, k.5, p.2, k.1, p.2, k.5, p.2, w.o.n., k.2, p.2, sl.1, k.2 tog., p.s.s.o., wl. fwd., k.2 tog., p.2, k.2, repeat from * to the last 22 sts., w.r.n., p.2, k.5, p.2, k.1, p.2, k.5, p.2, w.o.n., k.3.

12th ROW Sl.1, p.2, * 5 out of 1 (k.2, p.5 tog., k.2, 5 out of 1) twice, p.2, k.2, p.3, k.2, p.2, repeat from * to the last 24 sts., 5 out of 1, (k.2, p.5 tog., k.2, 5 out of 1) twice, p.2, k.1.

13th ROW Sl.1, k.2, * wl. fwd., k.5, (p.2, k.1, p.2, k.5) twice, wl. fwd., k.2, p.1, sl.1, k.2 tog., p.s.s.o., wl. fwd., k.2 tog., p.1, k.2, repeat from * to the last 28 sts., wl. fwd., k.5, (p.2, k.1, p.2, k.5) twice, wl. fwd., k.3.

14th ROW Sl.1, p.2, * k.1, p.5, (k.2, p.1, k.2, p.5) twice, k.1, p.2, k.1, p.3, k.1, p.2, repeat from * to the last 30 sts., k.1, p.5, (k.2, p.1, k.2, p.5) twice, k.1, p.2, k.1.

15th ROW Sl.1, k.2, * w.r.n., p.1, k.5, (p.2, k.1, p.2, k.5) twice, p.1, w.o.n., k.2, sl.1, k.2 tog., p.s.s.o., wl. fwd., k.2 tog., k.2, repeat from * to the last 30 sts., w.r.n., p.1, k.5, (p.2, k.1, p.2, k.5) twice, p.1, w.o.n., k.3.

16th ROW Sl.1, p.2, * k.2, p.5, k.2, (p.1, k.2, p.5, k.2) twice, p.7, repeat from * to the last 32 sts., k.2, p.5, k.2, (p.1, k.2, p.5, k.2) twice, p.2, k.1.

17th ROW Sl.1, k.2, * (p.2, k.5, p.2, k.1) 3 times, sl.1, k.2 tog., p.s.s.o., wl. fwd., k.2 tog., k.1, repeat from * to the last 32 sts., (p.2, k.5, p.2, k.1) 3 times, k.2.

18th ROW Sl.1, p.2, * (k.2, p.5 tog., k.2, p.1) 3 times, p.1, 5 out of 1, p.2, repeat from * to the last 32 sts., (k.2, p.5 tog., k.2, p.1) 3 times, p.1, k.1.

19th ROW Sl.1, k.2, * (p.2, k.1) 5 times, p.2, k.2, wl. fwd., k.5, wl. fwd., k.2, repeat from * to the last 20 sts., (p.2, k.1) 5 times, p.2, k.3.

20th ROW Sl.1, p.2, * (k.2, p.1) 5 times, k.2, p.2, k.1, p.5, k.1, p.2, repeat from * to the last 20 sts., (k.2, p.1) 5 times, k.2, p.2, k.1.

21st ROW Sl.1, k.2, * (p.2, k.1) twice, sl.1, k.2 tog., p.s.s.o., wl. fwd., k.2 tog., (k.1, p.2) twice, k.2, w.r.n., p.1, k.5, p.1, w.o.n., k.2, repeat from * to the last 20 sts., (p.2, k.1) twice, sl.1, k.2 tog., p.s.s.o., wl. fwd., k.2 tog., (k.1, p.2) twice, k.3.

22nd ROW Sl.1, p.2, * k.2, p.1, k.2, p.5, k.2, p.1, k.2, p.2, k.2, p.5, k.2, p.2, repeat from * to the last 18 sts., k.2, p.1, k.2, p.5, k.2, p.1, k.2, p.2, k.1.

23rd ROW Sl,1, k.2, * p.2, k.1, p.2, sl.1, k.2 tog., p.s.s.o., wl. fwd., k.2 tog., p.2, k.1, p.2, k.2, w.r.n., p.2, k.5, p.2, w.o.n., k.2, repeat from * to the last 18 sts., p.2, k.1, p.2, sl.1, k.2 tog., p.s.s.o., wl. fwd., k.2 tog., p.2, k.1, p.2, k.3.

24th ROW Sl.1, p.2, * k.2, p.1, k.2, p.3, k.2, p.1, k.2, p.2, 5 out of 1, k.2, p.5 tog., k.2, 5 out of 1, p.2, repeat from * to the last 16 sts., k.2, p.1, k.2, p.3, k.2, p.1, k.2, p.2, k.1.

25th ROW Sl.1, k.2, * p.2, k.1, p.1, sl.1, k.2 tog., p.s.s.o., wl. fwd., k.2 tog., p.1, k.1, p.2, k.2, wl. fwd., k.5, p.2, k.1, p.2, k.5, wl. fwd., k.2, repeat from * to the last 16 sts., p.2, k.1, p.1, sl.1, k.2 tog., p.s.s.o., wl. fwd., k.2 tog., p.1, k.1, p.2, k.3.

26th ROW Sl.1, p.2, * k.2, p.1, k.1, p.3, k.1, p.1, k.2, p.2, k.1, p.5, k.2, p.1, k.2, p.5, k.1, p.2, repeat from * to the last 14 sts., k.2, p.1, k.1, p.3, k.1, p.1, k.2, p.2, k.1.

27th ROW Sl.1, k.2, * p.2, k.1, sl.1, k.2 tog., p.s.s.o., wl. fwd., k.2 tog., k.1, p.2, k.2, w.r.n., p.1, k.5, p.2, k.1, p.2, k.5, p.1, w.o.n., k.2, repeat from * to the last 14 sts., p.2, k.1, sl.1, k.2 tog., p.s.s.o., wl. fwd., k.2 tog., k.1, p.2, k.3.

28th ROW Sl.1, p.2, * k.2, p.5, k.2, p.2, k.2, p.5, k.2, p.1, k.2, p.5, k.2, p.2, repeat from * to the last 12 sts., k.2, p.5, k.2, p.2, k.1.

29th ROW Sl.1, k.2, * p.2, sl.1, k.2 tog., p.s.s.o., wl. fwd., k.2 tog., p.2, k.2, w.r.n., p.2, k.5, p.2, k.1, p.2, k.5, p.2, w.o.n., k.2, repeat from * to the last 12 sts., p.2, sl.1, k.2 tog., p.s.s.o., wl. fwd., k.2 tog., p.2, k.3.

30th ROW Sl.1, p.2, * k.2, p.3, k.2, p.2 (5 out of 1, k.2, p.5 tog., k.2) twice, 5 out of 1, p.2 repeat from * to the last 10 sts., k.2, p.3, k.2, p.2, k.1.

31st ROW Sl.1, k.2, * p.1, sl.1, k.2 tog., p.s.s.o., wl. fwd., k.2 tog., p.1, k.2, wl. fwd., k.5, (p.2, k.1, p.2, k.5) twice, wl. fwd., k.2, repeat from * to the last 10 sts., p.1, sl.1, k.2 tog., p.s.s.o.. wl. fwd., k.2 tog., p.1, k.3.

32nd ROW Sl.1, p.2, * k.1, p.3, k.1, p.2, k.1, p.5, (k.2, p.1, k.2, p.5) twice, k.1, p.2, repeat from * to the last 8 sts., k.1, p.3, k.1, p.2, k.1.

33rd ROW Sl.1, k.2, * sl.1, k.2 tog., p.s.s.o., wl. fwd., k.2 tog., k.2, w.r.n., p.1, (k.5, p.2, k.1, p.2) twice, k.5, p.1, w.o.n., k.2, repeat from * to the last 8 sts., sl.1, k.2 tog., p.s.s.o., wl. fwd., k.2 tog., k.3.

34th ROW Sl.1, p.2, * p.5, (k.2, p.5, k.2, p.1) 3 times, p.1, repeat from * to the last 6 sts., p.5, k.1.

35th ROW Sl.1, k.1, * sl.1, k.2 tog., p.s.s.o., wl. fwd., k.2 tog., k.1, (p.2, k.5, p.2, k.1) 3 times, repeat from * to the last 7 sts., sl.1, k.2 tog., p.s.s.o., wl. fwd., k.2 tog., k.2.

36th ROW Sl.1, p.2, * 5 out of 1, p.2, (k.2, p.5 tog., k.2, p.1) 3 times, p.1, repeat from * to the last 4 sts., 5 out of 1, p.2, k.1.

These 36 rows form the pattern.

Repeat from the 1st to the 36th row (inclusive) once, then from the 1st to the 18th row (inclusive) once.

Shape the Armholes

1st ROW Cast off 10 sts., k.1 (making 2 sts. on the right hand needle) (p.2, k.1) twice, * p.2, k.2, wl. fwd., k.5, wl. fwd., k.2, (p.2, k.1) 5 times, repeat from * to the last 5 sts., p.2, k.3.

2nd ROW Cast off 10 sts., p.1, (making 2 sts. on the right hand needle), * (k.2, p.1) twice, k.2, p.2, k.1, p.5, k.1, p.2, (k.2, p.1) 3 times, repeat from * to the last st., k.1.

3rd ROW K.2 tog., p.2, * (k.1, p.2) twice, k.2, w.r.n., p.1, k.5, p.1, w.o.n., k.2, (p.2, k.1) twice, sl.1, k.2 tog., p.s.s.o., wl. fwd., k.2 tog., repeat from * to the last 27 sts., (k.1, p.2) twice, k.2, w.r.n., p.1, k.5, p.1, w.o.n., k.2, (p.2, k.1) twice, p.2, k.2 tog.

4th ROW K.2 tog., k.1, (p.1, k.2) twice, * p.2, k.2, p.5, k.2, p.2, k.2, p.1, k.2, p.5, k.2, p.1, k.2, repeat from * to the last 22 sts., p.2, k.2, p.5, k.2, p.2, (k.2, p.1) twice, k.1, k.2 tog.

5th ROW K.2 tog., (k.1, p.2) twice, * k.2, w.r.n., p.2, k.5, p.2, w.o.n., k.2, p.2, k.1, p.2, sl.1, k.2 tog., p.s.s.o., wl. fwd., k.2 tog., p.2, k.1, p.2, repeat from * to the last 21 sts., k.2, w.r.n., p.2, k.5, p.2, w.o.n., k.2, (p.2, k.1) twice, k.2 tog.

6th ROW K.2 tog., * k.2, p.1, k.2, p.2, 5 out of 1, k.2, p.5, tog., k.2, 5 out of 1, p.2, k.2, p.1, k.2, p.3, repeat from * to the last 27 sts., k.2, p.1, k.2, p.2, 5 out of 1, k.2, p.5 tog., k.2, 5 out of 1, p.2, k.2, p.1, k.2, k.2 tog.

7th ROW K.2 tog., * p.1, k.1, p.2, k.2, wl. fwd., k.5, p.2, k.1, p.2, k.5, wl. fwd., k.2, p.2, k.1, p.1, sl.1, k.2 tog., p.s.s.o., wl. fwd., k.2 tog., repeat from * to the last 29 sts., p.1, k.1, p.2, k.2, wl. fwd., k.5, p.2, k.1, p.2, k.5, wl. fwd., k.2, p.2, k.1, p.1, k.2 tog.

8th ROW K.2 tog., * p.1, k.2, p.2, k.1, p.5, k.2, p.1, k.2, p.5, k.1, p.2, k.2, p.1, k.1, p.3, k.1, repeat from * to the last 29 sts., p.1, k.2, p.2, k.1, p.5, k.2, p.1, k.2, p.5, k.1, p.2, k.2, p.1, k.2 tog.

9th ROW. K.2 tog., * p.2, k.2, w.r.n., p.1, k.5, p.2, k.1, p.2, k.5, p.1, w.o.n., k.2, p.2, k.1, sl.1, k.2 tog., p.s.s.o., wl. fwd., k.2 tog., k.1, repeat from * to the last 27 sts., p.2, k.2, w.r.n., p.1, k.5, p.2, k.1, p.2, k.5, p.1, w.o.n., k.2, p.2, k.2 tog.

10th ROW K.2 tog., k.1, * p.2, k.2, p.5, k.2, p.1, k.2, p.5, k.2, p.2, k.2, p.5, k.2, repeat from * to the last 26 sts., p.2, k.2, p.5, k.2, p.1, k.2, p.5, k.2, p.2, k.1, k.2 tog.

11th ROW K.2 tog., * k.2, w.r.n., p.2, k.5, p.2, k.1, p.2, k.5, p.2, w.o.n., k.2, p.2, sl.1, k.2 tog., p.s.s.o., wl. fwd., k.2 tog., p.2, repeat from * to the last 25 sts., k.2, w.r.n., p.2, k.5, p.2, k.1, p.2, k.5, p.2, w.o.n., k.2, k.2 tog.

Repeat from the 12th to the 36th row (inclusive) once, then from the 1st to the 35th row (inclusive) once.

NEXT ROW Sl.1, p.5, * (k.2, p.5 tog., k.2, p.1) 3 times, p.4, repeat from * to the last st. k.1.

Cast off.

THE RIGHT FRONT.

Cast on 72 sts.

1st ROW Sl.1, k.1, * p.1, k.1, repeat from * to end of row.

Repeat the 1st row once.

3rd ROW Sl.1, k.1, p.1, k.1, cast off 3 sts., * p.1, k.1, repeat from * to end of row.

4th ROW Sl.1, * k.1, p.1, repeat from * to the last 4 sts., cast on 3 sts. (p.1, k.1) twice.

Repeat the 1st row 20 times, the 3rd and 4th rows once, then the 1st row 4 times.

31st ROW Sl.1, (k.1, p.1) 4 times, * increase once in the next st., p.1, (k.1, p.1) 5 times, repeat from * to the last 3 sts., increase once in the next st., p.1, k.1 (78 sts.).

NEXT ROW Sl.1, p.2, * k.2, (p.1, k.2) 5 times, p.2, 5 out of 1, p.2, repeat from * to the last 9 sts., k.1, (p.1, k.1) 4 times.

Proceed as follows :—

1st ROW Sl.1, (k.1, p.1) 4 times, k.2, * wl. fwd., k.5, wl. fwd., k.2, (p.2, k.1) 5 times, p.2, k.2, repeat from * to the last st., k.1.

2nd ROW Sl.1, p.2, * (k.2, p.1) 5 times, k.2, p.2, k.1, p.5, k.1, p.2, repeat from * to the last 9 sts., k.1, (p.1, k.1) 4 times.

3rd ROW Sl.1, (k.1, p.1) 4 times, k.2, * w.r.n., p.1, k.5, p.1, w.o.n., k.2, p.2, k.1, p.2, k.1, sl.1, k.2 tog., p.s.s.o., wl. fwd., k.2 tog., (k.1, p.2) twice, k.2, repeat from * to the last st., k.1.

4th ROW Sl.1, p.2, * k.2, p.1, k.2, p.5, k.2, p.1, k.2, p.2, k.2, p.5, k.2, p.2, repeat from * to the last 9 sts., k.1, (p.1, k.1,) 4 times.

5th ROW Sl.1, (k.1, p.1) 4 times, k.2, * w.r.n., p.2, k.5, p.2, w.o.n., k.2, p.2, k.1, p.2, sl.1, k.2 tog., p.s.s.o., wl. fwd., k.2 tog., p.2, k.1, p.2, k.2, repeat from * to the last st., k.1,

6th ROW Sl.1, p.2, * k.2, p.1, k.2, p.3, k.2, p.1, k.2, p.2, 5 out of 1, k.2, p.5 tog., k.2, 5 out of 1, p.2, repeat from * to the last 9 sts., k.1, (p.1, k.1) 4 times.

7th ROW Sl.1, (k.1, p.1) 4 times, k.2, * wl. fwd., k.5, p.2, k.1, p.2, k.5, wl. fwd., k.2, p.2, k.1, p.1, sl.1, k.2 tog., p.s.s.o., wl. fwd., k.2 tog., p.1, k.1, p.2, k.2., repeat from * to the last st., k.1.

8th ROW Sl.1, p.2, * k.2, p.1, k.1, p.3, k.1, p.1, k.2, p.2, k.1, p.5, k.2, p.1, k.2, p.5, k.1, p.2, repeat from * to the last 9 sts., k.1, (p.1, k.1) 4 times.

9th ROW Sl.1, (k.1, p.1) 4 times, k.2, * w.r.n., p.1, k.5, p.2, k.1, p.2, k.5, p.1, w.o.n., k.2, p.2, k.1, sl.1, k.2 tog., p.s.s.o., wl. fwd., k.2 tog., k.1, p.2, k.2, repeat from * to the last st., k.1.

10th ROW Sl.1, p.2, * k.2, p.5, k.2, p.2, k.2., p.5, k.2, p.1, k.2, p.5, k.2, p.2, repeat from * to the last 9 sts., k.1, (p.1, k.1) 4 times.

11th ROW Sl.1, (k.1, p.1) 4 times, k.2, * w.r.n., p.2, k.5, p.2, k.1, p.2, k.5, p.2, w.o.n., k.2, p.2, sl.1, k.2 tog., p.s.s.o., wl. fwd., k.2 tog., p.2, k.2, repeat from * to the last st., k.1.

12th ROW Sl.1, p.2, * k.2, p.3, k.2, p.2, (5 out of 1, k.2, p.5, tog., k.2) twice, 5 out of 1, p.2, repeat from * to the last 9 sts., k.1, (p.1, k.1) 4 times.

13th ROW Sl.1, (k.1, p.1) 4 times, k.2, * wl. fwd., k.5, (p.2, k.1, p.2, k.5) twice, wl. fwd., k.2, p.,1 sl.1, k.2 tog., p.s.s.o., wl. fwd., k.2 tog., p.1, k.2, repeat from * to the last st., k.1.

14th ROW Sl.1, p.2, * k.1, p.3. k.1, p.2, k.1, p.5, (k.2, p.1, k.2, p.5) twice, k.1, p.2, repeat from * to the last 9 sts., k.1, (p.1, k.1) 4 times.

15th ROW Sl.1, k.1, p.1, k.1, cast off 3 sts., p.1, k.2, * w.r.n., p.1, k.5, (p.2, k.1, p.2, k.5) twice, p.1, w.o.n., k.2, sl.1, k.2 tog., p.s.s.o., wl. fwd., k.2 tog., k.2, repeat from * to the last st., k.1.

16th ROW Sl.1, p.2, * p.5, (k.2, p.5, k.2, p.1) 3 times, p.1, repeat from * to the last 6 sts., k.1, p.1, cast on 3 sts., (p.1, k.1) twice.

17th ROW Sl.1, (k.1, p.1) 4 times, k.2, * (p.2, k.5, p.2, k.1) 3 times, sl.1, k.2 tog., p.s.s.o., wl. fwd., k.2 tog., k.1, repeat from * to the last st., k.1.

18th ROW Sl.1, p.2, * 5 out of 1, p.2, (k.2, p.5, tog., k.2, p.1) 3 times, p.1, repeat from * to the last 9 sts., k.1 (p.1, k.1) 4 times.

19th ROW Sl.1, (k.1, p.1) 4 times, k.2, * (p.2, k.1) 5 times, p.2, k.2, wl. fwd., k.5, wl. fwd., k.2, repeat from * to the last st., k.1.

20th ROW. Sl.1, p.2, * k.1, p.5, k.1, p.2, (k.2, p.1) 5 times, k.2, p.2, repeat from * to the last 9 sts., k.1, (p.1, k.1) 4. imes.

21st ROW Sl.1, (k.1, p.1) 4 times, k.2, * (p.2, k.1) twice, sl.1, k.2 tog., p.s.s.o., wl. fwd., k.2 tog., (k.1, p.2) twice, k.2, w.r.n., p.1, k.5, p.1, w.o.n., k.2, repeat from * to the last st., k.1.

22nd ROW Sl.1, p.2, * k.2, p.5, k.2, p.2, k.2, p.1, k.2, p.5, k.2, p.1, k.2, p.2, repeat from * to the last 9 sts., k.1, (p.1, k.1) 4 times.

23rd ROW Sl.1, (k.1, p.1) 4 times, k.2, * p.2, k.1, p.2, sl.1, k.2, tog., p.s.s.o., wl. fwd., k.2 tog., p.2, k.1, p.2, k.2, w.r.n., p.2, k.5, p.2, w.o.n., k.2, repeat from * to the last st., k.1.

24th ROW Sl.1, p.2, * 5 out of 1, k.2, p.5 tog., k.2, 5 out of 1, p.2, k.2, p.1, k.2, p.3, k.2, p.1, k.2, p.2, repeat from * to the last 9 sts., k.1, (p.1, k.1) 4 times.

25th ROW Sl.1, (k.1, p.1) 4 times, k.2, * p.2, k.1, p.1, sl.1, k.2, tog., p.s.s.o., wl. fwd., k.2 tog., p.1, k.1, p.2, k.2, wl. fwd., k.5, p.2, k.1, p.2, k.5, wl. fwd., k.2, repeat from * to the last st., k.1.

26th ROW Sl.1, p.2, * k.1, p.5, k.2, p.1, k.2, p.5, k.1, p.2, k.2, p.1, k.1, p.3, k.1, p.1, k.2, p.2, repeat from * to the last 9 sts., k.1, (p.1, k.1) 4 times.

27th ROW Sl.1, (k.1, p.1) 4 times, k.2, * p.2, k.1, sl.1, k.2 tog., p.s.s.o., wl. fwd., k.2 tog., k.1, p.2, k.2, w.r.n., p.1, k.5, p.2, k.1, p.2, k.5, p.1, w.o.n., k.2, repeat from * to the last st., k.1.

28th ROW 1.S1, p.2, * k.2, p.5, k.2, p.1, (k.2, p.5, k.2, p.2) twice, repeat from * to the last 9 sts., k.1, (p.1, k.1) 4 times.

29th ROW Sl.1, (k.1, p.1) 4 times, k.2, * p.2, sl.1, k.2 tog., p.s.s.o., wl. fwd., k.2 tog., p.2, k.2, w.r.n., p.2, k.5, p.2, k.1, p.2, k.5, p.2, w.o.n., k.2, repeat from * to the last st., k.1.

30th ROW Sl.1, p.2, * 5 out of 1, (k.2, p.5 tog., k.2, 5 out of 1) twice, p.2, k.2, p.3, k.2, p.2, repeat from * to the last 9 sts., k.1, (p.1, k.1) 4 times.

31st ROW Sl.1, (k.1, p.1) 4 times, k.2, * p.1, sl.1, k.2 tog., p.s.s.o., wl.fwd., k.2 tog., p.1, k.2, wl. fwd., k.5, (p.2, k.1, p.2, k.5) twice, wl. fwd., k.2, repeat from * to the last st., k.1.

32nd ROW Sl.1, p.2, * k.1, p.5, (k.2, p.1, k.2, p.5) twice, k.1, p.2, k.1, p.3, k.1, p.2, repeat from * to the last 9 sts., k.1, (p.1, k.1) 4 times.

33rd ROW Sl.1, (k.1, p.1) 4 times, k.2, * sl.1, k.2 tog., p.s.s.o., wl. fwd., k.2 tog., k.2, w.r.n., p.1, (k.5, p.2, k.1, p2.) twice, k.5, p.1, w.o.n., k.2, repeat from * to the last st., k.1.

34th ROW Sl.1, p.2, * k.2, p.5, k.2, (p.1, k.2, p.5, k.2) twice, p.7, repeat from * to the last 9 sts., k.1, (p.1, k.1) 4 times.

35th ROW Sl.1, (k.1, p.1) 4 times, k.1, * sl.1, k.2 tog., p.s.s.o., wl. fwd., k.2 tog., k.1, (p.2, k.5, p.2, k.1) 3 times, repeat from * to the last 2 sts., k.2.

36th ROW Sl.1, p.2, * (k.2, p.5 tog., k.2, p.1) 3 times, p.1, 5 out of 1, p.2, repeat from * to the last 9 sts., k.1, (p.1, k.1) 4 times.

Repeat from the 1st to the 36th row (inclusive) once, omitting the buttonhole as worked in the 15th and 16th rows and working one (as before) in the 1st and 2nd rows and in the 23rd and 24th rows of pattern.

Repeat from the 1st to the 17th row (inclusive) once, working a buttonhole in the 9th and 10th row of pattern.

NEXT ROW Sl.1, p.5, (k.2, p.5 tog., k.2, p1.) 3 times, p.1, * 5 out of 1, p.2, (k.2, p.5 tog., k.2, p.1) 3 times, p.1, repeat from * to the last 9 sts., k.1, (p.1, k.1) 4 times.

NEXT ROW Sl.1, (k.1, p.1) 4 times, k.2, * (p.2, k.1) 5 times, p.2, k.2, wl. fwd., k.5, wl. fwd., k.2, repeat from * to the last 23 sts., (p.2, k.1) 5 times, p.2, k.6.

Shape the Armhole

1st ROW Cast off 10 sts., p.1 (making 2 sts. on the right hand needle), (k.2, p.1) 3 times, k.2, p.2, * k.1, p.5, k.1, p.2, (k.2, p.1) 5 times, k.2, p.2, repeat from * once, k.1, (p.1, k.1) 4 times.

2nd ROW Sl.1, (k.1, p.1) 4 times, k.2, * (p.2, k.1) twice, sl.1, k.2 tog., p.s.s.o., wl. fwd., k.2 tog., (k.1, p.2) twice, k.2, w.r.n., p.1, k.5, p.1, w.o.n., k.2, repeat from * once, (p.2, k.1) 3 times, p.2, k.2 tog.

3rd ROW K.2 tog., k.1, (p.1, k.2) 3 times, p.2, * k.2, p.5, k.2, p.2, k.2, p.1, k.2, p.5, k.2, p.1, k.2, p.2, repeat from * once, k.1, (p.1, k.1) 4 times.

4th ROW Sl.1, (k.1, p.1) 4 times, k.2, * p.2, k.1, p.2, sl.1, k.2 tog., p.s.s.o., wl. fwd., k.2 tog., p.2, k.1, p.2, k.2, w.r.n., p.2, k.5, p.2, w.o.n., k.2, repeat from * once, (p.2, k.1) 3 times, k.2 tog.

5th ROW K.2 tog., (k.2, p.1) 3 times, p.1, * 5 out of 1, k.2, p.5 tog., k.2, 5 out of 1, p.2, k.2, p.1, k.2, p.3, k.2, p.1, k.2, p.2, repeat from * once, k.1, (p.1, k.1) 4 times.

6th ROW Sl.1, (k.1, p.1) 4 times, k.2, * p.2, k.1, p.1, sl.1, k.2 tog., p.s.s.o., wl. fwd., k.2 tog., p.1, k.1, p.2, k.2, wl. fwd., k.5, p.2, k.1, p.2, k.5, wl. fwd., k.2, repeat from * once, (p.2, k.1) twice, p.1, k.2 tog.

7th ROW K.2 tog., (p.1, k.2) twice, p.2, * k. 1,p.5, k.2, p.1, k.2, p.5, k.1, p.2, k.2, p.1, k.1, p.3, k.1, p.1, k.2, p.2, repeat from * once, k.1, (p.1, k.1) 4 times.

8th ROW Sl.1, (k.1, p.1) 4 times, k.2, * p.2, k.1, sl.1, k.2 tog., p.s.s.o., wl. fwd., k.2 tog., k.1, p.2, k.2, w.r.n., p.1, k.5, p.2, k.1, p.2, k.5, p.1, w.o.n., k.2, repeat from * once, p.2, k.1, p.2, k.2 tog.

9th ROW K.2 tog., k.1, p.1, k.2, p.2, * k.2, p.5, k.2, p.1, (k.2, p.5, k.2, p.2) twice, repeat from * once, k.1, (p.1, k.1) 4 times.

10th ROW Sl.1, (k.1, p.1) 4 times, k.2, * p.2, sl.1, k.2 tog., p.s.s.o., wl. fwd., k.2 tog., p.2, k.2, w.r.n., p.2, k.5, p.2, k.1, p.2, k.5, p.2, w.o.n., k.2, repeat from * once, p.2, k.1, k.2 tog.

11th ROW K.2 tog., k.2, p.2, * 5 out of 1, (k.2, p.5 tog., k.2, 5 out of 1) twice, p.2, k.2, p.3, k.2, p.2, repeat from * once, k.1, (p.1, k.1) 4 times.

12th ROW Sl.1, k.1, p.1, k.1, cast off 3 sts., p.1, k.2, * p.1, sl.1, k.2 tog., p.s.s.o., wl. fwd., k.2 tog., p.1, k.2, wl. fwd., k.5, (p.2, k.1, p.2, k.5) twice, wl. fwd., k.2, repeat from * once, p.1, k.2 tog.

13th ROW K.2 tog., p.2, * k.1, p.5, (k.2, p.1, k.2, p.5) twice, k.1, p.2, k.1, p.3, k.1, p.2, repeat from * once, k.1, p.1, cast on 3 sts., (p.1, k.1) twice.

Repeat from the 33rd to the 36th row (inclusive) once, then from the 1st to the 18th row (inclusive) once, working another buttonhole (as before) in the 17th and 18th rows of pattern.

Shape the Neck

1st ROW Cast off 9 sts., k.1 (making 2 sts. on the right hand needle), * (p.2, k.1) 5 times, p.2, k.2, wl. fwd., k.5, wl. fwd., k.2, repeat from * once, k.1.

2nd ROW Sl.1, * p.2, k.1, p.5, k.1, p.2, (k.2, p.1) 5 times, k.2, repeat from * once, k.2 tog.

3rd ROW K.2 tog., p.1, k.1, * p.2, k.1, sl.1, k.2 tog., p.s.s.o., wl. fwd., k.2 tog., (k.1, p.2) twice, k.2, w.r.n., p.1, k.5, p.1, w.o.n., k.2, * p.2, k.1, repeat from * to * once, k.1. .

4th ROW Sl.1, p.2, * k.2, p.5, k.2, p.2, k.2, p.1, k.2, p.5, k.2, p.1, * k.2, p.2, repeat from * to * once, k.2 tog.

5th ROW K.2 tog., * p.2, sl.1, k.2 tog., p.s.s.o., wl. fwd., k.2 tog., p.2, k.1, p.2, k.2, w.r.n., p.2, k.5, p.2, w.o.n., k.2, * p.2, k.1, repeat from * to * once, k.1.

6th ROW Sl.1, p.2, * 5 out of 1, k.2, p.5 tog., k.2, 5 out of 1, p.2, k.2, p.1, k.2, p.3, * k.2, p.1, k.2, p.2, repeat from * to * once, k.1, k.2 tog.

7th ROW K.2 tog., k.2, * wl. fwd., k.2 tog., p.1, k.1, p.2, k.2, wl. fwd., k.5, p.2, k.1, p.2, k.5, wl. fwd., k.2, * p.2, k.1, p.1, sl.1, k.2 tog., p.s.s.o., repeat from * to * once, k.1.

8th ROW Sl.1, p.2, * k.1, p.5, k.2, p.1, k.2, p.5, k.1, p.2, k.2, p.1, k.1, p.3, * k.1, p.1, k.2, p.2, repeat from * to * once, k.2 tog.

9th ROW K.2 tog., k.2, p.1, * k.1, p.2, k.2, w.r.n., p.1, k.5, p.2, k.1, p.2, k.5, p.1, w.o.n., k.2, * p.2, k.1, sl.1, k.2 tog., p.s.s.o., wl. fwd., k.2 tog., repeat from * to * once, k.1.

10th ROW Sl.1, p.2, k.2, p.5, k.2, p.1, (k.2, p.5, k.2, p.2) twice (k.2, p.5, k.2, p.1) twice, p.1., k.2, p.1, k.1, p.1, k.2 tog.

11th ROW K.2 tog., p.1, k.1, * p 2, k.2, w.r.n., p.2, k.5, p.2, k.1, p.2, k.5, p.2, w.o.n., k.2, * p.2, k.1, sl.1, k.2 tog., p.s.s.o., wl. fwd., k.2 tog., repeat from * to * once, k.1.

12th ROW Sl.1, p.2, * 5 out of 1, (k.2, p.5 tog., k.2, 5 out of 1) twice, p.2, k.2, * p.3, k.2, p.2, repeat from * to * once, p.1, k.2 tog.

13th ROW K.2 tog., p.2, * k.2, wl. fwd., k.5, (p.2, k.1, p.2, k.5) twice, wl. fwd., k.2, * p.1. sl.1, k.2 tog., p.s.s.o., wl. fwd., k.2 tog., p.1, repeat from * to * once, k.1

14th ROW Sl.1, p.2, * k.1, p.5, (k.2, p.1, k.2, p.5) twice, k.1, p.2, k.1, * p.3, k.1, p.2, repeat from * to * once, k.2 tog.

15th ROW K.2 tog., k.2, * w.r.n., p.1, k.5, (p.2, k.1, p.2, k.5) twice, p.1, w.o.n., k.2, * sl.1, k.2 tog., p.s.s.o., wl. fwd., k.2 tog., k.2, repeat from * to * once, k.1.

Repeat from the 16th to the 35th row (inclusive) as given for the back once.

NEXT ROW Sl.1, p.5, (k.2, p.5 tog., k.2, p.1) 3 times, p.4, k.1.

Cast off.

THE LEFT FRONT

Cast on 72 sts.

1st ROW Sl.1, p.1, * k.1, p.1, repeat from * to the last 2 sts., k.2.

Repeat the 1st row 29 times.

31st ROW Sl.1, p.1, * increase once in the next st., p.1, (k.1, p.1) 5 times, repeat from * to the last 10 sts., increase once in the next st., (p.1, k.1) 4 times, k.1 (78 sts.).

NEXT ROW Sl.1, (p.1, k.1) 4 times, * p.2, 5 out of 1, p.2, k.2, (p.1, k.2), 5 times, repeat from * to the last 3 sts., p.2, k.1.

Proceed as follo ws :—

1st ROW Sl.1, k.2, * (p.2, k.1) 5 times, p.2, k.2, wl. fwd., k.5, wl. fwd., k.2, repeat from * to the last 9 sts., (p.1 k.1) 4 times, k.1.

2nd ROW Sl.1, (p.1, k.1) 4 times, * p.2, k.1, p.5, k.1, p.2, k.2, (p.1, k.2) 5 times, repeat from * to the last 3 sts., p.2, k.1.

3rd ROW Sl.1, k.2, * (p.2, k.1) twice, sl.1, k.2 tog., p.s.s.o., wl. fwd., k.2 tog., (k.1, p.2) twice, k.2, w.r.n., p.1, k.5, p.1, w.o.n., k.2, repeat from * to the last 9 sts., (p.1, k.1) 4 times k.1.

4th ROW Sl.1, (p.1, k.1) 4 times, * p.2, k.2, p.5, k.2, p.2, k.2, p.1, k.2, p.5, k.2, p.1, k.2, repeat from * to the last 3 sts., p.2, k.1.

5th ROW Sl.1, k.2, * p.2, k.1, p.2, sl.1, k.2 tog., p.s.s.o., wl. fwd., k.2 tog., p.2, k.1, p.2, k.2, w.r.n., p.2, k.5, p.2, w.o.n., k.2, repeat from * to the last 9 sts., (p.1, k.1) 4 times, k.1.

6th ROW Sl.1, (p.1, k.1) 4 times, * p.2, 5 out of 1, k.2, p.5 tog., k.2, 5 out of 1, p.2, k.2, p.1, k.2, p.3, k.2, p.1, k.2, repeat from * to the last 3 sts., p.2, k.1.

7th ROW Sl.1, k.2, * p.2, k.1, p.1, sl.1, k.2 tog., p.s.s.o., wl. fwd., k.2 tog., p.1, k.1, p.2, k.2, wl. fwd., k.5, p.2, k.1, p.2, k.5, wl. fwd., k.2, repeat from * to the last 9 sts., (p.1, k.1) 4 times,k .1.

8th ROW Sl.1, (p.1, k.1) 4 times, * p.2, k.1, p.5, k.2, p.1, k.2, p.5, k.1, p.2, k.2, p.1, k.1, p.3, k.1, p.1, k.2, repeat from * to the last 3 sts., p.2, k.1.

9th ROW Sl.1, k.2, * p.2, k.1, sl.1, k.2 tog., p.s.s.o., wl. fwd., k.2 tog., k.1, p.2, k.2, w.r.n., p.1, k.5, p.2, k.1, p.2, k.5, p.1, w.o.n., k.2, repeat from * to the last 9 sts., (p.1, k.1) 4 times, k.1.

10th ROW Sl.1, (p.1, k.1) 4 times, * p.2, k.2, p.5, k.2, p.1, k.2, p.5, k.2, p.2, k.2, p.5, k.2, repeat from * to the last 3 sts., p.2, k.1.

11th ROW Sl.1, k.2, * p.2, sl.1, k.2 tog., p.s.s.o., wl. fwd., k.2 tog., p.2, k.2, w.r.n., p.2, k.5, p.2, k.1, p.2, k.5, p.2, w.o.n., k.2, repeat from * to the last 9 sts., (p.1, k.1) 4 times, k.1.

12th ROW Sl.1, (p.1, k.1) 4 times, * p.2, (5 out of 1, k.2, p.5 tog., k.2) twice, 5 out of 1, p.2, k.2, p.3, k.2, repeat from * to the last 3 sts., p.2, k.1.

13th ROW Sl.1, k.2, * p.1, sl.1, k.2 tog., p.s.s.o., wl. fwd., k.2 tog., p.1, k.2, wl. fwd., k.5, (p.2, k.1, p.2, k.5) twice, wl. fwd., k.2, repeat from * to the last 9 sts., (p.1, k.1) 4 times, k.1.

14th ROW Sl.1, (p.1, k.1) 4 times, * p.2, k.1, p.5, (k.2, p.1, k.2, p.5) twice, k.1, p.2, k.1, p.3, k.1, repeat from * to the last 3 sts., p.2, k.1.

15th ROW Sl.1, k.2, * sl.1, k2. tog., p.s.s.o., wl. fwd., k.2 tog., k.2, w.r.n., p.1, (k.5, p.2, k.1, p.2) twice, k.5, p.1, w.o.n., k.2, repeat from * to the last 9 sts., (p.1, k.1) 4 times, k.1.

16th ROW Sl.1, (p.1, k.1) 4 times, * p.2, k.2, p.5, k.2 (p.1, k.2, p.5, k.2) twice, p.5, repeat from * to the last 3 sts., p.2, k.1.

17th ROW Sl.1, k.1, * sl.1, k.2 tog., p.s.s.o., wl. fwd., k.2 tog., (k.1, p.2, k.5, p.2) 3 times, k.1, repeat from * to the last 10 sts., k.1, (p.1. k.1) 4 times, k.1.

18th ROW Sl.1, (p.1, k.1) 4 times, * p.2, (k.2, p.5 tog., k.2, p.1) 3 times, p.1, 5 out of 1, repeat from * to the last 3 sts., p.2, k.1.

19th ROW Sl.1, k.2, * wl. fwd., k.5, wl. fwd., k.2, (p.2, k.1) 5 times, p.2, k.2, repeat from * to the last 9 sts., (p.1, k.1) 4 times, k.1.

20th ROW Sl.1, (p.1, k.1) 4 times, * p.2, (k.2, p.1) 5 times, k.2, p.2, k.1, p.5, k.1, repeat from * to the last 3 sts., p.2, k.1.

21st ROW Sl.1, k.2, * w.r.n., p.1, k.5, p.1, w.o.n., k.2, (p.2, k.1) twice, sl.1, k.2 tog., p.s.s.o., wl. fwd., k.2 tog., (k.1, p.2) twice, k.2, repeat from * to the last 9 sts., (p.1, k.1) 4 times, k.1.

22nd ROW Sl.1, (p.1, k.1) 4 times, * p.2, k.2, p.1, k.2, p.5, k.2, p.1, k.2, p.2, k.2, p.5, k.2, repeat from * to the last 3 sts., p.2, k.1.

23rd ROW Sl.1, k.2, * w.r.n., p.2, k.5, p.2, w.o.n., k.2, p.2, k.1, p.2, sl.1, k.2 tog., p.s.s.o., wl. fwd., k.2 tog., p.2, k.1, p.2, k.2, repeat from * to the last 9 sts., (p.1, k.1) 4 times, k.1.

24th ROW Sl.1, (p.1, k.1) 4 times, * p.2, k.2, pl., k.2, p.3, k.2, p.1, k.2, p.2, 5 out of 1, k.2, p.5 tog., k.2, 5 out of 1, repeat from * to the last 3 sts., p.2, k.1.

25th ROW Sl.1, k.2, * wl. fwd., k.5, p.2, k.1, p.2, k.5, wl. fwd., k.2, p.2, k.1, p.1, sl.1, k.2 tog., p.s.s.o., wl. fwd., k.2 tog., p.1, k.1, p.2, k.2, repeat from * to the last 9 sts., (p.1, k.1) 4 times, k.1.

26th ROW Sl.1, (p.1, k.1) 4 times, * p.2, k.2, p.1, k.1, p.3, k.1, p.1, k.2, p.2, k.1, p.5, k.2, p.1, k.2, p.5, k.1, repeat from * to the last 3 sts., p.2, k.1.

27th ROW Sl.1, k.2, * w.r.n., p.1, k.5, p.2, k.1, p.2, k.5, p.1, w.o.n., k.2, p.2, k.1, sl.1, k.2 tog., p.s.s.o., wl. fwd., k.2 tog., k.1, p.2, k.2, repeat from * to the last 9 sts., (p.1, k.1) 4 times, k.1.

28th ROW Sl.1, (p.1, k.1) 4 times, * (p.2, k.2, p.5, k.2) twice, p.1, k.2, p.5, k.2, repeat from * to the last 3 sts., p.2, k.1.

29th ROW Sl.1, k.2, * w.r.n., p.2, k.5, p.2, k.1, p.2, k.5, p.2, w.o.n., k.2, p.2, sl.1, k.2 tog., p.s.s.o., wl. fwd., k.2 tog., p.2, k.2, repeat from * to the last 9 sts., (p.1, k.1) 4 times, k.1.

30th ROW Sl.1, (p.1, k.1) 4 times, * p.2, k.2, p.3, k.2, p.2 (5 out of 1, k.2, p.5 tog., k.2) twice, 5 out of 1, repeat from * to the last 3 sts., p.2, k.1.

31st ROW Sl.1, k.2, * wl. fwd., k.5, (p.2, k.1, p.2, k.5) twice, wl. fwd., k.2, p.1, sl.1, k.2 tog., p.s.s.o., wl. fwd., k.2 tog., p.1, k.2, repeat from * to the last 9 sts., (p.1, k.1) 4 times, k.1.

32nd ROW Sl.1, (p.1, k.1) 4 times, * p.2, k.1, p.3, k.1, p.2, k.1, p.5, (k.2, p.1, k.2, p.5) twice, k.1, repeat from * to the last 3 sts., p.2, k.1.

33rd ROW Sl.1, k.2, * w.r.n., p.1, k.5, (p.2, k.1, p.2, k.5) twice, p.1, w.o.n., k.2, sl.1, k.2 tog., p.s.s.o , wl. fwd., k.2 tog., k.2, repeat from * to the last 9 sts., (p.1, k.1) 4 times, k.1.

34th ROW Sl.1, (p.1, k.1) 4 times, * p.7, (k.2, p.5, k.2, p.1) twice, k.2, p.5, k.2, repeat from * to the last 3 sts., p.2, k.1.

35th ROW Sl.1, k.2, * (p.2, k.5, p.2, k.1) 3 times, sl.1, k.2 tog., p.s.s.o., wl. fwd., k.2 tog., k.1, repeat from * to the last 9 sts., (p.1, k.1) 4 times, k.1.

36th ROW Sl.1, (p.1, k.1) 4 times, * p.2, 5 out of 1, p.1, (p.1, k.2, p.5 tog., k.2) 3 times, repeat from * to the last 3 sts., p.2, k.1.

Repeat from the 1st to the 36th row (inclusive) once, then from the 1st to the 17th row (inclusive) once.

NEXT ROW Sl.1, (p.1, k.1) 4 times, * p.2, (k.2, p.5 tog., k.2, p.1) 3 times, p.1, 5 out of 1, repeat from * once, p.2, (k.2, p.5 tog., k.2, p.1) 3 times, p.4, k.1.

Shape the Armhole

1st ROW Cast off 10 sts., k.1, (making 2 sts. on the right hand needle), (p.2, k.1) 3 times, p.2, k.2, * wl. fwd., k.5, wl. fwd., k.2, (p.2, k.1) 5 times, p.2, k.2, repeat from * once, (p.1, k.1) 4 times, k.1

2nd ROW Sl.1, (p.1, k.1) 4 times, * p.2, (k.2, p.1) 5 times, k.2, p.2, k.1, p.5, k.1, repeat from * once, p.2, (k.2, p.1) 3 times, k.2, k.2 tog.

3rd ROW K.2 tog., p.1, (k.1, p.2) 3 times, k.2, * w.r.n., p.1, k.5, p.1, w.o.n., k.2 (p.2, k.1) twice, sl.1, k.2 tog., p.s.s.o., wl. fwd., k.2 tog., (k.1, p.2) twice, k.2, repeat from * once, (p.1, k.1) 4 times, k.1.

4th ROW Sl.1, (p.1, k.1) 4 times, * p.2, k.2, p.1, k.2, p.5, k.2, p.1, k.2, p.2, k.2, p.5, k.2, repeat from * once, p.2, (k.2, p1) 3 times, k.2 tog.

5th ROW K.2 tog., (p.2, k.1) twice, p.2, k.2, * w.r.n., p.2, k.5, p.2, w.o.n., k.2, p.2, k.1, p.2, sl.1, k.2 tog., p.s.s.o., wl. fwd., k.2 tog., p.2, k.1, p.2, k.2, repeat from * once, (p.1, k.1) 4 times, k.1.

6th ROW Sl.1, (p.1, k.1) 4 times, * p.2, k.2, p.1, k.2, p.3, k.2, p.1, k.2, p.2, 5 out of 1, k.2, p.5, tog., k.2, 5 out of 1, repeat from * once p.2, k.2, p.1, k.2, p.1, k.1., k.2 tog.

7th ROW K.2 tog., (k.1, p.2) twice, k.2, * wl. fwd., k.5, p.2, k.1, p.2, k.5, wl. fwd., k.2, p.2, k.1, p.1, sl.1, k.2 tog., p.s.s.o., wl. fwd., k.2 tog., p.1, k.1, p.2, k.2, repeat from * once (p.1, k.1) 4 times, k.1.

8th ROW Sl.1, (p.1, k.1) 4 times, * p.2, k.2, p.1, k.1, p.3, k.1, p.1, k.2, p.2, k.1, p.5, k.2, p.1, k.2, p.5, k.1, repeat from * once, p.2, k.2, p.1, k.2, k.2 tog.

9th ROW K.2 tog., p.1, k.1, p.2, k.2, * w.r.n., p.1, k.5, p.2, k.1, p.2, k.5, p.1, w.o.n., k.2, p.2, k.1, sl.1, k.2 tog., p.s.s.o., wl. fwd., k.2 tog., k.1, p.2, k.2, repeat from * once, (p.1, k.1) 4 times, k.1.

10th ROW Sl.1, (p.1, k.1) 4 times, * (p.2, k.2, p.5, k.2) twice, p.1, k.2, p.5, k.2, repeat from * once, p.2, k.2, p.1, k.2 tog.

11th ROW K.2 tog., p.2, k.2, * w.r.n., p.2, k.5, p.2, k.1, p.2, k.5, p.2, w.o.n., k.2, p.2, sl.1, k.2 tog., p.s.s.o., wl. fwd., k.2 tog., p.2, k.2, repeat from * once, (p.1, k.1) 4 times, k.1.

12th ROW Sl.1, (p.1, k.1) 4 times, * p.2, k.2, p.3, k.2, p.2 (5 out of 1, k.2, p.5 tog., k.2) twice, 5 out of 1, repeat from * once, p.2, k.1, k.2 tog.

13th ROW K.2 tog., k.2, * wl. fwd., k.5, (p.2, k.1, p.2, k.5) twice, wl. fwd., k.2, p.1, sl.1, k.2 tog., p.s.s.o., wl. fwd., k.2 tog., p.1, k.2, repeat from * once (p.1, k.1) 4 times, k.1.

Repeat from the 32nd to the 36th row (inclusive) once, then from the 1st to the 17th row (inclusive) once.

Shape the Neck

1st ROW Cast off 9 sts., p.1 (making 2 sts. on the right hand needle), * (k2, p.5 tog., k.2, p.1) 3 times, p.1, 5 out of 1, p.2, repeat from * once, k.1.

2nd ROW Sl.1, * k.2, wl. fwd., k.5, wl. fwd., k.2, (p.2, k.1) 5 times, p.2, repeat from * once, k.2 tog.

3rd ROW K.2 tog., k.1, * (p.1, k.2) 5 times, p.2, k.1, p.5, k.1, p.2, * k.2, repeat from * to * once, k.1.

4th ROW Sl.1, * k.2, w.r.n., p.1, k.5, p.1, w.o.n., k.2, p.2, k.1, p.2, k.1, sl.1, k.2 tog., p.s.s.o., wl. fwd., k.2 tog., * (k.1, p.2) twice, repeat from * to * once, k.1, p.2, k.1, k.2 tog.

5th ROW K. 2 tog., * k.2, p.5, k.2, p.1, k.2, p.2, k.2, p.5, k.2, p.2, * k.2, p.1, repeat from * to * once, k.1.

6th ROW Sl.1, * k.2, w.r.n., p.2, k.5, p.2, w.o.n., k.2, p.2, k.1, p.2, sl.1, k.2 tog., p.s.s.o., wl. fwd., k.2 tog., * p.2, k.1, p.2, repeat from, * to * once, p.1, k.2 tog.

7th ROW K.2 tog., * p.3, k.2, p.1, k.2, p.2, 5 out of 1, k.2, p.5, tog., k.2 5 out of 1, p.2, * k.2, p.1, k.2, repeat from * to * once, k.1.

8th ROW Sl.1, * k.2, wl. fwd., k.5, p.2, k.1, p.2, k.5, wl. fwd.. k.2, p.2, k.1, p.1, sl.1, k.2 tog., p.s.s.o., * wl. fwd., k.2 tog., p.1, k.1, p.2, repeat from * to * once, k.2 tog.

9th ROW K.2 tog., * k.1, p.1, k.2, p.2, k.1, p.5, k.2, p.1, k.2, p.5, k.1, p.2, * k.2, p.1, k.1, p.3, repeat from * to * once, k.1.

10th ROW Sl.1, * k.2, w.r.n., p.1, k.5, p.2, k.1, p.2, k.5, p.1, w.o.n., k.2, p.2, k.1, * sl.1, k.2 tog., p.s.s.o., wl. fwd., k.2 tog. k.1, p.2, repeat from * to * once, k.2 tog.

11th ROW K.2 tog., * k.2, p.1, (p.1, k.2, p.5, k.2) twice. p.2, * k.2, p.5, repeat from * to * once, k.1.

12th ROW Sl.1, * k.2, w.r.n., p.2, k.5, p.2, k.1, p.2, k.5, p.2, w.o.n., k.2, * p.2, sl.1, k.2 tog., p.s.s.o., wl. fwd., k.2 tog., p.2, repeat from * to * once, p.1, k.2 tog.

13th ROW K.2 tog., * p.2, (5 out of 1, k.2, p.5 tog., k.2) twice, 5 out of 1, p.2, * k.2, p.3, k.2, repeat from * to * once, k.1.

Repeat from the 13th to the 35th row (inclusive) as given for the back once.

NEXT ROW Sl.1, p.5, (k.2, p.5 tog., k.2, p.1.) 3 times, p.4, k.1.

Cast off.

THE SLEEVES (Both alike)

Cast on 74 sts.

1st ROW Sl.1, k.1, * p.1, k.1, repeat from * to end of row.

Repeat the 1st row 13 times.

15th ROW Sl.1, k.1, p.1, * increase once in the next st., p.1, k.1, p.1 repeat from* to the last 3 sts., increase once in the next st., p.1, k.1 (92 sts.).

NEXT ROW Sl.1, * p.2, 5 out of 1, p.2, k.2, (p.1, k.2) 5 times, repeat from * to the last 3 sts., p.2, k.1.

Repeat from the 1st to the 35th row (inclusive) as given for the left front once, but omitting the 8 ribbed sts. of the border within the brackets.

NEXT ROW Sl.1, p.4, (p.1, k.2, p.5, tog., k.2) 3 times, * p.2, 5 out of 1, p.1, (p.1, k.2, p.5 tog., k.2) 3 times, repeat from * to the last 3 sts., p.2, k.1.

Shape the Top

1st ROW Cast off 5 sts. (p.2, k.1) 4 times, * p.2, k.2, wl. fwd., k.5, wl. fwd., k.2, (p.2, k.1) 5 times, repeat from * to the last 8 sts., p.2, k.6.

2nd ROW Cast off 5 sts., * k.2, (p.1, k.2) 5 times, p.2, k.1, p.5, k.1, p.2, repeat from * to the last 15 sts., (k.2, p.1) 5 times.

3rd ROW Cast off 1 st. p.1, k.1, * sl.1, k.2, tog., p.s.s.o., wl. fwd., k.2 tog. (k.1, p.2) twice, k.2, w.r.n., p.1, k.5, p.1, w.o.n., k.2, (p.2, k.1) twice, repeat from * to the last 12 sts., sl.1, k.2 tog., p.s.s.o., wl. fwd. k.2 tog., (k.1, p.2,) twice, k.1.

4th ROW Cast off 1 st., k.1, * p.1, k.2, p.5, k.2, p 1, k.2, p.2, k.2, p.5, k.2, p.2 k.2, repeat from * to the last 10 sts., p.1, k.2, p.5, k.2.

5th ROW Cast off 1 st., * sl.1, k.2 tog., p.s.s.o., wl. fwd., k.2 tog., p.2, k.1, p.2, k.2, w.r.n., p.2, k.5, p.2, w.o.n., k.2, p.2, k.1, p.2, repeat from * to the last 10 sts., sl.1, k.2 tog., p.s.s.o., wl. fwd., k.2 tog., p.,2 k.1, p.2.

6th ROW Cast off 1 st., * p.1, k.2, p.3, k.2, p.1, k.2, p.2, 5 out of 1, k.2, p.5 tog., k.2, 5 out of 1, p.2, k.2, repeat from * to the last 7 sts., p.1, k.2, p.3, k.1.

7th ROW * Sl.1, k.2 tog., p.s.s.o., wl. fwd., k.2 tog., p.1, k.1, p.2, k.2, wl. fwd., k.5, p.2, k.1, p.2, k.5, wl. fwd., k.2, p.2, k.1, p.1, repeat from * to the last 8 sts., sl.1, k.2 tog., p.s.s.o., wl. fwd. k.2 tog. p.1, k.1, p.1.

8th ROW Cast off 1 st., * k.1, p.3, k.1, p.1, k.2, p.2, k.1, p.5, k.2, p.1, k.2, p.5, k.1, p.2, k.2, p.1, repeat from * to the last 4 sts., k.1, p.3.

9th ROW Cast off 1 st., wl. fwd., k.2 tog., * k.1, p.2, k.2, w.r.n., p.1, k.5, p.2, k.1, p.2, k.5, p.1, w.o.n., k.2, p.2, k.1, sl.1, k.2 tog., p.s.s.o., wl. fwd. k.2 tog., repeat from * to the last last., k.1.

10th ROW Cast off 1 st., * p.3, k.2, p.2, k.2, p.5, k.2, p.1, k.2, p.5, (k.2, p.2) twice, repeat from * to the last 2 sts., p.1, k.1.

11th ROW Cast off 1 st., * wl. fwd., k.2 tog., p.2, k.2, w.r.n., p.2, k.5, p.2, k.1, p.2, k.5, p.2, w.o.n., k.2, p.2, sl.1, k.2 tog., p.s.s.o., repeat from * to the last st., k.1.

12th ROW Cast off 1 st., * k.2, p.2, (5 out of 1, k.2, p.5 tog., k.2) twice, 5 out of 1, p.2, k.2, p.3, repeat from * to end of row.

13th ROW Cast off 1 st., * wl. fwd., k.2 tog., p.1, k.2, wl. fwd., k.5, (p.2, k.1, p.2, k.5) twice, wl. fwd., k.2, p.1, sl.1, k.2 tog., p.s.s.o., repeat from * once, wl fwd., k.2 tog., p.1, k.2, wl. fwd., k.5, (p.2, k.1, p.2, k.5) twice, wl. fwd., k.2, p.2, k.1.

14th ROW Cast off 1 st., k.1, * p.2, k.1, p.5, (k.2, p.1, k.2, p.5) twice, k.1, p.2, k.1, p.3, k.1, repeat from * once, p.2, k.1, p.5, (k.2, p.1, k.2 p.5) twice, k.1, p.2 k.1, p.3.

15th ROW Cast off 1 st., * wl. fwd., k.2 tog., k.2, w.r.n., p.1, (k.5, p.2, k.1, p.2) twice, k.5, p.1, w.o.n., k.2, sl.1, k.2 tog., p.s.s.o., repeat from * once, wl. fwd., k.2 tog., k.2, w.r.n., p.1, (k.5, p.2, k.1, p.2) twice, k.5, p.1, w.o.n., k.2, p.2.

16th ROW Cast off 1 st., * p.2, k.2, p.5, k.2, (p.1, k.2, p.5, k.2) twice, p.5, repeat from * to end of row.

17th ROW Cast off 1 st., * wl. fwd., k.2 tog., (k.1, p.2, k.5, p.2) 3 times, k.1, sl.1, k.2 tog., p.s.s.o., repeat from * once, wl. fwd., k.2 tog., (k.1, p.2, k.5, p.2) 3 times, k.3.

18th ROW Cast off 1 st., p.1, * (k.2, p.5 tog., k.2, p.1) 3 times. p.1, 5 out of 1, p.2, repeat from * once, (k.2, p.5 tog., k.2, p.1) 3 times, p.3.

19th ROW Cast off 1 st., * k.2, (p.2, k.1) 5 times, p.2, k.2, wl. fwd., k.5, wl. fwd., repeat from * once, k.2, (p.2, k.1) 5 times, p.2, k.2.

20th ROW Cast off 1 st., * (k.2, p1.) 5 times, k.2, p.2, k.1, p.5, k.1, p.2, repeat from * once, (k.2, p.1) 5 times, k.2, p.2, k.1.

21st ROW Cast off 1 st., k.1, * (p.2, k.1) twice, sl.1, k.2 tog., p.s.s.o., wl. fwd., k.2 tog., (k.1, p.2) twice, k.2, w.r.n., p.1, k.5, p.1, w.o.n., k.2, repeat from * once, (p.2, k.1) twice, sl.1, k.2 tog., p.s.s.o., wl. fwd., k.2 tog., (k.1, p.2) twice, k.1.

22nd ROW Cast off 1 st. k.1, * p.1, k.2, p.5, k.2, p.1, k.2 ,p.2, k.2, p.5 k.2, p.2, k.2, repeat from * once, p.1, k.2, p.5, k.2, p.1, k.2 p.2

23rd ROW Cast off 1 st., * p.2, k.1, p.2, sl.1, k.2 tog., p.s.s.o., wl. fwd., k.2 tog., p.2, k.1, p.2, k.2, w.r.n., p.2, k.5, p.2, w.o.n., k.2, repeat from * once, p.2, k.1, p.2, sl.1, k.2 tog., p.s.s.o., wl. fwd., k.2 tog., p.2, k.1, p.2.

24th ROW Cast off 1 st., * p.1, k.2, p.3, k.2, p.1, k.2, p.2, 5 out of 1, k.2, p.5 tog. k.2. 5 out of 1. p.2, k.2. repeat from * once p.1, k.2, p.3, k.2, p.1, k.2, p.1.

25th ROW Cast off 1 st., p.1, * k.1, p.1, sl.1, k.2 tog., p.s.s.o., wl. fwd., k.2 tog., p.1, k.1, p.2, k.2, wl. fwd., k.5, p.2, k.1, p.2, k.5, wl. fwd., k.2, p.2, repeat from * once, k.1, p.1, sl.1, k.2 tog., p.s.s.o., wl. fwd., k.2 tog., p.1, k.1. p.1.

6th ROW Cast off 1 st., * k.1, p.3, k.1, p.1, k.2, p.2, k.1, p.5, k.2, p.1, k.2, p.5, k.1, p.2, k.2, p.1, repeat from * once, k.1, p.3, k.1, p.1, k.2.

27th ROW Cast off 1 st., * k.1, sl.1, k.2 tog., p.s.s.o., wl. fwd., k.2 tog., k1., p.2, k.2, w.r.n., p.1, k.5, p.2, k.1, p.2, k.5, p.1, w.o.n., k.2, p.2, repeat from * once, k.1, sl.1, k.2 tog., p.s.s.o., wl. fwd., k.2 tog., k.1.

28th ROW Cast off 1 st., p.3, * k.2, p.2, k.2, p.5, k.2, p.1, k.2, p.5, k.2, p.2, k.2, p.5, repeat from * once, k.1.

29th ROW Cast off 1 st., k.2 tog., * wl. fwd., k.2 tog., p.2, k.2, w.r.n., p.2, k.5, p.2, k.1, p.2, k.5, p.2, w.o.n., k.2, p.2, sl.1, k.2 tog., p.s.s.o., repeat from * once, wl. fwd., k.1.

30th ROW Cast off 1 st., p.1, * k.2, p.2 (5 out of 1, k.2, p.5 tog., k.2.) twice, 5 out of 1, p.2, k.2, p.3, repeat from * once, k.1.

31st ROW * Sl.1, k.2 tog., p.s.s.o., wl. fwd., k.2 tog., p.1, k.2, wl. fwd, k.5, (p.2, k.1, p.2, k.5) twice, wl. fwd., k.2, p.1, repeat from * once, sl.1, k.2 tog., p.s.s.o.

32nd ROW Cast off 1 st., * p.2, k.1, p.5, (k.2, p.1, k.2, p.5) twice, k.1, p.2, k.1, p.3, * k.1, repeat from * to * once.

33rd ROW Cast off 1 st., * wl. fwd., k.2 tog., k.2, w.r.n., p.1, k.5, (p.2, k.1, p.2, k.5) twice, p.1, w.o.n., k.2, * sl.1, k.2 tog., p.s.s.o., repeat from * to * once, k.1.

34th ROW Cast of 1 st., p.1, * (k.2, p.5, k.2, p.1) twice, k.2, p.5, k.2, * p.7, repeat from * to * once, p.5.

35th ROW Cast off 1 st., * wl. fwd., k.2 tog., k.1, (p.2, k.5, p.2, k.1) 3 times, * sl.1, k.2 tog., p.s s.o., repeat from * to * once, k.1.

36th ROW Cast off 1 st., * (k.2, p.5 tog., k.2, p.1) twice, k.2, p.5 tog., k.2, * p.5, repeat from * to * once, p.4.

Cast off.

THE COLLAR

Cast on 129 sts.

1st ROW Sl.1, k.2 tog., * p.1, k.1, repeat from * to the last 4 sts., p.1, k.2 tog., t.b.l., k.1.

2nd ROW Sl.1, * p.1, k.1, repeat from * to end of row.

3rd ROW Sl.1, p.2 tog., * k.1, p.1, repeat from * to the last 4 sts., k.1, p.2 tog., t.b.l., k.1.

4th ROW Sl.1, * k.1, p.1, repeat from * to the last 2 sts., k.2.

Repeat from the 1st to the 4th row (inclusive) 6 times (101 sts.).

Cast off.

TO MAKE UP THE CARDIGAN JUMPER

Press each piece separately on the wrong side under a damp cloth with a hot iron. Sew up the side, shoulder and sleeve seams. Sew in the sleeves, placing seam to seam. Sew the collar in position, the cast off edge to the neck and placing the ends 4 sts. from the edges of the fronts. Sew on buttons to correspond with the buttonholes.

Press all seams.

Golden Eagle 'Lady's Jumper'

MATERIALS

Biggan Design 4 ply 100% merino first cross pure new wool (180m/196yds per 50g ball)

6 (6, 7, 9, 10) balls shade 610 (Spruce) – MC
1 ball shade 915 (Vintage Rose) – A
1 ball shade 060 (Ghost Gum) – B
1 ball shade 925 (Rose) – C

1 pair 2.75mm (US #2) needles
1 2.75mm circular needle (Optional)
1 pair 3.25mm (US #3) needles
Stitch holders
3mm crochet hook
4 small buttons

TENSION

28 sts & 36 rows = 10cm (4in) using 3.25mm needles over stocking stitch

ABBREVIATIONS

See page 13 for standard abbreviations

SIZING

Measurements given in centimetres followed by inches in parentheses

To Fit	76–81 (30–32)	86–92 (34–36)	97–102 (38–40)	107–112 (42–44)	117–122 (46–48)
Finished Measurements					
Actual Bust Size	81 (32)	91½ (36)	100 (39½)	111½ (44)	120 (47¼)
Length to underarm	31 (12)	33½ (13)	35½ (14)	38 (15)	40 (16)
Armhole Depth	18 (7)	18 (7)	19 (7½)	20 (8)	21½ (8½)
Finished Length	49 (19)	51½ (20)	54½ (21½)	58 (23)	61½ (24½)
Shoulder to shoulder	32 (12½)	33 (13)	34 (13½)	35½ (14)	37 (14½)

Garment shown in photographs is for second size 86–92 (34–36)

FRONT

Using 2.75mm needles and MC, cast on 96 (112, 124, 140, 152) sts.

Row 1: K1, * K2, P2, repeat from * to last 3 sts, K3.

Row 2: K1, * P2, K2, repeat from * to last 3 sts, P2, K1.

Repeat these 2 rows until rib measures 9cm (3½in) ending with a WS row.

Change to 3.25mm needles and A. Commencing with a K row, work in stocking stitch from here onwards.

** **Row 1**: Kfb into each st along row (192, 224, 248, 280, 304 sts).

Row 2: P.

Row 3: K.

Rep rows 2 and 3, three more times. ***

Change to MC.

Row 10: * P2tog, repeat from * to end of row (96, 112, 124, 140, 152 sts).

Inc 1 st at each end of next and 4 foll 4th (6th, 6th, 6th, 6th) rows (106, 122, 134, 150, 162 sts).

Work 7 (3, 7, 11, 15) rows without shaping.

Change to B and work from ** to *** once. You will have

212 (244, 268, 300, 324) sts after the inc row.

Change to MC, and P2tog along row (106, 122, 134, 150, 162 sts).

Inc 1 st at each end of next and 2 foll 6th rows (112, 128, 140, 156, 168 sts).

Work 11 (15, 19, 23, 27) rows without shaping.

Change to C and work from ** to *** once. You will have 224 (256, 280, 312, 336) sts after the inc row.

Change to MC and P2tog along row (112, 128, 140, 156, 168 sts).

Work 2 rows without shaping.

Shape Armholes

Cast off 5 (8, 6, 6, 6) sts at beg of next 2 (2, 4, 6, 6) rows (102, 112, 116, 120, 132 sts).

Cast off 2 sts at beg of foll 2 rows (98, 108, 112, 116, 128 sts), then dec one st at each end of next and 3 (7, 7, 7, 11) foll alt rows (90, 92, 96, 100, 104 sts). ****

Work 15 (7, 9, 11, 7) rows in stocking stitch.

Change to A and work from ** to *** once. You will have 180 (184, 192, 200, 208) sts after inc row.

Change to MC and P2tog along row (90, 92, 96, 100, 104 sts). Work 8 rows in stocking stitch.

Divide for Neck
K25 (26, 28, 30, 32) sts, K across centre 40 sts and transfer these sts to holder or waste yarn, knit to end. Working on last 25 (26, 28, 30, 32) sts only, work 20 rows in stocking stitch.

Shape Shoulder
Row 1 (WS): Cast off 9 (9, 10, 10, 11), P to end.
Row 2: K.
Row 3: Cast off 8 (9, 9, 10, 11) sts, P to end.
Row 4: Cast off rem 8 (8, 9, 10, 10) sts.

With RS facing rejoin MC to remaining sts and commencing with a K row, work 19 rows in stocking stitch ending with a WS row.

Shape Shoulder
Row 1 (RS): Cast off 9 (9, 10, 10, 11), K to end.
Row 2: P.
Row 3: Cast off 8 (9, 9, 10, 11) sts, K to end.
Row 4: Cast off rem 8 (8, 9, 10, 10) sts.

BACK
Using 2.75mm needles and MC, cast on 96 (112, 124, 140, 152) sts.
Work as given for front until **** (90, 92, 96, 100, 104 sts).
Work 14 (6, 8, 10, 6) rows in stocking stitch.
Next row (WS): P42 (43, 45, 47, 49), K6, P42 (43, 45, 47, 49).

Divide for Back Neck
Change to A and work as folls:
Row 1: [Kfb] 42 (43, 45, 47, 49) times, K3, turn and work on these sts only, placing rem 87 (89, 93, 97, 101) sts on to stitch holder.
Row 2: K3, P to end.
Row 3: K.
Repeat row 2 and 3, three times more, then change to MC.
Row 10: K3, * P2tog, repeat from * to end (45, 46, 48, 50, 52 sts).
Row 11: K.
Row 12: K3, P to end.
Repeat last 2 rows 13 times more, then row 11 once more.
Next row (WS): Cast off 20 sts, P to end (25, 26, 28, 30, 32 sts).

Shape Shoulder
Row 1 (RS): Cast off 9 (9, 10, 10, 11), K to end.
Row 2: P.
Row 3: Cast off 8 (9, 9, 10, 11) sts, K to end.
Row 4: Cast off rem 8 (8, 9, 10, 10) sts.

With RS facing rejoin A to rem sts and work as folls:
Row 1: K3, [Kfb] to end (87, 89, 93, 97, 101 sts).
Row 2: P to last 3 sts, K3.
Row 3: K to end.
Repeat rows 2 and 3, three times more. Change to MC.
Row 10: * P2tog, repeat from * to last 3 sts, K3 (45, 46, 48, 50, 52 sts).
Row 11: K.
Row 12: P to last 3 sts, K3.
Repeat last 2 rows 13 times more.
Next row (RS): Cast off 20 sts, K to end (25, 26, 28, 30, 32 sts).

Shape Shoulder
Row 1 (WS): Cast off 9 (9, 10, 10, 11), P to end.
Row 2: K.
Row 3: Cast off 8 (9, 9, 10, 11) sts, P to end.
Row 4: Cast off rem 8 (8, 9, 10, 10) sts.

SLEEVES
Using 2.75mm needles cast on 80 (88, 92, 92, 96) sts in MC.
Row 1: K1, * K2, P2, repeat from * to last 3 sts, K3
Row 2: K1, * P2, K2, repeat from * to last 3 sts, P2, K1.
Rep these 2 rows a further 7 times.
Change to 3.25mm needles.
Commencing with a K row, work in stocking stitch, inc 1 st at each end of next and 5 (6, 7, 8, 9) foll 4th rows (92, 102, 108, 110, 116 sts).
Work 3 rows.
Change to C.
Next row: Kfb into each st along row (184, 204, 216, 220, 232 sts).
Next row: P.

Row 1 and every foll alt row: K.
Row 2: K18, [K2tog] twice, K24, [K2tog] twice, K36, [K2tog] twice, K24, [K2tog] twice, K18 (128 sts).
Row 4: K17, [K2tog] twice, K22, [K2tog] twice, K34, [K2tog] twice, K22, [K2tog] twice, K17 (120 sts).
Row 6: K16, [K2tog] twice, K20, [K2tog] twice, K32, [K2tog] twice, K20, [K2tog] twice, K16 (112 sts).
Cast off fairly loosely.

SLEEVE PADS
Make 2 sleeve pads (see 'Fit and Finish' chapter).

BOWS
Using 2.75mm needles and A, cast on 16 sts.
Knit 2 rows.
Row 3: K to last 4 sts, K2tog, K2.
Row 4: K2, P to last 2 sts, K2.
Row 5: K.
Row 6: As row 4.
Repeat from row 3 to 6, three times more (12 sts).
Work 4 rows without shaping.
Row 23: K to last 3 sts, Kfb, K2.
Row 24: As row 4.
Row 25: K.
Row 26: As row 4.
Repeat rows 23 to 26 twice, then row 23 once more (16 sts).
Knit 2 rows. Cast off.

BOW CENTRE
Cast on 10 sts and knit 16 rows. Cast off.

Work three further bows in A, B and C.

MAKING UP
Block each piece, taking care not to flatten rippled stripes. Sew side and sleeve seams together, matching stripes. Insert sleeves, matching centre of sleeve head to shoulder seam and matching side seams. Make each bow by sewing strips round centre, then sew in position down centre front, each bow matching the stripe.

BUTTON LOOPS
Make 4 button loops as shown in 'Fit and Finish' chapter. Sew buttons to correspond with button loops.

Sew sleeve pads inside top of sleeves. Darn in all ends.

Next row: K.
Rep last 2 rows, three more times.
Change to MC, and P2tog along row (92, 102, 108, 110, 116 sts).
Next row (RS): KFb, K to last st, Kfb (94, 104, 110, 112, 118 sts).
Work 3 rows without shaping.

Shape Sleeve Head
Continuing in stocking stitch and MC, cast off 2 sts at beg of next 19 (24, 27, 29, 36) rows (56, 56, 56, 54, 46 sts).
Work 1 (0, 1, 1, 0) row without shaping, thus ending with RS facing for next row.
Next row: Change to A. Kfb into each st along row (112, 112, 112, 108, 92 sts).
Next row: P.
Next row: K.
Rep last 2 rows, three more times.
Change to MC and P2tog along row (56, 56, 56, 54, 46 sts).
Dec 1 st at each end of next 7 rows (42, 42, 42, 40, 32 sts).
Work 1 row straight.
Next row: [K2tog] to end. Cast off rem sts.

NECKBAND (All sizes alike)
Join shoulder seams.
With RS facing, using 2.75mm circular needle and MC, commence at left back opening and pick up 20 sts up opening, pick up 28 sts along side of neck, K across 40 sts at front neck, pick up 28 sts on right side neck and then 20 sts down right back opening (136 sts).

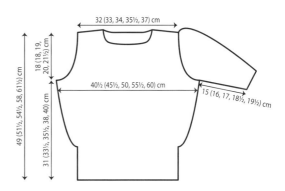

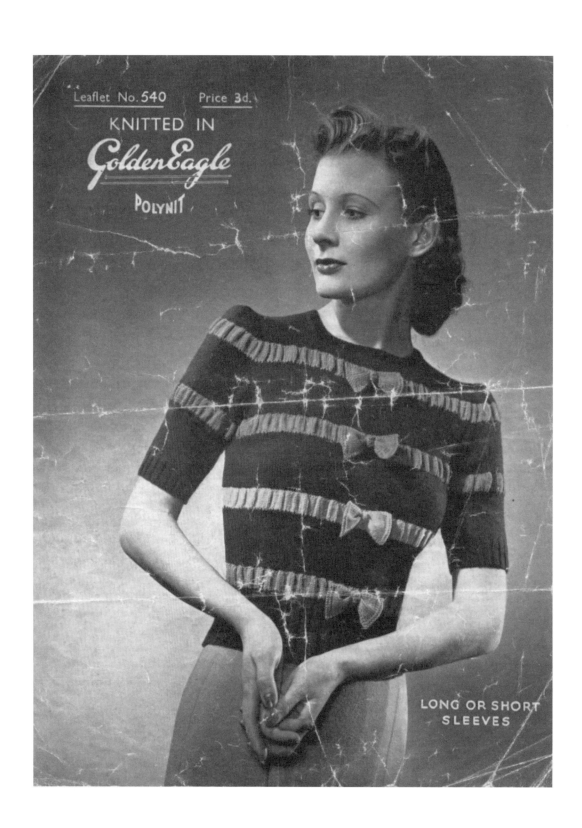

Golden Eagle Leaflet No. 540

Golden Eagle
LADY'S JUMPER
Long or Short Sleeves

YOU WILL NEED

Short Sleeves:
4 ozs. "POLYNIT" 3-ply Wool, Deep Blue, and a small ball each Hyacinth, Silver Grey, and Cerise.

Long Sleeves:
6 ozs. "POLYNIT" 3-ply Wool, Deep Blue, and a small ball each Hyacinth, Silver Grey, and Cerise.

(Or any other Colours included in the Shade Card.)

1 pair each No. 12 and No. 10 Knitting Needles. 4 Small Buttons.

MEASUREMENTS

Length, 18". To fit a 34/36" bust.
Short Sleeve seam, 5½".
Long Sleeve Seam, 20".

ABBREVIATIONS

K., knit; P., purl; tog., together; Rep., repeat; st., stitch; inc., increase; dec., decrease; st.st., stocking stitch, i.e., knit 1 row; purl 1 row.

TENSION

Work at a tension to produce 13 sts. to 2" in width, and 10 rows to 1" in depth approximately.

This design has been specially prepared for the quality, thickness, and twist of Golden Eagle POLYNIT Knitting Wool. The best and correct results will only be obtained if Golden Eagle POLYNIT is used.

CASTING ON.

Unless using the thumb method in casting on, work into the back of all cast on sts. to produce firm edges.

FRONT.

Using No. 12 needles, cast on 112 sts., using Blue wool.
1st row. K1, *K2, P2. Rep. from * to last 3 sts., K3.
2nd row. K1, *K2, P2, K2. Rep. from * to last 3 sts., P2, K1.
Rep. these 2 rows 19 times.
Change to No. 10 needles and Hyacinth wool.
1st row. Inc. once into each st. along row (224 sts.).
2nd row. Purl. **3rd row.** Knit.
Rep. 2nd and 3rd rows 3 times.
Change to Blue wool.
10th row. * P2 tog. Rep. from * to end of row (112 sts.).
Working in st.st., inc. once each end of needle in the next and every following 6th row till 122 sts.
Work 3 rows.
Change to Grey wool and work stripe exactly as given for Hyacinth stripe.
Change to Blue wool, P2 tog. along row (122 sts.).
Working in st.st., inc. once each end of needle in the next and each following 6th row till 128 sts.
Work 15 rows without shaping.
Change to Cerise wool and work as given for other stripes.
Change to Blue wool, P2 tog. along row (128 sts.).
Knit 1 row, purl 1 row.

Working in st.st., **Shape Armhole.**
Cast off 8 sts. at beginning of each of next 2 rows.
Cast off 2 sts. at beginning of next 2 rows.
Dec. once each end of needle in the next and every alternate row till 92 sts. remain.
Work 7 rows.

Change to Hyacinth wool and work as other stripe.
Change to Blue wool and work 19 rows st.st.

Divide for Neck. K26 sts., Cast off 40 sts., K25.
Work 20 rows st.st. on first 26 sts.
With wrong side facing :—
1st row. Cast off 9 sts., purl to end.
2nd row. Knit.
3rd row. As 1st row.
4th row. Cast off 8 sts.
Join wool at centre and work 19 rows st.st.

BACK.

Using No. 12 needles and Blue wool, cast on 112 sts.
Work exactly as given for front till 92 sts. on needle after armhole shaping.
Work 5 rows st.st.
With wrong side facing, P43, K6, P43.
Divide for vent and change to Hyacinth wool.
1st row. (Inc. once into st.) 43 times, K3, turn.
2nd row. K3, purl to end. **3rd row.** Knit.
Rep. 2nd and 3rd rows 3 times, then change to Blue wool.
10th row. K3, *P2 tog. Rep. from * to end.
11th row. Knit. **12th row.** K3, purl to end.
Rep. 11th and 12th rows 10 times, then 11th row once.
34th row. Cast off 20 sts., purl to end.
Change to No. 10 needles.

Shape Shoulder.
1st row. Cast off 9 sts., knit to end.
2nd row. Purl.
Rep. 1st and 2nd rows once. Cast off.
Join Hyacinth wool at centre.
Work as given for side just finished, reading each row backward to produce opposite effect from 1st row to end of 33rd row.

34th row. P26, cast off 20 sts.
35th row. Join wool and knit.
36th row. Cast off 9 sts., purl to end.
37th row. Knit.
38th row. As 36th row. Cast off.
Sew shoulder seams.

NECKBAND.

Using No. 12 needles and Blue wool.
With right side facing, commencing at back vent, pick up evenly 20 sts. along left side of vent, 28 sts. along side of neck, 40 sts. along front, 28 sts. along side, 20 sts. along right side of vent (136 sts.).
1st row and each alternate row. Knit.
2nd row. K18, (K2 tog.) twice, K24, (K2 tog.) twice, K36, (K2 tog.) twice, K24, (K2 tog.) twice, K18.
4th row. K17, (K2 tog.) twice, K22, (K2 tog.) twice, K34, (K2 tog.) twice, K22, (K2 tog.) twice, K17.

6th row. K16, (K2 tog.) twice, K20, (K2 tog.) twice, K32, (K2 tog.) twice, K20, (K2 tog.) twice, K16, cast off.

SHORT SLEEVES.

Using No. 12 needles, cast on 88 sts. in Blue wool.
1st row. K1, *K2, P2. Rep. from * to last 3 sts., K3.
2nd row. K1, *K2, P2, K2. Rep. from * to last 3 sts., P2, K1.
Rep. 1st and 2nd rows 7 times.
Change to No. 10 needles.
Working in st.st., inc. once each end of needle in the next and every following 4th row till 102 sts.
Work 3 rows.
Change to Cerise wool and work stripe as given for front Cerise stripe.
Change to Blue wool and P2 tog. along row (102 sts.).
Inc. in first st., knit to last st., inc. in last st (104 sts.).
Work 3 rows without shaping.

Shape Top of Sleeve.
Working in st.st., cast off 2 sts. at beginning of each row till 56 sts. Change to Hyacinth wool and work stripe as previous stripe. Change to Blue wool, P2 tog. along row.
Working in st.st., dec. once each end of needle in the next and every alternate row till 42 sts., ending in a purl row.
Next row. (K2 tog.) 21 times. Cast off.

SLEEVE PADS.

Using No. 10 needles and Blue wool, cast on 30 sts.
1st row. Knit. **2nd row.** Purl.
3rd row. Knit to within last 2 sts., turn.
4th row. Purl to within last 2 sts., turn.
Continue working 2 sts. less each side till 10 sts. remain in centre, turn. Now working from centre work 2 sts. extra each side till all sts. have been worked once more.
Knit 1 row. Cast off.

LONG SLEEVES.

Using No. 12 needles, cast on 52 sts.
1st row. K1, *K2, P2. Rep. from * to last 3 sts., K3.
2nd row. K1, *K2, P2, K2. Rep. from * to last 3 sts., P2, K1.
Rep. these 2 rows till work measures 3".
Change to No. 10 needles.
1st row. *K4, inc. in next st. Rep. from * to last 2 sts., K2 (62 sts.).
Working in st.st., inc. once each end of needle in every following 6th row till 68 sts.
Work 3 rows. Change to Cerise wool.
Work stripe exactly as given for front.
Change to Blue wool and P2 tog. along row (68 sts.).

Working in st.st., inc. once each end of needle in the next and every following 6th row till 76 sts.
Work 3 rows. Change to Hyacinth wool and work a stripe. Change to Blue wool and P2 tog. along row.
Working in st.st., inc. once each end of needle in the next and every following 4th row till 90 sts.
Work 3 rows.

Change to Grey wool and work a stripe.
Change to Blue wool and P2 tog. along row.
Working in st.st., inc. once each end of needle in the next and every following 4th row till 104 sts.
Work 3 rows.

Change to Cerise wool and work a stripe.
Change to Blue wool and P2 tog. along row.
Work 4 rows st.st.

Shape Top exactly as given for short sleeves.

2 extra ozs. of Blue wool and 1 oz. Hyacinth required.

BOWS.

Using No. 12 needles and Hyacinth wool, cast on 16 sts.
Knit 2 rows.
3rd row. Knit to last 4 sts., K2 tog., K2.
4th row. K2, purl to last 2 sts., K2.
5th row. Knit. **6th row.** As 4th row.
Rep. from 3rd to 6th rows 3 times.
Work 4 rows without shaping.
23rd row. Knit to last 3 sts., inc. in next st., K2.
24th row. As 4th row.
25th row. Knit.
26th row. As 4th row.
Rep. from 23rd to 26th rows twice, then 23rd row once.
Knit 2 rows. Cast off.
Cast on 10 sts., knit 16 rows. Cast off.
Work another Bow in Hyacinth, one in Silver Grey, and one in Cerise.

TO MAKE UP.

Press each piece with hot iron and damp cloth, taking care not to flatten rippled stripes. Sew side and sleeve seams, sewing each stripe with its own colour. Insert sleeves. Make each Bow by sewing strips round centre, then sew in position down centre front, each Bow matching the stripe. Make 4 loops at back vent and sew buttons to correspond. Stuff sleeve pads with cotton wool and sew inside top of sleeves.

It is essential to rinse every trace of soap from a hand-knitted garment before drying. **ALWAYS** dry very slowly.

TO OBTAIN THE CORRECT DIMENSIONS—

Be sure to check your Tension with the Measure down the edge of the back page.

HOW TO ALTER STANDARD SIZES TO O.S. OR SMALLER SIZES.

1. Divide extra amount needed for bust measurement by 2, adding half to front and half to back. For patterns work half the stitches of pattern at each end of original instruction row. (Reverse for smaller sizes.)

2. **Armhole Shaping.** Measure inches required across shoulders, calculate number of stitches from tension. Allow one-third of difference to each shoulder and neck. The difference between the number of stitches prior to shaping and as measured across shoulders is halved, and this number is cast off gradually at beginning and end of each row. (Same principle for smaller sizes.)

3. Usually with O.S. garments the front is required 2" or 3" longer than the back. Simplify this by "turning" after the welt is knitted. Begin by working to within 1" of end and continue turning, increasing amount at end and until there are about 5" in centre. This gives extra fullness to front.

A Snood For All Weathers

MATERIALS
Excelana 4 Ply Luxury Wool 100% pure new British wool (159m/174yds per 50g ball)
2 balls shade Ruby Red
1 pair 4mm (US #6) needles
1 pair 2.75mm (US #2) needles

TENSION
9 patt reps (36 sts) = 10cm (4in) using 4mm needles over stitch pattern

Standard Yarn Tension
28 sts & 36 rows = 10cm (4in) using 3mm needles over stocking stitch

ABBREVIATIONS
See page 13 for standard abbreviations

MEASUREMENTS
Circumference = 51cm (20in) when stretched over head

PATTERN NOTES
This snood is designed to be worn on back of head, as shown in photographs, and is a firm fit as a result of this.

Using 2.75mm needles, cast on 108 sts using alternate cable cast on (see 'Knitting Know How'). Work in rib as folls:
Next row (RS): * P1, K1, rep from * to end of row. Rep this row a further 26 times.
Next row (WS): * K1, Kfb, repeat from * to end (162 sts).
Change to 4mm needles and commence working in lace pattern as folls:
Row 1: K1, * YO, Sl1, K2tog, psso, YO, K1, repeat from * until 1 st rem, K1.
Row 2: P.
Row 3: K2tog, * YO, K1, YO, Sl1, K2tog, psso, repeat from * until 4 sts rem, YO, K1, YO, K2tog, K1.
Row 4: P.
These 4 rows form the pattern. Repeat these 4 rows a further 12 times, then rep rows 1–3 once more.
Next row (WS): P73, [P2tog] 8 times, P73 (154 sts).

MAKING UP
Place first 77 sts onto one needle and second 77 sts onto a second needle, and turn work RS together. Cast off using three needle cast off technique (see 'Knitting Know How'). Neatly sew up back seam, sewing up ribbing using a flat slip stitch. Darn in all ends.

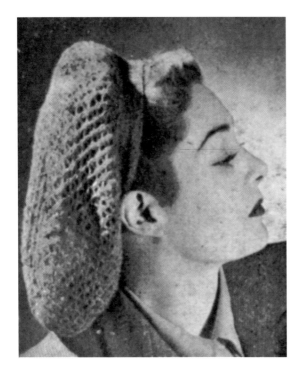

MATERIALS

*O*NE *ounce of Lister's Lavenda Wool, 2-ply ; a pair each of No. 8 and No. 13 knitting needles.*

TENSION AND MEASUREMENTS

*W*ORKED *at such a tension that 2 repeats of the open pattern measure 1¼ inches in width with No. 8 needles, the snood will measure 13 inches along the back seam, 10 inches from centre of head edge to back of snood, and 13 inches round the head edge, expanding to 18 inches.*

ABBREVIATIONS—TO BE READ BEFORE WORKING

*K*KNIT *plain ; p., purl ; st., stitch ; tog., together ; inc., increase (by working into the front and back of the same st.) ; sl., slip ; p.s.s.o., pass the slipped st. over ; m., make (by bringing the wool to the front of the needle and over it before knitting the next st.) ; single rib is k. 1 and p. 1 alternately.*

KNIT IT FOR THE HOLIDAYS

A Little Snood For All Weathers

TO WORK THE SNOOD

*B*EGIN at the head edge and with No. 13 needles cast on 108 sts.

Work 28 rows in single rib, working into the back of the sts. on the 1st row to give a neat edge.

Change to No. 8 needles and inc. thus :

INC. ROW : * K. 1, inc. in the next st. ; repeat from * to end. (162 sts.)

Now begin the lacy pattern as follows :

1ST ROW : K. 1, * m. 1, sl. 1, k. 2 tog., p.s.s.o., m. 1, k. 1 ; repeat from * until 1 st. remains, k. 1.

2ND ROW : All purl.

3RD ROW : K. 2 tog., * m. 1, k. 1, m. 1, sl. 1, k. 2 tog., p.s.s.o. ; repeat from * until 4 remain, m. 1, k. 1, m. 1, k. 2 tog., k. 1.

4TH ROW : All purl.

These 4 rows form the pattern, so repeat them 15 times more.

Now divide the sts. equally between two needles and cast off, taking 1 st. from each needle at a time, or an invisible join can be made by grafting the sts. together in the following way :

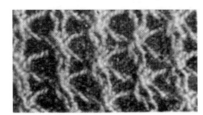

HOW TO GRAFT

*C*UT the wool, leaving about a yard hanging, thread this into a fine bodkin, and pass it through the first st. of the front row as if about to knit, draw the wool through and pass the st. off the needle ; pass the bodkin through the next st. along the front row as if about to purl, draw the wool through, but leave the st. on the needle. Now pass the bodkin *under* the front needle to the back and reverse the action thus : Pass the bodkin through the first st. purlwise and slip the st. off the needle, pass the bodkin through the next st. knitwise and leave the st. on the needle. Continue along the row until all the sts. are worked off, taking care not to draw up the wool too tightly, or the top will be puckered. Pass the cut end of the wool to the wrong side and fasten off. You can remember grafting by this little drill :

Front needle, k. and slip off, p. and keep on.

Back needle : P. and slip off, k. and keep on.

The k. and p. refer, of course, to the position of the bodkin when put into the stitch.

Sew the side seam with the same wool.

Victory Twinset Cardigan

MATERIALS
Fyberspates Scrumptious Lace 45% silk, 55% merino (1000m/1094yds per 100g skein)
2 (3, 3, 4, 4) skeins shade 508 (Midnight) – used double throughout – MC
1 (1, 1, 1, 1) skein shade 500 (Natural) – used double throughout – CC
1 pair 3.75mm (US #5) needles
Stitch holders
3 buttons

TENSION
41 sts & 34 rows = 10cm (4in) using 3.75mm needles over rib pattern (unstretched)

Standard Yarn Tension
25–30 sts & 37 rows = 10cm (4in) using 3mm needles over stocking stitch

ABBREVIATIONS
See page 13 for standard abbreviations

SIZING
Measurements given in centimetres followed by inches in parentheses

To Fit	76–81 (30–32)	86–92 (34–36)	97–102 (38–40)	107–112 (42–44)	117–122 (46–48)
Finished Measurements					
Actual Bust Size	50 (19½)	60 (23½)	70 (27½)	80 (31½)	90 (35½)
Length to underarm	36½ (14)	37 (14½)	38 (15)	39 (15½)	40½ (16)
Armhole Depth	18 (7)	19 (7½)	20 (8)	21½ (8½)	23 (9)
Finished Length	54½ (21½)	56 (22)	58 (23)	60½ (24)	63½ (25)
Sleeve Length	47 (18½)	47 (18½)	48 (19)	48 (19)	49½ (19½)
Shoulder to Shoulder	22 (8½)	27 (10½)	31 (12)	33 (13)	35½ (14)

Garment shown in photographs is for first size 76–81 (30–32)

PATTERN NOTES
Before commencing knitting wind each skein into two separate 50g balls, then use two strands of yarn throughout.

BACK
Using 3.75mm needles and MC doubled, cast on 102 (122, 142, 162, 182) sts.
Row 1 (RS): K2, * P2, K2, rep from * to end.
Row 2: P2 *K2, P2, rep from * to end.
Repeat these 2 rows a further 21 times (44 rows worked in total).
Next row (Inc): Kfb, patt to last st, Kfb (104, 124, 144, 164, 184 sts).
Patt 7 Rows.
Repeat last 8 rows a further 7 times (118, 138, 158, 178, 198 sts and a total of 108 rows worked).

Continue in pattern without further shaping for 16 (18, 22, 24, 30) more rows (work should measure 36½, 37, 38, 39, 40½ cm (14, 14½, 15, 15½, 16 in)), 124 (126, 130, 132, 138 rows) worked in total.

Shape Armholes
Cast off 6 (6, 7, 6, 8) sts at beg of the next 2 (2, 2, 4, 4) rows (106, 126, 144, 154, 166 sts).

Patt 2 sts tog at each end of next 8 (8, 8, 9, 10) rows (90, 110, 128, 136, 146 sts).
Continue without shaping for a further 52 (54, 58, 61, 64) rows (armhole should measure 18, 19, 20, 21½, 23 cm (7, 7½, 7¾, 8½, 9 in)), 186 (190, 198, 206, 216 rows) worked in total.

Shape Shoulders
Cast off 6 (9, 10, 11, 12) sts at beg of next 2 rows, then cast off 6 (9, 11, 11, 12) sts at beg of next 2 rows (66, 74, 86, 92, 98 sts).
Cast off 6 (9, 11, 12, 13) sts at beg of next 2 rows then cast off 8 (9, 11, 12, 13) sts at beg of next 2 rows (38, 38, 42, 44, 46 sts).
Cast off rem 38 (38, 42, 44, 46) sts loosely in rib.

POCKETS (Make two)
Using 3.75mm needles and MC doubled, cast on 26 sts.
Row 1 (RS): K2, * P2, K2, rep from * to end.
Row 2: P2 *K2, P2, rep from * to end.
Repeat these 2 rows a further 13 times. Leave sts on a spare needle or stitch holder.

V Neck Shaping

Row 75: Patt to last 4 sts, P2tog, K2 (61, 73, 81, 93, 101 sts).
Work 1 row straight.
Inc 1 st at beg of next and 3 foll 8th rows and
AT THE SAME TIME dec 1 st at end of 5th and 7 (7, 8, 8, 9) foll 6th rows 57 (69, 76, 88, 95) sts and 123 (123, 129, 129, 135) rows worked.

Work 1 (3, 1, 3, 3) rows without shaping 124 (126, 130, 132, 138) rows worked, work should measure 36½, 37, 38, 39, 40½ cm (14, 14½, 15, 15½, 16 in), ending with a WS row.

Shape Armhole

Cast off 6 (6, 7, 6, 8) sts at beg of next 1 (1, 1, 2, 2) rows, then dec 1 (1, 1, 0, 0) st at armhole edge on foll 1 (1, 1, 0, 0) rows (50, 62, 68, 76, 79 sts).

Cont to shape armhole by dec 1 st at armhole edge on next 7 (7, 7, 9, 10) rows, and AT THE SAME TIME, dec 1 st at neck edge of next and 10 (12, 11, 14, 12) foll 4th (4th, 4th, 4th, 6th) rows (32, 42, 49, 52, 56 sts).

When neck decreases are complete, continue without further shaping until work measures same as back to commencement of shoulder shaping, ending with a WS row.

Shape Shoulder

Cast off 6 (9, 10, 11, 12) sts at beg of next row and cast off 6 (9, 11, 11, 12) sts at beg of foll alt row (20, 24, 28, 30, 32 sts).
Cast off 6 (9, 11, 12, 13) sts at beg of foll alt row and cast off 8 (9, 11, 12, 13) sts at beg of next row, patt to end (6 sts).
Work on these 6 rem sts in rib for 18 (18, 22, 24, 26) rows.
Leave sts on safety pin (this makes up back neckband).

RIGHT FRONT

Using 3.75mm needles and MC doubled, cast on 58 (70, 78, 90, 98) sts.
Row 1 (RS): K2, * P2, K2, rep from * to end.
Row 2: P2 * K2, P2, rep from * to end.
Repeat these 2 rows a further 4 times.
Row 11 (buttonhole): K2, P1, cast off 3 sts, rib to end.
Row 12: Rib to cast off sts, cast on 3 sts, K1, P2.
Work 24 more rows in rib, then repeat two buttonhole rows once more.
Work 6 more rows in rib as set (44 rows worked in total).
Row 45 (RS): Patt 20 (32, 36, 44, 48), slip the next 26 sts onto a stitch holder, patt across sts from top of pocket, rib to last st, Kfb (59, 71, 79, 91, 99 sts).
Work 7 rows without shaping.
Inc 1 st at end of next row (60, 72, 80, 92, 100 sts).
Repeat last 8 rows once more (61, 73, 81, 93, 101 sts).
Work 1 row straight.
Work buttonhole over next 2 rows.
Work 4 more rows straight.
Inc 1 st at end of next row (62, 74, 82, 94, 102 sts).

LEFT FRONT

Using 3.75mm needles and MC doubled, cast on 58 (70, 78, 90, 98) sts.
Row 1 (RS): K2, * P2, K2, rep from * to end.
Row 2: P2 *K2, P2, rep from * to end.
Repeat these 2 rows a further 21 times (44 rows worked in total).
Row 45 (RS): Kfb, patt 11 (11, 15, 19, 23), slip the next 26 sts onto a stitch holder, patt across sts from top of pocket, rib to end (59, 71, 79, 91, 99 sts).
Work 7 rows without shaping.
Inc 1 st at beg of next row (60, 72, 80, 92, 100 sts).
Repeat last 8 rows 2 more times (62, 74, 82, 94, 102 sts).
Work 5 rows without shaping (74 rows worked in total and work should measure 21¾ (8½in)).

Work 5 rows without shaping (74 rows worked in total and work should measure 21¾cm (8½in)).

Complete to match left front, reversing all shaping.

SLEEVES
Using 3.75mm needles and MC doubled, cast on 54 (58, 62, 70, 74) sts.

Row 1 (RS): K2, * P2, K2, rep from * to end.

Row 2: P2, * K2, P2, rep from * to end.

Repeat these two rows twice more.

Change to CC doubled and rep rows 1 & 2 once.

** Change to MC doubled and rep rows 1 & 2 once.

Change to CC doubled and rep rows 1 & 2 once.

Rep from ** 4 times more.

Work in MC doubled only from this point.

Rib 4 rows.

Next row (Inc): Kfb of next st, patt until 1 st rems, Kfb (56, 60, 64, 72, 76 sts).

Patt 5 (5, 4, 4, 4) rows.

Work last 6 (6, 5, 5, 5) rows 16 (18, 21, 22, 25) more times, then work increase row once more (90, 98, 108, 118, 128 sts).

Continue without further shaping until sleeve measures 47 (47, 48, 48, 49½) cm (18½, 18½, 19, 19, 19½ in) ending with a WS row.

Shape Sleeve Head
Cast off 6 sts at beg of next 2 rows, then 0 (0, 3, 4, 6) sts at beg of foll 0 (0, 2, 2, 2) rows (78, 86, 90, 98, 104 sts). Dec 1 st at each end of next and every foll alt row until 22 (26, 30, 38, 44) sts rem, ending with a WS row. Cast off.

POCKET TOPS
Slip sts on holder onto 3.75mm needles with RS facing. Join CC doubled. Work in 2 row rib pattern as for back, change to MC and work a further 2 rows in rib. Cast off in rib using MC.

MAKING UP
Join shoulder seams. Sew up sleeve and side seams then set in sleeves, placing seam level with underarm and matching centre of sleeve head with shoulder seam. Slip stitch pocket linings into place on WS. Pin back neckband in position, and adjust length if necessary. Cast off sts and slip st into place. Sew on buttons. Darn in all ends. Do not press.

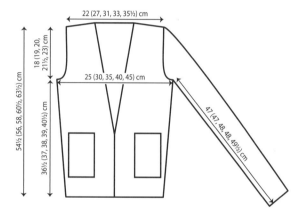

Victory Twinset Top

MATERIALS

Fyberspates Scrumptious Lace 45% silk, 55% merino (1000m/1094yds per 100g skein)
2 (2, 3, 3, 3) skeins shade 500 (Natural) – used double throughout – MC
1 (1, 1, 1, 1) skein shade 501 (Cherry) – used double throughout – CC
1 pair 3.75mm (US #5) needles

TENSION

41 sts & 34 rows = 10cm (4in) using 3.75mm needles over rib pattern (unstretched)

Standard Yarn Tension

25–30 sts & 37 rows = 10cm (4in) using 3mm needles over stocking stitch

ABBREVIATIONS

See page 13 for standard abbreviations

SIZING

Measurements given in centimetres followed by inches in parentheses

To Fit	76–81 (30–32)	86–92 (34–36)	97–102 (38–40)	107–112 (42–44)	117–122 (46–48)
Finished Measurements					
Actual Bust Size	56 (22)	67 (26½)	79 (31)	91 (36)	102½ (40)
Length to underarm	33 (13)	34½ (13½)	35½ (14)	37 (14½)	38 (15)
Armhole Depth	18 (7)	19 (7½)	20 (8)	21½ (8½)	23 (9)
Finished Length	51 (20)	53½ (21)	55½ (22)	58½ (23)	61 (24)
Shoulder to Shoulder	21½ (8½)	26½ (10½)	31 (12)	36 (14)	40½ (16)
Sleeve Length	14 (5½)	14 (5½)	14 (5½)	15 (6)	17 (6½)

Garment shown in photographs is for first size to fit 76–81 (30–32)

PATTERN NOTES

Before commencing knitting wind each skein into two separate 50g balls, then use two strands of yarn throughout.

FRONT AND BACK ALIKE

Using 3.75mm needles and MC doubled, cast on 98 (122, 146, 170, 194) sts.

Row 1 (RS): K2, * P2, K2, rep from * to end.

Row 2: P2 *K2, P2, rep from * to end.

Repeat these 2 rows a further 19 times.

Next row (Inc): Kfb, patt to last st, Kfb (100, 124, 148, 172, 196 sts).

Patt 7 Rows.

Repeat last 8 rows 6 times more, then the increase row only once more (114, 138, 162, 186, 210 sts).

Continue in pattern without further shaping until work measures 33 (34½, 35½, 37, 38) cm (13, 13½, 14, 14½, 15 in) ending with a WS row.

Shape Armholes

Cast off 6 (8, 10, 6, 7) sts at the beg of the next 2 (2, 2, 4, 4) rows (102, 122, 142, 162, 182 sts).

Patt 2 sts tog at each end of next 7 (7, 7, 7, 8) rows (88, 108, 128, 148, 166 sts).

Continue without shaping until work measures 38 (39½, 40½, 42, 43) cm (15, 15½, 16, 16,½, 17 in).

Change to CC doubled and patt 2 rows.

Change to MC and patt 4 rows.

Repeat last 6 rows a further 5 times.

Continue working in MC only until armhole measures 18 (19, 20, 21½, 23) cm (7, 7½, 8, 8½, 9 in) ending with a WS row.

Shape Shoulders

Cast off 8 (10, 12, 14, 16) sts at beg of next 4 rows.

Next row: Cast off rem 56 (68, 80, 92, 102) sts loosely in rib.

SLEEVES

Using 3.75mm needles and MC doubled cast on 78 (86, 94, 102, 110) sts.

Row 1 (RS): K2, * P2, K2, rep from * to end.

Row 2: P2 *K2, P2, rep from * to end.

Rep these 2 rows a further 6 times.

Next row (Inc): Kfb, patt to last st, Kfb (80, 88, 96, 104, 112 sts).

Patt 7 rows.

Rep last 8 rows twice more, then rep inc row only once more (86, 94, 102, 110, 118 sts).

Patt without further shaping until sleeve measures 14 (14, 14, 15, 17) cm (5½, 5½, 5½, 6, 6½ in) ending with a WS row.

Shape Sleeve Head

Cast off 6 (8, 10, 6, 7) sts at beg of next 2 (2, 2, 4, 4) rows (74, 78, 82, 86, 90 sts).

Cast off 4 sts at beg of foll 4 rows (58, 62, 66, 70, 74 sts) then dec 1 st at each end of next and every foll alt row until 40 (42, 44, 48, 50) sts rem. Cast off rem sts loosely in rib.

MAKING UP

Join shoulder seams. Sew up sleeve and side seams then set in sleeves, placing seam level with underarm and matching centre of sleeve head with shoulder seam. Darn in all ends. Do not press.

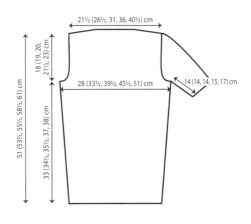

In Simple Ribbing

A quick-to-knit jumper and cardigan set for the smart woman

JUMPER

BACK AND FRONT ALIKE

WITH light wool, commence at lower edge, casting on 98 sts. **1st row**—K.2 (p. 2, k. 2) to end. **2nd row** —P. 2 (k. 2, p. 2) to end. Rep. these 2 rows 19 times. **41st row**—Inc., k. in rib till 1 rems., inc. **Next 7 rows**—Rib. Rep. last 8 rows 6 times, then rep. 41st row. (114 sts.). K. in rib till work measures 12 inches. Now shape armholes. **Next 2 rows**—Cast off 6, rib to end. **Next 7 rows**—Dec., rib till 2 rem., dec. (88 sts.). K. in rib till work measures 14 inches from lower edge. **Next 2 rows**—With dark, rib. **Next 4 rows**—With light, rib. Rep. last 6 rows 5 times. Break off dark wool. Now shape shoulders. **Next 6 rows**—Cast off 8, rib to end. Cast off loosely in rib.

SLEEVES (both alike)

With light wool, commence at lower edge, casting on 78 sts. Rep. 1st and 2nd rows of jumper 6 times. **13th row**—Inc., rib till 1 rems., inc. **Next 7 rows**—Rib. Rep. last 8 rows twice, then rep. 13th row (86 sts.). K. in rib till sleeve measures 5½ inches. Now shape top. **Next 12 rows**—Dec., rib to end. **Next 25 rows**—Dec., rib till 2 rem., dec. Cast off.

∽∽∽

TO MAKE .UP

Press each piece lightly on wrong side under a damp cloth with a hot iron.

Jumper.—Sew side, shoulder and sleeve seams. Sew in sleeves, placing seam level with underarm.

CARDIGAN

BACK

With dark wool, commence at lower edge, casting on 102 sts. **1st row**—K. 2 (p. 2, k. 2) to end. **2nd row**—P. 2 (k. 2, p. 2) to end. Rep. these 2 rows 21 times. **45th row**—Inc., rib till 1 rems., inc. **Next 7 rows**—Rib. Rep. last 8 rows 6 times, then rep. 45th row. (118 sts.). K. in rib till work measures 12 inches. Now shape armholes. **Next 2 rows**—Cast off 6, rib to end. **Next 8 rows**—Dec., rib till 2 rem., dec. (90 sts.). K. in rib till back measures 18½ inches. Now shape shoulders. **Next 6 rows**—Cast off 6, rib to end. **Next 2 rows**—Cast off 8, rib to end. Cast off.

POCKETS (both alike)

With dark, cast on 26 sts. Rep. 1st and 2nd rows of back 14 times. Leave until required.

MATERIALS

Femina Botany Fingering, 2-ply, 4 ozs. light and a small quantity dark for jumper; 5 ozs. dark and a small quantity light for cardigan. 2 Double Century knitting needles, No. 9.

3 buttons.

MEASUREMENTS

Jumper.—Shoulder to lower edge, 18½ inches; sleeve seam, 5½ inches; to fit a 32-34-inch bust.
Cardigan.—Shoulder to lower edge, 19 inches; sleeve seam, 18½ inches.

For abbreviations, see page 18.
Always work into back of each cast-on stitch.
Tension of knitting about 13 sts. and 19 rows to 2 inches.

Cast off 6, rib to end. **116th row**—Rib. **117th row**—K. 2 tog., rib to end. **118th row**—Rib till 2 rem., k. 2 tog., **119th row**—Dec., rib till 2 rem., dec. Rep. 118th and 117th rows twice. **124th row**—As 118th row. (71 sts.). **125th row**—Rib till 4 rem., p. 2 tog., k. 2. **Next 3 rows**—Rib. Rep. last 4 rows 9 times. K. in rib till front measures 18½ inches, ending at armhole edge. **Next row**—Cast off 8, rib to end. **Next row**—Rib. Rep. last 2 rows once. **Next row**—Cast off 10, rib 6. **Next 14 rows**—Rib. Leave sts.

RIGHT FRONT

With dark wool, commence at lower edge, casting on 58 sts. Rep. 1st and 2nd rows of back 5 times. **11th row**—K. 2, p. 1, cast off 3, rib to end. **12th row**—Rib till 3 rem., cast on 3, k. 1, p. 2. **Next 18 rows**—Rib. Rep. 11th and 12th rows. **Next 2 rows**—Rib. **35th row**—Rib 20, slip next 26 sts. on to a piece of wool, rib across pocket, rib 12. **Next 13 rows**—Rib. **49th row**—Rib till 1 rems., inc. **50th row**—Rib. Rep. 11th and 12th rows. **Next 4 rows**—Rib.

57th row—As 49th row. **Next 7 rows**—Rib. Continue as for left front from 65th row inclusive, but reading each row backwards.

POCKET TOPS (both alike)

Slip sts. for pocket top from wool to needle, point toward side seam. Join on light wool. K. 12 rows in rib thus—2 light; 2 dark; 2 light; 2 dark; 2 light; 2 dark. Cast off in rib.

SLEEVES (both alike)

With dark wool, commence at lower edge, casting on 54 sts. Rep. 1st and 2nd rows of back twice. Join on light wool.

Next 2 rows—With light, rib. **Next 2 rows**—With dark, rib. **Next 2 rows**—With light, rib. Rep. last 4 rows 4 times. Break off light wool. **Next 4 rows**—Rib. **Next row**—Inc., rib till 1 rems., inc. **Next 5 rows**—Rib. Rep. last 6 rows 17 times. (90 sts.). K. in rib till sleeve measures 18½ inches. **Next 16 rows**—Dec., rib to end. **Next 26 rows**—Dec., rib till 2 rem., dec. Cast off.

TO MAKE UP

Press each piece lightly on wrong side under a damp cloth with a hot iron.

Cardigan.—Sew down pockets and pocket tops. Sew side, shoulder and sleeve seams. Cast off the 2 sets of border sts. together, then sew border to back of neck. Sew in sleeves placing seam level with underarm. Sew on buttons.

LEFT FRONT

With dark wool, commence at lower edge, casting on 58 sts. Rep. 1st and 2nd rows of back 17 times. **35th row**—Rib 12, slip next 26 sts. on to a piece of wool for pocket top, rib across pocket sts., rib to end of row. **Next 13 rows**—Rib. **49th row**—Inc., rib to end. **Next 7 rows**—Rib. Rep. last 8 rows once.

65th row—Inc., rib till 4 rem., p. 2 tog., k. 2. **Next 5 rows**—Rib. **71st row**—Rib till 4 rem., p. 2 tog., k. 2. **72nd row**—Rib.

73rd row—As 49th row. **Next 3 rows**—Rib. **77th row**—As 71st row. **Next 3 rows**—Rib. **81st row**—As 49th row. **82nd row**—Rib. **83rd row**—As 71st row.

Next 5 rows—Rib. Rep. from 65th to 82nd row inclusive once. **107th row**—Rib till 4 rem., p. 2 tog., k. 2. **Next 5 rows**—Rib. **113th row**—As 71st row. **114th row**—Rib. Now shape armhole. **115th row**—

Lady's Ripple Jumper

MATERIALS
Jamieson's Spindrift 100% Shetland wool (105m per 25g ball)
6 (6, 8, 10) balls shade 435 (Apricot) – MC
2 (2, 3, 3) balls shade 630 (Dove) – A
2 (2, 3, 3) balls shade 308 (Tangerine) – B
1 pair 2.75mm (US #2) needles
1 pair 3.25mm (US #3) needles
3mm crochet hook
Stitch holders
5 knitted buttons (See 'Fit and Finish' chapter)
Ribbon

TENSION
27½ sts = 10cm (4in) over ripple pattern using 3.25mm needles
One patt rep (24 rows) = 6½cm (2½in) in height using 3.25mm needles

Standard Yarn Tension
30 sts & 32 rows = 10cm (4in) using 3.25mm needles over stocking stitch

ABBREVIATIONS
See page 13 for standard abbreviations

SIZING
Measurements given in centimetres followed by inches in parentheses

To Fit	81–86 (32–34)	92–97 (36–38)	102–106 (40–42)	112–117 (44–46)
Finished Measurements				
Actual Bust Size	88 (34½)	99 (39)	110 (43½)	121 (47½)
Length to underarm	29¾ (11¾)	33 (13)	36¼ (14¼)	39½ (15½)
Armhole Depth	16½ (6½)	16½ (6½)	19½ (7½)	19½ (7½)
Finished Length	46¼ (18¼)	49½ (19½)	55¾ (22)	59 (23¼)
Shoulder to Shoulder	30 (12)	36 (14)	39 (15½)	41¾ (16½)

Garment shown in photographs for second size 92–97 (36–38)

RIPPLE PATTERN
Row 1 (RS): Using A, K to end.
Row 2: Using A, K to end.
Row 3: Using MC, K to end.
Rows 4, 5 & 6: Using MC, P1, * YO, P2tog, rep from * to end.
Rows 7 & 8: Using A, K to end.
Row 9: Using MC, Kfb, K5, * K3tog, K4, Kfb into next 2 sts, K5, rep from * to last 9 sts, K3tog, K4, Kfb, K1.
(Please note: Incs and decs cancel each other out on this row, leaving stitch count the same).
Row 10: Using MC, P to end.
Row 11: As row 9.
Row 12: As row 10.
Rows 13 & 14: Using B, K to end.
Row 15: Using MC, K to end.
Rows 16, 17 & 18: Using MC, P1, * YO, P2tog, rep from * to end.
Rows 19 & 20: Using B, K to end.
Row 21: As row 9.
Row 22: Using MC, P to end.
Row 23: As row 9.
Row 24: Using MC, P to end.

These 24 rows set both stitch and colour repeat pattern. It is important to maintain colour pattern at all times. Rows should be matched when casting off for armhole shaping and before commencing shoulder shaping. Please note an extra 6 rows are worked on the front above the shoulder shaping that are not worked on the back. This allows for the gathering up of the front neck.

FRONT
Using 2.75mm needles and MC, cast on 113 (127, 141, 155) sts.
Row 1 (RS): * K1, P1, rep from * to last st, K1.
Row 2: * P1, K1, rep from * to last st, P1.
Row 3: * K1, P1, rep from * to last st, K1.
Repeat rows 2–3 until 10cm (4in) of ribbing have been

worked, ending with row 2.
Work short row shaping as folls:

2nd, 3rd and 4th sizes only
Rows 1 & 2: Rib to last (7, 14, 21) sts, turn.

All sizes
Rows 3 & 4: Rib to last 2 (9, 16, 23) sts, turn.
Rows 5 & 6: Rib to last 4 (11, 18, 25) sts, turn.
Rows 7 & 8: Rib to last 6 (13, 20, 27) sts, turn.
Rows 9 & 10: Rib to last 8 (15, 22, 29) sts, turn.
Cont in this manner working 2 fewer sts on every foll row until rows 55 & 56 have been worked (rib to last 54 (61, 68, 75) sts, turn). On row 56, only 5 rib stitches will be worked for all sizes.

Break off yarn, slip all sts onto one needle and turn to continue.

Change to 3.25mm needles and work 24 rows of ripple pattern as set above.
Next 2 rows: Work rows 1 and 2 of pattern.
Next row (Inc): Using MC, * K6, Kfb, repeat from * to last st, K1 (129, 145, 161, 177 sts).
Continue in pattern from row 4.
Noting that row 9 & rows worked as row 9, should now be worked as folls:
Using MC, Kfb, K6, * K3tog, K5, inc in each of the next 2 sts, K6, repeat from * to last 10 sts, K3tog, K5, Kfb, K1.

Continue in pattern without further shaping until 3 (3, 4, 4) full repeats of 24 row pattern have been worked, and then work 0 (13, 0, 13) rows of next pattern repeat.

Shape Armholes
Maintaining pattern, cast off 11 (11, 13, 15) sts at beg of next 2 rows (107, 123, 135, 147 sts), then K2tog at each end of every foll RS row until 83 (99, 107, 115) sts rem ending with a RS row. Work until armhole measures 16½ (16½, 19½, 19½) cm (6½, 6½, 7½, 7½ in).

Shape Shoulders and Neck
Next row: Using MC, K24 (32, 36, 40), [K2, Kfb] 11 times, K to last 6 (8, 9, 10) sts, turn (94, 110, 118, 126 sts).
Row 2: P to last 6 (8, 9, 10) sts, turn.
Row 3: K to last 12 (16, 18, 20) sts, turn.
Row 4: P to last 12 (16, 18, 20) sts, turn.
Row 5: K12 (16, 18, 20), [K3, Kfb] 11 times, knit to last 18 (24, 27, 30) sts, turn (105, 121, 129, 137 sts).
Row 6: P to last 18 (24, 27, 30) sts. Break yarn.
Slip all sts on to needle and with the RS facing proceed as folls:
Rows 1 & 2: Using B, K to end.
Row 3: Using MC, K to end.
Rows 4, 5 & 6: P1, * YO, P2tog, rep from * to end.
Row 7: Using B, K. Leave all sts on spare needle.

BACK
Using 2.75mm needles, and MC, cast on 103 (107, 121, 141) sts.
Row 1 (RS):* P1, K1, rep from * to last st, P1.
Row 2: * K1, P1, rep from * to last st, K1.
Row 3: * P1, K1, rep from * to last st, P1.
Repeat rows 2–3 until 10cm (4in) of ribbing has been worked, ending with row 3.
Next row (WS): * P9 (4, 5, 9), Kfb, repeat from * to last 3 (7, 1, 1) sts, P rem sts (113, 127, 141, 155 sts).
Change to 3.25mm needles and commencing with row 1, proceed in ripple pattern. Work without shaping until back measures same as front to armhole shaping and pattern matches.

Shape Armholes
Maintaining pattern, cast off 9 (9, 11, 13) sts at beginning of next 2 rows (95, 109, 119, 129 sts), then K2tog at each end of every foll RS row until 83 (99, 107, 115) sts rem, ending with a RS row. Work until armhole measures 6½ (6½, 9¾, 9¾) cm (2½, 2½ 3¾, 3¾ in), ending with a WS row.

Divide for Back Opening

Whilst maintaining pattern at all times, divide for back opening as folls:

Next row (RS): Patt 41 (49, 53, 57), place rem sts onto a stitch holder, turn.

Work without further shaping until back measures same as front to start of shoulder shaping, ending with a RS row.

Shape Shoulders

Using MC and stocking stitch work short row shaping as folls:

Row 1 (WS): P to last 6 (8, 9, 10) sts, turn.
Row 2: K to end.
Row 3: P to last 12 (16, 18, 20) sts, turn.
Row 4: K to end.
Row 5: P to last 18 (24, 27, 30) sts, turn.
Row 6: K to end.
Row 7: P to last 24 (32, 36, 40) sts, turn.
Row 8: K to end.

Cast off first 17 sts. Leave rem 24 (32, 36, 40) shoulder sts on spare needle or holder.

With RS facing, rejoin appropriate yarn to rem 42 (50, 54, 58) sts and work without further shaping until back measures same as front to start of shoulder shaping, ending with a WS row. Then work short row shaping as folls:

Row 1: K to last 6 (8, 9, 10) sts, turn.
Row 2: P to end.
Row 3: K to last 12 (16, 18, 20) sts, turn.
Row 4: P to end.
Row 5: K to last 18 (24, 27, 30) sts, turn.
Row 6: P to end.
Row 7: K to last 24 (32, 36, 40) sts, turn.
Row 8: P to end.

Cast off first 18 sts. Leave rem 24 (32, 36, 40) shoulder sts on spare needle or holder.

Casting Off Shoulders

Cast off using three needle cast off over first 24 (32, 36, 40) sts of front together with 24 (32, 36, 40) sts from back, cast off centre 57 sts on front neck, then cast off using three needle cast off across rem 24 (32, 36, 40) sts on front and back together.

SLEEVES

Using 2.75mm needles and MC, cast on 76 (88, 100, 100) sts.
Next row (RS); * K1, P1, rep from * to end.
Rep this row until work measures 2½cm (1in) ending with a RS row.

Next row: P4 (7, 1, 1) * Pfb, P7 (8, 10, 10) rep from * to end 85 (97, 109, 109 sts).

Change to 3.25mm needles and commencing with row 1, work in ripple pattern as set until one complete repeat has been worked noting that row 9 & rows worked as row 9, should be worked as folls:

Using MC, Kfb, K4, * K3tog, K3, inc in each of the next 2 sts, K4, repeat from * to last 8 sts, K3tog, K3, Kfb, K1.

Work rows 1 & 2 only of next repeat.
Next row (Inc): MC, * K5, Kfb, repeat from * to last st, K1 (99, 113, 127, 127 sts).

Continue in pattern from row 4, noting that row 9 & rows worked as row 9, should now be worked as folls:
Using MC, Kfb, K5, * K3tog, K4, inc in each of the next 2 sts, K5, repeat from * to last 9 sts, K3tog, K4, Kfb, K1.
Continue without further shaping until row 12 of third patt rep worked.

Shape Sleeve Head

Maintaining pattern, cast off 9 (9, 11, 11) sts at beginning of next 2 rows (81, 95, 105, 105 sts), then K2tog at each end of every foll RS row until 71 (85, 95, 95) sts rem ending with a RS row.
Continue without further shaping until row 20 of fifth patt rep worked.

Using MC and working in stocking stitch, cast off 6 (8, 7, 7) sts at beg of the next 6 (6, 8, 8) rows (35, 37, 39, 39 sts).
Cast off rem sts. Work another sleeve in the same manner.

TIE

Using 3.25mm needles and A, cast on 4 sts.
Row 1: Kfb to end (8 sts).
Row 2: * With yarn to the front Sl1 purlwise, take yarn to the back, K1, rep from * to end.
Repeat row 2 until the work measures 40½cm (16in).
Cast off working 2 sts tog along row.

SHOULDER PADS

Using MC, work shoulder pads as described in 'Fit and Finish' chapter.

BUTTONS

Using MC, A or B as preferred knit 5 buttons as described in 'Fit and Finish' chapter.

MAKING UP

Press pieces lightly under a damp cloth on WS of work.
Darn in all ends. Join side seams using neat back stitch,
carefully matching colour stripes. Sew up sleeve seams in
same way.

Using a long thread of MC sew a line of running stitches
across upper edge of each sleeve, knot each end of yarn and
gather up sleeve head. Pin sleeve head into position
carefully matching seams and stripes. Once position is
correct, sew into place using neat back stitch.

Using B and crochet hook, work 1 row of DC (SC) down
the right edge of the back opening, turn and work 5 button
loops at the equal distances apart along the same edge. ('Fit
and Finish' chapter). Work a row of DC (SC) along the left
side of the back opening.

Commencing at the point of the rib in the centre front and
finishing at the neck, run a thread of MC under the open
stitch stripe and over the smooth fabric stripe and draw up
to suit the wearer. Back stitch on the WS then bind the
gathering on the WS with a narrow piece of ribbon to keep
the gathers in position.

Make a bow of the tie and stitch to the top of the gathers,
at the neck, as shown in the photograph.

Attach the shoulder pads to the WS of the top of each
sleeve at the shoulder line. Sew buttons in place on back
opening.

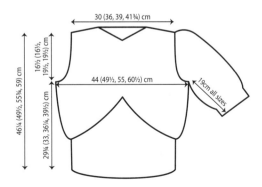

Copley's

LEAFLET No.
1552
Lady's Jumper
34 to 35 inch bust
PRICE 4d.

2-ply "EXCELSIOR" WOOL

L. COPLEY-SMITH & SONS LTD., MANCHESTER and LONDON

A suggestion of soft romantic pleats gathered up to a dainty bow gives a truly feminine charm to this model

MATERIALS : 4 oz. 2-ply "Excelsior" Shetland Wool, Lt. Clerical Grey, No. 1036.

1 oz. each 2-ply "Excelsior" Shetland Wool, Royal Blue No. 99 and Pilot Blue, No. 230.

1 pair No. 12 "Coploid" Knitting Needles.
1 pair No. 10 "Coploid" Knitting Needles.
1 No. 12 "Stratnoid" Crochet Hook.
5 Buttons.
2 Shoulder Pads.
A short length of narrow ribbon for binding.

MEASUREMENTS : Length from top of shoulder to lower edge, 18½ inches.
Width all round at underarm, to fit a 34—35 inch bust.
Length of sleeve seam, 6 inches.

TENSION : Using No. 10 Needles, work to produce 8 sts. and 10 rows to one square inch in smooth fabric (1 row K., 1 row P.).

ABBREVIATIONS : K.—knit. P.—purl. St.—stitch. Tog.—together.
W.r.n.—wool round needle. D.c.—double crochet.

THE FRONT.

Using No. 12 needles and Grey wool, cast on 127 sts.

1st Row.—Working into the back of the sts., * K.1, P.1. Repeat from * to the last st., K.1.

2nd Row.—* P.1, K.1. Repeat from * to the last st., P.1.

3rd Row.—* K.1, P.1. Repeat from * to the last st., K.1.

Repeat the 2nd and 3rd rows until 4 inches of ribbing have been worked, finishing at the end of a 2nd row.

Shape the front as follows :—

1st and 2nd Rows.—Rib to the last 7 sts., turn.
3rd and 4th Rows.—Rib to the last 9 sts., turn.
5th and 6th Rows.—Rib to the last 11 sts., turn.
7th and 8th Rows.—Rib to the last 13 sts., turn.
9th and 10th Rows.—Rib to the last 15 sts., turn.

Continue in this manner, working 2 sts. **less** on every following row, until the row " rib 5 sts. " has been worked. Break off wool.

Slip all the sts. on to one needle, turn.

Change to No. 10 needles and proceed in pattern for which 3 balls of wool will be required, 1 ball each of Grey, Royal and Pilot Blue, breaking off the colours at the completion of a group of stripes, but carrying the Grey wool up the side to avoid many ends.

1st and 2nd Rows.—Using Royal, knit.
3rd Row.—Using Grey, knit.
4th, 5th and 6th Rows.—Using Royal, knit. * w.r.n., P.2 tog. Repeat from * to the end.
7th and 8th Rows.—Using Royal, knit. Break off Royal.
9th Row.—Using Grey, increase 1 st. by knitting into the front and back of the first st., K.5, * K.3 tog., K.4, increase in each of the next 2 sts., K.5. Repeat from * to the last 9 sts., K.3 tog., K.4. increase in the next st., K.1.
10th Row.—Purl.
11th and 12th Rows.—As the 9th and 10th rows.
13th and 14th Rows.—Using Pilot Blue, knit.
15th—18th Rows.—As rows 3—6 inclusive.
19th and 20th Rows.—Using Pilot Blue, knit. Break off Pilot Blue.
21st—24th Rows.—As rows 9—12 inclusive.

These 24 rows form the order of the colouring.

Increase as follows :—

1st and 2nd Rows.—Using Royal, knit.
3rd Row.—Using Grey, * K.6, increase in the next st. Repeat from * to the last st., K.1. (145 sts. now on the needle.)
4th, 5th and 6th Rows.—P.1, * w.r.n., P.2 tog. Repeat from * to the end.
7th and 8th Rows.—Using Royal, knit.
9th Row.—Using Grey, increase in the first st., K.6, * K.3 tog., K.5, increase in each of the next 2 sts., K.6. Repeat from * to the last 10 sts., K.3 tog., K.5, increase in the next st., K.1.
10th Row.—Purl.
11th and 12th Rows.—As the 9th and 10th rows.
13th and 14th Rows.—Using Pilot Blue, knit.
15th Row.—Using Grey, knit.
16th—18th Rows.—As the 4th, 5th and 6th rows.
19th and 20th Rows.—Using Pilot Blue, knit.

Keeping the order of colouring correct, repeat rows 9—20 inclusive 3 times more, then repeat rows 9—12 inclusive. Break off Grey wool.

Shape the Armholes as follows :—

1st Row.—Using Pilot Blue, knit.
2nd Row.—Cast off 11 sts., K. to the last 11 sts., cast off the last 11 sts.
3rd Row.—Using Grey, K.2 tog., K. to the last 2 sts., K.2 tog.
4th, 5th and 6th Rows.—P.1, * w.r.n., P.2 tog. Repeat from * to the end.
7th Row.—Using Pilot Blue, K.2 tog., K. to the last 2 sts., K.2 tog.
8th Row.—Knit.
9th Row.—Using Grey, K.2 tog., K.1, * increase in the next st., K.6, K.3 tog., K.5, increase in the next st. Repeat from * to the last 4 sts., K.2, K.2 tog.
10th Row.—Purl.
11th Row.—K.2 tog., work as a 9th row from * to the last 3 sts., K.1, K.2 tog.
12th Row.—Purl.
13th Row.—Using Royal, K.2 tog., K. to the last 2 sts., K.2 tog.
14th Row.—Knit.
15th Row.—Using Grey, * K.6, K.2 tog. Repeat from * to the last st., K.1.

The armhole shaping is now completed and 99 sts. remain.

Now repeat 4—24 inclusive of the pattern rows as worked **above the ribbing**, then repeat rows 1—24 inclusive and finally rows 1—8 inclusive of the same instructions.

Shape the Shoulders and Neck as follows :—

1st Row.—Using Grey, K.32, (K.2, increase in the next st.) 11 times, K. to the last 8 sts., turn..
2nd Row.—P. to the last 8 sts., turn.
3rd Row.—K. to the last 16 sts., turn.
4th Row.—P. to the last 16 sts., turn.
5th Row.—K.16, (K.3, increase in the next st.) 11 times, K. to the last 24 sts., turn.
6th Row.—P. to the last 24 sts. Break off wool.

Slip all the sts. on to one needle and with the right side of the work facing, proceed as follows.

1st and 2nd Rows.—Using Pilot Blue, knit.
3rd Row.—Using Grey, knit.
4th, 5th and 6th Rows.—P.1, * w.r.n., P.2 tog. Repeat from * to the end. Break off Grey wool.
7th Row.—Using Pilot Blue, knit.

Cast off knitwise all across.

THE, BACK.

Using No. 12 needles and Grey wool, cast on 107 sts.

1st Row.—Working into the back of the sts., * P.1, K.1. Repeat from * to the last st., P.1.
2nd Row.—* K.1, P.1. Repeat from * to the last st., K.1.
3rd Row.—* P.1, K.1. Repeat from * to the last st., P.1.

Repeat the 2nd and 3rd rows until 4 inches of ribbing have been worked, finishing at the end of a 2nd row.

Next Row.—* P.4, increase in the next st. Repeat from * to the last 7 sts., P.7. (127 sts. now on the needle.)

Change to No. 10 needles and proceed in pattern for which 3 balls of wool will be required, 1 ball each of Grey, Royal and Pilot, breaking off the colours as before.

Repeat rows 1—24 inclusive **3 times** as worked **above the ribbing** on the Front, then repeat rows 1—12 inclusive of the same instructions. Break off Grey wool.

Shape the Armholes as follows :—

1st Row.—Using Pilot Blue, knit.
2nd Row.—Cast off 9 sts., K. to the last 9 sts., cast off the last 9 sts.
3rd Row.—Using Grey, K.2 tog., K. to the last 2 sts., K.2 tog.
4th, 5th and 6th Rows.—P.1, * w.r.n., P.2 tog. Repeat from * to the end.
7th Row.—Using Pilot Blue, K.2 tog., K. to the last 2 sts., K.2 tog.
8th Row.—Knit.
9th Row.—Using Grey, K.2 tog., K.1, * increase in the next st., K.5, K.3 tog., K.4, increase in the next st. Repeat from * to the last 4 sts., K.2, K.2 tog.
10th Row.—Purl.
11th Row.—K.2 tog., work as the 9th row from * to the last 3 sts., K.1, K.2 tog.
12th Row.—Purl.
13th Row.—Using Royal, K.2 tog., K. to the last 2 sts., K.2 tog.
14th Row.—Knit.

The armhole shaping is now completed and 99 sts. remain.

Now repeat 3—14 inclusive of the pattern rows as worked **above the ribbing** on the Front.

Divide for the Back Opening as follows :—

Next Row.—Using Grey, K.49 sts. Slip the remaining sts. on to a safety pin for the present, turn.

Proceed on the former set of sts. for the Right half of the Back as follows :—

1st Row.—P.1, * w.r.n., P.2 tog. Repeat from * to the end.
2nd and 3rd Rows.—As the 1st row.
4th and 5th Rows.—Using Pilot Blue, knit.
6th Row.—Using Grey, increase in the first st., K.5, * K.3 tog., K.4, increase in each of the next 2 sts., K.5. Repeat from * once more, K.3 tog., K.4, increase in the next st., K.7.
7th Row.—Purl.
8th and 9th Rows.—As the 6th and 7th rows.
10th and 11th Rows.—Using Royal, knit.
12th Row.—Using Grey, knit.

Keeping the order of colouring correct, repeat the last 12 rows twice more, then repeat rows 1—8 inclusive.

Shape the Shoulder as follows :—

1st Row.—Using Grey, P. to the last 8 sts., turn.
2nd Row.—K. to the neck.
3rd Row.—P. to the last 16 sts., turn.
4th Row.—K. to the neck.
5th Row.—P. to the last 24 sts., turn.
6th Row.—K. to the neck.
7th Row.—P. to the last 32 sts., turn.
8th Row.—K. to the neck.

Cast off purlwise all across.

Slip the sts. from the safety pin on to a No. 10 needle, the point to the centre, join on the Grey wool and casting on 1 st., proceed for the Left half of the Back as follows:—

1st Row.—Knit.
2nd, 3rd and 4th Rows.—P.1, * w.r.n., P.2 tog. Repeat from * to the end.
5th and 6th Rows.—Using Pilot Blue, knit.
7th Row.—Using Grey, K.8, * increase in the next st., K.5, K.3 tog., K.4, increase in the next st. Repeat from * twice more, K.1.
8th Row.—Purl.
9th and 10th Rows.—As the 7th and 8th rows.
11th and 12th Rows.—Using Royal, knit.

Keeping the order of colouring correct, repeat the last 12 rows twice more, then repeat rows 1—10 inclusive.

Shape the Shoulder as the instructions for the Right half of the Back, but reading K. for P. and P. for K. and casting off knitwise.

THE SLEEVE.

Using No. 12 needles and Grey wool, cast on 88 sts.

Working into the back of the sts. on the first row only, proceed in K.1, P.1 rib for 1 inch.

Next Row.—P.7, * increase in the next st., P.8. Repeat from * to the end. (97 sts. now on the needle.)

Change to No. 10 needles and proceed in pattern for which 3 balls of wool will be required as before.

1st and 2nd Rows.—Using Royal, knit.
3rd Row.—Using Grey, knit.
4th, 5th and 6th Rows.—P.1, * w.r.n., P.2 tog. Repeat from * to the end.
7th and 8th Rows.—Using Royal, knit.
9th Row.—Using Grey, increase in the first st. K.4, * K.3 tog., K.3, increase in each of the next 2 sts., K.4. Repeat from * to the last 8 sts., K.3 tog., K.3, increase in the next st., K.1.

10th Row.—Purl.
11th and 12th Rows.—As the 9th and 10th rows.
13th and 14th Rows.—Using Pilot Blue, knit.
15th—18th Rows.—As rows 3—6 inclusive.
19th and 20th Rows.—Using Pilot Blue, knit.
21st—24th Rows.—As rows 9—12 inclusive.
25th and 26th Rows.—As the 1st and 2nd rows.
27th Row.—Using Grey, * K.5, increase in the next st. Repeat from * to the last st., K.1. (113 sts. now on the needle.)

Now repeat 4—24 inclusive of the pattern rows as worked **above the ribbing** on the Front, then repeat rows 1—12 inclusive of the same instructions. Break off Grey wool.

Shape the Top as follows :—

Repeat rows 1—14 inclusive of the instructions for the **armhole shaping** on the Back, when 85 sts. will remain.

Now repeat 3—24 inclusive of the pattern rows as worked above the ribbing on the Front, then repeat rows 1—24 inclusive and finally rows 1—8 inclusive of the same instructions.

Proceed as follows :—

1st Row.—Using Grey, cast off 8 sts., K. to the end.
2nd Row.—Cast off 8 sts., P. to the end.

Repeat the last 2 rows twice more (37 sts. remain).

Cast off.

Work another sleeve in the same manner.

THE TIE.

Using No. 10 needles and Royal wool, cast on 4 sts.

1st Row.—K. into the front and back of every st. (8 sts. now on the needle.)
2nd Row.—Keeping the wool to the front of the needle slip 1 purlwise, wool to the back, K.1, * wool forward, slip 1 purlwise, wool to the back, K.1. Repeat from * to the end.

Repeat the 2nd row until the work measures 16 inches.

Cast off, knitting 2 sts. tog. whilst casting off.

MAKE-UP.

Stitch the 32 shoulder sts. of the Back to 32 sts. on each side of the cast-off edge of the Front.

Join the side and sleeve seams and stitch the sleeves into position, gathering up the fullness at the top of the sleeve to fit the armhole, care being taken to match the coloured stripes when joining all seams.

Using Grey wool and the crochet hook, work 1 row of d.c. down the edge of the Right side of the Back opening, turn and work 5 button loops at equal distances apart along the same edge.

Work a row of d.c. along the Left side of the opening.

Attach the buttons on to the Left side to correspond with the loops.

Complete the neck of the Back with a row of d.c. worked in Pilot Blue.

Commencing at the point of the rib in the centre Front and finishing at the neck, run a thread of Grey wool under the open stitch stripe and over the smooth fabric stripe and draw up to suit the wearer. Back stitch on the wrong side, then bind the gathering on the wrong side with a narrow piece of ribbon to keep the gathers in position.

Make a bow of the Tie and stitch to the top of the gathers, at the neck, as shown in the photograph.

Do not press the work at all.

Attach the shoulder pads to the wrong side of the top of each sleeve at the shoulder line.

Lady's Sleeveless Fair Isle Pullover

MATERIALS
Excelana 4 Ply Luxury Wool 100% pure new British wool (159m/174yds per 50g ball)
4 (5, 6, 7, 8) balls shade Saharan Sand – MC
1 (1, 1, 1, 2) balls each of Alabaster – B, Ruby Red – C, Nile Green – D, Persian Grey – E, Cornflower Blue – F
1 3.25mm (US #3) circular needles (length 80cm)
1 2.75mm (US #2) circular needles (length 60/80cm)
Stitch holder
2 stitch markers

TENSION
34 sts & 32 rows = 10 cm (4in) using 3.25mm needles over fair isle pattern

Standard Yarn Tension
28 sts & 36 rows = 10cm (4in) using 3mm needles over stocking stitch

ABBREVIATIONS
See page 13 for standard abbreviations

SIZING
Measurements given in centimetres followed by inches in parentheses

To Fit	81–86 (32–34)	92–97 (36–38)	102–107 (40–42)	112–117 (44–46)	122–127 (48–50)
Finished Measurements					
Actual Bust Size	85 (33½)	95 (37½)	106 (41¾)	116½ (46)	127 (50)
Length to underarm	28 (11)	31 (12¼)	33 (13)	34½ (13½)	35½ (14)
Armhole Depth	17½ (6¾)	20 (7¾)	22½ (8¾)	22½ (8¾)	25 (9¾)
Finished Length	45½ (17¾)	51 (20)	55½ (21¾)	57 (22¼)	60½ (23¾)
Shoulder to Shoulder	29½ (11½)	33 (13)	34½ (13½)	36½ (14½)	38 (15)

Garment shown in photographs is for first size 81–86 (32–34)

PATTERN NOTES
This pattern was originally written to be knitted in two separate pieces but in this particular instance, the design lends itself to be knitted in the round for the main body. Whilst working in the round the charts are read from right to left at all times, however when the work divides for the front and back and the work is then knitted in rows, remember to purl the wrong side rows but also to read the charts from left to right for these rows.

The motifs on the garment are knitted using traditional Fair Isle techniques of two colours per row with the colour not in use being carried fairly loosely behind the work until needed.

COLOURWORK PATTERN REPEAT
Work 3 (6, 7, 9, 11) rounds in MC.
Work 5 rounds of chart A.
Work 3 (6, 7, 7, 7) rounds in MC.
Work 13 rounds of chart B.
Work 3 (6, 7, 7, 7) rounds in MC.
Work 5 rounds of chart A.
Work 3 (6, 7, 7, 7) rounds in MC.
Work 13 rounds of chart C.
These 48 (60, 64, 66, 68) rounds set the colourwork pattern which is worked throughout.

BODY (knitted in one piece)
Using 2.75mm needles and MC, cast on 252 (288, 324, 360, 396) sts, placing a stitch marker after 126 (144, 162, 180, 198) sts. Join into round, taking care not to twist cast on edge and place a second marker.

Round 1: * K1, P1, rep from * to end.
Rep this round until work measures 7½ (7½, 7½, 8¾, 8¾) cm (3, 3, 3, 3¼, 3¼ in).
Change to 3.25mm needles and commence in main pattern as folls:
Knit 3 (6, 7, 9, 11) rounds using MC only.
Commencing with round 1 of chart A, and reading from right to left, work the 5 rounds of chart, repeating the 6-st motif 42 (48, 54, 60, 66) times in each round.
Knit 3 (6, 7, 7, 7) rounds using MC only.
Work 13 rounds of chart B, repeating the 18-st motif 14 (16, 18, 20, 22) times in each round.
Knit 2 (5, 6, 6, 6) rounds using MC only.

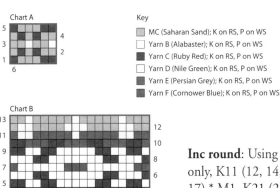

■ MC (Saharan Sand); K on RS, P on WS
□ Yarn B (Alabaster); K on RS, P on WS
■ Yarn C (Ruby Red); K on RS, P on WS
□ Yarn D (Nile Green); K on RS, P on WS
■ Yarn E (Persian Grey); K on RS, P on WS
■ Yarn F (Cornower Blue); K on RS, P on WS

Chart B

Chart C

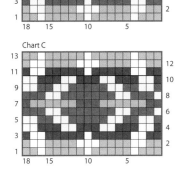

Inc round: Using MC only, K11 (12, 14, 15, 17) * M1, K21 (24, 27, 30, 33), rep from * to last 10 (12, 13, 15, 16) sts, M1, K10 (12, 13, 15, 16). (264, 300, 336, 372, 408 sts). Work 5 rounds of chart A, repeating the 6-st motif 44 (50, 56, 62, 68) times in each round.

Knit 2 (5, 6, 6, 6) rounds using MC only.
Inc round: Using MC only, K6 (12, 7, 2, 9) * M1, K11 (12, 14, 16, 17), rep from * to last 5 (12, 7, 2, 8) sts, M1, K5 (12, 7, 2, 8) (288, 324, 360, 396, 432 sts).
Work 13 rounds of chart C, repeating the 18-st motif 16 (18, 20, 22, 24) times in each round.
Continue in colourwork pattern as set until work measures 28 (31, 33, 34½, 35½) cm (11, 12¼, 13, 13½, 14 in).

Divide for Armholes
Next round: * Patt to 12 (12, 16, 17, 18) sts before marker, cast off 24 (24, 32, 34, 36) sts removing marker, rep from *
Stitches are now divided between front and back. Make a note of this chart and round number and also first stitch remaining on each section. Leave 120 (138, 148, 164, 180) sts on spare needle or on waste yarn and work on rem 120 (138, 148, 164, 180) sts only.

BACK
Maintaining colourwork pattern at all times, rejoin yarn to beginning of work with RS facing, and remembering to work in rows, dec 1 st at each end of next 10 (13, 15, 20, 25) rows (100, 112, 118, 124, 130 sts).
Work without further shaping until armhole measures 17½ (20, 22½, 22½, 25) cm (6¾, 7¾, 8¾, 8¾, 9¾ in), ending with a WS row.

Shape Shoulders
Cast off 10 (12, 12, 14, 14) sts at the beg of the next 4 (6, 2, 2, 6) rows, then 12 (0, 13, 13, 0) sts at the beg of the foll 2 (0, 4, 4, 0) rows. Leave rem 36 (40, 42, 44, 46) sts on a stitch holder.

FRONT
Return rem 120 (138, 148, 164, 180) sts to needle and rejoin yarn to work with RS facing. Again working in rows, and continuing from noted point on chart, work armhole shaping as for back (100, 112, 118, 124, 130 sts).
Work 4 (5, 7, 2, 3) rows without shaping.

Divide for Neck
Next row (RS): Patt 48 (54, 57, 60, 63), K2tog, slip rem 50 (56, 59, 62, 65) sts onto a stitch holder, turn work. Again make a note of chart and last st worked.
Next row (WS): Patt across rem 49 (55, 58, 61, 64) sts.
Dec 1 st at neck edge on next and on 16 (18, 19, 20, 21) foll alt rows (32, 36, 38, 40, 42 sts).
Continue without shaping until front measures same as back to start of shoulder shaping.

Shape Shoulders
Cast off 10 (12, 12, 14, 14) sts at the beg of next row.
Cast off 10 (12, 13, 13, 14) sts at start of foll alt row, then cast off rem 12 (12, 13, 13, 14) sts.
With RS facing, rejoin yarn at centre front, K2tog and patt to end (49, 55, 58, 61, 64 sts).
Work to match left front, reversing all shapings.

NECKBAND
Join shoulder seams. Using 2.75mm needle, MC, and with RS facing, knit across 36 (40, 42, 44, 46) sts on holder at back neck, pick up and K 36 (38, 40, 40, 42) sts down right front, M1 at centre front then pick up and K 35 (37,

39, 39, 41) sts up left front (108, 116, 122, 124, 130 sts).
Commence in rib as follows:

Round 1: K1, P1, to within 2 sts of centre K st, Sl1, K1, psso, K centre st, K2tog, P1, rib to end of round.

Round 2: Rib as sts presented on needle.

Round 3: Rib to within 2 sts of centre K st, P2togtbl, K centre st, P2tog, K1, rib to end.

Round 4: As round 2.

Repeat these 4 rounds once more (100, 108, 114, 116, 122 sts). Cast off loosely in rib.

ARMHOLE BANDS

Using 2.75mm needle, MC and with RS facing, pick up and knit 104 (116, 128, 128, 140) sts around armhole edge, evenly dividing stitches on each side of shoulder seam.

Round 1: * K1, P1, rep from * to end.

Repeat this round a further 7 times. Cast off loosely in rib.

MAKING UP

Press on WS of work using a damp cloth. Darn in all ends.

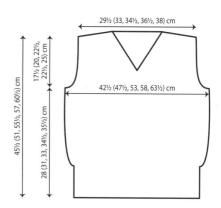

29½ (33, 34½, 36½, 38) cm

17½ (20, 22½, 22½, 25) cm

45½ (51, 55½, 57, 60½) cm

28 (31, 33, 34½, 35½) cm

42½ (47½, 53, 58, 63½) cm

4^D

1556

3-ply "EXCELSIOR" WOOL

LEAFLET No.
1556
Lady's Sleeveless
Fair isle Pullover
34 inch bust
PRICE 4d.

L. COPLEY-SMITH & SONS LTD., MANCHESTER and LONDON

No. 1556

LADY'S SLEEVELESS FAIR ISLE PULLOVER

Fair Isle gay and cheery, to make a really exciting sleeveless Pullover to wear with old or new blouses.

MATERIALS :
3 ozs. Copley's 3-ply " Excelsior " Wool, Limpid Blue No. 1136.

1 oz. each Copley's 3-ply " Excelsior " Wool, Riff Red No. 48, May Apple No. 1133, Shadow Rose No. 1135, Lt. Clerical Grey No. 1036, and about 20 yards Cowslip No. 1024.
1 set No. 12 " Coploid " Knitting Needles.
1 pair No. 9 " Coploid " Knitting Needles.

MEASUREMENTS :
Length from top of shoulder to lower edge, 18½ inches. Width all round at underarm, to fit a 34 inch bust.

TENSION :
Using No. 9 Needles, work to produce 8 sts. and 8 rows to one square inch, measuring over the Fair Isle pattern

ABBREVIATIONS :
K.—knit. P.—purl. St.—stitch. Tog.—together. Sl.—slip. P.s.s.o.—pass the slipped st. over.

Instructions

THE FRONT.

Using a pair of No. 12 needles and Limpid Blue wool, cast on 126 sts.

1st Row.—Working into the back of the sts., * K.1, P.1. Repeat from * to the end.

2nd Row.—* K.1, P.1. Repeat from * to the end.

Repeat the 2nd row until 3 inches of ribbing have been worked, **increasing** 1 st. by working into the front and back of the last st. on the last row. (127 sts. now on the needle.)

Change to No. 9 needles and proceed in pattern, carrying the colour not in use loosely along the back of the work and breaking off the colours last in use before commencing a new set.

N.B.—If when working with 2 colours, one colour is held in the right hand in the ordinary way and the other colour is held in the left hand, as if to crochet, the tiresome action of dropping and picking up when changing from one colour to another will be avoided.

1st Row.—Using Limpid Blue, knit.

2nd Row.—Using Limpid Blue, purl.

3rd Row.—As the 1st row.

4th Row.—Using Riff Red and Limpid Blue, P.2 R., * 3 L., 3 R. Repeat from * to the last 5 sts., 3 L., 2 R.

5th Row.—Using Riff Red and Limpid Blue, K.2 L., * 1 R., 1 L., 1 R., 3 L. Repeat from * to the last 5 sts., 1 R., 1 L., 1 R., 2 L.

6th Row.—Using May Apple and Limpid Blue, * P.1 M., 2 L. Repeat from * to the last st., 1 M.

7th-11th Rows.—As rows 5, 4, 3, 2, 1 respectively.

12th Row.—Using Limpid Blue and May Apple P.3 L., * 1 M., 5 L. Repeat from * to the last 4 sts., 1 M., 3 L.

13th Row.—Using Limpid Blue and May Apple, * K.2 L., 2 M., 4 L., 3 M., 4 L., 2 M., 1 L. Repeat from * to the last st., 1 L.

14th Row.—Using May Apple and Grey, * P.2 G., 2 M., 5 G., 1 M., 5 G., 2 M., 1 G. Repeat from * to the last st., 1 G.

15th Row.—Using Riff Red and Grey, * K.1 G., (2 R., 3 G) 3 times, 2 R. Repeat from * to the last st., 1 G.

16th Row.—Using Riff Red and Shadow Rose, * P.1 S., 2 R., 2 S., 2 R., 5 S., 2 R., 2 S., 2 R. Repeat from * to the last st., 1 S.

17th Row.—Using Riff Red and Shadow Rose, * K.1 R., 3 S., 2 R., 7 S., 2 R., 3 S. Repeat from * to the last st., 1 R.

18th Row.—Using Limpid Blue and Cowslip, P.2 C., * 6 L., 3 C. Repeat from * to the last 8 sts., 6 L., 2 C.

19th-24th Rows.—As rows 17, 16, 15, 14, 13 and 12 respectively.

25th and 26th Rows.—As the 1st and 2nd rows.

27th Row.—Still using Limpid Blue, K.11, * increase 1 st. by picking up the thread which lies between the st. just worked and the following st. and placing this on the left-hand needle, K. into the back of it (this action will be referred to as " M.1 "), K.21. Repeat from * to the last 11 sts., M.1, K.11. (133 sts. now on the needle.)

28th-34th Rows.—As rows 4-10 inclusive.

35th Row.—Still using Limpid Blue, K.6, * M.1, K.11. Repeat from * to the last 6 sts., M.1, K.6. (145 sts. now on the needle.)

36th Row.—Using Limpid Blue and Shadow Rose, P.3 L., * 1 S., 5 L. Repeat from * to the last 4 sts., 1 S., 3 L.

37th Row.—Using Limpid Blue and Shadow Rose, * K.2 L., 2 S., 4 L., 3 S., 4 L., 2 S., 1 L. Repeat from * to the last st., 1 L.

38th Row.—Using Shadow Rose and Riff Red, * P.2 R., 2 S., 5 R., 1 S., 5 R., 2 S., 1 R. Repeat from * to the last st., 1 R.

39th Row.—Using May Apple and Riff Red, * K.1 R., (2 M., 3 R) 3 times, 2 M. Repeat from * to the last st., 1 R.

40th Row.—Using May Apple and Grey, * P.1 G., 2 M., 2 G., 2 M., 5 G., 2 M., 2 G., 2 M. Repeat from * to the last st., 1 G.

41st Row.—Using May Apple and Grey, * K.1 M., 3 G., 2 M., 7 G., 2 M., 3 G. Repeat from * to the last st., 1 M.

42nd Row.—Using Limpid Blue and Cowslip, P.2 C., * L 6., 3 C. Repeat from * to the last 8 sts., 6 L., 2 C.

43rd-48th Rows.—As rows 41, 40, 39, 38, 37 and 36 respectively.

These 48 rows form the order of the colouring.

Now repeat rows 1-17 inclusive.

Shape the Armholes as follows :—

1st Row.—Using Limpid Blue, cast off 12 sts., P. the following 4 sts., there now being 5 sts. on the right-hand needle. Using Limpid Blue and Cowslip, * P.3 C., 6 L. Repeat from * to the last 20 sts., 3 C., 5 L., cast off the remaining 12 sts.

2nd Row.—Using Shadow Rose and Riff Red, K.2 tog. R., 1 R., * 3 S., 1 R., 3 S., 2 R., 7 S., 2 R. Repeat from * to the last 10 sts., 3 S., 1 R., 3 S., 1 R., 2 tog. R.

3rd Row.—P.2 tog. S., 1 S., * 2 R., 1 S., 2 R., 2 S., 2 R., 5 S., 2 R., 2 S. Repeat from * to the last 8 sts., 2 R., 1 S., 2 R., 1 S., 2 tog. S.

4th Row.—Using Riff Red and Grey, K.2 tog. G., * 2 R., 1 G., (2 R., 3 G.) 3 times. Repeat from * to the last 7 sts., 2 R., 1 G., 2 R., 2 tog. G.

5th Row.—Using Grey and May Apple, P.2 tog. M., * 3 G., 2 M., 5 G., 1 M., 5 G., 2 M. Repeat from * to the last 5 sts., 3 G., 2 tog. M.

6th Row.—Using May Apple and Limpid Blue, K.2 tog. L., 2 L. * 2 M., 4 L., 3 M., 4 L., 2 M., 3 L. Repeat from * to the last 19 sts., 2 M., 4 L., 3 M., 4 L., 2 M., 2 L., K.2 tog. L.

7th Row.—P.2 tog. L., * 1 M., 5 L. Repeat from * to the last 5 sts., 1 M., 5 L., 2 tog. L.

8th Row.—Using Limpid Blue, K.2 tog., K. to the last 2 sts., K.2 tog.

9th Row.—P.2 tog., P. to the last 2 sts., P.2 tog.

10th Row.—As the 8th row.

11th Row.—Using Limpid Blue and Riff Red, P.2 tog. L., * 3 R., 3 L. Repeat from * to the last 5 sts., 3 R., 2 tog. L. (101 sts. remain.)

12th Row.—Using Limpid Blue and Riff Red, * K.1 R., 3 L., 1 R., 1 L. Repeat from * to the last 5 sts., 1 R., 3 L., 1 R.

13th Row.—Using Limpid Blue and May Apple, * P.2 L., 1 M. Repeat from * to the last 2 sts., 2 L.

14th Row.—As the 12th row.

15th Row.—Using Limpid Blue and Riff Red, P.1 L., * 3 R., 3 L. Repeat from * to the last 4 sts., 3 R., 1 L.

Divide for the Neck as follows :—

Next Row.—Using Limpid Blue, K.49, K.2 tog. Slip the remaining 50 sts. on to a safety pin for the present, turn.

Proceed on the former set of 50 sts. for the Left side of the neck as follows :—

1st Row.—Using Limpid Blue, P. to the end.

2nd Row.—K. to the last 2 sts., K.2 tog.

3rd Row.—Using Shadow Rose and Limpid Blue, P.1 L., * 1 S., 5 L. Repeat from * to the end.

4th Row.—* K.4 L., 3 S., 4 L., 2 S., 3 L., 2 S. Repeat from * to the last 13 sts., 4 L., 3 S., 4 L., 2 tog. S.

5th Row.—Using Riff Red and Shadow Rose, P.1 S., * 5 R., 1 S., 5 R., 2 S., 3 R., 2 S. Repeat from * to the last 11 sts., 5 R., 1 S., 5 R.

6th Row.—Using Riff Red and May Apple, K.2 R., * (2 M., 3 R.) twice, 2 M., 1 R., 2 M., 3 R. Repeat from * to the last 10 sts., 2 M., 3 R., 2 M., 1 R., 2 tog. R.

7th Row.—Using May Apple and Grey, P.1 G., * 2 M., 5 G., 2 M., 2 G., 2 M., 1 G., 2 M., 2 G. Repeat from * to the last 10 sts., 2 M., 5 G., 2 M., 1 G.

8th Row.—* K. 2 M., 7 G., 2 M., 3 G., 1 M., 3 G. Repeat from * to the last 11 sts., 2 M., 7 G., 2 tog. M.

9th Row.—Using Limpid Blue and Cowslip, P.3 L., * 3 C., 6 L. Repeat from * to the last 7 sts., 3 C., 4 L.

10th Row.—Using May Apple and Grey, * K.2 M., 7 G., 2 M., 3 G., 1 M., 3 G. Repeat from * to the last 10 sts., 2 M., 6 G., 2 tog. G.

11th Row.—P.1 M., * 5 G., 2 M., 2 G., 2 M., 1 G., 2 M., 2 G., 2 M. Repeat from * to the last 8 sts., 5 G., 2 M., 1 G.

12th Row.—Using Riff Red and May Apple, K.2 R., * (2 M., 3 R) twice, 2 M., 1 R., 2 M., 3 R. Repeat from * to the last 7 sts., 2 M., 3 R., 2 tog. M.

13th Row.—Using Shadow Rose and Riff Red, P.2 R., * 1 S., 5 R., 2 S., 3 R., 2 S., 5 R. Repeat from * to the last 6 sts., 1 S., 5 R.

14th Row.—Using Shadow Rose and Limpid Blue, * K.4 L., 3 S., 4 L., 2 S., 3 L., 2 S. Repeat from * to the last 8 sts., 4 L., 2 S., 2 tog. S.

15th Row.—P.1 L., * 1 S., 5 L. Repeat from * to the end.

16th Row.—Using Limpid Blue, K. to the last 2 sts., K.2 tog.

17th Row.—P. to the end.

18th Row.—As the 16th row.

19th Row.—Using Limpid Blue and Riff Red, P.1 L., * 3 R., 3 L. Repeat from * to the last 4 sts., 3 R., 1 L.

20th Row.—* K.1 R., 3 L., 1 R., 1 L. Repeat from * to the last 5 sts., 1 R., 2 L., 2 tog. L.

21st Row.—Using May Apple and Limpid Blue, P.1 L., * 1 M., 2 L. Repeat from * to the end.

22nd Row.—Using Riff Red and Limpid Blue, * K.1 R., 3 L., 1 R., 1 L. Repeat from * to the last 4 sts., 1 R., 1 L., 2 tog. L.

23rd Row.—P.2 R., * 3 L., 3 R. Repeat from * to the last st., 1 L.

24th Row.—Using Limpid Blue, K. to the last 2 sts., K.2 tog.

25th Row.—P. to the end.

26th Row.—As the 24th row.

27th Row.—Using May Apple and Limpid Blue, P.1 L., * 1 M., 5 L. Repeat from * to the end.

28th Row.—K.4 L., 3 M., 4 L., 2 M., 3 L., 2 M., 4 L., 3 M., 4 L., 2 M., 3 L., 1 M., 2 tog. M.

29th Row.—Using May Apple and Grey, * P.2 M., 3 G., 2 M., 5 G., 1 M., 5 G. Repeat from * once more.

30th Row.—Using Riff Red and Grey, K.2 G., (2 R., 3 G.) twice, 2 R., 1 G., (2 R., 3 G.) 3 times, 2 R., 1 G., 1 R., 2 tog. R.

31st Row.—Using Riff Red and Shadow Rose, P.2 R., 1 S., 2 R., 2 S., 2 R., 5 S., 2 R., 2 S., 2 R., 1 S., 2 R., 2 S., 2 R., 5 S., 2 R., 1 S.

32nd Row.—K.2 R., 7 S., 2 R., 3 S., 1 R., 3 S., 2 R., 7 S., 2 R., 3 S., 1 R., 2 tog. S.

33rd Row.—Using Limpid Blue and Cowslip, * P.3 C., 6 L. Repeat from * to the last 7 sts., 3 C., 4 L.

34th Row.—Using Riff Red and Shadow Rose, K.2 R., 7 S., 2 R., 3 S., 1 R., 3 S., 2 R., 7 S., 2 R., 3 S., 2 tog. R.

35th Row.—P.1 S., 2 R., 2 S., 2 R., 5 S., 2 R., 2 S., 2 R., 1 S., 2 R., 2 S., 2 R., 5 S., 2 R., 1 S.

36th Row.—Using Riff Red and Grey, K.2 G., (2 R., 3 G.) twice, 2 R., 1 G., (2 R., 3 G.) 3 times, 1 R., 2 tog. R.

37th Row.—Using May Apple and Grey, P.1 G., 2 M., 5 G., 1 M., 5 G., 2 M., 3 G., 2 M., 5 G., 1 M., 5 G.

38th Row.—Using May Apple and Limpid Blue, K.4 L., 3 M., 4 L., 2 M., 3 L., 2 M., 4 L., 3 M., 4 L., 2 M., 1 L.

39th Row.—P.2 L., * 1 M., 5 L. Repeat from * to the end. (32 sts. remain.)

40th Row.—Using Limpid Blue, knit.

41st Row.—Purl.

42nd Row.—As the 40th row.

Shape the Shoulder as follows :—

1st Row.—Still using Limpid Blue, P. to the last 10 sts., turn.

2nd Row.—K. to the neck.

3rd Row.—P. to the last 20 sts., turn.

4th Row.—K. to the neck.

Cast off purlwise all across.

Slip the sts. from the safety pin on to a No. 9 needle, then slip them on to the second No. 9 needle, thus the point will be to the armhole edge, and proceed for the Right side of the Neck as follows :—

1st Row.—Using Limpid Blue, P. to the neck.

2nd Row.—Knit.

3rd Row.—P. to the last 2 sts., P. 2 tog.

Now continue as the instructions for the Left side of the neck, repeating rows 3-42 inclusive but reversing the instructions, i.e., reading K. for P. and P. for K.

Still reading K. for P. and P. for K., **shape the shoulder** as the instructions for the Left side.

Cast off knitwise.

THE BACK.

Using a pair of the No. 12 needles and Limpid Blue, cast on 108 sts.

Working into the back of the sts. on the first row only, proceed in K.1, P.1 rib, as on the Front, for 3 inches, **increasing** 1 st. at the end of the last row. (109 sts. now on the needle.)

Change to No. 9 needles and repeat 1-26 inclusive of the pattern rows as worked on the Front.

Next Row.—Still using Limpid Blue, K.9, * M.1, K.18. Repeat from * to the last 10 sts., M.1, K.10. (115 sts. now on the needle.)

Now repeat 4-10 inclusive of the pattern rows.

Next Row.—Still using Limpid Blue, K.7, * M.1, K.9. Repeat from * to the end. (127 sts. now on the needle.)

Now repeat 36-48 inclusive of the pattern rows, then repeat rows 1-17 inclusive.

Shape the Armholes as follows :—

1st Row.—Using Limpid Blue, cast off 8 sts., P. the following 8 sts. Using Limpid Blue and Cowslip, * P.3 C., 6 L. Repeat from * to the last 11 sts., 3 C., cast off the remaining 8 sts.

2nd Row.—Using Shadow Rose nd Riff Red, K.2 tog. S., * 3 S., * 2 R., 3 S., 1 R., 3 S., 2 R., 7 S. Repeat from * to the last 16 sts., 2 R., 3 S., 1 R., 3 S., 2 R., 3 S., 2 tog. S.

3rd Row.—P.2 tog. S., 1 S., * 2 R., 2 S., 2 R., 1 S., 2 R., 2 S., 2 R., 5 S. Repeat from * to the last 16 sts., 2 R., 2 S., 2 R., 1 S., 2 R., 2 S., 2 R., 1 S., 2 tog. S.

4th Row.—Using Riff Red and Grey, K.2 tog. R., 1 R., * 3 G., 2 R., 1 G., (2 R., 3 G.) twice, 2 R. Repeat from * to the last 14 sts., 3 G., 2 R., 1 G., 2 R., 3 G., 1 R., 2 tog. R.

5th Row.—Using Grey and May Apple, P.2 tog. G., 2 G., * 2 M., 3 G., 2 M., 5 G., 1 M., 5 G. Repeat from * to the last 11 sts., 2 M., 3 G., 2 M., 2 G., 2 tog. G.

6th Row.—Using May Apple and Limpid Blue, K.2 tog. L., 1 L., * 2 M., 3 L., 2 M., 4 L., 3 M., 4 L. Repeat from * to the last 10 sts., 2 M., 3 L., 2 M., 1 L., 2 tog. L.

7th Row.—P.2 tog. L., * 1 M., 5 L. Repeat from * to the last 3 sts., 1 M., 2 tog. L.

8th Row.—Using Limpid Blue, K.2 tog., K. to the last 2 sts., K.2 tog.

9th Row.—P.2 tog., P. to the last 2 sts., P.2 tog.

10th Row.—As the 8th row.

11th Row.—Using Limpid Blue and Riff Red, P.2 tog. R., 1 R., * 3 L., 3 R. Repeat from * to the last 6 sts., 3 L., 1 R., 2 tog. R.

The armhole shaping is now completed and 91 sts. remain.

Now repeat 5-11 inclusive of the pattern rows as worked on the Front, then repeat rows 36-48 inclusive and finally rows 1-24 inclusive of the same instructions.

Shape the Shoulders as follows :—

1st Row.—Using Limpid Blue, K. to the last 10 sts., turn.

2nd Row.—P. to the last 10 sts., turn.

3rd Row.—K. to the-last 20 sts., turn.

4th Row.—P. to the last 20 sts., turn.

5th Row.—K. to the last 32 sts., turn.

6th Row.—P. to the last 32 sts. Break off the wool.

Slip all the sts. on to one needle, rejoin the wool and cast off knitwise all across.

THE NECKBAND.

Join the shoulders of the Back to the same number of sts. as on the Front.

With the right side of the work facing, using the set of No. 12 needles and commencing at the Left shoulder, join the Limpid Blue wool and **knit up** an even number of sts. to the centre V (working through the 2nd st. from the edge), then **knit up** the centre st. **which always remains a K. st.**, continue round the neck, finishing at the Left shoulder. (On the original 162 sts. in all were knitted up.)

Proceed to work in rounds as follows :—

1st Round.—Work in K.1, P.1 rib to within 2 sts. of the centre st., sl.1, K.1, p.s.s.o., K. the centre st., K.2 tog., commencing with P.1, continue in rib to the end of the round.

2nd Round.—Work in rib to within 2 sts. of the centre st., sl.1, K.1, p.s.s.o., K.1, P.2 tog., continue in rib to the end of the round.

Repeat the 1st and 2nd rounds 3 times more. Cast off in rib.

THE ARMHOLE BAND.

With the right side of the work facing, using a pair of No. 12 needles, join the Limpid Blue wool and **knit up** an even number of sts. along the armhole edge. (On the original 166 sts. were knitted up.)

Proceed in K.1, P.1 rib for 8 rows.

Cast off in rib.

Complete the second armhole in the same manner.

MAKE-UP.

Omitting the ribbing, press the work on the wrong side, using a hot iron and a damp cloth.

Firmly knot all ends of wool, then join the side seams, working in the loose ends with the seam or if preferred leaving the ends loose on the wrong side, after neatly trimming same.

Press all seams.

Lady's Evening Jumper

MATERIALS
Fyberspates Scrumptious Lace 45% silk/55% merino (1000m/1094yds per 100g skein)
2 skeins shade 505 (purple) for all sizes
1 pair 3mm (US #2–3) needles
1 2.5mm (US #1–2) circular needle (80cm)
3 press studs

TENSION
Stitches – 1 patt rep (33 sts) = 9cm (3½in) using 3mm needles over stitch pattern after blocking
Rows – 1 patt rep (24 rows) = 6¼cm (2½in) using 3mm needles over stitch pattern after blocking

Standard Yarn Tension
25–30 sts & 37 rows = 10cm (4in) using 3mm needles over stocking stitch

ABBREVIATIONS
See page 13 for standard abbreviations

SIZING
Measurements given in centimetres followed by inches in parentheses

To Fit	76–81 (30–32)	86–92 (34–36)	97–102 (38–40)	107–112 (42–44)	117–122 (46–48)
Finished Measurements					
Actual Bust Size	84½ (33½)	94½ (37)	103 (40½)	113½ (44½)	123 (48½)
Length to underarm	32½ (13)	32½ (13)	38½ (15)	38½ (15)	38½ (15)
Armhole Depth	18 (7)	18 (7)	20½ (8)	20½ (8)	23 (9)
Finished Length	50½ (20)	50½ (20)	59 (23)	59 (23)	61½ (24)
Shoulder to Shoulder	31 (12¼)	33 (13)	35½ (14)	38 (15)	41 (16)
Sleeve Length	32½ (12¾)	32½ (12¾)	32½ (12¾)	32½ (12¾)	32½ (12¾)

Garment shown in photographs for first size 76–81 (30–32)

FRONT
Using 3mm needles, cast on 104 (122, 138, 158, 176) sts.
Knit 1 row, then work in pattern as folls:
Row 1 (RS): K1, reading from right to left and starting and ending as indicated, work from chart A row 1, repeating marked section 3 (3, 3, 4, 4) times, K1.
Row 2 (WS): K1, reading from left to right and starting and ending as indicated, work from chart A row 2, repeating marked section 3 (3, 3, 4, 4) times, K1.
These 2 rows set selvedge sts and chart pattern, which is worked throughout the garment.
Work a further 54 rows in pattern from chart, thus ending on chart row 8 **

The following 2 rows form the front darts. 34 extra sts (one whole pattern repeat) are cast on over each set of cast off stitches to create more fabric. This is then gathered and sewn in when making up the finished garment.
Next row (chart row 9): Work first 18 (27, 35, 45, 54) sts in pattern as set, cast off 17 sts, work in pattern until you have 34 sts on right hand needle after those cast off, cast off 16 sts, work in pattern as set to end of row.
Next row (chart row 10): Work in pattern as set, casting on 50 sts over the first set of cast off stitches that you reach, and casting on 51 sts over the second set (172, 190, 206, 226, 244 sts).

Starting from row 11, work a further 66 (66, 90, 90, 90) rows in pattern, thus ending on chart row 4.

Shape Armholes
Keeping lace pattern correct, cast off 15 (17, 19, 12, 14) sts at the start of the next 2 (2, 2, 4, 4) rows (142, 156, 168, 178, 188 sts).
Dec 1 st at each end of next 19 (22, 24, 24, 24) rows (104, 112, 120, 130, 140 sts).
Work a further 31 (28, 26, 24, 24) rows in pattern without further shaping, thus ending on chart row 8.

Shape Neck
Next row (chart row 9): Work 43 (47, 51, 56, 61) sts in lace pattern as set (and slip these sts onto a holder), cast off centre 18 sts, work in pattern to end of row (43, 47, 51, 56, 61 sts).
Keeping lace pattern correct, dec 1 stitch at neck edge of next 7 (8, 9, 10, 12) rows, thus ending with chart row 16 (17, 18, 19, 21) (36, 39, 42, 46, 49 sts).
Work 8 (7, 16, 15, 23) more rows in pattern without further shaping, thus ending with chart row 24 (24, 10, 10, 20).

Chart A (Front and Back)

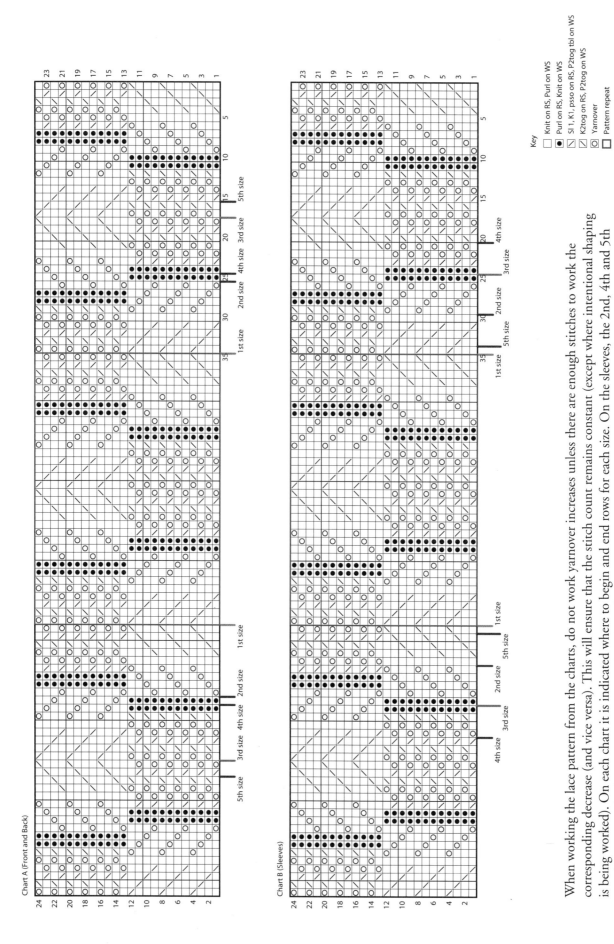

Chart B (Sleeves)

Key
☐ Knit on RS, Purl on WS
● Purl on RS, Knit on WS
⟋ Sl 1, K1, psso on RS, P2tog tbl on WS
⟍ K2tog on RS, P2tog on WS
○ Yarnover
☐ Pattern repeat

When working the lace pattern from the charts, do not work yarnover increases unless there are enough stitches to work the corresponding decrease (and vice versa). This will ensure that the stitch count remains constant (except where intentional shaping is being worked). On each chart it is indicated where to begin and end rows for each size. On the sleeves, the 2nd, 4th and 5th sizes have unmatched increases/decreases at the edges. If in doubt about how to keep the stitch count constant, place stitch makers at each side of the marked pattern repeat, and work the edge stitches in plain stocking stitch.

Shape Shoulder
Row 1 (RS): Pattern 26 (28, 30, 32, 34) sts, turn leaving rem sts unworked.
Row 2: Pattern to end.
Row 3: Pattern 12 (13, 14, 15, 16) sts, turn.
Row 4: Pattern to end.
Cast off rem sts knitwise.

With WS facing, slip the sts from the holder on to 3mm needle, rejoin the wool and proceed for the left side of the neck as folls:
Keeping lace pattern correct, dec 1 st at neck edge of next 7 (8, 9, 10, 12) rows, thus ending with chart row 16 (17, 18, 19, 21) (36, 39, 42, 46, 49 sts). Work 9 (8, 17, 16, 24) more rows in pattern without further shaping, thus ending with chart row 1 (1, 11, 11, 21).

Shape Shoulder
Row 1 (WS): Pattern 26 (28, 30, 32, 34) sts, turn leaving rem sts unworked.
Row 2: Pattern to end.
Row 3: Pattern 12 (13, 14, 15, 16) sts, turn.
Row 4: Pattern to end.
Cast off rem sts purlwise.

BACK
Work as the instructions for the Front up to **

The following 2 rows form the back dart. 34 extra sts (one whole pattern repeat) are cast on over the cast off stitches to create more fabric. This is then gathered and sewn in when making up the finished garment.
Next row (chart row 9): Work 35 (44, 52, 62, 71) sts in pattern, cast off 33 sts, pattern to end.
Next row (chart row 10): Work in pattern, casting on 67 sts over those cast off on the previous row (138, 156, 172, 192, 210 sts).
Keeping pattern correct, work a further 66 (66, 90, 90, 90) rows in pattern, thus ending with chart row 4.

Shape Armholes
Keeping lace pattern correct, cast off 6 (7, 9, 7, 9) sts at the start of the next 2 (2, 2, 4, 4) rows (126, 142, 154, 164, 174 sts).
Dec 1 st at each end of next 11 (15, 17, 17, 17) rows, thus ending on chart row 17 (21, 24, 1, 1) (104, 112, 120, 130, 140 sts).
Work a further 51 (47, 55, 53, 63) rows in pattern as set, thus ending on chart row 20 (20, 6, 6, 16).

Shape Shoulder
Row 1: Pattern to last 10 (11, 12, 14, 15) sts, turn leaving rem sts unworked.
Row 2: Pattern to last 10 (11, 12, 14, 15) sts, turn leaving rem sts unworked.
Row 3: Pattern to last 24 (26, 28, 31, 33) sts, turn.
Row 4: Pattern to last 24 (26, 28, 31, 33) sts, turn.
Break off wool.

Slip all the sts on to one needle rejoin the wool and cast off all rem sts knitwise.

THREE-QUARTER SLEEVES
Using 3mm needles cast on 70 (80, 90, 98, 106) sts. K 1 row.
Row 1 (RS): K1, reading from right to left and starting and ending as indicated, work from chart B row 1, repeating marked section 2 (2, 2, 2, 3) times, K1.
Row 2 (WS): K1, reading from left to right and starting and ending as indicated, work from chart B row 2, repeating marked section 2 (2, 2, 2, 3) times, K1.
Working pattern as set by last 2 rows work a further 34 rows in pattern, thus ending with chart row 12.
Next row (chart row 13): Pattern 18 (23, 28, 32, 36) sts, cast off 34 sts, pattern to end.
Next row (chart row 14): Work in pattern, casting on 102 sts over those cast off on previous row (138, 148, 158, 166, 174 sts).
Work a further 86 rows in pattern, thus ending on chart row 4.

Shape Sleeve Head
Keeping lace pattern correct, cast off 15 (17, 19, 12, 14) sts at the start of the next 2 (2, 2, 4, 4) rows (108, 114, 120, 118, 118 sts).
Dec 1 st at each end of next 19 (22, 25, 24, 24) rows, thus ending on chart row 1 (70 sts all sizes).

Now work 47 (44, 49, 50, 60) more rows in pattern thus ending on chart row 24 (24, 8, 10, 20). Cast off. Work another sleeve in the same manner.

MAKING UP

Block all pieces to specified dimensions before commencing sewing up.

Sew up front darts by gathering up the cast on sts in the centre of the front until these measure the same as the cast off edges directly below and then stitch the 2 edges together on the WS. Complete the darts on the back and sleeves in the same manner.

Join the right shoulder of the back and front together.

Neckband

Using 2.5mm circular needle, and with RS facing, commence at left front shoulder and pick up and K 34 (37, 40, 44, 47) sts across shoulder, then 21 (21, 29, 29, 37) sts down left side neck, 18 sts across front neck, 21 (21, 29, 29, 37) sts up right side neck, 34 (36, 38, 40, 44) sts across back neck and 34 (37, 40, 44, 47) sts across left back shoulder (162, 170, 194, 204, 230 sts).

K 3 rows then cast off loosely. Join side and sleeve seams. Place the left shoulder of the Front over the back and stitch the armhole edge of the shoulder for 1½cm.

Gather Sleeve Head

Mark 7½cm (3in) below the casting off at each side of the top of the sleeves. Gather up the sleeve between the points marked until the sleeve top is the correct size to fit the armhole.

Stitch the sleeves into position, taking care to match centre of sleeve head with shoulder seam and matching side seams. Stitch 3 press studs to the left shoulder to close the neck. Attach shoulder pads to WS of the top of each sleeve at the shoulder line if required (see 'Fit and Finish' chapter). Darn in all ends.

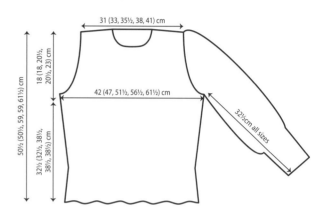

6D

1547

Copley's

Lady's Evening Jumper
LEAFLET NO.   PRICE
1547   6D.
Three-quarter or
short sleeves
34-inch bust

2-ply "EXCELSIOR" Shetland WOOL

L. COPLEY-SMITH & SONS LTD., MANCHESTER and LONDON

Copley's Leaflet No. 1547

LADY'S EVENING JUMPER

with three-quarter or short sleeves

MATERIALS :   5 ozs. Copley's 2-ply " Excelsior " Shetland Wool.

I pair No. 11 " Coploid " Knitting Needles.

I pair No. 10 " Coploid " Knitting Needles.

I No. 12 " Stratnoid " Crochet Hook.

6 Small Hooks and Eyes.

2 Shoulder Pads.

MEASUREMENTS : Length from top of shoulder to lower edge, 19 inches.

Width all round at underarm, to fit a 34 inch bust.

Length of sleeve seam, three-quarter 12 inches, short 7 inches.

TENSION :   Using No. 10 Needles, work to produce 8 sts. and 10 rows to one square inch in smooth fabric (1 row K., 1 row P.).

ABBREVIATIONS : K.—knit. P.—purl. St.—stitch. Tog.—together. Sl.—slip Wl.fwd.—wool forward. W.r.n.—wool round needle. P.s.s.o.—passed the slipped st. over. D.C.—double crochet.

Instructions

THE FRONT

Using No. 11 needles, cast on 104 sts.

Working into the back of the sts., K. one row.

Now proceed in pattern as follows :—

1st Row.—K.1, * K.3, K.2 tog., K.4, wl.fwd., w.r.n., P.2, (K.2, wl.fwd., sl.1, K.1, p.s.s.o.) 3 times, P.2, keeping the wool to the front of the needle, K.1 (thus making a st.), K.3, sl.1, K.1, p.s.s.o., K.3. Repeat from * to the last st., K.1.

2nd Row.—K.1, * P.2, P.2 tog. through the back of the sts., P.4, w.r.n., P.1, K.2, (P.2, w.r.n., P.2 tog.) 3 times, K.2, P.1, w.r.n., P.4, P.2 tog., P.2. Repeat from * to the last st., K.1.

3rd Row.—K.1, * K.1, K.2 tog., K.4, wl.fwd., K.2, P.2, (K.2, wl.fwd., sl.1, K.1, p.s.s.o.) 3 times, P.2, K.2, wl.fwd., K.4, sl.1, K.1, p.s.s.o., K.1. Repeat from * to the last st., K.1.

4th Row.—K.1, * P.2 tog. through the back of the sts., P.4, w.r.n., P.3, K.2, (P.2, w.r.n., P.2 tog.) 3 times, K.2, P.3, w.r.n., P.4, P.2 tog. Repeat from * to the last st., K.1.

5th-12th Rows.—Repeat rows 1-4 inclusive twice.

13th Row.—K.1, * wl.fwd., sl.1, K.1, p.s.s.o., K.2, wl.fwd., sl.1, K.1, p.s.s.o., P.2, keeping the wool to the front of the needle K.4, sl.1, K.1, p.s.s.o., K.6, K.2 tog., K.4, wl.fwd., w.r.n., P.2, K.2, wl.fwd., sl.1, K.1, p.s.s.o., K.2. Repeat from * to the last st., K.1.

14th Row.—K.1, wl.fwd., * w.r.n., P.2 tog., P.2, w.r.n., P.2 tog., K.2, P.1, w.r.n., P.4, P.2 tog., P.4, P.2 tog. through the back of the sts., P.4, w.r.n., P.1, K.2, P.2, w.r.n., P.2 tog. P.2. Repeat from * to the last st., K.1.

15th Row.—K.1, * wl.fwd., sl.1, K.1, p.s.s.o., K.2, wl.fwd., sl.1, K.1, p.s.s.o., P.2, K.2, wl.fwd., K.4, sl.1, K.1, p.s.s.o., K.2, K.2 tog., K.4, wl.fwd., K.2, P.2, K.2, wl.fwd., sl.1, K.1, p.s.s.o., K.2. Repeat from * to the last st., K.1.

16th Row.—K.1, wl.fwd., * w.r.n., P.2 tog., P.2, w.r.n., P.2 tog., K.2, P.3, w.r.n., P.4, P.2 tog. through the back of the sts., P.4, w.r.n., P.3, K.2, P.2, w.r.n., P.2 tog. P.2. Repeat from * to the last st., K.1.

17th-24th Rows.—Repeat rows 13-16 inclusive twice.

These 24 rows form the pattern which is worked throughout the garment.

Change to No. 10 needles and repeat rows 1-24 inclusive once more, then repeat rows 1-4 inclusive **twice**. * *

Next Row.—K.4, K.2 tog., K.4, wl.fwd., w.r.n., P.2, K.2, wl.fwd., sl.1, K.1, p.s.s.o., K.2, cast off the following 17 sts., K. the following 2 sts. there now being 3 sts. on the right-hand needle after the casting-off, K.2 tog., K.4, wl.fwd., w.r.n., P.2, (K.2, wl.fwd., sl.1, K.1, p.s.s.o.) 3 times, P.2, keeping the wool etc. K.4, sl.1, K.1, p.s.s.o., K.3, cast off the following 16 sts., the st. on the right-hand needle after the second casting-off, counting as K.1, wl.fwd., sl.1, K.1, p.s.s.o., K.2, wl.fwd., sl.1, K.1, p.s.s.o., P.2, keeping the wool etc. K.4, sl.1, K.1, p.s.s.o., K.4.

Next Row.—K.1, P.2, P.2 tog. through the back of the sts., P.4, w.r.n., P.1, K.2, P.2, w.r.n., P.2 tog., P.3, turn and cast on 50 sts., turn. P.2, P.2 tog. through the back of the sts., P.4, w.r.n., P.1, K.2, (P.2, w.r.n., P.2 tog.) 3 times, K.2, P.1, w.r.n., P.4, P.2 tog., P.2, turn and cast on 51 sts., turn, P.4, w.r.n., P.2 tog., K.2, P.1, w.r.n., P.4, P.2 tog., P.2, K.1, (172 sts. now on the needle.)

Working into the back of the cast-on sts. on the first row only, repeat the 3rd and 4th rows of the original pattern.

Now repeat 13-24 inclusive of the pattern rows, then repeat rows 1-24 inclusive **twice** and finally rows 1-4 inclusive.

Shape the Armholes as follows :—

1st Row.—Cast off 15 sts., K. the following 2 sts. Work as a 13th pattern row from * to the last 18 sts., wl.fwd., sl.1, K.1, p.s.s.o., K.2, wl.fwd., sl.1, K.1, p.s.s.o., K.2, keeping the wool etc. K.4, sl.1, K.1, p.s.s.o., K.4.

2nd Row.—Cast off 15 sts., P. the following 2 sts. Work as a 14th pattern row from * to the last 3 sts., P.3.

3rd Row.—K.2 tog., K.1. Work as a 15th pattern row from * to the last 3 sts., K.1, K.2 tog.

4th Row.—P.2 tog. Work as a 16th pattern row from * to the last 2 sts., P.2 tog.

5th Row.—K.2 tog., K.3, wl.fwd., sl.1, K.1, p.s.s.o., P.2, keeping the wool etc. K.4, sl.1, K.1, p.s.s.o., K.3. Work as a 1st pattern row from * to the last 18 sts., K.3, K.2 tog., K.4, wl.fwd., w.r.n., P.2, K.2, wl.fwd., sl.1, K.1, p.s.s.o., K.1, K.2 tog.

6th Row.—P.2 tog., P.2, w.r.n., P.2 tog., K.2, P.1, w.r.n., P.4, P.2 tog., P.2. Work as a 2nd pattern row from * to the last 17 sts., P.2, P.2 tog. through the back of the sts., P.4, w.r.n., P.1, K.2, P.2, w.r.n., (P.2 tog.) twice.

7th Row.—K.2 tog., K.1, wl.fwd., sl.1, K.1, p.s.s.o., P.2, K.2, wl.fwd., sl.1, K.1, p.s.s.o., K.1. Work as a 3rd pattern row from * to the last 16 sts., K.1, K.2 tog., K.4, wl.fwd., K.2, P.2, K.2, wl.fwd., sl.1, K.1, **K.2 tog.**, p.s.s.o.

8th Row.—P.2 tog., w.r.n., P.2 tog., K.2, P.3, w.r.n., P.2 tog. Work as a 4th pattern row from * to the last 15 sts., P.2 tog. through the back of the sts., P.4, w.r.n., P.3, K.2, P.2, P.2 tog.

9th Row.—K.2 tog., K.4, P.2, K.2, wl.fwd., sl.1, K.1, p.s.s.o., K.2. Work as a 13th pattern row from * to the last 14 sts., wl.fwd., sl.1, K.1, p.s.s.o., K.2, wl.fwd., sl.1, K.1, p.s.s.o., P.2, K.4, K.2 tog.

10th Row.—P.2 tog., P.3, K.2, P.2, w.r.n., P.2 tog., P.2. Work as a 14th pattern row from * to the last 13 sts., w.r.n., P.2 tog., P.2, w.r.n., P.2 tog., K.2, P.3, P.2 tog.

11th Row.—K.2 tog., K.2, P.2, K.2, wl.fwd., sl.1, K.1, p.s.s.o., K.2. Work as a 15th pattern row from * to the last 12 sts., wl.fwd., sl.1, K.1, p.s.s.o., K.2, wl.fwd., sl.1, K.1, p.s.s.o., P.2, K.2, K.2 tog.

12th Row.—P.2 tog., P.1, K.2, P.2, w.r.n., P.2 tog., P.2. Work as a 16th pattern row from * to the last 11 sts., w.r.n., P.2 tog., P.2, w.r.n., P.2 tog., K.2, P.1, P.2 tog.

13th Row.—K.2 tog., P.2, K.2, wl.fwd., sl.1, K.1, p.s.s.o., K.2. Work as a 13th pattern row from * to the last 10 sts., wl.fwd., sl.1, K.1, p.s.s.o., K.2, wl.fwd., sl.1, K.1, p.s.s.o., P.2, K.2 tog.

14th Row.—K.2 tog., K.1, P.2, w.r.n., P.2 tog., P.2. Work as a 14th pattern row from * to the last 9 sts., w.r.n., P.2 tog., P.2, w.r.n., P.2 tog., K.1, K.2 tog.

15th Row.—P.2 tog., K.2, wl.fwd., sl.1, K.1, p.s.s.o., K.2. Work as a 15th pattern row from * to the last 8 sts., wl.fwd., sl.1, K.1, p.s.s.o., K.2, wl.fwd., sl.1, K.1, p.s.s.o., P.2 tog.

16th Row.—P.2 tog., P.1, w.r.n., P.2 tog., P.2. Work as a 16th pattern row from * to the last 7 sts., w.r.n., P.2 tog., P.3, P.2 tog.

17th Row.—K.2 tog., wl.fwd., sl.1, K.1, p.s.s.o., K.2. Work as a 13th pattern row from * to the last 6 sts., wl.fwd., sl.1, K.1, p.s.s.o., K.2, K.2 tog.

18th Row.—P.2 tog., P.3. Work as a 14th pattern row from * to the last 5 sts., w.r.n., P.2 tog., P.1, P.2 tog.

19th Row.—K.2 tog., K.2. Work as a 15th pattern row from * to the last 4 sts., wl.fwd., sl.1, K.1, p.s.s.o., K.2 tog.

20th Row.—P.2 tog., P.1. Work as a 16th pattern row from * to the last 3 sts., P.1, P.2 tog.

21st Row.—K.2 tog. Work as a 1st pattern row from * to the last 2 sts., K.2 tog.

The armhole shaping is now completed and 104 sts. remain.

Now repeat 2-24 inclusive of the pattern rows, then repeat rows 1-4 inclusive **twice** more.

Shape the Neck as follows :—

Next Row.—K.4, K.2 tog., K.4, wl.fwd., w.r.n., P.2, (K.2, wl.fwd., sl.1, K.1, p.s.s.o.) 3 times, keeping the wool etc. K.4, sl.1, K.1, p.s.s.o., K.11, cast off the following 18 sts., K. the following 10 sts., K.2 tog., K.4, wl.fwd., w.r.n., P.2, (K.2, wl.fwd., sl.1, K.1, p.s.s.o.) 3 times, P.2, keeping the wool etc. K.4, sl.1, K.1, p.s.s.o., K.4.

Next Row.—K.1, P.2, P.2 tog. through the back of the sts., P.4, w.r.n., P.1, K.2, (P.2, w.r.n., P.2 tog.) 3 times, K.2, P.1, w.r.n., P.4, P.2 tog., P.4, P.2 tog. through the back of the sts., P.4. Slip the remaining sts. on to a safety pin for the present, turn.

Proceed on the former set of sts. for the Right side of the neck as follows :—

1st Row.—K.4, sl.1, K.1, p.s.s.o., K.2, K.2 tog., K.4, wl.fwd., K.2, P.2 (K.2, wl.fwd., sl.1, K.1, p.s.s.o.) 3 times, P.2, K.2, wl.fwd., K.4, sl.1, K.1, p.s.s.o., K.2.

2nd Row.—K.1, P.2 tog. through the back of the sts., P.4, w.r.n., P.3, K.2, (P.2, w.r.n., P.2 tog.) 3 times, K.2, P.3, w.r.n., P.4, P.2 tog., P.2 tog., through the back of the sts., P.4.

3rd Row.—K.2 tog., K.1, (K.2, wl.fwd., sl.1, K.1, p.s.s.o.) **twice**, P.2, keeping the wool etc. K.4, sl.1, K.1, p.s.s.o., K.6, K.2 tog., K.4, wl.fwd., w.r.n., P.2, K.2, wl.fwd., sl.1, K.1, p.s.s.o., K.3.

4th Row.—K.1, wl.fwd., w.r.n., P.2 tog., P.2 w.r.n., P.2 tog., P.2, P.1, w.r.n., P.4, P.2 tog., P.4, P.2 tog. through the back of the sts., P.4, w.r.n., P.1, K.2, (P.2, w.r.n., P.2 tog.) **twice**, P.2 tog.

5th Row.—K.2 tog., K.1, wl.fwd., sl.1, K.1, p.s.s.o., K.2, wl.fwd., sl.1, K.1, p.s.s.o., P.2, K.2, wl.fwd., K.4, sl.1, K.1, p.s.s.o., K.2, K.2 tog., K.4, wl.fwd., K.2, P.2, K.2, wl.fwd., sl.1, K.1, p.s.s.o., K.3.

6th Row.—K.1, wl.fwd., w.r.n., P.2 tog., P.2, w.r.n., P.2 tog., K.2, P.3, w.r.n., P.4, P.2 tog., P.2 tog. through the back of the sts., P.4, w.r.n., P.3, K.2, P.2, w.r.n., P.2 tog., P.2, P.2 tog. (36 sts. remain.)

Now repeat 13-16 inclusive **twice** of the pattern rows.

Shape the Shoulder as follows :—

1st Row.—K.4, K.2 tog., K.4, wl.fwd., w.r.n., P.2, (K.2, wl.fwd., sl.1, K.1, p.s.s.o.) 3 times, P.2, turn.

2nd Row.—K.2, (P.2, w.r.n., P.2 tog.) 3 times, K.2, P.1, w.r.n., P.4, P.2 tog., P.2, K.1.

3rd Row.—K.2, K.2 tog., K.4, wl.fwd., K.2, P.2, turn.

4th Row.—K.2, P.3, w.r.n., P.4, P.2 tog., K.1.

Cast off knitwise all across.

Slip the sts. from the safety pin on to a No. 10 needle, the point to the centre, rejoin the wool and proceed for the Left side of the neck as follows :—

1st Row.—P.4, P.2 tog., P.4, P.2 tog. through the back of the sts., P.4, w.r.n., P.1, K.2, (P.2, w.r.n., P.2 tog.) 3 times, K.2, P.1, w.r.n., P.4, P.2 tog., P.2, K.1.

2nd Row.—K.2, K.2 tog., K.4, wl.fwd., K.2, P.2, (K.2, wl.fwd., sl.1, K.1, p.s.s.o.) 3 times, P.2, K.2, wl.fwd., K.4, sl.1, K.1, p.s.s.o., K.2, K.2 tog., K.4.

3rd Row.—P.4, P.2 tog., P.2 tog. through the back of the sts., P.4, w.r.n., P.3, K.2, (P.2, w.r.n., P.2 tog.) 3 times, K.2, P.3, w.r.n., P.4, P.2 tog., K.1.

4th Row.—K.1, wl.fwd., sl.1, K.1, p.s.s.o., K.2, wl.fwd., sl.1, K.1, p.s.s.o., P.2, keeping the wool etc. K.4, sl.1, K.1, p.s.s.o., K.6, K.2 tog., K.4, wl.fwd., w.r.n., P.2, (K.2, wl.fwd., sl.1, K.1, p.s.s.o.) twice, K.1, K.2 tog.

5th Row.—P.2 tog., (P.2, w.r.n., P.2 tog.) twice, K.2, K.2 tog., K.4, P.2 tog., P.4, P.2 tog. through the back of the sts., P.4, w.r.n., P.1, K.2, P.2, w.r.n., P.2 tog., P.2, K.1.

6th Row.—K.1, wl.fwd., sl.1, K.1, p.s.s.o., K.2, wl.fwd., sl.1, K.1, p.s.s.o., K.2, wl.fwd., K.4, sl.1, K.1, p.s.s.o., K.2, K.2 tog., K.4, wl.fwd., K.2, P.2, K.2, wl.fwd., sl.1, K.1, p.s.s.o., K.3, K.2 tog.

7th Row.—P.2 tog., w.r.n., P.2, P.2, w.r.n., P.2 tog., K.2, P.3, w.r.n., P.4, P.2 tog., P.2 tog. through the back of the sts., P.4, w.r.n., P.3, K.2, P.2, w.r.n., P.2 tog., K.1. (36 sts. remain.)

Now repeat 13-16 inclusive **twice** of the pattern rows then repeat the 1st row.

Shape the Shoulder as follows :—

1st Row.—K.1, P.2, P.2 tog. through the back of the sts., P.4, w.r.n., P.1, K.2, (P.2, P.2 tog.) 3 times, K.2, turn.

2nd Row.—P.2, (K.2, wl.fwd., sl.1, K.1, p.s.s.o.) 3 times, P.2, K.2, wl.fwd., K.4, sl.1, K.1, p.s.s.o., K.2.

3rd Row.—K.1, P.2 tog. through the back of the sts., P.4, w.r.n., P.3, K.2, turn.

4th Row.—P.2, K.10.

Cast off purlwise all across.

THE BACK.

Work as the instructions for the Front up to * *.

Next Row.—K.1, * K.3, K.2 tog., K.4, wl.fwd., w.r.n., P.2, (K.2, wl.fwd., sl.1, K.1, p.s.s.o.) 3 times, P.2, keeping the wool etc. K.4, sl.1, K.1, p.s.s.o., K.3, * cast off the following 33 sts., the st. on the right-hand needle after the casting off counting as K.1, repeat from * to * once more, K.1.

Next Row.—K.1, * P.2, P.2 tog. through the back of the sts., P.4, w.r.n., P.1, K.2, (P.2, w.r.n., P.2 tog.) 3 times, K.2, P.1, w.r.n., P.4, P.2 tog., P.2, * P.1, turn and cast on 67 sts., turn and repeat from * to * once more, K.1. (138 sts. now on the needle.)

Working into the back of the cast-on sts. on the first row only, repeat the 3rd and 4th rows of the original pattern.

Now repeat 13-24 inclusive of the pattern rows, then repeat rows 1-24 inclusive **twice** and finally repeat rows 1-4 inclusive.

Shape the Armholes as follows:—

1st Row.—Cast off 6 sts., K. the following 3 sts., P.2, K.2, wl.fwd., sl.1, K.1, p.s.s.o., K.2. Work as a 13th pattern row from * to the last 18 sts., wl.fwd., sl.1, K.1, p.s.s.o., K.2, wl.fwd., sl.1, K.1, p.s.s.o., P.2, K.10.

2nd Row.—Cast off 6 sts., P. the following 3 sts., K.2, P.2, w.r.n., P.2 tog., P.2. Work as a 14th pattern row from * to the last 12 sts., w.r.n., P.2 tog., P.2, w.r.n., P.2 tog., K.2, P.4.

3rd Row.—K.2 tog., K.2, P.2, K.2, wl.fwd., sl.1, K.1, p.s.s.o., K.2. Work as a 15th pattern row from * to the last 12 sts., wl.fwd., sl.1, K.1, p.s.s.o., K.2, wl.fwd., sl.1, K.1, p.s.s.o., P.2, K.2, K.2 tog.

4th Row.—P.2 tog., P.1, K.2, P.2, w.r.n., P.2 tog., P.2. Work as a 16th pattern row from * to the last 11 sts., w.r.n., P.2 tog., P.2, w.r.n., P.2 tog., K.2, P.1, P.2 tog.

5th Row.—K.2 tog., P.2, K.2, wl.fwd., sl.1, K.1, p.s.s.o., K.2. Work as a 13th pattern row from * to the last 10 sts., wl.fwd., sl.1, K.1, p.s.s.o., K.2, wl.fwd., sl.1, K.1, p.s.s.o., P.2, K.2 tog.

6th Row.—K.2 tog., K.1, P.2, w.r.n., P.2 tog., P.2. Work as a 14th pattern row from * to the last 9 sts., w.r.n., P.2 tog., P.2, K.1, K.2 tog.

7th Row.—P.2 tog., K.2, wl.fwd., sl.1, K.1, p.s.s.o., K.2. Work as a 15th pattern row from * to the last 8 sts., wl.fwd., sl.1, K.1, p.s.s.o., K.2, wl.fwd., sl.1, K.1, p.s.s.o., P.2 tog.

8th Row.—P.2 tog., P.1, w.r.n., P.2 tog., P.2. Work as a 16th pattern row from * to the last 7 sts., w.r.n., P.2 tog., P.2, w.r.n., **P.3 tog.**

9th Row.—K.2 tog., K.4. Work as a 1st pattern row from * to the last 6 sts., K.4, K.2 tog.

10th Row.—P.2 tog., P.3. Work as a 2nd pattern row from * to the last 5 sts., P.3, P.2 tog.

11th Row.—K.2 tog., K.2. Work as a 3rd pattern row from * to the last 4 sts., K.2, K.2 tog.

12th Row.—P.2 tog., P.1. Work as a 4th pattern row from * to the last 3 sts., P.1, P.2 tog.

13th Row.—K.2 tog. Work as a 1st pattern row from * to the last 2 sts., K.2 tog.

The armhole shaping is now completed and 104 sts. remain.

Now repeat 6-24 inclusive of the pattern rows, then repeat rows 1-24 inclusive once more and finally repeat rows 1-4 inclusive **twice**.

Shape the Shoulder as follows :—

1st Row.—K.1. Work as a 1st pattern row, from * to the last 35 sts., K.3, K.2 tog., K.4, wl.fwd., w.r.n., P.2, (K.2, wl.fwd., sl.1, K.1, p.s.s.o.) 3 times, P.2, turn.

2nd Row.—K.2, (P.2, w.r.n., P.2 tog.) 3 times, K.2, P.1, w.r.n., P.4, P.2 tog., P.2. Work as a 2nd pattern row from * to the last 35 sts., P.2, P.2 tog. through the back of the sts., P.4, w.r.n., P.1, K.2, (P.2, w.r.n., P.2 tog.) 3 times, K.2, turn.

3rd Row.—P.2, (K.2, wl.fwd., sl.1, K.1, p.s.s.o.) 3 times, P.2, K.2, wl.fwd., K.4, sl.1, K.1, p.s.s.o., K.1. Work as a 3rd pattern row from * to the last 35 sts., K.1, K.2 tog., K.4, wl.fwd., K.2, P.2, turn.

4th Row.—K.2, P.3, w.r.n., P.4, P.2 tog. Work as a 4th pattern row from * to the last 35 sts., P.2 tog. through the back of the sts., P.4, w.r.n., P.3, K.2, turn. Break off the wool.

Slip all the sts. on to one needle, rejoin the wool and cast off knitwise all across.

THE THREE-QUARTER SLEEVE.

Using No. 11 needles, cast on 70 sts.

Working into the back of the sts. K. one row.

Now repeat 1-24 inclusive of the original pattern rows, then repeat rows 1-12 inclusive.

Next Row.—K.1, wl.fwd., sl.1, K.1, p.s.s.o., K.2, wl.fwd., sl.1, K.1, p.s.s.o., P.2, keeping the wool etc. K.4, sl.1, K.1, p.s.s.o., K.3, cast off the following 34 sts., K. the following 2 sts., K.2 tog., K.4, wl.fwd., w.r.n., P.2, K.2, wl.fwd., sl.1, K.1, p.s.s.o., K.3.

Next Row.—K.1, wl.fwd., w.r.n., P.2 tog., P.2, w.r.n., P.2 tog., K.2, P.1, w.r.n., P.4, P.2 tog., P.2, turn, cast on 102 sts., turn, P.2, P.2 tog. through the back of the sts., P.4, w.r.n., P.1, K.2, P.2, w.r.n., P.2 tog., P.2, K.1. (138 sts. now on the needle.)

Working into the back of the cast-on sts. on the first row only, repeat the 15th and 16th rows of the pattern. * * *

Change to No. 10 needles and repeat 13-16 inclusive twice of the pattern rows, then repeat rows 1-24 inclusive 3 times, and finally rows 1-4 inclusive of the same instructions.

Shape the Top as follows :—

Repeat rows 1-21 inclusive of the instructions for the **armhole shaping** on the **Front,** when 70 sts. remain.

Now repeat 2-24 inclusive of the pattern rows, then repeat rows 1-24 inclusive once more.

Cast off.

Work another sleeve in the same manner.

THE SHORT SLEEVE.

Work as the instructions for the three-quarter sleeve up to * * *. Change to No. 10 needles and repeat 13-16 inclusive twice of the pattern rows, then repeat rows 1-24 inclusive once and finally rows 1-4 inclusive of the same instructions.

Shape the Top and complete as the instructions for the three-quarters sleeve.

Work another sleeve in the same manner.

MAKE-UP.

Gather up the cast-on sts. in the centre of the Front until these measure the same as the cast-off edges and then stitch the two edges together on the wrong side.

Complete the casting-on in the centre of the Back and sleeves in the same manner.

Stitch the 36 sts. on the Right shoulder of the Back and Front together.

Lightly press the work on the wrong side, using a warm iron and a damp cloth.

Using the crochet hook, work a row of d.c. along the Left shoulder of the Back, round the neck and along the shoulder of the Front, turn and work a second row in the same manner.

Join the side and sleeve seams.

Place the Left shoulder of the Front over that of the Back and stitch the armhole edge of the shoulder for ½-inch.

Mark 3 inches below the casting-off at each side of the top of the sleeves. Gather up the material between the points marked until the sleeve top is the correct size to fit the armhole.

Stitch the sleeves into position.

Stitch the hooks and eyes to the Left shoulder to close the neck.

Attach the shoulder pads to the wrong side of the top of each sleeve at the shoulder line.

Sporting Affair

MATERIALS
Excelana 4 Ply Luxury Wool 100% pure new British wool (159m/174yds per 50g ball)
2 balls shade Cornflower Blue – MC
2 balls shade Powdered Egg – CC

Scarf
1 pair 3.75mm (US #5) needles

Gloves
First Size – 1 set 2.75mm (US #2) Double Pointed Needles (DPNs)
Second Size – 1 set 3mm (US #3) DPNs

TENSION
32 sts & 40 rows = 10cm (4in) using 2.75mm needles over stocking stitch
28 sts & 36 rows = 10cm (4in) using 3mm needles over stocking stitch

ABBREVIATIONS
See page 13 for standard abbreviations

SIZING
Scarf
Length = 101½cm (40in)

Gloves
First size to fit small-medium lady's hand – circumference 16¼cm (6½in)
Second size to fit medium-large lady's hand – circumference 18½cm (7¼in)

PATTERN NOTES
When changing yarn, weave ends on wrong side of work for approx 6 sts. This can be done during knitting or if preferred can be done when scarf is completed with a sewing up needle. Do not carry ends up sides of scarf as they will be visible.

Scarf

Using 3.75mm needles and MC, cast on 56 sts.
Row 1: K.
Row 2: K.
Row 3: P.
Rows 4 & 5: As rows 2 & 3.
Row 6: P.
Row 7: K.
Row 8: P.
Change to CC.
Rows 9 & 10: K.
Row 11: P.
Row 12: K.
Row 13: P.
Change to MC.
Row 14: P.
Row 15: K.
Rows 16 & 17: As rows 14 & 15.
Row 18: K.
Row 19: P.
Rows 20 & 21: As rows 18 & 19.
Change to CC.
Row 22: P.

Row 23: K.
Row 24: P.
These 24 rows form pattern. Repeat until scarf measures 101½cm (40in) approx, ending with row 21. Cast off fairly loosely.

Gloves

LEFT HAND
Using 2.75 (3) mm needles and MC, cast on 60 sts. Join into round taking care not to twist cast on edge. Work cuff as folls:
Rounds 1–4: K.
Rounds 5–8: P.
Change to CC
Rounds 9–11: K.
Change to MC
Round 12: K.
Rounds 13–16: P.
Rounds 17–19: K.
Change to CC
Round 20: K.
Rounds 21–24: P.

Rep rounds 1–23 once more.
Next round (Dec): * P3, P2tog, rep from * to end (48 sts).

Divide for Palm

Working in CC only from this point, slip first 26 sts on 1 needle for palm, leaving rem 22 sts on spare needle for back of hand. Continue on these 26 sts only, now working back and forth.
Row 1: K.
Row 2: P.
Rep these 2 rows twice more.
Row 7: K24, Kfb, K to end.
Row 8: P.
Rep these last two rows until 42 sts on needle, ending with a RS row.

Divide for Thumb

Next row (WS): P1, and place this stitch on a safety pin, P16, cast on 4, and leave rem 25 sts on holder.
K one row, then join 20 thumb sts into a round, and now K for 25 rounds or required length (see 'Fit and Finish' chapter).
Next round: [K2tog] rep to end of round (10 sts).
Next round: [K2tog] rep to end of round (5 sts).
Draw through rem sts and fasten off.

Rejoin CC to work at base of thumb. Take st from safety pin, then pick up and K 4 sts from cast on at base of thumb, and P 25 sts on holder (30 sts). Work back and forth in stocking stitch for 20 rows or required length then place sts on holder.

Back

Take 22 sts from spare needle and with RS facing, join in MC and work as for scarf commencing with row 13. Work a further complete patt rep and then a further 20 rows. Working in CC only from this point, K one row, then K across sts on holder (52 sts).

First Finger

K7 from back sts, cast on 4, place next 36 sts onto spare needle, then K rem 9 sts from palm. Join into a round and K 30 rounds or required length (20 sts). Finish off as for thumb.

Second Finger

Using CC, pick and K 3 sts from cast on edge at base of preceding finger, K5 from back of hand, cast on 3 and K7 from palm (18 sts). K 37 rounds or required length. Finish off as for thumb.

Third Finger

Work as for second finger but only K 34 rounds.

Fourth Finger

Pick up and K 3 sts from cast on edge at base of third finger, K rem 12 sts (15 sts). K 29 rounds or required length. Finish as for thumb.

RIGHT HAND

Work to correspond with left hand, but in the palm reverse position of thumb by increasing in the 25 st from end each time, and dividing sts on RS instead of WS. Divide for fingers by reading all rounds from back to front.

MAKING UP

Press scarf lightly with a damp cloth. Press the gloves well but avoid the cuffs. Join the edges of the back neatly to palm edges on WS. Darn in all ends.

Sporting Affairs

Angora Striped Scarf & Gloves

VARY the stripes in this attractive scarf and glove set. Two shades of red were used together for this copy, but there is no reason why you cannot use any scraps of wool you have about so long as you remember to knit to the correct tension. The gloves have plain palms and fingers and neat little striped gauntlet cuffs.

MATERIALS: 3 (½-oz.) balls Beryl Fine-Spun Angora and 2 ozs. Patons Super, or Beehive, Scotch Fingering, 3-ply. Original uses dark red angora with light red fingering. A pair No. 9 and a set of four No. 12 "Beehive" needles.

MEASUREMENTS: SCARF: Width, 8 inches; length, 40 inches when stretched. GLOVES: To fit size 6¼–7-inch hand.

TENSION: 7 stitches to 1 inch on No. 9 needles; 8 stitches to 1 inch on No. 12 needles.

SCARF

With No. 9 needles and angora, cast on 56 stitches. 1ST ROW: Knit. 2ND ROW: Knit. 3RD ROW: Purl. Repeat these 2 rows once. 6TH ROW: Purl. 7TH ROW: Knit. 8TH ROW: Purl.

Change to fingering. (Break the thread each time when changing the wool and weave the end in on wrong side for 6 stitches, in order to keep the edge tidy.) 9TH AND 10TH ROWS: Knit. 11TH ROW: Purl. 12TH ROW: Knit. 13TH ROW: Purl.

Change to angora. 14TH ROW: Purl. 15TH ROW: Knit. Repeat last 2 rows once. 18TH ROW: Knit. 19TH ROW: Purl. Repeat last 2 rows once.

Change to fingering. 22ND ROW: Purl. 23RD ROW: Knit. 24TH ROW: Purl. Change to angora.

Repeat these 24 rows of pattern until scarf measures 40 inches, when stretched, ending with 21st row. Cast off.

GLOVES

LEFT HAND: With No. 12 needles and angora, cast on 60 stitches (20–20–20), join into a round and work as follows:—1ST, 2ND, 3RD, AND 4TH ROUNDS: Knit. 5TH, 6TH, 7TH, AND 8TH ROUNDS: Purl.

Change to fingering. 9TH, 10TH, AND 11TH ROUNDS: Knit.

Change to angora. 12TH ROUND: Knit. 13TH, 14TH, 15TH, AND 16TH ROUNDS: Purl. 17TH, 18TH, AND 19TH ROUNDS: Knit.

Change to fingering. 20TH ROUND: Knit. 21ST, 22ND, 23RD, AND 24TH ROUNDS: Purl. Work rounds 1–23 inclusive again. 48TH ROUND: Purl, working together every 4th and 5th stitch.

Now divide stitches for palm. Slip first 26 stitches on to 1 needle for palm and leave remaining 22 stitches on spare needle for back. Continue on 26 palm stitches. 1ST ROW: Knit. 2ND ROW: Purl. Repeat these 2 rows twice. 7TH ROW: k. 24, knit twice into next stitch, knit to end. 8TH ROW: Purl. Repeat 7th and 8th rows until there are 42 stitches on needle, then divide for thumb (wrong side facing).

NEXT ROW: p. 1, and leave on safety pin, p. 16, cast on 4, and leave remaining 25 stitches on holder. Join the 20 thumb stitches into a round and continue in rounds of plain knitting for 30 rounds. NEXT 2 ROUNDS: k. 2 tog. all round and fasten off.

Return to main work. Take the stitch from safety pin, pick up and knit 4 stitches out of those cast on for thumb, and purl 25 stitches from holder. Continue back and forth in stocking-stitch for 20 rows, then leave on holder whilst you work the back.

Take the 22 stitches from spare needle, join in angora, and with right side facing, start pattern as given for scarf, starting with the 13th row. Complete this pattern, work the next, and 20 rows of the following pattern (7 purl stripes). Break angora and join in fingering; knit 1 row, then knit across palm stitches on holder, so that the stitches are in a round once more. Here divide for fingers:—

FOREFINGER: k. 7 from back, cast on 3, leave next 36 stitches on spare needles, knit the remaining 9 stitches from palm. Join into a round and work 34 rounds plain knitting on these 19 stitches. Finish as for thumb.

MIDDLE FINGER: Pick up and knit 3 out of those cast on for forefinger, k. 5 from back of hand, cast on 3 and k. 7, from palm. Work 37 rounds on these 18 stitches, and finish as before.

THIRD FINGER: As for middle finger, but work 34 rounds.

LITTLE FINGER: Pick up and knit 3 out of those cast on for third finger; knit the remaining 12 stitches. Work 29 rounds on these 15 stitches, and finish as before.

RIGHT HAND: Work to correspond with left hand, but in the palm reverse position of thumb by increasing in the 25th stitch from end each time, and dividing stitches with right instead of wrong side facing. Divide for fingers by reading all rounds from back to front.

TO MAKE UP

Press scarf lightly with a damp cloth. Press the gloves well, but the cuffs only lightly. Join the edges of back neatly to palm edges on wrong side.

Fair Isle Jumper

MATERIALS
Excelana Luxury 4 Ply Wool 100% pure new British wool (159m/174yds per 50g ball)
4 (5, 6, 6, 7, 8) balls shade Nile Green – MC
1 (1, 2, 2, 2, 2) balls shade Persian Grey – A
1 ball (all sizes) shades Powdered Egg – B, Alabaster – C, Cornflower Blue – D, French Rose – E
1 pair 2.75mm (US #2) needles
1 pair 3.25mm (US #3) needles
Stitch holder

TENSION
30 sts & 30 rows = 10cm (4in) using 3.25mm needles over Fair Isle pattern

Standard Yarn Tension
28 sts & 36 rows = 10cm (4in) using 3mm needles over stocking stitch

ABBREVIATIONS
See page 13 for standard abbreviations

SIZING
Measurements given in centimetres followed by inches in parentheses

To Fit	71–76 (28–30)	81–86 (32–34)	92–97 (36–38)	102–106 (40–42)	112–117 (44–46)	117–122 (48–50)
Finished Measurements						
Actual Bust Size	81 (32)	91 (36)	102 (40)	112½ (44½)	123½ (48½)	134 (53)
Length to underarm	30 (12)	32½ (12¾)	32½ (12¾)	33½ (13¼)	35½ (14)	36½ (14½)
Armhole Depth	17 (6½)	17 (6½)	18 (7)	19½ (7½)	20½ (8)	21½ (8½)
Finished Length	47 (18½)	49½ (19½)	50½ (20)	53 (21)	56 (22)	58 (23)
Shoulder to Shoulder	33 (13)	35 (14)	37 (14½)	39 (15½)	42 (16½)	44½ (17½)
Sleeve Length	16½ (6½)	16½ (6½)	16½ (6½)	16½ (6½)	16½ (6½)	16½ (6½)

Garment shown in photographs is for the second size 81–86 (32–34)

PATTERN NOTES
This jumper was designed to be worn with the cardigan shown next. Designed as a twin set, they have interchangeable sleeves, meaning either can be made long or short sleeved. Remember, if you add long sleeves to the jumper, you will need extra yarn in the main colour. Both are also designed to have knitted shoulder pads. If knitting both cardigan and sweater to be worn together, I would recommend only having shoulder pads in one of the two garments.

BACK
Using 2.75mm needles and MC, cast on 111 (127, 143, 159, 175, 191) sts. Work in rib as folls:

Next row (RS): * K1, P1, rep from * to last st, K1.

Next row: * P1, K1, rep from * to last st, P1.

Rep these 2 rows until work measures 7½ (10, 10, 10, 10, 10) cm (3, 4, 4, 4, 4, 4 in) from cast on, ending with a WS row.

Next row (Inc): Inc 10 sts evenly across row (121, 137, 153, 169, 185, 201 sts).

Change to 3.25mm needles and still working in MC, P 1 row.

Row 1 (RS): Work all sts from chart row 1, repeating marked section 6 (7, 8, 9, 10, 11) times, and reading from right to left.

Row 2 (WS): Work all sts from chart row 2, repeating marked section 6 (7, 8, 9, 10, 11) times, and reading from left to right.

Work from chart, as set by last 2 rows, until 68 (68, 68, 70, 76, 80) rows in Fair Isle pattern have been worked (last row is row 16 (16, 16, 18, 24, 2 of chart)).

Shape Armholes
Whilst maintaining pattern as set by chart, cast off 6 (8, 10, 11, 13, 15) sts at beg of next 2 rows, cast off 3 (4, 5, 7, 8, 9) sts at beg of foll 2 rows, then cast off 1 (2, 2, 2, 2, 2) sts at beg of next 4 (4, 6, 8, 8, 10) rows (99, 105, 111, 117, 127, 133 sts) ending with row 24 (24, 26, 4, 10, 16) of chart.

Continue in patt for 30 (30, 28, 32, 26, 20) rows thus ending with chart row 2 (2, 2, 10, 10, 10). ***

Change to MC and commencing with a K row work in stocking stitch until armhole measures 15½ (15½, 16½, 18, 19, 20) cm (6, 6, 6½, 7, 7½, 8 in), ending with a WS row.

Shape Shoulders
Cast off 5 (6, 7, 8, 9, 10) sts at beg of the next 6 rows, then cast off the rem 69 (69, 69, 69, 73, 73) sts.

FRONT
Work as for back to *** (99, 105, 111, 117, 127, 133 sts).

5th & 6th sizes only
Change to MC and commencing with a K row, work (8, 10) rows in stocking stitch.

All sizes
Change to MC, work in stocking stitch as folls:
Row 1 (RS): K27 (30, 33, 36, 41, 44), turn, leaving the rem 72 (75, 78, 81, 86, 89) sts unworked on a holder.
Commencing with a P row, work straight in stocking stitch until armhole measures 18 (18, 19, 20½, 21½, 22½) cm (7, 7, 7½, 8, 8½, 9 in) ending with a WS row.

Shape Shoulder
Cast off 5 (6, 7, 8, 9, 10) sts at beg of next and foll 2 alt rows.
Cast off 6 (6, 6, 6, 7, 7) sts at beg of foll 2 alt rows.

With RS facing rejoin MC to 72 (75, 78, 81, 86, 89) rem sts, cast off centre 45 sts and K to end of row (27, 30, 33, 36, 41, 44 sts).
Commencing with a P row work straight in stocking stitch, until armhole measures 18 (18, 19, 20½, 21½, 22½) cm (7, 7, 7½, 8, 8½, 9 in) ending with a RS row.

Shape Shoulder
Cast off 5 (6, 7, 8, 9, 10) sts at beg of next and foll 2 alt rows.
Cast off 6 (6, 6, 6, 7, 7) sts at beg of foll 2 alt rows.

SLEEVES
Using 2.75mm needles and MC, cast on 87 (91, 95, 99, 103, 107) sts.
Next row (RS): K1, * P1, K1, rep from * to end.
Next row: P1, * K1, P1, rep from * to end.
Rep these 2 rows until work measures 5½cm (2in) ending with a WS row.
Change to 3.25mm needles and commencing with a K row, work 4 rows in stocking stitch, then inc 1 st at each end of next row and every foll 6th row, until 93 (97, 101, 105, 109, 113 sts), ending with a RS row. Work 5 rows without shaping.

Chart

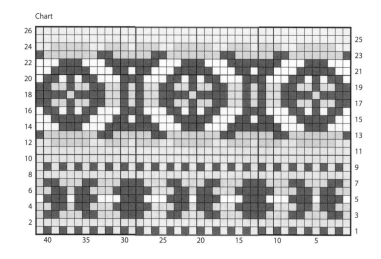

Key
- ☐ MC (Nile Green); K on RS, P on WS
- ■ A (Persian Grey); K on RS, P on WS
- ☐ B (Powdered Egg); K on RS, P on WS
- ☐ C (Alabaster); K on RS, P on WS
- ■ D (Cornower Blue); K on RS, P on WS
- ▨ E (French Rose); K on RS, P on WS
- ☐ Pattern repeat

Shape Sleeve Head

Dec 1 st at the beg of every row until 53 sts rem.

Work 10 rows straight, then cast off 16 sts at beg of the next 2 rows (21 sts).

On these centre 21 sts work 16 rows straight, then cast off. Work a second sleeve in the same way.

NECKBAND

With RS facing and using MC and 2.75mm needles, pick up and knit 45 sts along front neck edge.

Row 1 (WS): P2tog, * K1, P1, rep from * to last 3 sts, K1, P2tog (43 sts).

Row 2: K1, * P1, K1, rep from * to end.

Rep these 2 rows 3 times more, then cast off rem 37 sts loosely in rib.

Join shoulder seams. With RS facing and using MC and 2.75mm needles, pick up and knit 32 (32, 38, 38, 46, 66) sts up right side of neck, 42 sts along back of neck and 32 (32, 38, 38, 46, 66) sts down left side of neck (106, 106, 118, 118, 134, 174 sts).

Working in single rib, dec 1 st at each end of next row and every foll alt row (98, 98, 110, 110, 126, 166 sts). Work one row. Cast off loosely in rib.

SHOULDER PADS (Optional)

See 'Fit and Finish' chapter.

MAKING UP

Press all pieces on WS using a damp cloth. Sew mitred edges of neckband together using flat slip stitch. Press again if necessary. Darn in all ends. Join side seams, taking care to match pattern.

Make box head at top of sleeves as explained in 'Fit and Finish' chapter. Sew up sleeve seam and set in sleeve, taking care to match centre of box head to shoulder seam. Sew in shoulder pads to extend from armhole seam into box head.

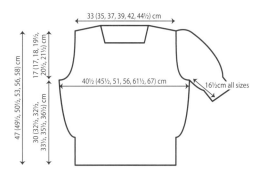

BESTWAY LEAFLET 1480 3d

FAIR ISLE JUMPER
(3-ply)

INSTRUCTIONS FOR CARDIGAN ARE
PUBLISHED IN BESTWAY LEAFLET No. 1481

Instructions for
MATCHING CARDIGAN
LEAFLET 1481

FAIR ISLE JUMPER

Instructions for Cardigan to match
appear in Bestway Leaflet No. 1481

MATERIALS.—4ozs. of Sirdar Super Shetland Wool, 3-ply, in natural and 1 oz. each of the same wool in the following colours : red, brown, blue, green and yellow ; a pair each of No. 12, No. 10 and No. 9 knitting needles ; shoulder pads. For the Cardigan to match the Jumper, instructions for which are given in Bestway Leaflet No. 1481, get 8 ozs. of the same wool in natural, with oddments of the same wool in red, brown, blue, green and yellow, left over from the Jumper.

TENSION AND MEASUREMENTS.— Worked at a tension of 8 sts. to the inch in width on the Fair Isle pattern with No. 9 needles, the measurements on the diagram are attained after light pressing.

ABBREVIATIONS.—TO BE READ BEFORE WORKING. K., knit plain ; p., purl ; st., stitch ; tog., together ; inc., increase (by working into the front and back of the same st.) ; dec., decrease (by working 2 sts. tog.) ; s.-s., stocking-st. (k. on the right side and p. back) ; single rib is k. 1 and p. 1 alternately ; n., natural ; br., brown ; r., red ; b., blue ; g., green ; y., yellow. Directions in brackets are worked the number of times stated after the last bracket.

TWO-COLOUR KNITTING.—For this either of the following two methods may be used : After knitting with the

The Shape and Measurements

first colour, join on the second colour, leaving the first colour at the back of the work. This must be carried along so as to be in position when next required, but care must be taken not to draw up the strands too tightly, or the work will be puckered and the size contracted. On the purl side leave the strands at the front of the work. The second method which is really the better one, as there are no loose threads, is known as " weaving in." For this the wool out of action is passed once over the working thread before working each stitch with the second colour, so that the spare thread is caught at the back of the work with every stitch.

Some workers find a difficulty in working in the spare thread on the purl side, in which case the loose strands can be left on the purl side of the work, weaving in on the knit rows only.

TO WORK THE BACK.
Begin at the lower edge by casting on 127 sts. with No. 12 needles and N wool. Work 36 rows in single rib, working into the back of the sts. on the first row to give a neat edge.

Inc. row : Inc. in every 12th st. until 10 sts. are added, k. 7. (137 sts.).

Change to No. 10 needles and purl 1 row, then begin the Fair Isle pattern as follows :

1st row (Right side) : K. 1 N, * 1 B, 1 N ; repeat from * to the end of the row.

2nd row : With N wool all purl.

3rd row : K. 1 Y, 2 B, 3 Y, 2 B, * 3 Y, 3B, (3 Y, 2 B) twice ;

repeat from * until 1 st. remains, 1 Y.

4th row : P. 2 Y, 2 B, 1 Y, 2 B, * 3 Y, 5 B, 3 Y, 2 B,1 Y, 2 B ; repeat from * until 2 sts. remain, 2 Y.

5th row : K. 1 R, 3 G, 1 R, * 3 G, (3 R, 3 G) twice, 1 R ; repeat from * until 4 sts. remain, 3 G, 1 R.

Repeat the 4th, 3rd, 2nd, 1st and 2nd rows once more.

11th row : All k. with N wool.

12th row : P. 2 N, 5 Br, 2 N, * 3 Br, 1 N, 3 Br, 2 N, 5 Br, 2 N ; repeat from * to the end.

13th row : K. 1 G, 7 Br, 2 G, * 5 Br, 2 G, 7 Br ; repeat from * ending the last repeat with 1 G instead of 2 G.

14th row : P. 3 R, 3 G, 3 R, * 7 G, 3 R, 3 G, 3 R ; repeat from * to the end of the row.

15th row : K. 2 R, 5 G, 3 R, * 2 G, 1 R, 2 G, 3 R, 5 G, 3 R ; repeat from *, ending the last repeat with 2 R instead of 3 R.

16th row : P. 1 R, 2 B, 1 R, 1 B, 1 R, 2 B, 3 R, * 3 B, 3 R, 2 B, 1 R, 1 B, 1 R, 2 B, 3 R ; repeat from *, ending the last repeat with 1 R instead of 3 R.

17th row : K. 2 B, 2 Y, 1 B, 2 Y, 2 B, 2 Y, * 1 B, 1 Y, 1 B, 2 Y, 2 B, 2 Y, 1 B, 2 Y, 2 B, 2 Y ; repeat from *, omitting the 2 Y, at the end of the last repeat.

18th row : P. 4 B, 1 Y, 4 B, 2 Y, * 1 B, 1 Y, 1 B, 2 Y, 4 B, 1 Y, 4 B, 2 Y ; repeat from *, omitting the 2 Y at the end of the last repeat. Now work from the 17th row **back** to the 12th row.

25th row : With N. wool all k.

26th row : With N wool all p. These 26 rows form the Fair Isle pattern. Change to No. 9 needles and repeat these 26 rows once more, then work the first 16 rows

of the next pattern to the armholes.

TO SHAPE THE ARMHOLES.

1st row : With Y cast off 8 sts., (1 st. on needle) 2 Y, * 1 B, 1 Y, 1 B, 2 Y, 2 B, 2 Y, 1 B, 2 Y, 2 B, 2 Y ; repeat from * omitting the 2 Y at end of last repeat.

2nd row : With Y cast off 8 sts., (1 st. on needle) 2 Y, * 1 B, 1 Y, 1 B, 2 Y, 4 B, 1 Y, 4 B, 2 Y ; repeat from * until 6 sts. remain, then 1 B, 1 Y, 1 B, 2 Y, 1 B.

3rd row : With B cast off 4 sts., (1 st. on needle) 1 B, 2 Y, 2 B, 2 Y, 1 B, 2 Y, 2 B, 2 Y, * 1 B, 1 Y, 1 B, 2 Y, 2 B, 2 Y ; repeat from * until 6 sts. remain, 1 B, 1 Y, 1 B, 2 Y, 1 B.

4th row : With B cast off 4, (1 st. on needle) 1 B, 3 R, 2 B, 1 R, 1 B, 1 R, 2 B, 3 R, * 3 B, 3 R, 2 B, 1 R, 1 B, 1 R, 2 B, 3 R ; repeat from * until 2 remain, 2 B.

5th row : With R cast off 2, (1 st. on needle) 3 R, 5 G, 3 R, * 2 G, 1 R, 2 G, 3 R, 5 G, 3 R ; repeat from * until 3 remain, 2 G, 1 R.

6th row : With G cast off 2, (1 st. on needle) 1 G, 3 R, 3 G, 3 R, * 7 G, 3 R, 3 G, 3 R ; repeat from * until 2 remain, 2 R.

7th row : With G cast off 2 (1 st. on needle) 7 Br, 2 G, * 5 Br, 2 G, 7 Br, 2 G ; repeat from * until 1 st. remains, 1 Br.

8th row : With N cast off 2, (1 st. on needle) 1 N, 5 Br, 2 N, * 3 Br, 1 N, 3 Br, 2 N, 5 Br, 2 N ; repeat from * to end. (105 sts.)

9th row : With N all k.

10th row : With N all p.

Now work 28 rows straight in Fair Isle pattern, beginning with the 1st pattern row as at the beginning. After which work 16 rows in s.-s.

entirely with N colour wool to bring the work to the shoulderline.

TO SLOPE THE SHOULDERS.

Cast off 10 sts. at the beginning of the next 6 rows, then cast off the remaining sts.

THE FRONT.
Work this exactly the same as the Back until the 10 rows of armhole shaping have been finished and 105 sts. remain, then continue as follows :

Work 28 rows straight in Fair Isle pattern, beginning with the 1st pattern row, then continue in s.-s. entirely with N colour wool, and divide the sts. for the neck thus :

THE LEFT HALF FRONT.
1st row : K. 30, turn, leaving the remaining 75 sts. unworked.

** Work 25 rows straight in s.-s., beginning with a purl row, to bring the work to the shoulder-line. (Work 1 row more here on the right half front.)

TO SLOPE THE SHOULDER.

Cast off 6 sts. at the beginning of the next row and following 4 alternate rows. Fasten off.

THE RIGHT HALF FRONT.
Return to the 75 sts. left unworked and cast off 45 sts. for front neck, then k. to the end of the row. (30 sts.)

Now repeat from ** on the Left Half Front to the end, noting the item in brackets.

THE SLEEVES.
Begin at the arm edge by casting on 91 sts. with No. 12 needles and N wool. Work 20 rows in single rib.

Change to No. 9 needles and work 4 rows in s.-s., then inc. 1 st. at both ends of the next row and every following 6th row, until the 3rd inc. row has been worked. (97 sts.) Work 5 rows straight.

TO SHAPE THE SLEEVE TOP.
Dec. 1 st. at the beginning only of every row, until 53 sts. remain.

Work 10 rows straight, then cast off 16 sts. at the beginning of the next 2 rows. (21 sts.)

On these centre 21 sts. work 16 rows straight, then cast off. Work a second sleeve in the same way.

THE FRONT NECK-BAND.
Holding the work with the right side facing, and using No. 12 needles and N wool, pick up and rib (k 1 and p. 1 alternately) 45 sts. along the front neck edge.

Work 8 rows in single rib, decreasing 1 st. at both ends of the next row and every following alternate row. (37 sts.)
Cast off loosely in rib.

THE SIDE AND BACK NECK-BAND.
First join the shoulder-seams, beginning at the armhole edge and taking 1 st. from each side at a time. With the right side of work facing, and using No. 12 needles and N colour wool, pick up and rib 32 sts. along the row ends at side of neck, 42 sts. along back neck edge and 32 sts. along the row ends at opposite side of neck. (106 sts.)

Work 8 rows in single rib, decreasing 1 st. at both ends of the next row and every following alternate row. (98 sts.)
Cast off loosely in rib.

TO MAKE UP THE JUMPER.
First press all parts, except the ribbing, with a hot iron over a damp cloth on the wrong side. Sew the row ends of the last 16 rows at sleeve top to the cast-off edges of the sts. cast off at each side, then set the sleeves into the armholes. Join the sleeve and side seams in one line and press. Sew the mitred edges of neck band and stroke these seams flat with the tip of a thimble. Sew in shoulder pads.

Fair Isle Cardigan

MATERIALS
Excelana Luxury 4 Ply Wool 100% pure new British wool (159m/174yds per 50g ball)
6 (7, 8, 9, 10, 11) balls shade Nile Green – MC
1 ball (all sizes) shades Persian Grey – A, Powdered Egg – B, Alabaster – C, Cornflower Blue – D, French Rose – E
1 pair 2.75mm (US #2) needles
1 pair 3.25mm (US #3) needles
8 buttons

TENSION
26 sts & 36 rows = 10cm (4in) using 3.25mm needles over stocking stitch

Standard Yarn Tension
28 sts & 36 rows = 10cm (4in) using 3mm needles over stocking stitch

ABBREVIATIONS
See page 13 for standard abbreviations

SIZING
Measurements given in centimetres followed by inches in parentheses

To Fit	71–76 (28–30)	81–86 (32–34)	92–97 (36–38)	102–106 (40–42)	112–117 (44–46)	117–122 (48–50)
Finished Measurements						
Actual Bust Size	89 (35)	100½ (39½)	109½ (43)	119½ (47)	129 (51)	140½ (55)
Length to underarm	30½ (12)	33 (13)	34 (13½)	35½ (14)	37 (14½)	38 (15)
Armhole Depth	18 (7)	19 (7½)	20 (8)	21½ (8½)	23 (9)	24 (9½)
Finished Length	48½ (19)	52 (20½)	54 (21½)	57 (22½)	60 (23½)	62 (24½)
Shoulder to Shoulder	31 (12½)	36½ (14½)	41 (16)	45 (17½)	48 (19)	52 (20½)
Sleeve Length	47 (18½)	47 (18½)	47 (18½)	48 (19)	48 (19)	49 (19½)

Garment shown in photographs is for second size 81–86 (32–34)

PATTERN NOTES
This cardigan was designed to be worn with the jumper shown previously. Designed as a twin set, they have interchangeable sleeves, meaning either can be made long or short sleeved. Remember, if you add long sleeves to the jumper, you will need extra yarn in the main colour. Both are also designed to have knitted shoulder pads. If knitting both cardigan and sweater to be worn together, I would recommend only having shoulder pads in one of the two garments.

BACK
Using 2.75mm needles and MC, cast on 101 (115, 127, 141, 153, 167) sts. Work in rib as folls:
Next row (RS): * K1, P1, rep from * to last st, K1.
Next row: * P1, K1, rep from * to last st, P1.
Rep these 2 rows until work measures 10cm (4in) from cast on edge.
Change to 3.25mm needles and commencing with a K row, work 4 rows in stocking stitch. Inc 1 st at each end of next row and on 7 foll 6th rows (117, 131, 143, 157, 169, 183 sts).
Continue without further shaping until work measures 30½ (33, 34, 35½, 37, 38) cm (12, 13, 13½, 14, 14½, 15 in) ending with a WS row.

Shape Armholes
Cast off 4 (4, 4, 6, 6, 8) sts at beg of next 2 rows, then dec 1 st at each end of foll 14 (14, 14, 14, 16, 16) rows (81, 95, 107, 117, 125, 135 sts).

Work without further shaping until armhole measures 18 (19, 20, 21½, 23, 24) cm (7, 7½, 8, 8½, 9, 9½ in).

Shape Shoulders
Cast off 7 (7, 9, 9, 10, 11) sts at beg of next 4 rows (53, 67, 71, 81, 85, 91 sts).
Cast off 6 (7, 8, 9, 10, 10) sts at beg of next 4 rows (29, 39, 39, 45, 45, 51 sts). Cast off rem 29 (39, 39, 45, 45, 51) sts.

LEFT FRONT
Using 2.75mm needles and MC, cast on 49 (57, 63, 69, 75, 83) sts.
Next row: * K1, P1, rep from * to last st, K1.
Next row: * P1, K1, rep from * to last st, P1.
Rep these 2 rows until work measures 10cm (4in) from cast on edge.
Change to 3.25mm needles and commencing with a K row, work 4 rows in stocking stitch, then inc 1 st at beg

(armhole edge) of next and 7 foll 6th rows (57, 65, 71, 77, 83, 91 sts).

Work without further shaping until front measures 30½ (33, 34, 35½, 37, 38) cm (12, 13, 13½, 14, 14½, 15 in) ending with a WS row.

Shape Armhole
Cast off 5 (5, 5, 7, 7, 9) sts at beg of next row (52, 60, 66, 70, 76, 82 sts).

Dec 1 st at armhole edge of foll 14 (14, 14, 14, 16, 16) rows, and at the same time dec 1 st at front edge (for the front slope) on 2nd and 5 foll 4th rows, (32, 40, 46, 50, 54, 60 sts).

2nd, 3rd, 4th and 5th sizes only
Dec 1 st at front edge of (1, 2, 3, 4) foll 4th rows (39, 44, 47, 50 sts).

6th size only
Dec 1 st at front edge of 2 foll 4th rows (58 sts).
†Work 1 row straight.
Dec 1 st at front edge of next row.
Work 3 rows straight.
Dec 1 st at front edge of next row.
Repeat from † once more (54 sts).

All sizes
Continuing in stocking stitch, work without further shaping until front measures 36 rows less than back to start of shoulder shaping (if row tension is correct, there should only be 1–3 rows to work), ending with a WS row (32, 39, 44, 47, 50, 54 sts). Now work from chart A as foll:
Start each RS row at stitch 1, and work from right to left to the coloured outline for your size. Only work decreases marked when they are in the same colour as your size outline. Start WS rows at the coloured line for your size and read from left to right, ending row at stitch 1 of chart.

Work from chart A until row 36 is complete (26, 28, 34, 36, 40, 42 sts).

Shape Shoulder
Working in MC only, cast off 7 (7, 9, 9, 10, 11) sts at beg of next and foll alt row (12, 14, 16, 18, 20, 20 sts).
Cast off 6 (7, 8, 9, 10, 10) sts at beg of 2 foll alt rows.

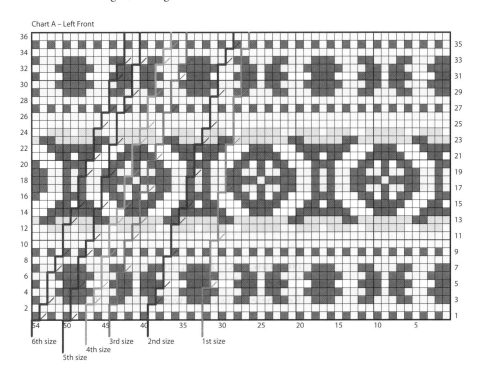

Chart A – Left Front

Key
☐ MC (Nile Green); K on RS, P on WS
■ A (Persian Grey); K on RS, P on WS
☐ B (Powdered Egg); K on RS, P on WS
☐ C (Alabaster); K on RS, P on WS
■ D (Cornower Blue); K on RS, P on WS
☐ E (French Rose); K on RS, P on WS
◪ K2tog (only work when colour of symbol matches your size)
◩ Sl 1, K1, psso (only work when colour of symbol matches your size)

54   50   45   40   35   30   25   20   15   10   5
6th size
5th size
4th size
3rd size   2nd size   1st size

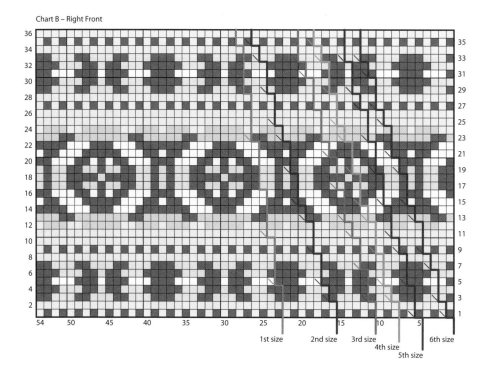

Chart B – Right Front

RIGHT FRONT

Using 2.75mm needles and MC, cast on 49 (57, 63, 69, 75, 83) sts.

Next row: * K1, P1, rep from * to last st, K1.

Next row: * P1, K1, rep from * to last st, P1.

Rep these 2 rows until work measures 10cm (4in) from cast on edge.

Change to 3.25mm needles and commencing with a K row, work 4 rows in stocking stitch, then inc 1 st at end (armhole edge) of next and 7 foll 6th rows (57, 65, 71, 77, 83, 91 sts).

Work without further shaping until front measures 30½ (33, 34, 35½, 37, 38) cm (12, 13, 13½, 14, 14½, 15 in) ending with a RS row.

Shape Armhole

Cast off 5 (5, 5, 7, 7, 9) sts at beg of next row (52, 60, 66, 70, 76, 82 sts).

Dec 1 st at armhole edge of foll 14 (14, 14, 14, 16, 16) rows, at the same time dec 1 st at front edge (for the front slope) on next and 5 foll 4th rows, (32, 40, 46, 50, 54, 60 sts).

2nd, 3rd, 4th and 5th sizes only

Dec 1 st at front edge of (1, 2, 3, 4) foll 4th rows (39, 44, 47, 50 sts).

6th size only

Dec 1 st at front edge of 2 foll 4th rows (58 sts).

† Work 1 row straight.

Dec 1 st at front edge of next row.

Work 3 rows straight.

Dec 1 st at front edge of next row.

Repeat from † once more (54 sts).

All sizes

Continuing in stocking stitch, work without further shaping until front measures 36 rows less than back to start of shoulder shaping (if row tension is correct, there should only be 1–3 rows to work), ending with a WS row (32, 39, 44, 47, 50, 54 sts).

Now work from chart B as foll:

Start each RS row at stitch to left of coloured outline for your size and work from right to left to the end of the chart. Only work decreases marked when they are in the same colour as your size outline. Start WS rows at stitch 54 of the chart and read from left to right, ending at coloured line for your size.

Work from chart A until row 36 is complete (26, 28, 34, 36, 40, 42 sts).

Work 1 row without shaping

Shape Shoulder

Working in MC only, cast off 7 (7, 9, 9, 10, 11) sts at beg of next and foll alt row (12, 14, 16, 18, 20, 20 sts).

Cast off 6 (7, 8, 9, 10, 10) sts at beg of 2 foll alt rows.

SLEEVES

Using 2.75mm needles and MC cast on 51 (55, 59, 63, 67, 71) sts.

Next row: * K1, P1, rep from * to last st, K1.

Next row: * P1, K1, rep from * to last st, P1.

Rep these 2 rows until work measures 10cm (4in) from cast on edge. Change to 3.25mm needles and commencing with a K row, work 6 rows in stocking stitch, then inc 1 st at each end of next row and every foll 6th row until 93 (97, 101, 105, 109, 113) sts (21 inc rows worked).

Work without further shaping until sleeve measures 47 (47, 47, 48, 48, 49½) cm (18½, 18½, 18½, 19, 19, 19½ in) from cast on edge.

Shape Sleeve Head
Dec 1 st at beg of every row, until 53 sts rem.
Work 12 rows straight then cast off 16 sts at beg of next
2 rows (21 sts).
On the centre 21 sts work 18 rows straight. Cast off.

BUTTONHOLE BAND
Using 2.75mm needles and MC cast on 13 sts. Work 10
rows in single rib, then work a buttonhole as folls:
Row 1: Rib 6, cast off 4, rib 2.
Row 2: Work in rib, casting on 4 sts over those cast off on
previous row.
Work 14 rows in single rib then rep the 2 buttonhole rows
again.
Repeat the last 16 rows 6 times more when there will be 8
buttonholes altogether.
Work straight for length required to complete the two
fronts and back neck. Do not cast off until strip is sewn on
so that the length can be adjusted as required.

SHOULDER PADS
See 'Fit and Finish' chapter.

MAKING UP
Press work through a damp cloth on the WS of work. Join
shoulder seams. Join sleeve and side seams. Make box head
at top of sleeves as explained in 'Fit and Finish' chapter.
Sew up sleeve seam and set in sleeve, taking care to match
centre of box head to shoulder seam. Sew in shoulder pads
to extend from armhole seam into box head. Sew the
buttonhole band to the fronts and back neck beginning at
the lower edge of the right front with band slightly
stretched, using a flat slip stitch (see 'Fit and Finish'
chapter). Adjust to fit if necessary and cast off sts. Sew
buttons to the left front to correspond with the
buttonholes. Sew in shoulder pads if required (see 'Fit and
Finish' chapter). Darn in all ends.

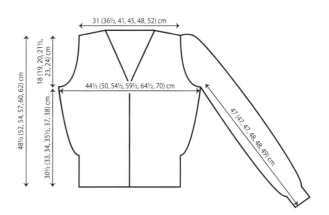

BESTWAY LEAFLET 3ᵈ 1481

FAIR ISLE CARDIGAN
(3-ply)

INSTRUCTIONS FOR JUMPER ARE
PUBLISHED IN BESTWAY LEAFLET No. 1480

FAIR ISLE CARDIGAN

Instructions for the Matching Jumper
appear in Bestway Leaflet No. 1480

MATERIALS. 8 ozs. of *Sirdar Super Shetland Wool*, 3 ply, in natural, with oddments in the following shades : red, brown, blue, green and yellow, for the Fair Isle yoke on each Front (if you are knitting the matching jumper, instructions for which are given in Bestway Leaflet No. 1480, get 4 ozs. of the main colour, and 1 oz. each of the same wool in red, brown, blue, green and yellow ; the oddments left over from these colours will be sufficient for the Fair Isle yoke of the cardigan) ; *a pair each of No. 12 and No. 9 knitting needles ; 8 buttons ; shoulder pads.*

TENSION AND MEASUREMENTS. Worked at a tension of $7\frac{1}{2}$ sts. to the inch in width on the stocking-stitch with No. 9 needles, the measurements on the diagram are attained after light pressing.

ABBREVIATIONS. TO BE READ BEFORE WORKING. K., knit plain ; p., purl ; st., stitch ; tog. together ; inc., increase (by working into the front and back of the same st.) ; dec., decrease (by working 2 sts. tog.) ; s.-s., stocking-st. (k. on the right side and p. back) ; single rib is k. 1 and p. 1 alternately ; N, natural ; Br., brown ; R, red ; B, blue ; G, green ; Y, yellow. Directions in brackets are worked the number of times stated after the last bracket.

TWO - COLOUR KNITTING. For this either of the following two methods may

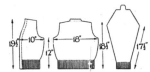

The Shape and Measurements.

be used : After knitting with the first colour, join on the second colour, leaving the first colour at the back of the work. This must be carried along so as to be in position when next required, but care must be taken not to draw up the strands too tightly or the work will be puckered and the size contracted. On the purl side leave the strands at the front of the work. The second method, which is really the better one, as there are no loose threads, is known as "weaving in." For this the wool out of action is passed once over the working thread before working each stitch with the second colour, so that the spare thread is caught at the back of the work with every stitch. Some workers find a difficulty in working in the spare thread on the purl side, in which case the loose strands can be left on the purl side of the work, weaving in on the knit rows only.

TO WORK THE BACK. Begin at the lower edge by casting on 115 sts. with No. 12 needles and N wool. Work 40 rows in single rib, working into the back of the sts. on the first row to give a neat edge.

Change to No. 9 needles and work 4 rows in s.-s., then inc. 1 st. at both ends of the next row and every following 6th row, until the 8th inc. row has been worked. (131 sts.)

Work 25 rows more to the armholes.

TO SHAPE THE ARMHOLES. Cast off 4 sts. at the beginning of the next 2 rows, then dec. 1 st. at both ends of the following 14 rows. (95 sts.)

Work 40 rows straight to bring the work to the shoulder-line.

TO SLOPE THE SHOULDERS. Cast off 7 sts. at the beginning of the next 6 rows, then cast off the remaining sts.

THE LEFT FRONT. Begin at the lower edge by casting on 57 sts. with No. 12 needles and N wool.

Work 40 rows in single rib.

Change to No. 9 needles and work 4 rows in s.-s., then inc. 1 st. at the *beginning* (seam end) of the next row and every following 6th row, until the 8th inc. row has been worked. (65 sts.)

Work 25 rows straight to the armhole.

** TO SHAPE THE ARMHOLE. Cast off 5 sts. at the beginning (armhole end) of the next row, then dec. 1 st. (armhole end) on the following 14 rows, *at the same time* decreasing 1 st. (front edge) for the front slope on the 1st, 5th, 9th and 13th of these rows. (42 sts.)

Work 11 rows, working straight at armhole end, but still decreasing for the front slope on every 4th row following the previous dec. (39 sts.)
Now begin the Fair Isle yoke as follows :

1st row (right side) : K. 1 N, * 1 B, 1 N ; repeat from * to the end.

2nd row : P. with N wool.

3rd row : K. 2 B, * 3 Y, (2 B, 3 Y) twice, 3 B ; repeat from * once more, then 3 Y, k. 2 tog. Y.

4th row : P. 3 Y, * 5 B, 3 Y, 2 B, 1 Y, 2 B, 3 Y ; repeat from * once more, 3 B.

5th row : K. 2 G, (3 R, 3 G, 1 R, 3 G, 3 R, 3 G) twice, 2 R, k. 2 tog. R.

6th row : P. 2 Y, (5 B, 3 Y, 2 B, 1 Y, 2 B, 3 Y) twice, 3 B.

7th row : K. 2 B, * (3 Y, 2 B) twice, 3 Y, 3 B ; repeat from * once more, 3 Y.

8th row : All purl with N wool.

9th row : K. 1 N, * 1 B, 1 N ; repeat from * until 2 sts. remain, k. 2 tog. B.

10th row : All p. with N wool.

11th row : All k. with N wool.

12th row : P. 3 Br, 1 N, (3 Br, 2 N, 5 Br, 2 N, 3 Br, 1 N) twice.

13th row : K. 3 Br, (2 G, 7 Br, 2 G, 5 Br) twice, ending the last repeat with 4 Br, k. 2 tog. Br. instead of 5 Br.

14th row : P. 6 G, * 3 R, 3 G, 3 R, 7 G ; repeat from *, ending the last repeat with 4 G, instead of 7 G.

15th row : K. 1 R, (2 G, 3 R, 5 G, 3 R, 2 G, 1 R) twice, k. 2 tog. G.

16th row : P. (3 B, 3 R, 2 B, 1 R, 1 B, 1 R, 2 B, 3 R) twice, 2 B.

17th row : K. 1 Y, 1 B, (2 Y, 2 B, 2 Y, 1 B, 2 Y, 2 B, 2 Y, 1 B, 1 Y, 1 B) twice.

18th row : P. 1 B, 1 Y, (1 B, 2 Y, 4 B, 1 Y, 4 B, 2 Y, 1 B, 1 Y) twice.

19th row : K. (1 Y, 1 B, 2 Y, 2 B, 2 Y, 1 B, 2 Y, 2 B, 2 Y, 1 B) twice, k. 2 tog. Y.

20th row : P. 2 B, * 3 R, 2 B, 1 R, 1 B, 1 R, 2 B, 3 R, 3 B ; repeat from *, ending last repeat with 2 B, instead of 3 B.

21st row : K. (1 R, 2 G, 3 R, 5 G, 3 R, 2 G) twice, 1 R.

22nd row : K. 4 G., * 3 R, 3 G, 3 R, 7 G ; repeat from *, ending the last repeat with 4 G, instead of 7 G.

23rd row : K. 3 Br, * 2 G, 7 Br, 2 G, 5 Br ; repeat from *, ending the last repeat with 1 Br, k. 2 tog. Br. instead of 5 Br.

24th row : P. 3 Br, 2 N, 5 Br, 2 N, 3 Br 1 N, 3 Br, 2 N, 5 Br, 2 N, 3 Br, 1 N.

25th row : With N wool k. until 2 sts remain, k. 2 tog.

26th row : All p. with N wool.

27th row : K. 1 N, * 1 B, 1 N ; repeat from * to the end.

28th row : All p. with N wool.

29th row : K. 2 B, 3 Y, (2 B, 3 Y) twice, 3 B, 3 Y, 2 B, 3 Y, 2 B, 1 Y, k. 2 tog. Y.

30th row : P. 3 Y, 2 B, 1 Y, 2 B, 3 Y, 5 B, 3 Y, 2 B, 1 Y, 2 B, 3 Y, 3 B.

31st row : K. 2 G, 3 R, 3 G, 1 R, 3 G, (3 R, 3 G) twice, 1 R, 3 G, 2 R.

32nd row : As 30th row.

33rd row : K. 2 B, 3 Y, (2 B, 3 Y) twice, 3 B, 3 Y, 2 B, 3 Y, 2 B, k. 2 tog. Y.

34th row : All p. with N wool.

35th row : As 27th row.

36th row : All p. with N wool.
(On Right Front k. 1 row more with N wool here.)

TO SLOPE THE SHOULDER. Continue entirely with N wool and cast off 7 sts. at the beginning of the next row and following 3 alternate rows. Pass 1 st. over the other and fasten off.

THE RIGHT FRONT. Begin at the lower edge by casting on 57 sts. with No. 12 needles and N wool. Work 40 rows in single rib.

Change to No. 9 needles and work 4 rows in s.-s., then inc. 1 st. at the *end* of the next row and every following 6th row, until the 8th inc. row has been worked. (65 sts.)

Work 26 rows straight to the armhole then repeat from ** on the Left Front to the end, but work all the Fair-Isle pattern rows backwards : the 1st row will read thus ; * 1 N, 1 B ; repeat from * until 1 st. remains, 1 N. Also note the item in brackets before sloping the shoulder.

THE SLEEVES. Begin at the wrist edge by casting on 55 sts. with No. 12 needles and N wool. Work 30 rows in single rib.

Change to No. 9 needles and work 6 rows in s.-s., then inc. 1 st. at both ends of the next row and every following 6th row, until the 21st inc. row has been worked. (97 sts.)
Work 9 rows straight.

TO SHAPE THE SLEEVE TOP. Dec. 1 st. at the beginning only of every row, until 53 sts. remain.
Work 12 rows straight, then cast off 16 sts. at the beginning of the next 2 rows. (21 sts.)
On the centre 21 sts. work 18 rows straight. Cast off.
Work a second sleeve in the same way.

THE BUTTONHOLE BAND. With No. 12 needles and N wool cast on 13 sts. Work 10 rows in single rib, then work a buttonhole thus :

1st buttonhole row : Rib 6, cast off 4 (1 st. on needle), rib 2.

2nd buttonhole row : Work in single rib, casting on 4 sts. over those cast off to complete the buttonhole.
Work 14 rows in single rib, then repeat the 2 buttonhole rows again.
Repeat the last 16 rows 6 times more, when there will be 8 buttonholes altogether.
Work straight for length required to complete the two fronts and back neck. Do not cast off until strip is sewn on, then the length can be adjusted as required.

TO MAKE UP THE CARDIGAN. Press all parts, except the ribbing, with a hot iron over a damp cloth on the wrong side. Join the shoulder seams, beginning at the armhole end and taking 1 st. from each side at a time. Sew the row ends of the last 18 rows at sleeve top to the cast-off edge of the 16 sts. cast off at each side, then set the sleeves into the armholes and press these seams. Join the sleeve and side seams in one line and press these seams. Sew the buttonhole band to the Fronts and back neck, beginning at the lower edge of the Right Front, and stretching a little round the back of the neck. Cast off the opposite end, when the sewing is nearly finished. Sew buttons to the Left Front to correspond with the buttonholes. Sew in shoulder pads.

Pinafore Frock and Jumper

MATERIALS
Jamieson's Spindrift 100% Shetland wool (105m per 25g ball)

Pinafore
9 (10, 11, 11, 12, 13) balls shade 1160 (Scotch Broom) – MC
3 (3, 4, 4, 4, 4) balls shade 1290 (Loganberry) – CC
1 pair 2.75mm (US #2) needles
1 pair 3mm (US #2–3) needles
Stitch markers
Crochet hook
4 buttons
4 press studs

Jumper
5 (6, 6, 7, 7, 8) balls shade 1290 (Loganberry) – MC
4 (5, 5, 6, 6, 7) balls shade 1160 (Scotch Broom) – CC

TENSION
30 sts & 36 rows using 3mm needles over stocking stitch
30 sts & 60 rows using 2.75mm needles over garter stitch

ABBREVIATIONS
See page 13 for standard abbreviations

JUMPER SIZING
Measurements given in centimetres followed by inches in parentheses

To Fit Bust	81 (32)	86 (34)	91 (36)	97 (38)	101 (40)	107 (42)
Finished Measurements *Dimensions given are unstretched*						
Actual Bust Size	62 (24½)	67 (26½)	72 (28½)	77 (30½)	82 (32½)	87 (34½)
Length to underarm	31½ (12½)	33½ (13)	33½ (13)	35 (14)	36½ (14½)	36½ (14½)
Armhole Depth	16½ (6½)	18 (7)	18 (7)	19 (7½)	20 (8)	20 (8)
Finished Length	48 (19)	51½ (20½)	51½ (20½)	54 (21½)	56½ (22½)	56½ (22½)
Shoulder to Shoulder	24 (9½)	25½ (10)	27½ (11)	29 (11½)	31 (12)	33 (13)
Sleeve Length	10 (4)	10 (4)	10 (4)	10 (4)	10 (4)	10 (4)

PINAFORE FROCK SIZING

To Fit Waist	61 (24)	66 (26)	71 (28)	76 (30)	81 (32)	86 (34)
Finished Measurements						
Length of Skirt	60 (23½)	60 (23½)	65 (25½)	65 (25½)	65 (25½)	70½ (28)
Waist	68 (27)	73 (28½)	78½ (31)	84 (33)	88 (34½)	93½ (37)

Pinafore frock shown in photographs is for fourth size 76 (30) and Jumper shown is for third size 91 (36)

PATTERN NOTES
Pinafore is knitted in two main separate pieces, for front and back, commencing at garter stitch edge at bottom of skirt. The bib is worked with the front and then an additional facing is knitted. The back skirt is knitted to the top of the waistband only. The Coordinating jumper is worked from side to side.

Pinafore

FRONT
Using 3mm needles and CC, cast on 226 (234, 242, 250, 256, 264) sts and knit 6 rows.
Change to MC and knit 4 rows.
Repeat last 10 rows once more, then first 6 rows again.
Commencing with a K row and using MC, work in stocking stitch, decreasing in next row as folls:
[K2tog, K40 (42, 43, 45, 46, 48)] twice, K2tog, PM, K54 (54, 58, 58, 60, 60) (centre panel), PM, K2tog, [K40 (42, 43, 45, 46, 48), K2tog] twice (220, 228, 236, 244, 250, 258 sts).
Work 11 rows straight.
Row 13: K2tog, K38 (40, 41, 43, 44, 46), K2tog, K39 (41, 42, 44, 45, 47), K2tog, K54 (54, 58, 58, 60, 60), K2tog, K39 (41, 42, 44, 45, 47), K2tog, K38 (40, 41, 43, 44, 46), K2tog (214, 222, 230, 238, 244, 252 sts).
Work 11 rows straight.
Row 25: [K2tog, K37 (39, 40, 42, 43, 45)] twice, K2tog, K54 (54, 58, 58, 60, 60), K2tog, [K37 (39, 40, 42, 43, 45), K2tog] twice (208, 216, 224, 232, 238, 246 sts).
Work 9 rows straight.

Row 35: K2tog, K35 (37, 38, 40, 41, 43), K2tog, K36 (38, 39, 41, 42, 44), K2tog, K54 (54, 58, 58, 60, 60), K2tog, K36 (38, 39, 41, 42, 44), K2tog, K35 (37, 38, 40, 41, 43), K2tog (202, 210, 218, 226, 232, 240 sts).
Continue as set, dec 6 sts on every 8th (8th, 10th, 10th, 10th, 12th) row and keeping centre panel straight until 142 (150, 158, 166, 172, 180) sts rem, ending with a WS row.

Shape Hips

Next row: K2tog, K40 (44, 46, 50, 52, 56), K2tog, K54 (54, 58, 58, 60, 60), K2tog, K40 (44, 46, 50, 52, 56), K2tog (138, 146, 154, 162, 168, 176 sts).
Work 7 rows straight.
Next row: K2tog, K38 (42, 44, 48, 50, 54), K2tog, K54 (54, 58, 58, 60, 60), K2tog, K38 (42, 44, 48, 50, 54), K2tog (134, 142, 150, 158, 164, 172 sts).
Cont as set, dec at each end of row and at each side of centre panel in every foll 8th row until there are 102 (110, 118, 126, 132, 140) sts.
Work straight until skirt measures 60 (60, 65, 65, 65, 70½) cm (23½, 23½, 25½, 25½, 25½, 28 in) from cast on edge.

WAISTBAND

Using 2.75mm needles, knit 26 rows in colours as for hem. †

BIB

Change to 3mm needles and using MC, cast off 26 sts at beg of next 2 rows (50, 58, 66, 74, 80, 88 sts), then commencing with a K row continue in stocking stitch on rem sts, inc 1 st at each end of 7th (3rd, 3rd, 7th, 7th, 7th) and every foll 4th (6th, 6th, 6th, 6th, 6th) row until 80 (88, 96, 104, 110, 118) sts. Work straight in stocking stitch until bib measures 24½ (26, 26, 27, 28½, 30) cm (9½, 10, 10, 10½, 11, 12 in), ending with a WS row. Cast off.

BIB FACING

Using 3mm needles and CC, cast on 50 (58, 66, 74, 80, 88) sts. Commencing with a K row, work in stocking stitch, inc 1 st at each end of 7th (3rd, 3rd, 7th, 7th, 7th) and every foll 4th (6th, 6th, 6th, 6th, 6th) row until 80 (88, 96, 104, 110, 118) sts. Work straight in stocking stitch until bib measures 24½ (26, 26, 27, 28½, 30) cm (9½, 10, 10, 10½, 11, 12 in), ending with a WS row. Cast off.

SKIRT BACK

Work as for pinafore front to †.
Cast off all sts.

STRAPS (Make two)

Using 3mm needles and CC, cast on 30 sts. Commencing with a K row work in stocking stitch for 31½ (33, 34, 35½, 37, 38) cm (12½, 13, 13½, 14, 14½, 15 in), ending with a RS row. Leave sts on waste yarn.

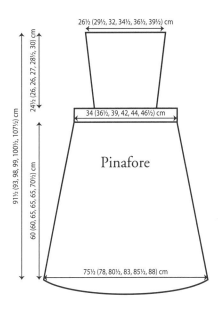

26½ (29½, 32, 34½, 36½, 39½) cm

24½ (26, 26, 27, 28½, 30) cm

34 (36½, 39, 42, 44, 46½) cm

91½ (93, 98, 99, 100½, 107½) cm

60 (60, 65, 65, 65, 70½) cm

Pinafore

75½ (78, 80½, 83, 85½, 88) cm

Jumper

BACK

(Worked sideways, commences at left side back edge)

Work throughout in garter stitch (every row knit) with 2 rows in CC followed by 2 rows in MC.

Please note: Increases and decreases worked at start of WS rows will shape the hem end of the piece, and those worked at start of RS rows will shape the armhole/neck end.

Using 3mm needles and CC, cast on 14 (16, 12, 13, 14, 10) sts. Working in patt as set, cast on 4 sts at beg of foll 6 (6, 7, 7, 7, 8) WS rows (38, 40, 40, 41, 42, 42 sts).

Next row (RS): Kfb, K to end.

Next row (WS): Cast on 4 sts, K to end.

Repeat last 2 rows 4 (5, 5, 6, 7, 7) more times (63, 70, 70, 76, 82, 82 sts).

Shape Armhole and Waist

Next row (RS): Cast on 44 (48, 48, 50, 52, 52) sts for armhole, K to end (107, 118, 118, 126, 134, 134 sts).

Next row (WS): Cast on 36 sts for waist, K to end (143, 154, 154, 162, 170, 170 sts).

Work 11 (13, 11, 15, 13, 17) rows without shaping.

Next row (WS): Patt to last st, Kfb (144, 155, 155, 163, 171, 171 sts).

Work 11 (11, 13, 13, 15, 15) rows without shaping.

Next row (WS): Patt to last st, Kfb (145, 156, 156, 164, 172, 172 sts).

Work last 12 (12, 14, 14, 16, 16) rows twice more (147, 158, 158, 166, 174, 174 sts) ††

Work 48 (50, 52, 56, 60, 64) rows without shaping for back neck.

††† **Next row** (RS): K2tog, patt to end (146, 157, 157, 165, 173, 173 sts)

Work 11 (11, 13, 13, 15, 15) rows without shaping.

Work these 12 (12, 14, 14, 16, 16) rows twice more (144, 155, 155, 163, 171, 171 sts).

Next row (RS): K2tog, patt to end (143, 154, 154, 162, 170, 170 sts).

Work 11 (13, 11, 15, 13, 17) rows without shaping.

Next row (RS): Cast off 36 sts for waist, K to end (107, 118, 118, 126, 134, 134 sts).

Next row (WS): Cast off 44 (48, 48, 50, 52, 52) sts for armhole, K to end (63, 70, 70, 76, 82, 82 sts).

Next row (RS): K2tog, K to end.

Next row (WS): Cast off 4 sts, K to end.

Work these 2 rows 4 (5, 5, 6, 7, 7) more times (38, 40, 40, 41, 42, 42 sts).

Cast off 4 sts at start of 6 (6, 7, 7, 7, 8) foll WS rows (14, 16, 12, 13, 14, 10 sts). Cast off rem sts.

FRONT

Work as for back to ††

Shape V Neck

Next row (RS): Cast off 10 sts, K to end (137, 148, 148, 156, 164, 164 sts)

Next row: K.

Cast off 3 sts at beg of next and foll 5 (5, 5, 5, 6, 6) alt rows (119, 130, 130, 138, 143, 143 sts).

Next row (WS): K.

K2tog at neck edge on every row 12 (13, 14, 16, 16, 18) times (107, 117, 116, 122, 127, 125 sts).

Inc 1 st at neck edge on every foll row 12 (13, 14, 16, 16, 18) times (119, 130, 130, 138, 143, 143 sts).

Next row (RS): Cast on 3 sts, K to end.

Cast on 3 sts at start of 5 (5, 5, 5, 6, 6) foll RS rows (137, 148, 148, 156, 164, 164 sts). Patt one row. Cast on 10 sts at neck edge of next row (147, 158, 158, 166, 174, 174 sts).

Next row (WS): K to end.

Complete front as for back from †††

SLEEVES

Using 3mm needles, cast on 30 sts, beg at side seam.

Work 4 (6, 8, 10, 12, 14) rows straight in garter stitch stripe patt, then inc 1 st on every row at end of RS and beg of WS rows, until there are 74 (78, 78, 80, 82, 82) sts.

Work 17 (19, 21, 23, 25, 27) rows without shaping. Dec 1 st at same edge of every row until 30 sts. Work 4 (6, 8, 10, 12, 14) rows without shaping. Cast off.

Using 2.75mm needles, MC and with WS facing, pick up and knit 68 (76, 80, 86, 92, 96) sts along bottom edge of sleeve.

Next row (RS): P. Change to 3mm needles.

Continue in reverse stocking stitch until work measures 4cm (1½in).

Change to garter st and knit 2 rows CC, 2 rows MC, 1 row CC, then cast off loosely using CC.

COLLAR

Using MC cast on 102 (106, 108, 114, 122, 128) sts.

Row 1: K98 (102, 104, 110, 118, 124), w&t.

Row 2: P94 (98, 100, 106, 114, 120), w&t.

Row 3: K90 (94, 96, 102, 110, 116), w&t.

Row 4: P86 (90, 92, 98, 106, 112), w&t.

Cont to work 4 sts fewer on every row for 12 more rows.

Row 17: Kfb, K32 (36, 38, 44, 52, 58), Kfb, w&t.

Row 18: P32 (36, 38, 44, 52, 58), w&t.

Row 19: K28 (32, 34, 40, 48, 54), w&t.

Row 20: P24 (28, 30, 36, 44, 50), w&t.

Cont to work 4 sts fewer on every row for 2 (4, 6, 6, 8, 8) more rows.

Row 27: K to end, working wraps with sts as necessary.

Row 28: P to end, working wraps with sts as necessary.

Row 29: Slip first 8 sts to RH needle, then change to CC and knit to last 8 sts (no need to w&t when working in garter st).

Row 30: Using CC, knit to last 8 sts, slip rem sts to RH needle without working them.

Using MC, knit 3 full rows.

Cast off all sts.

MAKING UP

Press skirt pieces on WS under a damp cloth. Block collar and cuffs of jumper.

Pinafore

Join right side seam. Place skirt on a flat surface RS up. Place cast on edges of straps onto cast off edge of bib with RS against RS of bib and tack in place. Place bib facing over bib and straps RS down, matching all seams. Sew around both sides and top edge through all layers. Turn work to RS. Ease bib facing into position at waistband, pin and then slip stitch into place. Adjust straps to fit and cast off sts on waste yarn. With RS together sew up left side seam leaving waistband and the top 7cm (3in) of seam unstitched. Sew press studs in place, 2 on waistband and a further 2 press studs on open seam. Using crochet hook and MC work a chain button loop at each corner of cast off edge of each strap (see 'Fit and Finish' chapter). Cross straps over and mark button position on back waistband. Sew buttons in place and button straps in place. Darn in all ends.

Jumper

Join shoulder seams. Sew side and sleeve seams. Fold back cuff, over RS of sleeve, concealing seam. Catch stitch in place if necessary. Insert sleeves, matching centre of sleeve head and shoulder seam and matching side seams. Sew collar into place using a flat slip stitch along cast on edge of collar (see 'Fit and Finish' chapter). Match centre back of collar to centre back neck and ensure collar ends meet at centre front. Darn in all ends.

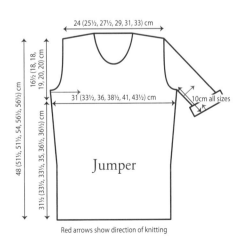

Red arrows show direction of knitting

MATERIALS

MATERIALS: *For pinafore frock:* 7 ozs. Patons Beehive Fingering, 2-ply ("Patonised" shrink-resist finish) in main shade and 1 oz. in contrast. *For jumper:* 3 ozs. each of main and contrast shades. A pair No. 11 and No. 12 "Beehive" needles. Braid or webbing and two buttons.

MEASUREMENTS: *Pinafore:* From waist to hem, 25 inches; from waist to top of bib, 9 inches. *Jumper:* Length from top of shoulders, 19 inches; to fit 32-34-inch bust; sleeve seam, 4½ inches. TENSION: 8 stitches to an inch.

PINAFORE

With No. 11 needles and contrast wool, cast on 250 sts. and knit 6 rows. Change to main shade and knit 4 rows. Repeat last 10 rows once more, then first 6 rows again.

Change to stocking-stitch, decreasing in next row, thus:—(k. 2 tog., k. 45) twice, k. 2 tog., k. 58 (centre panel), k. 2 tog., (k. 45, k. 2 tog.) twice (244 sts.).

Work 11 rows straight.
13TH ROW: k. 2 tog., k. 43, k. 2 tog., k. 44, k. 2 tog., k. 58, k. 2 tog., k. 44, k. 2 tog., k. 43, k. 2 tog. (238 sts.). Work 11 rows straight. 25TH ROW: (k. 2 tog., k. 42) twice, k. 2 tog., k. 58, k. 2 tog., (k. 42, k. 2 tog.) twice (232 sts.). Work 9 rows straight.
35TH ROW: k. 2 tog., k. 40, k. 2 tog., k. 41, k. 2 tog., k. 58, k. 2 tog., k. 41, k. 2 tog., k. 40, k. 2 tog. Work 9 rows straight. Continue thus, decreasing 6 sts. every 10 rows, keeping centre panel straight until 166 sts. remain.

Shape for hips:—k. 2 tog., k. 50, k. 2 tog., k. 58, k. 2 tog., k. 50, k. 2 tog. Work 7 rows straight. NEXT ROW: k. 2 tog., k. 48, k. 2 tog., k. 58, k. 2 tog., k. 48, k. 2 tog. Continue thus, decreasing at each end of needle and at each side of centre panel in every following 8th row until there are 126 sts.

Work straight until skirt is required length to waist. *Waist-band:* With No. 12 needles, work 26 rows as for hem. Start bib. With No. 11 needles, cast off 26 at beginning of next 2 rows, then continue in stocking-stitch on centre 74, increasing at side edge in 7th and every following 6th row until there are 104 sts. Cast off. Cast on 74 sts. and work another piece for bib facing, exactly the same.

For back of skirt, work as for front but cast off when waist-band is finished.

STRAPS

With main shade and No. 11 needles, cast on 30 sts. and work in stocking-stitch two lengths to reach from top of bib over to centre back. Cast off.

JUMPER

BACK

N.B.—Worked sideways in garter-stitch, 2 rows main shade, 2 rows contrast, on No. 11 needles, throughout.

Start at left-hand back edge by casting on 12 sts., main shade. Working in pattern, cast on 4 at beginning of next 7 alternate rows. Continue to increase in this way at same edge but increase once at other end of needle on next 6 alternate rows (154 sts.).

At beginning of next row, cast on 48 to bring you to top of shoulder. Work back to other edge and cast on 36 to bring you to bottom edge of jumper (154 sts.).

* Work 12 rows straight, increasing in last stitch at shoulder edge; repeat from * 3 times more, working 14 rows straight instead of 12. Now work 52 rows straight for back of neck (158 sts.).

Work second side to correspond with first, decreasing instead of increasing. You will find the stripes a great help to count by.

FRONT

Work to end of first shoulder as for back, then shape for V neck. Cast off 10, work to end and back. Cast off 3 at beginning of next 6 alternate rows (*i.e.*, at neck edge), then k. 2 tog. at neck edge on every row 14 times (116 sts.).

Work other half of front to correspond, decreasing instead of increasing, and *vice versa*.

SLEEVES

Cast on 30 sts. at side seam. Shapings come at left side. Work 8 rows straight, then increase 1 st. every row at left edge, until there are 78 sts. Work 21 rows straight, then work second half to correspond, decreasing instead of increasing.

With wrong side of work facing, pick up and knit 80 sts. round bottom edge with main shade. Purl back, then continue in stocking-stitch for 1½ inches. Change to garter-stitch and knit 2 rows main shade, 2 rows contrast, 1 row main shade, and cast off, *very loosely*, with double wool.

COLLAR

With main shade, cast on 168 sts. and, working in stocking-stitch, leave last 4 sts. on each row unworked every row. When there are 8 groups of 4 unworked at each end of needle, knit twice into every 20th st. to increase for collar turnover.

Continue to leave 4 more sts. unworked every row until there are 14 groups unworked each end, then on next row increase in every 10th st. Continue as before until there are 18 unworked groups at each end.

Now knit 2 rows over all sts., then with contrast wool, knit 2 rows, but start and finish 8 sts. in from either end. Knit 3 rows main shade over all sts. and cast off.

TO MAKE UP

Press all stocking-stitch parts carefully on wrong side under a damp cloth, but leave garter-stitch unpressed.

Pinafore: Join side seams, leaving opening at left side. Join two bib pieces together neatly all round, purl sides facing inwards. Fit petersham to waistband and ease on bib to fit. Finish side opening with zip- or press-studs.

Stitch shoulder-straps over braid or webbing, so that seam comes down centre back on strap and will not show. Strengthen top of bib and sides with braid and sew on straps at each top corner. Make a strong loop at end of each strap and cross at back to fit comfortably, sewing on buttons in strategic places at back of waist.

Jumper: Join side, shoulder, and sleeve seams. Turn back cuffs and catch in place. Insert sleeves. Sew on collar.

Pinafore Frock and Jumper on front cover

Stitchcraft April 1945

Box Coat

MATERIALS
Knitshop Tundra 100% wool (60m per 100g skein)
17 (20, 22, 25, 28) skeins shade 026
1 pair 7mm (US #10.5) needles
1 button
1 large press stud

TENSION
13 sts and 19 rows = 10cm (4in) using 7mm needles over 4 row pattern (stitch count measured across row 4).

ABBREVIATIONS
See page 13 for standard abbreviations

SIZING
Measurements given in centimetres followed by inches in parentheses

To Fit	71–76 (28–30)	81–86 (32–34)	92–97 (36–38)	102–107 (40–42)	112–117 (44–46)
Finished Measurements					
Actual Bust Size	100 (39½)	111 (43½)	120 (47½)	129 (51)	138 (54½)
Length to underarm	43½ (17)	46 (18)	48 (19)	50 (19½)	52 (20½)
Armhole Depth	19 (7½)	19 (7½)	21½ (8½)	24 (9½)	26½ (10½)
Finished Length	62½ (24½)	65 (25½)	69½ (27½)	74 (29)	78½ (81)
Shoulder to Shoulder	37 (14½)	41½ (16¼)	46 (18)	51 (20)	55½ (22)

Garment shown in photographs is for second size 81–86 (32–34)

PATTERN NOTES
This boxy coat is worked with an interesting yoke panel on the upper back of the garment, which is used to stabilise the garment and prevent stretch. The side stitches of the yoke are brought forward over the shoulder and also attached to the straight cast off edges of the front neck to further reinforce the coat. The sleeves of the coat are constructed with a box sleeve head which is explained further in the 'Fit and Finish' chapter.

BACK
Using 7mm needles, cast on 66 (72, 78, 84, 90) sts.
Row 1 (RS): K1, * knit next st, wrapping wool around needle twice, K2, repeat from * to last 2 sts, knit next st, wrapping wool around needle twice, K1.
Row 2: P1, * Sl1 purlwise, dropping the extra loop, P2, repeat from * to last 2 sts, Sl1 purlwise, dropping the extra loop, P1.
Row 3: K1, * Sl1 purlwise, K2, repeat from * to last 2 sts, Sl1, K1.
Row 4: K1, * P1, K2, repeat from * to last 2 sts, P1, K1.
Repeat these 4 rows (pulling down work to adjust long sts) until work measures 43½ (46, 48, 50, 52) cm (17, 18, 19, 19½, 20½ in) from cast on, ending on row 3.

Shape Armholes
Cast off 5 sts at the beginning of the next 2 rows (56, 62, 68, 74, 80 sts) then dec 1 st each end of 4 foll alt rows (48, 54, 60, 66, 72 sts).
Cont without further shaping until armholes measure 13 (13, 15, 18, 20) cm (5, 5, 6, 7, 8 in), ending with row 3.

Next row (WS): Patt 9 (9, 12, 15, 18) sts, place these sts onto a holder, cast off the next 30 (36, 36, 36, 36) sts, patt rem 9 (9, 12, 15, 18) sts.
Continue in patt on these 9 (9, 12, 15, 18) sts only until armhole measures 19 (19, 21½, 24, 26½) cm (7½, 7½, 8½, 9½, 10½ in), ending with row 3. Cast off.
With RS facing, rejoin 9 (9, 12, 15, 18) sts sts on holder and work to match first side.

LEFT FRONT
Using 7mm needles, cast on 42 (45, 48, 51, 54) sts. Work as for back until work measures 43½ (46, 48, 50, 52) cm (17, 18, 19, 19½, 20½ in), ending on row 4.

Shape Armhole
Next row (RS): Cast off 5 sts, patt to end (37, 40, 43, 46, 49 sts).
Dec 1 st at armhole edge on 4 foll alt rows (33, 36, 39, 42, 45 sts).
Continue without further shaping until armhole measures 13 (13, 15, 18, 20) cm (5, 5, 6, 7, 8 in), ending on row 3.

Shape Neck

Next row (WS): Cast off 24 (27, 27, 27, 27) sts, patt 9 (9, 12, 15, 18).

Continue without further shaping on rem sts until armhole measures 19 (19, 21½, 24, 26½) cm (7½, 7½, 8½, 9½, 10½ in), ending with row 3. Cast off.

RIGHT FRONT

Using 7mm needles, cast on 42 (45, 48, 51, 54) sts. Work as for back until work measures 43½ (46, 48, 50, 52) cm (17, 18, 19, 19½, 20½ in), ending on row 3.

Shape Armhole

Next row (WS): Cast off 5 sts, patt to end (37, 40, 43, 46, 49 sts).

Dec 1 st at armhole edge on 3rd row and 3 foll alt rows (33, 36, 39, 42, 45 sts).

Continue without further shaping until armhole measures 10 (10, 13, 15, 18) cm (4, 4, 5, 6, 7 in), ending on row 4.

Next row (RS buttonhole): Patt 3 sts, cast off 3 sts, patt to end.
Next row: Patt to cast off sts, cast on 3 sts, patt 3 sts.

Work without further shaping until right front measures same as left to commencement of neck shaping ending on row 4.

Shape Neck

Next row (RS): Cast off 24 (27, 27, 27, 27) sts, patt 9 (9, 12, 15, 18).

Continue without further shaping on rem sts until armhole measures 19 (19, 21½, 24, 26½) cm 7½ (7½, 8½, 9½, 10½ in), ending with row 4. Cast off.

SLEEVES

Using 7mm needles, cast on 39 (42, 45, 48, 51) sts.
Work in patt as for back, inc 1 st at each end of 6 foll 14th rows (51, 54, 57, 60, 63 sts).

Cont in patt without further shaping, until sleeve measures 46 (48, 48, 48, 49½) cm (18, 19, 19, 19, 19½ in) from cast on edge.

Shape Sleeve Head

Cast off 5 sts at the beginning of each of the next 2 rows (41, 44, 47, 50 53 sts), then dec 1 st at each end of every foll alt row twice (37, 40, 43, 46, 49 sts) then dec 1 st each end of every 4th row, 5 times (27, 30, 33, 36, 39 sts).

Continue in patt without further shaping until work measures 14 (14, 16½, 18, 21½) cm (4½, 5½, 6½, 7, 8½ in) from first decrease.

Cast off 7 (8, 10, 11, 13) sts at beg of each of the next 2 rows (13, 14, 13, 14, 13 sts). Work on these rem sts for 8 rows. Cast off.

neck stretching to fit, then sew cast off sts at each end of yoke over cast off neck sts of front. Attach pockets, positioning bottom edge of pocket to cast on edge of coat and lining up pattern whilst positioning pocket as close to side edge as pattern matching will allow. Sew around all sides. Sew on button to left front. Attach press stud to underside of right front. Darn in all ends.

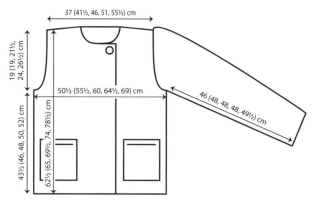

POCKETS
Using 7mm needles, cast on 24 sts.
Work in patt as for back for 14cm (5½in), ending on row 4.
Next row: Patt 6 sts, cast off 12, patt 6 sts.
Next row: Patt 6 sts, cast on 12, patt 6 sts.
Work 4 rows without shaping. Cast off.

BACK YOKE
Using 7mm needles, cast on 30 (36, 36, 36, 36) sts.
Work in patt as for back for 9cm (3½in), ending on row 3.
Next row: Patt 7 (9, 9, 9, 9, 9) sts place these onto a st holder, cast off 16 (18, 18, 18, 18) sts, patt 7 (9, 9, 9, 9, 9) sts, turn.
Continue working in patt on these 7 (9, 9, 9, 9, 9) sts only, until work measures 13 (13, 15½, 18, 20½) cm, (5, 5, 6, 7, 8 in) ending on row 3. Cast off.
With RS facing, rejoin 7 (9, 9, 9, 9, 9) sts on holder and work to match first side. Cast off.

MAKING UP
Join shoulder seams. Make box sleeve head by sewing 7 (8, 10, 11, 13) cast off sts at top of sleeve head to 8 straight rows worked (see 'Fit and Finish' chapter). Sew up side and sleeve seams. Inset sleeves, matching centre of box head to shoulder seam and matching side seams. Sew cast on sts of back yoke over cast off back neck sts, matching pattern. Sew sides of yoke across side back neck and side front

Box Coat

For quick knitting. You'll like this loose fitting box coat for so many occasions. Use either Monarch Jumbo or Monarch Speedway as desired. Two patch pockets with unusual opening. Interesting pattern carried throughout.

Size 16

MEASUREMENTS OF FINISHED GARMENT WHEN BLOCKED: All around at underarm, 40 inches. Length from shoulder to lower edge, 25½ inches. Length of sleeve at underarm seam, 18 inches.

TENSION OF STITCH—4 sts. = 1 inch. 23 rows = 4 inches.

Materials Used

MONARCH JUMBO	or	MONARCH SPEEDWAY
10 Balls Valley Green		10 Skeins River Blue
1 Pair No. 4 Needles		1 Large Crochet Hook

BACK—Starting at lower edge, cast on 72 sts.
1ST ROW (Right Side)—K1, * knit next st., wrapping wool around needle twice (instead of once), K2, repeat from *, ending K1.
2ND ROW—P1, * S1, as if to purl, dropping the extra loop, P2, repeat from *, ending P1.
3RD ROW—K1, * slip 1, as if to purl, K2, repeat from *, ending S1, K1.
4TH ROW—K1, * P1, K2, repeat from *, ending P1, K1.
Repeat these 4 rows (pulling down work to adjust long sts.) until work measures 18 inches from beginning, ending with 3rd pattern row.
SHAPE ARMHOLES by casting off 5 sts. at the beginning of each of the next 2 rows. Decrease 1 st. each end of needle every 2nd row, 4 times (54 sts. on needle).
Continue evenly until armhole measures 4½ inches from first decreasing, ending with 3rd pattern row.
NEXT ROW (Wrong Side)—Pattern 9 sts., place these sts. on to a stitch holder, cast off the next 36 sts., pattern to end.
Continue working on these 9 sts. until armhole measures 7½ inches from first decreasing, ending with 3rd pattern row. Cast off.
Take 9 sts. from stitch holder, join at neck edge, work on these 9 sts. in same manner as other side. Cast off.

LEFT FRONT—Starting at lower edge, cast on 45 sts.
Work in pattern same as back, until work measures 18 inches from beginning, ending with 4th pattern row.
SHAPE ARMHOLE:
NEXT ROW (Right Side)—Cast off 5 sts., pattern to end.
Decrease 1 st. (armhole edge) every 2nd row, 4 times (36 sts. on needle).
Continue evenly until armhole measures 5 inches from first decreasing, ending with 3rd pattern row.
SHAPE NECK:
NEXT ROW (Wrong Side)—Cast off 27 sts., pattern to end.
Continue working on these 9 sts. until armhole measures 7½ inches from first decreasing, ending with 3rd pattern row. Cast off.

RIGHT FRONT—Starting at lower edge, cast on 45 sts.
Work to correspond with left front, reversing all shapings, until armhole measures 3¾ inches from first decreasing, ending with 4th pattern row.
NEXT ROW (Front Edge)—Pattern 3 sts., cast off 3 sts., pattern to end.
NEXT ROW—Pattern to "cast-off" sts., cast on 3 sts., pattern 3 sts.
Work 5 rows even.
NEXT ROW—Pattern 9 sts., cast off 27 sts., join at neck edge, pattern on these 9 sts. until armhole measures 7½ inches from first decreasing. Cast off.

SLEEVES—Starting at cuff, cast on 42 sts.
Work in pattern, same as back, increasing 1 st. each end of needle every 16th row, 6 times (54 sts. on needle).
Continue evenly until sleeve measures 18 inches from beginning.
Cast off 5 sts. at the beginning of each of the next 2 rows.
Decrease 1 st. each end of needle every 2nd row, twice.
Decrease 1 st. each end of needle every 4th row, 5 times (30 sts. on needle).
Continue evenly until work measures 5½ inches from first decreasing.
Cast off 8 sts. at the beginning of each of the next 2 rows.
Work on remaining 14 sts. for 10 rows. Cast off.

COLLAR—Starting at lower edge, cast on 36 sts.
Work in pattern same as back for 3 inches, ending with 3rd pattern row.
NEXT ROW—Pattern 9 sts., place these sts. on to a stitch-holder, cast off 18 sts., pattern 9 sts., turn.
Continue in pattern on these 9 sts. until work measures 5½ inches from beginning, ending with 3rd pattern row. Cast off.
Take 9 sts. from stitch-holder, join at neck edge, work on these 9 sts. to correspond with other side. Cast off.

POCKETS—Starting at lower edge, cast on 24 sts. Work in pattern same as back for 5½ inches, ending with 4th pattern row.
NEXT ROW—Pattern 6 sts., cast off 12 sts., pattern 6 sts.
NEXT ROW—Pattern 6 sts., cast on 12 sts., pattern 6 sts.
Work 6 rows even. Cast off.

TO FINISH—Sew seams. Sew "cast-off" sts. at top of sleeves to edges of insert for 1½ inches.
Join wool at neck edge of left side of collar, working from right side, work 1 row s.c. around collar, working 2 s.c. in each corner st. Sew "cast-on" sts. of collar to "cast-off" sts. on back, matching patterns and leaving s.c. edge loose. Sew sides to collar over garment, holding in 13 "cast-off" sts. of each front to 9 "cast-off" sts. of collar.
Work 1 row s.c. around entire coat, keeping edges flat, working 2 s.c. in each corner. Sew pockets on as illustrated, sewing around the 4 edges, matching patterns. Bind buttonhole. Sew on button, matching buttonhole.

A Warm Jacket with an unusual bubble-stitch yoke

MATERIALS
Jamieson's Spindrift 100% Shetland wool (105m per 25g ball)
12 (14, 16, 18, 20, 22) balls shade 462 (Ginger)
1 pair 2.75mm (US #2) needles
1 pair 3mm (US #2–3) needles
1 set 3.25mm (US #3) DPNs or 1 3.25mm (US #3) circular needle
Stitch holders
12 buttons

TENSION
37 sts & 36 rows = 10cm (4in) using 3mm needles over K1, P1, rib

Standard Yarn Tension
30 sts & 32 rows = 10cm (4in) using 3.25mm needles over stocking stitch

ABBREVIATIONS
See page 13 for standard abbreviations

SIZING
Measurements given in centimetres followed by inches in parentheses

To Fit	76–81 (30–32)	86–92 (34–36)	97–102 (38–40)	107–112 (42–44)	117–122 (46–48)	127–132 (50–52)
Finished Measurements						
Actual Bust Size	81 (32)	92 (36)	103 (40½)	113½ (44½)	124½ (49)	135 (53)
Length to underarm	33 (13)	35½ (14)	38 (15)	40½ (16)	43 (17)	45½ (18)
Armhole Depth	24 (9½)	26 (10)	27 (10½)	28 (11)	28½ (11¼)	30 (12)
Finished Length	57 (22½)	61½ (24)	65 (25½)	68½ (27)	71½ (28)	75½ (30)
Sleeve Length	46 (18)	47 (18½)	47 (18½)	48 (19)	48 (19)	48 (19)

Garment shown in photographs is for first size 76–81 (30–32)

BACK
Using 2.75mm needles cast on 130 (150, 170, 190, 210, 230) sts and work in rib as folls:

Next row (RS): * K1, P1, rep from * to end.

Rep this row until work measures 10cm (4in) ending with a WS row.

Change to 3mm needles, and continuing in rib, inc 1 st at each end of next and every foll 8th row until 150 (170, 190, 210, 230, 250) sts.

Work straight until side edge measures 33 (35½, 38, 40½ 43, 45½) cm (13, 14, 15, 16, 17, 18 in) ending with a WS row.

Shape Armholes
Cast off 10 (14, 10, 11, 14, 16) sts at beg of next 2 (2, 4, 4, 4, 4) rows (130, 142, 150, 166, 174, 186 sts) then K2tog at each end of every foll alt row until 120 (128, 136, 152, 160, 168) sts rem.

Next row (RS): Rib 56 (60, 64, 72, 76, 80), turn, rib back, leaving remaining 64 (68, 72, 80, 84, 88) sts unworked and on a stitch holder.

Next row: Rib 52 (56, 60, 68, 72, 76), turn, rib to end.

Next row: Rib 48 (52, 56, 64, 68, 72), turn, rib to end.

Continue working 4 sts less every alternate row until only 4 sts are left unworked. Leave all 56 (60, 64, 72, 76, 80) sts on a stitch holder.

With WS facing, rejoin yarn to opposite armhole edge, rib 56 (60, 64, 72, 76, 80), turn, leaving central 8 sts unworked and on a holder. Then continue working short rows in same way as first side. Leave all 120 (128, 136, 152, 160, 168) back sts on spare needle or stitch holder (56, 60, 64, 72, 76, 80 sts from each side plus 8 sts in the centre).

LEFT FRONT
Using 2.75mm needles, cast on 74 (84, 94, 104, 114, 124) sts, and work in rib as for back until work measures 10cm (4in) ending with a WS row. Change to 3mm needles, and continuing in rib, inc 1 st at side edge on next and every following 8th row until 84 (94, 104, 114, 124, 134) sts. Work without further shaping until side edge measures 33 (35½, 38, 40½ 43, 45½) cm (13, 14, 15, 16, 17, 18 in) ending with a WS row.

Shape Armhole
Cast off 10 (14, 10, 11, 14, 16) sts at beg of next and 0 (0, 1, 1, 1, 1) foll alt row (74, 80, 84, 92, 96, 102 sts).

Then K2tog on every foll alt row at side edge until 64 (68, 72, 80, 84, 88) sts rem, ending with a WS row.

Next row (RS): Rib 56 (60, 64, 72, 76, 80), turn, rib back, leaving remainder on spare needle.

Next row: Rib 52 (56, 60, 68, 72, 76), turn, rib to end.

Next row: Rib 48 (52, 56, 64, 68, 72), turn, rib to end.

Continue working 4 sts less every alternate row until only 4 sts are left unworked. Leave all 64 (68, 72, 80, 84, 88) sts on a stitch holder.

RIGHT FRONT

Using 2.75mm needles, cast on 74 (84, 94, 104, 114, 124) sts, and work 4 (4, 4, 4, 8, 4) rows in K1, P1 rib as for back.

Make Buttonhole

Next row (RS): Rib 3, cast off foll 3 sts, patt to end.

Next row: Patt to cast off sts, turn, cast on 3 sts, turn, patt to end.

Continue working in rib until work measures 10cm (4in) and at same time as all foll instructions work buttonholes on every 15th (17th, 17th, 19th, 19th, 21st) & (16th, 18th, 18th, 20th, 20th, 22nd) rows until a further 8 buttonholes worked up to commencement of the yoke.

Change to 3mm needles, working in rib and continuing to place buttonholes as indicated, inc 1 st at side edge on next and every following 8th row until 84 (94, 104, 114, 124, 134) sts.

Work without further shaping until side edge measures 33 (35½, 38, 40½ 43, 45½) cm (13, 14, 15, 16, 17, 18 in) ending with a RS row.

Shape Armhole

Cast off 10 (14, 10, 11, 14, 16) sts at beg of next and 0 (0, 1, 1, 1, 1) foll alt row (74, 80, 84, 92, 96, 102 sts).

Then K2tog on every foll alt row at side edge until 64 (68, 72, 80, 84, 88) sts rem ending with a RS row.

Next row (WS): Rib 56 (60, 64, 72, 76, 80), turn, rib back, leaving rem 8 sts on spare needle.

Next row: Rib 52 (56, 60, 68, 72, 76), turn, rib to end.

Next row: Rib 48 (52, 56, 64, 68, 72), turn, rib to end.

Continue working 4 sts less every alternate row until only 4 sts are left unworked. Leave all 64 (68, 72, 80, 84, 88) sts on a stitch holder.

SLEEVES

Using 2.75mm needles, cast on 64 (70, 74, 78, 80, 86) sts and work 7½cm (3in) in K1, P1 rib as for back.

Change to 3mm needles, and continuing in rib, inc 1 st at each end of 5th and every 6th row until 104 (110, 114, 118, 120, 126) sts.

Work without further shaping until sleeve measures 46 (47, 47, 48, 48, 48) cm (18, 18½, 18½, 19, 19, 19 in).

Shape Sleeve Head

Cast off 7 sts at beg of next two rows (90, 96, 100, 104, 106, 112 sts) then K2tog at each end of every foll alt row until 42 sts rem. Leave sts on a spare needle or a stitch holder.

YOKE

Using 3.25mm circular or DPNs, and with RS of work facing pick up stitches for yoke commencing at front edge of right front as folls:

Next row (RS): Rib 10 (9, 11, 12, 11, 10), P54 (59, 61, 68, 73, 78), P across 42 sts of one sleeve, then across 120 (128, 136, 152, 160, 168) sts of back, 42 sts of second sleeve, 54 (59, 61, 68, 73, 78) sts from left front, then rib last 10 (9, 11, 12, 11, 10) sts (332, 348, 364, 396, 412, 428 sts).

Row 2: Rib 10 (9, 11, 12, 11, 10), K312 (330, 342, 372, 390, 408), rib 10 (9, 11, 12, 11, 10).

Row 3: Rib 10 (9, 11, 12, 11, 10), P312 (330, 342, 372, 390, 408), rib 10 (9, 11, 12, 11, 10).

Row 4: As row 3.

Row 5: Rib 10 (9, 11, 12, 11, 10), * (P1, K1) into next st, (K1, P1) into next st, P4, rep from * to last 10 (9, 11, 12, 11, 10) sts, rib to end.

Row 6: Rib 10 (9, 11, 12, 11, 10), * K4, P4, rep from * to last 10 (9, 11, 12, 11, 10) sts, rib to end.

Row 7: Rib 10 (9, 11, 12, 11, 10), * (P1, K1) into next st, K2, (K1, P1) into next st, P4, rep from * to last 10 (9, 11, 12, 11, 10) sts, rib to end.

Row 8: Rib 10 (9, 11, 12, 11, 10), * K4, P6, rep from * to last 10 (9, 11, 12, 11, 10) sts, rib to end.

Row 9: Rib 10 (9, 11, 12, 11, 10), * (P1, K1) into next st, K4, (K1, P1) into next st, P4, rep from * to last 10 (9, 11, 12, 11, 10) sts, rib to end.

Row 10: Rib 10 (9, 11, 12, 11, 10), * K4, P8, rep from * to last 10 (9, 11, 12, 11, 10) sts, rib to end.

Row 11: Rib 10 (9, 11, 12, 11, 10), * Sl1, K1, psso, K4, K2tog, P4, rep from * to last 10 (9, 11, 12, 11, 10) sts, rib to end.

Row 12: As row 8.

Row 13: Rib 10 (9, 11, 12, 11, 10), * Sl1, K1, psso, K2, K2tog, P4, rep from * to last 10 (9, 11, 12, 11, 10) sts, rib to end.

Row 14: As row 6.

Row 15: Rib 3, cast off 3 for buttonhole, rib 4 (3, 5, 6, 5, 4), * Sl1, K1, psso, K2tog, P4, rep from * to last 10 (9, 11, 12, 11, 10) sts, rib to end (332, 348, 364, 396, 412, 428 sts).

Row 16: Rib 10 (9, 11, 12, 11, 10), * K4, P2, rep from * to last 10 (9, 11, 12, 11, 10) sts, rib 4 (3, 5, 6, 5, 4), cast on 3 sts over those cast off, rib to end.

Row 17: Rib 10 (9, 11, 12, 11, 10), * P2tog, P2, rep from * to last 10 (11, 13, 12, 13, 10) sts, P0 (2, 2, 0, 2, 0), rib to end (254, 266, 279, 303, 315, 326 sts).

Row 18: Rib 10 (9, 11, 12, 11, 10), K1 (3, 3, 1, 3, 1), * K1, K2tog, rep from * to last 12 (11, 13, 14, 13, 12) sts, K2tog, rib to end (176, 184, 194, 210, 218, 224 sts).

Row 19: Rib 10 (9, 11, 12, 11, 10), P0 (2, 0, 2, 0, 0), * (P1, K1) into next st, (K1, P1) into next st, P2, rep from * to last 10 (9, 11, 12, 11, 10) sts, rib to end.

Row 20: Rib 10 (9, 11, 12, 11, 10), * K2, P4, rep from * to last 10 (13, 11, 14, 11, 10) sts, K0 (2, 0, 2, 0, 0), rib to end.

Row 21: Rib 10 (9, 11, 12, 11, 10), P0 (2, 0, 2, 0, 0), * (P1, K1) into next st, K2, (K1, P1) into next st, P2, rep from * to last 10 (9, 11, 12, 11, 10) sts, rib to end.

Row 22: Rib 10 (9, 11, 12, 11, 10), * K2, P6, rep from * to last 10 (13, 11, 14, 11, 10) sts, K0 (2, 0, 2, 0, 0), rib to end.

Row 23: Rib 10 (9, 11, 12, 11, 10), P0 (2, 0, 2, 0, 0), * (P1, K1) into next st, K4, (K1, P1) into next st, P2, rep from * to last 10 (9, 11, 12, 11, 10) sts, rib to end.

Row 24: Rib 10 (9, 11, 12, 11, 10), * K2, P8, rep from * to last 10 (13, 11, 14, 11, 10) sts, K0 (2, 0, 2, 0, 0), rib to end.

Row 25: Rib 10 (9, 11, 12, 11, 10), P0 (2, 0, 2, 0, 0), * Sl1, K1, psso, K4, K2tog, P2, rep from * to last 10 (9, 11, 12, 11, 10) sts, rib to end.

Row 26: As row 22.

Row 27: Rib 10 (9, 11, 12, 11, 10), P0 (2, 0, 2, 0, 0), * Sl1, K1, psso, K2, K2tog, P2, rep from * to last 10 (9, 11, 12, 11, 10) sts, rib to end.

Row 28: As row 20.

Row 29: Rib 3, cast off 3, rib 4 (3, 5, 6, 5, 4), P0 (2, 0, 2, 0, 0), * Sl1, K1, psso, K2tog, P2, rep from * to last 10 (9, 11, 12, 11, 10) sts, rib to end.

Row 30: Rib 10 (9, 11, 12, 11, 10), * K2, P2, rep from * to last 10 (13, 11, 14, 11, 10) sts, K0 (2, 0, 2, 0, 0), rib to end, casting on 3 as before (176, 184, 194, 210, 218, 224 sts).

Row 31: Rib 10 (9, 11, 12, 11, 10), P0 (1, 0, 1, 0, 0), * P2tog, P2, rep from * to last 10 (10, 11, 13, 11, 10) sts, P0 (1, 0, 1, 0, 0), rib to end (137, 143, 151, 164, 169, 173 sts).

Row 32: Rib 10 (9, 11, 12, 11, 10), K0 (1, 0, 1, 0, 0), * K2tog, K1, rep from * to last 10 (10, 11, 13, 11, 10) sts, K0 (1, 0, 1, 0, 0), rib to end (98, 102, 108, 118, 120, 122 sts).

Row 41: Rib 10 (9, 11, 12, 11, 10), P2 (0, 2, 2, 2, 2), * Sl1, K1, psso, K2, K2tog, P2, rep from * to last 10 (9, 11, 12, 11, 10) sts, rib 10 (9, 11, 12, 11, 10).
Row 42: As row 34.
Row 43: Rib 10 (9, 11, 12, 11, 10), P2 (0, 2, 2, 2, 2), * Sl1, K1, psso, K2tog, P2, rep from * to last 10 (9, 11, 12, 11, 10) sts, rib 10 (9, 11, 12, 11, 10) (98, 102, 108, 118, 120, 122 sts).
Row 44: Rib 10 (9, 11, 12, 11, 10), * K2, P2, rep from * to last 12 (9, 13, 14, 13, 12) sts, K2 (0, 2, 2, 2, 2), rib to end.
Row 45: Change to 2.75mm needles, rib 3, cast off 3, rib 4 (3, 5, 6, 5, 4), purl to last 10 (9, 11, 12, 11, 10) sts, rib to end.
Row 46: Rib 10 (9, 11, 12, 11, 10), knit to last 10 (9, 11, 12, 11, 10) sts, rib to end, casting on 3 sts as before.
Row 47: Work in single rib.
Cast off in rib.

MAKING UP

Do not press work. Join side and sleeve seams; sew in sleeves. Sew on buttons. Darn in all ends.

Row 33: Rib 10 (9, 11, 12, 11, 10), P2 (0, 2, 2, 2, 2), * (P1, K1) into next st, (K1, P1) into next st, P2, rep from * to last 10 (9, 11, 12, 11, 10) sts, rib to end.
Row 34: Rib 10 (9, 11, 12, 11, 10), * K2, P4, rep from * to last 12 (9, 13, 14, 13, 12) sts, K2 (0, 2, 2, 2, 2), rib to end.
Row 35: Rib 10 (9, 11, 12, 11, 10), P2 (0, 2, 2, 2, 2), * (P1, K1) into next st, K2, (K1, P1) into next st, P2, rep from * to last 10 (9, 11, 12, 11, 10) sts, rib to end.
Row 36: Rib 10 (9, 11, 12, 11, 10), * K2, P6, rep from * to last 12 (9, 13, 14, 13, 12) sts, K2 (0, 2, 2, 2, 2), rib to end.
Row 37: Rib 10 (9, 11, 12, 11, 10), P2 (0, 2, 2, 2, 2), * (P1, K1) into next st, K4, (K1, P1) into next st, P2, rep from * to last 10 (9, 11, 12, 11, 10) sts, rib 10 (9, 11, 12, 11, 10).
Row 38: Rib 10 (9, 11, 12, 11, 10), * K2, P8, rep from * to last 12 (9, 13, 14, 13, 12) sts, K2 (0, 2, 2, 2, 2), rib to end.
Row 39: Rib 10 (9, 11, 12, 11, 10), P2 (0, 2, 2, 2, 2), * Sl1, K1, psso, K4, K2tog, P2, rep from * to last 10 (9, 11, 12, 11, 10) sts, rib 10 (9, 11, 12, 11, 10).
Row 40: As row 36.

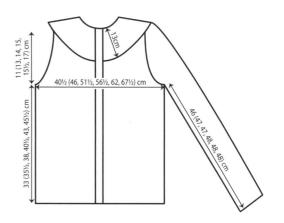

A warm Jacket
with an
unusual bubble-stitch yoke

MATERIALS: 10 ozs. Patons Beehive Finger-ing, 3-ply ("Patonised" shrink-resist finish). A pair each No. 11 and No. 12 "Beehive" needles. A set of four No. 10 needles, pointed both ends. Twelve buttons.

MEASUREMENTS: To fit 34–36-inch bust; length from top of shoulders, 21 inches; sleeve seam, 18½ inches.

TENSION: 10½ stitches to an inch over ribbing on No. 11 needles, unstretched.

BACK

With No. 12 needles, cast on 130 sts. and work 4 inches k. 1, p. 1 rib. Change to No. 11 needles and continue in rib, increasing at each end of next and every following 8th row until there are 150 sts.

Work straight until side edge measures 13 inches, then shape armholes by casting off 10 at beginning of next 2 rows, and k. 2 tog. at each end of every alternate row until 120 remain.

NEXT ROW: Rib 56, turn and rib back, leaving remainder on a spare needle. NEXT ROW: Rib 52, turn, rib to end. NEXT ROW: Rib 48, turn, rib to end. Continue thus, working 4 sts. less every alternate row until 4 are left unworked. Leave these 56 on a safety-pin.

Join wool at armhole side of remaining 64 sts., rib 56, turn and continue working other half in same way, leaving all 64 on spare needle.

FRONTS

Left: With No. 12 needles, cast on 74 sts. and work 4 inches k. 1, p. 1 rib. Change to No. 11 needles and continue in rib, increasing at side edge on next and every following 8th row until there are 84 sts.

Work straight until side edge measures 13 inches, then cast off 10 at side edge for armhole and k. 2 tog. at same side until 64 remain. Work yoke shaping as for first half of back, then leave all 64 on spare needle.

Right: Work to correspond with left, working yoke as for second half of back, and making button-holes up front edge. The first hole comes in 5th and 6th rows, and remaining ones in following 17th and 18th rows.

To make a buttonhole:—Rib 3, cast off 3, work to end and back, casting on 3 over those cast off in previous row.

SLEEVES

With No. 12 needles, cast on 64 sts. and work 3 inches k. 1, p. 1 rib. Change to No. 11 needles and continue in rib, increasing at each end of every 6th row until there are 104 sts.

Work straight until side edge measures required length, then cast off 7 at beginning of next two rows, then k. 2 tog. at each end of every alternate row until 42 remain. Leave these sts. on a spare needle, and make another sleeve.

YOKE

With right side of work facing and set of four No. 10 needles, start at straight edge of right front.

From spare needle, rib 10, purl 54, purl across 42 sts. of one sleeve, then across 120 sts. of back, 42 of second sleeve, 54 from left front, and rib last 10 sts. Arrange sts. on 3 needles to simplify working.

2ND ROW: Rib 10, k. 312, rib 10. 3RD ROW: Rib 10, p. 312, rib 10. 4TH ROW: As 3rd.

5TH ROW: Rib 10, * (p. 1, k. 1) into next st., (k. 1, p. 1) into next st., p. 4; repeat from * to last 10 sts., rib 10. 6TH ROW: Rib 10, * k. 4, p. 4; repeat from * to last 10 sts., rib 10.

7TH ROW: Rib 10, * (p. 1, k. 1) into next st., k. 2, (k. 1, p. 1) into next st., p. 4; repeat from * to last 10 sts., rib 10. 8TH ROW: Rib 10, * k. 4, p. 6; repeat from * to last 10 sts., rib 10.

9TH ROW: Rib 10, * (p. 1, k. 1) into next st., k. 4, (k. 1, p. 1) into next st., p. 4; repeat from * to last 10 sts., rib 10. 10TH ROW: Rib 10, * k. 4, p. 8; repeat from * to last 10 sts., rib 10. 11TH ROW Rib 10, * slip 1, k. 1, pass slipped stitch over k. 4, k. 2 tog., p. 4; repeat from * to last 10 sts., rib 10.

12TH ROW: As 8th. 13TH ROW: Rib 10, * slip 1, k. 1, p.s.s.o., k. 2, k. 2 tog., p. 4; repeat from * to last 10 sts., rib 10. 14TH ROW: As 6th.

15TH ROW: Rib 3, cast off 3 for buttonhole, rib 4, * slip 1, k. 1, p.s.s.o., k. 2 tog., p. 4; repeat from * to last 10 sts., rib 10. 16TH ROW: Rib 10, * k. 4, p. 2; repeat from * to last sts., rib 4, cast on 3 sts. over those cast off, rib 3.

17TH ROW: Rib 10, * p. 2 tog., p. 2; repeat from * to last 10 sts., rib 10. 18TH ROW: Rib 10, k. 1, * k. 1, k. 2 tog.; repeat from * to last 12 sts., k. 2 tog., rib 10. 19TH ROW: Rib 10 * (p. 1, k. 1) into next st., p. 2; repeat from * to last 10 sts., rib 10.

20TH ROW: Rib 10, k. 2, * p. 2, k. 2; repeat from * to last 10 sts., rib 10. 21ST ROW: Rib 10, * (p. 1, k. 1) into next st., k. 2, (k. 1, p. 1) into next st., p. 2; repeat from * to last 10 sts., rib 10.

22ND ROW: Rib 10, * k. 2, p. 4; repeat from * to last 10 sts., rib 10. 23RD ROW: Rib 10, * (p. 1, k. 1) into next st., k. 2, (k. 1, p. 1) into next st., p. 2; repeat from * to last 10 sts., rib 10.

24TH ROW: Rib 10, * k. 2, p. 6; repeat from * to last 10 sts., rib 10. 25TH ROW: Rib 10, * (p. 1, k. 1) into next st., k. 4, (k. 1, p. 1) into next st., p. 2 repeat from * to last 10 sts., rib 10.

26TH ROW: Rib 10, * k. 2, p. 8; repeat from * to last 10 sts., rib 10. 27TH ROW: Rib 10, * slip 1, k. 1, p.s.s.o., k. 4, k. 2 tog., p. 2; repeat from * to last 10 sts., rib 10. 28TH ROW: Rib 10, * k. 2, p. 6; repeat from * to last 10 sts., rib 10.

29TH ROW: Rib 10, * slip 1, k. 1, p.s.s.o., k. 2, k. 2 tog., p. 2; repeat from * to last 10 sts., rib 10. 30TH ROW: Rib 10, * k. 2, p. 4; repeat from * to last 10 sts., rib 10.

31ST ROW: Rib 3, cast off 3, rib 4, * slip 1, k. 1, p.s.s.o., k. 2 tog., p. 2; repeat from * to last 10 sts., rib 10. 32ND ROW: Rib 10, * k. 2, p. 2; repeat from * to last 10 sts., rib 10, casting on 3 as before. 33RD ROW: Rib 10, p. 1, * p. 2, p. 2 tog.; repeat from * to last 11 sts., p. 1, rib 10.

34TH ROW: Rib 10, k. 1, * k. 2 tog., k. 1; repeat from * to last 11 sts., k. 1, rib 10. 35TH ROW: Rib 10, p. 2, * (p. 1, k. 1) into next st., p. 2; repeat from * to last 10 sts., rib 10.

36TH ROW: Rib 10, k. 2, * p. 4, k. 2; repeat from * to last 10 sts., rib 10. 37TH ROW: Rib 10, p. 2, * (p. 1, k. 1) into next st., k. 2, (k. 1, p. 1) into next st., p. 2; repeat from * to last 10 sts., rib 10.

38TH ROW: Rib 10, * k. 2, p. 6; repeat from * to last 10 sts., rib 10. 39TH ROW: Rib 10, p. 2, * (p. 1, k. 1) into next st., k. 4, (k. 1, p. 1) into next st., p. 2; repeat from * to last 10 sts., rib 10.

40TH ROW: Rib 10, k. 2, * p. 8, k. 2; repeat from * to last 10 sts., rib 10.

41ST ROW: Rib 10, p. 2, * slip 1, k. 1, p.s.s.o., k. 4, k. 2 tog., p. 2; repeat from * to last 10 sts., rib 10. 42ND ROW: Rib 10, k. 2, * p. 6, k. 2; repeat from * to last 10 sts., rib 10.

43RD ROW: Rib 10, p. 2, * slip 1, k. 1, p.s.s.o., k. 2, k. 2 tog., p. 2; repeat from * to last 10 sts., rib 10. 44TH ROW: Rib 10, k. 2, * p. 4, k. 2; repeat from * to last 10 sts., rib 10.

45TH ROW: Rib 10, p. 2, * slip 1, k. 1, p.s.s.o., k. 2 tog., p. 2; repeat from * to last 10 sts., rib 10. 46TH ROW: Rib 10, k. 2, * p. 2, k. 2; repeat from * to last 10 sts., rib 10. 47TH ROW: With No. 12 needles, rib 3, cast off 3, rib 4, purl to last 10 sts, rib 10. 48TH ROW: Rib 10, knit to last 10 sts., rib 10, casting on 3 sts., as before. 49TH ROW: As 47th. Cast off

TO MAKE UP

Do not press work. Join side and sleeve seams; sew in sleeves. Sew on buttons.

So Neat and Sweet in her Simple V-Necked Jersey

MATERIALS
Jamieson's Spindrift 100% Shetland wool (105m per 25g ball)
13 (14, 16, 18, 20, 23, 25) balls shade 764 (Cloud)
1 pair 2.75mm (US #2) needles
1 pair 3.25mm (US #3) needles
Stitch markers

TENSION
28 sts & 36 rows = 10cm (4in) using 3.25mm needles over stitch pattern

Standard Yarn Tension
30 sts & 32 rows = 10cm (4in) using 3.25mm needles over stocking stitch

ABBREVIATIONS
See page 13 for standard abbreviations

SIZING
Measurements given in centimetres followed by inches in parentheses

To Fit	76–81 (30–32)	86–92 (34–36)	97–102 (38–40)	107–112 (42–44)	117–122 (46–48)	127–132 (50–52)	137–142 (54–56)
Finished Measurements							
Actual Bust Size	90 (35½)	100 (39½)	110 (43½)	120 (47)	130 (51)	140 (55)	150 (59)
Length to underarm	35 (13¾)	36½ (14½)	38½ (15)	40 (15¾)	41½ (16½)	43½ (17)	45 (17¾)
Armhole Depth	16½ (6½)	18½ (7)	20 (8)	22 (8½)	23½ (9¼)	25 (10)	26½ (10½)
Finished Length	51½ (20¼)	55 (21½)	58½ (23)	62 (24½)	65 (25½)	68½ (27)	71½ (28)
Shoulder to Shoulder	35 (13¾)	38 (15)	40 (15¾)	43 (17)	45 (17¾)	48 (19)	50 (19½)
Sleeve Length	46 (18)	47½ (18¾)	47½ (18¾)	49 (19¼)	49 (19¼)	51 (20)	51 (20)

Garment shown in photographs is for first size 76–81 (30–32)

PATTERN NOTES
Stitch counts vary over this 6 row pattern depending on row you have just completed. Row 1 increases 2 sts for every (K1, P1, K1) into next st worked and on row 6, the same number of sts are decreased. The stitch counts shown in the pattern reflect which row you should have just completed. The number of rows worked over the left and right fronts after dividing for the neck should be noted.

BACK
Using 2.75mm needles, cast on 126 (140, 154, 168, 182, 196, 210) sts.
Next row (RS): * K1, P1, rep from * to end of row.
Rep this row until work measures 10cm (4in).
Change to 3.25mm needles and work in pattern as folls:
Row 1: (RS) K1, * P2, (K1, P1, K1) into next st, P2, K2, repeat from * ending last rep with K1 (162, 180, 198, 216, 234, 252, 270 sts).
Row 2: P1, * K2, P3, K2, P2, repeat from * ending last rep with P1.
Row 3: K1, * P2, K3, P2, K2, repeat from * ending last rep with K1.
Repeat rows 2 and 3 once more.
Row 6: P1, * K2, Sl 2 over 1 thus: Sl 2nd and 3rd sts on LH needle over first, then purl the rem st, K2, P2, repeat from * ending the last rep with P1 (126, 140, 154, 168, 182, 196, 210 sts).

These 6 rows form patt, rep a further 14 (15, 16, 17, 18, 19, 20) times (until work measures 35 (36½, 38½, 40, 41½, 43½, 45) cm (13¾, 14½, 15, 16, 16½, 17, 18 in)).

Shape Armholes
Place markers at each end of the central 98 (106, 112, 120, 126, 134, 140) sts. For the duration of the armhole shaping, the 14 (17, 21, 24, 28, 31, 35) sts at each end of the row will be worked in rib as set without working any (K1, P1, K1) into next stitch increases. In the central section the stitch pattern will be maintained as normal.

Maintain patt as described, cast off 5 (8, 5, 7, 7, 8, 9) sts at beg of next 2 (2, 4, 4, 4, 4, 4) rows.
Dec 1 st at each end of next 5 (5, 5, 7, 7, 8, 9) rows, then dec 1 st at each end of foll 4 (4, 6, 3, 7, 7, 8) alt rows, then work 3 (3, 3, 1, 5, 4, 1) rows without shaping, ending with row 6 (98, 106, 112, 120, 126, 134, 140 sts).

Remove markers and work in pattern over all sts without further shaping until armhole measures 16½ (18½, 20, 22, 23½, 25, 26½ cm) (6½, 7¼, 8, 8½, 9, 10, 10½ in), ending with a pattern row 6.

Shape Shoulders

Place markers at each end of the central 38 (38, 46, 46, 56, 56, 60) sts. For the duration of the shoulder shaping, the 30 (34, 33, 37, 35, 39, 40) sts at each end of the row will be worked in rib as set without working any (K1, P1, K1) into next stitch increases. In the central section the stitch pattern will be maintained as normal.

Cast off 10 (11, 11, 12, 11, 13, 13) sts at beg of next 6 (4, 6, 4, 2, 6, 4) rows then 0 (12, 0, 13, 12, 0, 14) at the beg of foll 0 (2, 0, 2, 4, 0, 2) rows. Cast off rem 38 (38, 46, 46, 56, 56, 60) sts.

FRONT

Using 2.75mm needles, cast on 126 (140, 154, 168, 182, 196, 210) sts.

Next row (RS): * K1, P1, rep from * to end of row.
Rep this row until work measures 10cm (4in).
Change to 3.25mm needles and work in pattern as for back until 13 (14, 15, 16, 17, 18, 19) pattern reps have been worked (31½, 33½, 35, 36½, 38½, 40, 41½ cm (12½, 13, 13¾, 14½, 15, 15¾, 16½ in)), ending with a row 6.

Divide for Neck and Shoulders

Next row (RS): K1, [P2, (K1, P1, K1) into next st, P2, K2] 8 (9, 10, 11, 12, 13, 14) times, P2, (K1, P1, K1) into next st, P2, K1, turn leaving 63 (70, 77, 84, 91, 98, 105) sts on spare needle for right front.

Left Front

Maintaining continuity of pattern, dec 1 st at neck edge of next and 2 foll 4th rows. Work 2 rows straight, thus ending with row 6 of patt (60, 67, 74, 81, 88, 95, 102 sts).

Shape Armhole

Place markers 14 (17, 21, 24, 28, 31, 35) sts from armhole edge and 5 (5, 6, 5, 8, 8, 8) sts from neck edge. For the duration of the following shaped section, the central 41 (45, 47, 52, 52, 56, 59) sts will be worked in stitch pattern as normal, and the edge sts at each end will be worked in rib as set, with no (K1, P1, K1) into same stitch increases. Maintaining pattern as described, cast off 5 (8, 5, 7, 7, 8, 9) sts at beg of next row, then cast off 0 (0, 5, 7, 7, 8, 9) sts at beg of foll alt row, dec 1 st at armhole edge of foll 5 (5, 5, 7, 7, 8, 9) rows, then dec 1 st at armhole edge of 4 (4, 6, 3, 7, 7, 8) foll alt rows, and AT THE SAME TIME, dec 1 st at neck edge of 2nd row and 4 (4, 5, 4, 7, 7, 7) foll 4th rows (thus continuing from earlier neck decreases). Work 0 (0, 2, 0, 0, 0, 0) rows without further shaping, thus ending on row 6 of pattern (41, 45, 47, 52, 52, 56, 59 sts).

**Remove marker(s), and place new marker 3 sts from neck edge – do not work stitch pattern increases on these 3 sts. Work 0 (0, 1, 0, 0, 0, 0) row straight. Dec 1 st at neck edge of next and 2 foll 4th rows. Work 3 (3, 2, 3, 3, 3, 3) rows

straight, thus ending on row 6 of pattern (38, 42, 44, 49, 49, 53, 56 sts).
Repeat from ** 1 (1, 2, 2, 2, 2, 3) more times (35, 39, 38, 43, 43, 47, 47 sts).

1st, 2nd, 4th, 5th, 6th and 7th sizes only

Remove marker and place new marker 1 (2, 0, 2, 1, 2, 1) sts from neck edge – do not work stitch pattern increases on these sts. Dec 1 st at neck edge of next and 0 (1, 0, 1, 0, 1, 0) foll 4th row. Work 5 (1, 0, 1, 5, 1, 5) rows straight, thus ending on row 6 of pattern (34, 37, 0, 41, 42, 45, 46 sts).

All sizes

Remover any remaining markers and work straight in pattern for a further 0 (6, 0, 6, 0, 6, 0) rows (34, 37, 38, 41, 42, 45, 46 sts).

Shape Shoulder

Place marker 30 (34, 33, 37, 35, 39, 40) sts from armhole edge. These sts will be worked in rib with no increases, while the normal stitch pattern will be maintained over the 4 (3, 5, 4, 7, 6, 6) neck edge sts.
Cast off 10 (11, 11, 12, 11, 13, 13) sts at beg of next row. Work 1 row straight.
Cast off 10 (11, 11, 12, 12, 13, 13) sts at beg of next row. Work 1 row straight.
Cast off 10 (12, 11, 13, 12, 13, 14) sts at beg of next row. Cast off remaining sts.

Right Front

With RS facing rejoin yarn to rem 63 (70, 77, 84, 91, 98, 105) sts at neck edge, and patt to end.
Maintaining continuity of pattern, dec 1 st at neck edge of next and 2 foll 4th rows. Work 2 rows straight, thus ending with row 6 of patt (60, 67, 74, 81, 88, 95, 102 sts).
Place markers 14 (17, 21, 24, 28, 31, 35) sts from armhole edge and 5 (5, 6, 5, 8, 8, 8) sts from neck edge. For the duration of the following shaped section, the central 41 (45, 47, 52, 52, 56, 59) sts will be worked in stitch pattern as normal, and the edge sts at each end will be worked in rib as set, with no (K1, P1, K1) into same stitch increases. Work 1 row in pattern as described (with no increases on the sts outside of the marked section).

Shape Armhole

Maintaining pattern as described, cast off 5 (8, 5, 7, 7, 8, 9) sts at beg of next row, then cast off 0 (0, 5, 7, 7, 8, 9) sts at beg of foll alt row, dec 1 st at armhole edge of foll 5 (5, 5, 7, 7, 8, 9) rows, then dec 1 st at armhole edge of 4 (4, 6, 3, 7, 7, 8) foll alt rows, and AT THE SAME TIME, dec 1 st at neck edge of next row and 4 (4, 5, 4, 7, 7, 7) foll 4th rows (thus continuing from earlier neck decreases). Work 0 (0, 2, 0, 0, 0, 0) rows without further shaping, thus ending on row 6 of pattern (41, 45, 47, 52, 52, 56, 59 sts).

** Remove marker(s), and place new marker 3 sts from neck edge – do not work stitch pattern increases on these 3 sts. Work 0 (0, 1, 0, 0, 0, 0) row straight. Dec 1 st at neck edge of next and 2 foll 4th rows. Work 3 (3, 2, 3, 3, 3, 3)

rows straight, thus ending on row 6 of pattern (38, 42, 44, 49, 49, 53, 56 sts).
Repeat from ** 1 (1, 2, 2, 2, 2, 3) more times (35, 39, 38, 43, 43, 47, 47 sts).

1st, 2nd, 4th, 5th, 6th and 7th sizes only
Remove marker and place new marker 1 (2, 0, 2, 1, 2, 1) sts from neck edge – do not work stitch pattern increases on these sts. Dec 1 st at neck edge of next and 0 (1, 0, 1, 0, 1, 0) foll 4th row. Work 5 (1, 0, 1, 5, 1, 5) rows straight, thus ending on row 6 of pattern (34, 37, 0, 41, 42, 45, 46 sts).

All sizes
Remove any remaining markers and work straight in pattern for a further 0 (6, 0, 6, 0, 6, 0) rows (34, 37, 38, 41, 42, 45, 46 sts).
Place marker 30 (34, 33, 37, 35, 39, 40) sts from armhole

edge. These sts will be worked in plain rib with no increases, while the normal stitch pattern will be maintained over the 4 (3, 5, 4, 7, 6, 6) neck edge sts. Work 1 row in pattern as described.

Shape Shoulder
Cast off 10 (11, 11, 12, 11, 13, 13) sts at beg of next row.
Work 1 row straight.
Cast off 10 (11, 11, 12, 12, 13, 13) sts at beg of next row.
Work 1 row straight.
Cast off 10 (12, 11, 13, 12, 13, 14) sts at beg of next row.
Cast off remaining sts.

SLEEVES
Using 2.75mm needles, cast on 70 (78, 84, 92, 98, 106, 112) sts. Work in rib as for back until work measures

7½cm (3in) ending with a WS row, dec 0 (1, 0, 1, 0, 1, 0) st at end of last row (70, 77, 84, 91, 98, 105, 112 sts).

Change to 3.25mm needles and work 18 rows in pattern as set for back. Cont in patt, inc 1 st at each end of the next and every foll 8th row until the 14th inc row has been worked, working the extra sts in K2, P2 rib until enough sts increased to work into pattern. When increases are complete, work 1 more row in pattern (a row 6) (98, 105, 112, 119, 126, 133, 140 sts).

Work 4 (5, 5, 6, 6, 7, 7) more repeats of the stitch pattern, without further shaping, ending with a row 6. Work should measure 46 (47½, 47½, 49, 49, 51, 51) cm (18, 18¾, 18¾, 19¼, 19¼, 20, 20 in).

Shape Sleeve Head
Place stitch markers around the central 60 (67, 74, 81, 88, 95, 102) sts. The 19 sts at each end of the row will be worked in rib with no (K1, P1, K1) into next stitch increases.

Maintaining continuity of pattern as described, cast off 9 sts at beg of next 4 rows, then dec 1 st at each end of next row. Work 1 row straight (row 6 of pattern) (60, 67, 74, 81, 88, 95, 102 sts).

*** Place markers 3 sts from each end of the row. These 3 sts will be worked in simple rib, with the normal stitch pattern worked over the central sts. Dec 1 st at each end of next and 2 foll alt rows. Work 1 row straight (54, 61, 68, 75, 82, 89, 96 sts).

Rep from *** 4 (5, 6, 7, 8, 9, 10) more times (30, 31, 32, 33, 34, 35, 36 sts). Cast off rem sts taking 2 sts together along row.

NECKBAND
Using 2.75mm needles, cast on 3 sts and knit 1 row. Cont in garter st, inc 1 st at the beg of next and every alt row until there are 12 sts. Work 258 (258, 262, 262, 266, 266, 270) rows on these sts, then dec 1 st at the shaped edge on every alt row until 3 sts rem. Cast off.
Sew neckband all round neck edge using a flat slip stitch, with the mitred edges sewn together at the front.

MAKING UP
Block pieces to size on the WS using a damp cloth. Join the shoulder seams. Join sleeve and side seams. Set sleeves into armholes matching centre of sleeve head with shoulder seam and matching side seams. Darn in all ends.

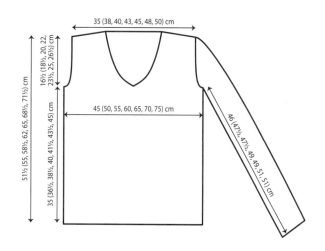

35 (38, 40, 43, 45, 48, 50) cm

16½ (18¾, 20, 22, 23½, 25, 26½) cm

45 (50, 55, 60, 65, 70, 75) cm

46 (47½, 47½, 49, 49, 51, 51) cm

51½ (55, 58½, 62, 65, 68½, 71½) cm

35 (36½, 38½, 40, 41½, 43½, 45) cm

SO NEAT AND SWEET IN HER SIMPLE V-NECKED JERSEY

Susan Shaw, young star of the J. Arthur Rank Organisation, demonstrates the charm of this jersey with a scarf tucked into the neckline.

Grey Jersey With Daffodil Yellow Scarf—Bottle Green With Nasturtium Colour—Or Warm Brown Jersey With Scarf Of Hyacinth Blue

MATERIALS: *Six ounces of Patons Beehive Fingering 2-ply ('Patonised' Shrink-resist finish), or five ounces if short sleeves are worked; a pair each of No. 10 and No. 13 knitting needles.*

TENSION AND MEASUREMENTS: *Worked at a tension of two repeats of the pattern to 1⅓ inches in width with No. 10 needles, the measurements on the diagram on page 44 are attained after very light pressing, but the jersey will comfortably expand to 36 inches round the bust.*

ABBREVIATIONS—To Be Read Before Working—K., knit plain; p., purl; st., stitch; tog., together; inc., increase (by working into the back and front of the same st.); dec., decrease (by taking 2 sts. tog.); single rib is k. 1 and p. 1 alternately; sl., slip; garter-st. is k. plain on every row. Directions in brackets are worked the number of times stated after the last bracket.

TO WORK THE BACK

BEGIN at the lower edge and using No. 13 needles, cast on 126 sts.

Work 50 rows in single rib.

Change to No. 10 needles and work the pattern as follows:

1st row: (Right side). K. 1, * p. 2, work 3 in 1, thus: cast on 2 sts., k. into back of the next st., p. into the 2nd, then k. into the next st., p. 2, k. 2; repeat from *, ending the last repeat with k. 1 (162 sts.).

2nd row: * P. 1, * k. 2, p. 3, k. 2, p. 2; repeat from *, ending the last repeat with p. 1.

3rd row: K. 1, * p. 2, k. 3, p. 2, k. 2; repeat from *, ending the last repeat with p. 1.

Repeat the 2nd and 3rd row once more.

6th row: * P. 1, * k. 2, sl. 2 over 1, thus: sl. 2nd and 3rd sts. on left-hand needle over the first, then p. the remaining st., k. 2, p. 2; repeat from *, ending the last repeat with p. 1 (126 sts.).

These 6 rows form one pattern, so repeat them 14 times more to the armholes.

To SHAPE THE ARMHOLES.—*1st row:* Cast off 5, (1 st. on needle and likewise on following row) k. 2, * p. 2, 3 in 1, p. 2, k. 2; repeat from * until 6 sts. remain, (p. 2, k. 1) twice.

2nd row: Cast off 5, * p. 2, k. 2, p. 3, k. 2; repeat from * until 3 remain, p. 2, k. 1.

Dec. 1 st. at each end of the next 3 rows.

6th row: K. 2 tog., * sl. 2 over 1, k. 2, p. 2, k. 2; repeat from * until 5 remain, sl. 2 over 1, k. 2 tog.

7th row: K. 2 tog., * p. 2, k. 2, p. 2, 3 in 1; repeat from *, ending the last repeat with k. 2 tog. instead of 3 in 1.

Dec. 1 st. at each end of the next 2 alternate rows.

12th row: K. 1, * p. 2, k. 2, sl. 2 over 1, k. 2; repeat from *, ending the last repeat with k. 2, p. 1.

13th row: K. 1, * p. 2, k. 2, k. 1, p. 2, 3 in 1; repeat from *, ending last repeat with k. 1, k. 2 tog.

Dec. 1 st. at each end of the next 2 alternate rows.

Work 1 row straight, then dec. 1 st. at each end of the next row.

Repeat 4th to the 6th row as on the back (98 sts.), then 7 complete patterns more.

To SLOPE THE SHOULDERS.—Cast off 13 sts. at the beginning of the next 6 rows.

Cast off remaining sts.

THE FRONT

WORK as for the back until 13 patterns have been worked after the ribbing.

Divide the sts. for the neck and shoulders on the next row as follows:

1st pattern row: K. 1, (p. 2, 3 in 1, p. 2, k. 2) 8 times, p. 2, 3 in 1, p. 2, k. 1, turn, leaving remaining 63 sts. on a spare needle for Right Front Shoulder.

THE LEFT FRONT SHOULDER.—Work 4 rows in pattern, decreasing 1 st. at beginning of the 1st row.

6th row: P. 1, (k. 2, sl. 2 over 1, k. 2, p. 2) 8 times, k. 2, sl. 2 over 1, k. 2, p. 1, (3 in 1, p. 2, k. 2, p. 2) 8 times, 3 in 1, p. 2, k. 1.

7th row: P. 1, (3 in 1, p. 2, k. 2, p. 2) 8 times, 3 in 1, p. 2, k. 1.

Work 2 rows straight in pattern.

10th row: K. 2 tog., pattern to the end.

Work 1 row more.

12th row: K. 2 tog., (k. 2, sl. 2 over 1, k. 2, p. 2) sl. 2 over 1) 8 times, k. 2, p. 1.

To SHAPE THE ARMHOLE.—*1st row:* Cast off 5, (1 st. on needle) (k. 2, p. 2, 3 in 1, p. 2) 7 times, k. 2, p. 2, k. 1.

2nd row: K. 2 tog., pattern to the end.

Dec. 1 st. at the arm end of the next 3 rows.

6th row: K. 2 tog., (p. 2, k. 2, sl. 2 over 1, k. 2, p. 2) k. 2 tog.

7th row: K. 1, (p. 2, k. 2, p. 2, 3 in 1) 6 times, p. 2, k. 2, p. 2, k. 2 tog.

Pattern 2 rows, decreasing 1 st. at arm end of 2nd row.

10th row: P. 2 tog., pattern to end.

11th row: P. 2 tog., pattern to end.

12th row: K. 1, (p. 2, k. 2, sl. 2 over 1, k. 2) 6 times, p. 2, k. 1.

13th row: K. 2, (p. 2, 3 in 1, p. 2) 6 times, k. 1, k. 2 tog.

Dec. 1 st. at the end of each of the next 2 rows (54 sts.).

Work 2 rows straight.

18th row: P. 1, (k. 2, sl. 2 over 1, k. 2, p. 2) 5 times, k. 2, sl. 2 over 1, k. 1, k. 2 tog. (41 sts.).

24th row: P. 1, (k. 2, sl. 2 over 1, k. 2, p. 2) 5 times, k. 2, sl. 2 over 1, k. 1.

25th row: P. 1, k. 1, (p. 2, k. 2, p. 2, 3 in 1) 5 times, p. 2, k. 1.

Work 4 rows in pattern, decreasing 1 st. at the beginning of the 3rd row.

30th row: P. 1, (k. 2, sl. 2 over 1, k. 2, p. 2) 5 times, k. 1, k. 2 tog.

Work 20 rows in pattern, decreasing 1 st. at the beginning (neck edge) of every 4th row. Work 3 rows straight.

54th row: Sl. 3 over 1, thus : sl. the 2nd, 3rd and 4th sts. on left-hand needle over the first st., then p. the remaining st., (k. 2, p. 2, k. 2, sl. 2 over 1) 4 times, k. 2, p. 1.

55th row: K. 1, (p. 2, 3 in 1, p. 2, k. 2) 4 times, p. 2, k. 1.

Work 7 rows decreasing 1 st. at beginning of 3rd row (39 sts.).

To SLOPE THE SHOULDER.—Cast off 13 sts. at the beginning of the next row and following alternate row.

4th row: K. 2, p. 2, k. 2, p. 3, k. 2, p. 2.

THE RIGHT FRONT SHOULDER.—Rejoin wool to neck end of remaining 63 sts., and work as follows:

1st row: K. 1, (p. 2, 3 in 1, p. 2, k. 2) 8 times, p. 2, 3 in 1, p. 2, k. 1.

Work 4 rows in pattern, decreasing 1 st. at the end of the 1st row.

6th row: P. 1, (k. 2, sl. 2 over 1, k. 2, p. 2) 8 times, k. 2, sl. 2 over 1, k. 2 tog.

7th row: P. 1, (3 in 1, p. 2, k. 2, p. 2) 8 times, 3 in 1, p. 2, k. 1.

Work 2 rows straight.

10th row: Pattern until 2 remain, p. 2 tog.

Work 1 row more.

12th row: P. 1, (k. 2, sl. 2 over 1, k. 2, p. 2) 8 times, k. 2, sl. 2 over 1, k. 2 tog.

13th row: P. 1, (3 in 1, p. 2, k. 2, p. 2, 3 in 1) twice.

To SHAPE THE ARMHOLE.—*2nd pattern row:* Cast off 5, pattern until 2 sts. remain, p. 2 tog.

Dec. 1 st. at the arm end of the next 3 rows.

6th row: K. 2 tog., (sl. 2 over 1, k. 2, p. 2, k. 2, p. 2, k. 1) twice.

7th row: P. 1, k. 2, p. 2, (3 in 1, p. 2, k. 2, p. 2) 6 times, k. 2, p. 2, k. 2 tog.

Pattern 2 rows, decreasing 1 st. at arm end of 2nd row.

THE SLEEVES

BEGIN at the wrist edge by casting on 70 sts. with No. 13 needles.

Work 34 rows in single rib.

Change to No. 10 needles and work 3 patterns as on back.

Continue in pattern, increasing 1 st. at each end of the 14th inc. row has been worked, working the extra sts. in k. 2, p. 2 rib until there are 7 more at each end, making another 2 repeats of the pattern.

Work 33 rows straight, finishing with the 6th row of the 26th pattern from beginning (98 sts.).

To SHAPE THE SLEEVE TOP.—*1st row:* P. 3 tog., k. 1, * p. 2, k. 2, p. 2, k. 2, 3 in 1; repeat from *, until 10 remain, p. 2, k. 2, p. 2, k. 1, p. 3 tog.

Dec. 1 st. at each end of the next 5 rows.

7th row: P. 2 tog., p. 1, k. 1, * p. 2, k. 2, p. 2, 3 in 1; repeat from *, ending the last repeat with k. 2 tog.

Dec. 1 st. at each end of the next 5 rows.

Dec. 1 st. at each end of the next 2 rows.

19th row: K. 2 tog., k. 1, * p. 2, 3 in 1, p. 2, k. 2; repeat from *, ending the last repeat with k. 1, k. 2 tog.

Dec. 1 st. at each end of the next 3 rows.

Take 3 sts. tog. at each end of the next 2 rows.

25th row: P. 2 tog., * p. 2, 3 in 1, p. 2; repeat from * until 4 remain, k. 2, p. 2 tog.

Dec. 1 st. at each end of the next 4 rows.

30th row: Sl. 3 over 1, * k. 2, p. 2, k. 2, sl. 2 over 1; repeat from *, ending the last repeat with sl. 3 over 1.

31st row: K. 1, * p. 2, 3 in 1, p. 2, k. 2, 3 in 1; repeat from *, ending the last repeat with k. 1 instead of 3 in 1.

Dec. 1 st. at each end of the next row and following alternate rows (30 sts.). Cast off remaining sts., taking 2 sts. tog. along row.

FOR SHORT SLEEVES

BEGIN at the arm edge by casting on 88 sts. with No. 13 needles.

Work 11 rows in single rib.

Inc. row: (Wrong side) K. 8, (inc., k. 7) 10 times (98 sts.).

Change to No. 10 needles and work 7 patterns as on the back.

Shape the top as given for long sleeves.

TO MAKE UP THE JERSEY

PRESS all parts except the ribbing very lightly on the wrong side with a hot iron over a damp cloth, and a thick blanket underneath. Join the shoulder seams, taking 1 st. from each side at a time. Set sleeves into armholes and press these seams. Join sleeve and side seams in one line and press.

THE NECK BAND

WITH No. 13 needles cast on 3 sts. and k. 1 row.

Continue in garter-st. increasing 1 st. at the beginning of the next row and every alternate row until there are 12 sts. Join the shaped 258 rows on these sts. (129 ridges), then dec. 1 st. at the shaped edge on every alternate row until 3 sts. remain. Cast off.

Sew the neck band all round neck edge, with the mitred edges sewn together at the front.

SLEEVE · FRONT · BACK · NECK BAND · 19 · 16½ · 13

The Shape and Measurements of the Jersey.

Bonnet and Mittens – On the Cover

MATERIALS
Excelana 4 Ply Luxury Wool 100% pure new British wool (159m/174yds per 50g ball)
3 balls shade Persian Grey – MC
1 balls shade Ruby Red – A
1 balls shade Nile Green – B
1 pair 3mm (US #2–3) needles
Set of 3mm (US #2–3) DPNs

TENSION
32 sts & 32 rows = 10cm (4in) using 3mm needles over fair isle pattern

Standard Yarn Tension
28 sts & 36 rows = 10cm (4in) using 3mm needles over stocking stitch

ABBREVIATIONS
See page 13 for standard abbreviations

SIZING

Bonnet To fit average ladies head

Mittens To fit Medium–Large ladies hand
Circumference at palm = 24cm (9½in) approx
Length of hand (without gauntlet) = 20cm (8in)

Bonnet

BACK
Using 3mm needles and MC, cast on 29 sts.
Row 1: K.
Row 2: P.
Row 3: Work from chart A row 1, starting at first stitch of chart and reading from right to left, repeating the marked 6-stitch motif 4 times in total and ending with stitch 11.
Row 4: Work from chart A row 2 starting with stitch 11 and reading from left to right, then repeating the motif 4 times in total, and ending with sts 4–1.
Rows 3 and 4 set chart pattern. Taking incs into pattern, and repeating the 6-row motif as necessary, inc 1 st at each end of the following rows of colourwork pattern: 3, 5, 7, 9, 12, 15, 17, 19, 22, 26, 31 (51 sts).
Then, keeping pattern correct, dec 1 st at each end of the following rows of colourwork pattern: 43, 46, 49, then every row from 51 to 59 inclusive (27 sts).
Dec 2 sts at each end of next 3 rows (K3tog on RS rows, P3tog on WS rows) (15 sts).
Dec 1 st at each end of next row (13 sts).
Cast off all sts.

FRONT
Using 3mm needles and MC, cast on 176 sts.
Row 1 (RS): Reading from right to left, work all sts from chart B row 1, repeating the marked section 8 times.
Row 2 (WS): Reading from left to right, work all sts from chart B row 2, repeating marked section 8 times.
Rows 1 & 2 set chart pattern. Continue to work from chart until row 39 is complete.
Row 40 (WS): Using MC, purl to last st, Pfb (177 sts).

Next row (RS): Reading from right to left, work all sts from chart C row 1, repeating the marked section 29 times.
Next row (WS): Reading from left to right, work all sts from chart C row 2, repeating the marked section 29 times.
Work from chart C as set until row 6 is complete.
Work 2 more rows in stocking stitch using MC. Cast off.

TIES
Make 2 lengths of crochet chain in each colour approx 30cm (12in) long. Pin one end of each coloured chain together and work into a plait (as shown on photo). Knot at end. Neaten ends.

MAKING UP
Press pieces on wrong side under a damp cloth. Turn back pattern C on to WS and hem using slip stitch for turnback. Stitch front to back, easing in any excess fabric on front, then using MC, work a row of DC (SC) all round bottom of bonnet. Sew ties into place along bottom edge, approx 6cm (2.5in) from front of bonnet.

Chart A (Bonnet)

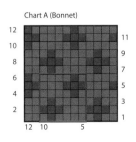

Key
- MC (Persian Grey); Knit on RS, Purl on WS
- Yarn A (Ruby Red); Knit on RS, Purl on WS
- Yarn B (Nile Green); Knit on RS, Purl on WS
- Pattern repeat

Mittens

CUFF

Using 3mm needles and MC cast on 92 sts.

Row 1 (RS): Reading from right to left work all sts from chart D row 1, repeating marked motif 15 times.

Row 2 (WS): Reading from left to right, work row 2 of chart D.

Work as set until chart row 6 is complete.

Next row: Work all sts from chart B row 1, repeating the marked section 4 times in each row.

Work from chart B as set until row 40 is complete.

Next row: With MC, * K5, K2tog, rep from * to last 8 sts, K5, K3tog (78 sts).

Work 1 row purl.

RIGHT HAND

Next row (RS): Reading from right to left, work all sts from row 1 chart E, repeating the marked section12 times.

Next row (WS): Reading from left to right, work all sts from row 2 chart E, repeating the marked section 12 times.

Work 18 more rows in colourwork pattern as set by last 2 rows.

Row 21 (RS): Work 40 sts in pattern, slip next 12 sts to waste yarn for thumb, cast on 12 sts in pattern, cont in pattern to end of row.

Work 28 more rows in pattern as set.

Row 50 (WS): P2tog, pattern 36 sts, slip last 37 sts to waste yarn, cast off 2 sts, pattern 36 sts, P2tog tbl (37 sts).

Dec 1 st at each end 7 foll alt rows (23 sts).

Dec 1 st at each end of next 5 rows (13 sts).

Cast off rem sts.

Rejoin yarn to other side of mitten and complete to match first side.

LEFT HAND

Work as for right hand, with the exception of row 21 which is worked as foll:

Row 21 (RS): Work 26 sts in pattern, slip next 12 sts to waste yarn for thumb, cast on 12 sts in pattern, cont in pattern to end of row.

Complete left hand as for right hand.

THUMB (both worked alike)

Return to sts on waste yarn for thumb, join in A, pick up 2 from side of opening, pick up and knit 12 sts across cast on edge, then 2 more from other side of opening (28 sts).

Using DPNs and A, work in rounds until thumb measures 6cm (2½in) or required length.

Next row: K2tog all round (14 sts).

Break off yarn and run end through sts. Draw up tightly and fasten off.

MAKING UP

Darn in all ends. Back stitch seams together, then turn over first 6 rows at lower edge of mitts to WS and slip stitch in place for hem.

Chart B (Bonnet and Mittens)

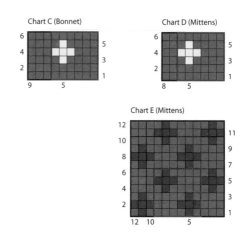

Chart C (Bonnet)

Chart D (Mittens)

Chart E (Mittens)

Stitchcraft February 1943

Bonnet and mittens - on the Cover

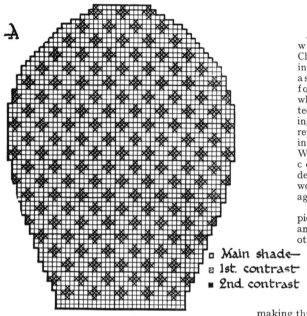

A

cast on 29 sts.

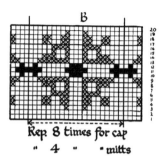

B

20 19 18 17 16 15 14 13 12 11 10 9 8 7 6 5 4 3 2 1

Rep. 8 times for cap
" 4 " " mitts

□ Main shade—
☒ 1st. contrast
■ 2nd. contrast

Hand: Now work from Chart D, leaving 12 sts. on a spare needle for thumb where indicated and casting on 12 to replace them in next row. When you come to decrease at top, cast off the 2 centre sts. and work on last 38 for palm, then join wool again to other 38 and work to correspond.

Return to sts. on spare needle for thumb, pick up 2 from side of opening, pick up and knit 12 cast-on sts., then 2 more from other side of opening. With four needles, work in rounds, using contrast wool and work for 2½ inches. NEXT ROW: k. 2 tog. all round. Break off wool and run end through sts.; draw up tightly and fasten off. Work other mitt to correspond, making thumb as indicated by dotted lines on chart. Turn in 6 ins. of top of cuff and hem, and thread round elastic through wrist to reqd. size. Join seams neatly.

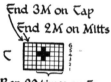

End 3M on Cap
End 2M on Mitts

C

6 5 4 3 2 1

Rep. 29 times on Cap
" 15 " " Mitts

CUFF: With main wool, cast on 92 sts. and work pattern from Chart C as indicated for 6 rows. Now work Chart B twice in same way as for bonnet.

NEXT ROW: With main shade, * k. 5, k. 2 tog.; repeat from * all along, ending k. 3 tog. (78 sts.). Work 1 row purl.

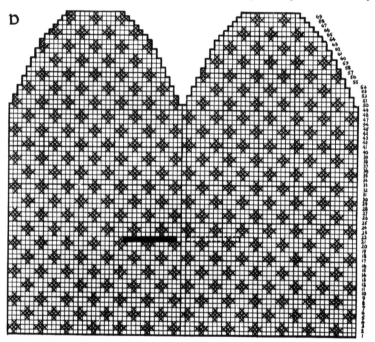

D

MATERIALS: *Bonnet:* 1 oz. Patons Beehive Fingering, 3-ply, and ½ oz. each of two contrasting shades. *Mitts:* 2 ozs. main shade, 1 oz. first and ½ oz. second contrasting shades. A pair No. 11 "Beehive" needles. A medium-sized crochet hook.

MEASUREMENTS: *Bonnet:* From top to bottom of back piece, 7 inches; from back to front of brim, 4½ inches; all round face, 18 inches. *Mitts:* Width all round hand, 8 inches; from tip to top of cuffs, 11½ inches.

TENSION: 10½ sts. to an inch.

BACK

With main shade, cast on 29 sts. and work from Chart A, working in stocking-stitch, and using one contrast shade for diamond pattern.

FRONT

With main wool, cast on 176 sts. and work from Chart B. Repeat pattern again, reversing the contrasting colours, and increase in last st.

Now work pattern C from chart, then 2 more rows stocking-stitch in main shade. Cast off.

STRINGS

Make lengths of crochet chain in each colour and plait, stitching ends together neatly.

TO MAKE UP

Press pieces on wrong side under a damp cloth. Turn back pattern C and hem neatly for turnback. Stitch front to back, then work a row of double crochet all round bottom of bonnet.

Jacket and Hood for Weekend Sports

MATERIALS
New Lanark Mills Silk & Wool DK 90% pure new wool/10% silk (120m/132yds per 50g ball)

Jacket
10 (11, 13, 15, 16) balls shade Lovage

Hood
2 balls shade Lovage
1 pair 2.75mm (US #2) needles
1 pair 3.75mm (US #5) needles
46cm (18in) open end zip
2 short close end zips (Finished length approx 11cm (4½in))

TENSION
24 sts & 28 rows = 10cm (4in) using 3.75mm needles over 6 row pattern

ABBREVIATIONS
See page 13 for standard abbreviations

SIZING
Measurements given in centimetres followed by inches in parentheses

To Fit	76–81 (30–32)	86–92 (34–36)	97–102 (38–40)	107–112 (42–44)	117–122 (46–48)
Finished Measurements					
Actual Bust Size	91 (36)	103 (40½)	117 (46)	128 (50½)	136½ (54)
Length to underarm	36½ (14½)	36½ (14½)	38 (15)	39 (15½)	41 (16)
Finished Length	54½ (21½)	55½ (22)	58 (23)	60½ (24)	64 (25)
Armhole Depth	18 (7)	19 (7½)	20 (8)	21½ (8½)	23 (9)

Garment shown in photographs for first size 76–81 (30–32)

Jacket

BACK
Using 2.75mm needles, cast on 100 (112, 128, 144, 156) sts and work as folls:

Next row: * K2, P2, rep from * to end.

Rep this row until work measures 10cm (4in) ending with a RS row.

Next row (WS): Working in rib, inc 2 (2, 4, 0, 0) sts evenly across row (102, 114, 132, 144, 156 sts).

Change to 3.75mm needles and work in patt as folls:

Row 1 (RS): * K5, P1, repeat from * to end.

Row 2: * P5, K1, repeat from * to end.

Row 3: K1, P1 * K5, P1, repeat from * to last 4 sts, K4.

Row 4: P3, K1, * P5, K1, repeat from * to last 2 sts, P2.

Row 5: K3, P1, * K5, P1, repeat from * to last 2 sts, K2.

Row 6: P1, K1, * P5, K1, repeat from * to last 4 sts, P4.

These 6 rows form patt. Continue in patt as set until work measures 36½ (36½, 38, 39, 41) cm (14½, 14½, 15, 15½, 16 in) ending with a WS row.

Shape Armholes
Maintaining patt, cast off 9 (10, 12, 8, 8) sts at beg of next 2 (2, 2, 4, 4) rows then dec 1 st at each end of next 3 (4, 6, 7, 10) rows (78, 86, 96, 98, 104 sts).

Continue in pattern without further shaping until armhole measures 18 (19, 20, 21½, 23) cm (7, 7½, 8, 8½, 9 in).

Shape Shoulders
Cast off 8 (10, 11, 11, 12) sts at beg of next 4 rows, then cast off 9 (9, 9, 10, 10) sts at beg of foll 2 rows (28, 28, 34, 34, 36 sts). Cast off rem sts.

LEFT FRONT
Using 2.75mm needles, cast on 58 (66, 74, 82, 86) sts.

Row 1 (RS): P2, * K2, P2, repeat from * till 4 sts rem, K4.

Row 2: K6, * P2, K2, repeat from * to end.

Repeat these 2 rows until work measures 10cm (4in) ending with row 2.

Change to 3.75mm needles and work in patt as folls:

Row 1 (RS): K0 (1, 3, 0, 3), P0 (1, 1, 0, 1), * K5, P1, repeat from * to last 4 sts, K4.

Row 2: K4, P1, K1, * P5, K1, repeat from * to last 4 (0, 2, 4, 2) sts, P4 (0, 2, 4, 2).

Row 3: K3 (0, 1, 3, 1), P1 (0, 1, 1, 1), * K5, P1, repeat from * to last 6 sts, K6.

Row 4: K4, P3, K1, * P5, K1, repeat from * to last 2 (4, 0, 2, 0) sts, P2 (4, 0, 2, 0).

Row 5: K1 (3, 0, 1, 0), P1 (1, 0, 1, 0), * K5, P1, repeat from * to last 8 sts, K8.

Row 6: K4, * P5, K1, repeat from * to last 0 (2, 4, 0, 4) sts, P0 (2, 4, 0, 4).

These 6 rows form patt. Rep 6 rows of patt, 3 times more. The following two rows place pocket. If pockets are not required, simply omit these two rows.

Next row (RS, place pocket): Work 18 (22, 26, 30, 32) sts in patt, cast off 25, pattern to end.

Next row: Work in patt, casting on 25 sts over those cast off in previous row.

Continue working in patt until work measures same as back to start of armhole shaping ending with a WS row.

Shape Armhole

Maintaining patt, cast off 9 (10, 12, 8, 8) sts at beg of next row and foll alt row 0 (0, 0, 1, 1) time (49, 56, 62, 66, 70 sts), patt one row, then dec 1 st at armhole edge of foll 3 (4, 6, 7, 10) rows (46, 52, 56, 59, 60 sts).

Continue in patt without further shaping until armhole measures 12 (12½, 13, 13½, 14) cm (4½, 5, 5, 5½, 5½ in) ending with a RS row.

Shape Neck

Cast off 8 sts at beg of next row (38, 44, 48, 51, 52 sts) then dec 1 st at neck edge of 13 (15, 17, 19, 18) foll rows (25, 29, 31, 32, 34 sts). Work without further shaping until front matches back to beg of shoulder shaping, ending with a WS row.

Shape Shoulder

Cast off 8 (10, 11, 11, 12) sts at beg of next and foll alt row. Cast off rem 9 (9, 9, 10, 10) sts.

RIGHT FRONT

Using 2.75mm needles cast on 58 (66, 74, 82, 86) sts.

Row 1 (RS): K4, P2, * K2, P2, repeat from * to end.
Row 2: * P2, K2, repeat from * to last 6 sts, K6.
Repeat these 2 rows until work measures 10cm (4in) ending with a WS row.
Change to 3.75mm needles and work in patt as folls:

Row 1 (RS): K4, * K5, P1, repeat from * to last 0 (2, 4, 0, 4) sts, K0 (2, 4, 0, 4).
Row 2: P0 (1, 3, 0, 3), K0 (1, 1, 0, 1), * P5, K1, repeat from * to last 4 sts, K4.
Row 3: K5, * P1, K5, repeat from * to last 5 (1, 3, 5, 3) sts, P1, K4 (0, 2, 4, 2).
Row 4: P3 (5, 1, 3, 1), * K1, P5, repeat from * to last 7 sts, K1, P2, K4.
Row 5: K7, * P1, K5, repeat from * to last 3 (5, 1, 3, 1) sts, P1, K2 (4, 0, 2, 0).
Row 6: P1 (3, 0, 1, 0), K1 (1, 0, 1, 0), * P5, K1, repeat from * to last 8 sts, P4, K4.

These 6 rows form patt. Rep until work measures same as back to armhole shaping, ending with a RS row.

Shape Armhole

Cast off 9 (10, 12, 8, 8) sts at beg of next row and foll alt row 0 (0, 0, 1, 1) time, then dec 1 st at armhole edge of next 3 (4, 6, 7, 10) rows (46, 52, 56, 59, 60 sts).

Continue in patt for 5 (5, 4, 5, 4) more rows.

Next row (RS, pocket placement): Patt 14 (16, 20, 22, 22), cast off 25 sts, patt to end.

Next row: Work in patt, casting on 25 sts over those cast off in previous row.

Continue in pattern until armhole measures 12 (12½, 13, 13½, 14) cm (4½, 5, 5, 5½, 5½ in) ending with a WS row.

Shape Neck

Cast off 8 sts at beg of next row (38, 44, 48, 51, 52 sts), then dec 1 st at neck edge of 13 (15, 17, 19, 18) foll rows (25, 29, 31, 32, 34 sts). Work without further shaping until front matches back to beg of shoulder shaping, ending with a RS row.

Next row: * K2, P2, rep from * to end. Continue in rib until work measures 10cm (4in) ending on a WS row, increasing 0 (2, 0, 2, 0) sts evenly on last row (60, 66, 72, 78, 84 sts). Change to 3.75mm needles and working in patt as for back, inc 1 st each end of 4th (4th, 6th, 8th, 8th) and 11 foll 8th rows (84, 90, 96, 102, 108 sts). Work without further shaping until sleeve measures 46 (47, 48, 48, 49½) cm (18, 18½, 19, 19, 19½ in).

Shape Sleeve Head
Cast off 5 (6, 7, 8, 8) sts at beg of next 2 rows (74, 78, 82, 86, 92 sts), then dec 1 st at each end of every row until 34 (36, 36, 36, 38) sts rem. Cast off rem sts.

COLLAR
Using 3.75mm needles, cast on 136 (140, 144, 152, 156) sts and proceed as folls:

Next row: * K2, P2, rep from * to end. Rep this row a further 19 times.

Row 1: Rib 40 (40, 40, 44, 44), [K2, P2tog] 4 times, rib 22 (26, 30, 30, 34), [P2tog, K2] 4 times, rib 42 (42, 42, 46, 46) (128, 132, 136, 144, 148 sts).

Row 2: Rib 44 (44, 44, 48, 48), [K1, P2] 4 times, rib 20 (24, 28, 28, 32), [K1, P2] 4 times, rib 40 (40, 40, 44, 44).

Row 3: Rib 40 (40, 40, 44, 44), [K2, P1] 4 times, rib 20 (24, 28, 28, 32), [K2, P1] 4 times, rib 44 (44, 44, 48, 48).

Repeat last 2 rows 3 more times then repeat row 2 once more.

Row 11: Rib 40 (40, 40, 44, 44), [K2, P1] 4 times, [K2, P2tog] 5 (6, 7, 7, 8) times, [K2, P1] 4 times, rib 44 (45, 46, 50, 53) (123, 126, 129, 137, 140 sts)

Row 12: Rib 44 (44, 44, 48, 48), [K1, P2] 13 (14, 15, 15, 16) times, rib 40 (40, 40, 44, 44).

Row 13: Rib 40 (40, 40, 44, 44), [K2, P1] 13 (14, 15, 15, 16) times, rib 44 (44, 44, 48, 48).

Repeat last 2 rows twice.

Keeping rib patt correct, cast off 10 sts at beg of next 10 rows (23, 26, 29, 37, 40 sts).

Cast off rem sts.

Shape Shoulder
Cast off 8 (10, 11, 11, 12) sts at beg of next and foll alt row. Cast off rem 9 (9, 9, 10, 10) sts.

POCKETS (Make two)
Using 3.75mm needles, cast on 25 sts.
Commencing with a K row, work in stocking stitch until work measures 7½cm (3in).
Cast off.

SLEEVES
Using 2.75mm needles cast on 60 (64, 72, 76, 84) sts and work in rib as folls:

MAKING UP

Press work lightly through a damp cloth. Join shoulder seams. Join side and sleeve seams. Set in sleeves taking care to match centre of sleeve head to shoulder seam. Stitch zip up centre and sew collar in place using a flat slip stitch (See 'Fit and Finish' chapter). Sew zips into each pocket and attach pocket linings to WS of jacket over each zip.

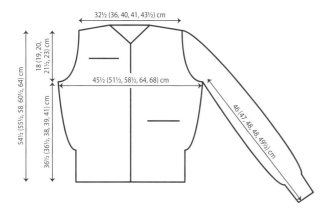

Hood

Using 2.75mm needles cast on 50 sts.
Row 1 (RS): K2, * P2, K2, rep from * to end.
Row 2 (WS): P2, * K2, P2, rep from * to end.
These 2 rows set rib. Work a further 12 rows as set, place marker at beg of last row.
Change to 3.75mm needles and continue in rib until work measures 28cm (11in). Place marker at beg of last row to show end of first side, continue in rib until 2nd side measures same to lower marker, change to 2.75mm needles and work 14 more rows. Cast off in rib.

STRAPS

Using 3.75mm needles, cast on 32 sts and work in K2, P2 rib as set above for 32cm (12½in). Cast off in rib using 2.75mm needles. Make another strip the same.

MAKING UP

Fold hood in half at centre marker and with RS together, sew up back seam. Sew one strap at cast off edge to each side of lower front edge of hood. Darn in all ends. Press.

MATERIALS

Kelpie Knitting Wool: 14 ozs. for Jacket and 5 ozs. for Hood.
2 No. 12 and 2 No. 8 Abel Morrall's "Aero" knitting needles.
2 No. 9 Abel Morrall's "Aero" knitting needles (for Hood).
Zipp fastener, 18 ins. long.
2 Zipp fasteners, 4 in. long.

To obtain the best results it is essential that you use the exact materials mentioned on the left

MEASUREMENTS

Round Jacket, below armholes, 36 inches. Shoulder to lower edge, 20 inches. Sleeve seam, 19 inches.

Tension on No. 8 needles about 6 stitches and 8 rows to one inch.

Jacket and

For golf, hiking and flying—a long-sleeved Jacket to keep you warm and a smart new knitted Hood to slip over your curls

6 times, k. 8. (46 sts.) **6th row**—As 6th pattern row.

Rep. rows 1–6 inclusive of pattern 6 more times, then rep. 1st row again. (Work should measure exactly 18 inches.) Now shape neck and shoulders:

1st row—Cast off 8, p. 3, k. 1, (p. 5, k. 1) 5 times, p. 4. ** Work 13 rows in pattern knitting 2 tog. at neck edge of every row. (25 sts.) Work 3 rows in pattern, then cast off 8 sts. at the beginning of the next 2 rows that start at armhole edge. Cast off remaining 9 sts.

The Back

USING No. 12 needles cast on 100 sts. and work in rib of k. 2, p. 2 for 4 inches, increasing 1 st. each end of the last row. Change to No. 8 needles and work in pattern as follows:

1st row—* K. 5, p. 1, rep. from * to end of row. **2nd row**—* P. 5, k. 1, rep. from * to end of row. **3rd row**—K. 1, p. 1, * k. 5, p. 1, rep. from * till 4 sts. remain, k. 4. **4th row**—P. 3, k. 1, * p. 5, k. 1, rep. from * till 2 sts. remain, p. 2.

5th row—K. 3, p. 1, * k. 5, p. 1, rep. from * till 2 sts. remain, k. 2.

6th row—P. 1, k. 1, * p. 5, k. 1, rep. from * till 4 sts. remain, p. 4. These 6 rows form the pattern. Rep. these 6 rows 14 more times. (90 rows, and work should measure about 14¼ inches.) Now shape for armholes:

1st row—Cast off 9, k. 2, p. 1, * k. 5, p. 1, rep. from * to end of row.

2nd row—Cast off 9, p. 2, k. 1, * p. 5, k. 1, rep. from * till 3 sts. remain, p. 3.

3rd row—K. 2 tog., k. 2, * p. 1, k. 5, rep. from * till 2 sts. remain, p. 2 tog.

4th row—P. 2 tog., p. 3, k. 1, * p. 5, k. 1, rep. from * till 4 sts. remain, p. 2, p. 2 tog. **5th row**—K. 2 tog., k. 2, p. 1, * k. 5, p. 1, rep. from * till 3 sts. remain, k. 2 tog., k. 1. (78 sts.)

6th row—As 6th pattern row. Rep. the 6 rows of pattern 8 more times. Now shape shoulders by casting off 8 sts. at the beginning of the next 4 rows, then 9 sts. at the beginning of the following 2 rows. Cast off remaining 28 sts.

The Left Front

Using No. 12 needles cast on 58 sts.
1st row—P. 2, * k. 2, p. 2, rep. from * till 4 sts. remain, k. 4. **2nd row**—K. 6, * p. 2, k. 2, rep. from * to end of row. Rep. these 2 rows for 4 inches, ending with the 2nd row. Change to No. 8 needles and work in pattern as follows:

1st row—* K. 5, p. 1, rep. from * till 4 sts. remain, k. 4. **2nd row**—K. 4, p. 1, k. 1, * p. 5, k. 1, rep. from * till 4 sts. remain, p. 4. **3rd row**—K. 3, p. 1, * k. 5, p. 1, rep. from * till 6 sts. remain, k. 6. **4th row**—K. 4, p. 3, k. 1, * p. 5, k. 1, rep. from * till 2 sts. remain, p. 2.

5th row—K. 1, p. 1, * k. 5, p. 1, rep. from * till 8 sts. remain, k. 8.

6th row—K. 4, * p. 5, k. 1, rep. from * to end of row. These 6 rows form the pattern. Rep. pattern 3 more times.

25th row—(K. 5, p. 1) 3 times, cast off 25, k. 4, p. 1, k. 5, p. 1, k. 4.

26th row—K. 4, p. 1, k. 1, p. 5, k. 1, p. 3, cast on 25 and p. these 25 sts., p. 1, k. 1, (p. 5, k. 1) twice, p. 4.

Rep. rows 3–6 inclusive of pattern, then rep. rows 1–6 inclusive of pattern 10 more times. (90 rows, and work should measure about 14¼ inches.) Now shape for armhole:

1st row—Cast off 9, k. 2, p. 1, (k. 5, p. 1) 7 times, k. 4. **2nd row**—K. 4, p. 1, k. 1, (p. 5, k. 1) 7 times, p. 1.

3rd row—K. 2 tog., k. 4, p. 1, (k. 5, p. 1) 6 times, k. 6. **4th row**—K. 4, p. 3, k. 1, (p. 5, k. 1) 6 times, p. 2, p. 2 tog.

5th row—K. 2 tog., p. 1, (k. 5, p. 1)

The Right Front

Using No. 12 needles cast on 58 sts.
1st row—K. 4, p. 2, * k. 2, p. 2, rep. from * to end of row. **2nd row**—* K. 2, p. 2, rep. from * till 6 sts. remain, k. 6. Rep. these 2 rows for 4 inches, ending with the 2nd row. Change to No. 8 needles and work in pattern as follows:

1st row—K. 4, * k. 5, p. 1, rep. from * to end of row. **2nd row**—* P. 5, k. 1,

Hood

for WEEK-END SPORTS

rep. from * till 4 sts. remain, k. 4.

3rd row—K. 5, * p. 1, k. 5, rep. from * till 5 sts. remain, p. 1, k. 4. **4th row**—P. 3 * k. 1, p. 5, rep. from * till 7 sts. remain, k. 1, p. 2, k. 4. **5th row**—K. 7, * p. 1, k. 5, rep. from * till 3 sts. remain, p. 1, k. 2. **6th row**—P. 1, k. 1, * p. 5, k. 1, rep. from * till 8 sts. remain, p. 4, k. 4. These 6 rows form the pattern. Rep. pattern 14 more times, and work 1st row of next pattern. (91 rows, and work should measure 14¼ inches.) Now shape for armhole :

1st row—Cast off 9, p. 2, k. 1, (p. 5, k. 1) 7 times, k. 4. **2nd row**—(K. 5, p. 1) 7 times, k. 5, k. 2 tog. **3rd row**—P. 2 tog., p. 3, (k. 1, p. 5) 6 times, k. 1, p. 2, k. 4. **4th row**—K. 7, (p. 1, k. 5) 6 times, p. 1, k. 1, k. 2 tog. (46 sts.)

5th row—As 6th pattern row. Work rows 1–4 inclusive of pattern.

10th row—K. 7, p. 1, k. 5, p. 1, cast off 25, k. 4, p. 1, k. 2. **11th row**—P. 1, k. 1, p. 5, cast on 25 sts. and p. across these sts., p. 5, k. 1, p. 4, k. 4.

Rep. rows 1–6 inclusive of pattern 5 more times. (Work should measure

18 inches.) **Next row**—Cast off 8, k. 1, p. 1, (k. 5, p. 1) 6 times. Now rep. from ** of Left Front.

The Pockets (two alike)

Cast on 25 sts. **1st row**—Knit. **2nd row**—Purl. Rep. these 2 rows for 3 inches. Cast off. Make another piece the same.

The Sleeves (both alike)

Using No. 12 needles cast on 60 sts. and work in rib of k. 2, p. 2 for 4 inches. Change to No. 8 needles and work rows 1–6 of pattern as given for Back. Continue in pattern increasing 1 st. each end of the 4th row and every 10th row after till 84 sts. are on needle. Work straight till sleeve is required length. Cast off 5 sts. at the beginning of the next 2 rows, then k. 2 tog. each end of every row till 30 sts. remain. Cast off.

The Collar

Using No. 8 needles cast on 136 sts. and work in rib of k. 2, p. 2 for 20 rows.

21st row—Rib 40, (k. 2, p. 2 tog.) 4 times, rib 22, (p. 2 tog., k. 2) 4 times, rib 42. **22nd row**—Rib 44, (k. 1, p. 2) 4 times, rib 20, (k. 1, p. 2) 4 times, rib 40

23rd row—Rib 40, (k. 2, p. 1) 4 times, rib 20, (k. 2, p. 1) 4 times, rib 44. Rep. last 2 rows 3 times, then rep. 22nd row again. **31st row** —Rib 40, (k. 2, p. 1) 4 times, (k. 2, p. 2 tog.) 5 times, (k. 2,

p. 1) 4 times, rib 44. **32nd row**—Rib 44, (k. 1, p. 2) 13 times, rib 40.

33rd row—Rib 40, (k. 2, p. 1) 13 times, rib 40. Rep. last 2 rows twice.

Next row—Cast off 10 in rib, work in rib pattern to end of row. Rep. this row 9 more times. (23 sts.) Cast off.

TO MAKE UP

Press work lightly with a warm iron over a damp cloth. Join shoulder seams and sew in sleeves. Join side and sleeve seams. Stitch Zipp up centre and sew cast off edge of collar round neckline, so that the wrong side is the decreased side. Sew Zipps into each pocket opening and sew pocket linings down on the wrong side of work over zipps. Press all seams

HOOD

Using No. 12 needles cast on 88 sts. and work in rib of k. 2, p. 2 for 14 rows. Change to No. 9 needles and continue in rib till work measures 11 inches. Cast off in rib. Make another piece the same.

The Straps

Using No. 9 needles cast on 32 sts. and work in rib of k. 2, p. 2 for 12½ inches. Cast off in rib with No. 12 needles. Make another strip the same. Join one side seam of two main pieces, and join both cast-off edges together. Now sew cast-off edge of each strap to lower side edges of hood. Do not press work.

Looped Bed Jacket

MATERIALS
Jamieson's Spindrift 100% Shetland wool (105m per 25g ball)
18 (21, 25, 29, 33, 37) balls shade 440 (Peach)
1 pair 4.5mm (US #7) needles
3mm crochet hook
1m of 5cm wide ribbon

TENSION
18 sts & 30 rows = 10cm (4in) using 4.5mm needles over stitch pattern

Standard Yarn Tension
30 sts & 32 rows = 10cm (4in) using 3.25mm needles over stocking stitch

ABBREVIATIONS
See page 13 for standard abbreviations

SIZING
Measurements given in centimetres followed by inches in parentheses

To Fit	81–86 (32–34)	92–97 (36–38)	102–106 (40–42)	112–117 (44–46)	122–127 (48–50)	132–137 (52–54)
Finished Measurements						
Actual Bust Size	96 (38)	103½ (40¾)	114½ (45)	123½ (48½)	134½ (53)	143½ (56½)
Length to underarm	25½ (10)	28 (11)	30½ (12)	33 (13)	34½ (14)	37½ (15)
Armhole Depth	20 (8)	21½ (8½)	23 (9)	24 (9½)	25½ (10)	26½ (10½)
Finished Length	45½ (18)	49½ (19½)	53½ (21)	57 (22½)	60 (23½)	64 (25)
Shoulder to Shoulder	35 (14)	37 (14½)	40½ (16)	43 (17)	46 (18)	48 (19)
Sleeve Length	19 (7½)	20 (8)	21½ (8½)	23 (9)	24 (9½)	25½ (10)

Garment shown in photographs is for first size 81–86 (32–34)

LEFT FRONT
Using 4.5mm needles, cast on 45 (49, 55, 59, 65, 69) sts and work in patt as folls:
Row 1 (RS): K.
Row 2: P.
Row 3: K.
Row 4: K2, * put needle in next st as if to knit, then wind wool twice round RH needle and 2 fingers of left hand, winding it in the opposite direction to knitting, then take it over needle again, and draw all 3 loops through the st on LH needle, then put these 3 loops on LH needle and knit all 4 sts together as 1 st, repeat from * to last 2 sts, K2.

These 4 rows form the pattern. Repeat them 18 (20, 22, 24, 25, 27) times more, ending with RS facing.

Shape Armholes
Note on shaping: If you have to dec a st at start or end of a 4th patt row, just knit 2 sts together in ordinary way. But if you have to cast off sts at start of 4th patt row, work each sts as you would normally do on a 4th pattern row, before casting it off.

Maintaining pattern, cast off 7 (9, 10, 10, 7, 8) sts at beginning of next and foll 0 (0, 0, 0, 1, 1) alt row (38, 40, 45, 49, 51, 53 sts) then dec 1 st at armhole edge on each of the next 3 rows (35, 36, 40, 42, 46, 48 sts). Now continue in patt without further shaping until you have worked the 3rd row of the 32nd (35th, 38th, 41st, 43rd, 46th) patt from cast on.

Shape Neck
Maintaining pattern, cast off 10 (10, 11, 11, 13, 13) sts at beg of next row (25, 26, 29, 31, 33, 35 sts), then dec 1 st at neck edge of every row until 20 (22, 24, 26, 28, 30) sts remain. Continue in pattern without further shaping, until 34th (37th, 40th, 43rd, 45th, 48th) patt from beg is completed. Cast off.

RIGHT FRONT
Using 4.5mm needles, cast on 45 (49, 55, 59, 65, 69) sts and work 4 row patt 18 (20, 22, 24, 25, 27) times, then work 3 rows of 19th (21st, 23rd, 25th, 26th, 28th) patt rep ending with a RS row.

Shape Armhole
Maintaining patt, cast off 7 (9, 10, 10, 7, 8) sts at beginning of next and foll 0 (0, 0, 0, 1, 1) alt row (38, 40, 45, 49, 51, 53 sts) then dec 1 st at armhole edge on each of the next 3 (4, 5, 7, 5, 5) rows (35, 36, 40, 42, 46, 48 sts). Continue in patt without further shaping until 32nd (35th,

and work 4 row patt, 4 times, then dec 1 st at each end of next and every foll 8th row until 65 (69, 73, 77, 81, 85) sts rem, then work straight until 14th (15th, 16th, 17th, 18th, 19th) patt from beg worked.

Shape Sleeve Head
Maintaining patt, cast off 7 (9, 10, 10, 7, 8) sts at beg of next 2 (2, 2, 2, 4, 4) rows (51, 51, 53, 57, 53, 53 sts), then dec 1 st at each end of next and 14 (12, 12, 15, 13, 12) foll alt rows and then dec 1 st at each end of 0 (2, 3, 2, 3, 4) foll 4th rows (21, 21, 21, 21, 19, 19 sts). Work 8 rows without shaping. Cast off.

MAKING UP
Join shoulder seams then join side and sleeve seams. Inset sleeves into armhole. If preferred, work 1 row of double crochet (single crochet) using a 3mm crochet hook around neck and down front edges, spacing the sts evenly to keep the work flat. Cut ribbon in two and sew one piece to each side of front at neck. Darn in all ends.

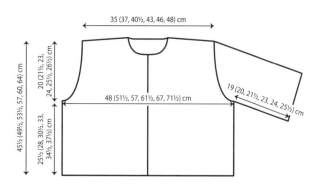

38th, 41st, 43rd, 46th) patt from beg completed ending with RS facing.

Shape Neck
Maintaining patt, cast off 10 (10, 11, 11, 13, 13) sts at beg of next row (25, 26, 29, 31, 33, 35 sts), then dec 1 st at neck edge of every row until 20 (22, 24, 26, 28, 30) sts remain. Continue in pattern without further shaping, until 34th (37th, 40th, 43rd, 45th, 48th) patt from beg completed. Cast off.

BACK
Using 4.5mm needles, cast on 83 (93, 103, 111, 121, 129) sts and work in 4 row patt 18 (20, 22, 24, 25, 27) times, then work 3 rows of 19th (21st, 23rd, 25th, 26th, 28th) patt rep.

Shape Armholes
Maintaining patt, cast off 7 (9, 10, 10, 7, 8) sts at beg of next 2 (2, 2, 2, 4, 4) rows (69, 75, 83, 91, 93, 97 sts) then dec 1 st at each end of next 3 (4, 5, 7, 5, 5) rows (63, 67, 73, 77, 83, 87 sts). Continue in patt without further shaping until you have worked 3rd row of 33rd (36th, 39th, 42nd, 44th, 47th) patt from cast on.
Next row: Patt 22 (24, 26, 28, 30, 32) sts, cast off next 19 (19, 21, 21, 23, 23) sts then work rem 22 (24, 26, 28, 30, 32) sts. Put first set of 22 (24, 26, 28, 30, 32) sts on stitch holder and work on rem 22 (24, 26, 28, 30, 32) sts as folls:
** Dec 1 st at neck edge of next 2 rows (20, 22, 24, 26, 28, 30 sts), then work 2 rows without further shaping. Cast off. **
With RS facing, rejoin yarn to neck edge of rem 22 (24, 26, 28, 30, 32) sts and work as for first side from ** to **.

SLEEVES
Using 4.5mm needles, cast on 75 (79, 83, 87, 91, 95) sts

WELDONS
LEAFLET 3d
No. 489

LOOPED BED-JACKET
Quickly and Simply Knitted
8 oz. of 3-ply

THIS adorable bed-jacket is so light and warm to wear. It has the appearance of swansdown, and the fascinating loop stitch in which it is knitted is quick, simple to work and very effective.

DAINTY BED-JACKET
Knitted in Loop Stitch
To Fit Average Women's Size

MATERIALS: *8 ozs. of Patons Beehive Baby Wool, 3-ply ('Patonised' Shrink-resist finish): 1 pair of No. 5 knitting needles, 1 yard of ribbon, a medium size crochet hook.*

TENSION: *5 sts. to 1 inch in width, and 12 rows (3 patterns) to 2 inches in depth.*

MEASUREMENTS: *Round underarms, about 35 inches. Length from shoulder, 14 inches. Sleeves down underarms, 9½ inches.*

ABBREVIATIONS: *K., knit: p., purl: st., stitch: sts., stitches: rep., repeat: tog., together: dec., decrease.*

LEFT FRONT

Cast on 45 sts. and work in pattern :

1st row (right side): K.

2nd row: P. **3rd row:** K.

4th row: K. 2, * put needle in next st. as if to k., then wind wool twice round right-hand needle and 2 fingers of left hand, winding it in the opposite direction to knitting, then take it over needle again, and draw all 3 loops through the st. on left-hand needle, then put these 3 loops on left-hand needle and k. all 4 sts. tog. as 1 st. Rep. from * to last 2 sts., k. 2.

These 4 rows form the pattern. Rep. them 12 times more, and then you are ready to begin armhole shapings.

Note on shapings: If you have to dec. a st. at start or end of a 4th pattern row, just knit 2 sts. tog. in the ordinary way. But if you have to cast off sts. at start of a 4th pattern row, work each st. as you would normally do on a 4th pattern row, before casting it off.

To shape armhole, proceed as follows :

Cast off 7 sts. at beginning of next row, then dec. 1 st. at armhole edge on each of the next 3 rows. Now proceed in pattern as original pattern rows until you have worked the 3rd row of the 19th pattern from start. To shape neck, cast off 10 sts. at beginning of next row, then dec. 1 st. at neck edge of every row until 20 sts. remain. Work a few rows without dec. until you have completed 21st pattern from start. Cast off.

RIGHT FRONT

Work as given for left front until you have finished 3rd row of 13th pattern from start. To shape armhole, cast off 7 sts. at start of next row, then dec. 1 st. at armhole edge on each of the next 3 rows. Work next row as an ordinary 4th pattern row, and continue in pattern until you have completed 19th pattern from start. To shape neck, cast off 10 sts. at beginning of next row, then dec. 1 st. at neck edge of every row until 20 sts. remain. Work a row or two without dec. until you have completed 21st pattern from start. Cast off.

BACK

Cast on 83 sts. and work in pattern as given for left front until you have worked 3rd row of 13th pattern from start. To shape armholes, cast off 7 sts. at beginning of next 2 rows, then dec. 1 st.

at each end of next 3 rows. Proceed in pattern until you have worked 3rd row of 20th pattern from start.

Next row: Work in pattern over 22 sts., cast off next 19 sts., then work remaining 22 sts. Put first set of 22 sts. on st.-holder and proceed over 2nd set thus:

Work 4 rows on these sts., but dec. 1 st. at inner (neck) edge of first 2 rows. Cast off.

Join wool to inner end of the 22 sts. for other side and work to match 1st side from ** to **.

SLEEVES (both alike)

Cast on 75 sts. and work in pattern as for left front for 4 patterns, then dec. 1 st. at each end of next row, and every following 8th row until 65 sts. remain, then work straight until you have completed 14th pattern from start. To shape top, cast off 7 sts. at beginning of next 2 rows, then dec. 1 st. at each end of next row. Work next row (a loop row) without dec.

Dec. 1 st. at each end of next 3 rows, then work next row without dec. Rep. last 4 rows 3 times. Work 8 rows (2 patterns) straight. Cast off.

TO MAKE UP

Join shoulder seams and sew sleeves into armholes. Join side and sleeve seams. Work 1 row of double crochet round neck and down front edges, spacing the sts. evenly to keep the work flat. Cut ribbon in two and sew one piece to each side of front at neck.

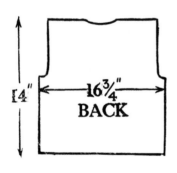

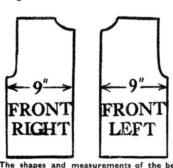

The shapes and measurements of the bed-jacket are clearly shown in this diagram.

Feather Stitch Scarf

MATERIALS
J C Rennie Lambswool 100% lambswool (246m/270yds per 50g ball)
1 ball each of shades: 200 (Winter white) – MC, 777 (Lush) – A, 1424 (Carnation) – B, 364 (Pagan) – C
1 pair 3.75mm (US #5) needles

TENSION
1 patt rep = 4cm (1½in) using 3.75mm needles & 28 rows = 10cm (4in) using 3.75mm needles over feather pattern

ABBREVIATIONS
See page 13 for standard abbreviations

SIZING
Finished length 131cm (51½in), width 30cm (12in)

Using 3.75mm needles and MC, cast on 75 sts, and work in patt as folls:
Row 1: K2, K2tog, (K3, YO, K1, YO, K3, K3tog) to last 11 sts, K3, YO, K1, YO, K3, K2tog, K2.
Row 2: K.

These 2 rows form pattern. Rep them 5 times more and then continue in patt in colour sequence as folls:

** 2 rows A
2 rows B
10 rows C
8 rows MC
6 rows A
2 rows B
2 rows A
4 rows B
2 rows A

2 rows B
6 rows A
8 rows MC
8 rows C
2 rows B
2 rows A
12 rows MC
2 rows A
12 rows MC

Rep this 92 row colour sequence from ** three times more, but on final rep omit the final 2 rows A and 12 rows MC from end of sequence. Cast off loosely.

MAKING UP
Dampen scarf, with WS upmost, block out to correct measurements and steam gently. Leave to dry before removing pins.

THE SCARF

MATERIALS : 1 oz. of Copley's 2-ply "Excelsior" Super Fingering in main colour and ¼ oz. each of dark green, light green and yellow, or 2 ozs. if making scarf in one colour 1 pair of No. 7 knitting needles.

TENSION : 15 sts. to 2 inches and 23 rows to 3 inches, after pressing.

MEASUREMENTS : Width, 10 inches ; length, 38 inches.

ABBREVIATIONS : M, main colour ; D, dark green ; L, light green ; Y, yellow. For other "Abbreviations" see page 2.

TO MAKE

With M wool, cast on 75 sts. and work in pattern thus :

1st pattern row : K. 2, k. 2 tog., (k. 3, w.fd., k. 1, w.fd., k. 3, k. 3 tog.) to last 11 sts., k. 3, w.fd., k. 1, w.fd., k. 3, k. 2 tog., k. 2. **2nd row:** K.

These 2 rows form the pattern. Rep. them 5 times more, then continue in pattern in the following colour sequence.

* 2 rows Y, 2 M, 2 L, 2 M, 8 D, 8 Y, 6 L, 2 M, 2 L, 4 M, 2 L, 2 M, 6 L, 8 Y, 8 D, 2 M, 2 L, 2 M, 2 Y, 12 M, 2 L, 12 M.*

Rep. from * to * twice, but omit the last 2 L and 12 M from end of 2nd rep. Cast off.

TO COMPLETE

Darn in the ends of wool. Press with a warm iron over a damp cloth.

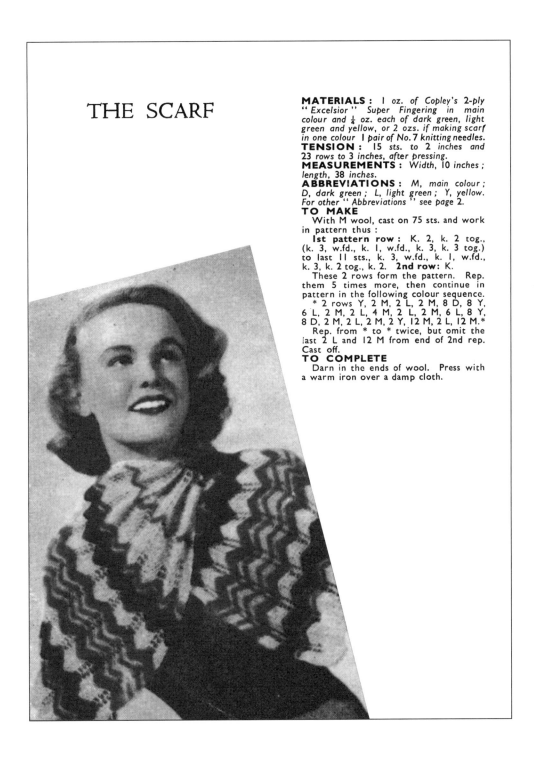

Plaid Jacket and Cap

MATERIALS

Jamieson's Spindrift 100% Shetland wool (105m per 25g ball)

Jacket
10 (12, 13, 15, 17) balls shade 105 (Eesit) – MC
1 (1, 2, 2, 2) balls shade 788 (Leaf) – A
1 (1, 1, 1, 2) balls shade 525 (Crimson) – B

Cap
2 balls shade 105 (Eesit) – MC
Small quantities of shades 788 (Leaf) A and 525 (Crimson) B for contrasts
1 pair 2.75mm (US #2) needles
1 pair 3.25mm (US #3) needles
8 buttons
1 feather
1m of Petersham or Buckram (optional)

TENSION

26 sts & 32 rows = 10cm (4in) using 3.25mm needles over stripe pattern

Standard Yarn Tension

30 sts & 32 rows = 10cm (4in) using 3.25mm needles over stocking stitch

ABBREVIATIONS

See page 13 for standard abbreviations

SIZING

Measurements given in centimetres followed by inches in parentheses

To Fit	76–81 (30–32)	86–92 (34–36)	97–102 (38–40)	107–112 (42–44)	117–122 (46–48)
Finished Measurements					
Actual Bust Size	84 (33)	96 (38)	104 (41)	116 (45½)	124 (49)
Length to underarm	34½ (13½)	35½ (14)	37 (14½)	38 (15)	39½ (15½)
Armhole Depth	16 (6¼)	18½ (7¼)	19½ (7½)	19½ (7½)	21½ (8½)
Finished Length	50½ (20)	54 (21¼)	57½ (22½)	57½ (22½)	61 (24)
Shoulder to Shoulder	35 (14)	39½ (15½)	42½ (16¾)	46 (18)	47½ (18¾)
Sleeve Length	45¾ (18)	47 (18½)	47 (18½)	48 (19)	49½ (19½)

Garment shown in photographs is for first size 76–81 (30–32)

STRIPE PATTERN (Worked in stocking stitch throughout)
Work 31 rows MC,
1 row A,
3 rows MC,
1 row B,
1 row MC,
1 row A
These 38 rows form pattern.

Jacket

LEFT FRONT

Using 2.75mm needles and A, cast on 54 (62, 68, 74, 80) sts. Commencing with a K row work 9 rows in stocking stitch. Change to 3.25mm needles and MC, and work one K row (this denotes hem line).

Commencing with a K row and row 1 of stripe pattern, work in stocking stitch until work measures 2½cm (1in) from hemline, ending with a WS row. Dec 1 st at beg of next row and foll 8th row (52, 60, 66, 72, 78 sts). Work without further shaping until front measures 10cm (4in) ending with a WS row. Inc 1 st at beg of next row and every foll 6th row until there 62 (70, 76, 82, 88) sts. Work without further shaping until work measures 34½ (35½, 37, 38, 39½ cm (13½, 14, 14½, 15, 15½ in) from hemline, ending with a WS row.

Shape Armhole

Cast off 5 (7, 8, 6, 7) sts at beg of next and 0 (0, 0, 1, 1) foll alt row, then 3 sts on foll alt row (54, 60, 65, 67, 71 sts), then dec 1 st at beg of each row at armhole edge until 49 (55, 60, 62, 66) sts rem, ending with a RS row.

Row 14 (RS): K4, cast off next 3 sts, K to end.
Row 15: P to cast off sts, cast on 3, P4.

Whilst maintaining pattern as set below, work 7 further buttonholes on every foll 13th (13th, 13th, 13th, 15th) & 14th (14th, 14th, 14th, 16th) rows. If row tension is correct, last buttonhole should fall before the end of armhole shaping.

Work without further shaping until front measures 10cm (4in) ending with a RS row. Inc 1 st at beg of next row and every foll 6th row until there 62 (70, 76, 82, 88) sts. Work without further shaping until work measures 34½ (35½, 37, 38, 39½) cm (13½, 14, 14½, 15, 15½ in) from hemline, ending with a RS row.

Shape Armhole

Cast off 5 (7, 8, 6, 7) sts at beg of next and 0 (0, 0, 1, 1) foll alt row, then 3 sts on foll alt row (54, 60, 65, 67, 71 sts), then dec 1 st at beg of each row at armhole edge until 49 (55, 60, 62, 66) sts rem, ending with a WS row.

Shape Neck

Dec 1 st at beg of next and every foll 4th row until 44 (50, 55, 57, 61) sts rem, then dec 1 st on every foll alt row until 31 (35, 39, 43, 43) sts rem, ending at armhole edge.

Shape Shoulder and Neck

Cast off 7 (8, 9, 10, 10) sts at beg of next and foll 3 alt rows and at same time dec 1 st at beg of every row at neck edge 3 times.

Shape Neck

Dec 1 st at beg of next and every foll 4th row until 44 (50, 55, 57, 61) sts rem, then dec 1 st on every foll alt row until 31 (35, 39, 43, 43) sts rem, ending at armhole edge. Work 0 (4, 6, 8, 6) rows without shaping.

Shape Shoulder and Neck

Cast off 7 (8, 9, 10, 10) sts at beg of next and foll 3 alt rows and at same dec 1 st at beg of every row at neck edge 3 times.

RIGHT FRONT

Using 2.75mm needles and A, cast on 54 (62, 68, 74, 80) sts. Commencing with a K row work 9 rows in stocking stitch. Change to 3.25mm needles and MC, and work one K row (this denotes hem line).

Commencing with a K row and row 1 of stripe pattern, work in stocking stitch until work measures 2½cm (1in) from hemline, ending with a RS row.
Row 1 (WS): Dec 1 st at beg of row.
Work 7 rows straight.
Row 9: Dec 1 st at beg of row (52, 60, 66, 72, 78 sts).
Work 4 rows straight.

BACK

Using 2.75mm needles and A, cast on 93 (109, 119, 135, 145) sts. Commencing with a K row work 9 rows in stocking stitch. Change to 3.25mm needles and MC, and work one K row (this denotes hem line).

Commencing with a K row and row 1 of stripe pattern, work in stocking stitch until work measures 2½cm (1in) from hemline, ending with a WS row. Dec 1 st at each end of next row and foll 8th row (89, 105, 115, 131, 141 sts). Work without further shaping until back measures 10cm (4in) from hemline, ending with a WS row. Inc 1 st at each end of next row and every foll 6th row until 109 (125, 135, 151, 161) sts. Work without further shaping until work measures same as left front to start of armhole shaping ending with a WS row.

Shape Armhole

Cast off 5 (7, 8, 6, 7) sts at beg of next 2 (2, 2, 4, 4) rows (99, 111, 119, 127, 133 sts) then 3 sts at beg of foll 2 rows (93, 105, 113, 121, 127 sts), then dec 1 st at beg of each row at armhole edge until 91 (103, 111, 119, 123) sts rem. Work without further shaping until armhole measures same as left front to start of shoulder shaping, ending with a WS row.

Shape Shoulder

Cast off 7 (8, 9, 10, 10) sts at beg of next 8 rows (35, 39, 39, 39, 43 sts). Cast off rem sts.

SLEEVE

Using 2.75mm needles and A, cast on 49 (55, 61, 67, 73) sts. Commencing with a K row work 9 rows in stocking stitch. Change to 3.25mm needles and MC, and work one K row (this denotes hem line).

Commencing with row 1 of stripe pattern and a K row, work until sleeve measures 5cm (2in) from hem line. Inc 1 st at each end of next and every foll 8th row until 69 (75, 81, 87, 93) sts, then inc 1 st at each end of every foll 6th row until 79 (85, 91, 97, 103) sts.

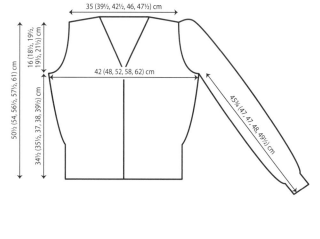

Work without further shaping until sleeve measures 45¾ (47, 47, 48, 49½) cm (18, 18½, 18½, 19, 19½ in) from hem line.

Shape Sleeve Head

Cast off 6 (7, 8, 9, 10) sts at beg of next 2 rows (67, 71, 75, 79, 83 sts) then dec 1 st at each end of every foll alt row until 53 sts rem. Work without further shaping for 32 rows then cast off 6 sts at beg of every row until 29 sts rem. Cast off rem sts.

MAKING UP

Press pieces on WS of work through a damp cloth.

Vertical Stripes

These are worked in chain stitch embroidery (See 'Fit and Finish' chapter) and positioned as folls:

Fronts

Commence stripes on fronts by counting 5 rows in from centre front and placing a pin through centre of 6th row of sts to mark position of first row of chain st. Work a vertical row of chain st in B, carrying st over 2 knit sts in length. Miss 5 rows, then work a second row of chain st using A.
At side edge count 2 rows in from edge of shoulder seam and place pin through centre of 3rd row. Work a row in A, miss 4 rows, work a row in B, miss 5 rows, work a row in A.

Back

Line up back piece to respective fronts and mark position of stripes at side edge and work 3 stripes at each side to correspond. Find centre row of back and work a row of chain st in B, then work a stripe in A on either side of this stripe, missing 5 rows and working on 6th.

Sleeves

Find centre st and work a row in B, then work a stripe in A on either side of this stripe, again missing 5 rows and working on 6th.

Sleeve Pads (Make two)

See 'Fit and Finish' chapter.

Join shoulder seams. Join side and sleeve seams matching stripes carefully. Set in sleeves, taking care to match centre of sleeve head to shoulder seam and matching side seams. Using first vertical stripe at centre front as edge, fold first 5 rows of centre fronts to WS and slip stitch in place. Fold hems to WS and stitch in place.

Neck
Turn over cast off edge of back neck sts to WS and slip stitch in place.

Reinforce button band on left front with ribbon on right or wrong side of work as preferred. Buttonholes can be reinforced using buttonhole st in contrast yarn of choice if preferred. Darn in all ends. Attach buttons, and sew sleeve pads into position.

Cap

BRIM
Using 3.25mm needles and MC, cast on 21 sts. Commencing with a K row, work in stripe pattern as set for jacket and at same time inc 1 st at beg of every foll row until 61 sts. Work without further shaping until work measures 42cm (16½in) from cast on edge. Dec 1 st at beg of every row until 21 sts rem. Cast off.

Crown (worked in A throughout)
Using 3.25mm needles and A, cast on 10 sts.
Work in moss st as folls and at same time inc 1 st at beg of every row until 48 sts.
Row 1: * K1, P1, rep from * to end.
Row 2: * P1, K1, rep from * to end.

Work without shaping until crown measures 23cm (9in) from cast on. Dec 1 st at beg of every row until 20 sts rem. Cast off.

MAKING UP
Press pieces using a damp cloth. Work vertical stripes of chain stitch as shown in photographs. Fold brim in half, lengthways and sew edges together. This shaped edge is top of brim. Sew lower edge of brim (folded edge) to crown with tapered ends of brim meeting at middle of the 10 cast on crown sts at centre back. Sew the 2 short ends of brim together. Draw feather through crown and brim at back, fit cap on head and work into shape. Attach Petersham or Buckram to inside of brim if required.

Plaid Jacket and Cap

MATERIALS.—12 oz. of Patons & Baldwins' Super or Beehive Scotch Fingering 4-ply wool in grey with red, green and lemon fleck (shade 7273), 2 oz. in green and 1 oz. in red. 1 pair of needles size 9. 1 medium crochet hook, 9 buttons, 1 pair of shoulder pads and 1 feather.

MEASUREMENTS.—Bust : 32 ins. Length : 19½ ins.

TENSION.—7 sts. and 9 rows to 1 in., measured over st. 1.

STITCHES.—(1) Jacket and brim of cap are worked in stocking st. which is k. 1 row, p. 1 row repeated throughout. The horizontal stripes are worked into this st. in the following way : * work 31 rows fleck, 1 row green, 3 rows fleck, 1 row red, 1 row fleck, 1 row green and rep. from * to end. (N.B.—Wool must be broken at end of every stripe and each fresh colour must be joined at beg. of every stripe.) Vertical stripes are embroidered on at end of work and instructions for this will be given later. (2) Crown of cap is worked in moss st. in the following way : *1st row.*—* K. 1, p. 1 and rep. from * to end. *2nd and every following row.*— K. the k. and p. the p. sts. of preceding row.

JACKET

LEFT FRONT.—With flecked wool cast on 54 and k. back into back of sts. Work in st. 1. Work 1 in., ending with a p. row. Dec. 1 st. at beg. of next row (side edge) and again 8 rows afterwards. Work without further shaping on 52 sts. until front measures 4 ins. from beg., ending with a p. row. Inc. 1 st. at beg. of next row and at this same edge every 6th row afterwards until there are 62 sts. Work without further shaping to end of 32nd row of 3rd set of stripes. Shape armholes. Cast off at beg. of next and following row at this edge, 5 once and 3 once then dec. 1 st. at beg. of every row at armhole edge until there are 49 sts. left, ending at centre-front edge. Shape neck. Dec. 1 st. at beg. of next row and every 4th row afterwards until there are 44 left, then every alternate row afterwards until there are 31 left, ending at armhole edge. Shape shoulder and continue to shape neck in the following way : cast off 7 at beg. of every row at armhole edge and dec. 1 st. at beg. of every row at neck edge until all sts. are eliminated.

RIGHT FRONT.—Follow instructions for left front

but, in order to reverse shaping, read " p." for " k." and " k." for " p." and beg. armhole after end of 33rd row of 3rd set of stripes. Also add 9 buttonholes by marking position of buttons on left front and making buttonholes to correspond on right front in following way : in a row which begins at centre-front edge, work 2, cast off 3, work to end. In following row, cast on 3 above cast-off sts.

BACK.—With flecked wool, cast on 93 and k. back into back of sts. Work in st. 1. Work 1 in. Dec. 1 st. at each end of next row and again 8 rows afterwards. Work without further shaping until back measures 4 ins. from beg. Inc. 1 st. at each end of next row and every 6th row afterwards until there are 109 sts., then work without further shaping to end of 32nd row of 3rd set of stripes. Shape armholes. Cast off at beg. of next and following rows, 4 twice and 2 twice, then dec. 1 st. at beg. of every row until there are 91 left. Work without further shaping until armholes measure same as those of fronts. Shape shoulders. Cast off 7 at beg. of every row until there are 35 left. Cast off.

SLEEVES.—With flecked wool cast on 49 and k. back into back of sts. Work in st. 1. Work 2 ins. Inc. 1 st. at each end of next row and every 8th row afterwards until there are 69 sts., then every 6th row afterwards until there are 79 sts. Work without further shaping to end of 32nd row of 4th set of stripes. Shape top of sleeve. Cast off 6 at beg. of each of next 2 rows then dec. 1 st. at beg. of every row until there are 53 left. Work without further shaping for 32 rows then cast off 6 at beg. of every row until there are 29 left. Cast off.

VERTICAL STRIPES.—These are worked in chain-st. embroidery. The stripes are placed as follows : left and right fronts.—Miss 5 sts. at centre-front edge, work red stripe up next row of sts., miss 5 fleck sts., work green stripe up next row of sts. Miss 24 fleck sts. then work 1 green, miss 4, work 1 red, miss 5, work 1 green. Back.—Work a group of stripes each side to meet front stripes at shoulders and make one central group of stripes as follows : work a red stripe up row of sts. at centre-back, miss 5 fleck sts. each side and then work a green stripe each side. Sleeves.— With right side of work towards you, miss 18 fleck sts. at right-hand bottom edge, work green stripe up next row of sts., miss 5 fleck sts., work red stripe up next row of sts., miss 5 fleck sts., work green stripe up next row of sts.

TO MAKE UP.—Sew side, shoulder and sleeve seams, matching stripes, and set in sleeves, easing in fulness across top. Work 2 rows of double crochet in fleck wool round all edges. Buttonhole st. round buttonholes, sew buttons on left front, sew in shoulder pads and press well.

CAP

BRIM.—With flecked wool cast on 21 and k. back into back of sts. Work in st. 1. Inc. 1 st. of every row until there are 61 sts. Work without further shaping until work measures 16½ ins. from beg. Dec. 1 st. at beg. of every row until there are 21 left. Cast off. Work 1 green stripe up work, leaving 11 fleck sts. between green stripe and side edge at widest part of work, then miss 5 fleck sts. and work 1 red stripe.

CROWN.—With green wool cast on 10 and k. back into back of sts. Work in st. 2. Inc. 1 st. at beg. of every row until there are 48 sts. Work without further shaping until crown measures 9 ins. from beg. Dec. 1 st. at beg. of every row until there are 20 sts. left. Cast off.

TO MAKE UP.—Fold brim in half lengthways and sew edges tog. This shaped edge is top of brim. Sew lower edge of brim (folded edge) to crown with tapered ends of brim meeting at middle of the 10 cast-on crown sts. at centre-back. Sew the 2 short ends of brim tog. Draw feather through crown and brim at back, fit cap on head and work into shape.

Warm Jumper

MATERIALS
Excelana 4 Ply Luxury Wool 100% pure new British wool (159m/174yds per 50g ball)
6 (6, 8, 9) balls shade Cornflower Blue
1 pair 3.25mm (US #3) needles
1 pair 4mm (US #6) needles
1 3.25mm (US #3) circular needle or 4 double pointed needles of same size
2 cable needles or double pointed needles
Stitch holder
2 stitch markers

TENSION
22 sts & 30 rows = 10 cm (4in) using 4mm needles over pattern
1 pattern repeat of 12 sts = 3cm (1¼in).

Standard Yarn Tension
28 sts & 36 rows = 10cm (4in) using 3mm needles over stocking stitch

ABBREVIATIONS
See page 13 for standard abbreviations

SIZING
Measurements given in centimetres followed by inches in parentheses

To Fit	81–91 (32–36)	86–102 (34–40)	107–117 (42–46)	122–137 (48–54)
Finished Measurements				
Actual Bust Size	98 (38½)	98 (38½)	120 (47)	142 (56)
Length to underarm	32 (12½)	35½ (14)	39½ (15½)	47 (18½)
Finished Length	48½ (19)	54 (21¼)	60 (23½)	67 (26½)
Armhole Depth	16½ (6½)	18½ (7¼)	20½ (8)	22 (8½)
Back Neck Width	14½ (5¾)	14½ (5¾)	16½ (6½)	16½ (6½)
Sleeve Length	46½ (18¼)	47 (18½)	48 (19)	49½ (19½)
Shoulder to shoulder	40 (15½)	40 (15½)	47 (18½)	50 (19½)

Garment shown in photographs for first size 81–91 (32–36)

PATTERN NOTES
Work tension square by casting on 36 sts using 4mm needles and working pattern as for back until one pattern repeat completed. The tension should be measured over block of purl stitches flattened under your hand, with rows measured along stocking stitch column.

The sizing of the first 2 sizes overlap due to the amount of stretch in this garment. The finished dimensions will fit a wide range of sizes but the length of the 1st size makes it only suitable for a petite fit. If you are small framed but longer in the body I would recommend the 2nd size.

BACK
Using 3.25mm needles, cast on 84 (84, 108, 132) sts and work as follows:
Row 1 (RS): K1, * P2, K2, rep from * to last 3 sts, P2, K1.
Row 2: P1, * K2, P2, rep from * to last 3 sts, K2, P1.
Repeat these 2 rows 3 times more then change to 4mm needles.
Work 22 row pattern repeat as follows:
Row 1 (RS): K1, * P10, K2, rep from * to last 11 sts, P10, K1.
Row 2: P1, * K10, P2, rep from * to last 11 sts, K10, P1.

Rep last 2 rows twice more.
Row 7: K1, * P2, K2, rep from * to last 3 sts, P2, K1.
Row 8: P1, * K2, P2, rep from * to last 3 sts, K2, P1.
Rep last 2 rows 3 times more.
Row 15: K1, * P2, slip the next 2 sts onto a cable needle and leave at front of work; then slip the following 2 sts onto a 2nd cable needle and leave at back work; K the next 2 sts from LH needle, P the 2 sts on needle at back of work, then K the 2 sts on needle at front of work, P2, K2, rep from * to end, finishing last repeat with K1 instead of K2.
Row 16: As row 8.

FRONT

Work as for back until armhole shaping has been completed and there are 88 (88, 104, 116) sts on needle.

Shape Neck

Next row (RS): Patt 42 (42, 50, 56) sts, patt 2 tog, turn. Leaving rem 44 (44, 52, 58) sts on spare needle, continue on these 43 (43, 51, 57) sts only.

Dec 1 st at neck edge on every 4th row 8 (12, 0, 3) times, then on every 3rd row 4 (0, 17, 14) times (31, 31, 34, 40 sts).
Work 0 (2, 0, 0) rows without shaping.

Shape Shoulders

1st & 2nd sizes only
Next row (RS): Cast off 7 sts, patt to last 2 sts, K2tog.
Next row: Patt to end.
Repeat last 2 rows twice more, then cast off rem 7 sts.

3rd size only
Cast off 10 sts at beg of next row and 8 sts at beg of foll 3 alt rows.

4th size only
Cast off 10 sts at beg of next and foll 3 alt rows.

All sizes
With RS facing, rejoin yarn to 44 (44, 52, 58) sts at neck edge.
Next row: Patt 2 tog, patt to end (43, 43, 51, 57).
Work to match first side, reversing all shapings.

Rep rows 7 and 8 three times more. These 22 rows complete one pattern repeat. Continue in pattern, and at the same time, inc 1 st at each end of the next and every following 5th row until 108 (108, 132, 156) sts, working extra sts into pattern.

Continue without further shaping until row 22 (10, 22, 22) of the 4th (5th, 5th, 6th) pattern repeat is complete.

Shape Armholes

Whilst maintaining pattern, cast off 6 (6, 7, 6) sts at beg of next 2 (2, 2, 4) rows, then 2 sts at beg of foll 4 (4, 7, 8) rows (88, 88, 104, 116 sts).

Continue without further shaping until row 6 (22, 16, 22) of the 7th (7th, 8th, 9th) pattern repeat has been completed.

Shape Shoulders

Cast off 7 (7, 10, 10) sts at beg of next 2 rows, then cast off 7 (7, 8, 10) sts at beg of next 6 rows (32, 32, 36, 36 sts).

Breaking off yarn, slip rem 32 (32, 36, 36) sts onto a stitch holder and put work to one side.

SLEEVES

Using 3.25mm needles, cast on 48 (52, 56, 60) sts and work as folls:
Row 1 (RS): K1, * P2, K2, rep from * to last 3 sts, P2, K1.
Row 2: P1, * K2, P2, rep from * to last 3 sts, K2, P1.
Repeat these 2 rows 3 (3, 3, 5) times more.

Change to 4mm needles and work one complete 22 row pattern repeat. Whilst maintaining pattern, inc 1 st at each end of next and every foll 8th row until 68 (72, 76, 84) sts. Continue without shaping until sleeve measures 46½ (47, 48, 49½) cm (18¼, 18½, 19, 19½ in) ending with a WS row.

Shape Sleeve Head

Cast off 6 sts at beg of next 2 rows (56, 60, 64, 72 sts) then dec 1 st at beg of every row until 26 (26, 28, 32) sts rem.
Cast off 4 sts at beg of next 4 rows (10, 10, 12, 16 sts).
Cast off rem sts.

NECKBAND

Join shoulder seams using a neat back stitch. Using
3.25mm circular needle, and commencing at back neck
with RS facing, knit across 32 (32, 36, 36) sts on holder,
pick up and K 50 (54, 54, 58) sts down left front neck,
PM, pick up and K 50 (54, 54, 58) sts up right front neck
(132, 140, 144, 152 sts), PM (start of round).

Next Round: P1, * K2, P2, rep from * to last 3 sts, K2, P1.

Next 7 rounds: Rib as set to within 2 sts of 1st marker, work
2 sts tog, SM, work next 2 sts tog, patt to end of round
marker (118, 126, 130, 138 sts). Cast off fairly loosely in rib.

MAKING UP

Sew up side and sleeve seams. Insert sleeves, carefully
matching centre of sleeve head to shoulder seam. Darn in
all ends. Do not press.

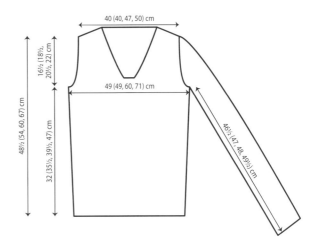

40 (40, 47, 50) cm

16½ (18½, 20½, 22) cm

49 (49, 60, 71) cm

48½ (54, 60, 67) cm

32 (35½, 39½, 47) cm

46½ (47, 48, 49½) cm

WELDONS LEAFLET 3d. No. 290

WARM JUMPER
14 ozs. Yarn (Less than 100 yards to the oz.)

1st row of 7th pattern : Cast off 7, then work to last 2 sts., and take 2 tog. **2nd row :** Work without shaping. Rep. last 2 rows twice. Cast off remaining 7 sts.

Join yarn to inner end of sts. for other side, and work thus :—

7th row of 5th pattern—2nd side: Take 2 tog., work to end. Continue to dec. 1 st. at neck edge of every 3rd row from previous dec. row until 21st row of 6th pattern is finished. (31 sts.)

Next row : Cast off 7, and work to end. **Next row :** Take 2 tog., and work to end.

Rep. last 2 rows twice more ; then cast off remaining 7 sts.

2nd pattern row : P. 1, * k. 10, p. 2 ; rep. from * to last 11 sts., k. 10, p. 1. Rep. the 1st and 2nd pattern rows twice more.

7th pattern row : K. 1, * p. 2, k. 2 ; rep. from * to last 3 sts., p. 2, k. 1.

8th pattern row : P. 1, * k. 2, p. 2 ; rep. from * to last 3 sts., k. 2, p. 1. Rep. the 7th and 8th pattern rows 3 times more.

15th pattern row : K. 1, * p. 2, slip the next 2 sts. on to a spare double pointed needle and leave at front of work ; slip the next 2 sts. on to another spare double pointed needle and place at back of work ; k. the next 2 sts., then p. the 2 sts. from spare needle at back of work, then k. the 2 sts. from spare needle at front of work ; p. 2, k. 2 ; rep. from * to end, finishing last rep. with k. 1, instead of k. 2.

16th pattern row : As 8th. Rep. the 7th and 8th pattern rows 3 times. These 22 rows form one pattern. Rep. them, but being careful to keep the continuity of the pattern, inc. 1 st. at each end of the next row, and every following 5th row of knitting until there are 108 sts. on the needle, gradually working the extra sts., into pattern. Continue without further inc. until 4 complete patterns have been worked from start.

To shape armholes, cast off 6 sts. at the beginning of the next 2 rows, and 2 sts. at the beginning of next 4 rows (88 sts.).

Continue without further dec. until 20th row of 6th pattern has been worked from start.

To shape shoulders, cast off 7 sts. at the beginning of the next 8 rows. Break off yarn, slip the remaining 32 centre sts. on to a st. holder and leave for the present.

THE FRONT

Work as given for the back until the armhole shapings have been completed and 88 sts. remain. Now shape the neck thus :

Next row : Pattern 42 sts., take 2 tog., turn. Leaving the remaining sts. on a spare needle for time being, continue only on the first set of 43 sts. as follows :—

Dec. 1 st. at the neck edge on every 3rd row from previous dec. row, until 21st row of 6th pattern has been worked (31 sts. remain.) Work one row straight.

THE SLEEVES (both alike)

Cast on 48 sts. using two No. 8 needles and work the 2 rib rows as given at start of back for 8 rows. Change to No. 6 needles and work one pattern. Keeping the continuity of pattern, inc. 1 st. at each end of the next row, and every following 8th row of knitting until there are 68 sts. Continue without inc. until 5 patterns have been worked from start.

To shape top, cast off 6 sts. at the beginning of the next 2 rows, then dec. 1 st. at the beginning of every row until 26 sts. remain. Cast off 4 sts. at the beginning of the next 4 rows. Cast off.

NECK RIBBING

Join the shoulder seams. Slip the 32 back neck sts. on to a No. 8 needle and with right side of work towards you, rib these sts., then using a 2nd No. 8 needle pick up and k. 50 sts. down the left front neck to centre front. With a 3rd No. 8 needle pick up and k. 50 sts. up the other side of front neck to right shoulder seam (132 sts.). Using a 4th No. 8 needle work in rounds as follows :

1st round—starting from right shoulder : P. 1, * k. 2, p. 2 ; rep. from * to last 3 sts., k. 2, p. 1.

Continue in rib for 7 rounds, in each round taking last 2 sts. of 2nd needle tog., and first 2 sts. of 3rd needle tog., for centre front "V." Cast off.

TO MAKE UP

Pin out the work to measurements required, wrong side up, place a damp cloth on top and pass a warm iron lightly over without actually pressing it. Sew in the sleeves, then join the side and sleeve seams.

CABLED JUMPER
In the New Yarn

THIS warm, quickly knitted Jumper was made in yarn (under 100 yards per oz.).

MATERIALS : The original garment took seven 2-oz. hanks of yarn, with approximately 144 yards to the 2-oz. hank ; one pair of No. 6 knitting needles, and one set of four No. 8 knitting needles, pointed at both ends.

TENSION : On No. 6 needles, 5½ sts. to 1 inch in width (measured over a P. block in the pattern), and 13 rows to 2 inches in depth.

MEASUREMENTS : To fit a 34-38 inch bust size. Length from shoulder to lower edge, 21 inches. Length of sleeve seam, 18 inches.

ABBREVIATIONS : K., knit ; P., purl ; st., stitch ; sts., stitches ; rep., repeat ; tog., together ; inc., increase ; dec., decrease.

NOTE : To dec. 1 st., take 2 sts. tog. To inc. 1 st., work into the front and then into the back of the same st. before slipping it off left-hand needle.

THE BACK

Using two No. 8 needles cast on 84 sts. and work in rib thus :—

1st rib row—right side : K. 1, * p. 2, k. 2 ; rep. from * to last 3 sts., p. 2, k. 1.

2nd rib row : P. 1, * k. 2, p. 2 ; rep. from * to last 3 sts., k. 2, p. 1. Rep. these 2 rib rows 3 times more. Change to No. 6 needles.

1st pattern row : K. 1, * p. 10, k. 2 ; rep. from * to last 11 sts., p. 10, k. 1.

Colourful Winter Sports Outfit

MATERIALS
Fyberspates Scrumptious 4ply 45% silk/55% merino (365m per 100g skein)

Jumper
2 (3, 3, 4) skeins shade 310 (Natural) – MC
1 (all sizes) skein shade 302 (Gold) – A
2 (all sizes) skeins shade 309 (Midnight) – B
1 pair 2.75mm (US #2) needles
1 pair 3.25mm (US #3) needles

Mittens
2 skeins shade 309 (Midnight) – B
1 skein shade 310 (Natural) – MC
1 skein shade 302 (Gold) – A
1 pair 2.75mm (US #2) needles
1 pair 3.75mm (US #5) needles
stitch markers

Beret
1 skein shade 309 (Midnight) – B
1 skein shade 310 (Natural) – MC
1 skein shade 302 (Gold) – A
1 pair 2.75mm (US #2) needles
1 pair 3.75mm (US #5) needles

Only 1 skein of 302 (Gold) is needed to knit both mittens and beret

TENSION
30 sts & 32 rows = 10cm (4in) using 3.25mm needles over Fair Isle pattern
34 sts & 32 rows = 10cm (4in) using 3.75mm needles over rib pattern (yarn doubled)

Standard Yarn Tension
28 sts & 37 rows = 10cm (4in) using 3.5mm needles over stocking stitch

ABBREVIATIONS
See page 13 for standard abbreviations

JUMPER SIZING
Measurements given in centimetres followed by inches in parentheses

To Fit	76–81 (30–32)	86–92 (34–36)	97–102 (38–40)	107–112 (42–44)
Finished Measurements				
Actual Bust Size	86 (34)	98 (38½)	107½ (42½)	117 (46)
Length to underarm	35 (14)	37½ (15)	41½ (16½)	43 (17)
Armhole depth	21½ (8½)	24 (9½)	26½ (10½)	27½ (11)
Finished length	56½ (22)	61½ (24)	68 (27)	70½ (28)
Shoulder to shoulder	33½ (13)	38½ (15)	41½ (16½)	44½ (17½)
Sleeve length	44½ (17½)	44½ (17½)	45½ (18)	45½ (18)

Jumper shown in photographs for first size 76–81 (30–32)

BERET One Size – To fit head circumference approx 58 (23)

MITTENS One size (circumference 27 (10¾)) – To fit medium/large adult female hand

Jumper
FRONT
Using 3.25mm needles and MC, cast on 97 (115, 129, 143) sts.
Knit 2 rows, change to A and knit 2 rows, then change to B and knit a further 2 rows.
Now work from chart A as folls:
Row 1 (RS): Reading from right to left and starting and ending as indicated, work from row 1 chart A, repeating marked section 4 (5, 6, 7) times.
Row 2 (WS): Reading from left to right and starting and ending as indicated, work from row 2 chart A, repeating marked section 4 (5, 6, 7) times.
Work from chart A as set by last 2 rows until row 26 is complete.

2nd size only
Work rows 15 to 18 (inclusive) of chart A again.

3rd and 4th sizes only
Work rows 15 to 24 (inclusive) of chart A again.

All sizes
Change to 2.75mm needles.
Knit 2 rows using A, then knit 2 rows using B.
Rep these 4 rows for 5cm (2in) ending on WS.

Note: In the following section chart B is worked over 36 (40, 42, 44) rows, depending on which size you are making. It is recommended that you clearly mark which rows you need to follow, on a working copy of this chart before you start to knit. Rows 1 & 2 are shown in dark brown, and are only worked by 4th size. Rows 31 & 32 are shown in light brown and are only worked by 3rd & 4th sizes. Rows 41 to 44 are shown in pale yellow and blue and are only worked by 2nd, 3rd and 4th sizes.

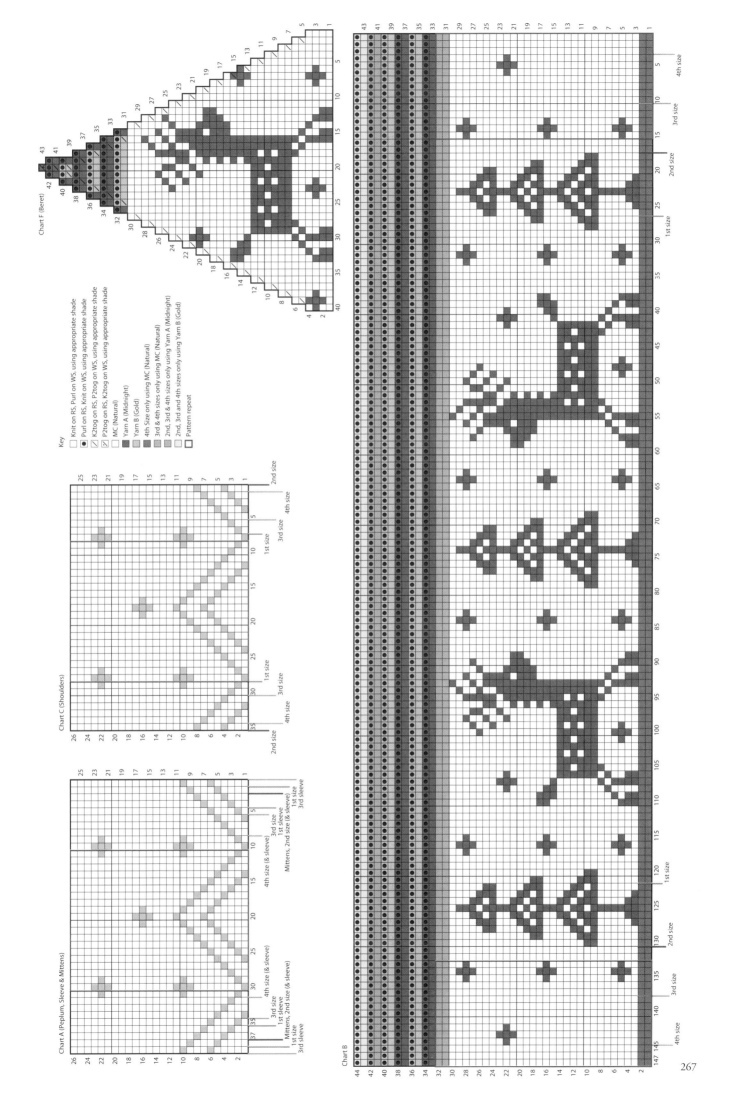

Chart F (Beret)

Key

☐ Knit on RS, Purl on WS, using appropriate shade
⦿ Purl on RS, Knit on WS, using appropriate shade
◢ K2tog on RS, P2tog on WS, using appropriate shade
◣ P2tog on RS, K2tog on WS, using appropriate shade
☐ MC (Natural)
■ Yarn A (Midnight)
▨ Yarn B (Gold)
▨ 4th Size only using MC (Natural)
▨ 3rd & 4th sizes only using MC (Natural)
▨ 2nd, 3rd & 4th sizes only using Yarn A (Midnight)
▨ 2nd, 3rd and 4th sizes only using Yarn B (Gold)
☐ Pattern repeat

Chart C (Shoulders)

Chart A (Peplum, Sleeve & Mittens)

Chart B

Change to 3.25mm needles, join in MC, break off A and cont in pattern with MC and B as folls:

Row 1 (RS): Kfb using MC, reading from right to left, and starting and ending as indicated work 95 (113, 127, 141) sts from row 3 (3, 3, 1) of chart B, Kfb using MC (99, 117, 131, 145 sts).

Row 2 (WS): P2 MC, reading from left to right over the same sts as last row, work from row 4 (4, 4, 2) of chart B, P2 MC.

Cont to work in pattern from chart as set, inc 1 st at each end of every 4th row 15 more times [working next inc on row 7 (7, 7, 5)]. Take increased sts into chart pattern (largest sizes will need to repeat the marked spot motif sections as required), only working additional spot motifs when sufficient sts are present to work the whole motif (129, 147, 161, 175 sts).

Cont to work straight until 64 (68, 72, 76) rows of chart B are completed (last row will be chart row 30 (30, 32, 32)).

Shape Armholes

Keeping chart pattern correct, cast off 6 (6, 8, 9) sts at beg of next 2 rows (117, 135, 145, 157 sts).

Dec 1 st at each end of next 8 (10, 10, 12) rows (101, 115, 125, 133 sts).

Keeping chart pattern correct, work a further 34 (40, 42, 42) rows from chart B (last row will be chart row 40 (44, 44, 44). †

Commencing with row 1, work from chart C beginning and ending rows as indicated, and working marked section 5 (5, 6, 6) times. Work from chart C until row 12 (12, 18, 18) is completed.

Shape Neck

Next row: Maintaining chart C pattern, work 37 (42, 45, 47) sts turn, leaving rem 64 (73, 80, 86) sts on a holder. Keeping pattern correct (repeating rows 15–26 as required), dec 1 st at neck edge of next 7 (7, 7, 9) rows (30, 35, 38, 38 sts).

Change to B and work 4 rows in garter st, ending with a WS row.

Shape Shoulder

Next row: Cast off 8 (9, 10, 10), K to end.

Next row: K.

Repeat last 2 rows twice more.

Cast off rem 6 (8, 8, 8) sts.

With RS facing, rejoin MC and A to 37 (42, 45, 47) sts at shoulder (leaving 27 (31, 35, 39) sts in centre on a holder for neckband) and work in pattern to end of row. Working in patt, dec 1 st at neck edge on foll 7 (7, 7, 9) rows (30, 35, 38, 38 sts). Change to B and work 3 rows in garter stitch, ending with a RS row.

Shape Shoulder

Next row: Cast off 8 (9, 10, 10), K to end.

Next row: K.

Repeat last 2 rows twice more.
Cast off rem 6 (8, 8, 8) sts.

BACK

Work exactly as for Front to † (101, 115, 125, 133 sts). Commencing with row 1, work from chart C beginning and ending rows as indicated, and working marked section 5 (5, 6, 6) times. Work from chart C until row 20 (20, 26, 26) is complete.

4th size only

Work rows 15 & 16 of chart C once more.

All sizes

Work 2 rows in garter st in B.

Next row (RS): K36 (41, 44, 46), K2tog, turn. Work on these 37 (42, 45, 47) sts only.

Next row: K2tog, K to end (36, 41, 44, 46 sts).

Next row: Cast off 8 (9, 10, 10), K to last 2 sts, K2tog (28, 32, 34, 36 sts).

Next row: K2tog, K to end.

Repeat last 2 rows twice more.

Cast off rem 7 (9, 9, 11) sts.

Slip centre 25 (29, 33, 37) sts on to stitch holder. With RS facing, rejoin B to rem 38 (43, 46, 48) sts at neck edge, K2tog then knit to end (37, 42, 45, 47 sts).

Next row: Cast off 8 (9, 10, 10), K to last 2 sts, K2tog (28, 32, 34, 36 sts).

Next row: K2tog, K to end.

Repeat these 2 rows twice. Cast off rem 8 (10, 10, 11) sts.

NECKBAND

Join right shoulder seam. With RS of work facing and using 2.75mm needles and B, and starting at left side of neck at front, knit 21 (21, 21, 23) sts down left side of neck, 27 (31, 35, 39) sts across front neck, 21 (21, 21, 23) sts up right side of neck, 14 sts along side of back neck, 25 (29, 33, 37) sts across back neck, and 14 sts along second side of back neck (122, 130, 138, 150 sts).

Next row (WS): *K1, P1, rep from * to end of row. Rep this row until rib measures 7½cm (3in). Cast off loosely with 3.25mm needle.

SLEEVES

Using 2.75mm needle and B, cast on 65 (69, 73, 77) sts and work in rib as folls:

Row 1 (RS): K1, * P1, K1, rep from * to end.

Row 2: P1, * K1, P1, rep from * to end.

Rep these 2 rows until work measures 6½cm (2½in) ending with a WS row.

Change to 3.25mm needles and A:

Using A, K 2 rows, inc 1 st at each end of 1st row (67, 71, 75, 79 sts).

Using B, K 2 rows.

Using A, K 2 rows.

Using B, K 2 rows, inc 1 st at each end of 1st row (69, 73, 77, 81 sts).

Using A, K 2 rows.
Using B, K 2 rows.
Using MC, K 2 rows, inc 1 st at each end of 1st row (71, 75, 79, 83 sts).
Break off B and using MC and A, work from chart A as foll: Starting and ending rows as indicated for sleeves, work from chart A until row 26 is complete.
Repeating rows 15 to 26 inclusive, inc 1 st at each end of next and 10 foll 8th rows, taking extra sts into spot pattern (93, 97, 101, 105 sts). Maintaining patt, work straight until sleeve measures 44½ (44½, 45½, 45½) cm (17½, 17½, 18, 18 in).

Shape Sleeve Head
Whilst maintaining spot patt, dec 1 st at each end of every foll alt row until 49 sts rem. Cast off 5 sts at beg of next 6 rows (19 sts). Cast off rem sts.

MAKING UP
Press all work lightly on WS through a damp cloth. Join remaining shoulder seam. To create 'rolled' neckband, turn neckband over to RS and over sew in place from WS. Alternatively fold in half for polo neck. Join side and sleeve seams. Set sleeves into place taking care to match centre of sleeve head to shoulder seams and matching side seams. Darn in all ends.

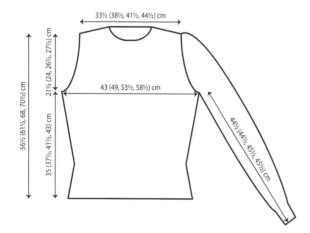

Mittens
Work using yarn doubled throughout.

RIGHT HAND
Using 3.75mm needles and double MC, cast on 75 sts and knit 2 rows.
Join in double B and knit 2 rows.
Join in double A and knit 2 rows.
Repeat last 4 rows once, then work 2 rows in stocking stitch using MC, then place chart as folls:
Row 1 (RS): Reading from right to left and starting and ending as indicated, work from row 1 chart A, repeating marked section 3 times.
Row 2 (WS): Reading from left to right and starting and ending as indicated, work from row 2 chart A, repeating marked section 3 times.
Cont to work from chart A as set until row 26 is complete.
Next 2 rows: Using B, K.
Next 2 rows: Using A, K.
Repeat last 4 rows once, inc 1 st at end of last row (76 sts).
Change to 2.75mm needles and B and work in rib as folls:
Next row: * K1, P1, rep from * to end.
Rep this row until rib measures 6½cm (2½in) ending with a WS row.

Shape Thumb
Row 1 (RS): Rib 37, PM, Kfb, K1, Kfb, PM, rib to end (78 sts).
Row 2 (and every foll alt row): Rib to end, allowing for inc sts.

Row 3: Rib to marker, SM, Kfb, P1, K1, P1, Kfb, SM, rib to end (80 sts).

Row 5: Rib to marker, SM, Kfb, rib to last st before marker, Kfb, SM, rib to end (82 sts).

Inc 1 st at each end of thumb on foll 6 alt rows (94 sts). You should now have 21 sts between the thumb markers.

Row 18: As row 2.

Row 19: Rib 58, turn, cast on 2 sts.

Next row: Rib 23, turn, cast on 2 sts.

Working on these 25 sts only, complete thumb as folls:

Work 4 rows in rib.

Row 5: K2tog, rib to last 2 sts, K2tog (23 sts).

Repeat last 5 rows until 19 sts rem then if necessary cont in rib until thumb measures 6½cm (2½in) or required length, ending with a WS row.

Shape Top

Row 1: * Rib 1, work 2 tog, repeat from * to last st, rib 1 (13 sts).

Row 2: Rib to end.

Row 3: [K2tog] 6 times, K1 (7 sts).

Break off yarn, and thread through rem sts, draw up and fasten off, then sew thumb seam.

With RS facing, rejoin yarn to RS of work and pick up and knit 3 sts at base of thumb, rib to end (76 sts).

Work 1 row in rib then, using A, shape as folls:

Row 1: K1, K2tog, K32, K2tog, K2, K2tog, K32, K2tog, K1 (72 sts).

Row 2: Using A, K.

Row 3: Using B, K1, K2tog, K30, K2tog, K2, K2tog, K30, K2tog, K1 (68 sts).

Row 4: Using B, K.

Row 5: Using A, K1, K2tog, K28, K2tog, K2, K2tog, K28, K2tog, K1 (64 sts).

Row 6: Using A, K.

Row 7: Using B, K.

Row 8: As row 7.

Row 9: Using MC, K.

Row 10: Using MC, P.†

Hand

Now work from chart E as folls:

Row 1 (RS): Reading from right to left, work all sts from row 1 chart E.

Row 2 (WS): Reading from left to right, work all sts from row 2 chart E.

Work in patt from chart as set. Work decreases as indicated, until row 38 is completed (20 sts).

Cast off in A.

LEFT HAND MITTEN

Work as for right hand mitten to † (64 sts).

Now work from chart D as foll:

Row 1 (RS): Reading from right to left, work all sts from row 1 chart D.

Row 2 (WS): Reading from left to right, work all sts from row 2 chart D.

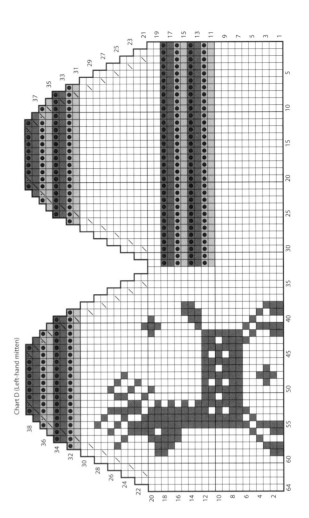

Chart D (Left-hand mitten)

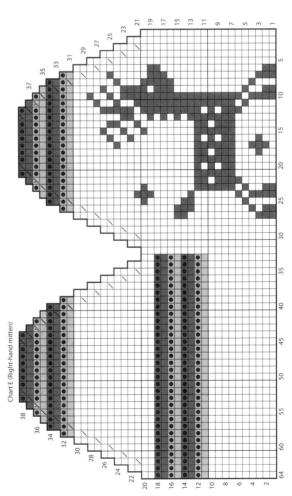

Chart E (Right-hand mitten)

Work in patt from chart as set. Work decreases as indicated, until row 38 is complete (20 sts).
Cast off in A.

MAKING UP
Press work lightly on WS through a damp cloth. Darn in all ends. Join sides and top seams, matching stripes and patt neatly.

Beret
Work with yarn doubled throughout.

Using 2.75mm needles and B doubled, cast on 98 sts.
Work in rib as folls:
Next row: * K1, P1, rep from to end.
Rep this row once more.
Next row: K1, * work twice into next st, repeat from * to end (195 sts).
Change to 3.75mm needles.

Using A, knit 2 rows.
Using B, knit 2 rows.
Rep last 4 rows twice more, working incs across final row as folls:
Using B, * Kfb, K38, rep from * 4 more times (200 sts).

Now work pattern from chart F as foll:
Row 1 (RS): Reading from right to left, work all sts from row 1 chart F, repeating them 5 times in each row.
Row 2 (WS): Reading from left to right, work all sts from row 2 chart F, repeating them 5 times in each row.
Work in patt from chart as set. Work decreases as indicated, until row 43 is complete (5 sts).
Draw yarn through remaining sts and fasten off.

MAKING UP
Press work lightly on WS through a damp cloth. Join back seam neatly, matching patt. Darn in all ends. Press seam lightly using a damp cloth.

COLOURFUL WINTER SPORTS OUTFIT

PUBLICATION 1008

Colourful Winter Sports Outfit

The JERSEY

FRONT

With No. 9 needles and Grey wool cast on 115 sts., k. 2 rows.

Change to Red wool and k. 2 rows.

Change to Blue wool and k. 2 rows.

Change to Grey wool and work 2 rows in st.-st., ending p. row.

Break off Blue wool, cont. in patt. with Grey and Red wools thus :

1st row : K.3 G., 1 R., 3 G., * 1 R., 3 G., 1 R., 11 G., 1 R., 3 G. Rep. from * to last 8 sts., 1 R., 3 G., 1 R., 3 G.

2nd row : P.2 G., 1 R., 3 G., 1 R., * 1 G., 1 R., 3 G., 1 R., 9 G., 1 R., 3 G., 1 R. Rep. from * to last 5 sts., 1 G., 1 R., 3 G., 1 R., 2 G.

3rd row : K.1 G., * 1 R. (3 G., 1 R.) 3 times, 7 G. Rep. from * to last 14 sts., 1 R. (3 G., 1 R.) 3 times, 1 G.

4th row : * P.1 R., 3 G., 1 R., 5 G. Rep. from * to last 5 sts., 1 R., 3 G., 1 R.

5th row : * K.3 G., 1 R., 7 G., 1 R. (3 G., 1 R.) twice. Rep. from * to last 15 sts., 3 G., 1 R., 7 G., 1 R., 3 G.

6th row : P.2 G., * 1 R., 9 G., 1 R., 3 G., 1 G., 1 R., 3 G. Rep. from * to last 13 sts., 1 R., 9 G., 1 R., 2 G.

7th row : K.1 G., * 1 R., 11 G., 1 R., 3 G., 1 R., 3 G. Rep. from * to last 14 sts., 1 R., 11 G., 1 R., 1 G.

8th row : P.1 R., * 13 G., 1 R., 5 G., 1 R. Rep. from * to last 14 sts., 13 G., 1 R.

9th row : * K.7 G., 1 R., 7 G., 1 R., 3 G. Rep. from * to last 15 sts., 7 G., 1 R., 7 G.

10th row : P.6 G., * 3 R., 7 G., 1 R., 1 G., 1 R., 7 G. Rep. from * to last 9 sts., 3 R., 6 G.

11th row : K.7 G., * 1 R., 9 G. Rep. from * to last 8 sts., 1 R., 7 G.

12th-14th rows : Work 3 rows in st.-st. with G. wool, ending p. row.

15th row : K.17 G., * 1 R., 19 G. Rep. from * ending 17 G. instead of 19.

16th row : P.16 G., * 3 R., 17 G. Rep. from * ending 16 G. instead of 17.

17th row : As 15th row.

18th-20th rows : With G. wool work 3 rows in st.-st., ending p. row.

21st row : K.7 G., * 1 R., 19 G. Rep. from * to last 8 sts., 1 R., 7 G.

22nd row : P.6 G., * 3 R., 17 G. Rep. from * to last 9 sts., 3 R., 6 G.

23rd row : As 21st row.

24th-26th rows : With G. wool work 3 rows in st.-st., ending p. row.

Rep. rows 15 to 18 inclusive. (Work measures 4 ins.).

Change to No. 12 needles.

With Red wool k. 2 rows.

With Blue wool k. 2 rows.

Rep. these 4 rows for 2 ins., ending row on wrong side. (6 ins. from lower edge).

Change to No. 9 needles, join in Grey wool, break off Red wool and cont. in stag patt. with Grey and Blue wools thus :

Now work in patt. as given on the stitch diagram, using G. and B. wools : a guide to the colour of the wools is given with the diagram. One square of the diagram represents 1 st. or 1 row, the odd rows will be k. rows and worked from right to left, the uneven rows p. rows and worked from left to right.

There are 113 sts. in the patt. panel, the two extra sts. on needle (i.e., 115 sts. on needle) are to be worked in G. st.-st. throughout, one at each end of row. Always work these sts. before and after the patt. rows, they will afterwards be used for seam sts. in sewing up.

Now work patt. rows 1 to 24 inclusive from patt. chart, at the same time inc. 1 st. both ends of 1st and every following 4th row for side shaping, working these extra sts. in G. st.-st. before and after working patt. rows. Thus **1st row** will read : K. twice into first st. G., 3 G., 1 R., 3 G., 1 R., 2 B., 12 G., 2 B., 1 G., * 5 B., 12 G., 2 B., 1 G., 2 B., 12 G., 2 B., 1 G., 2 B., 12 G. Rep. from * once, 5 B., 3 G., k. twice into next st. G.

2nd row : P.6 G., 3 B., 7 G., 1 B., 5 G., 2 B., 1 G., 2 B., 5 G., 1 B., 6 G., 2 B., 1 G., 2 B., 4 G., 1 B., 8 G., 3 B., 8 G., 1 B., 4 G., 2 B., 1 G., 2 B., 6 G., 1 B., 5 G., 2 B., 1 G., 2 B., 5 G., 1 B., 7 G., 3 B., 6 G.

Cont. in this way to the end of the 24th patt. row. 127 sts.).

25th patt. row : K. twice into first st. G., k.2 G., 1 B., 3 G., work as 25th patt. row to last 7 sts., 3 G., 1 B., 2 G., k. twice into last st. G.

Now rep. patt. rows 26 to 28 inclusive once.

This completes the " stag " panel.

With B. wool work 2 rows in g.-st., inc. 1 st. both ends of 1st row.

With R. wool work 2 rows in g.-st.

Rep. last 4 rows twice more (135 sts.).

Now rep. the " stag " panel once more, working patt. in side thus :

1st row : K. twice into first st. G., k.10 G., work as 1st patt. row to last 11 sts., k.10 G., k. twice into last st.

2nd row : P.8 G., 1 B., 3 G., work as 2nd patt. row to last 12 sts., p.3 G., 1 B., 8 G.

3rd row : K.7 G., 3 B., 2 G., work as 3rd patt. row to last 12 sts., k.2 G., 3 B., 7 G.

4th row : P.8 G., 1 B., 3 G., work as 4th patt. row to last 12 sts., p.3 G., 1 B., 8 G.

Now cont. in patt. on centre 113 sts., beg. at 5th patt. row, keeping side sts. in G. st.-st. for 8 rows, inc. 1 st. both ends of next row and following 4th row (141 sts.).

Next row : K. twice into first st. G., k.9 G., 1 B., 3 G., work as 13th patt. row to last 14 sts., k.3 G., 1 B., 9 G., k. twice into last st. G.

Next row : P.10 G., 3 B., 2 G., work as 14th patt. row to last 15 sts., p.2 G., 3 B., 10 G.

Next row : K.11 G., 1 B., 3 G., work as 15th patt. row to last 15 sts., k.3 G., 1 B., 11 G.

Work 3 rows in patt. on centre 113 sts. with side sts. in G. st.-st., inc. 1 st. both ends of the 2nd row.

Next row : K.3 G., 1 B., 12 G., work as 19th patt. row to last 16 sts., k.12 G., 1B., 3 G.

Next row : P.2 G., 3 B., 11 G., work as 20th patt. row to last 16 sts., p.11 G., 3 B., 2 G.

Next row : K. twice into first st. G., k.2 G., 1 B., 12 G., work as 21st patt. row to last 16 sts., k.12 G., 1 B., 2 G., k. twice into last st. G. (This completes side shapings). (147 sts.).

Now cont. in patt. on centre 113 sts. with side sts. in G. st.-st. (with spots to fit in as before on the 25th, 26th and 27th patt. rows) to the end of the 28th patt. row.

SHAPE ARMHOLES

With B. wool work 2 rows in g.-st., casting off 6 sts. at beginning of each row.

With R. wool work 2 rows in g.-st., dec. 1 st. each end of each row.

With B. wool work 2 rows in g.-st., dec. 1 st. each end of each row.

Rep. last 4 rows once, then work 2 more rows in R. g.-st. dec. 1 st. at each end of each row. (115 sts.).

Now rep. the patt. panel of 28 rows again, using G. and B. wool and keeping an odd st. at each end of every row in G. st.-st. as explained in earlier paragraph.

Next 2 rows : Work 2 rows in g.-st. with B. wool.

Next 2 rows : Work 2 rows in g.-st. with R. wool.

Rep. last 4 rows twice.

Now using G. and R. wool rep. patt. rows 1 to 11 inclusive, as given for lower edge border, once.

SHAPE NECK THUS :

With G. wool p. 1 row.

Next row : K.42, turn.

Work 7 rows in patt. on 42 sts. using G. and R. wool, keeping regularity of spots, dec. 1 st. at neck edge on each row (35 sts.).

Change to B. wool and work 4 rows in g.-st., thus ending armhole edge.

SHAPE SHOULDER

Next row : Cast off 9, k. to end.

Next row : K. to end.

Rep. last 2 rows twice.

Cast off remaining sts.

Rejoin wools at neck edge and work to match first side on last 42 sts., leaving centre 31 sts. on spare needle, thus ending with a p. row in G. Work only 3 rows in g.-st. to armhole edge instead of 4 rows before shoulder shaping.

BACK

Work exactly as for Front to end of 20th patt. row in top border, omitting Neck shaping, thus ending p. row.

Change to B. wool and shape for Neck and Shoulders thus :

Work 2 rows in g.-st. in B. wool.

Next row : K.41, k.2 tog., turn. Work on these 42 sts. only.

Next row : K.2 tog., k. to end.

Next row : Cast off 9, k. to last 2 sts., k.2 tog.

Next row : K.2 tog., k. to end.

Rep. last 2 rows twice.

Cast off remaining sts.

Slip centre 29 sts. on spare needle, rejoin wool to remaining sts. at neck edge and k. 1 row, then work to match first side.

NECK BAND

Backstitch right shoulder seam.

With right side of work facing and using No. 12 needles and B. wool k. up 21 sts. along front neck edge, 31 sts. from spare needle, 21 sts. along front neck edge to shoulder seam, 14 sts. along back of neck edge, 29 sts. from spare needle, 14 sts. along back neck edge to shoulder edge.

Work in k.1, p.1 rib for 3 ins.

Cast off loosely with a No. 9 needle.

SLEEVES

With No. 12 needles and B. wool cast on 69 sts. and work 2½ ins. in k.1, p.1 rib.

Change to No. 9 needles.

Work 2 rows in g.-st. with R. wool, inc. 1 st. both ends of 1st row.

Work 2 rows g.-st. with B. wool.

Work 2 rows g.-st. with R. wool.

Work 2 rows g.-st. with B. wool, inc. 1 st. both ends of 1st row.

Work 2 rows g.-st. with R. wool.

Work 2 rows g.-st. with B. wool.

Work 2 rows st.-st. with G. wool, inc. 1 st. both ends of k. row (75 sts.).

Break off B. wool and, using G. and R. wool, rep. patt. rows 1 to 26 inclusive as given for lower edge border, once.

Cont. in spot patt., rep. patt. rows 15 to 26 inclusive, inc. 1 st. both ends of first row and every 8th row until work measures 17½ ins., working extra sts. gradually into patt. (97 sts.).

SHAPE TOP

Cont. in patt., dec. 1 st. both ends of every alternate row until 49 sts. remain.

Cast off 5 sts. beg. of next 6 rows.

Cast off remaining sts.

MAKE UP

Press all work lightly on wrong side with hot iron over damp cloth.

Backstitch shoulder seam, oversewing neck band on reverse side to turn over on to right side of work.

Join side seams, matching patt. panels carefully.

Join sleeve seams and backstitch sleeves into armholes, matching seams.

Press seams.

The
MITTENS

Work with double wool throughout, giving a tension of approximately 6 sts. to 1 in. on No. 9 needles.

RIGHT HAND MITTEN

With No. 9 needles and double G. wool cast on 75 sts. and k. 2 rows.

Join in double B. wool and k. 2 rows.

Join in double R. wool and k. 2 rows.

Rep. last 4 rows once, then work 2 rows in st.-st. with G. wool.

Now, using G. and R. wools, rep. the 26 patt. rows as given for lower edge of Jersey, once. (Work now measures 4 ins.).

Next 2 rows : With B. wool, k.

Next 2 rows : With R. wool, k.

Rep. last 4 rows once, inc. 1 st. at end of last row (76 sts.).

Change to No. 12 needles and, using B. wool, work in k.1, p.1 rib for 2½ ins., ending row on wrong side.

SHAPE FOR THUMB

1st row : Rib 37, k. twice into next st., k.1, k. twice into next st., rib to end.

2nd and each alternate row : Rib to end, allowing for inc. sts.

3rd row : Rib 37, k. twice into next st., p.1, k.1, p.1, k. twice into next st., rib to end.

5th row : Rib 37, k. twice into next st., rib 5, k. twice into next st., rib to end.

7th row : Rib 37, k. twice into next st., rib 7, k. twice into next st., rib to end.

9th row : Rib 37, k. twice into next st., rib 9, k. twice into next st., rib to end.

11th row : Rib 37, k. twice into next st., rib 11, k. twice into next st., rib to end.

13th row : Rib 37, k. twice into next st., rib 13, k. twice into next st., rib to end.

15th row : Rib 37, k. twice into next st., rib 15, k. twice into next st., rib to end.

17th row : Rib 37, k. twice into next st., rib 17, k. twice into next st., rib to end.

19th row : Rib 58, turn, cast on 2 sts.

Next row : Rib 23, turn, cast on 2 sts.

Work on these 25 sts. for thumb thus :

Work 4 rows in rib.

5th row : K.2 tog., rib to last 2 sts., k.2 tog.

Rep. these 5 rows until 19 sts. remain, then, if necessary, cont. in rib until thumb measures 2¼ ins., ending row on wrong side.

SHAPE TOP

1st row : * Rib 1, work 2 tog. Rep. from * to last st., rib 1.

2nd row : Rib to end.

3rd row : (K.2 tog.) 6 times, k.1.

Break off wool, thread ends through remaining sts., draw up and fasten off, then sew down side edges to base of thumb.

With right side of work facing, rejoin wool to right hand needle and k. up 3 sts. at base of thumb, rib to end (76 sts.).

Work 1 row in rib then, using R. wool, shape thus :

1st row : K.1, k.2 tog., k.32, k.2 tog., k.2, k.2 tog., k.32, k.2 tog., k.1.

2nd row : With R. k.

3rd row : With B. k.1, k.2 tog., k.30, k.2 tog., k.2, k.2 tog., k.30, k.2 tog., k.1.

4th row : With B. k.

5th row : With R. k.1, k.2 tog., k.28, k.2 tog., k.2, k.2 tog., k.28, k.2 tog., k.1.

6th row : With R. k.

7th row : With B. k.

8th row : As 7th row.

9th row : With G. k.

10th row : With G. p.

Now cont. in st.-st. in G. wool working one "stag" panel from Jersey patt. diagram on the centre 22 sts. for back of mitten thus :

1st patt. row : K.5 G., 2 B., 1 G., 2 B., 12 G., 2 B., 1 G., 2 B., 37 G.

2nd patt. row : P.37 G., 2 B., 1 G., 2 B., 5 G., 1 B., 6 G., 2 B., 1 G., 2 B., 5 G.

Cont. thus, starting at the 72nd stitch in the patt. panel on k. rows and 21st stitch in patt. panel on p. rows. Cont. in this way until 10 patt. rows are completed.

Join in R. wool.

11th row : K.9 G., 2 B., (1 G., 3 B.) 3 times, 9 G., 32 R.

12th row : K.32 R., p.9 G., 14 B., 9 G.

13th row : K.9 G., 4 B., 10 G., 3 B., 6 G., 32 B.

14th row : K.32 B., p.5 G., 3 B., 12 G., 3 B., 9 G.

15th row : K.9 G., 4 B., 12 G., 2 B., 5 G., 32 R.

16th row : K.32 R., p.20 G., 5 B., 7 G.

17th row : K.6 G., 7 B., 19 G., 32 B.

18th row : K.32 B., p.20 G., 7 B., 5 G.

19th row : K.5 G., 3 B., 1 G., 4 B., 10 G., 1 B., 40 G.

20th row : P.39 G., 3 B., 7 G., 1 B., 2 G., 5 B., 7 G.

SHAPE TOP

21st row : K.1, k.2 tog., k.5 G., 3 B., 2 G., 1 B., 9 G., 1 B. With G., k.5, k.2 tog., k.2, k.2 tog., k.26, k.2 tog., k.1.

22nd row : P.45 G., 1 B., 2 G., 2 B., 1 G., 2 B., 7 G.

23rd row : K.1, k.2 tog., k.4 G., 2 B., 1 G., 2 B., 1 G., 1 B. With G. k.13, k.2 tog., k.2, k.2 tog., k.24, k.2 tog., k.1.

24th row : P.41 G., 1 B., 2 G., 1 B., 1 G., 2 B., 2 G., 1 B., 5 G.

25th row : K.1, k.2 tog., k.1 G., 1 B., 2 G., (1 B., 1 G.) 3 times, 1 B. With G. k.11, k.2 tog., k.2, k.2 tog., k.22, k.2 tog., k.1.

26th row : P.40 G., (1 B., 2 G.) twice, 1 B., 5 G.

27th row : K.1, k.2 tog., k.4 G., 1 B. With G. k.15, k.2 tog., k.2, k.2 tog., k.20, k.2 tog., k.1.

28th row : P.42 G., 1 B., 5 G.

29th row : With G. k.1, k.2 tog., k.18, k.2 tog., k.2, k.2 tog., k.18, k.2 tog., k.1.

30th row : With G. p.

31st row : With R. k.1, k.2 tog., k.16, k.2 tog., k.2, k.2 tog., k.16, k.2 tog., k.1.

32nd row : With R. k.

33rd row : With B. k.1, k.2 tog., k.14, k.2 tog., k.2, k.2 tog., k.14, k.2 tog., k.1.

34th row : With B. k.

35th row : With R. k.1, k.2 tog., k.12, k.2 tog., k.2, k.2 tog., k.12, k.2 tog., k.1.

36th row : With R. k.1, k.2 tog., k.10, k.2 tog., k.2, k.2 tog., k.10, k.2 tog., k.1.

37th row : With B. k.1, k.2 tog., k.8, k.2 tog., k.2, k.2 tog., k.8, k.2 tog., k.1.

38th row : With B. k.1, k.2 tog., k.6, k.2 tog., k.2, k.2 tog., k.6, k.2 tog., k.1.

Cast off in R.

LEFT HAND MITTEN

Work as for right hand mitten to the beg. of the "stag" panel, finishing at the end of the 10th row (64 sts.).

Now cont. as given in st.-st. in G. wool with the "stag" panel on centre 22 sts. for back of hand reversed thus :

1st row : K.37 G., 2 B., 1 G., 2 B., 12 G., 2 B., 1 G., 2 B., 5 G.

2nd row : P.5 G., 2 B., 1 G., 2 B., 6 G., 1 B., 5 G., 2 B., 1 G., 2 B., 37 G.

Cont. in this way to the end of the 10th patt. row, then reverse the g.-st. stripes and shapings to match with right hand mitten.

MAKE UP

Press work lightly on wrong side with hot iron over damp cloth.

Join side and top seams, matching stripes and patt. neatly.

Press seams.

The
BERET

Work with double wool throughout.

Using No. 12 needles and double wool cast on 98 sts. loosely with B.

Work ½ in. in k.1, p.1 rib.

Next row : K.1, * work twice into next st. Rep. from * to end (195 sts.).

Change to No. 9 needles.

Using R. wool k. 2 rows.

Using B. wool k. 2 rows.

Using G. wool work 2 rows st.-st., ending p. row.

Now rep. patt. rows 1 to 12 inclusive, as given for front of Jersey, once.

13th row : With G. * k.38, k. twice into next st. Rep. from * to end (200 sts.).

14th row : With G. p.

Using R. k. 2 rows.

Using B. k. 2 rows.

Rep. last 4 rows twice.

Now cont. in G. st.-st. with 5 stags taken from jersey patt. diagram thus :

Using G., work 2 rows in st.-st., ending p. row.

Now work from the stitch diagram for Jersey, starting at the 61st stitch on odd rows (which will be k. rows) and at the 14th stitch on even rows (which will be p. rows) and working across the following 40 sts. Thus 1st and 2nd rows will be :

1st row : * K.11 G., 2 B., 1 G., 2 B., 12 G., 2 B., 1 G., 2 B., 7 G. Rep. from * 4 times.

2nd row : * P.1 G., 1 B., 5 G., 2 B., 1 G., 2 B., 5 G., 1 B., 6 G., 2 B., 1 G., 2 B., 4 G., 1 B., 6 G. Rep. from * 4 times.

Work 3rd and 4th rows from stitch diagram in same way, then shape thus :

5th row : K.2 tog., k.12 G., 1 B., 1 G., 1 B., 11 G., 1 B., 1 G., 1 B., 7 G., k.2 tog. G., turn.

Cont. on these 38 sts. for one panel thus :

6th row : P.9 G., 1 B., 1 G., 1 B., 9 G., 1 B., 1 G., 1 B., 14 G.

Cont. in this way, working from 7th row of stitch diagram and allowing for dec. sts., dec. 1 st. at both ends of every k. row to the end of the 28th patt. row from diagram (16 sts.).

29th row : With G. k.2 tog., k. to last 2 sts., k.2 tog.

30th row : With G. p.

31st row : K.1 B., with R. k.2 tog., k. to last 3 sts., k.2 tog., k.1 B.

32nd row : K.1 B., with R. k. to last st., k.1 B.

33rd row : With B. k.1, k.2 tog., k. to last 3 sts., k.2 tog., k.1.

34th row : With B. k.

Rep. last 4 rows once.

39th row : K.1 B., with R. (k.2 tog.) twice, k.1 B.

40th row : K.1 B., 2 R., 1 B.

41st row : With B. k.1, k.2 tog., k.1.

42nd row : K.3 B.

43rd row : K.3 tog. B. and fasten off.

** Now, with right side of work facing, rejoin wools to main sts. and work on the next 40 sts. in same way as for first panel, repeating rows 5 to 43 inclusive.**

Rep. from ** to ** 3 times more.

MAKE UP

Press work lightly on wrong side with hot iron over damp cloth.

Join each panel seam neatly, matching patt., then join back seam.

Press seams.

1950s

With prosperity, came variety and change. Yarns in alpaca, silk, mohair, cashmere and angora as well as artificial fibres containing Courtelle, Orlon and Nylon, could be purchased in a rainbow of colours.

Knitting remained popular but with improved wages and cheap mass produced clothing widely available it now had a lot of competition. Knitting magazines such as "Stitchcraft", "Needlework Illustrated" and "Vogue Knitting" styled their models like film stars, using exaggerated poses to emphasize the 'haughty' look seen in fashion magazines and on the Paris catwalk. Ensembles of jumper, hat, gloves and even hand bags were offered, sometimes with very complex constructions.

Twin sets became increasingly popular, often featuring very high neck lines on both jumper and cardigan, with the jumper requiring a zip at the back neck to gain access. Angora jumpers abounded, worn tightly over swelling, pointed breasts tucked into tiny-waisted full skirts, to create the perfect hour glass shape.

As the decade progressed the influence of sportswear and the new social group, the 'teenager' began to influence hand knitting. Now teamed with capri pants or jeans and ballet pumps, casual wear and long-line, over-sized jumpers and cardigans became increasingly popular, laying the foundations for how many of us wear our knitwear to this day.

Middy Jacket

MATERIALS

Excelana Luxury 4 Ply wool 100% pure new British wool (159m/174yds per 50g ball)
7 (8, 8, 9, 10, 11, 11, 12) balls shade Persian Grey – MC
2 (2, 2, 2, 2, 2, 3, 3) balls shade Nile Green – CC
1 pair 2.25mm (US #1) needles
1 button

TENSION

30 sts & 66 rows = 10cm (4in) using 2.25mm needles over garter stitch

Standard Yarn Tension

28 sts & 36 rows = 10cm (4in) using 3mm needles over stocking stitch

ABBREVIATIONS

See page 13 for standard abbreviations

SIZING

Measurements given in centimetres followed by inches in parentheses

To Fit	81 (32)	86 (34)	92 (36)	97 (38)	102 (40)	106 (42)	112 (44)	117 (46)
Finished Measurements								
Actual Bust Size	85 (33½)	90½ (35½)	96 (38)	101 (40)	106½ (42)	112 (44)	117 (46)	122½ (47½)
Length to underarm	32 (12½)	33 (13)	34 (13½)	35½ (14)	37 (14½)	38 (15)	39 (15½)	40½ (16)
Armhole Depth	15 (6)	16½ (6½)	18 (7)	19 (7½)	20 (8)	21½ (8½)	23 (9)	24 (9½)
Finished Length	47 (18½)	49½ (19½)	52 (20½)	54½ (21½)	57 (22½)	59½ (23½)	62 (24½)	64½ (25½)
Shoulder to Shoulder	31½ (12½)	34 (13½)	36½ (14½)	39½ (15½)	40½ (16)	42 (16½)	43 (17)	44½ (17½)

Garment shown in photographs is for fourth size 97 (38)

PATTERN NOTES

Garment fronts are worked in two colours throughout, using Intarsia method. Take care to cross yarns over each other at back of work when changing from one colour to the other to avoid leaving a hole.

LEFT FRONT

Using 2.25mm needles, cast on 30 sts in CC and 39 (43, 47, 51, 55, 59, 63, 67) sts in MC (69, 73, 77, 81, 85, 89, 93, 97 sts). Work in patt as folls:

Row 1 (RS): K39 (43, 47, 51, 55, 59, 63, 67) in MC, K30 in CC.
Row 2: K30 in CC, K39 (43, 47, 51, 55, 59, 63, 67) in MC.
Row 3: P39 (43, 47, 51, 55, 59, 63, 67) in MC, P30 in CC.
Row 4: P30 in CC, P39 (43, 47, 51, 55, 59, 63, 67) in MC.
These 4 rows form patt. Repeat these four rows twice more.

Cont in patt as set, shaping panel at front edge of next row as folls:
Next row (RS): K39 (43, 47, 51, 55, 59, 63, 67) in MC, K2tog in CC, K28 in CC.
Cont dec 1 st at beg of CC panel on every foll 4th row until 54 (58, 62, 66, 70, 74, 78, 82) sts rem.
Maintaining patt, work without further shaping until front measures 15 (15½, 16, 16½, 17, 17½, 18, 18½) cm (6, 6¼, 6¼, 6½, 6¾, 6¾, 7, 7¼ in) ending with a WS row.
With RS facing cont in patt, inc 1 st at beg of CC panel on next and every foll 4th row until 69 (73, 77, 81, 85, 89, 93, 97) sts.
Work without further shaping until front measures 32 (33, 34, 35½, 37, 38, 39, 40½) cm 12½ (13, 13½, 14, 14½, 15, 15½, 16 in) ending with a WS row.

Shape Armhole

With RS facing, cast off 6 sts at beg of next row (63, 67, 71, 75, 79, 83, 87, 91 sts).

7th and 8th sizes only

Work 1 row without shaping.
Cast off 6 sts at beg of next row (81, 85 sts).

All Sizes

Cast off 2 sts at beg of next 2 (2, 2, 2, 3, 4, 2, 3) RS rows (59, 63, 67, 71, 73, 75, 77, 79 sts), then K2tog at same edge on foll 2 alt rows (57, 61, 65, 69, 71, 73, 75, 77 sts).
Work straight until armhole measures 15 (16½, 18, 19, 20, 21½, 23, 24) cm (6, 6½, 7, 7½, 8, 8½, 9, 9½ in) ending with a WS row.

Shape Shoulder

Cast off 7 (8, 9, 10, 14, 11, 11, 12) sts at beg of next and foll 3 (3, 3, 3, 2, 3, 2, 3) alt rows, then cast off 0 (0, 0, 0, 0, 0, 13, 0) sts on foll alt row 0 (0, 0, 0, 0, 0, 1, 0) times (29 sts).

Collar

Cont in patt on rem 29 sts, dec 1 st at each end of next and every foll 4th row until 3 sts rem. Cast off rem sts.

RIGHT FRONT

Using 2.25mm needles, cast on 39 (43, 47, 51, 55, 59, 63, 67) sts in MC and 30 sts in CC (69, 73, 77, 81, 85, 89, 93, 97 sts). Work in patt as folls:

Row 1 (RS): K30 in CC, K39 (43, 47, 51, 55, 59, 63, 67) in MC.

Row 2: K39 (43, 47, 51, 55, 59, 63, 67) in MC, K30 in CC.

Row 3: P30 in CC, P39 (43, 47, 51, 55, 59, 63, 67) in MC.

Row 4: P39 (43, 47, 51, 55, 59, 63, 67) in MC, P30 in CC.

These 4 rows form patt. Repeat these four rows twice more.

Cont in patt as set, shaping panel at front edge of next row as folls:

Next row (RS): K28 in CC, K2tog in CC, K39 (43, 47, 51, 55, 59, 63, 67) in MC.

Cont dec 1 st at end of CC panel on every foll 4th row until 54 (58, 62, 66, 70,74, 78, 82) sts rem.

Maintaining patt, work without further shaping until front measures 13½ (14, 14½, 15, 15½, 16, 16½, 17) cm (5, 5½, 5¾, 6, 6, 6¼, 6½, 6¾ in), ending with a WS row.

Next row (RS buttonhole): Patt 5, cast off 5, patt to end.

Next row: Patt to cast off sts, cast on 5, patt to end.

Continue without further shaping until front measures 15 (15½, 16, 16½, 17, 17½, 18, 18½) cm (6, 6¼, 6¼, 6½, 6¾, 6¾, 7, 7¼ in) ending with a WS row.

Cont in pattern and inc 1 st at end of CC panel on next and every foll 4th row until 69 (73, 77, 81, 85, 89, 93, 97) sts. Work without further shaping until front measures 32 (33, 34, 35½, 37, 38, 39, 40½) cm (12½, 13, 13½, 14, 14½, 15, 15½, 16 in) ending with a RS row.

Shape Armhole

With WS facing, cast off 6 sts at beg of next row (63, 67, 71, 75, 79, 83, 87, 91 sts).

7th and 8th sizes only

Work 1 row without shaping.

Cast off 6 sts at beg of next row (81, 85 sts).

All sizes

Cast off 2 sts at beg of next 2 (2, 2, 2, 3, 4, 2, 3) WS rows (59, 63, 67, 71, 73, 75, 77, 79 sts), then K2tog at same edge on foll 2 alt rows (57, 61, 65, 69, 71, 73, 75, 77 sts).

Work straight until armhole measures 15 (16½, 18, 19, 20, 21½, 23, 24) cm (6, 6½, 7, 7½, 8, 8½, 9, 9½ in) ending with a RS row.

Shape Shoulder

Cast off 7 (8, 9, 10, 14, 11, 11, 12) sts at beg of next and foll 3 (3, 3, 3, 2, 3, 2, 3) alt rows, then cast off 0 (0, 0, 0, 0, 0, 13, 0) sts on foll alt row 0 (0, 0, 0, 0, 0, 1, 0) times (29 sts).

Collar

Cont in patt on rem 29 sts dec 1 st at each end of next and every foll 4th row until 3 sts rem. Cast off rem sts.

BACK

Using 2.25mm needles and MC, cast on 118 (126, 134, 142, 150, 158, 166, 174) sts, and work straight in ridged patt as folls:

Row 1 (RS): K.

Row 2: K.

Row 3: P.

Row 4: P.

These 4 rows form patt. Rep until back measures 32 (33, 34, 35½, 37, 38, 39, 40½) cm (12½, 13, 13½, 14, 14½, 15, 15½, 16 in) ending with a WS row.

Shape Armholes

Cast off 6 sts at beg of next 2 (2, 2, 2, 2, 2, 4, 4) rows, (106, 114, 122, 130, 138, 146, 142, 150 sts), then cast off 2 sts at beg of next 4 (4, 4, 4, 6, 8, 4, 6) rows (98, 106, 114, 122, 126, 130, 134, 138 sts),

Shape Sleeve Head

Cast off 6 sts at beg of next 2 rows (84, 88, 92, 96, 100, 104, 108, 112) sts, then 2 sts at beg of foll 4 rows (76, 80, 84, 88, 92, 96, 100, 104 sts), then dec 1 st at each end of next and every foll 4th row until 38 (38, 36, 36, 38, 36, 36, 36) sts rem.
Cast off rem sts.

MAKING UP

Join shoulder, side and sleeve seams. Insert sleeves, easing sleeve head into place. Place inside edge of pointed collar from left front across back of neck, taking care not to stretch edge of knitting (this piece should fit to within 4cm (1½in) of right shoulder seam) and sew in position using a flat slip stitch. Place right collar on top of left across back of neck in the same way and sew in position. Sew button at waist to match buttonhole. Darn in all ends.

then K2tog at beg of foll 4 rows (94, 102, 110, 118, 122, 126, 130, 134 sts).
Maintaining patt, work without further shaping until armhole measures 15 (16½, 18, 19, 20, 21½, 23, 24) cm (6, 6½, 7, 7½, 8, 8½, 9, 9½ in) ending with a WS row.

Shape Shoulders

With RS facing, cast off 7 (8, 9, 10, 14, 11, 11, 12) sts at beg of next 8 (8, 8, 8, 6, 8, 6, 8) rows and cast off 0 (0, 0, 0, 0, 0, 13, 0) sts at beg of next 0 (0, 0, 0, 0, 0, 2, 0) rows.
Cast off rem 38 sts.

SLEEVES

Using 2.25mm needles and MC, cast on 56 (60, 64, 68, 72, 76, 80, 84) sts and commencing with row 1, work in ridge patt as for back until work measures 11½cm (4½in) ending with a WS row. Cont in patt, inc 1 st at each end of next and every foll 4th row until there are 96 (100, 104, 108, 112, 116, 120, 124) sts.
Work without further shaping until sleeve measures 34½cm (13½in).

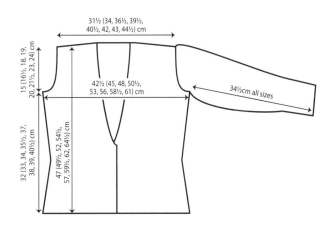

Middy jacket

Materials: Of Patons Beehive Fingering 3-ply, Patonised, 9 ozs. Storm Grey 155 and 2 ozs. Chartreuse 163. A pair No. 12 "Beehive" needles. One decorative button.

Measurements: To fit 35–36 inch bust; length from top of shoulders, 22 inches; sleeve seam, 13½ inches.

Tension: 8½ stitches to an inch.

FRONTS

Left: Cast on 30 sts. in Chartreuse and 51 sts. in Grey, and work in pattern as follows, twisting wools at back of work when changing colour to avoid a hole:—1ST ROW: right side facing, knit, 51 Gr., 30 C. 2ND ROW: Knit, 30 C., 51 Gr. 3RD ROW: Purl, 51 Gr., 30 C. 4TH ROW: Purl, 30 C., 51 Gr. These 4 rows form pattern. Repeat them twice more.

Continue in pattern, shaping in light panel at front edge as follows:—NEXT ROW: k. 51 Gr., k. 2 tog. C., k. 28 C. Continue decreasing 1 stitch thus at beginning of light panel on every following 4th row until 66 sts. remain on needle. Work straight in pattern until front measures 6½ inches.

With right side facing, continue in pattern, increasing 1 stitch at beginning of light panel on next and every following 4th row until there are again 81 sts. on needle.

Work straight until front measures 14 inches.

With right side facing, shape armhole by casting off 6 sts. at beginning of next row, 2 sts. at beginning of following 2 alternate rows, then k. 2 tog. at this edge on following 2 alternate rows (69 sts.). Work straight until front measures 21½ inches.

With right side facing, shape shoulder by casting off 10 sts. at beginning of next and following 3 alternate rows, armhole edge. Continue in pattern on remaining 29 sts., decreasing 1 stitch at each end of next and every following 4th row until 3 sts. remain. Cast off.

Right: Cast on 51 sts. in Gr. and 30 sts. in C. Work to correspond with left front, reversing shapings and working a buttonhole at waist in 101st and 102nd rows. To make a buttonhole:—With right side facing, pattern 5, cast off 5, pattern to end and back, casting on 5 over those cast off.

BACK

With Grey, cast on 142 sts. and work straight in ridged pattern as for front until back measures 14 inches. With right side facing, shape armholes by casting off 6 sts. at beginning of next 2 rows, 2 sts. at beginning of next 4 rows, then k. 2 tog. at beginning of following 4 rows (118 sts.). Work straight in pattern until back measures 21½ inches.

With right side facing, shape shoulders by casting off 10 sts. at beginning of next 8 rows. Cast off remaining stitches.

SLEEVES

With Grey cast on 68 sts. and work 4½ inches straight in ridged pattern. Continue in pattern, increasing 1 stitch at each end of next and every following 4th row until there are 108 sts. Work straight until sleeve measures 13½ inches.

With right side facing, shape top by casting off 6 sts. at beginning of next 2 rows, 2 sts. at beginning of following 4 rows, then k. 2 tog. at beginning of every row until 34 sts. remain. Cast off.

TO MAKE UP

Press work lightly on wrong side under a damp cloth. Join shoulder, side and sleeve seams; insert sleeves, matching ridges. Place inside edge of pointed collar from left front across back of neck, taking care not to stretch edge of knitting (this piece should fit to within 1¼ inches of right shoulder seam); sew in position. Now place right collar on top of left across back of neck in the same way and sew in position. Sew button at waist to match buttonhole. Press seams.

Jumper with Collar and Flowers

MATERIALS
Knitshop 4ply Cotton 100% mercerised cotton (125m per 50g ball)
5 (6, 6, 7, 7, 8, 9, 9) balls shade Shell Pink – MC
3 (3, 3, 4, 4, 4, 4, 4) balls shade Arctic White – A
1 ball shade Canary Yellow – B
1 pair 2.75mm (US #2) needles
1 pair 3mm (US #2–3) needles
2mm crochet hook
Sewing thread and needle
Stitch holders

TENSION
27 sts & 36 rows = 10cm (4in) using 3mm needles over stocking stitch

ABBREVIATIONS
See page 13 for standard abbreviations

SIZING
Measurements given in centimetres followed by inches in parentheses

To Fit	81 (32)	86 (34)	92 (36)	97 (38)	102 (40)	107 (42)	112 (44)	117 (46)
Finished Measurements								
Actual Bust Size	86 (34)	92 (36)	96½ (38)	102 (40)	106½ (42)	112½ (44½)	118½ (46½)	121½ (48)
Length to underarm	30½ (12)	30½ (12)	32 (12½)	33 (13)	33 (13)	34 (13½)	35½ (14)	35½ (14)
Armhole Depth	16½ (6½)	16½ (6½)	18 (7)	18 (7)	20½ (8)	20½ (8)	23 (9)	23 (9)
Finished Length	47 (18½)	47 (18½)	50 (19½)	51 (20)	53½ (21)	54½ (21½)	58½ (23)	58½ (23)
Shoulder to shoulder	32 (12½)	35 (14)	37 (14½)	39¼ (15½)	40 (15¾)	41½ (16¼)	43 (17)	44½ (17½)
Sleeve Length	4 (1½)	4 (1½)	4 (1½)	4 (1½)	4½ (1¾)	5 (2)	5 (2)	5 (2)

Garment shown in photographs is for fourth size 96 (38)

BACK
Using 2.75mm needles and MC, cast on 94 (102, 110, 118, 122, 130, 138, 142) sts and work in rib as folls:
Next row (RS): K2, * P2, K2, rep from * to end.
Next row: P2, * K2, P2, rep from * to end.
Rep these 2 rows until rib measures 10cm (4in) ending with a WS row, and increasing 2 (2, 0, 0, 2, 2, 2, 2) sts on final row (96, 104, 110, 118, 124, 132, 140, 144 sts).
Next row (Inc): K24 (26, 27, 29, 31, 33, 35, 36), M1, K48 (52, 56, 60, 62, 66, 70, 72), M1, K to end.
Work 5 rows straight.
Next row (Inc): K25 (27, 28, 30, 32, 34, 36, 37), M1, K48 (52, 56, 60, 62, 66, 70, 72), M1, K to end.
Work 5 rows straight.
Next row (Inc): K26 (28, 29, 31, 33, 35, 37, 38), M1, K48 (52, 56, 60, 62, 66, 70, 72), M1, K to end.
Work 5 rows straight.
Cont inc on every 6th row until there are 116 (124, 130, 138, 144, 152, 160, 164) sts, then work without further shaping until back measures 30½ (30½, 32, 33, 33, 34, 35½, 35½) cm (12, 12, 12½, 13, 13, 13½, 14, 14 in) from cast on, ending with a WS row **

Shape Armholes
Cast off 3 (3, 3, 3, 4, 5, 6, 6) sts at beg of next 4 rows (104, 112, 118, 126, 128, 132, 136, 140 sts), then K2tog at each end of next and every foll RS row until 86 (94, 100, 106, 108, 112, 116, 120) sts rem. Work without further shaping until armhole measures 16½ (16½, 18, 18, 20½, 20½, 23, 23) cm (6½, 6½, 7, 7, 8, 8, 9, 9 in) ending with a WS row.

Shape Shoulders
Cast off 9 (10, 10, 10, 10, 10, 11, 12) sts at beg of next 4 (4, 6, 6, 4, 4, 6, 4) rows then cast off 8 (8, 0, 0, 11, 11, 0, 10) sts at beg of next 2 (2, 0, 0, 2, 2, 0, 2) rows.
Cast off rem 34 (38, 40, 46, 46, 50, 50, 52) sts.

FRONT
Work exactly as for back until **

Shape Armholes and Divide for Neck
Next row (RS): Cast off 3 (3, 3, 3, 4, 5, 6, 6) sts, knit to 45 (47, 49, 50, 52, 53, 56, 57) sts on right needle, cast off 20 (24, 26, 32, 32, 36, 36, 38) sts, K48 (50, 52, 53, 56, 58, 62, 63). Place 45 (47, 49, 50, 52, 53, 56, 57) sts on holder and continue on last 48 (50, 52, 53, 56, 58, 62, 63) sts only.

Next row (WS): Cast off 3 (3, 3, 3, 4, 5, 6, 6) sts, P to last 2 sts, P2tog (44, 46, 48, 49, 51, 52, 55, 56 sts).
Next row: K2tog, K to end (43, 45, 47, 48, 50, 51, 54, 55 sts).
Next row: Cast off 3 (3, 3, 3, 4, 5, 6, 6), P to last 2 sts, P2tog (39, 41, 43, 44, 45, 45, 47, 48 sts).
Dec 1 st at neck edge on next 4 rows and at armhole edge on next 9 (9, 9, 10, 10, 10, 10, 10) alt rows (26, 28, 30, 30, 31, 31, 33, 34 sts).
Work without further shaping until armhole measures 16½ (16½, 18, 18, 20½, 20½, 23, 23) cm (6½, 6½, 7, 7, 8, 8, 9, 9 in) ending with a RS row.

Shape Shoulder
Cast off 9 (10, 10, 10, 10, 10, 11, 12) sts at beg of next and foll 1 (1, 2, 2, 1, 1, 2, 1) alt rows, then 8 (8, 0, 0, 11, 11, 0, 10) sts at beg of foll 1 (1, 0, 0, 1, 1, 0, 1) alt row.

With WS facing, rejoin yarn to rem 45 (47, 49, 50, 52, 53, 56, 57) sts.
Next row: P2tog, P to end.
Next row: Cast off 3 (3, 3, 3, 4, 5, 6, 6), K to last 2 sts, K2tog (40, 42, 44, 45, 46, 46, 48, 49 sts).
Dec 1 st at neck edge on next 5 rows and at armhole edge on next 9 (9, 9, 10, 10, 10, 10, 10) alt rows (26, 28, 30, 30, 31, 31, 33, 34 sts) ending with a WS row.

Shape Shoulder
Cast off 9 (10, 10, 10, 10, 10, 11, 12) sts at beg of next and foll 1 (1, 2, 2, 1, 1, 2, 1) alt rows, then 8 (8, 0, 0, 11, 11, 0, 10) sts at beg of foll 1 (1, 0, 0, 1, 1, 0, 1) alt row.

SLEEVES
Using 3mm needles and MC, cast on 92 (96, 100, 104, 108, 112, 116, 120) sts and K one row for hem line.
Commencing with a K row (K row is RS of work), work in stocking stitch for 4 (4, 4, 4, 4½, 5, 5, 5) cm (1½, 1½, 1½, 1½, 1¾, 2, 2, 2 in) ending with a WS row.

Shape Sleeve Head
Cast off 3 (3, 3, 3, 4, 5, 6, 6) sts at beg of next 4 rows (80, 84, 88, 92, 92, 92, 92, 96 sts), then K2tog at each end of next and every foll RS row until 54 (54, 50, 50, 46, 46, 42, 42) sts rem, then at each end of every foll row until 20 sts rem. Cast off.

CUFFS
Using 3mm needles and A, cast on 30 sts and K 1 row.
Next row: K2tog, K27, Kfb.
Next row: Kfb, K27, K2tog.
Repeat these 2 rows until cuff fits along sleeve edge.
Cast off.
Make another piece the same.

COLLAR
Using 3mm needles and A, cast on 50 sts and work as for cuff until piece measures 54½ (56½, 61, 63½, 69½, 71½, 77½, 78) cm (21½, 22, 24, 25, 27½, 28, 30½, 30¾ in).
Cast off.

FLOWERS
Using 3mm needles and A, cast on 15 sts.
** **Row 1** (RS): K.
Row 2: K.
Row 3: K12, turn and K to end.
Row 5: K.
Row 6: Cast off 10, K to end (5 sts).
Row 7: K5, cast on 10 (15 sts).
Row 8: K. **
Repeat from ** to ** until there are 15 petals.
Cast off.
Make 2 more flowers in the same way.

STAMENS (Make three)
Using 2mm crochet hook and B, ch 60, then fold to make 3 loops, and sew together. Draw through final chain and fasten off.

Run a gathering thread through straight edge of flower, gather and bind round stamens, sew firmly in positions. Work 2 rem flowers in the same way.

MAKING UP
Crochet edgings

Join collar and cuffs into rounds and using a 2mm crochet hook, work a row of DC (SC) all around one edge.

Next Round: * 6 ch, miss 1 DC (SC), [1 DC (SC) into next st] twice, repeat from * to end.

Next Round: 3 DC (SC) into first loop, * 5 ch, 1 DC (SC) into next loop, repeat from * to end. Fasten off.

Press body pieces lightly on WS under a damp cloth. Join right shoulder seam, then with RS facing, and using 2.75mm needles and A, pick up and K 166 (174, 186, 202, 214, 222, 238, 242) sts all round neck. Work in rib as folls:

Next row (WS): * K2, P2, rep from * to last 2 sts, K2.

Next row: * P2, K2, rep from * to last 2 sts, P2.

Rep these 2 rows until ribbing measures 2½cm (1in). Cast off in rib.

Join left shoulder, side and sleeve seams. Set in sleeves taking care to match centre of sleeve head to shoulder seam and matching side seams. Press collar and cuff firmly using spray on starch to stiffen fabric. Sew cuffs in position, turn back and press again. Sew collar to lower edge of neck ribbing on WS, using a flat slip stitch, bringing narrower ends of collar over to RS of collar, then sew collar ends together. Pin flowers in position as shown in photograph. Sew in place securely. Darn in all ends.

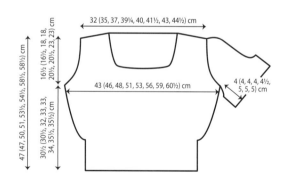

A delightfully feminine affair for dressy occasions. The demure and becoming neck has a posy of knitted flowers. A charming jumper to wear when you want to look your prettiest.

JUMPER WITH COLLAR AND FLOWERS

MATERIALS: Of Patons Beehive Fingering 2-ply, Patonised, 4 ozs. main shade and 1 oz. contrast. For flowers, 1 oz. contrast and 6 yards yellow wool for centres. A pair each No. 12 and No. 11 "Queen Bee" needles. A No. 13 crochet hook.

MEASUREMENTS: To fit 33-34-inch bust; length from top of shoulders, 19½ inches; sleeve seam, cuff turned back, 1½ inches.

TENSION: 8½ sts. and 10½ rows to an inch.

BACK

With No. 12 needles and main shade, cast on 118 sts. and work 4 inches k. 2, p. 2 rib, rows on right side having a k. 2 at each end. Change to No. 11 needles and stocking-stitch and work 10 rows straight, starting with a knit row.

Next row: k. 29, increase 1 by picking up and knitting into back of horizontal thread before next stitch, k. 60, pick up and knit into back of horizontal thread before next stitch, k. 29. Work 5 rows straight in stocking-stitch.

Next row: k. 30, increase as before, k. 60, increase as before, k. 30. Work 5 rows straight. Next row: k. 31, increase as before, k. 60 increase as before, k. 31. Work 5 rows straight. Continue increasing thus on every 6th row until there are 138 sts., then work straight until back measures 12 inches at centre.

With right side facing, shape armholes by casting off 3 sts. at beginning of next 4 rows, then k. 2 tog. at each end of every knit row until 106 sts. remain. Work straight until armhole measures 7 inches.

With right side facing, shape shoulders by casting off 10 sts. at beginning of next 6 rows. Cast off.

FRONT

Work exactly as for back until front measures 12 inches at centre. Here shape armholes and neck. Next row: Cast off 3, k. 50, cast off 32, k. 53. Slip 50 sts. for left shoulder on to a spare needle and continue on last 53 sts.

Next row: Cast off 3, k. 48, p. 2 tog. Next row: k. 2 tog., knit to end. Next row: Cast off 3, purl to last 2 sts., p. 2 tog. Now decrease 1 stitch at neck edge on next 5 rows and at armhole edge on next 10 alternate rows (30 sts.).

Work straight until armhole measures 7 inches, then with wrong side facing, shape shoulder by casting off 10 sts. at beginning of next and following 2 alternate rows, armhole edge.

Rejoin wool to remaining sts. at neck edge. Next row: p. 2 tog., purl to end. Next row: Cast off 3, knit to last 2 sts., k. 2 tog. Now work to correspond with right shoulder.

SLEEVES

With No. 11 needles and main shade, cast on 104 sts. and knit 1 row. Work straight in stocking-stitch for 1½ inches, starting with a knit row. With right side facing, shape top by casting off 3 sts. at beginning of next 4 rows. Now k. 2 tog. at each end of every following knit row until 50 sts. remain, then at each end of every row until 20 sts. remain. Cast off.

COLLAR AND CUFFS

Cuffs: With No. 11 needles and contrast wool, cast on 30 sts. and k. 1 row. Next row: k. 2 tog., k. 27, knit twice into last stitch. Next row: Knit twice into first stitch, k. 27, k. 2 tog. Repeat these 2 rows until cuff fits along sleeve edge. Cast off. Make another piece the same. *Collar:* Cast on 50 sts. and work in the same way until piece measures 25 inches. Cast off.

Crochet edgings: Join collar and cuffs into rounds and work a row of double-crochet all round one edge. Next round: * 6 ch., miss 1 st., (1 d.c. into next stitch) twice; repeat from * to end. Next round: 3 d.c. into first loop, * 5 ch., 1 d.c. into next loop; repeat from * to end. Fasten off.

FLOWERS

With contrast wool and No. 11 needles, cast on 15 sts. ** 1st row: Knit. 2nd row: Knit. 3rd row: k. 12, turn and knit to end. 5th row: Knit. 6th row: Cast off 10, knit to end. 7th row: k. 5, cast on 10. 8th row: Knit. ** Repeat from ** to ** until there are 15 petals. Cast off. Make 2 more pieces the same.

Wind 2 yards of yellow wool round a piece of cardboard 1-inch wide; slip off cardboard and bind in centre, then cut one end to form stamens. Run a gathering thread through straight edge of flower, gather and bind round stamens; sew firmly in position. Work two remaining flowers in the same way. Sew a small safety-pin to back of each flower.

TO MAKE UP

Press pieces lightly on wrong side under a damp cloth. Join right shoulder seam, then with right side facing. No. 12 needles and main shade, pick up and k. 202 sts. all round neck. Work ¾-inch in k. 2, p. 2 rib. Cast off in rib. Join left shoulder, side and sleeve seams; insert sleeves. Sew cuffs in position, turn back and press. Sew collar to lower edge of neck ribbing on wrong side, having join at back. Press seams. Pin flowers in position as shown in photograph.

Blouse with Gathered Neckline

MATERIALS
Posh Yarns Valerie hand dyed merino/silk blend (1200m per 100g skein)
1 (2, 2, 2, 2, 2) skeins
1 pair 2.25mm (US #1) needles
2 press studs

TENSION
40 sts & 51 rows = 10cm (4in) using 2.25mm needles over stitch pattern

ABBREVIATIONS
See page 13 for standard abbreviations

Specific abbreviations for this pattern
3L – (K1, P1, K1) into next st, winding yarn around needle twice for each st worked
Sl3L – With yarn at front of work Sl3 purlwise, dropping extra loops worked

SIZING
Measurements given in centimetres followed by inches in parentheses

To Fit	81–86 (32–34)	86–92 (34–36)	92–97 (36–38)	102–106 (40–42)	106–112 (42–44)	112–117 (44–46)
Finished Measurements						
Actual Bust Size	85 (33½)	92 (36)	99 (39)	106 (41¾)	113 (44½)	120 (47)
Length to underarm	30½ (12)	32 (12½)	33 (13)	35½ (14)	35½ (14)	37 (14½)
Armhole Depth	18 (7)	19 (7½)	20 (8)	20 (8)	21½ (8½)	23 (9)
Finished Length	48½ (19)	51 (20)	53 (21)	55½ (22)	57 (22½)	60 (23½)
Shoulder to shoulder	33½ (13)	34½ (13½)	37 (14½)	38 (15)	39 (15½)	41½ (16½)
Sleeve Length	15 (6)	15 (6)	15 (6)	15 (6)	15 (6)	15 (6)

Garment shown in photographs for first size 81–86 (32–34)

PATTERN NOTES
Stitch counts do not include any increased stitches formed as part of the loop motif. If in doubt, complete partial motifs and then count stitches.

Stitches are increased at armhole edges on upper front body after armhole shaping has been completed. This is necessary to provide room at front neck.

BACK
Using 2.25mm needles, cast on 130 (144, 158, 172, 186, 200) sts and work in rib as folls:
Next row (RS): * K1, P1, rep from * to end of row.
Rep this row until work measures 7½cm (3in) ending with a RS row.
Next row (Inc): Rib 10 (0, 2, 4, 6, 8), * Kfb, rib 9 (11, 12, 13, 14, 15), rep from * 9 more times (142, 156, 170, 184, 198, 212 sts).

Place Pattern
Row 1 (RS): Working from right to left, work row 1 of chart, rep marked section 9 (10, 11, 12, 13, 14) times.
Row 2: Working from left to right, work row 2 of chart, rep marked section 9 (10, 11, 12, 13, 14) times.
Continue as set repeating 32 rows of pattern throughout garment, and at same time, inc at each end of 7th and 13 foll 6th rows, working extra sts into pattern, thus ending on chart row 21 (170, 184, 198, 212, 226, 240 sts). Once all extra sts increased, marked section will repeat 11 (12, 13, 14, 15, 16) times across row.

Maintaining pattern, continue without further shaping until work measures 30½ (32, 33, 35½, 35½, 37) cm (12, 12½, 13, 14, 14, 14½ in) ending with a WS row, but not a chart row 4, 8, 12, 20, 24 or 28 (as these rows have extra motif sts).

Shape Armholes
Throughout the shaping sections, omit loop motifs where there will not be sufficient stitches and/or rows to complete the motif, replacing the loop stitch with stocking stitch.

Cast off 4 (5, 6, 4, 5, 6) sts at beg of next 2 (2, 2, 4, 4, 4) rows (162, 174, 186, 196, 206, 216 sts), then dec 1 st at each end of next 14 (18, 19, 22, 25, 25) rows (134, 138, 148, 152, 156, 166 sts after completion of any partial motifs) **

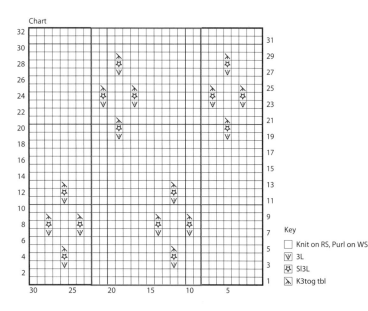

Chart

Key
- ☐ Knit on RS, Purl on WS
- Ⅴ 3L
- ⊕ Sl3L
- ⋋ K3tog tbl

Continue without further shaping until work measures 36 (38½, 40½, 43, 44½, 47½) cm (14, 15, 16, 17, 17½, 18¾ in) ending with a WS row but not a chart row 4, 8, 12, 20, 24 or 28 (as these rows have extra motif sts).

Divide for Back Opening

Next row: Patt 72 (74, 79, 81, 83, 88) sts, turn, leaving rem 62 (64, 69, 71, 73, 78) sts on a stitch holder. Continue in pattern, on these 72 (74, 79, 81, 83, 88) sts until armhole measures 18 (19, 20, 20, 21½, 23) cm (7, 7½, 8, 8, 8½, 9 in), ending with a WS row but not a chart row 4, 8, 12, 20, 24 or 28 (as these rows have extra motif sts).

Shape Neck and Shoulder

Row 1 (RS): Cast off 9 (9, 10, 10, 10, 11) sts, patt to end (63, 65, 69, 71, 73, 77 sts).
Row 2: Cast off 22 (23, 24, 26, 28, 28) sts for neck, patt to end (41, 42, 45, 45, 45, 49 sts).
Row 3: Cast off 9 (9, 10, 10, 10, 11) sts, patt to last 2 sts, K2tog (31, 32, 34, 34, 34, 37 sts).
Row 4: P2tog, patt to end.
Rep the last 2 rows once more, then row 3 once again (9, 10, 10, 10, 10, 11 sts rem).
Row 8: P to end.
Cast off rem sts.
With RS facing, rejoin yarn to rem 62 (64, 69, 71, 73, 78) sts, and cast on 10 sts (for button band) (72, 74, 79, 81, 83, 88 sts).
Working 10 sts in garter st for button band throughout, work in patt until armhole measures 18 (19, 20, 20, 21½, 23) cm (7, 7½, 8, 8, 8½, 9 in) ending with a RS row, but not a chart row 3, 7, 11, 19, 23 or 27 (as these rows have extra motif sts).

Shape Neck and Shoulder

(remembering to work button band sts in garter st)
Row 1: Cast off 9 (9, 10, 10, 10, 11) sts, patt to last 10 sts, K10 (63, 65, 69, 71, 73, 77 sts).
Row 2: Cast off 22 (23, 24, 26, 28, 28) sts for neck, patt to end (41, 42, 45, 45, 45, 49 sts).
Row 3: Cast off 9 (9, 10, 10, 10, 11) sts, patt to last 2 sts, P2tog (31, 32, 34, 34, 34, 37 sts).
Row 4: K2tog, K to end.
Rep the last 2 rows once more, then row 3 once again (9, 10, 10, 10, 10, 11 sts).
Row 8: K.
Cast off rem sts.

FRONT

Work as given for back until **
Continue without shaping until work measures 36¾ (39, 41, 44, 45, 48) cm (14½, 15¼, 16, 17¼, 17¾, 19 in) ending with a WS row.
Throughout the shaping sections, omit loop motifs where there will not be sufficient stitches and/or rows to complete the motif, replacing the loop stitch with stocking stitch.
Inc 1 st at each end of next and 7 foll 4th rows (150, 154, 164, 168, 172, 182 sts). Continue in pattern, without further shaping until work measures 43 (45½, 47½, 50, 51½, 54½) cm (17, 18, 19, 19½, 20, 21½ in) ending with a WS row.

Shape Neck

Next row: Kfb, patt 60 (62, 67, 69, 71, 75) (62, 64, 69, 71, 73, 77 sts on needle), place these sts on holder, cast off the next 28 (28, 28, 28, 28, 30) sts, patt to last st, Kfb.
Work in patt on rem 62 (64, 69, 71, 73, 77) sts, inc 1 st at armhole edge on 6 foll 4th rows and AT THE SAME TIME dec 1 st at neck edge on 23 (25, 25, 27, 29, 28) foll rows (45, 45, 50, 50, 50, 55 sts).
Continue without further shaping until armhole measures 18 (19, 20, 20, 21½, 23) cm (7, 7½, 8, 8, 8½, 9 in) ending with a RS row.

Shape Shoulders

Cast off 9 (9, 10, 10, 10, 11) sts at beg of next and 4 foll alt rows (all sts now cast off).
With WS facing, rejoin to rem 62 (64, 69, 71, 73, 77) sts and work to match right shoulder, reversing all shapings.

SLEEVES

Using 2.25mm needles, cast on 107 (115, 123, 127, 137, 147) sts and commencing with a K row, work 16 rows in stocking stitch.
Next row (Make picot): K1, * YO, K2tog, rep from * to end.
Next row: P2tog, P to end (106, 114, 122, 126, 136, 146 sts).
Commencing with a K row, work in stocking stitch for 16 rows.

Work in pattern as folls:
Row 1 (RS): Kfb, K3 (7, 4, 6, 4, 2), rep marked section of row 1 of chart 7 (7, 8, 8, 9, 10) times, K3 (7, 4, 6, 4, 2), Kfb (108, 116, 124, 128, 138, 148 sts).
Row 2 (WS): P5 (9, 6, 8, 6, 4), rep marked section of row 2 of chart 7 (7, 8, 8, 9, 10) times, P5 (9, 6, 8, 6, 4).
Continue working from chart as set, inc 1 st at each end of 6 foll 6th rows (120, 128, 136, 140, 150, 160 sts), working inc sts into pattern as pattern allows. Continue without further shaping until sleeves measures 15cm (6in) from picot row, ending with a WS row but not a chart row 4, 8, 12, 20, 24 or 28 (as these rows have extra motif sts).

Shape Sleeve Head
Please Note: Throughout the shaping sections, omit loop motifs where there will not be sufficient stitches and/or rows to complete the motif, replacing the loop stitch with stocking stitch.
Cast off 4 (5, 6, 4, 5, 6) sts at beg of next 2 (2, 2, 4, 4, 4) rows (112, 118, 124, 124, 130, 136 sts), dec 1 st at each end of 10 foll rows (92, 98, 104, 104, 110, 116 sts), then dec 1 st at each end of 29 (32, 35, 35, 38, 41) foll alt rows (34 sts).
Cast off 4 sts at beg of next 4 rows (18 sts).
Cast off rem sts.

NECKBAND
Using 2.25mm needles, cast on 147 (149, 153, 163, 171, 171) sts and commencing with a K work 10 rows in stocking stitch.
Next row: K1, * YO, K2tog rep from * to end.
Next row: P.
Commencing with a K row work 9 rows in stocking stitch.
Cast off.

NECK BOW
Using 2.25mm needles, cast on 101 sts and commencing with a K row, work 6 rows in stocking stitch.
Row 7: K1, * YO, K2tog, rep from * to end.
Row 8: P.
Commencing with a K row, work 10 rows in stocking stitch, then rep rows 7 and 8 once more.
Work 4 more rows in stocking stitch. Cast off.

MAKING UP
Press work lightly on WS, through a damp cloth. Join side, shoulder and sleeve seams. Sew sleeves into armholes, matching seams to underarm seams and easing fullness at shoulder. Turn up the 16 rows at lower edge of sleeve to form a hem and stitch neatly on the wrong side. Run a thread through front of neck edge and gather up to fit neckband. Pin centre of cast on edge of neckband to centre front of neck with RS tog. Sew into position using back stitch, matching edges of back opening to ends of band. Fold band in half with RS tog, and join back opening edges of band using back stitch. Turn to RS, folded at picot and sew the cast off edge in place using a loose slip stitch. Neaten lower edge of back opening.
Fold bow into shape and stitch to front of neck. Sew on press studs to back opening. Darn in all ends.

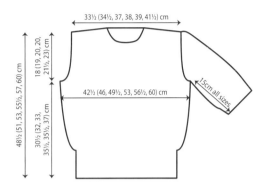

BLOUSE with gathered neckline

MATERIALS

2 hanks (approx. 4 oz.) Anny Blatt fine 1-ply wool.
2 No. 13 and 2 No. 14 knitting needles.
Press studs for back opening.

MEASUREMENTS

Bust—36 ins.   Length—19 ins.   Sleeve seam—5 ins.

TENSION

Using No. 13 needles : 10 sts. to 1 inch.

ABBREVIATIONS

k.—knit, p.—purl, st.—stitch, sl.—slip, tog.—together, inc.—increase, dec.—decrease, Rep.—repeat, ins.—inches, g.st.—garter stitch (every row k.), st.st.—stocking stitch (1 row k., 1 row p.), wl.fwd.—wool forward, wl.bk.—wool back, patt.—pattern, rem.—remain, beg.—beginning, p.w.—purlwise, cont.—continue.

BACK

Using No. 14 needles cast on 130 sts. and work in k.1, p.1 rib for 3 ins.

Next row—Rib 2, * inc. (by knitting into front and back of st.), rib 6.

Rep. from * until 2 sts. rem., inc. p.1 (149 sts.).

Change to No. 13 needles and work in patt. thus :—

1st row—k. to end.

2nd row—p. to end.

3rd row—k.11, * work 3 long sts. into next st. thus: winding wool twice instead of once round needle for each st. work k.1, p.1, k.1 into this st., k.13. Rep. from * ending k.11, instead of k.13.

4th row—p.11, *keeping wool to front of work sl.3 p.w. dropping extra loops (always drop extra loops whenever slipping sts.) p.13. Rep. from * ending p.11, instead of p.13.

5th row—k.11, *k.3 tog. through back of loops (when working patt. always knit sts. tog. through back of loops) k.13. Rep. from * ending k.11 instead of k.13.

6th row—p. to end.

7th row—k.9, * work 3 long sts. into next st., k.3, work 3 long sts. into next st., k.9. Rep. from * to end.

8th row—p.9, * sl. 3 p.w., p.3, sl. 3 p.w., p.9. Rep. from * to end.

9th row—k.9, * k.3 tog., k.3, k.3 tog., k.9. Rep. from * to end.

10th to 14th rows—Rep. rows 2 to 6 inclusive.

15th to 18th rows—Rep. 1st and 2nd rows twice.

19th row—k.4, * work 3 long sts. into next st., k.13. Rep. from * ending k.4 instead of k.13.

20th row—p.4 * sl. 3 p.w., p.13.   Rep. from * ending p.4 instead of p.13.

21st row—k.4, * k.3 tog., k.13.   Rep. from * ending k.4 instead of k.13.

22nd row—p. to end.

23rd row—k.2, * work 3 long sts. into next st., k.3, work 3 long sts. into next st., k.9.   Rep. from * ending k.2 instead of k.9.

24th row—p.2, * sl. 3 p.w., p.3, sl. 3 p.w., p.9.   Rep. from * ending p.2 instead of p.9.

25th row—k.2, * k.3 tog., k.3, k.3 tog., k.9.   Rep. from * ending k.2, instead of k.9.

26th to 30th rows—Rep. rows 18 to 22 inclusive.

31st and 32nd rows—As 1st and 2nd rows.

These 32 rows form the patt.

Cont. in patt. inc. 1 st. at both ends of 7th and every following 6th row until there are 177 sts. working extra sts. into patt.

D. H. Evans of Oxford St, London

Cont. straight until work measures 12 ins., ending with a row on wrong side.

SHAPE ARMHOLES

Cast off 4 sts. at the beg. of next 2 rows, then dec. 1 st. at both ends of every row until 135 sts. rem. Cont. straight until work measures 14 ins., ending with a row on wrong side.

DIVIDE FOR BACK OPENING

Next row—patt. 72 sts., turn.

Leaving rem. 63 sts. on a spare needle cont. in patt. on these 72 sts. until work measures 19 ins., ending with a row on wrong side.

SHAPE NECK AND SHOULDER

1st row—Cast off 9 sts., patt. to end (when casting off the long loops must be counted as one st.).

2nd row—Cast off 22 sts., p. to end.

3rd row—Cast off 9 sts., patt. to last 2 sts., k.2 tog.

4th row—p.2 tog., p. to end.

Rep. the last 2 rows once more, then the 3rd row once again.

8th row—p. to end.

Cast off rem. sts.

Rejoin wool at needle point to the rem. 63 sts., cast on 9 sts. for underwrap.

Work to match first side, reversing neck and shoulder shapings and keeping the 9 cast on sts. in g.st.

FRONT

Work exactly as given for back until armhole shapings are completed.

Cont. straight until work measures 14½ ins., ending with a row on wrong side.

Now inc. 1 st. at both ends of next and every following 4th row until there are 151 sts., ending with 3 rows worked after the last inc. row. (Work should measure about 17 ins.).

SHAPE NECK

Next row—inc. in 1st st., patt. 60 (62 sts. on needle), cast off the next 29 sts., patt. to last st., inc. in last st. Work in patt. on the last set of 62 sts., still inc. every 4th row at armhole edge and at the same time dec. 1 st. on every row at neck edge until 23 sts. in all have been dec. at this edge. Work 1 more inc. at armhole edge (45 sts.).

Cont. straight if necessary until work measures 19 ins., ending with a row on right side.

SHAPE SHOULDER

Cast off 9 sts. at beg. of next and every alternate row until all sts. have been cast off.

Rejoin wool at neck edge to the rem. 62 sts. and work to match right shoulder.

SLEEVES

Using No. 14 needles cast on 107 sts. and work 16 rows in st.st. thus ending with a p. row.

Next row—k.1, * m.1, k.2 tog. Rep. from * to end.

Next row—p. to end.

Now work in patt. as for back for 16 rows.

Change to No. 13 needles and cont. in patt. inc. 1 st. at both ends of next and every following 6th row until there are 121 sts. Cont. straight until work measures 6 ins., ending with a row on wrong side.

SHAPE TOP

Cast off 4 sts. at the beg. of next 2 rows, then dec. 1 st. at both ends of every row until 93 sts. rem. Now dec. 1 st. at both ends of every alternate row until 35 sts. rem. Cast off 4 sts. at beg. of next 4 rows. Cast off rem. sts.

POCKET

Using No. 13 needles cast on 34 sts. and work in st.st., inc. 1 st. at both ends of every row until there are 50 sts. Cont. straight until work measures 3 ins. Cast off.

POCKET BORDER

Using No. 14 needles cast on 41 sts. and work 6 rows in st.st.

Next row—k.1, * m.1, k.2 tog. Rep. from * to end.

Next row—p. to end.

Work 5 rows in st.st. Cast off.

POCKET BOW

Using No. 14 needles cast on 61 sts. and work 4 rows in st.st.

5th row—k.1, * m.1, k.2 tog. Rep. from * to end.

6th row—p. to end.

Work 6 rows in st.st. then rep. rows 5 and 6 once more.

Work 2 more rows in st.st. Cast off.

NECK BOW

Using No. 13 needles cast on 101 sts. and work 6 rows in st.st.

7th row—k.1, * m.1, k.2 tog. Rep. from * to end.

8th row—p. to end.

Work 10 rows in st.st., then rep. rows 7 and 8 once more.

Work 4 more rows in st.st. Cast off.

NECKBAND

Using No. 13 needles cast on 147 sts. and work 4 rows in st.st.

Change to No. 14 needles and work 6 more rows in st.st.

Next row—k.1, * m.1, k.2 tog. Rep. from * to end.

Next row—p. to end.

Work 5 rows in st.st., then change to No. 13 needles and work 4 more rows in st.st. Cast off.

MAKE UP

Press all work lightly on wrong side, using a hot iron over a damp cloth. Join side, shoulder and sleeve seams. Sew sleeves into armholes, matching seams to under-arm seams and easing fullness at shoulder.

Turn up the first 16 rows at lower edge of sleeve to form a hem and stitch neatly on the wrong side.

Run a thread through front of neck edge and draw up to about 8 ins. Pin centre of cast-on edge of neck border to centre front of neck and sew into position to edges of back opening.

Fold over in half and sew the cast-off edge down to form a hem. Neaten lower edge of back opening. Sew cast-on edge of pocket border to the cast-off edge of pocket, easing in fullness, then fold over and hem to match neck border. Sew the pocket to front of blouse. Press all seams. Stitch bows to front of neck and centre of pocket top. Sew on press studs to fasten back opening.

Bobble Topper

MATERIALS
Rooster Almerino DK 50% baby alpaca/50% merino wool (113m/124yds per 50g ball)
2 balls shade 203
1 pair 3.75mm (US #5) needles
1 set of 3.75mm (US #5) Double Pointed Needles (DPNs)

TENSION
23 sts & 31 rows 10cm (4in) using 3.75mm needles over stitch pattern

Standard Yarn Tension
21 sts & 28 rows = 10cm (4in) using 4mm needles over stocking stitch

ABBREVIATIONS
See page 13 for standard abbreviations

Specific abbreviations for this pattern
MB (make Bobble): (P1, K1, P1, K1) all into next st, turn, K4, turn, [P2tog] twice, slip the first P2tog over the 2nd.

FINISHED SIZE
Hat Circumference = 53cm (21in) approx

PATTERN NOTES
The main body of the hat is knitted on the bias, with decs and incs worked at the beg and end of rows respectively and tucks worked on every 8th row.

MAIN BODY AND BRIM
Using 3.75mm needles, cast on 61 sts.
Row 1 (RS): K2tog, K to last st, Kfb.
Row 2: P.
Row 3: As row 1.
Row 4: P.
Row 5: P2tog, P4, [MB, P5] 4 times, MB, P3, K to last st, Kfb.
Row 6: P28, K33.
Row 7: P2tog, P31, K to last st, Kfb.
Row 8 (Tuck): P29, then pick up 32 sts along the 4th pattern row below next 32 sts on needle, and make a tuck by purling together 1 st from each needle across all 32 stitches.
These 8 rows form pattern. Rep them a further 19 times. Cast off. Join cast off edge to cast on edge.

CROWN
Using 3.75mm DPNs and with RS facing, pick up and K 60 sts around top of hat (tucked edge). Knit 3 rounds.
Rounds 4, 8 & 12: * K5, MB, rep from * to end.
Round 5: [K8, K2tog] 6 times (54 sts).
Rounds 6 & 10: K.
Round 7: [K7, K2tog] 6 times (48 sts).
Round 9: [K6, K2tog] 6 times (42 sts).
Round 11: [K5, K2tog] 6 times (36 sts).
Round 13: [K4, K2tog] 6 times (30 sts).
Round 14: [K3, K2tog] 6 times (24 sts).
Round 15: [K2, K2tog] 6 times (18 sts).
Round 16: [K1, K2tog] 6 times (12 sts).
Draw yarn through rem sts and fasten off.

MAKING UP
Press brim only, folding brim in half to WS, slip stitching brim into place along edge of tucks. Darn in all ends.

Materials: 4 ozs. Patons Double Quick Knitting Italian Pink 3179. A pair No. 9 "Queen Bee" needles. A set of four No. 9 "Queen Bee" needles pointed both ends; a spare No. 12 needle pointed both ends. ¾ yard 1-inch wide petersham ribbon.

Measurements: To fit an average head.

Tension: 11½ sts. and 15½ rows measure 2 ins. over stocking-stitch on No. 9 needles.

Main Part and Brim: With two No. 9 needles, cast on 61 sts. fairly loosely. 1ST ROW: right side facing, k. 2 tog., knit to last stitch, increase in last stitch. 2ND ROW: Purl. 3RD ROW: As 1st. 4TH ROW: Purl.

5TH ROW: p. 2 tog., p. 4, * make a bobble thus: (p. 1, k. 1, p. 1, k. 1) all into next stitch, turn, k. 4, turn, (p. 2 tog.) twice, slip the 1st p. 2 tog. over the 2nd p. 2 tog., p. 5; repeat from * 3 times more, make a bobble in next stitch as before, p. 3, knit to last stitch, increase in last stitch.

k 60 sts. (20 on each of 3 needles) round top of hat, *i.e.,* tucked edge. Knit 3 rounds.

4TH ROUND: * k. 5, make a bobble in next stitch as before; repeat from * to end. 5TH ROUND: (k. 8, k. 2 tog.) 6 times. 6TH ROUND: Knit. 7TH ROUND: (k. 7, k. 2 tog.) 6 times. 8TH ROUND: As 4th.

9TH ROUND: (k. 6, k. 2 tog.) 6 times. 10TH ROUND: Knit. 11TH ROUND: (k. 5, k. 2 tog.) 6 times. 12TH ROUND: As 4th. 13TH ROUND: (k. 4, k. 2 tog.) 6 times. 14TH ROUND: (k. 3, k. 2 tog.) 6 times.

15TH ROUND: (k. 2, k. 2 tog.) 6 times. 16TH ROUND: (k. 1, k. 2 tog.) 6 times. Draw thread through remaining stitches and fasten off.

To make up: Press brim only. Fold brim in half to wrong side and slip hem along to edge of tucks, then cut petersham ribbon to fit head and sew inside hat round hem-line. Slip hem other edge fairly loosely.

6TH ROW: p. 28, k. 33. 7TH ROW: p. 2 tog., p. 31, knit to last stitch, increase in last stitch. 8TH ROW: p. 29, now with the spare No. 12 needle, pick up 32 sts. below the next 32 sts., along the 4th pattern row, and make a tuck by purling together 1 stitch from each needle.

These 8 rows form pattern. Repeat them 19 times more. Cast off. Join cast-on edge to cast-off edge.

Crown: With right side facing and the set of four No. 9 needles, pick up and

Bobble topper stays put and keeps out the wind!

Lavenda Droplet Bolero

MATERIALS
Biggan Design 4 ply 100% merino first cross pure new wool (180m/196yds per 50g ball)
5 (6, 7, 7, 8, 9, 10, 11, 12) balls shade 435 (Light Olive)
1 pair 3.25mm (US #3) needles
1 pair 2.75mm (US #2) needles

TENSION
28½ sts & 34 rows = 10cm (4in) using 3.25mm needles over stocking stitch
1 droplet pattern repeat = 3 × 3 cm (1¼ × 1¼ in) using 3.25mm needles

ABBREVIATIONS
See page 13 for standard abbreviations

Specific abbreviations for this pattern
Make 5 from 1: (K1, P1, K1, P1, K1) into next stitch

SIZING
Measurements given in centimetres followed by inches in parentheses

To Fit	81 (32)	86 (34)	92 (36)	97 (38)	102 (40)	107 (42)	112 (44)	117 (46)	122 (48)
Finished Measurements									
Actual Bust Size	75 (29½)	82 (32)	89 (35)	96 (38)	103 (40½)	110 (43½)	117 (46)	124 (49)	131 (51½)
Length to underarm *	18 (7)	19 (7½)	20½ (8)	21½ (8½)	23 (9)	24 (9½)	25½ (10)	26½ (10½)	28 (11)
Armhole Depth	18¾ (7¼)	19½ (7½)	20 (7¾)	21½ (8½)	23 (9)	24½ (9½)	26½ (0½)	27½ (10¾)	28 (11)
Finished Length *	36¾ (4½)	38½ (15)	40½ (15¾)	43 (17)	46 (18)	48½ (19)	52 (20½)	54 (21¼)	56 (22)
Shoulder to Shoulder	30 (12)	32 (12½)	34 (13½)	36 (14¼)	38 (15)	40 (15¾)	41¾ (16¾)	44 (17½)	46½ (18¼)
Sleeve Length	47 (18½)	47 (18½)	48 (19)	48 (19)	48 (19)	48 (19)	49 (19½)	49 (19½)	49 (19½)

* Garment length does not include ribbed edgings
Garment shown in photographs is for third size 92 (36)

PATTERN NOTES
Both the jumper and bolero are worked in stocking stitch until the droplet yoke is commenced. Background stitches within the yoke sections and throughout the sleeves of the jumper, are worked in reverse stocking stitch. The long and short sleeves of the bolero and jumper are interchangeable, so the jumper could be made with long sleeves or the bolero with short for example. Please bear in mind that changing the sleeve lengths will alter the amount of yarn used.

BACK
Using 3.25mm needles, cast on 107 (117, 127, 137, 147, 157, 167, 177, 187) sts and commencing with a K row, work in stocking stitch until work measures 18 (19, 20½, 21½, 23, 24, 25½, 26½, 28) cm (7, 7½, 8, 8½, 9, 9½, 10, 10½, 11 in) from cast on, ending with a WS row.

Shape Armholes
Cast off 4 (5, 7, 10, 10, 5, 5, 5, 5) sts at beg of next 4 (4, 2, 2, 2, 4, 4, 4, 4) rows (91, 97, 113, 117, 127, 137, 147, 157, 167 sts).
Then dec 1 st at each end of the next 3 (3, 8, 7, 9, 11, 14, 16, 17) rows (85, 91, 97, 103, 109, 115, 119, 125, 133 sts).
Cont in stocking stitch without further shaping until armhole measures 18¾ (19½, 20, 21½, 23, 24½, 26½, 27½, 28) cm (7¼, 7½, 7¾, 8½, 9, 9½, 10½, 10¾, 11 in) ending with a WS row.

Shape Shoulders
Cast off 9 (10, 11, 11, 12, 12, 13, 14, 15) sts at beg of next 6 (6, 6, 4, 6, 4, 6, 6, 6) rows and 0 (0, 0, 12, 0, 14, 0, 0, 0) sts at beg of next 0 (0, 0, 2, 0, 2, 0, 0, 0) rows. Cast off rem 31 (31, 31, 35, 37, 39, 41, 41, 43) sts.

LEFT FRONT
Using 3.25mm needles, cast on 22 (26, 30, 34, 36, 38, 42, 44, 46) sts.
Starting with a knit row, work in stocking stitch and inc 1 st at front edge (end of RS rows and beg of WS rows) of next 26 (26, 26, 26, 28, 30, 30, 32, 34) rows and AT THE SAME TIME inc 1 st at the side edge (beg of RS rows) of 7th and 4 (5, 6, 7, 8, 9, 10, 11, 12) following 6th rows (53, 58, 63, 68, 73, 78, 83, 88, 93 sts).

Cont without further shaping until work measures 18 (19, 20½, 21½, 23, 24, 25½, 26½, 28) cm (7, 7½, 8, 8½, 9, 9½, 10, 10½, 11 in) from commencement ending with a WS row.

Chart A (Left front)

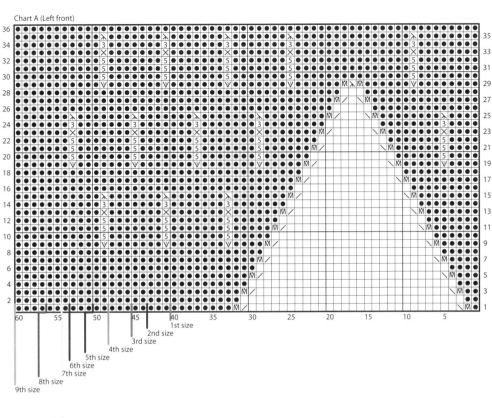

Chart B (Right front)

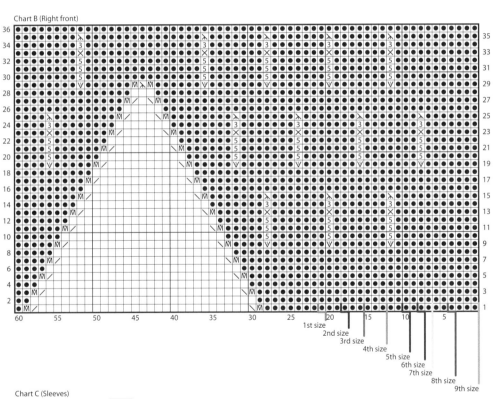

Chart C (Sleeves)

Key

☐ Knit on RS, Purl on WS
● Purl on RS, Knit on WS
◣ Sl1, K1, psso on RS
◢ K2tog on RS
人 Sl 1, K2tog, psso
▽ Make 5 from 1
5 K5 on RS, P5 on WS
3 K3 on RS, P3 on WS
✕ Sl1, K1, psso, K1, K2tog
Ⓜ M1P
☐ Pattern repeat

Shape Armhole and Front Edge

Cast off 4 (5, 7, 10, 10, 5, 5, 5, 5) sts at beg of next and 1 (1, 0, 0, 0, 1, 1, 1, 1) alt rows then dec 1 st at armhole edge of the next 3 (3, 8, 7, 9, 11, 14, 16, 17) rows and AT THE SAME TIME dec 1 st at neck edge of next and 1 (1, 2, 2, 2, 3, 4, 4, 5) foll 4th rows (40, 43, 45, 48, 51, 53, 54, 57, 60 sts). Work 0 (0, 1, 1, 0, 0, 1, 1, 1) rows straight, thus ending with a WS row.

Yoke

Omit droplets where there will not be sufficient stitches and/or rows to complete the droplet motif, and replace with reverse stocking stitch.

Work from chart as set below, and AT THE SAME TIME dec 1 st at neck edge on chart row 3 (3, 3, 3, 1, 3, 3, 1, 3) and on 12 (12, 11, 13, 14, 14, 14, 14, 14) foll 4th rows.
Row 1 (RS): Reading chart from right to left, starting at st 1 and ending as indicated (dec for 5th & 8th sizes), work from row 1 chart A.
Row 2 (WS): Reading chart from left to right, starting as indicated and ending at st 1, work from row 2 chart A. When all 36 rows of chart A are complete, continue to work in droplet stitch pattern as set.

Continue in droplet stitch pattern without further shaping, until front matches back to start of shoulder shaping, ending with a WS row after completion of droplet motif (27, 30, 33, 34, 36, 38, 39, 42, 45 sts).

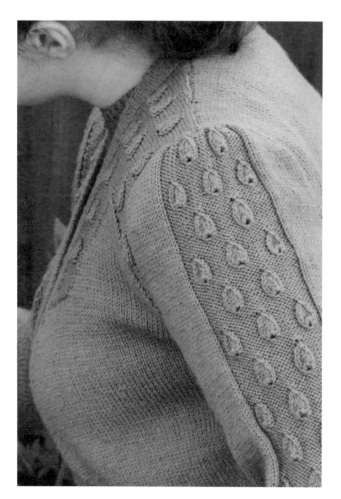

Shape Shoulder

Working in reverse stocking stitch, cast off 9 (10, 11, 11, 12, 12, 13, 14, 15) sts at beg of next and foll 2 (2, 2, 1, 2, 1, 2, 2, 2) alt rows, then cast off 0 (0, 0, 12, 0, 14, 0, 0, 0) sts at beg of next 0 (0, 0, 1, 0, 1, 0, 0, 0) alt row.

RIGHT FRONT

Using 3.25mm needles, cast on 22 (26, 30, 34, 36, 38, 42, 44, 46) sts.
Starting with a knit row, work in stocking stitch and inc 1 st at front edge (beg of RS rows and end of WS rows) of next 26 (26, 26, 26, 28, 30, 30, 32, 34) rows and AT THE SAME TIME inc 1 st at the side edge (end of RS rows) of 7th and 4 (5, 6, 7, 8, 9, 10, 11, 12) following 6th rows (53, 58, 63, 68, 73, 78, 83, 88, 93 sts).

Cont without further shaping until work measures 18 (19, 20½, 21½, 23, 24, 25½, 26½, 28) cm (7, 7½, 8, 8½, 9, 9½, 10, 10½, 11 in) from commencement ending with a WS row.

Shape Armhole and Front Edge

Dec 1 st at neck edge of next and 1 (1, 2, 2, 2, 3, 4, 4, 5) foll 4th rows and AT THE SAME TIME cast off 4 (5, 7, 10, 10, 5, 5, 5, 5) sts at beg of 2 (2, 1, 1, 1, 2, 2, 2, 2) foll alt rows then dec 1 st at armhole edge of the next 3 (3, 8, 7, 9, 11, 14, 16, 17) rows (40, 43, 45, 48, 51, 53, 54, 57, 60 sts). Work 1 (1, 0, 1, 1, 1, 0, 0, 1) rows straight, ending with a WS row.

Yoke

Omit droplets where there will not be sufficient stitches and/or rows to complete the droplet motif, and replace with reverse stocking stitch.

Work from chart as set below, and AT THE SAME TIME decrease 1 st at neck edge on chart row 1 (1, 3, 3, 1, 1, 3, 1, 3) and on 12 (12, 11, 13, 14, 14, 14, 14, 14) foll 4th rows.
Row 1 (RS): Reading chart from right to left, starting as indicated and ending on st 60, work from row 1 chart B.
Row 2 (WS): Reading chart from left to right, starting on st 60 and ending as indicated, work from row 2 chart B. When all 36 rows of chart A are complete, continue to work in droplet stitch pattern as set.

Continue in droplet stitch pattern without further shaping, until front matches back to start of shoulder shaping, ending with a RS row that completes a droplet motif (27, 30, 33, 34, 36, 38, 39, 42, 45 sts).

Shape Shoulder

Working in reverse stocking stitch, cast off 9 (10, 11, 11, 12, 12, 13, 14, 15) sts at beg of next and foll 2 (2, 2, 1, 2, 1, 2, 2, 2) alt rows, then cast off 0 (0, 0, 12, 0, 14, 0, 0, 0) sts at beg of next 0 (0, 0, 1, 0, 1, 0, 0, 0) alt row.

SLEEVES

Using 2.75mm needles, cast on 50 (58, 66, 74, 82, 90, 98, 106, 114) sts and work as folls:

Next row (RS): * K1, P1, rep from * to end.

Rep this row until rib measures 7½cm (3in), ending with a RS row.

Next row (WS): Work in rib as above to last st, Pfb (51, 59, 67, 75, 83, 91, 99, 107, 115 sts).

Change to 3.25mm needles and work as folls:

Next row (RS): K14 (18, 22, 26, 26, 30, 30, 34, 34), reading from right to left, work all sts from row 1 of chart C, repeating marked section 2 (2, 2, 2, 3, 3, 4, 4, 5) times, K14 (18, 22, 26, 26, 30, 30, 34, 34).

Next row: P14 (18, 22, 26, 26, 30, 30, 34, 34), reading from left to right, work all sts from row 2 of chart C, repeating marked section 2 (2, 2, 2, 3, 3, 4, 4, 5) times, P14 (18, 22, 26, 26, 30, 30, 34, 34).

These 2 rows set position of droplet pattern with a border of stocking stitch on each side. Continue as set, working from chart C across 23 (23, 23, 23, 23, 23, 31, 31, 39) sts of centre panel and at same time inc 1 st at each end of 7th and every foll 8th row until (79, 87, 95, 103, 111, 119, 127, 135, 143) sts (working all incs in stocking stitch).

Continue without further shaping, and maintaining centre panel of droplet pattern, until work measures 47 (47, 48, 48, 48, 48, 49, 49, 49) cm (18½, 18½, 19, 19, 19, 19, 19½, 19½, 19½ in) ending with a WS row.

Shape Sleeve Head

When the shaping reaches the droplet panel, omit droplet motifs if there will not be sufficient stitches and/or rows to complete the motif, replacing the droplet with rev st st.

Maintaining patt, cast off 5 (5, 5, 5, 5, 5, 5, 7, 7) sts at beg of next 2 (2, 2, 2, 4, 4, 4, 4, 4) rows (69, 77, 85, 93, 91, 99, 107, 107, 115 sts) then K2tog at beg of every row until 45 (53, 53, 53, 53, 53, 53, 53, 53) sts rem.

Cont in patt on these sts until work measures 10 (11, 11½, 13, 14½, 16, 18, 19, 19½) cm (4, 4¼, 4½, 5, 5¾, 6¼, 7, 7½, 7¾ in) from commencement of sleeve head shaping ending with a WS row. K2tog at each end of next 10 rows (25, 33, 33, 33, 33, 33, 33, 33, 33 sts).

Next row (RS): K1, * K2tog, rep from * to end (13, 17, 17, 17, 17, 17, 17, 17, 17 sts). Cast off rem sts.

RIBBED BAND

Using 3.25mm needles, cast on 12 sts and work as folls:

Next row (RS): * K1, P1, rep from * to end.

Rep this row until work measures 116 (125, 134½, 144½, 155, 164½, 175½, 185, 194½) cm (45½, 49, 53, 57, 61, 64¾, 69, 73, 76½ in). Leave sts on spare needle.

MAKING UP

Press all pieces lightly on WS through a damp cloth. Join shoulder seams, then side and sleeve seams. Set in sleeves, matching centre of sleeve head with shoulder seam and matching side seams. Commencing at centre back and cast on end of ribbed band, slip stitch band down left front, across lower edge, up right front, finishing at centre back. Adjust band to fit and cast off sts. Sew ends of band together using a flat slip stitch. Darn in all ends.

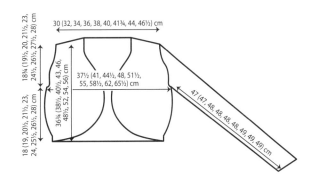

Lavenda Droplet Jumper

MATERIALS
Biggan Design 4 ply 100% merino first cross pure new wool (180m/196yds per 50g ball)
5 (6, 6, 7, 8, 8, 9, 10, 11) balls shade 435 (Light Olive)
1 pair 3.25mm (US #3) needles
1 pair 2.75mm (US #2) needles
2 buttons

TENSION
28½ sts & 34 rows = 10cm (4in) using 3.25mm needles over stocking stitch
1 droplet pattern repeat = 3 × 3 cm (1¼ × 1¼ in) using 3.25mm needles

ABBREVIATIONS
See page 13 for standard abbreviations

Specific abbreviations for this pattern
Make 5 from 1: (K1, P1, K1, P1, K1) into next stitch

SIZING
Measurements given in centimetres followed by inches in parentheses

To Fit	81 (32)	86 (34)	92 (36)	97 (38)	102 (40)	107 (42)	112 (44)	117 (46)	122 (48)
Finished Measurements									
Actual Bust Size	75 (29½)	82 (32)	89 (35)	96 (38)	103 (40½)	110 (43½)	117 (46)	124 (49)	131 (51½)
Length to underarm	30½ (12)	32 (12½)	33 (13)	34½ (13½)	35½ (14)	37 (14½)	38 (15)	39½ (15½)	40½ (16)
Armhole Depth	19½ (7½)	19½ (7½)	20 (7¾)	20 (7¾)	20½ (8)	21½ (8½)	22½ (8¾)	23 (9)	23 (9
Finished Length	50 (19½)	51½ (20½)	53 (21)	54½ (21½)	56 (22)	58½ (23)	60½ (23¾)	62½ (24½)	63½ (25)
Shoulder to Shoulder	30 (12)	32 (12½)	34 (13½)	36 (14¼)	38 (15)	40 (15¾)	41¾ (16¾)	44 (17½)	46½ (18½)
Sleeve Length	17 (6½)	17 (6½)	17 (6½)	17 (6½)	17 (6½)	17 (6½)	17 (6½)	22½ (8¾)	22½ (8¾)

Garment shown in photographs is for third size 92 (36)

PATTERN NOTES
Both the jumper and bolero are worked in stocking stitch until the droplet yoke is commenced. Background stitches within the yoke sections and throughout the sleeves of the jumper, are worked in reverse stocking stitch. The long and short sleeves of the bolero and jumper are interchangeable, so the jumper could be made with long sleeves or the bolero with short for example. Please bear in mind that changing the sleeve lengths will alter the amount of yarn used.

BACK
Using 2.75mm needles cast on 86 (94, 102, 110, 118, 126, 134, 142, 150) sts and work in rib as folls:
Next row (RS) * K1, P1, rep from * to end.
Rep this row until rib measures 10cm (4in) from cast on ending with a RS row.
Next row (WS): P2, * Pfb, P3, repeat from * to end (107, 117, 127, 137, 147, 157, 167, 177, 187 sts).
Change to 3.25mm needles and commencing with a K row, work in stocking stitch until work measures 30½ (32, 33, 34½, 35½, 37, 38, 39½, 40½) cm (12, 12½, 13, 13½, 14, 14½, 15, 15½, 16 in) ending with a WS row.

Shape Armholes
Cast off 5 (7, 7, 10, 10, 5, 5, 5, 5) sts at beg of next 2 (2, 2, 2, 2, 4, 4, 4, 4) rows, then K2tog at each end of the next 6 (6, 8, 7, 9, 11, 14, 16, 17) rows (85, 91, 97, 103, 109, 115, 119, 125, 133 sts).

Yoke
Row 1 (RS): Reading from right to left and starting and ending as indicated, work from row 1 chart A, and repeat the marked section 1 (1, 1, 3, 3, 3, 3, 3, 3) times.
Row 2 (WS): Reading from left to right and starting and ending as indicated, work from row 2 chart A and repeat the marked section 1 (1, 1, 3, 3, 3, 3, 3, 3) times.
Continue to work from chart A as set until row 36 is complete **

Divide for Back Opening
Next row (RS): P41 (44, 47, 50, 53, 56, 58, 61, 65), K3, turn. Place rem 41 (44, 47, 50, 53, 56, 58, 61, 65) sts on holder, and continue working on these 44 (47, 50, 53, 56, 59, 61, 64, 68) sts only.
Next row (WS): K.
Row 1 (RS): Reading from right to left, starting as indicated and ending at st 23 on left of chart, and repeating marked section 4 (4, 4, 5, 5, 6, 6, 6, 7) times, work from row 1 chart B, K3.

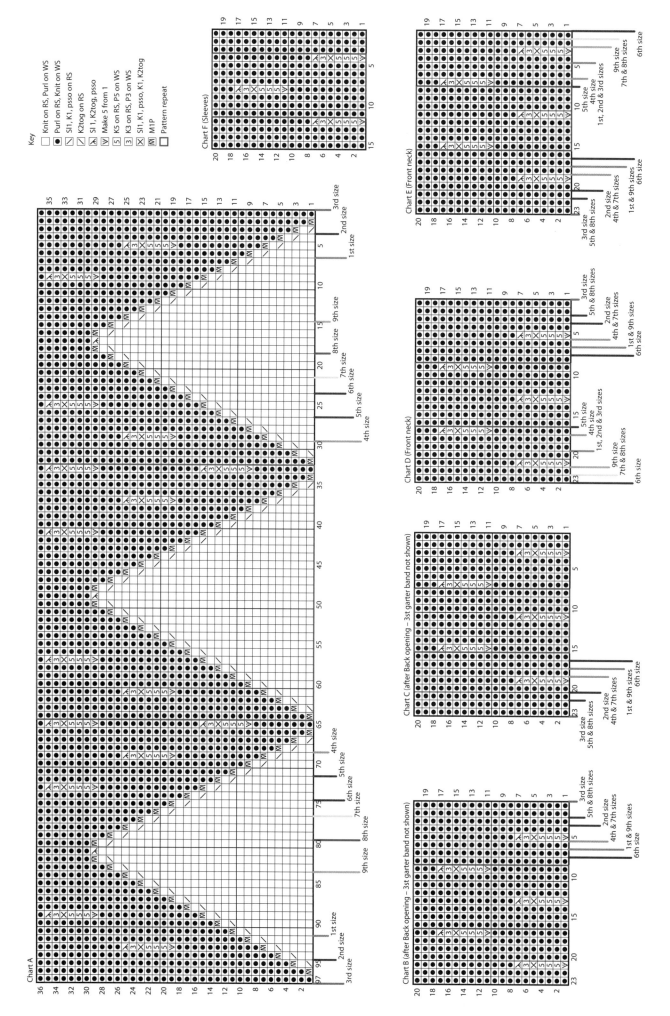

Key

□ Knit on RS, Purl on WS
● Purl on RS, Knit on WS
⟋ Sl1, K1, psso on RS
╱ K2tog on RS
⋏ Sl 1, K2tog, psso
∨ Make 5 from 1
5 K5 on RS, P5 on WS
3 K3 on RS, P3 on WS
⊠ Sl1, K1, psso, K1, K2tog
Μ M1P
□ Pattern repeat

Chart A

Chart B (after Back opening – 3st garter band not shown)

Chart C (after Back opening – 3st garter band not shown)

Chart D (Front neck)

Chart E (Front neck)

Chart F (Sleeves)

Row 2 (WS): K3, reading from left to right, starting at st 23 on left of chart, and ending as indicated, and repeating marked section 4 (4, 4, 5, 5, 6, 6, 6, 7) times, work from row 2 chart B.

Continue to work from chart B as set until row 20 is complete, maintaining 3 sts in garter st at back opening as set.

Shape Shoulder

Next row (RS): Cast off 9 (10, 11, 11, 12, 12, 13, 14, 15) sts, P to last 3 sts, K3 (35, 37, 39, 42, 44, 47, 48, 50, 53 sts).

Next row: K.

Next row: Cast off 9 (10, 11, 11, 12, 12, 13, 14, 15) sts, P to last 3 sts, YO, K2tog, K1 (26, 27, 28, 31, 32, 35, 35, 36, 38 sts).

Next row: K.

Next row: Cast off 9 (10, 11, 12, 12, 14, 13, 14, 15) sts, P to last 3 sts, K3 (17, 17, 17, 19, 20, 21, 22, 22, 23 sts).

Leave rem 17 (17, 17, 19, 20, 21, 22, 22, 23) sts on a holder.

Using 3.25mm needles and with RS facing, rejoin yarn to rem sts. Cast on 3 sts, K across these 3 sts, P to end (44, 47, 50, 53, 56, 59, 61, 64, 68 sts).

Next row (WS): K.

Row 1 (RS): K3, work from row 1 chart C, starting at st 1, ending as indicated, and repeating marked section 4 (4, 4, 5, 5, 6, 6, 6, 7) times.

Row 2 (WS): Work from row 2 chart C, starting as indicated and ending at st 1 on right of chart, and repeating marked section 4 (4, 4, 5, 5, 6, 6, 6, 7) times, K3. Continue to work from chart C as set until row 19 is complete, maintaining 3 sts in garter st at back opening as set.

Shape Shoulder

Next row (WS): Cast off 9 (10, 11, 11, 12, 12, 13, 14, 15) sts, K to end (35, 37, 39, 42, 44, 47, 48, 50, 53 sts).

Next row: P.

Next row: Cast off 9 (10, 11, 11, 12, 12, 13, 14, 15) sts, K to end (26, 27, 28, 31, 32, 35, 35, 36, 38 sts).

Next row: P.

Next row: Cast off 9 (10, 11, 12, 12, 14, 13, 14, 15) sts, K to end (17, 17, 17, 19, 20, 21, 22, 22, 23 sts).

Leave rem 17 (17, 17, 19, 20, 21, 22, 22, 23) sts on a holder.

FRONT

Work as for back until **

Next row (RS): P.

Next row: K.

Shape Neck

Omit droplet motifs where there will not be sufficient stitches and/or rows to complete the motif, replacing the droplet stitch with reverse stocking stitch.

Next row (RS): Reading from right to left and starting and ending as indicated, work in patt from row 1 chart D over next 37 (40, 43, 44, 46, 48, 49, 52, 55) sts repeating marked section 4 (4, 4, 5, 5, 5, 5, 5, 6) times, turn and work on these sts only, leaving rem sts on a holder.

Row 2 (WS): Work 2 sts together, then keeping pattern lined up with previous row, work in patt from row 2 of chart D to end (as indicated).

Cont to work in patt from chart D as set, dec 1 st at neck edge of foll 9 rows (27, 30, 33, 34, 36, 38, 39, 42, 45 sts). Maintaining patt from chart D, work without further shaping until front measures same as back to commencement of shoulder shaping, ending with a chart row 18 or 20 (WS row).

Shape Shoulder

Working in reverse stocking stitch, cast off 9 (10, 11, 11, 12, 12, 13, 14, 15) sts at beg of next and foll 2 (2, 2, 1, 2, 1, 2, 2, 2) alt rows and cast off 0 (0, 0, 12, 0, 14, 0, 0, 0) sts at beg of next alt row.

Using 3.25mm needles and with RS facing, place centre 11 (11, 11, 15, 17, 19, 21, 21, 23) sts on holder, and rejoin yarn to rem sts.

Next row (RS): Reading from right to left and starting and ending as indicated, work from row 1 chart E, repeating marked section 4 (4, 4, 5, 5, 5, 5, 5, 6) times.

Next row (WS): Keeping pattern lined up as before and remembering to omit droplet motifs where necessary, work from row 2 of chart E, dec 1 st at neck edge.

Cont to work in patt from chart E as set, decreasing 1 st at neck edge of foll 9 rows (27, 30, 33, 34, 36, 38, 39, 42, 45 sts).

Continue in patt from chart E, without further shaping until front measures same as back to commencement of shoulder shaping, ending with a chart row 17 or 19 (RS row).

Shape Shoulder

Working in reverse stocking stitch, cast off 9 (10, 11, 11, 12, 12, 13, 14, 15) sts at beg of next and foll 2 (2, 2, 1, 2, 1, 2, 2, 2) alt rows and cast off 0 (0, 0, 12, 0, 14, 0, 0, 0) sts at beg of next alt row.

SLEEVES

Using 2.75mm needles, cast on 64 (70, 76, 84, 90, 96, 102, 108, 116) sts and work as folls:

Next row (RS): * K1, P1, rep from * to end.

Rep this row until rib measures 5cm (2in) ending with a RS row.

Next row (Inc): K4 (2, 0, 8, 6, 4, 2, 0, 8) * K3, Kfb, repeat from * to end (79, 87, 95, 103, 111, 119, 127, 135, 143 sts).

Change to 3.25mm needles and commencing with row 1 work from chart F as folls:

Row 1 (RS): Reading from right to left, work all sts from row 1 chart F, repeating marked section 9 (10, 11, 12, 13, 14, 15, 16, 17) times.

Row 2 (WS): Reading from left to right, work all sts from row 2 chart F, repeating marked section 9 (10, 11, 12, 13, 14, 15, 16, 17) times.

These 2 rows set position of droplet pattern. Continue working from chart F until 2 (2, 2, 2, 2, 2, 2, 3, 3) reps have been worked in total.

Shape Sleeve Head
Omit droplet motifs where there won't be sufficient stitches and/or rows to complete the motif (and replace the droplet st with rev st st.

Whilst continuing to maintain patt, cast off 5 (5, 5, 5, 5, 5, 5, 7, 7) sts at beg of next 2 (2, 2, 2, 4, 4, 4, 4, 4) rows (69, 77, 85, 93, 91, 99, 107, 107, 115 sts) then K2tog at beg of every row until 45 (53, 53, 53, 53, 53, 53, 53, 53) sts rem. Cont in patt on these sts until work measures 10 (11, 11½, 13, 14½, 16, 18, 19, 19½) cm (4, 4¼, 4½, 5, 5¾, 6¼, 7, 7½, 7¾ in) from commencement of sleeve head shaping ending with a WS row. K2tog at each end of next 10 rows (25, 33, 33, 33, 33, 33, 33, 33, 33 sts).
Next row (RS): K1, * K2tog, rep from * to end (13, 17, 17, 17, 17, 17, 17, 17, 17 sts). Cast off rem sts.

NECKBAND
Join both shoulder seams. With RS facing, and using 2.75mm needles, commence at LH side of back opening as folls:
Next row: K across 17 (17, 17, 19, 20, 21, 22, 22, 23) sts from holder, pick up and K 27 sts around left side neck to front neck sts, K across 11 (11, 11, 15, 17, 19, 21, 21, 23)

sts from front holder, pick up and K 26 sts around right side neck, then K across 17 (17, 17, 19, 20, 21, 22, 22, 23) sts on holder for right back neck (98, 98, 98, 106, 110, 114, 118, 118, 122 sts).
Next row (WS): * K1, P1, rep from * to end.
Rep this row a further 5 times.
Next row: Patt to last 3 sts, YO, K2tog, P1.
Work 2 rows more in rib. Cast off loosely in rib.

MAKING UP
Press all pieces lightly through a damp cloth. Join side and sleeve seams. Set in sleeves matching centre of sleeve head to shoulder seam and matching side seams. Slip stitch cast on sts at back neck into position behind buttonhole band and sew buttons in position. Darn in all ends.

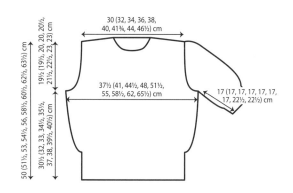

Jumper and Bolero

in Lister's Lavenda 3 Ply or Lavenda Crepe

Materials

						Lister's
Jumper	..	..	..	..	7 ozs.	Lavenda
Bolero	..	..	..	..	8 ozs.	3 ply
Set	..	..	..	..	15 ozs.	
						or
Jumper	..	..	..	..	9 ozs.	Lavenda
Bolero	..	..	..	..	10 ozs.	Crepe
Set	..	..	..	..	19 ozs.	

Pair each needles Nos. 10 and 12.
4 buttons for Jumper.
3 safety pins.

Measurements

To fit 34 ins. Bust measurement.

Jumper:

Length from shoulder	..	..	20 ins.
Length of undersleeve seam	..	..	6 ins.

Bolero:

Length from shoulder	..	..	15 ins.
Length of undersleeve seam	..	..	17½ ins.

N.B.—Always count ' K5IN ' as one st. when increasing and decreasing.

Tension

7½ sts. and 10 rows equal one inch (No. 10 needles).

N.B. The tension of the knitting controls the size of the finished garment. Before commencing, cast on 15 sts. and work in one row knit, one row purl for 20 rows. If you sample has less sts. per inch than our tension, try again with smaller needles and vice-versa, then work the garment on the needles which produce our tension.

JUMPER

BACK

Using No. 12 needles cast on 102 sts. and work in k1, p1 rib for 4 ins.

Increase row.—P2, * P2IN, p3, repeat from * to end (127 sts.).

Change to No. 10 needles and st.st. (1st row—knit) until work measures 13 ins., ending with a purl row.

SHAPE ARMHOLES

Cast off 7 sts. at beginning of next 2 rows, then k2tog. at each end of next 8 rows (97 sts.).

NOW WORK YOKE

1st row.—(P1, PL, SKPO, k27, k2tog., PL) three times, p1.
2nd row.—(K2, p29, k1) three times, k1.
3rd row.—(P2, PL, SKPO, k25, k2tog., PL, p1) three times, p1.
4th row.—(K3, p27, k2) three times, k1.
5th row.—(P3, PL, SKPO, k23, k2tog., PL, p2) three times, p1.
6th row.—(K4, p25, k3) three times, k1.
7th row.—(P4, PL, SKPO, k21, k2tog., PL, p3) three times, p1.
8th row.—(K5, p23, k4) three times, k1.
9th row.—P5, PL, SKPO, k19, k2tog., (PL, p4, K5IN, p4, PL, SKPO, k19, k2tog.) twice, PL, p5.
10th row.—K6, p21, (k5, p5, k5, p21) twice, k6.
11th row.—P6, PL, SKPO, k17, k2tog., (PL, p5, k5, p5, PL, SKPO, k17, k2tog.) twice, PL, p6.
12th row.—K7, p19, (k6, p5, k6, p19) twice, k7.
13th row.—P7, PL, SKPO, k15, k2tog., (PL, p6, SKPO, k1, k2tog., p6, PL, SKPO, k15, k2tog.) twice, PL, p7.
14th row.—K8, p17 (k7, p3, k7, p17) twice, k8.
15th row.—P8, PL, SKPO, k13, k2tog., (PL, p7, S.K2tog.PO, p7, PL, SKPO, k13, k2tog.) twice, PL, p8.
16th row.—K9, (p15, k17) twice, p15, k9.
17th row.—P9, PL, SKPO, k11, k2tog. (PL, p17, PL, SKPO, k11, k2tog.) twice, PL, p9.
18th row.—K10, (p13, k19) twice, p13, k10.
19th row.—(P4, K5IN, p5, PL, SKPO, k9, k2tog. PL, p5, K5IN, p3), three times p1.
20th row.—(K4, p5, k6, p11, k6, p5, k3), three times k1.
21st row.—(P4, k5, p6, PL, SKPO, k7, k2tog., PL, p6, k5, p3), three times p1.
22nd row.—(K4, p5, k7, p9, k7, p5, k3), three times k1.
23rd row.—(P4, SKPO, k1, k2tog., p7, PL, SKPO, k5, k2tog., PL, p7, SKPO, k1, k2tog., p3), three times p1.
24th row.—(K4, p3, k8, p7, k8, p3, k3), three times k1.
25th row.—(P4, S.K2tog.PO, p8, PL, SKPO, k3, k2tog., PL, p8, S.K2tog.PO, p3), three times p1.
26th row.—K14, (p5, k27) twice, p5, k14.

27th row.—(P14, PL, SKPO, k1, k2tog., PL, p13), three times p1.
28th row.—K15, (p3, k29) twice, p3, k15.
29th row.—P8, K5IN, p6, PL, S.K2tog.PO, (PL, p6, PL, p6, K5IN, p7, K5IN, p6, PL, S.K2tog.PO) twice, PL, p6, K5IN, p8.
30th row.—K8, p5, (k15, p5, k7, p5, k7, p5) twice, k15, p5, k8.
31st row.—P8, k5, (p15, k5, p7, k5, p7, k5) twice, p15, k5, p8.
32nd row.—As 30th row.
33rd row.—P8, SKPO, k1, k2tog. (p15, [SKPO, k1, k2tog., p7] twice, SKPO, k1, k2tog.), twice, p15, SKPO, k1, k2tog., p8.
34th row.—K8, p3,(k15, p3, k7, p3, k7, p3)twice, k15, p3, k8.
35th row.—P8, S.K2tog.PO, (p15, [S.K2tog.PO, p7] twice, S.K2tog.PO), twice, p15, S.K2tog.PO, p8.
36th row.—Knit. **

DIVIDE FOR BACK OPENING

37th row.—P47, k3, turn.   **38th row.**—Knit.
39th row.—P4, (K5IN, p7) five times, K5IN, p2, k3.
40th row.—K5, (p5, k7) five times, p5, k4.
41st row.—P4, (k5, p7) five times, k5, p2, k3.
42nd row.—As 40th row.
43rd row.—P4, (SKPO, k1, k2tog., p7) five times, SKPO, k1, k2tog., p2, k3.
44th row.—K5, (p3, k7) five times, p3, k4.
45th row.—P4, (S.K2tog.PO, p7) five times, S.K2tog.PO, p2, m1, k2tog., k1.   **46th row.**—Knit.
47th row.—P47, k3.   **48th row.**—As 46th row.
49th row.—P8, (K5IN, p7) four times, K5IN, p6, k3.
50th row.—K9 (p5, k7) four times, p5, k8.
51st row.—P8, (k5, p7) four times, k5, p6, k3.
52nd row.—As 50th row.
53rd row.—P8, (SKPO, k1, k2tog., p7) four times, SKPO, k1, k2tog., p6, m1, k2tog., k1.
54th row.—K9, (p3, k7) four times, p3, k8.
55th row.—P8, (S.K2tog.PO, p7) four times, S.K2tog.PO, p6, k3.   **56th row.**—Knit.
57th row.—P47, k3.   **58th row.**—As 56th row.

SHAPE SHOULDERS

Next row.—Cast off 11 sts., p35, k3.
Next-row.—Knit.
Next row.—Cast off 11 sts., p24, m1, k2tog., k1.
Next row.—Knit.
Next row.—Cast off 11 sts, p13, k3.
Leave these 17 sts. on a safety pin.
Return to remaining sts., rejoin wool, cast on 3 sts., and purl to end of row.
38th row.—Knit.
39th row.—K3, p2, (K5IN, p7) five times, K5IN, p4.
40th row.—K4, (p5, k7) five times, k5, k5.
Now work to match first side omitting buttonholes.

Hand Knitwear in Lavenda

Abbreviations

k = Knit. p = Purl. sts. = Stitches.
ins. = Inches. tog. = Together.
SKPO = Slip one, knit one, pass slipped st. over, i.e. into front and then into back of st.
K2IN = Knit twice into st., i.e. into front and then into back of st.
PL = Pick up and purl the loop before the next st., thus making a st.
St.st. = Stocking st., which is the smooth side of one row knit, one row purl.
S.K2tog.PO = Slip one, k2tog., pass slipped st. over.
K5IN = K1, p1, k1, p1, k1, into next st., counting the "bud" as one st.
P2IN = Purl twice into st., i.e. into front and then into back of st.
M = Make a st., by bringing wool to front of work before a knit st., and by wrapping wool round needle before a purl st.

Cast On—Thumb Method

2 yards from the end, twist the wool round the left thumb to make a loop and knit this loop on to the needle from the ball of wool. Repeat till required number of sts. are on the needle, making the loop from the 2 yards and knitting from the ball. This method of casting on should always be used.

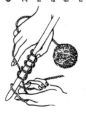

FRONT

Work as Back as far as **.
Next row.—Pattern 43 turn.
37th row.—Purl. 38th row.—Knit.

SHAPE NECK

Next row.—...
Continue in pattern on these sts. decreasing one st. at neck edge on next 10 rows. Continue in pattern on these sts. for 9 more rows.

SHAPE SHOULDER

Cast off 11 sts. at beginning of next and each alternate row three times.
Return to remaining sts., slip first 11 sts. on to a safety pin, rejoin wool at neck edge and work to match first side to end.

SLEEVES

Using No. 12 needles cast on 76 sts. and work in k1, p1 rib for 2 ins.
Increase row.—* K3, K2IN (K5IN, p7) eleven times, K5IN, p3.
Change to No. 10 needles and work as follows:
1st row.—P3, (K5IN, p7) eleven times, K5IN, p3.
2nd row.—K3, (p5, k7) eleven times, p5, k3.
3rd row.—P3, (K5, p7) eleven times, K5, p3.
4th row.—As 2nd row.
5th row.—P3, (SKPO, k1, k2tog., p7) eleven times, SKPO, k1, k2tog., p3.
6th row.—(p7, SKPO, k1, k2tog.) eleven times, p7.
7th row.—P3, (S.K2tog.PO, p7) eleven times, S.K2tog.PO, p3.
8th row.—Knit. 9th row.—Purl.
10th row.—(P7, K5IN) eleven times, p7.
11th row.—(P7, p5, k7) eleven times, k7.
12th row.—(K7, p5) eleven times, k7.
13th row.—As 12th row.
14th row.—As 2nd row.
15th row.—(P7, SKPO, k1, k2tog.) eleven times, p7.
16th row.—(K7, p3) eleven times, k7.
17th row.—(P7, S.K2tog.PO) eleven times, p7.
18th row.—Knit. 19th row.—Purl.
20th row.—Knit.
Repeat these 20 rows once more.

SHAPE HEAD Keeping in pattern:

Cast off 5 sts. at beginning of next 2 rows, then k2tog. at beginning of every row until 53 sts. remain. Continue in pattern on these sts. until work measures 4½ ins. from commencement of Head Shaping.
Now k2tog. at each end of next 10 rows.
Next row.—K1, * K2tog., pass first st. over second. Repeat from * to end.

NECKBAND

Join both shoulder seam. With right side of work facing and commencing at left-hand side of back opening, rejoin wool and using No. 12 needles (k1, p1) eight times, k1, across 17 sts. on safety pin; pick up and knit 27 sts. to sts. on safety pin; (k1, p1) five times, k1, across these 11 sts.; pick up and knit 26 sts. to right shoulder; and finally (p1, k1) eight times, p1, across 17 sts. on safety pin (98 sts.).
Work 5 rows in k1, p1 rib.
6th row.—Rib to within 3 sts., m1, k2tog., p1.
Work 2 rows more in rib.
Cast off loosely in rib.

BOLERO

BACK.

Using No. 10 needles cast on 127 sts. and work in k1, p1 (1st row—knit) until work measures 8 ins from commencement.

SHAPE ARMHOLES

Cast off 7 sts. at beginning of next 2 rows, then k2tog. at each end of next 8 rows (97 sts.).
Continue on these sts. until work measures 7 ins. from commencement of armhole shaping.

SHAPE SHOULDERS

Cast off 11 sts. at beginning of next 6 rows. Cast off remaining sts.

LEFT FRONT

Using No. 10 needles cast on 30 sts.
1st row.—Knit to within one st., K2IN (Front Edge).
2nd row.—P2IN, purl to end.
Repeat last 2 rows twice more.
7th row.—K2IN, knit to within one st., K2IN.
8th row.—As 2nd row. 10th row.—As 2nd row.
9th row.—As 1st row.
*** Continue in st.st. increasing one st. at Front Edge on next 16 rows, at the same time increasing one st. at side edge on every 6th row from previous increase. Continue increasing at side edge as before until there are 63 sts. on needle.
Continue on these sts. until work measures 8 ins. from commencement.***

SHAPE ARMHOLES AND FRONT EDGE

Right side facing.
Next row.—Cast off 7 sts., knit to within 2 sts., k2tog.
Next row.—Purl.
Next row.—K2tog., knit to end.
Next row.—Purl to within 2 sts., p2tog.
Next row.—K2tog., knit to within 2 sts., k2tog.
Next row.—Purl to within 2 sts., p2tog.
Next row.—K2tog., knit to end.
Next row.—Purl to within 2 sts., p2tog.
Next row.—K2tog., knit to within 2 sts., k2tog.
Next-row.—Purl to within 2 sts., p2tog. (45 sts.).

NOW WORK YOKE

1st row.—P1, PL, SKPO, k27, k2tog., PL, p13.
2nd row.—K14, p29, k2.
3rd row.—P2, PL, SKPO, k25, k2tog., PL, p12, p2tog.
4th row.—K14, p27, k3.
5th row.—P3, PL, SKPO, k23, k2tog., PL, p14.
6th row.—K15, p25, k4.
7th row.—P4, PL, SKPO, k21, k2tog., PL, p13, p2tog.
8th row.—K15, p23, k5.
9th row.—P5, PL, SKPO, k19, k2tog., PL, p4, K5IN, p10.
10th row.—K10, p5, k5, p21, k6.
11th row.—P6, PL, SKPO, k17, k2tog., PL, p5, k5, p8, p2tog.
12th row.—K7, p5, k6, p19, k7.
13th row.—P7, PL, SKPO, k15, k2tog., PL, p6, SKPO, k1, k2tog., p9.
14th row.—K9, p3, k7, p17, k8.
15th row.—P8, PL, SKPO, k13, k2tog., PL, p7, S.K2tog.PO, p7, p2tog. 16th row.—K17, p15, k9.
17th row.—P9, PL, SKPO, k11, k2tog., PL, p1.
18th row.—K18, p13, k10.
19th row.—P4, K5IN, p5, PL, SKPO, k9, k2tog., PL, p5, K5IN, p10, p2tog.
20th row.—K11, p5, k6, p11, k6, p5, k4.
21st row.—P4, k5, p6, PL, SKPO, k7, k2tog., PL, p6, k5, p11.
22nd row.—K11, p5, k7, p9, k7, p5, k4.
23rd row.—P4, SKPO, k1, k2tog., p7, PL, SKPO, k5, k2tog., PL, p7, SKPO, k1, k2tog., p9, p2tog.
24th row.—K10, p3, k8, p7, k8, p3, k4.
25th row.—P4, S.K2tog.PO, p8, PL, SKPO, k3, k2tog., PL, p8, S.K2tog.PO, p10. 26th row.—K20, p5, k14.
27th row.—P14, PL, SKPO, k1, k2tog., PL, p18, p2tog.
28th row.—K20, p3, k15.
29th row.—P8, K5IN, p6, PL, S.K2tog.PO, PL, p6, K5IN, p7, K5IN, p5.
30th row.—K5, p5, k15, p5, k8.
31st row.—P8, k5, p15, k5, p5, p2tog.
32nd row.—K4, p5, k7, p15, k7, p5, k8.
33rd row.—P8, SKPO, k1, k2tog., p15, SKPO, k1, k2tog., p7, SKPO, k1, k2tog., p4.
34th row.—K4, p3, k7, p3, k15, p3, k8.
35th row.—P8, S.K2tog.PO, p15, S.K2tog.PO, p2, p2tog.
36th row.—Knit. 37th row.—Purl.
38th row.—Knit.
39th row.—P4, (K5IN, p7) three times, K5IN, p5, p2tog.
40th row.—K6, (p5, k7) three times, p5, k4.
41st row.—P4, (k5, p7) three times, k5, p6.
42nd row.—As 40th row.
43rd row.—P4, (SKPO, k1, k2tog. p7), three times, SKPO, k1, k2tog., p4, p2tog.
44th row.—K5, (p3, k7) three times, p3, k4.
45th row.—P4, (S.K2tog.PO, p7) three times, S.K2tog.PO, p5.
46th row.—Knit.
47th row.—Purl to within 2 sts., p2tog. (33 sts.).
48th row.—Knit.
49th row.—P8, (K5IN, p7) three times, p1.
50th row.—K8, (p5, k7) three times, p1.
51st row.—P8, (k5, p7) three times, p1.
52nd row.—As 50th row.
53rd row.—P8, (SKPO, k1, k2tog., p7) three times, p1.
54th row.—K8, (p3, k7) three times, k1.
55th row.—P8, (S.K2tog.PO, p7) three times, p1.
56th row.—Knit. 57th row.—Purl.
58th row.—Knit.

SHAPE SHOULDER

Cast off 11 sts. at beginning of next and each alternate row three times.

RIGHT FRONT

Using No. 10 needles cast on 30 sts.
1st row.—K2IN, knit to end.
2nd row.—Purl to within one st., P2IN.
Repeat last 2 rows twice more.
7th row.—K2IN, knit to within one st., K2IN.
8th row.—As 2nd row. 9th row.—As 2nd row.
10th row.—As 2nd row.
Work as Left Front from *** to ***.

SHAPE ARMHOLE AND FRONT EDGE

Right side facing.
Next row.—K2tog., knit to end.
Next row.—Cast off 7 sts., purl to end.
Next row.—Knit to within 2 sts., k2tog.
Next row.—P2tog., purl to end.
Next row.—K2tog., knit to within 2 sts., k2tog.
Next row.—P2tog., purl to end.
Repeat last 4 rows once more.

NOW WORK YOKE

1st row.—P13, PL, SKPO, k27, k2tog., PL, p5.
2nd row.—K2, p29, k14.
3rd row.—P12, PL, SKPO, k25, k2tog., PL, p2.
4th row.—K3, p27, k14.
5th row.—P14, PL, SKPO, k23, k2tog., PL, p3.
6th row.—K4, p25, k15.
7th row.—P2tog., p13, PL, SKPO, k21, k2tog., PL, p4.
8th row.—K5, p23, k15.
9th row.—P10, K5IN, p4, PL, SKPO, k19, k2tog., PL, p5.
10th row.—K6, p21, k5, p5, k10.
Continue to match other side, decreasing as before at Front Edge.

LONG SLEEVES

Using No. 12 needles cast on 66 sts. and work in k1, p1 rib for 3 ins, increasing one st. at end of last row.
Change to No. 10 needles and work as follows:
1st row.—K22, p3, (K5IN, p7) twice, K5IN, p3, k22.
2nd row.—P22, k3, (p5, k7) twice, p5, k3, p22.
3rd row.—K22, p3, (k5, p7) twice, k5, p3, k22.
4th row.—As 2nd row.
5th row.—K22, p3, (SKPO, k1, k2tog., p7) twice, SKPO, k1, k2tog., p3, k22.
6th row.—P22, k3, (p3, k7) twice, p3, k2, p22.
7th row.—K22, p3, k21, (S.K2tog.PO, p7) twice, S.K2tog.PO, p3, k21, K2IN.
8th row.—P23, k21, K21N.
9th row.—K23, p23, k23.
9th row.—As 8th row.
10th row.—K23, (p7, K5IN) twice, p7, k23.
11th row.—K23, (p7, p5) twice, k7, p23.
12th row.—K23, (k7, p5) twice, k7, k23.
13th row.—K23, (k7, k5) twice, k7, k23.
14th row.—As 12th row.
15th row.—K22, K22, (p7, SKPO, k1, k2tog.) twice, p7, k22, K2IN.
16th row.—P24, (k7, p3) twice, k7, p24.
Keeping centre panel of 23 sts. correct, continue in pattern increasing one st. at each end of every 8th row from previous increase, until there are 95 sts. on needle.
Continue on these sts. until work measure 17½ ins.

SHAPE HEAD

As Short Sleeves.

RIBBED BAND

Using No. 12 needles cast on 12 sts. and work in k1, p1 rib until work measures 53 ins. Cast off.

TO MAKE UP

Pin out and press each piece on wrong side under a damp cloth, avoiding ribbed welts.
Jumper.—Join side and sleeve seams. Sew in sleeves, placing centre of head of sleeve to shoulder seam. Sew 3 sts. in position at Back Opening. Sew on buttons to correspond with buttonholes. Press all seams.
Bolero.—Join side, shoulder and sleeve seams. Sew in sleeves, placing centre of head of sleeve to shoulder seam. Commencing at centre back of neck, sew band down Left Front, across lower edge of Back, up Right Front to centre back of neck. Press all seams.

Ribbon Threaded Jumper

MATERIALS
Knitshop Pima Cotton 60% cotton/40% wool (225m per 100g ball)
4 (4, 5, 6, 6, 6, 7, 8, 9) balls shade Apricot
1 pair 2.75mm (US #2) needles
1 pair 3.25mm (US #3) needles
1 2.75mm (US #2) circular needle
3m of 7½mm (¼in) wide ribbon

TENSION
25 sts & 36 rows = 10cm (4in) using 3.25mm needles over stitch pattern

ABBREVIATIONS
See page 13 for standard abbreviations

SIZING
Measurements given in centimetres followed by inches in parentheses

To Fit	76 (30)	81–86 (32–34)	92 (36)	97 (38)	102–107 (40–42)	102 (44)	117 (46)	122 (48)	127 (50)
Finished Measurements									
Actual Bust Size	85 (33½)	91 (36)	97½ (38½)	104 (41)	110½ (43½)	117 (46)	123 (48½)	129½ (51)	136 (53½)
Length to underarm	28½ (11¼)	32 (12½)	35½ (14)	35½ (14)	35½ (14)	38½ (15)	38½ (15)	42 (16½)	42 (16½)
Armhole Depth	16½ (6½)	16½ (6½)	20 (8)	20 (8)	20 (8)	20 (8)	23½ (9¼)	23½ (9¼)	26½ (10½)
Finished Length	45 (17¾)	48½ (19)	55½ (22)	55½ (22)	55½ (22)	58½ (23)	62 (24¼)	65½ (25¾)	68½ (27)
Yoke Circumference	49½ (19½)	53½ (21)	58 (23)	62½ (24½)	66½ (26)	71 (28)	75 (29½)	79 (31)	83½ (32½)
Sleeve Length	9 (3½)	9 (3½)	12½ (5)	12½ (5)	12½ (5)	12½ (5)	16 (6½)	16 (6½)	19 (7½)

Garment shown in photographs is for fifth size 102–107 (40–42)

BACK
Using 2.75mm needles, cast on 94 (102, 110, 118, 126, 134, 142, 150, 158) sts and work in rib as folls:
Next row (RS): * K1, P1, rep from * to end.
Rep this row until 40 rows have been worked **
Next row (RS): Rib 2 (1, 0, 4, 1, 2, 1, 0, 2), [rib 17 (19, 21, 22, 24, 25, 27, 29, 30), Kfb] 4 times, rib 20 (21, 22, 25, 28, 29, 30, 32) (98, 106, 114, 122, 130, 138, 146, 154, 162 sts).
Change to 3.25mm needles and purl 1 row, then work in lace patt (also shown on chart) as folls:
Row 1 (RS): K1, * K1, YO, Sl1, K1, psso, K3, K2tog, YO, rep from * to last st, K1.
Row 2 and all foll alt rows: P.
Row 3: K1, * K1, YO, K1, Sl1, K1, psso, K1, K2tog, K1, YO, rep from * to last st, K1.
Row 5: K1, * K1, YO, K2, Sl1, K2tog, psso, K2, YO, rep from * to last st, K1.
Row 7: K1, * K2, K2tog, YO, K1, YO, Sl1, K1, psso, K1, rep from * to last st, K1.
Row 9: K1, * K1, K2tog, [K1, YO] twice, K1, Sl1, K1, psso, rep from * to last st, K1.
Row 11: K1, K2tog, * K2, YO, K1, YO, K2, Sl1, K2tog, psso, rep from * to last 7 sts, K2, YO, K1, YO, K2, Sl1, K1, psso.

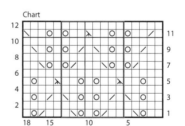

Row 12: P.
These 12 rows form patt. Work 5 (6, 7, 7, 7, 8, 8, 9, 9) complete patts, decreasing 1 st each end of the last purl row (96, 104, 112, 120, 128, 136, 144, 152, 160 sts). Leave sts on a spare needle.

FRONT
Using 2.75mm needles cast on 94 (102, 110, 118, 126, 134, 142, 150, 158) sts and work as given for back to **
Next row (RS): K5 (9, 3, 6, 0, 4, 8, 1, 5), * K3 (3, 3, 4, 4, 5, 5, 5, 6, 6), Kfb, rep from * to last 9 (13, 7, 12, 6, 10, 14, 9, 13) sts, knit to end (114, 122, 130, 138, 146, 154, 162, 170, 178 sts).
Change to 3.25mm needles and purl one row, then work in patt as given for back until row 10 of 5th (6th, 7th, 7th, 7th, 8th, 8th, 9th, 9th) patt row has been worked.

Next row: K1, [K1 (1, 0, 0, 0, 0), Kfb] 2 (8, 2, 6, 9, 13) times, [K2 (2, 1, 1, 1, 1), Kfb] 23 (16, 43, 40, 39, 36) times, [K1 (1, 0, 0, 0, 0), Kfb] 2 (8, 2, 6, 9, 13) times, K1 (1, 0, 1, 0, 1) (106, 114, 138, 146, 154, 162 sts).

All sizes
Change to 3.25mm needles.
Proceed in patt as given for back until row 11 of 2nd (2nd, 3rd, 3rd, 3rd, 3rd, 4th, 4th, 5th) patt row has been worked.
Next row (WS): Cast off 9 sts, P to end.
Leave (89, 97, 105, 113, 121, 129, 137, 145, 153) sts on spare needle.

RIGHT SLEEVE
Work exactly as for left sleeve until row 10 of 2nd (2nd, 3rd, 3rd, 3rd, 3rd, 4th, 4th, 5th) patt row has been worked.
Next row (RS): Cast off 9 sts, patt to end.
Next row: P.
Leave (89, 97, 105, 113, 121, 129, 137, 145, 153) sts on a spare needle.

YOKE
Using 2.75mm circular needle, place sts onto needle as follows: Return 96 (104, 112, 120, 128, 136, 144, 152, 160) sts from back to circular needle, then place 89 (97, 105, 113, 121, 129, 137, 145, 153) sts from one sleeve onto needle with unshaped edge next to back sts. Next place 96 (104, 112, 120, 128, 136, 144, 152, 160) front sts onto needle and finally 89 (97, 105, 113, 121, 129, 137, 145, 153) sts from second sleeve with shaped edge next to front (370, 402, 434, 466, 498, 530, 562, 594, 626 sts).

Maintaining patt, cast off 9 sts at beginning of next 2 rows (96, 104, 112, 120, 128, 136, 144, 152, 160 sts). Leave sts on spare needle.

LEFT SLEEVE
Using 2.75mm needles cast on 76 (79, 82, 85, 88, 91, 94, 97, 100) sts and work in rib as folls:
Next row (RS): * K1, P1, rep from * to last 0 (1, 0, 1, 0, 1, 0, 1, 0) sts, K0 (1, 0, 1, 0, 1, 0, 1, 0).
Next row (WS): P0 (1, 0, 1, 0, 1, 0, 1, 0), * K1, P1, rep from * to end.
Rep these 2 rows once more.
Next row: K1, [K1, YO, K2tog] to end.
Work 2 rows more in rib.

1st, 4th and 5th sizes only
Next row: K4 (4, 2) * K2 (1, 1), Kfb, rep from * to last 6 (7, 2) sts, K6 (7, 2) (98, 122, 130 sts).

With RS facing, reposition sts on needle and rejoin yarn to back sts so that you have 6 (7, 7, 8, 8, 9, 9, 10, 10) reps of back lace patt on right needle tip side and 6 (6, 7, 7, 8, 8, 9, 9, 10) reps of back lace patt on left needle tip (for 1st, 3rd, 5th, 7th and 9th sizes, this is centre back, all other sizes, this is before the central lace pattern motif) and commence working in patt as folls:
Row 1: Cast on 1 st onto left needle, K1 (stitch just cast on), [K1, YO, Sl1, K1, psso, K3, K2tog, YO] 6 (6, 7, 7, 8, 8, 9, 9, 10) times, K2tog, YO, Sl1, K1, psso, K3, K2tog, YO, [K1, YO, Sl1, K1 psso, K3, K2tog, YO] 32 (35, 38, 41, 44, 47, 50, 53, 56) times, K1, YO, Sl1, K1, psso, K3, K3tog, YO, [K1, YO, Sl1, K1, psso, K3, K2tog, YO] 5 (6, 6, 7, 7, 8, 8, 9, 9) times, K1, YO, Sl1, K1, psso, K4, Kfb (stitch count has not changed).
By working back and forth over all stitches, you will now create the yoke, with an opening at the back (which is later sewn shut). Cont in patt across all sts, as given for back, until 2 (2, 3, 3, 3, 3, 4, 4, 5) complete patt reps have been worked.

Shape Yoke

Next row: K1, * K2tog, YO, K2tog, rep from * to last st, K1 (278, 302, 326, 350, 374, 398, 422, 446, 470 sts).

Next row: P.

Work yoke pattern as folls:

Row 1: * P2, K2, YO, K2tog, rep from * to last 2 sts, P2.

Row 2: * K2, P2, YO, P2tog, rep from * to last 2 sts, K2.

Rep 2 rows 4 more times.

Row 11: * P2tog, K2, YO, K2tog, rep from * to last 2 sts, P2tog (231, 251, 271, 291, 311, 331, 351, 371, 391 sts).

Row 12: * K1, P2, YO, P2tog, rep from * to last st, K1.

Row 13: * P1, K2, YO, K2tog, rep from * to last st, P1.

Rep last 2 rows 3 more times, then row 12 once again.

Row 21: * K2tog, K1, YO, K2tog, rep from * to last st, K1 (185, 201, 217, 233, 249, 265, 281, 297, 313 sts).

Row 22: K1, * P2, YO, P2tog, rep from * to end.

Row 23: * K2, YO, K2tog, rep from * to last st, K1.

Rep last 2 rows 3 more times.

Next row: P.

Next row: [K1, YO, K2tog] to last 2 (0, 1, 2, 0, 1, 2, 0, 1) sts, K2 (0, 1, 2, 0, 1, 2, 0, 1) (124, 134, 145, 156, 166, 177, 188, 198, 209 sts).

Next row: P.

Cast off.

MAKING UP

Press the work lightly through a damp cloth, avoiding ribbing. Sew together the cast off edges of sleeve and underarm. Sew up sleeve and side seams. Sew up back opening. Darn in all ends. Thread ribbon through eyelets at top of yoke and through eyelets on sleeves. Draw up to required size and tie bows.

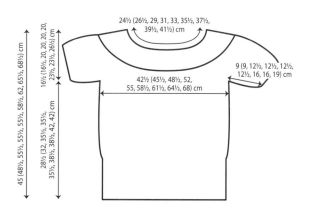

Ribbon-threaded Jumper

MATERIALS : — Seven ounces of Strutt's Milford Knitting Cotton No. 8; two No. 13 and two No. 14 and a set of four long No. 12 Milward's 'Phantom' Knitting Pins; one card Strutt's Elastic Thread to match Cotton as nearly as possible; 4 yards narrow velvet ribbon.

MEASUREMENTS.—To fit a 34 to 36-inch bust figure; length from shoulder, 18½ inches; sleeve seam, 4 inches.

TENSION.—About 7 stitches and 12 rows to one inch measured over the pattern.

ABBREVIATIONS.—Please see page 30.

Black velvet ribbons thread yoke and sleeves of this picture-style Jumper. Both the leaf-lace pattern and open-rib yoke are knitted.

BACK.—With No. 14 needles cast on 126 sts. and work in k. 1, p. 1 rib for 2 rows. Next row—Work in k. 1, p. 1 rib but weave in the Elastic Thread thus: Holding elastic in left hand and keeping it at back of work, (k. 1 putting needle under elastic, p. 1 putting needle over elastic) to end. (Elastic should be slightly stretched whilst working.) Work 2 rows in rib without elastic. Next row—Keeping elastic at front of work, (k. 1 putting needle over elastic, p. 1 putting needle under elastic) to end. Continue in this way, weaving in elastic on one side of work on every 3rd row, till 40 rows have been worked from start. Next row—K. 1, (rib 24, inc.) 4 times, rib 25. (130 sts.) Change to No. 12 needles and purl one row, then work in patt. as follows: 1st row—K. 1, * k. 1, m. 1, s. 1, k. 1, p.s.s.o., k. 3, k. 2 tog., m. 1; rep. from * to last st., k. 1. 2nd and every alternate row—P. 3rd row—K. 1, * k. 1, m. 1, k. 1, s. 1, k. 1, p.s.s.o., k. 1, k. 2 tog., k. 1, m. 1, rep. from * to last st., k. 1. 5th row—K. 1, * k. 1, m. 1, k. 2, s. 1, k. 2 tog., p.s.s.o., k. 2, m. 1; rep. from * to last st., k. 1. 7th row—K. 1, * k. 2, k. 2 tog., m. 1, k. 1, m. 1, s. 1, k. 1, p.s.s.o., k. 1; rep. from * to last st., k. 1. 9th row—K. 1, * k. 1, k. 2 tog., (k. 1, m. 1) twice, k. 1, s. 1, k. 1, p.s.s.o.; rep. from * to last st. k., 1. 11th row—K. 1, * k. 2, m. 1, k. 1, m. 1, k. 2, s. 1, k. 2 tog., p.s.s.o.; rep. from * till 7 rem., k. 2, m. 1, k. 1, m. 1, k. 2, s. 1, k. 1, p.s.s.o. 12th row—P. These 12 rows form pattern. Work 7 complete patts., decreasing one st. each end of the last p. row. Leave sts. on a spare needle.

FRONT.—With No. 14 needles cast on 126 sts. and work the welt as given for Back. Next row—(K. 5, inc.) to last 6 sts., k 6. (146 sts.) Change to No. 12 needles and purl one row, then work in pattern as given for Back until 10th row of 7th patt. has been worked. Cast off 9 sts. at beg. of next 2 rows. Leave sts. on a spare needle.

LEFT SLEEVE.—With No. 14 needles cast on 88 sts. and work 4 rows in k. 1, p. 1 rib weaving in the elastic on the 1st and 4th rows. Next row—K. 1, (k. 1, m. 1, k. 2 tog.) to end. Work 2 more rows in rib. Next row—K. 2, (k. 1, inc.) to last 2 sts., k. 2. (130 sts.) Change to No. 12 needles. Proceed in patt. as given for Back until 11th row of 3rd patt. has been worked. Next row—Cast off 9 sts., p. to end. Leave sts. on a spare needle.

RIGHT SLEEVE.—Work exactly as for Left Sleeve until 10th row of 3rd patt. has been worked Next row—Cast off 9 sts., patt. to end. Next row—P. Leave sts. on a spare needle.

YOKE.—This is worked on four No. 12 needles, the opening at centre back. Divide Back sts. on to two needles, 64 sts. on each, then place the 121 sleeve sts., straight edge to side edge of Back, on to outer ends of needles holding Back sts., then place the Front 128 sts. on to one needle (the shaped edges of Front and Sleeves will come together when working across all sts.). With right side of work facing, join cotton to centre Back and cast on 1. Now commence patt. as follows: 1st row—K. 1, (k. 1, m. 1, s. 1, k. 1, p.s.s.o., k. 3, k. 2 tog., m. 1) 8 times, k. 2 tog., m. 1, s. 1, k. 1, p.s.s.o., k. 3, k. 2 tog., m. 1, (k. 1, m. 1, s. 1, k. 1, p.s.s.o., k. 3, k. 2 tog., m. 1) 44 times, k. 1, m. 1, s. 1, k. 1, p.s.s.o., k. 3, k. 3 tog., m. 1, (k. 1, m. 1, s. 1, k. 1, p.s.s.o., k. 3, k. 2 tog., m. 1) 7 times, k. 1, m. 1, s. 1, k. 1, p.s.s.o., k. 3, k. 1, inc. (498 sts.) Continue in patt. across all sts., as given for Back, until 2 complete patts. have been worked. Next row—K. 1, * k. 2 tog., m. 1, k. 2 tog., rep. from * to last st., k. 1. (374 sts.) Next row—P. Change to No. 13 needles and work as follows: 1st row—* P. 2, k. 2, m. 1, k. 2 tog., rep. from * to last 2 sts., p. 2. 2nd row—* K. 2, p. 2, m. 1 by putting cotton over needle, p. 2 tog., rep. from * to last 2 sts., k. 2. Rep. last 2 rows 4 more times.

11th row—* P. 2 tog., k. 2, m. 1, k. 2 tog., rep. from * to last 2 sts., p. 2 tog. 12th row—* K. 1, p. 2, m. 1, p. 2 tog., rep. from * to last st., k. 1. 13th row—* P. 1, k. 2, m. 1, k. 2 tog., rep. from * to last st., p. 1. Rep. last 2 rows 3 more times, then rep. 12th row. 21st row—* K. 2 tog., k. 1, m. 1, k. 2 tog., rep. from * to last st., k. 1. 22nd row—K. 1, * p. 2, m. 1, p. 2 tog., rep. from * to end. 23rd row—* K. 2, m. 1, k. 2 tog., rep. from * to last st., k. 1. Rep. last 2 rows 3 more times. Next row—P. Next row—(K. 1, m. 1, k. 2 tog.) to end. Next row—P. Cast off, using a No. 12 needle.

TO MAKE UP.—Press the work lightly under a damp cloth with a hot iron, avoiding ribbing. Sew together the cast-off edges of sleeve and underarm. Sew sleeve and side seams. Sew up back opening. Thread ribbon through slots top and bottom of yoke and through slots on sleeves; draw up to required size and tie bows.

Dainty leaf pattern for the ribbon-threaded Jumper.

Fiesta Cap and Gloves

MATERIALS
J C Rennie Castle Collection 4 ply 58% lambswool/42% silk (154m/169yds per 50g ball)
2 balls shade 013 (Carsluith)
1 pair 3mm (US #2–3) needles
1 set 3mm (US #2–3) Double Pointed Needles (DPNs)
Stitch marker

TENSION
25 sts & 36 rows = 10cm (4in) using 3mm needles over stocking stitch

ABBREVIATIONS
See page 13 for standard abbreviations

SIZING
Cap Circumference = 53cm (21in)

Gloves circumference = 21cm (8½in) – to fit medium ladies hand

Cap

Using 3mm DPNs, cast on 144 sts, placing 48 sts on each of three needles. Join into round, placing a marker to mark end of round, taking care not to twist cast on edge and work in rib as folls:
Next round: * K1, P1, rep from * to end of round.
Rep this round a further 9 times. Now K every round until work measures 14cm (5½in) from cast on edge.

Shape Crown
Round 1: [K1, K2tog] to end of round (96 sts).
K 5 rounds, then rep last 6 rounds once more (64 sts).
Round 13: K1, * K2tog, K1, rep from * to end of round (43 sts).
K 5 rounds.
Round 19: Work as for round 13 (29 sts).
Round 20: K.
Round 21: K2tog, * K1, K2tog, rep from * to end of round (19 sts). Break off yarn, leaving a long end. Thread through rem sts, draw up and fasten off securely. Darn in all ends.

Gloves

LEFT HAND
Using 3mm needles, cast on 74 sts and work as folls:
Row 1 (RS): P1, [K1, P1] 21 times, K31.
Row 2: P31, K1, [P1, K1] to end.
Rep these 2 rows twice more.
** Continue as set, dec 1 st at each end of next and every foll 4th row until 58 sts rem. Work 1 row.
Next row (Dec): K3, [K2tog, K8] 5 times, K2tog, K3 (52 sts). Commencing with a P work in stocking stitch from this point for 5cm (2in) ending with a P row **

Thumb
Row 1: K26, turn, slipping rem 26 sts onto waste yarn.
Row 2: Cast on 11 sts, P21, turn, slipping rem 16 sts onto a separate piece of waste yarn.
Row 3: K21 †
Work without shaping until thumb measures 5¾cm (2¼in) or required length (see 'Fit and Finish' chapter), ending with a WS row.

Shape Thumb
Row 1: K1, K2tog, K6, K3tog, K6, K2tog, K1 (17 sts).
Row 2: P.
Row 3: K1, K2tog, K4, K3tog, K4, K2tog, K1 (13 sts).
Break off yarn leaving a long end, draw through rem sts, and fasten securely, then join thumb seam.

With RS of work facing, rejoin yarn to base of thumb and pick and K 10 sts across thumb cast on, then K 26 sts from waste yarn.
Next row (WS): P36, then P 16 sts from rem waste yarn (52 sts).
*** Commencing with a K row, work in stocking stitch for 5cm (2in) ending with a WS row.

SHAPE FINGERS

Finger 1
Row 1: K34, turn, slip rem 18 sts onto waste yarn.
Row 2: Cast on 3 sts, P19, turn and slip rem 18 sts onto second piece of waste yarn.
Work until finger measures 5¾cm (2¼in) or required length ending with a WS row.

Shape Top

Row 1 (RS): K1, K2tog, K5, K3tog, K5, K2tog, K1 (15 sts).
Row 2: P.
Row 3: K1, K2tog, K3, K3tog, K3, K2tog, K1 (11 sts). Break off yarn leaving a long end, draw through rem sts, and fasten securely, then join seam.

Finger 2

With RS facing, rejoin yarn to base of preceding finger and pick up and K 4 sts across cast on, then K 6 sts from left hand sts held on waste yarn, turn.
Next row: Cast on 3 sts, P13, then P 6 sts from second set of sts on waste yarn, turn. Work in stocking stitch for 7½cm (3in) or required length. Now shape top as for first finger.

Finger 3

Work as for second finger but work straight for 7cm (2¼in) or required length before shaping top.

Finger 4

With RS facing, rejoin yarn to base of preceding finger and pick up and K 3 sts across cast on, then K rem 6 sts from first waste yarn.
Next row: P9, then P rem 6 sts from rem waste yarn (15 sts). Work in stocking stitch until finger is required length ending with a WS row.

Shape Top

Row 1 (RS): K1, K2tog, K3, K3tog, K3, K2tog, K1 (11 sts).
Row 2: P.

Row 3: K1, K2tog, K1, K3tog, K1, K2tog, K1 (7 sts). Break off yarn leaving a long end, draw through rem sts, and fasten securely, then join seam from top of finger then down side seam to cast on edge ***

RIGHT HAND

Using 3mm needles, cast on 74 sts and work as folls:
Row 1 (RS): K31, P1, * K1, P1, rep from * to end.
Row 2: K1, [P1, K1] 21 times, P31.
Rep these 2 rows twice more. Now work as given for left glove from ** to ** then place thumb as folls:

Thumb

Row 1 (RS): K36, turn, slipping rem 16 sts onto waste yarn.
Row 2: Cast on 11 sts, P21, turn slipping rem 26 sts on to waste yarn.
Now complete thumb as given for left glove, commencing from † (row 3).
With RS facing, rejoin yarn to base of thumb and pick up and K 10 sts from cast on edge, then K 16 sts from left hand waste yarn.
Next row (WS): P26, then P 26 sts from second set of sts on waste yarn (52 sts).
Now proceed as given for left glove from *** to ***

MAKING UP

Press work lightly on WS using a damp cloth. Do not press ribbing on cuff. Turn over approx 3 or 4 rows of knitting at wrist edge and slip stitch into place on WS of work. Darn in all ends.

CAP AND GLOVE SET

To Fit Average Size

The Set in "Fiesta" Wool

MATERIALS.—Allow 3 ozs. of Penelope's W.B. Fiesta for the set ; 1 pair of No. 11 knitting needles and a set of four No. 11 needles, pointed at both ends.

TENSION.—Over the stocking-stitch, 17 stitches and 21 rows to 2 inches.

MEASUREMENTS :—**Cap**—To suit an average head size.

Gloves—Width all round hand above thumb division, 6 inches ; overall length, about 10¼ inches.

ABBREVIATIONS.—K., knit ; p., purl ; st., stitch ; sts., stitches ; rep., repeat ; tog., together ; dec., decrease; (by taking 2 sts. tog.) ; st.-st., stocking-stitch (1 row k. and 1 row p. alternately when working in rows, but every round k. when working in rounds).

Stitches in brackets must be worked along row or round to the extent stated after 2nd bracket.

THE CAP
TO MAKE

Using the set of four No. 11 needles, cast on 144 sts., putting 48 sts. on each of 3 needles. With 4th needle, work 10 rounds in k. 1, p. 1 rib. Now proceed in st.-st. until work measures 5½ inches from cast-on edge, then shape top.

1st top shaping round : (K. 1, k. 2 tog.) to end of round.

Next 5 rounds : K. to end. Rep. the last 6 rounds once.

13th round : K. 1, (k. 2 tog., k. 1) to end of round.

Next 5 rounds : K. to end.

19th round : As 13th round.

20th round : K. to end.

21st round : K. 2 tog., (k. 1, k. 2 tog.) to end of round.

Break off wool, leaving a longish end, which run through remaining sts., draw up and fasten off securely.

Press work lightly with a warm iron over a damp cloth, avoiding the ribbing.

THE GLOVES
LEFT GLOVE

Using the pair of No. 11 needles, cast on 74 sts. and work in rib and st.-st. as follows :

1st row—right side : P. 1, (k. 1, p. 1) 21 times, k. 31.

2nd row : P. 31, k. 1, (p. 1, k. 1) to end.

Rep. these 2 rows twice more.

** Continue with sts. as now set, but dec. 1 st. at each end of next row and every following 4th row until 58 sts. remain ; work 1 row straight. Proceed in st.-st. over all sts., but dec. on next row thus :

Dec. row : K. 3, (k. 2 tog., k. 8) 5 times, k. 2 tog., k. 3.

Work 2 inches in st.-st. on remaining 52 sts., finishing with a

p. row.** Now proceed for thumb as follows :

The Thumb—1st row : K. 26 sts. ; turn, slipping remaining 26 sts. on to a piece of thread.

2nd row : Cast on 11 sts., p. 21 ; turn, slipping remaining 16 sts. on to another thread.

3rd row : K. 21. Work 2¼ inches in st.-st. on these 21 sts., finishing with a p. row. Now shape top.

1st top shaping row : K. 1, 2 tog., k. 6, k. 3 tog., k. 6, k. 2 tog., k. 1.

2nd row : P. 17.

3rd row : K. 1, k. 2 tog., k. 4, k. 3 tog., k. 4, k. 2 tog., k. 1.

Break off wool, leaving a longish end, which run through remaining 13 sts., draw up and fasten off securely, then join seam of thumb.

With right side of work facing you, join wool to base of thumb and pick up and k. 10 sts. from those cast-on, then k. the 26 sts. from left-hand thread.

Next row : P. 36, then p. the 16 sts. from 2nd thread.

*** Work 2 inches in st.-st. on these 52 sts., finishing with a p. row. Now commence fingers.

1st finger—1st row : K. 34 sts., turn, slipping remaining 18 sts. on to a piece of thread.

2nd row : Cast on 3 sts., p. 19 ; turn, slipping remaining 18 sts. on to another thread.

Work 2¾ inches in st.-st. on these 19 sts., finishing with a p. row.

Now shape top.

1st top shaping row : K. 1, k. 2 tog., k. 5, k. 3 tog., k. 5, k. 2 tog., k. 1.

2nd row : P. 15.

3rd row : K. 1, k. 2 tog., k. 3, k. 3 tog., k. 3, k. 2 tog., k. 1.

Break off wool, leaving a longish end, which run through remaining 11 sts., draw up and fasten off securely, then join seam of finger.

2nd finger : With right side of work towards you, join wool to base of preceding finger and pick up and k. 4 sts. from those cast-on, then k. 6 sts. from left-hand thread ; turn.

Next row : Cast on 3 sts., p. 13, then p. 6 sts. from other thread ; turn. Work 3¼ inches in st.-st. on these 19 sts., finishing with a p. row. Now shape top and join seam as given for 1st finger.

3rd finger : Proceed as given for 2nd finger, but only work 2¾ inches in st.-st., instead of 3¼ inches before shaping top.

4th finger : With right side of work towards you, join wool to base of preceding finger and pick up and k. 3 sts. from those cast-on, then k. the remaining 6 sts. from 1st thread.

Next row : P. 9, then p. remaining 6 sts. from other thread. Work 2 inches in st.-st. on these 15 sts., finishing with a p. row. Now shape top.

Now shape top.

1st top shaping row : K. 1, k. 2 tog., k. 3, k. 3 tog., k. 3, k. 2 tog., k. 1.

2nd row : P. 11.

3rd row : K. 1, k. 2 tog., k. 1, k. 3 tog., k. 1, k. 2 tog., k. 1.

Break off wool, leaving a longish end, which run through remaining 7 sts., draw up and fasten off securely, then join seam from tip of finger to wrist edge.***

RIGHT GLOVE

Using the pair of No. 11 needles, cast on 74 sts. and work in st.-st. and rib as follows :

1st row—right side : K. 31, p. 1, (k. 1, p. 1) to end.

2nd row : K. 1, (p. 1, k. 1) 21 times, p. 31.

Rep. these 2 rows twice more. Now work as given for left glove from ** to **, then commence thumb.

The Thumb—1st row : K. 36 sts. ; turn, slipping remaining 16 sts. on to a piece of thread.

2nd row : Cast on 11 sts., p. 21 ; turn, slipping remaining 26 sts. on to a piece of thread.

Now complete thumb as given for left glove. Starting with the 3rd row.

With right side of work facing you, join wool to base of thumb and pick up and k. 10 sts. from those cast-on, then k. the 16 sts. from left-hand thread.

Next row : P. 26, then p. the 26 sts. from 2nd thread.

Now proceed as given for left glove from *** to ***.

TO COMPLETE

Press work lightly on wrong side with a warm iron over a damp cloth, avoiding the ribbing at wrist. Turn over 3 rows of knitting at wrist edge and catch-stitch down on wrong side.

Tyrolean Jumper Coat

MATERIALS
Excelana 4 Ply Luxury Wool 100% pure new British wool (159m/174yds per 50g ball)
6 (7, 9, 10, 11) balls shade French Rose
1 pair 3mm (US #2–3) needles
1 pair 2.75mm (US #2) needles
Cable needle (CN)
9 buttons
Embroidery threads in 4 colours

TENSION
34 sts & 36 rows = 10cm (4 in) using 3mm needles worked over sample pattern of reverse stocking stitch and C6B cable

Standard Yarn Tension
28 sts and 36 rows = 10cm (4in) over stocking stitch using 3mm needles

ABBREVIATIONS
See page 13 for standard abbreviations

Specific abbreviations for this pattern
C6B: Sl3 onto CN and hold at back of work, K3, then K 3 held sts
T4B: Sl1 st onto CN and hold at back of work, K3, then P held st
T4F: Sl3 sts onto CN and hold at front, P next st, then K 3 held sts
T5B: Sl2 sts onto CN and hold at back of work, K3, then P2 held sts
T5F: Sl3 sts onto CN and hold at front, P2, then K 3 held sts

SIZING
Measurements given in centimetres followed by inches in parentheses

To Fit	71–76 (28–30)	81–86 (32–34)	92–97 (36–38)	102–107 (40–42)	112–117 (44–46)
Finished Measurements					
Actual Bust Size	83 (32½)	92½ (36½)	102 (40)	111 (43½)	120½ (47½)
Length to underarm	31¾ (12½)	31¾ (12½)	34¾ (13½)	37 (14½)	38 (15)
Armhole Depth	17¾ (7)	19½ (7¾)	23 (9)	24 (9½)	25½ (10)
Finished Length	49½ (19½)	51¼ (20¼)	57¾ (22½)	61 (24)	63½ (25)
Shoulder to shoulder	26½ (10½)	31 (12)	36 (14)	40½ (16)	45½ (18)
Sleeve Length	43 (17)	44½ (17½)	45½ (18)	47 (18½)	48 (19)

Garment shown in photographs is for third size 92–97 (36–38)

PATTERN NOTES
The shoulders of this garment are worked using short row shaping. There are various ways of working wrap and turns, see the 'Fit and Finish' chapter for a suggested method.

RIGHT FRONT
Using 3mm needles, cast on 49 (57, 65, 73, 81) sts and work in cable patt (also shown on chart A) as folls:
Row 1 (RS): * P2, K6, repeat from * to last st, P1.
Rows 2, 4, 6, 8 & 10: K1, * P6, K2, repeat from * to end.
Row 3: * P2, K6, repeat from * to last st, P1.
Row 5: * P2, C6B, repeat from * to last st, P1.
Row 7: As row 3.
Rows 8–10: Repeat rows 6–7, then repeat row 6 only, once more.
Rows 5–10 inclusive form the cable pattern.
Repeat rows 5–10 inclusive 6 times more, then repeat row 5 only once more.

Proceed in main cable patt as folls:
Row 1 (WS): Work from chart B row 1, and reading from left to right, start as indicated for your size, then repeat marked section 1 (1, 2, 2, 2) times, ending row with stitches 13 to 1 inclusive. **Note**: 2nd and 5th sizes start as indicated and work 20 sts of the marked section before repeating the whole marked repeat.
Row 2 (RS): Work from chart B row 2, and reading from right to left, work sts 1 to 13 inclusive, then repeat marked section 1 (1, 2, 2, 2) times, ending row as indicated for your size. **Note**: 2nd and 5th sizes work 20 sts of the marked section thus ending as indicated.
These 2 rows set position of chart B.

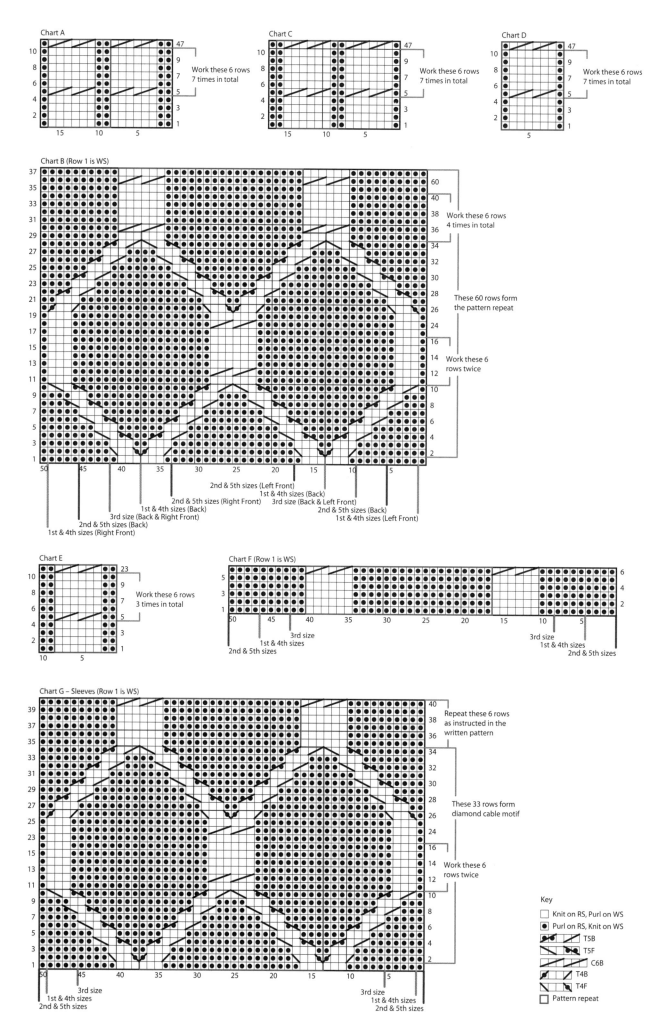

Continue working from chart B, inc 1 st at side edge of row 4 and every foll 3rd row until 71 (79, 87, 95, 103) sts, taking increased sts into pattern, working further repeats of the marked section when enough sts. (Where there are insufficient sts remaining to complete a cable, work knit or purl stitches as appropriate instead). **Please note**: Incs will be worked at beg of WS rows and end of RS rows.

When row 61 of chart completed return to row 2 and continue working from chart until all incs worked. Continue working from chart without further shaping until work measures 31¾ (31¾, 34¾, 37, 38) cm (12½, 12½, 13½, 14½, 15 in) ending with a RS row.

Shape Armhole
Keeping pattern correct, cast off 11 sts at start of next row (60, 68, 76, 84, 92 sts).
Dec 1 st at armhole edge of next 14 rows (46, 54, 62, 70, 78 sts).
Work without shaping until armhole measures 11¾ (11¾, 15¼, 16¼, 16¼) cm (4½, 4½, 6, 6½, 6½ in), ending with a WS row.

Shape Neck
From this point onwards, if necessary complete current diamond cable, then continue to repeat next 6-row straight cable pattern, and do not work any further diamond cables. Keeping pattern correct, cast off 9 (12, 12, 12, 12) sts at beg of next row (37, 42, 50, 58, 66 sts).
Dec 1 st at neck edge of next and 5 (6, 6, 12, 18) foll alt rows (31, 35, 43, 45, 47 sts).
Work without further shaping until armhole measures 17¾ (19½, 23, 24, 25½) cm (7, 7¾, 9, 9½, 10 in), ending with a WS row.

Shape Shoulder
Next row (RS): Patt 21 (24, 29, 30, 32) sts, w&t.
Next row: Patt to end.
Next row: Patt 11 (12, 15, 15, 16) sts, w&t.
Next row: Patt to end.
Cast off all sts.

LEFT FRONT
Using 3mm needles, cast on 49 (57, 65, 73, 81) sts and work in cable patt (also shown on chart C) as folls:
Row 1 (RS): P1, * K6, P2, repeat from * to end.
Rows 2, 4 & 6: * K2, P6, repeat from * to last st, K1.
Row 3: P1, * K6, P2, repeat from * to end.
Row 5: P1, * C6B, P2, repeat from * to end.
Row 7: As row 3.
Rows 8–10: Repeat rows 6–7 and then row 6 again.
Rows 5–10 inclusive form cable pattern.
Repeat rows 5–10 inclusive 6 times more, then repeat row 5.

Proceed in main cable patt as folls:
Row 1 (WS): Work from chart B row 1, and reading from left to right, work sts 50 to 38 inclusive, then repeat marked section 1 (1, 2, 2, 2) times, then work to end as indicated for your size. **Note**: 2nd and 5th sizes work 20 sts

of the marked section thus ending as indicated.
Row 2 (RS): Work from chart B row 2, and reading from right to left, start as indicated for your size, then repeat marked section 1 (1, 2, 2, 2) times, ending row with sts 38 to 50 inclusive. **Note**: 2nd and 5th sizes start as indicated and work 20 sts of the marked section before repeating the whole marked repeat.
These 2 rows set position of chart B.

Whilst working from chart B (at end of row 61 of chart, return to row 2), increase 1 st at side seam edge (start of RS rows, and end of WS rows) of row 4 and every foll 3rd row until you have 71 (79, 87, 95, 103) sts, taking increased sts into pattern, working further repeats of the marked section when you have enough sts. Where there are insufficient sts remaining to complete a cable, work knit or purl stitches as appropriate instead.
Continue working from chart without further shaping until work measures 31¾ (31¾, 34¾, 37, 38) cm (12½, 12½, 13½, 14½, 15 in) ending with a WS row.

Shape Armhole
Keeping pattern correct, cast off 11 sts at start of next row (60, 68, 76, 84, 92 sts).
Dec 1 st at armhole edge of next 14 rows (46, 54, 62, 70, 78 sts).
Work without shaping until armhole measures 11¾ (11¾, 15¼, 16¼, 16¼) cm (4½, 4½, 6, 6½, 6½ in), ending with a RS row.

Shape Neck

From this point onwards, if necessary complete current diamond cable, then continue to repeat next 6-row straight cable pattern, and do not work any further diamond cables. Keeping pattern correct, cast off 9 (12, 12, 12, 12) sts at start of next row (37, 42, 50, 58, 66 sts). Dec 1 st at neck edge of next and 5 (6, 6, 12, 18) foll alt rows (31, 35, 43, 45, 47 sts). Work without further shaping until armhole measures 17¾ (19½, 23, 24, 25½) cm (7, 7¾, 9, 9½, 10 in), ending with a RS row.

Shape Shoulder

Next row (WS): Patt 21 (24, 29, 30, 32) sts, w&t.
Next row: Patt to end.
Next row: Patt 11 (12, 15, 15, 16) sts, w&t.
Next row: Patt to end. Cast off all sts.

BACK

Using 3mm needles, cast on 96 (112, 128, 144, 160) sts and work in cable patt (also shown on Chart D) as folls:
Row 1: * P1, K6, P1, repeat from * to end.
Rows 2, 4 & 6: * K1, P6, K1, repeat from * to end.
Row 3: * P1, K6, P1, repeat from * to last st, P1.
Row 5: * P1, C6B, P1, repeat from * to end.
Row 7: As row 3.
Rows 8–10: Repeat rows 6–7, then 6 again.
Rows 5–10 inclusive form cable patt.
Repeat rows 5–10 inclusive 6 times more, then repeat row 5 once more.

Proceed in main cable patt as folls:
Row 1 (WS): Work from chart B row 1, and reading from left to right, start and end as indicated and repeat marked section 4 (4, 5, 6, 6) times.
Row 2 (RS): Work from chart B row 2, and reading from right to left, start and end as indicated and repeat marked section 4 (4, 5, 6, 6) times.
These 2 rows set position of chart B.

Whilst working from chart B (at end of row 61 of chart, return to row 2), increase 1 st at both ends of row 4 and every foll 3rd row until you have 140 (156, 172, 188, 204) sts, taking increased sts into pattern, working further repeats of the marked section when you have enough sts. Where there are insufficient sts remaining to complete a cable, work knit or purl stitches as appropriate instead. Work without shaping until back measures same as front to commencement of armhole shaping, ending with a WS row.

Shape Armholes

Cast off 11 sts at start of next 2 rows (118, 134, 150, 166, 182 sts).
Dec 1 st at each end of next 14 rows (90, 106, 122, 138, 154 sts).

Work without further shaping until armhole measures 11¾ (11¾, 15¼, 16¼, 16¼) cm (4½, 4½, 6, 6½, 6½ in). If necessary complete current diamond cable, and then continue to repeat next 6-row straight cable pattern without working any further diamond cables (as for the fronts). Work until back measures same as front to start of shoulder shaping ending with a WS row.

Shape Shoulders

Next row (RS): Patt 80 (95, 108, 123, 139) sts, w&t.
Row 2: Patt 70 (84, 94, 108, 124) sts, w&t.
Row 3: Patt 60 (72, 80, 93, 108) sts, w&t.
Row 4: Patt 50 (60, 66, 78, 92) sts, w&t.
Row 5: Patt 39 (48, 51, 63, 76) sts, w&t.
Row 6: Patt 28 (36, 36, 48, 60) sts. Break off wool.
Slip all the sts on 1 needle, rejoin the wool and with RS facing cast off all sts.

SLEEVES

Using 3mm needles, cast on 42 (50, 58, 66, 74) sts and work in cable patt (also shown on chart E) as folls:
Row 1: * P2, K6, repeat from * to last 2 sts, P2.
Rows 2, 4 & 6: * K2, P6, repeat from * to last 2 sts, K2.
Row 3: * P2, K6, repeat from * to last 2 sts, P2.
Row 5: * P2, C6B repeat from * to last 2 sts, P2.
Row 7: As row 3.
Rows 8–10: Repeat rows 6–7, then 6 again.
Rows 11–23: Repeat rows 5–10 inclusive twice, then repeat 5 again.

Proceed in cable patt as folls:
Row 1 (WS): Work from chart F row 1, and reading from left to right, start and end as indicated for your size, and repeat marked section 1 (1, 2, 2, 2) times.
Row 2 (RS): Work from chart F row 2, and reading from right to left, start and end as indicated and repeat marked section 1 (1, 2, 2, 2) times.
These 2 rows set position for chart F. Repeat 6 rows of chart throughout following increase section.

Keeping the cables correct and working the inc sts in reverse stocking stitch, inc 1 st at both ends of row 6 and on 11 (7, 15, 11, 7) foll 4th rows to (66, 66, 90, 90, 90) sts.

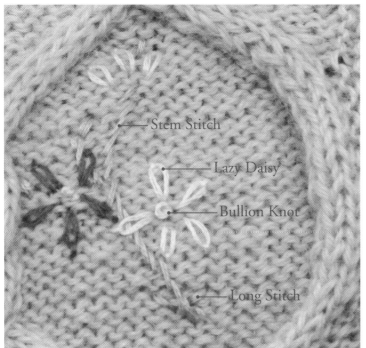

Stem Stitch

Lazy Daisy

Bullion Knot

Long Stitch

Keeping cables correct and working inc sts in stocking stitch, inc at both ends of every foll 4th row until 6 more sets of inc have been worked and there are 78 (78, 102, 102, 102) sts.

Keeping cable correct cont to inc 1 st at both ends of every foll 4th row, working the inc sts in reverse stocking stitch until 9 (13, 5, 9, 13) more sets of inc have been worked and there are 96 (104, 112, 120, 128) sts.

Keeping cables correct proceed without further shaping until work measures 38 (39½, 40½, 42, 43) cm (15, 15½, 16, 16½, 17 in) from commencement, ending with a cable row.

Proceed as foll:

Row 1 (WS): K0 (3, 0, 0, 3), work from chart G row 1, and reading from left to right, start and end as indicated for your size, repeating marked section 3 (3, 4, 4, 4) times, K0 (3, 0, 0, 3).

Row 2 (RS): P0 (3, 0, 0, 3), work from chart G row 2, and reading from right to left, start and end as indicated for your size, repeating marked section 3 (3, 4, 4, 4) times, P0 (3, 0, 0, 3).

These 2 rows set position of chart G for diamond cable pattern (with rev st st at edges in 2nd and 5th sizes).

Cont to work in pattern as set, until you have worked 18 rows of diamond cable pattern, ending with a RS row.

Shape Sleeve Head

Keeping diamond cable pattern correct, cast off 7 sts at beg of next 2 rows (82, 90, 98, 106, 114 sts).

Dec 1 st at each end of next and every foll alt row to 52 (60, 68, 68, 68) sts. When diamond cable motif is complete, return to working straight cables as shown on rows 35–40 of chart G. Work 1 row.

Now decrease at both ends of every row, until 26 sts rem. Cast off.

MAKING UP

Press lightly on WS through damp cloth. Embroider diamond shaped portion of the work with a flower spray as shown in the photograph using sts as explained in 'Fit and Finish' chapter. Press embroidery lightly on the WS. Join shoulders.

NECKBAND

Using 2.75mm needles and with RS facing, pick up and K 9 (12, 12, 12, 12) sts across right front neck, 14 (18, 22, 24, 32) sts up right side neck, 28 (36, 36, 48, 60) sts across back neck, 14 (18, 22, 24, 32) sts down left side neck and 9 (12, 12, 12, 12) sts across left front neck (74, 96, 104, 120, 148 sts). Work in garter stitch for 6 rows. Cast off knitwise.

Join sleeve and side seams. Stitch the sleeves into position, taking care to match the pattern wherever possible and matching centre of sleeve head with shoulder seam.

BUTTON BAND

Using 2.75mm needles, with RS facing and commencing at top edge of neckband, pick up and K 130 (134, 154, 166, 174) sts down left front. Work in garter stitch for 8 rows. Cast off knitwise. Mark position of 9 buttons with top button level with neckband and bottom button approx 2½cm (1in) from bottom edge, and remaining 7 buttons spread out evenly between.

BUTTONHOLE BAND

Using 2.75mm needles, with RS facing and commencing at lower edge of right front, pick up and K 130 (134, 154, 166, 174) sts. K 3 rows.

Next row (RS): K and at the same time work buttonholes to match marked positions on left front, casting off 2 sts as required.

Next row: * K to cast off sts, turn, cast on 2, turn, rep from * across row, then K to end.

K 3 more rows.

Cast off knitwise.

Sew buttons in place. Darn in all ends.

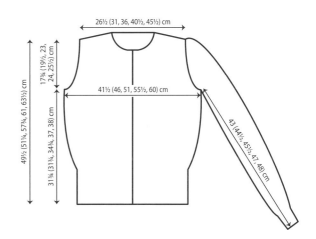

26½ (31, 36, 40½, 45½) cm

17¾ (19½, 23, 24, 25½) cm

41½ (46, 51, 55½, 60) cm

49½ (51¼, 57¾, 61, 63½) cm

31¾ (31¾, 34¾, 37, 38) cm

43 (44½, 45½, 47, 48) cm

6ᴰ

3-ply "EXCELSIOR" SUPER FINGERING

LADY'S TYROLEAN JUMPER COAT

No. 1928

MATERIALS :	9 ozs. Copley's 3-ply "Excelsior" Super Fingering, Pale Blue No. 80. A small quantity of Medium Pink ; Medium Blue ; Yellow, Lt. and Dk. Green wools for the embroidery. 1 pair No. 11 "Coploid" Knitting Needles. 1 No. 12 "Stratnoid" Crochet Hook. 9 Buttons. Approx. equivalent American and Continental size needles, 3.
MEASUREMENTS :	Length from top shoulder to lower edge, 21 inches. Width all round at underarm, to fit a 34 inch bust. Length of sleeve seam, 18 inches.
TENSION :	Work to produce 8 sts. and 10 rows to one square inch in smooth fabric (1 row K., 1 row P.).
ABBREVIATIONS :	K.—knit. P.—Purl. St.—stitch. Tog.—together. Sl.—slip. P.s.s.o.—pass the slipped st. over. T.b.s.—through back of sts.

THE RIGHT FRONT.

Cast on 65 sts.

1st Row.—Working into the back of the sts., * P.2, K.6, repeat from * to the last st., P.1.

2nd Row.—K.1, * P.6, K.2, repeat from * to the end.

3rd Row.—* P.2, K.6, repeat from * to the last st., P.1.

4th Row.—As the 2nd row.

5th Row.—*P.2, slip the next 3 sts. on to a spare needle and leave at the back of the work, K. the next 3 sts., bring forward the slipped sts. and K. them (this action will be referred to as " Cable 6—C.6 "), repeat from * to the last st., P.1.

6th Row.—K.1, * P.6, K.2, repeat from * to the end.

7th Row.—*P.2, K.6, repeat from * to the last st., P.1.

8th—10th Rows.—Repeat the 6th and 7th rows, then repeat the 6th row.
Rows 5—10 inclusive form the cable.
Repeat rows 5—10 inclusive 6 times more, then repeat the 5th row.
Proceed in pattern, increasing as follows :—

1st Row.—K.1, (P.6, K.18) twice, P.6, K.10.

2nd Row.—P.9, slip the next st. on to the spare needle and leave at the **back** of the work, K. the next 3 sts., bring forward the slipped st. and **P.** it (this action will be referred to as " Back Cable 4—B. C. 4 "), slip the next 3 sts. on to the spare needle and bring to the **front** of the work, P. the following st. take back the slipped sts. and **K.** them (this action will be referred to as " Front Cable 4—F. C. 4 "), P.16, B.C.4, F.C.4, P.16, B.C.4, F.C.4.

3rd Row.—(P.3, K.2, P.3, K.16) twice, P.3, K.2, P.3, K.9.

4th Row.—P.7, slip the next 2 **sts.**, on to the spare needle and leave at the back of the work, K. the next 3 sts., bring forward the slipped sts. and P. them (this action will be referred to as " **Back Cable 5—B.C.5**"), P.2, slip the next 3 sts. on to the spare needle and bring to the front of the work, P. the following **2 sts.**, take back the slipped sts. and K. them (this action will be referred to as **Front Cable 5—F.C.5**"), P.12, B.C.5, P.2, F.C.5, P.12, B.C.5, P.3, K.1, increase by working into the front and back of the last st.

5th Row.—P.2, K.6, (P.3, K.12, P.3, K.6) twice, P.3, K.7.

6th Row.—P.5, (B.C.5, P.6, F.C.5, P.8) twice, B.C.5, P.7, K.1.

7th Row.—Increase in the first st., K.9, (P.3, K.8, P.3, K.10) twice, P.3, K.5.

8th Row.—P.3, (B.C.5, P.10, F.C.5, P.4) twice, B.C.5, P.11.

9th Row.—K.13, (P.3, K.4, P.3, K.14) twice, P.3, K.3.

10th Row.—P.1, (B.C.5, P.14, F.C.5) twice, B.C.5, P.12, increase in the last st.

11th Row.—K.16, (P.6, K.18) twice, P.3, K.1.

12th Row.—P.1, K.3, (P.18, C.6) twice, P.16.

13th Row.—Increase in the first st., K.15, (P.6, K.18) twice, P.3, K.1.

14th Row.—P.1, K.3, (P.18, K.6) twice, P.17.

15th Row.—K.17, (P.6, K.18) twice, P.3, K.1.

16th Row.—P.1, K.3, (P.18, K.6) twice, P.16, increase in the last st.

17th Row.—K.18, (P.6, K.18) twice, P.3, K.1.

18th Row.—P.1, K.3, (P.18, C.6) twice, P.18.

19th Row.—Increase in the first st., K.17, (P.6, K.18) twice, P.3, K.1.

20th Row.—P.1, K.3, (P.18, K.6) twice, P.19.

21st Row.—K.19, (P.6, K.18) twice, P.3, K.1.

22nd Row.—P.1, K.3, (P.18, K.6) twice, P.18, increase in the last st.

23rd Row.—K.20, (P.6, K.18) twice, P.3, K.1.

24th Row.—P.1, K.3, (P.18, C.6) twice, P.20.

25th Row.—Increase in the first st., K.19, (P.6, K.18) twice, P.3, K.1.

26th Row.—P.1, (F.C.4, P.16, B.C.4) twice, F.C.4, P.17, K.3.

27th Row.—K.1, (P.3, K.16, P.3, K.2) 3 times.

28th Row.—(P.2, F.C.5, P.12, B.C.5) 3 times, increase in the last st.

29th Row.—K.4, (P.3, K.12, P.3, K.6) twice, P.3, K.12, P.3, K.4.

30th Row.—P.4, (F.C.5, P.8, B.C.5, P.6) twice, F.C.5, P.8, B.C.5, P.4.

31st Row.—Increase in the first st., K.5, (P.3, K.8, P.3, K.10) twice, P.3, K.8, P.3, K.6.

32nd Row.—P.6, (F.C.5, P.4, B.C.5, P.10) twice, F.C.5, P.4, B.C.5, P.7.

33rd Row.—K.9, (P.3, K.4, P.3, K.14) twice, P.3, K.4, P.3, K.8.

34th Row.—P.8, (F.C.5, B.C.5, P.14) twice, F.C.5, B.C.5, P.8, increase in the last st.

35th Row.—K.12, (P.6, K.18) twice, P.6, K.10.

36th Row.—P.10, (C.6, P.18) twice, C.6, P.12.

37th Row.—Increase in the first st., K.11, (P.6, K.18) twice, P.6, K.10.

38th Row.—P.10, (K.6, P.18) twice, K.6, P.13.

39th Row.—K.13, (P.6, K.18) twice, P.6, K.10.

40th Row.—P.10, (K.6, P.18) twice, K.6, P.12, increase in the last st.

41st Row.—K.14, (P.6, K.18) twice, P.6, K.10.

42nd Row.—P.10, (C.6, P.18) twice, C.6, P.14.

43rd Row.—Increase in the first st., K.13, (P.6, K.18) twice, P.6, K.10.

44th Row.—P.10, (K.6, P.18) twice, K.6, P.15.

45th Row.—K.15, (P.6, K.18) twice, P.6, K.10.

46th Row.—P.10, (K.6, P.18) twice, K.6, P.14, increase in the last st.

47th Row.—K.16, (P.6, K.18) twice, P.6, K.10.

48th Row.—P.10, (C.6, P.18) twice, C.6, P.16.

49th Row.—Increase in the first st., K.15, (P.6, K.18) twice, P.6, K.10.

50th Row.—P.10, (K.6, P.18) twice, K.6, P.17.

51st Row.—K.17, (P.6, K.18) twice, P.6, K.10.

52nd Row.—P.10, (K.6, P.18 twice, K.6, P.16, increase in the last st.

53rd Row.—K.18, (P.6, K.18) twice, P.6, K.10.

54th Row.—P.10, (C.6, P.18) twice, C.6, P.18.

55th Row.—Increase in the first st., K.17, (P.6, K.18) twice, P.6, K.10.

56th Row.—P.10, (K.6, P.18) twice, K.6, P.19.

57th Row.—K.19, (P.6, K.18) twice, P.6, K.10.

58th Row.—P.10, (K.6, P.18) twice, K.6, P.18, increase in the last st.

59th Row.—K.20, (P.6, K.18) twice, P.6, K.10.

60th Row.—P.10, (C.6, P.18) twice, C.6, P.19, K.1.

61st Row.—Increase in the first st., P.1, (K.18, P.6) 3 times, K.10.

62nd Row.—P.9, (B.C.4, F.C.4, P.16) 3 times, B.C.4.

63rd Row.—K.1, (P.3, K.16, P.3, K.2) 3 times, P.3, K.9.

64th Row.—P.7, (B.C.5, P.2, F.C.5, P.12) 3 times, B.C.5, increase in the last st.

65th Row.—K.4, (P.3, K.12, P.3, K.6) 3 times, P.3, K.7.

66th Row.—P.5, (B.C.5, P.6, F.C.5, P.8) 3 times, B.C.5, P.4.

67th Row.—Increase in the first st., K.5, (P.3, K.8, P.3, K.10) 3 times, P.3, K.5. (87 sts. now on the needle.}

68th Row.—P.3, (B.C.5, P.10, F.C.5, P.4) 3 times, B.C.5, P.7.

69th Row.—K.9, (P.3, K.4, P.3, K.14) 3 times, P.3, K.3.

70th Row.—P.1, (B.C.5, P.14, F.C.5) 3 times, B.C.5, P.9.

71st Row.—K.11, (P.6, K.18) 3 times, P.3, K.1.

72nd Row.—P.1, K.3, (P.18, C.6) 3 times, P.11.

73rd Row.—K.11, (P.6, K.18) 3 times, P.3, K.1.

74th Row.—P.1, K.3, (P.18, K.6) 3 times, P.11.

75th—77th Rows.—Repeat the 73rd and 74th rows, then repeat the 73rd row.

78th Row.—P.1, K.3, (P.18, C.6) 3 times, P.11.

Shape the Armhole as follows :—

1st Row.—Cast off 11 sts., P. the following 5 sts., there now being 6 sts. on the right-hand needle after the casting-off, (K.18, P.6) twice, K.18, P.3, K.1.

2nd Row.—P.1, K.3, (P.18, K.6) twice, P.18, K.4, sl.1, K.1, p.s.s.o.

3rd Row.—P.2 tog.t.b.s., P.3, (K.18, P.6) twice, K.18, P.3, K.1.

4th Row.—P.1, K.3, (P.18, K.6) twice, P.18, K.2, sl.1, K.1, p.s.s.o.

5th Row.—P.2 tog.t.b.s., P.1, (K.18, P.6) twice, K.18, P.3, K.1.

6th Row.—P.1, K.3, (P.18, C.6) twice, P.18, sl.1, K.1, p.s.s.o.

7th Row.—K.2 tog., K.17, (P.6, K.18) twice, P.3, K.1.

8th Row.—P.1, (F.C.4, P.16, B.C.4) twice, F.C.4, P.15, P.2 tog.

9th Row.—K.2 tog., K.14, P.3, K.2, (P.3, K.16, P.3, K.2) twice.

10th Row.—(P.2, F.C.5, P.12, B.C.5) twice, P.2, F.C.5, P.11, P.2 tog.

11th Row.—K.2 tog., K.10, P.3, (K.6, P.3, K.12, P.3) twice, K.4.

12th Row.—P.4, (F.C.5, P.8, B.C.5, P.6) twice, F.C.5, P.7, P.2 tog.

13th Row.—K.2 tog., K.6, P.3, (K.10, P.3, K.8, P.3) twice, K.6.

14th Row.—P.6, (F.C.5, P.4, B.C.5, P.10) twice, F.C.5, P.3, P.2 tog.

15th Row.—K.2 tog., K.2, P.3, (K.14, P.3, K.4, P.3) twice, K.8.
The armhole shaping is now completed and 62 sts. remain.
Proceed as follows :—

***1st Row.**—P.8, (F.C.5, B.C.5, P.14) twice, F.C.5, P.1.

2nd Row.—K.1, P.3, (K.18, P.6) twice, K.10.

3rd Row.—P.10, (C.6, P.18) twice, K.3, P.1.

4th Row.—K.1, P.3, (K.18, P.6) twice, K.10.

5th Row.—P.10, (K.6, P.18) twice, K.6, P.10.

6th—8th Rows.—Repeat the 4th and 5th rows, then repeat the 4th row.

9th—28th Rows.—Repeat rows 3—8 inclusive 3 times, then repeat the 3rd and 4th rows.

29th Row.—P.9, (B.C.4, F.C.4, P.16) twice, B.C.4, P.1.

30th Row.—K.2, (P.3, K.16, P.3, K.2) twice, P.3, K.9.

31st Row.—P.7, B.C.5, P.2, (F.C.5, P.12, B.C.5, P.2) twice.

32nd Row.—K.4, (P.3, K.12, P.3, K.6) twice, P.3, K.7.

33rd Row.—P.5, B.C.5, (P.6, F.C.5, P.8, B.C.5) twice, P.4.

34th Row.—K.6, (P.3, K.8, P.3, K.10) twice, P.3, K.5.

35th Row.—P.3, B.C.5, (P.10, F.C.5, P.4, B.C.5) twice, P.6.

36th Row.—K.8, (P.3, K.4, P.3, K.14) twice, P.3, K.3.

37th Row.—P.1, B.C.5, (P.14, F.C.5, B.C.5) twice, P.8.

38th Row.—K.10, (P.6, K.18) twice, P.3, K.1.

39th Row.—P.1, K.3, (P.18, C.6) twice, P.10.

40th Row.—As the 38th row.***

Shape the Neck as follows :—

1st Row.—Cast off 12 sts., P. the following 9 sts., there now being 10 sts. on the right-hand needle after the casting-off, K.6, P.18, K.6, P.10.

2nd Row.—K.10, P.6, K.18, P.6, K.8, sl.1, K.1, p.s.s.o.

3rd Row.—P.9, K.6, P.18, K.6, P.10.

4th Row.—K.10, P.6, K.18, P.6, K.7, sl.1, K.1, p.s.s.o.

5th Row.—P.8, C.6, P.18, C.6, P.10.

6th Row.—K.10, P.6, K.18, P.6, K.6, sl.1, K.1, p.s.s.o.

7th Row.—P.7, K.6, P.18, K.6, P.10.

8th Row.—K.10, P.6, K.18, P.6, K.5, sl.1, K.1, p.s.s.o.

9th Row.—P.6, K.6, P.18, K.6, P.10.

10th Row.—K.10, P.6, K.18, P.6, K.4, sl.1, K.1, p.s.s.o.

11th Row.—P.5, C.6, P.18, C.6, P.10.

12th Row.—K.10, P.6, K.18, P.6, K.3, sl.1, K.1, p.s.s.o.

13th Row.—P.4, K.6, P.18, K.6, P.10.

14th Row.—K.10, P.6, K.18, P.6, K.2, sl.1, K.1, p.s.s.o. (43 sts. remain.)

15th Row.—P.3, K.6, P.18, K.6, P.10.

16th Row.—K.10, P.6, K.18, P.6, K.3.

17th Row.—P.3, C.6, P.18, C.6, P.10.

18th Row.—K.10, P.6, K.18, P.6, K.3.

19th Row.—P.3, K.6, P.18, K.6, P.10.

20th—22nd Rows.—Repeat the 18th and 19th rows, then repeat the 18th row.

23rd—28th Rows.—As rows 17—22 inclusive.

Shape the Shoulder as follows :—

1st Row.—P.3, C.6, P.18, K.2, turn.

2nd Row.—P.2, K.18, P.6, K.3.

3rd Row.—P.3, K.6, P.6, turn.

4th Row.—K.6, P.6, K.3.
Cast off.

THE LEFT FRONT.

Cast on 65 sts.

1st Row.—Working into the back of the sts., P.1,* K.6, P.2, repeat from * to the end.

2nd Row.—*K.2, P.6, repeat from * to the last st., K.1.

3rd Row.—P.1, * K.6, P.2, repeat from * to the end.

4th Row.—As the 2nd row.

5th Row.—P.1, * C.6, P.2, repeat from * to the end.

6th Row.—*K.2, P.6, repeat from * to the last st., K.1.

7th Row.—P.1, * K.6, P.2, repeat from * to the end.

8th—10th Rows.—Repeat the 6th and 7th rows, then repeat the 6th row.
Rows 5—10 inclusive form the cable.
Repeat rows 5—10 inclusive 6 times more than repeat the 5th row.

Proceed in pattern, increasing as follows :—

1st Row.—K.10, (P.6, K.18) twice, P.6, K.1.

2nd Row.—(B.C.4, F.C.4, P.16) twice, B.C.4, F.C.4, P.9.

3rd Row.—K.9, (P.3, K.2, P.3, K.16) twice, P.3, K.2, P.3.

4th Row.—Increase in the first st., K.1, P.3, (F.C.5, P.12, B.C.5, P.2) twice, F.C.5, P.7.
Now repeat rows 5—78 inclusive of the increase rows on the Right Front, but reading the rows from the **end** to the **beginning**, also F.C. for B.C. and B.C. for F.C., thus the 5th and 6th rows will read :—
5th Row.—K.7, P.3, (K.6, P.3, K.12, P.3) twice, K.6, P.2. **6th Row.**—K.1, P.7, F.C.5, (P.8, B.C.5, P.6, F.C.5) twice, P.5.

Shape the Armhole as follows :—

1st Row.—K.1, P.3, (K.18, P.6) 3 times, cast off the remaining sts. Break off wool.

2nd Row.—Rejoin the wool ; K.2 tog., K.4, P.18, (K.6, P.18) twice, K.3, P.1.

3rd Row.—K.1, P.3, K.18, (P.6, K.18) twice, P.3, P.2 tog.

4th Row.—K.2 tog., K.2, P.18, (K.6, P.18) twice, K.3, P.1.

5th Row.—K.1, P.3, K.18, (P.6, K.18) twice, P.1, P.2 tog.

6th Row.—K.2 tog., P.18, (C.6, P.18) twice, K.3, P.1.

7th Row.—K.1, P.3, (K.18, P.6) twice, K.17, sl.1, K.1, p.s.s.o.

8th Row.—P.2 tog.t.b.s., P.15, B.C.4, (F.C.4, P.16, B.C.4) twice, P.1.

9th Row.—(K.2, P.3, K.16, P.3) twice, K.2, P.3, K.14, sl.1, K.1, p.s.s.o.

10th Row.—P.2 tog.t.b.s., P.11, B.C.5, P.2, (F.C.5, P.12, B.C.5, P.2) twice.

11th Row.—K.4, (P.3, K.12, P.3, K.6) twice, P.3, K.10, sl.1, K.1, p.s.s.o.

12th Row.—P.2 tog.t.b.s., P.7, B.C.5, (P.6, F.C.5, P.8, B.C.5) twice, P.4.

13th Row.—K.6, (P.3, K.8, P.3, K.10) twice, P.3, K.6, sl.1, K.1, p.s.s.o.

14th Row.—P.2 tog.t.b.s., P.3, B.C.5, (P.10, F.C.5, P.4, B.C.5) twice, P.6.

15th Row.—K.8, (P.3, K.4, P.3, K.14) twice, P.3, K.2, sl.1, K.1, p.s.s.o.
The armhole shaping is now completed and 62 sts. remain.

Now proceed as the instructions for the Right Front from *** to ***, but reading the rows from the **end** to the **beginning** also B.C. for F.C. and F.C. for B.C.

Shape the Neck as follows :—

1st Row.—P.10, K.6, P.18, K.6, P.10, cast off the remaining sts. Break off wool.

2nd Row.—Rejoin the wool; K.2 tog., K.8, P.6, K.18, P.6, K.10.

3rd Row.—P.10, K.6, P.18, K.6, P.9.

4th Row.—K.2 tog., K.7, P.6, K.18, P.6, K.10.

5th Row.—P.10, C.6, P.18, C.6, P.8.

6th Row.—K.2 tog., K.6, P.6, K.18, P.6, K.10.

7th Row.—P.10, K.6, P.18, K.6, P.7.

8th Row.—K.2 tog., K.5, P.6, K.18, P.6, K.10.

9th Row.—P.10, K.6, P.18, K.6, P.6.

10th Row.—K.2 tog., K.4, P.6, K.18, P.6, K.10.

11th Row.—P.10, C.6, P.18, C.6, P.5.

12th Row.—K.2 tog., K.3, P.6, K.18, P.6, K.10.

13th Row.—P.10, K.6, P.18, K.6, P.4.

14th Row.—K.2 tog., K.2, P.6, K.18, P.6, K.10. (43 sts. remain.)

15th Row.—P.10, K.6, P.18, K.6, P.3.

16th Row.—K.3, P.6, K.18, P.6, K.10.

17th Row.—P.10, C.6, P.18, C.6, P.3.

18th Row.—K.3, P.6, K.18, P.6, K.10.

19th Row.—P.10, K.6, P.18, K.6, P.3.

20th—22nd Rows.—Repeat the 18th and 19th rows, then repeat the 18th row.

23rd—28th Rows.—As rows 17—22 inclusive.

29th Row.—P.10, K.6, P.18, C.6, P.3.

Shape the Shoulder as follows :—

1st Row.—K.3, P.6, K.18, P.2, turn.

2nd Row.—K.2, P.18, K.6, P.3.

3rd Row.—K.3, P.6, K.6, turn.

4th Row.—P.6, K.6, P.3.
Cast off.

THE BACK

Cast on 128 sts.

1st Row.—Working into the back of the sts., * P.1, K.6, P.1, repeat from * to the end.

2nd Row.—*K.1, P.6, K.1, repeat from * to the end.

3rd Row.—*P.1, K.6, P.1, repeat from * to the end.

4th Row.—As the 2nd row.

5th Row.—*P.1, C.6, P.1, repeat from * to the end.

6th Row.—*K.1, P.6, K.1, repeat from * to the end.

7th Row.—*P.1, K.6, P.1, repeat from * to the end.

8th—10th Rows.—Repeat the 6th and 7th rows, then repeat the 6th row.
Rows 5—10 inclusive form the cable.
Repeat rows 5—10 inclusive 6 times more, then repeat the 5th row.

Proceed in pattern, increasing as follows :—

1st Row.—K.1, (P.6, K.18) 5 times, P.6, K.1.

2nd Row.—(B.C.4, F.C.4, P.16) 5 times, B.C.4, F.C.4.

3rd Row.—(P.3, K.2, P.3, K.16) 5 times, P.3, K.2, P.3.

4th Row.—Increase in the first st., K.1, P.3, (F.C.5, P.12, B.C.5, P.2) 5 times, P.1, K.1, increase in the last st.

5th Row.—P.2, K.6, (P.3, K.12, P.3, K.6) 5 times, P.2.

6th Row.—K.1, P.7, (F.C.5, P.8, B.C.5, P.6) 5 times, P.1, K.1.

7th Row.—Increase in the first st., K.9, (P.3, K.8, P.3, K.10) 4 times, P.3, K.8, P.3, K.9, increase in the last st.

8th Row.—P.11, (F.C.5, P.4, B.C.5, P.10) 4 times, F.C.5, P.4, B.C.5, P.11.

9th Row.—K.13, (P.3, K.4, P.3, K.14) 4 times, P.3, K.4, P.3, K.13.

10th Row.—Increase in the first st., P.12, (F.C.5, B.C.5, P.14) 4 times, F.C.5, B.C.5, P.12, increase in the last st.

11th Row.—K.16, (P.6, K.18) 4 times, P.6, K.16.

12th Row.—P.16, (C.6, P.18) 4 times, C.6, P.16.

13th Row.—Increase in the first st., K.15, (P.6, K.18) 4 times, P.6, K.15, increase in the last st.

14th Row.—P.17, (K.6, P.18) 4 times, K.6, P.17.

15th Row.—K.17, (P.6, K.18) 4 times, P.6, K.17.

16th Row.—Increase in the first st., P.16, (K.6, P.18) 4 times, K.6, P.16, increase in the last st.

17th Row.—(K.18, P.6) 5 times, K.18.

18th Row.—(P.18, C.6) 5 times, P.18.

19th Row.—Increase in the first st., K.17, (P.6, K.18) 4 times, P.6, K.17, increase in the last st.

20th Row.—P.19, (K.6, P.18) 4 times, K.6, P.19.

21st Row.—K.19, (P.6, K.18) 4 times, P.6, K.19.

22nd Row.—Increase in the first st., (P.18, K.6) 5 times, P.18, increase in the last st.

23rd Row.—K.20, (P.6, K.18) 4 times, P.6, K.20.

24th Row.—K.1, P.1, (P.18, C.6) 5 times, P.19, K.1.

25th Row.—Increase in the first st., P.1, (K.18, P.6) 5 times, K.18, P.1, increase in the last st.

26th Row.—(F.C.4, P.16, B.C.4) 6 times.

27th Row.—K.1, (P.3, K.16, P.3, K.2) 5 times, P.3, K.16, P.3, K.1.

28th Row.—Increase in the first st., (F.C.5, P.12, B.C.5, P.2) 5 times, F.C.5, P.12, B.C.5, increase in the last st.

29th Row.—K.4, (P.3, K.12, P.3, K.6) 5 times, P.3, K.12, P.3, K.4.

30th Row.—P.4, (F.C.5, P.8, B.C.5, P.6) 5 times, F.C.5, P.8, B.C.5, P.4.

31st Row.—Increase in the first st., K.5, (P.3, K.8, P.3, K.10) 5 times, P.3, K.8, P.3, K.5, increase in the last st.

32nd Row.—P.7, (F.C.5, P.4, B.C.5, P.10) 5 times, F.C.5, P.4, B.C.5, P.7.

33rd Row.—K.9, (P.3, K.4, P.3, K.14) 5 times, P.3, K.4, P.3, K.9.

34th Row.—Increase in the first st., P.8, (F.C.5, B.C.5, P.14) 5 times, F.C.5, B.C.5, P.8, increase in the last st.

35th Row.—K.12, (P.6, K.18) 5 times, P.6, K.12.

36th Row.—P.12, (C.6, P.18) 5 times, C.6, P.12.

37th Row.—Increase in the first st., K.11, (P.6, K.18) 5 times, P.6, K.11, increase in the last st.

38th Row.—P.13, (K.6, P.18) 5 times, K.6, P.13.

39th Row.—K.13, (P.6, K.18) 5 times, P.6, K.13.

40th Row.—Increase in the first st., P.12, (K.6, P.18) 5 times, K.6, P.12, increase in the last st.

41st Row.—K.14, (P.6, K.18) 5 times, P.6, K.14.

42nd Row.—P.14, (C.6, P.18) 5 times, C.6, P.14.

43rd Row.—Increase in the first st., K.13, (P.6, K.18) 5 times, P.6, K.13, increase in the last st.

44th Row.—P.15, (K.6, P.18) 5 times, K.6, P.15.

45th Row.—K.15, (P.6, K.18) 5 times, P.6, K.15.

46th Row.—Increase in the first st., P.14, (K.6, P.18) 5 times, K.6, P.14, increase in the last st.

47th Row.—K.16, (P.6, K.18) 5 times, P.6, K.16.

48th Row.—P.16, (C.6, P.18) 5 times, C.6, P.16.

49th Row.—Increase in the first st., K.15, (P.6, K.18) 5 times, P.6, K.15, increase in the last st.

50th Row.—P.17, (K.6, P.18) 5 times, K.6, P.17.

51st Row.—K.17, (P.6, K.18) 5 times, P.6, K.17.

52nd Row.—Increase in the first st., P.16, (K.6, P.18) 5 times, K.6, P.16, increase in the last st.

53rd Row.—(K.18, P.6) 6 times, K.18.

54th Row.—(P.18, C.6) 6 times, P.18.

55th Row.—Increase in the first st., K.17, (P.6, K.18) 5 times, P.6, K.17, increase in the last st.

56th Row.—P.1, (P.18, K.6) 6 times, P.19.

57th Row.—K.1, (K.18, P.6) 6 times, K.19.

58th Row.—Increase in the first st., (P.18, K.6) 6 times, P.18, increase in the last st.

59th Row.—K.2, (K.18, P.6) 6 times, K.20.

60th Row.—K.1, P.19, (C.6, P.18) 5 times, C.6, P.19, K.1.

61st Row.—Increase in the first st., P.1, (K.18, P.6) 6 times, P.18, K.1, increase in the last st.

62nd Row.—(F.C.4, P.16, B.C.4) 7 times.

63rd Row.—K.1, (P.3, K.16, P.3, K.2) 6 times, P.3, K.16, P.3, K.1.

64th Row.—Increase in the first st., (F.C.5, P.12, B.C.5, P.2) 6 times, F.C.5, P.12, B.C.5, increase in the last st.

65th Row.—K.4, (P.3, K.12, P.3, K.6) 6 times, P.3, K.12, P.3, K.4.

66th Row.—P.4, (F.C.5, P.8, B.C.5, P.6) 6 times, F.C.5, P.8, B.C.5, P.4.

67th Row.—Increase in the first st., K.5, (P.3, K.8, P.3, K.10) 6 times, P.3, K.8, P.3, K.5, increase in the last st. (172 sts. now on the needle.)

68th Row.—P.7, (F.C.5, P.4, B.C.5, P.10) 6 times, F.C.5, P.4, B.C.5, P.7.

69th Row.—K.9, (P.3, K.4, P.3, K.14) 6 times, P.3, K.4, P.3, K.9.

70th Row.—P.9, (F.C.5, B.C.5, P.14) 6 times, F.C.5, B.C.5, P.9.

71st Row.—K.11, (P.6, K.18) 6 times, P.6, K.11.

72nd Row.—P.11, (C.6, P.18) 6 times, C.6, P.11.

73rd Row.—K.11, (P.6, K.18) 6 times, P.6, K.11.

74th Row.—P.11, (K.6, P.18) 6 times, K.6, P.11.

75th—77th Rows.—Repeat the 73rd and 74th rows, then repeat the 73rd row.

78th Row.—As the 72nd row.

Shape the Armholes as follows :—

1st Row.—Cast off 11 sts., P. the following 5 sts., there now being 6 sts. on the right-hand needle after the casting-off, (K.18, P.6) 6 times, cast off the remaining sts. Break off wool.

2nd Row.—Rejoin the wool ; K.2 tog., K.4, (P.18, K.6) 5 times, P.18, K.4, sl.1, K.1, p.s.s.o.

3rd Row.—P.2 tog.t.b.s., P.3, (K.18, P.6) 5 times, K.18, P.3, P.2 tog.

4th Row.—K.2 tog., K.2, (P.18, K.6) 5 times, P.18, K.2, sl.1, K.1, p.s.s.o.

5th Row.—P.2 tog.t.b.s., P.1, (K.18, P.6) 5 times, K.18, P.1, P.2 tog.

6th Row.—K.2 tog., (P.18, C.6) 5 times, P.18, sl.1, K.1, p.s.s.o.

7th Row.—K.2 tog., K.17, (P.6, K.18) 4 times, P.6, K.17, sl.1, K.1, p.s.s.o.

8th Row.—P.2 tog.t.b.s., P.15, (B.C.4, F.C.4, P.16) 4 times, B.C.4, F.C.4, P.15, P.2 tog.

9th Row.—K.2 tog., K.14, (P.3, K.2, P.3, K.16) 4 times, P.3, K.2, P.3, K.14, sl.1, K.1, p.s.s.o.

10th Row.—P.2 tog.t.b.s., P.11, (B.C.5, P.2, F.C.5, P.12) 4 times, B.C.5, P.2, F.C.5, P.11, P.2 tog.

11th Row.—K.2 tog., K.10, (P.3, K.6, P.3, K.12) 4 times, P.3, K.6, P.3, K.10, sl.1, K.1, p.s.s.o.

12th Row.—P.2 tog.t.b.s., P.7, (B.C.5, P.6, F.C.5, P.8) 4 times, B.C.5, P.6, F.C.5, P.7, P.2 tog.

13th Row.—K.2 tog., K.6, (P.3, K.10, P.3, K.8) 4 times, P.3, K.10., P.3, K.6, sl.1, K.1, p.s.s.o.

14th Row.—P.2 tog.t.b.s., P.3, (B.C.5, P.10, F.C.5, P.4) 4 times, B.C.5, P.10, F.C.5, P.3, P.2 tog.

15th Row.—K.2 tog., K.2, (P.3, K.14, P.3, K.4) 4 times, P.3, K.14, P.3, K.2, sl.1, K.1, p.s.s.o.

The armhole shaping is now completed and 122 sts. remain.

Proceed as follows :—

1st Row.—P.1, (B.C.5, P.14, F.C.5) 5 times, P.1.

2nd Row.—K.1, P.3, (K.18, P.6) 4 times, K.18, P.3, K.1.

3rd Row.—P.1, K.3, (P.18, C.6) 4 times, P.18, K.3, P.1.

4th Row.—K.1, P.3, (K.18, P.6) 4 times, K.18, P.3, K.1.

5th Row.—P.1, K.3, (P.18, K.6) 4 times, P.18, K.3, P.1.

6th—8th Rows.—Repeat the 4th and 5th rows, then repeat the 4th row.

9th—28th Rows.—Repeat rows 3—8 inclusive 3 times, then repeat the 3rd and 4th rows.

29th Row.—P.1, (F.C.4, P.16, B.C.4) 5 times, P.1.

30th Row.—(K.2, P.3, K.16, P.3) 5 times, P.1.

31st Row.—(P.2, F.C.5, P.12, B.C.5) 5 times, P.2.

32nd Row.—K.4, (P.3, K.12, P.3, K.6) 4 times, P.3, K.12, P.3, K.4.

33rd Row.—P.4, (F.C.5, P.8, B.C.5, P.6) 4 times, F.C.5, P.8, B.C.5, P.4.

34th Row.—K.6, (P.3, K.8, P.3, K.10) 4 times, P.3, K.8, P.3, K.6.

35th Row.—P.6, (F.C.5, P.4, B.C.5, P.10) 4 times, F.C.5, P.4, B.C.5, P.6.

36th Row.—K.8, (P.3, K.4, P.3, K.14) 4 times, P.3, K.4, P.3, K.8.

37th Row.—P.8, (F.C.5, B.C.5, P.14) 4 times, F.C.5, B.C.5, P.8.

38th Row.—K.10, (P.6, K.18) 4 times, P.6, K.10.

39th Row.—P.10, (C.6, P.18) 4 times, C.6, P.10.

40th Row.—K.10, (P.6, K.18) 4 times, P.6, K.10.

41st Row.—P.10, (K.6, P.18) 4 times, K.6, P.10.

42nd—44th Rows.—Repeat the 40th and 41st rows, then repeat the 40th row.

45th—59th Rows.—Repeat rows 39—44 inclusive twice, then repeat rows 39—41 inclusive.

60th Row.—As the 40th row.

Shape the Shoulders as follows :—

1st Row.—P.10, (K.6, P.18) 4 times, K.2, turn.

2nd Row.—P.2, (K.18, P.6) 3 times, K.18, P.2, turn.

3rd Row.—K.2, (P.18, C.6) 3 times, P.6, turn.

4th Row.—K.6, (P.6, K.18) twice, P.6, K.6, turn.

5th Row.—P.6, K.6, P.18, K.6, P.15, turn.

6th Row.—K.15, P.6, K.15. Break off wool.

Slip all the sts. on to one needle, rejoin the wool and with the right side of the work facing, cast off all across.

THE SLEEVE.

Cast on 58 sts.

1st Row.—Working into the back of the sts., * P.2, K.6, repeat from * to the last 2 sts., P.2.

2nd Row.—*K.2, P.6, repeat from * to the last 2 sts., K.2.

3rd Row.—*P.2, K.6, repeat from * to the last 2 sts., P.2.

4th Row.—As the 2nd row.

5th Row.—*P.2, C.6, repeat from * to the last 2 sts., P.2.

6th Row.—*K.2, P.6, repeat from * to the last 2 sts., K.2.

7th Row.—*P.2, K.6, repeat from * to the last 2 sts., P.2.

8th—10th Rows.—Repeat the 6th and 7th rows, then repeat the 6th row.

11th—23rd Rows.—Repeat rows 5—10 inclusive twice, then repeat the 5th row.

Proceed to increase as follows :—

1st Row.—K.2, (P.6, K.18) twice, P.6, K.2.

2nd Row.—P.2, (K.6, P.18) twice, K.6, P.2.

3rd—5th Rows.—Repeat the 1st and 2nd rows, then repeat the 1st row.

6th Row.—Increase in the first st., P.1, (C.6, P.18) twice, C.6, P.1, increase in the last st.

Keeping the cables correct and working the increased sts. in **reversed** smooth fabric, continue increasing 1 st. at both ends of every following 4th row until 15 more sets of increases have been worked and there are 90 sts. on the needle.

Keeping the cables correct and working the increased sts. in smooth fabric, increase at both ends of every following 4th row until 6 more sets of increases have been worked and there are 102 sts. on the needle.

Keeping the cables correct, continue increasing 1 st. at both ends of every following 4th row, working the increased sts. in **reversed** smooth fabric, until 5 more sets of increases have been worked and there are 112 sts. on the needle.

Keeping the cables correct, proceed without further shaping until the work measures 16 inches from the commencement, finishing at the end of a cable row.

Proceed as follows :—

1st Row.—K.5, (P.6, K.18) 4 times, P.6, K.5.

2nd Row.—P.4, (B.C.4, F.C.4, P.16) 4 times, B.C.4, F.C.4, P.4.

3rd Row.—K.4, (P.3, K.2, P.3, K.16) 4 times, P.3, K.2, P.3, K.4.

4th Row.—P.2, (B.C.5, P.2, F.C.5, P.12) 4 times, B.C.5, P.2, F.C.5, P.2.

5th Row.—K.2, (P.3, K.6, P.3, K.12) 4 times, P.3, K.6, P.3, K.2.

6th Row.—(B.C.5, P.6, F.C.5, P.8) 4 times, B.C.5, P.6, F.C.5.

7th Row.—P.3, K.10, (P.3, K.8, P.3, K.10) 4 times, P.3.

8th Row.—K.2, P.11, (F.C.5, P.4, B.C.5, P.10) 4 times, P.1, K.2.

9th Row.—P.1, K.14, (P.3, K.4, P.3, K.14) 4 times, P.1.

10th Row.—P.15, (F.C.5, B.C.5, P.14) 4 times, P.1.

11th Row.—K.17, (P.6, K.18) 3 times, P.6, K.17.

12th Row.—P.17, (C.6, P.18) 3 times, C.6, P.17.

13th Row.—K.17, (P.6, K.18) 3 times, P.6, K.17.

14th Row.—P.17, (K.6, P.18) 3 times, K.6, P.17.

15th—17th Rows.—Repeat the 13th and 14th rows, then repeat the 13th row.

18th Row.—As the 12th row.

Shape the Top as follows :—

1st Row.—Cast off 7 sts., K. the following 9 sts., there now being 10 sts. on the right-hand needle after the casting-off, (P.6, K.18) 3 times, P.6, K.10, cast off the remaining sts. Break off wool.

2nd Row.—Rejoin the wool ; P.10, (K.6, P.18) 3 times, K.6, P.10.

3rd Row.—K.2 tog., K.8, (P.6, K.18) 3 times, P.6, K.8, sl.1, K.1, p.s.s.o.

4th Row.—P.9, (K.6, P.18) 3 times, K.6, P.9.

5th Row.—K.2 tog., K.7, (P.6, K.18) 3 times, P.6, K.7, sl.1, K.1, p.s.s.o.

6th Row.—K.8, (C.6, P.18) 3 times, C.6, P.8.

7th Row.—K.2 tog., K.6, (P.6, K.18) 3 times, P.6, K.6, sl.1, K.1, p.s.s.o.

8th Row.—P.6, B.C.4, (F.C.4, P.16, B.C.4) 3 times, F.C.4, P.6.

9th Row.—K.2 tog., K.4, P.3, K.2, (P.3, K.16., P.3, K.2) 3 times, P.3, K.4, sl.1, K.1, p.s.s.o.

10th Row.—P.3, B.C.5, P.2, (F.C.5, P.12, B.C.5, P.2) 3 times, F.C.5, P.3.

11th Row.—K.2 tog., K.1, P.3, K.6, (P.3, K.12, P.3, K.6) 3 times, P.3, K.1, sl.1, K.1, p.s.s.o.

12th Row.—B.C.5, P.6, (F.C.5, P.8, B.C.5, P.6) 3 times, F.C.5.

13th Row.—P.2 tog., P.1, K.10, (P.3, K.8, P.3, K.10) 3 times, P.1, P.2 tog.t.b.s.

14th Row.—K.1, P.11, (F.C.5, P.4, B.C.5, P.10) 3 times, P.1, K.1.

15th Row.—K.2 tog., K.12, (P.3, K.4, P.3, K.14) twice, P.3, K.4, P.3, K.12, sl.1, K.1, p.s.s.o.

16th Row.—P.13, (F.C.5, B.C.5, P.14) twice, F.C.5, B.C.5, P.13.

17th Row.—K.2 tog., K.13, (P.6, K.18) twice, P.6, K.13, sl.1, K.1, p.s.s.o.

18th Row.—P.14, (C.6, P.18) twice, C.6, P.14.

19th Row.—K.2 tog., K.12, (P.6, K.18) twice, P.6, K.12, sl.1, K.1, p.s.s.o.

20th Row.—P.13, (K.6, P.18) twice, K.6, P.13.

Keeping the cables correct, continue decreasing 1 st. at both ends of the next and every alternative row, until 68 sts. remain.

Work 1 row.

Now decrease at both ends of every row, until 26 sts. remain.

Cast off.

Work another sleeve in the same manner.

MAKE-UP

Press the work lightly on the wrong side, using a warm iron and a damp cloth.

Embroider each diamond-shaped portion of the work with a flower spray as shown in the photograph, using the sts. illustrated in the diagram.

Press the embroidery lightly on the wrong side.

Join the shoulders of the Back and Fronts together.

Join the side and sleeve seams.

Stitch the sleeves into position, care being taken to match the pattern wherever possible.

Using the crochet hook and with the right side of the work facing, join the wool to the lower edge and work 1 row of d.c. up the edge of the Right Front, finishing at the neck and missing the edge of every 3rd row (on the original 120 sts. were worked), now work in d.c. round the neck, working st. into st. and working 3 d.c. into the corner sts. Finally work in d.c. down the Left Front, finishing at the lower edge, missing the edge of every 3rd row., 1 ch., turn. Working through both top loops of the sts. of the previous row and working 3 d.c. into each corner st. work 3 more rows in d.c., turning at the end of each row with 1 ch.

Next Row.—Work 7 d.c., * 4 ch., miss the following 4 sts., 1 d.c. into the following 10 sts., repeat from * 7 times more, 4 ch., miss the following 4 sts., working 3 d.c. into the corner sts., continue in d.c. to the end of the row., 1 ch., turn.

Work 3 more rows in d.c. Fasten off.

Press all seams and the crochet edges.

Attach the buttons on to the Left Front to correspond with the buttonholes.

Long st.

Lazy Daisy st.

French knot

Stem st.

Springtime Bolero

MATERIALS
Excelana 4 Ply Luxury Wool 100% pure new British wool (159m/174yds per 50g ball)
5 (5, 5, 6, 6) balls shade Powdered Egg
1 pair 2.75mm (US #2) needles

TENSION
30 sts & 50 rows = 10cm (4in) using 2.75mm needles over moss stitch
9 stitches in rib = 2½cm (1in) unstretched using 2.75mm needles

Standard Yarn Tension
28 sts & 36 rows = 10cm (4in) using 3mm needles over stocking stitch

ABBREVIATIONS
See page 13 for standard abbreviations

SIZING
Measurements given in centimetres followed by inches in parentheses

To Fit	76–81 (30–32)	86–92 (34–36)	92–97 (36–38)	97–102 (38–40)	102–106 (40–42)
Finished Measurements					
Actual Bust Size (twice back width)	85 (33½)	91 (36)	96 (38)	101 (40)	107 (42)
Length to underarm	24 (9½)	24 (9½)	24 (9½)	25 (10)	25 (10)
Armhole Depth	19 (7½)	19 (7½)	20½ (8)	20½ (8)	22 (8½)
Finished Length	43 (17)	43 (17)	44½ (17½)	45½ (18)	47 (18½)
Shoulder to Shoulder	32 (12½)	34½ (13½)	36½ (14½)	38½ (15)	40½ (16)

Garment shown in photographs is for first size 76–81 (30–32)

PATTERN NOTES
The fronts of the bolero are shaped using a combination of short rows and decrease rows, with the fronts beginning at centre front. The short rows are worked using Yarn Over Method (see 'Knitting Know How'). Additional decrease rows are also worked which alter the rib worked on each subsequent decrease from K4, P2 down to K1, P1, reducing the number of stitches as you work towards the armhole from the centre front. On the right front, decreases are worked on rows when the shoulder edge of the work is the beginning of the row (this is the RS of the work). The back is worked in moss st from bottom to top.

BACK
Using 2.75mm needles, cast on 100 (108, 116, 124, 132) sts.
Row 1 (RS): * K1, P1, rep from * to end.
Row 2 (WS): * P1, K1, rep from * to end.
These 2 rows set moss stitch pattern. Cont in patt, inc 1 st at each end of 4th row and 13 foll 6th rows (128, 136, 144, 152, 160 sts).
Cont without shaping until work measures 24 (24, 24, 25, 25) cm (9½, 9½, 9½, 10, 10 in) from beginning.

Shape Armholes
Cast off 6 (6, 7, 8, 9) at beg of next 2 rows and 2 sts at beg of foll 2 rows (116, 124, 130, 136, 142 sts). Dec 1 st at each end of every alt row until 96 (104, 110, 116, 122) sts. Cont on these sts until work measures 19 (19, 20½, 20½, 22) cm (7½, 7½, 8, 8, 8½ in) from beg of armhole shaping.

Shape Shoulders
Cast off 11 (12, 13, 13, 14) sts at beg of next 6 rows.

Cast off rem 30 (32, 32, 38, 38) sts.

LEFT FRONT
Using 2.75mm needles, and commencing at front edge, cast on 216 (222, 228, 234, 240) sts.
Work in rib as folls:
Row 1 (RS): * K4, P2, rep from * to end.
Row 2: * K2, P4, rep from * to end.
Rep these 2 rows until work measures 4cm (1½in) ending with row 2.

Commence Short Row Shaping
Rows 1 & 2: Rib 30 (30, 31, 31, 32), turn, YO, work to end in rib as set.
Rows 3 & 4: Rib 30 (30, 31, 31, 32), work the YO and next st together to prevent hole, rib 29 (29, 30, 30, 31), turn, YO, work to end in rib as set.
Rows 5 & 6: Rib 60 (60, 62, 62, 64), work the YO and the

next st together to prevent hole, rib 29 (29, 30, 30, 31), turn, YO, work to end in rib as set.

Rows 7 & 8: Rib 90 (90, 93, 93, 96), work the YO and next st together to prevent hole, rib 29 (29, 30, 30, 31), turn, YO, work to end in rib as set.

Continue as set working 30 (30, 31, 31, 32) more sts on each pair of rows until 4 more pairs of rows have been worked. The final pair will leave 6 (12, 11, 17, 16) sts unworked at shoulder.

Work 2 rows over all sts in rib, finishing at side edge.
Next row (RS): * K2, K2tog, P2, rep from * to end (180, 185, 190, 195, 200 sts).
Next row: * K2, P3, rep from * to end.
Next row: * K3, P2, rep from * to end.
Repeat last 2 rows until work measures 6½cm (2½in) at shoulder edge, ending at side edge.
Next pair of rows: Rib 25 (25, 26, 26, 27) sts, turn, YO, work back.

Remembering to work sts together as before, work 6 more pairs of rows – 25 (25, 26, 26, 27) more sts are worked in rib on each pair of rows. The final pair will leave 5 (10, 8, 13, 11) sts unworked at shoulder.

Work 2 rows over all sts, finishing at side edge.
Next row: * K1, K2tog, P2, rep from * to end, (144, 148, 152, 156, 160 sts).
Next row: * K2, P2, rep from * to end.
Repeat this row until shoulder edge measures 9cm (3½in) ending at side edge.

Next row: Rib 20 (20, 21, 21, 22) sts turn, YO, work back. Working sts together as before, work 6 more pairs of rows – (20, 20, 21, 21, 22) more sts are worked in rib on each pair of rows. The final pair will leave 4 (8, 5, 9, 6) sts unworked at shoulder. Work 2 rows over all sts finishing at side edge.
Next row (RS): * K2tog, P2, repeat from * to end (108, 111, 114, 117, 120 sts).
Next row: * K2, P1, repeat from * to end.
Next row: * K1, P2, repeat from * to end.
Repeat last 2 rows until shoulder edge measures 11½ (11½, 11½, 12½, 12½) cm (4½, 4½, 4½, 5, 5 in) ending at side edge.
Next row: * K1, P2tog, rep from * to end (72, 74, 76, 78, 80 sts).
Next row: * K1, P1, rep from * to end.
Rep this row until shoulder edge measures 13 (13½, 13½, 14½, 14½) cm (5, 5¼, 5¼, 5¾, 5¾ in).
Cast off loosely in rib.

RIGHT FRONT
Work to match Left Front, commencing each pair of short rows on WS of work and starting decrease rows with shoulder edge of rows facing.

MAKING UP
Press pieces lightly on WS through a damp cloth. Join shoulder and side seams. Darn in all ends.

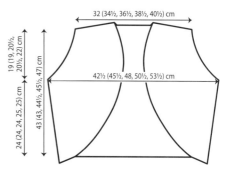

BOLERO

MATERIALS.—6 (6, 7, 7, 8) ounces of W.G. "Springtime" Wool and Tinsel Boucle. No. 12 needles. Medium crochet hook.

MEASUREMENTS.—To fit a 30 (32, 34, 36, 38) inch bust. The figures in brackets refer to the 32, 34, 36, 38 inch sizes.

TENSION.—9 sts. over rib; 8 sts. over moss st.=1 inch.

BACK.—Cast on 100 (108, 116, 124, 132) sts. Work in moss st. Inc. 1 st. at both ends every ½ inch, 14 times, 128 (136, 144, 152, 160) sts. Continue without further shaping until work measures 8 (8, 8½, 8½, 9) in. from beg. **Shape Armholes**—Cast off 6 (6, 7, 8, 9) sts. at beg. of next 2 rows, and 2 sts. at beg. of foll. 2 rows. Dec. 1 st. at both ends of every alt. row until there are 96 (104, 110, 116, 122) sts. Continue on these sts. until work measures 7½ (7½, 8, 8, 8½) in. from beg. of armhole shaping. **Shape Shoulders**—Cast off 11 (12, 13, 13, 14) sts. at beg. of next 6 rows. Cast off.

LEFT FRONT.—Com. at front edge cast on 216 (222, 228, 234, 240) sts. Work in rib as follows: **Row 1**—* k.4, p.2, rep. from * to end. **Row 2**—* k.2, p.4, rep. from * to end. Rep. these 2 rows until work measures 1½ in., ending with a 2nd row. **Commence Shaping**—**Row 1**—Rib 30 (30, 31, 31, 32) sts. turn, M.1, work back. **Row 3**—Rib 30 (30, 31, 31, 32) sts., work the M.1 and next st. tog., to prevent hole, then rib 29 (29, 30, 30, 31) sts., turn, M.1, work back. Cont. in this way working 30 (30, 31, 31, 32) sts. more on next and every alt. row, 5 times more; turn, M.1, work back, thus leaving 6 (12, 11, 17, 16) sts. unworked at shoulder. Work 2 rows over all sts. in rib thus finishing at side edge. **Next row**—* k.2, k.2 tog., p.2, rep. from * to end. 180 (185, 190, 195, 200) sts. **Next row**—* k.2, p.3, rep. from * to end. **Next row**—* k.3, p.2, rep. from * to end. Rep. last 2 rows until work measures 2½ in. at shoulder edge, finishing at side edge. **Next row**—Rib 25 (25, 26, 26, 27) sts., turn, M.1, work back. Cont. working sts. tog. as before, and working 25 (25, 26, 26, 27) sts. more on next and every alt. row, 6 times more, thus leaving 5 (10, 8, 13, 11) sts. unworked at shoulder. Work 2 rows over all sts., thus finishing at side edge. **Next row**—* k.1, k.2 tog., p.2, rep. from * to end, 144 (148, 152, 156, 160) sts. Work in k.2, p.2 rib until shoulder edge measures 3½ in., finishing at side edge. **Next row**—Rib 20 (20, 21, 21, 22) sts., turn, M.1, work back. Cont. working sts. tog. as before, and working 20 (20, 21, 21, 22) sts. more on next and every alt. row 6 times more, thus leaving

4 (8, 5, 9, 6) sts. unworked at shoulder. Work 2 rows over all sts. thus finishing at side edge. **Next row**—* k.2 tog., p.2, rep. from * to end, 108 (111, 114, 117, 120) sts . **Next row**—* k.2, p.1, rep. from * to end. **Next row**—* k.1, p.2, rep. from * to end. Rep. last 2 rows until shoulder edge measures 4¼ (4½, 4½, 5, 5) in., finishing at side edge. **Next row**—* k.1, p.2 tog., rep. from * to end, 72 (74, 76, 78, 80) sts. Work in k.1, p.1 rib until shoulder edge measures 5 (5¼, 5¼, 5¼, 5¾) in. Cast off loosely in rib.

RIGHT FRONT.—Work to match Left Front, commencing turning rows on wrong side of work and decreases at shoulder edge.

Sew shoulder and underarm seams, easing in if necessary. Work 1 row of double crochet around all edges. Press.

ABBREVIATIONS

Alt., alternate; beg., beginning; ch., chain; cl., cluster; c.o.h., cotton over hook; ctn., cotton; c.o., cotton over; cont., continue; sc., single crochet; dc., double crochet; dec., decrease (by taking 2 stitches together); foll., following; inc., increase (by working into the front and then into the back of a stitch); K. k, knit; lp(s), loop(s); P, p, purl; p., picot; p.s.s.o., pass slip stitch over; patt., pattern; M.S., moss stitch (every row *k 1, p. 1, rep. from * to last st., k. 1); rem., remaining; rep., repeat; sp., space; shl., shell; st(s)., stitches; ST. st., S.S., stocking stitch (knit one row, purl one row alternately); sl.s, slip; sl. st., s.s., slip stitch; sp.n., spare needle; tr., treble; Half tr., hf.tr., half treble; d.tr., double treble; trip.tr., triple treble; quad. tr., quadruple treble; tog., together; th.fd., thread forward; t.b.l., through back of loops; wl.fwd., wool forward; w.r.n., wool round needle; w.o.n., wool over needle; wl.bk., wool back.

Directions are given for making this smart bolero in 5 sizes

Majestic Jumper with Gloves

MATERIALS
Biggan Design 4 ply 100% merino first cross pure new wool (180m/196yds per 50g ball)
Jumper
7 (8, 9, 9, 10, 10, 11, 12, 12) balls shade 755 (Sky Blue)
Gloves
2 balls shade 755 (Sky Blue)
1 pair 2.75mm (US #2) needles
1 pair 3mm (US #2–3) needles
1 pair 3.25mm (US #3) needles
3mm crochet hook
5 buttons

TENSION
30 sts & 36 rows = 10cm (4in) using 3.25mm needles over stocking stitch & double moss stitch pattern

ABBREVIATIONS
See page 13 for standard abbreviations

SIZING
Measurements given in centimetres followed by inches in parentheses

To Fit	86 (34)	92 (36)	97 (38)	102 (40)	107 (42)	112 (44)	117 (46)	122 (48)	127 (50)
Finished Measurements									
Actual Bust Size	87 (34¼)	92½ (36½)	97½ (38½)	103 (40½)	108½ (42½)	113½ (44½)	119 (47)	124½ (49)	129½ (51)
Length to underarm	35½ (14)	37 (14½)	38 (15)	39½ (15½)	40 (15¾)	40½ (16)	41 (16¼)	42 (16½)	42½ (16¾)
Armhole Depth	19 (7½)	20 (7¾)	20½ (8)	21 (8¼)	21½ (8½)	22¼ (8¾)	22¾ (9)	23½ (9¼)	24 (9½)
Finished Length	54½ (21½)	57 (22½)	58½ (23)	60½ (23¾)	61½ (24¼)	62¾ (24½)	63¾ (25)	65½ (25¾)	66½ (26)
Shoulder to shoulder	34½ (13½)	36 (14)	37½ (14¾)	37½ (14¾)	38½ (15)	40 (15¾)	41½ (16½)	42½ (16¾)	44 (17½)
Sleeve length	47 (18½)	47 (18½)	48 (18¾)	48 (18¾)	48 (18¾)	48 (18¾)	48 (18¾)	49½ (19½)	49½ (19½)

Garment shown in photographs is for second size 92 (36)

Jumper

BACK
Using 2.75mm needles, cast on 108 (116, 124, 132, 140, 148, 156, 164, 172) sts and work in rib as folls:
Next row (RS): * K1, P1, rep from * to end of row.
Rep this row until work measures 9cm (3½in) ending with a WS row.
Change to 3.25mm needles and commencing with a K row, work in stocking stitch inc 1 st at each end of 7th and every foll 6th row until 130 (138, 146, 154, 162, 170, 178, 186, 194) sts.
Work without further shaping until work measures 35½ (37, 38, 39½, 40, 40½, 41, 42, 42½) cm (14, 14½, 15, 15½, 15¾, 16, 16¼, 16½, 16¾ in).

Shape Armholes
Cast off 4 (6, 8, 6, 7, 8, 9, 10, 11) sts at beg of next 2 (2, 2, 4, 4, 4, 4, 4, 4) rows (122, 126, 130, 130, 134, 138, 142, 146, 150 sts), then dec 1 st at each end of next 9 rows (104, 108, 112, 112, 116, 120, 124, 128, 132 sts).

Work without shaping until armhole measures 5¼ (6¼, 6¾, 7½, 7¾, 8½, 9, 9¾, 10¼) cm (2, 2¼, 2½, 2¾, 3, 3¼, 3½, 3¾, 4 in) ending with a WS row.

Divide for Back Neck
Next row: K52 (54, 56, 56, 58, 60, 62, 64, 66), turn, and leave rem sts on a spare needle.
Work without shaping until armhole measures 19 (20, 20½, 21, 21½, 22¼, 22¾, 23½, 24) cm (7½, 7¾, 8, 8¼, 8½, 8¾, 9, 9¼, 9½ in), ending with a WS row.

Shape Shoulder
Cast off 8 (9, 9, 9, 10, 10, 11, 11, 11) sts at beg of next and foll 3 (2, 3, 3, 2, 3, 2, 2, 3) alt rows and 0 (7, 0, 0, 8, 0, 9, 9, 0) sts at beg of next foll alt row (20, 20, 20, 20, 20, 20, 20, 22, 22 sts). Cast off rem sts.

With RS facing, rejoin yarn to neck edge, casting on 4 sts for button band (56, 58, 60, 60, 62, 64, 66, 68, 70 sts).
Row 1 (RS): [K1, P1] twice, K52 (54, 56, 56, 58, 60, 62, 64, 66).

Row 2: P52 (54, 56, 56, 58, 60, 62, 64, 66), [K1, P1] twice.
Row 3: [P1, K1] twice, K52 (54, 56, 56, 58, 60, 62, 64, 66).
Row 4: P52 (54, 56, 56, 58, 60, 62, 64, 66), [P1, K1] twice.
Rep these 4 rows until work measures same as first side to start of shoulder shaping.

Shape Shoulder

Whilst maintaining continuity of double moss stitch border, cast off 8 (9, 9, 9, 10, 10, 11, 11, 11) sts at beg of next and foll 3 (2, 3, 3, 2, 3, 2, 2, 3) alt rows and 0 (7, 0, 0, 8, 0, 9, 9, 0) sts at beg of next foll alt row (24, 24, 24, 24, 24, 24, 24, 26, 26 sts). Cast off rem sts.

FRONT

Using 2.75mm needles cast on 108 (116, 124, 132, 140, 148, 156, 164, 172) sts and work in rib as folls:
Next row (RS): * K1, P1, rep from * to end of row.
Rep this row until work measures 9cm (3½in) ending with a RS row.
Next row: Rib to last st, Pfb (109, 117, 125, 133, 141, 149, 157, 165, 173 sts).
Change to 3.25mm needles and set pattern as folls:
Row 1 (RS): K21 (25, 29, 33, 37, 41, 45, 49, 53), [P1, K1] 10 times, P1, K25, [P1, K1] 10 times, P1, K21 (25, 29, 33, 37, 41, 45, 49, 53).
Row 2: P21 (25, 29, 33, 37, 41, 45, 49, 53), [K1, P1] 10 times, K1, P25, [K1, P1] 10 times, K1, P21 (25, 29, 33, 37, 41, 45, 49, 53).
Row 3: K21 (25, 29, 33, 37, 41, 45, 49, 53), [K1, P1] 10 times, K26, [K1, P1] 10 times, K22 (26, 30, 34, 38, 42, 46, 50, 54).
Row 4: P21 (25, 29, 33, 37, 41, 45, 49, 53), [P1, K1] 10 times, P26, [P1, K1] 10 times, P22 (26, 30, 34, 38, 42, 46, 50, 54).

These 4 rows set patt, rep these rows and at the same time inc 1 st at each end of 3rd and every foll 6th row until 131 (139, 147, 155, 163, 171, 179, 187, 195) sts, taking inc sts into stocking stitch. Work without further shaping until front measures same as back to commencement of armhole shaping.

Shape Armholes

Cast off 4 (6, 8, 6, 7, 8, 9, 10, 11) sts at beg of next 2 (2, 2, 4, 4, 4, 4, 4, 4) rows (123, 127, 131, 131, 135, 139, 143, 147, 151 sts), then dec 1 st at each end of next 2 rows (119, 123, 127, 127, 131, 135, 139, 143, 147 sts).
Now continue with armhole shaping and commence yoke:
Row 1: K2tog, K24 (26, 28, 28, 30, 32, 34, 36, 38), [P1, K1] 33 times, P1, K24 (26, 28, 28, 30, 32, 34, 36, 38), K2tog.
Row 2: P2tog, P23 (25, 27, 27, 29, 31, 33, 35, 37), [K1, P1] 33 times, K1, P23 (25, 27, 27, 29, 31, 33, 35, 37), P2tog.
Row 3: K2tog, K22 (24, 26, 26, 28, 30, 32, 34, 36), [K1, P1] 33 times, K23 (25, 27, 27, 29, 31, 33, 35, 37), K2tog.
Row 4: P2tog, P21 (23, 25, 25, 27, 29, 31, 33, 35), [P1, K1] 33 times, P22 (24, 26, 26, 28, 30, 32, 34, 36), P2tog.
Row 5: K2tog, K20 (22, 24, 24, 26, 28, 30, 32, 34), [P1, K1] 33 times, P1, K20 (22, 24, 24, 26, 28, 30, 32, 34), K2tog.
Row 6: P2tog, P19 (21, 23, 23, 25, 27, 29, 31, 33), [K1, P1] 33 times, K1, P19 (21, 23, 23, 25, 27, 29, 31, 33), P2tog.
Row 7: K2tog, K18 (20, 22, 22, 24, 26, 28, 30, 32), [K1, P1] 33 times, K19 (21, 23, 23, 25, 27, 29, 31, 33), K2tog.
This completes the armhole shaping (105, 109, 113, 113, 117, 121, 125, 129, 133 sts).
Next row: P19 (21, 23, 23, 25, 27, 29, 31, 33), [P1, K1] 33 times, P20 (22, 24, 24, 26, 28, 30, 32, 34).
Next row: K19 (21, 23, 23, 25, 27, 29, 31, 33), [P1, K1] 33 times, P1, K19 (21, 23, 23, 25, 27, 29, 31, 33).

Next row: P19 (21, 23, 23, 25, 27, 29, 31, 33), [K1, P1] 33 times, K1, P19 (21, 23, 23, 25, 27, 29, 31, 33).
Now work in double moss stitch over all sts as folls:
Row 1: [P1, K1] to last st, P1.
Row 2: [K1, P1] to last st, K1.
Row 3: As row 2.
Row 4: As row 1.
Repeat these 4 rows until front measures 18 (18, 18, 18, 20, 20, 22, 22, 24) rows less than back to start of shoulder shaping, ending with a WS row.

Shape Neck
Maintaining continuity of patt, shape neck as folls:
Next row (RS): Patt 44 (46, 48, 48, 50, 52, 54, 54, 56) sts, turn. Leaving rem sts on a spare needle, work on first set of sts as folls:
Dec 1 st at neck edge on each of the next 12 rows (32, 34, 36, 36, 38, 40, 42, 42, 44 sts). Work 5 (5, 5, 5, 7, 7, 9, 9, 11) rows straight.

Shape Shoulder
Cast off 8 (9, 9, 9, 10, 10, 11, 11, 11) sts at beg of next and foll 3 (2, 3, 3, 2, 3, 2, 2, 3) alt rows and 0 (7, 0, 0, 8, 0, 9, 9, 0) sts at beg of next foll alt row.

With RS facing, rejoin yarn to rem sts and cast off centre 17 (17, 17, 17, 17, 17, 17, 21, 21) sts, then patt to end of row (44, 46, 48, 48, 50, 52, 54, 54, 56 sts). Work 1 row straight, then dec 1 st at neck edge on each of next 12 rows (32, 34, 36, 36, 38, 40, 42, 42, 44 sts). Work 5 (5, 5, 5, 7, 7, 9, 9, 11) rows straight.

Shape Shoulder
Work as for first side.

SLEEVES
Using 2.75mm needles, cast on 56 (60, 64, 68, 72, 76, 80, 84, 88) sts and work in rib as folls:

Next row (RS): * K1, P1, rep from * to end of row.
Rep this row until work measures 7½cm (3in) ending with a WS row.
Change to 3.25mm needles and commencing with a K row working in stocking stitch, inc 1 st at each end of 7th and every foll 6th row until 94 (98, 102, 106, 110, 114, 118, 122, 126) sts.
Work without shaping until sleeve measures 47 (47, 48, 48, 48, 48, 48, 49½, 49½) cm (18½, 18½, 18¾, 18¾, 18¾, 18¾, 18¾, 19½, 19½ in).

Shape Sleeve head
Cast off 4 (6, 8, 6, 7, 8, 9, 10, 11) sts at beg of next 2 rows (86, 86, 86, 94, 96, 98, 100, 102, 104 sts), then dec 1st at each end of next row and every foll alt row until 54 sts rem.
Work 1 row straight.
Now dec 1 st at each end of next 10 rows (34 sts), then cast off 3 sts at beg of next 4 rows (22 sts).
Cast off rem 22 sts.

NECKBAND
Join shoulder seams. With RS facing, rejoin yarn to neck at top of left side of back opening and using 2.75mm needles pick up and K28 (28, 28, 28, 28, 28, 28, 30, 30) sts along neck to left shoulder, 25 (25, 25, 25, 25, 25, 27, 27, 27) sts along left side of front neck and 16 (16, 16, 16, 16, 16, 16, 20, 20) sts from those cast off at centre front, then pick up and K 25 (25, 25, 25, 25, 25, 27, 27, 27) along other side of front neck and 24 (24, 24, 24, 24, 24, 24, 26, 26) sts along right side of back neck (118, 118, 118, 118, 118, 118, 122, 130, 130 sts).
Next 2 rows: * K1, P1, rep from * to end of row.
Next row: Rib 57 (57, 57, 57, 57, 57, 59, 63, 63) turn, and leaving rem sts on spare needle, work on these sts only.
Dec 1 st at beg of next and foll 3 alt rows (53, 53, 53, 53, 53, 53, 55, 59, 59 sts).
Work 1 row straight. Cast off rem sts in rib.
With WS facing, rejoin yarn to inner end of 61 (61, 61, 61, 61, 61, 63, 67, 67) sts on spare needle and work in rib as folls:
Next row (WS): P1, * K1, P1, rep from * to end of row.
Now dec 1 st at end of next and foll 3 alt rows (57, 57, 57,

57, 57, 57, 59, 63, 63 sts).
Work 1 row straight. Cast of rem sts in rib.

MAKING UP

Press work lightly on WS through a damp cloth, avoiding the ribbing. Join side and sleeve seams. Set in sleeves, carefully matching centre of sleeve head with shoulder seam and matching side seams. Stitch down base of button band at back on WS of work.

Crochet a row of DC (SC) along both sides of back opening, making 5 buttonhole loops on right hand side with top loop on back neckband (see 'Fit and Finish' chapter). Sew buttons in place. Darn in all ends.

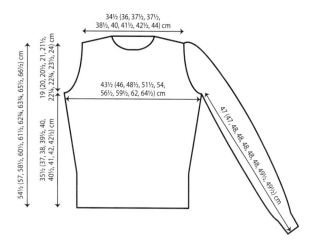

Gloves

RIGHT

Using 2.75mm needles, cast on 58 sts and work in rib as folls:
Next row (RS): * K1, P1, rep from * to end of row.
Rep this row until work measures 6½cm (2½in), ending with a WS row.
Commencing with a K row, work in stocking stitch for 6 rows, ending with a P row.

Place Thumb

Place pattern as folls, working double moss stitch on back of hand, stocking stitch on palms and fingers:
Row 1: [K1, P1] 15 times, PM, Kfb, K2, Kfb, PM, K24 (60 sts).
Row 2: P30, [K1, P1] 15 times.
Row 3: [P1, K1] 15 times, K30.
Row 4: P30, [P1, K1] 15 times.
Row 5 (Thumb inc): [K1, P1] 15 times, Kfb, K4, Kfb, K24 (62 sts).
Row 6: P32, [K1, P1] 15 times.
Row 7: [P1, K1] 15 times, K32.
Row 8: P32, [P1, K1] 15 times.
Row 9 (Thumb inc): [K1, P1] 15 times, Kfb, K6, Kfb, K24 (64 sts).
Row 10: P34, [K1, P1] 15 times.
Row 11: [P1, K1] 15 times, K34.

Row 12: P34, [P1, K1] 15 times.
Row 13 (Thumb inc): [K1, P1] 15 times, Kfb, K8, Kfb, K24 (66 sts).
Row 14: P36, [K1, P1] 15 times.
Row 15: [P1, K1] 15 times, K36.
Row 16: P36, [P1, K1] 15 times.
Row 17 (Thumb inc): [K1, P1] 15 times, Kfb, K10, Kfb, K24 (68 sts).
Row 18: P38, [K1, P1] 15 times.
Row 19: [P1, K1] 15 times, K38.
Row 20: P38, [P1, K1] 15 times.
Row 21 (Thumb inc): [K1, P1] 15 times, Kfb, K12, Kfb, K24 (70 sts).
Row 22: P40, [K1, P1] 15 times.
Row 23: [P1, K1] 15 times, K40.
Row 24: P40, [P1, K1] 15 times.
Row 25 (Thumb inc): [K1, P1] 15 times, Kfb, K14, Kfb, K24 (72 sts).
Row 26: P42, [K1, P1] 15 times.
Row 27: [P1, K1] 15 times, K42.
Row 28: P42, [P1, K1] 15 times.

Divide for Thumb.

Next row: [K1, P1] 15 times, K18, turn, slipping rem sts on to a piece of yarn.

THUMB

Row 1: Cast on 2 sts, P20, turn, slipping rem sts on to another piece of yarn (20 sts).
Next row: Cast on 2 sts, K22 (22 sts).
Commencing with a P row, work 25 rows (or required length – see 'Fit and Finish' chapter) on these 22 sts, ending with a WS row.

Shape Top

Row 1: [K1, K2tog] to last st, K1 (15 sts).
Row 2: P.
Row 3: [K2tog] to last st, K1 (8 sts).
Break yarn, leaving longish end, draw through rem sts and fasten off securely, then with RS together sew up seam of thumb.
With RS facing, rejoin yarn to base of thumb and pick up and knit 4 sts from those cast on at base of thumb, then K24 sts of palm.
Next row: P28, then maintaining existing double moss st, patt across 30 sts for back of hand (58 sts).
Keeping back of hand in double moss stitch and palm in stocking stitch work 18 rows without shaping.

** Now working all sts in stocking stitch, commence fingers as folls:

Finger 1

Row 1: K37, turn, slipping rem sts on to a piece of yarn.
Row 2: Cast on 1 st, P17, turn, slipping rem sts, on to another piece of yarn.

Row 3: Cast on 1 st, K18 (18 sts).
Commencing with a P row, work 29 rows (or required length) on these 18 sts.

Shape Top
Row 1: [K1, K2tog] to end (12 sts).
Row 2: P.
Row 3: [K2tog] to end (6 sts).
Break yarn, draw through rem sts and fasten off securely, then join seam as for thumb.

Finger 2
Row 1 (RS): Rejoin yarn and pick up and K 2 sts from cast on sts at base of preceding finger, K7 over palm, turn.
Row 2: Cast on 1 st, P10, P7 from back (17 sts).
Row 3: Cast on 1 st, K18. Commencing with a P row work 33 rows (or for required length) on these 18 sts, shape top, draw up and join seam as for finger 1.

Finger 3
Proceed as given for finger 2, but work only 29 rows instead of 33 rows before shaping top.

Finger 4
Row 1 (RS): Rejoin yarn and pick up and K 2 sts from cast on sts at base of preceding finger, knit rem sts from palm.
Row 2: P9, P rem sts from back (16 sts).
Work 20 rows on these 16 sts, shape top and draw up as for thumb, join seam and side seam. Darn in all ends **

LEFT
Using 2.75mm needles, cast on 58 sts and work in rib as folls:
Next row (RS): * K1, P1, rep from * to end of row.
Rep this row until work measures 6½cm (2½in), ending with a WS row.
Commencing with a K row, work in stocking stitch for 6 rows, ending with a P row.

Place Thumb.
Next row: K24, PM, Kfb, K2, Kfb, PM, [P1, K1] 15 times.
Continue working increases as for right hand until 28 rows have been worked and 72 sts on needle.

Divide for thumb
K42, turn, slip rem 30 sts on to a piece of yarn.
Commencing with row 1 work thumb as for right hand.

With RS facing, rejoin yarn and pick up and K 4 sts from those cast on at base of thumb, then work across sts of back of hand in double moss stitch as before.
Next row: [P1, K1] 15 times, P4, P24 sts from palm of hand.
Keeping palm sts in stocking stitch and back sts in double moss st, work 18 rows straight on these 58 sts.
Work fingers and finishing as given for right glove from ** to **

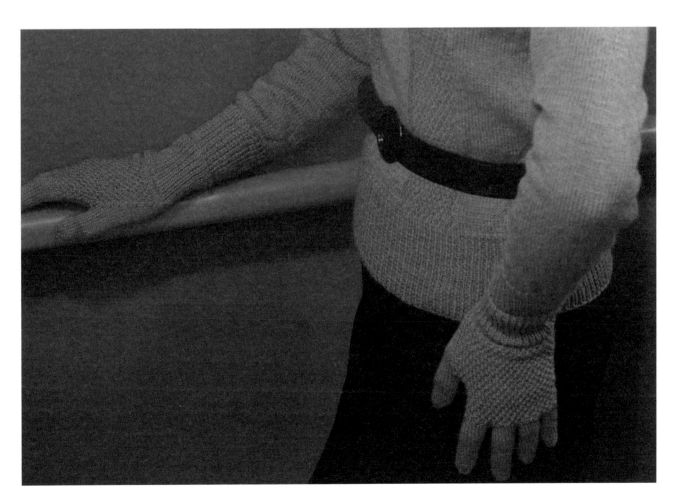

JUMPER, GLOVES & HAT

KNITTED IN 3-PLY WOOL

MATERIALS: *12 ozs. of Sirdar Majestic Wool, 3-ply for the set, (approximately 8 ozs. for the jumper; 1½ ozs. for the gloves and 2½ ozs. for the hat). You will also require 1 pair each of Nos. 10, 11 and 12 knitting needles; 4 small buttons for the jumper; ¾ yard of narrow elastic for the hat; a medium size crochet hook.*

TENSION: *Over the stocking-stitch on No. 10 needles, 8 stitches and 10 rows to 1 inch. On No. 11 needles, 17 stitches to 2 inches and 11 rows to 1 inch and on No. 12 needles, 9 stitches and 12 rows to 1 inch.*

MEASUREMENTS: The Jumper—*To suit a 34 to 36 inch bust size; length from shoulder, about 20½ inches; sleeve seam, 18 inches.*

The Gloves—*Width all round hand above thumb division, 6½ inches; length, about 9½ inches.*

The Hat—*To suit an average head size.*

ABBREVIATIONS: *K., knit; p., purl; st., stitch; sts., stitches; rep., repeat; tog., together; inc., increase (by working twice into same st.); dec., decrease (by taking 2 sts. tog.); st.-st., stocking-stitch (1 row k. and 1 row p. alternately); m.-st., moss-stitch. Stitches in brackets must be worked along row to the extent stated after 2nd bracket.*

THE JUMPER

THE BACK

With No. 12 needles, cast on 116 sts. and work in k. 1, p. 1 rib for 3½ inches.

Change to No. 10 needles and proceed in st.-st., but inc. 1 st. at each end of the 7th row and every following 6th row until there are 138 sts. Work 33 rows straight after last inc. row.

To shape armholes, cast off 6 sts. at start of next 2 rows, then dec. 1 st. at each end of the next 9 rows. Work 13 rows straight ending with a p. row. Now divide sts.

Next row: K. 54 sts.; turn. Leaving remaining sts. on a spare needle, continue on the first set of sts. as follows:

Work 47 rows straight. To shape shoulder, cast off 9 sts. at start of next row and the following two alternate rows and 8 sts. at start of the following alternate row. Cast off remainder.

With right side of work facing you, join wool to inner end of sts. on spare needle, cast on 4 sts. for underwrap, then work as follows:

1st row: (K. 1, p. 1) twice, k. 54.
2nd row: P. 54, (k. 1, p. 1) twice.
3rd row: (P. 1, k. 1) twice, k. 54.
4th row: P. 54, (p. 1, k. 1) twice.

Rep. these 4 rows 11 times, then work 1st row again.

Now keeping the continuity of the double m.-st. for underwrap, shape shoulder. Cast off 9 sts. at start of next row and the following 2 alternate rows and 8 sts. at start of the following alternate row. Cast off remainder.

THE FRONT

With No. 12 needles, cast on 116 sts. and work in k. 1, p. 1 rib for 3½ inches, increasing 1 st. at end of last row.

Change to No. 10 needles and proceed in st.-st. with double m.-st. panels thus:

1st pattern row: K. 25, (p. 1, k. 1) 10 times, p. 1, k. 25, (p. 1, k. 1) 10 times, p. 1, k. 25.

2nd row: P. 25, (k. 1, p. 1) 10 times, k. 1, p. 25, (k. 1, p. 1) 10 times, k. 1, p. 25.

3rd row: K. 25, (k. 1, p. 1) 10 times, k. 26, (k. 1, p. 1) 10 times, k. 26.

4th row: P. 25, (p. 1, k. 1) 10 times, p. 26, (p. 1, k. 1) 10 times, p. 26.

These 4 rows form the pattern for st.-st. with double m.-st. panels. Rep. the 1st and 2nd rows again, then keeping the continuity of the patterned panels, inc. 1 st. at each end of next row and every following 6th row until there are 139 sts. Work 33 rows straight after last inc. row.

To shape armholes, cast off 6 sts. at start of next 2 rows, then dec. 1 st. at each end of the following 2 rows. Now continue armhole shaping and commence yoke.

5th armhole shaping row: K. 2 tog., k. 26, (p. 1, k. 1) 33 times, p. 1, k. 26, k. 2 tog.

6th row: P. 2 tog., p. 25, (k. 1, p. 1) 33 times, k. 1, p. 25, p. 2 tog.

7th row: K. 2 tog., k. 24, (k. 1, p. 1) 33 times, k. 25, k. 2 tog.

8th row: P. 2 tog., p. 23, (p. 1, k. 1) 33 times, p. 24, p. 2 tog.

9th row: K. 2 tog., k. 22, (p. 1, k. 1) 33 times, p. 1, k. 22, k. 2 tog.

10th row: P. 2 tog., p. 21, (k. 1, p. 1) 33 times, k. 1, p. 21, p. 2 tog.

11th row: K. 2 tog., k. 20, (k. 1, p. 1) 33 times, k. 21, k. 2 tog.

This completes the armhole shapings.

Next row: P. 21, (p. 1, k. 1) 33 times, p. 22.

Next row: K. 21, (p. 1, k. 1) 33 times, p. 1, k. 21.

Next row: P. 21, (k. 1, p. 1) 33 times, k. 1, p. 21.

Now proceed in double m.-st. over all sts. as follows:

1st double m.-st. row: (P. 1, k. 1) to last st., p. 1.
2nd row: (K. 1, p. 1) to last st., k. 1.
3rd row: As 2nd row.
4th row: As 1st row.

Rep. these 4 rows 9 times more, then work 1st and 2nd rows once again. Now keeping the continuity of the double m.-st., shape neck.

Next row: Pattern 47 sts.; turn. Leaving remaining sts. on a spare needle, continue on this first set of sts. thus:

* Dec. 1 st. at neck edge on each of the next 12 rows. Work 5 rows straight. To shape shoulder, cast off 9 sts. at start of next row and the following 2 alternate rows; then work 1 row straight; cast off remainder *.

With right side of work facing you, join wool to inner end of sts. on spare needle and cast off the next 15 sts., then pattern to end of row.

Work 1 row straight, then proceed as for first side from * to *.

THE SLEEVES (both alike)

With No. 12 needles, cast on 60 sts. and work in k. 1, p. 1 rib for 3 inches.

Change to No. 10 needles and proceed in st.-st., but inc. 1 st. at each end of the 7th row and every following 6th row until there are 98 sts. Work 33 rows straight after last inc. row.

To shape top, cast off 6 sts. at start of next 2 rows, then dec. 1 st. at each end of next row and every following alternate row until 54 sts. remain. Work 1 row straight. Now dec. 1 st. at each end of the next 10 rows. Cast off 3 sts. at start of next 4 rows. Cast off remainder.

THE NECKBAND

Join shoulder seams. With right side of work facing you, join wool to neck at top of left side of back opening and using a No. 12 needle pick up and k. 28 sts. along neck to left shoulder, 25 sts. along left side of front neck and 16 sts. from those cast-off at centre front, then pick up and k. 25 sts. along other side of front neck and 24 sts. along right side of back neck.

Work 2 rows in k. 1, p. 1 rib on these 118 sts.

Next row: Rib 57 sts.; turn. Leaving remaining sts. on a spare needle, continue on this first set of sts. thus:

Dec. 1 st. at start of next row and the following 3 alternate rows.

Work 1 row straight. Cast off ribwise.

With wrong side of work facing you, join wool to inner end of sts. on spare needle, and rib to end of row.

Now dec. 1 st. at end of next row and the following 3 alternate rows.

Work 1 row straight. Cast off.

TO COMPLETE JUMPER

Press work lightly on wrong side with a warm iron over a damp cloth, avoiding the ribbing. Set in sleeves, then join side and sleeve seams. Stitch down base of underwrap at back on wrong side. Work a row of double crochet along both sides of back opening, making 4 buttonhole loops of chain on right-hand side. Add buttons.

THE GLOVES

THE RIGHT GLOVE

With No. 12 needles, cast on 58 sts. and work 2¼ inches in k. 1, p. 1 rib.

Change to st.-st. and work 6 rows straight, ending with a p. row.

Now work in double m.-st. on back hand sts. and st.-st. on front hand sts. and at the same time commence thumb increases thus:

1st thumb inc. row: (K. 1, p. 1) 15 times, inc. in next st., k. 2, inc. in next st., k. 24.
2nd row: P. 30, (k. 1, p. 1) 15 times.
3rd row: (P. 1, k. 1) 15 times, k. 30.
4th row: P. 30, (p. 1, k. 1) 15 times.
5th row—2nd thumb inc. row: (K. 1, p. 1) 15 times, inc. in next st., k. 4, inc. in next st., k. 24.
6th row: P. 32, (k. 1, p. 1) 15 times.
7th row: (P. 1, k. 1) 15 times, k. 32.
8th row: P. 32, (p. 1, k. 1) 15 times.
9th row—3rd thumb inc. row: (K. 1, p. 1) 15 times, inc. in next st., k. 6, inc. in next st., k. 24.
10th row: P. 34, (k. 1, p. 1) 15 times.
11th row: (P. 1, k. 1) 15 times, k. 34.
12th row: P. 34, (p. 1, k. 1) 15 times.
13th row—4th thumb inc. row: (K. 1, p. 1) 15 times, inc. in next st., k. 8, inc. in next st., k. 24.
14th row: P. 36, (k. 1, p. 1) 15 times.
15th row: (P. 1, k. 1) 15 times, k. 36.
16th row: P. 36, (p. 1, k. 1) 15 times.
17th row—5th thumb inc. row: (K. 1, p. 1) 15 times, inc. in next st., k. 10, inc. in next st., k. 24.
18th row: P. 38, (k. 1, p. 1) 15 times.
19th row: (P. 1, k. 1) 15 times, k. 38.
20th row: P. 38, (p. 1, k. 1) 15 times.
21st row—6th thumb inc. row: (K. 1, p. 1) 15 times, inc. in next st., k. 12, inc. in next st., k. 24.
22nd row: P 40, (k 1, p. 1) 15 times.
23rd row: (P. 1, k. 1) 15 times, k. 40.
24th row: P. 40, (p. 1, k. 1) 15 times.
25th row—7th thumb inc. row: (K. 1, p. 1) 15 times, inc. in next st., k. 14, inc. in next st., k. 24.
26th row: P. 42, (k. 1, p. 1) 15 times.
27th row: (P. 1, k. 1) 15 times, k. 42.
28th row: P. 42, (p. 1, k. 1) 15 times.

Now divide sts. for thumb.

Next row: (K. 1, p. 1) 15 times, k. 18; turn, slipping remaining sts. on to a piece of thread.

The Thumb—1st row: Cast on 2, p. 20; turn, slipping remaining sts. on to another thread. **Next row:** Cast on 2, k. 22.

Starting with a p. row, work 25 rows in st.-st. on these sts. Now shape top.

1st top shaping row: (K. 1, k. 2 tog.) to last st., k. 1. **2nd row:** P. **3rd row:** (K. 2 tog.) to last st., k. 1.

Break wool, leaving a longish end, run it through remaining sts., draw up and fasten off securely, then join seam of thumb.

With right side of work facing you, join on wool and pick up and k. 4 sts. from those cast-on at base of thumb, then k. the 24 sts. on left-hand thread.

Next row: P. 28, then work over the sts. on remaining thread thus: (k. 1, p.1) 15 times.

Still keeping the back hand sts. in double m.-st. and the front hand sts. in st.-st., work 18 rows straight on these 58 sts.

** Now working in st.-st., commence fingers as follows:

1st finger—1st row: K. 37 sts.; turn, slipping remaining sts. on to a piece of thread.

2nd row: Cast on 1, p. 17; turn, slipping remaining sts. on to another thread.

3rd row: Cast on 1, k. 18.

Starting with a p. row, work 29 rows on these 18 sts., then shape top.

1st top shaping row: (K. 1, k. 2 tog.) to end. **2nd row:** P. **3rd row:** (K. 2 tog.) to end. Break wool, run end through remaining sts., draw up and join seam as for thumb.

2nd finger—1st row: With right side of work facing you, join on wool and pick up and k. 2 sts. from those cast-on at base of preceding finger, then k. 7 sts. from left-hand thread: turn.

2nd row: Cast on 1, p. 10, then p. 7 sts. from other thread. **3rd row:** Cast on 1, k. 18. Starting with a p. row work 33 rows on these 18 sts., then shape top, draw up and join seam as for 1st finger.

3rd finger: Proceed as given for 2nd finger, but work only 29 rows instead of 33 rows before shaping top.

4th finger—1st row: With right side of work facing you, join on wool and pick up and k. 2 sts. from those cast-on at base of preceding finger, then k. remaining sts. from left-hand thread.

2nd row: P. 9, then p. remaining sts. from other thread.

Work 16 rows on these 16 sts., then shape top and draw up as for thumb, then join seam, continuing this down to wrist **.

THE LEFT GLOVE

With No. 12 needles, cast on 58 sts. and work 2¼ inches in k. 1, p. 1 rib then work 6 rows st.-st., ending with a p. row.

Now, beginning with 1st thumb inc. row, work the next 28 rows of right glove, but read each of these rows backwards. Thus 1st thumb inc. row will read: "K. 24, inc. in next st., k. 2, inc. in next st., (p. 1, k. 1) 15 times." When the 28 rows are completed, divide sts. for thumb, as follows:

Next row: K. 42 sts.; turn, slipping remaining sts. on to a piece of thread. Now work thumb as given for right glove, starting with its 1st row.

With right side of work facing you, join on wool and pick up and k. 4 sts. from those cast-on at base of thumb, then work over sts. on left-hand thread, thus: (p. 1, k. 1) 15 times.

Next row: (P. 1, k. 1) 15 times, p. 4, then p. the 24 sts. on remaining thread.

Still keeping the front hand sts. in st.-st. and the back hand sts. in double m.-st. work 18 rows straight on these 58 sts.

Now work fingers as given for right glove from ** to **.

THE HAT

THE CROWN

With No. 11 needles, cast on 20 sts. and k. 1 row and p. 1 row.

Continuing in st.-st., cast on 5 sts. at start of next 4 rows.

7th row: K. 4, inc. in next st., k. to last 5 sts., inc. in next st., k. 4.

8th row: P. 4, inc. in next st., p. to last 5 sts., inc. in next st., p. 4. **9th row:** K.

10th row: As 8th row. **11th row:** K. to last 4 sts.; turn. **12th row:** P. to last 4 sts.; turn.

13th row: K. to end. **14th row:** As 8th row. Rep. the 9th to 14th rows inclusive 5 times more, then work the 9th and 10th rows once again. There are now 70 sts.

47th row: (K. 6, inc. in next st.) to last 7 sts., k. 7. **48th row:** P. 79. **49th row:** As 7th row. **50th row:** P. **51st row:** K.

52nd row: As 8th row. **53rd row:** K.

54th row: P. Rep. the 49th to 52nd rows inclusive once. Work 33 rows straight on these 87 sts. **92nd row:** P. 4, p. 2 tog., p. to last 6 sts., p. 2 tog., p. 4. **93rd row:** K.

94th row: P. **95th row:** K. 4, k. 2 tog., k. to last 6 sts., k. 2 tog., k. 4.

96th row: P. **97th row:** K.

Rep. the 92nd to 96th rows inclusive once.

103rd row: (K. 6, k. 2 tog.) to last 7 sts., k. 7. **104th row:** P. **105th row:** As 95th row. **106th row:** P. to last 4 sts.; turn.

107th row: K. to last 4 sts.; turn.

108th row: P. **109th row:** As 95th row.

110th row: P.

Rep. the 105th to 110th rows inclusive 5 times. **141st row:** As 95th row.

142nd row: P. **143rd row:** As 95th row.

144th row: As 92nd row.

Cast off 5 sts. at start of next 4 rows. Cast off remaining 20 sts.

THE BAND

With No. 11 needles, cast on 37 sts. and work in double m.-st. thus:

1st double m.-st. row: (K. 1, p. 1) to last st., k. 1. **2nd row:** (P. 1, k. 1) to last st., p. 1. **3rd row:** As 2nd row.

4th row: As 1st row.

Rep. these 4 rows 109 times. Cast off.

TO COMPLETE HAT

Press work lightly on wrong side with a warm iron over a damp cloth. Turn under ½ inch all round outer edge of crown and slip-stitch down on wrong side, to form a casing for elastic, leaving a small opening to take the elastic. Cut the elastic to your head measurement and thread through the casing; join ends together and finish hem. Join the long side edges of band together, then fold strip so that the seam comes to the middle of the under side and tack in position. Now pin the centre of the strip to the centre of the cast-off edge of crown, take the ends round towards front, and cross them, folding right-hand end under left-hand end. Tack ends in position under the band, about 2½ inches each side of centre back, then slip-stitch the seam of band (except overlapping portions) to hem of the crown all round on wrong side.

Weldons Knitwear Leaflet No. B1249

'Trimmed with Roses' Twinset Cardigan

MATERIALS
Jamieson & Smith 2 ply Jumper Yarn 100% Shetland wool (115m/125yds per 25g ball)
12 (13, 15, 17, 19, 21) balls shade FC43 – MC
Jamieson's Spindrift 100% Shetland wool (105m per 25g ball)
1 (1, 1, 1, 2, 2) balls each of shade 526 – A, shade 788 – B and shade 242 – C
1 pair 2.75mm (US #2) needles
1 pair 3.25mm (US #3) needles
7 buttons

TENSION
26 sts & 36 rows = 10cm (4in) using 3.25mm needles over stocking stitch

ABBREVIATIONS
See page 13 for standard abbreviations

SIZING
Measurements given in centimetres followed by inches in parentheses

To Fit	76–81 (30–32)	86–92 (34–36)	97–102 (38–40)	107–112 (42–44)	117–122 (46–48)	127–132 (50–52)
Finished Measurements						
Actual Bust Size	91 (36)	101½ (40)	112½ (44)	123 (48½)	132½ (52)	141½ (55½)
Length to underarm	33 (13)	34 (13½)	35½ (14)	37 (14½)	38 (15)	39½ (15½)
Armhole Depth	18½ (7¼)	19 (7½)	20 (8)	21½ (8½)	23 (9)	24 (9½)
Finished Length	51½ (20¼)	53 (21)	55½ (22)	58½ (23)	61 (24)	63½ (25)
Shoulder to shoulder	35½ (14)	39 (15½)	43 (17)	47 (18½)	51 (20)	54½ (21½)
Sleeve length	46 (18)	46 (18)	48 (19)	48 (19)	49½ (19½)	49½ (19½)

Garment shown in photographs is for second size 86–92 (34–36)

LEFT FRONT
Using 2.75mm needles and MC, cast on 53 (60, 67, 74, 80, 86) sts and work in rib as folls:
Next row (RS): P1 (0, 1, 0, 0, 1), * K1, P1, rep from * to end.
Next row (WS): * K1, P1, rep from * to last 1 (0, 1, 0, 0, 1) st, K1 (0, 1, 0, 0, 1).
Rep these 2 rows until work measures 9cm (3½in) from cast on edge, ending with a WS row.
Change to 3.25mm needles and commencing with a K row work in stocking stitch, inc 1 st at beg of 5th and on 10 foll 6th rows (64, 71, 78, 85, 91, 97 sts).

Work straight until piece measures 26½ (26½, 26½, 27, 27, 27½) cm (10¼, 10¼, 10¼, 10½, 10½, 11 in) ending with a RS row.

Front Neck Shaping
Dec 1 st at neck edge of next and 5 (6, 7, 8, 9, 10) foll 4th rows (58, 64, 70, 76, 81, 86 sts). Work 3 rows without shaping, thus ending with a WS row. If tension is correct, piece should measure approx 33 (34, 35½, 37, 38, 39½) cm (13, 13½, 14, 14½, 15, 15½ in).

Shape Armhole
Dec 1 st at neck edge of next and 14 (15, 16, 17, 18, 19) foll 4th rows, and AT THE SAME TIME work armhole shaping, stripe and chart patterns as described below:
Cast off 7 (8, 9, 10, 10, 11) sts at beg of next row, then dec 1 st at armhole edge of next 6 (7, 8, 9, 10, 10) rows, then P 1 (0, 1, 0, 1, 1) row (43, 47, 50, 54, 58, 62 sts).

With RS facing and still working decs at front edge work stripes as folls:
Work 2 rows in A, 2 rows in MC then a further 2 rows in A. Change back to MC and work 4 rows in stocking stitch (40, 44, 48, 52, 55, 59 sts).

Yoke
Work rose motif in a combination of Fair Isle and intarsia techniques, carrying colours across single motifs but not from one motif to the next, using separate small balls of yarn for each motif.
Row 1: Using MC, K9 (1, 2, 4, 6, 8), work all sts from chart, repeating marked section 1 (2, 2, 2, 2, 2) times, using MC, K9 (1, 2, 4, 7, 9), [K2tog] 0 (0, 1, 1, 0, 0) times (neck dec) (40, 44, 47, 51, 55, 59 sts).
Row 2: Using MC, P9 (1, 3, 5, 7, 9), work all sts from chart, repeating marked section 1 (2, 2, 2, 2, 2) times, using MC, P9 (1, 2, 4, 6, 8).

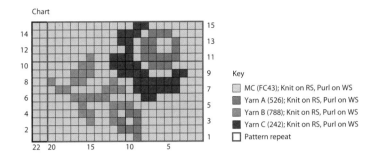

Chart

Key
- ☐ MC (FC43); Knit on RS, Purl on WS
- ▨ Yarn A (526); Knit on RS, Purl on WS
- ▧ Yarn B (788); Knit on RS, Purl on WS
- ■ Yarn C (242); Knit on RS, Purl on WS
- ☐ Pattern repeat

Continuing to work front decs as set, work from chart until row 15 is completed, then continue in MC only until neck decs arc complete (30, 33, 36, 39, 42, 45 sts).

Work straight until armhole measures 18½ (19, 20, 21½, 23, 24) cm (7¼, 7½, 8, 8½, 9, 9½ in) ending with a WS row.

Shape Shoulder
Cast off 10 (11, 12, 13, 14, 15) sts at beg of next and foll 2 alt rows.

RIGHT FRONT
Using 2.75mm needles and MC, cast on 53 (60, 67, 74, 80, 86) sts and work in rib as folls:
Next row (RS): P1 (0, 1, 0, 0, 1), * K1, P1, rep from * to end.
Next row (WS): * K1, P1, rep from * to last 1 (0, 1, 0, 0, 1) sts, K1 (0, 1, 0, 0, 1).
Rep these 2 rows until work measures 9cm (3½in) from cast on edge, ending with a WS row.
Change to 3.25mm needles and commencing with a K row work in stocking stitch, inc 1 st at end of 5th and on 10 foll 6th rows (64, 71, 78, 85, 91, 97 sts).

Work straight until piece measures 26½ (26½, 26½, 27, 27, 27½) cm (10¼, 10¼, 10¼, 10½, 10½, 11 in) ending with a WS row.

Front Neck Shaping
Dec 1 st at neck edge of next and 5 (6, 7, 8, 9, 10) foll 4th rows (58, 64, 70, 76, 81, 86 sts). Work 2 rows without shaping, thus ending with a RS row. If tension is correct, piece should measure approx 33 (34, 35½, 37, 38, 39½) cm (13, 13½, 14, 14½, 15, 15½ in).

Shape Armhole
Dec 1 st at neck edge of 2nd and 14 (15, 16, 17, 18, 19) foll 4th rows, and AT THE SAME TIME work armhole shaping, stripe and chart patterns as described below:
Cast off 7 (8, 9, 10, 10, 11) sts at beg of next row, then dec 1 st at armhole edge of next 6 (7, 8, 9, 10, 10) rows, then P 2 (1, 2, 1, 2, 2) rows (43, 47, 50, 54, 58, 62 sts).

With RS facing and still working decs at front edge work stripes as folls:
Work 2 rows in A, 2 rows in MC then a further 2 rows in A. Change back to MC and work 4 rows in stocking stitch (40, 44, 48, 52, 55, 59 sts).

Yoke
Work rose motif in a combination of Fair Isle and intarsia techniques, carrying colours across single motifs but not from one motif to the next, using separate small balls of yarn for each motif.
Row 1: Using MC, [K2tog] 0 (0, 1, 1, 0, 0) times (neck dec), K9 (1, 2, 4, 7, 9), work all sts from chart, repeating marked section 1 (2, 2, 2, 2, 2) times, using MC, K9 (1, 2, 4, 6, 8) (40, 44, 47, 51, 55, 59 sts).

Row 2: Using MC, P9 (1, 2, 4, 6, 8), work all sts from chart, repeating marked section 1 (2, 2, 2, 2, 2) times, using MC, P9 (1, 3, 5, 7, 9).
Continuing to work front decs as set, work from chart until row 15 is completed, then continue in MC only until neck decs are complete (30, 33, 36, 39, 42, 45 sts).

Work straight until armhole measures 18½ (19, 20, 21½, 23, 24) cm (7¼, 7½, 8, 8½, 9, 9½ in) ending with a RS row.

Shape Shoulder
Cast off 10 (11, 12, 13, 14, 15) sts at beg of next and foll 2 alt rows.

BACK
Using 2.75mm needles and MC, cast on 98 (112, 126, 140, 152, 164) sts and work in rib as folls:
Next row (RS): * K1, P1, rep from * to end.
Rep this row until work measures 9cm (3½in) from cast on edge.
Change to 3.25mm needles and commencing with a K row work in stocking stitch, inc 1 st at beg of 5th and every foll 6th row until 118 (132, 146, 160, 172, 184) sts.

Work without further shaping until back measures same as front to start of armhole shaping, ending with a WS row.

Shape Armholes
Cast off 7 (8, 9, 10, 10, 11) sts at beg of next 2 rows (104, 116, 128, 140, 152, 162 sts), then K2tog at each end of every row until 92 (102, 112, 122, 132, 142) sts rem ending with a WS row. With RS facing work stripes as folls: Work 2 rows in A, 2 rows in MC then a further 2 rows in A. Change back to MC and work 4 rows in stocking stitch.

Yoke
Next row (RS): Using MC, K5 (0, 5, 0, 5, 0), work all sts from row 1 of chart, repeating marked section 4 (5, 5, 6, 6, 7) times, using MC, K5 (0, 5, 0, 5, 0).
Next row (WS): Using MC, P5 (0, 5, 0, 5, 0), work all sts from row 2 of chart, repeating marked section 4 (5, 5, 6, 6, 7) times, using MC, P5 (0, 5, 0, 5, 0).
Work from chart as set, until row 15 is complete. Then work straight in stocking stitch, using MC only, until back measures same as front to start of shoulder seams, ending with a WS row.

Shape Shoulders

Cast off 10 (11, 12, 13, 14, 15) sts at beg of next 6 rows (32, 36, 40, 44, 48, 52 sts).
Cast off rem sts.

SLEEVES

Using 2.75mm needles and MC cast on 52 (60, 66, 74, 80, 86) sts and work in rib as folls:

Next row (RS): * K1, P1, rep from * to end.

Rep this row until work measures 7½cm (3in) from cast on edge.

Change to 3.25mm needles and commencing with a K row work in stocking stitch, inc at each end of 5th and every foll 6th row until 90 (98, 104, 112, 118, 124) sts.

Work straight until sleeve measures 46 (46, 48, 48, 49½, 49½) cm (18, 18, 19, 19, 19½, 19½ in) ending with a WS row.

Shape Sleeve Head

Cast off 4 (4, 5, 5, 5, 6) sts at beg of next 2 rows (82, 90, 94, 102, 108, 112 sts), then dec 1 st at beg of next 8 rows (74, 82, 86, 94, 100, 104 sts).

Continue to dec 1 st at beg of next 8 rows whilst working stripes as folls (66, 74, 78, 86, 92, 96 sts):

Work 2 rows in A
Work 2 rows in MC
Work 2 rows in A
Work 4 rows in MC

Place chart as folls:

Next row (RS): K2tog, K0 (4, 6, 0, 3, 5), work all sts from row 1 of chart repeating marked section 3 (3, 3, 4, 4, 4) times, K0 (4, 6, 0, 3, 5), K2tog (64, 72, 76, 84, 90, 94 sts).

Next row (WS): P1 (5, 7, 1, 4, 6), work all sts from row 2 of chart repeating marked section 3 (3, 3, 4, 4, 4) times, P1 (5, 7, 1, 4, 6).

Work until chart is complete, continuing to dec 1 st at each end of every knit row (50, 58, 62, 70, 76, 80 sts). Change to MC, now dec 1 st at each end of every row until 18 sts rem. Cast off rem sts.

FRONT BAND

Join shoulder seams. Using 2.75mm needles and MC, cast on 11 sts and work in rib as folls:

Row 1 (RS): * K1, P1, rep from * to last st, K1.

Row 2: * P1, K1, rep from * to last st, P1.

Work 4 rows, then work buttonhole as folls:

Next row (RS): Rib 4, cast off 3, rib to end.

Next row: Rib to cast off sts, cast on 3, rib to end.

Continue in rib, working 6 further buttonholes on every foll 15th & 16th rows.

Continue in rib until band fits, when slightly stretched, up right front across back neck and down left front. Place sts on safety pin.

MAKING UP

Press all pieces on WS under damp cloth, avoiding ribbing. Join side and sleeve seams, insert sleeves, taking care to match centre of sleeve head with shoulder seam, and to match side seams. Sew band in place, using flat slip stitch, stretching band slightly as sewn in place and adjusting to fit (see 'Fit and Finish' chapter). Cast off sts once fit corrected. Sew buttons in place. Darn in all ends.

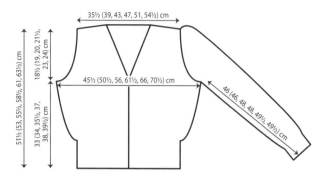

'Trimmed with Roses' Twinset Jumper

MATERIALS
Jamieson & Smith 2 ply Jumper Yarn 100% Shetland wool (115m/125yds per 25g ball)
6 (7, 8, 9, 10, 11) balls shade FC43 – MC
Jamieson's Spindrift 100% Shetland wool (105m per 25g ball)
2 (2, 3, 3, 4, 4) balls shade 526 – A,
1 (1, 1, 1, 2, 2) balls each of shade 788 – B and shade 242 – C
1 pair 2.75mm (US #2) needles
1 pair 3.25mm (US #3) needles
1 short zip, approx 13cm (5in) long
Stitch holders

TENSION
26 sts & 36 rows = 10cm (4in) using 3.25mm needles over stocking stitch

ABBREVIATIONS
See page 13 for standard abbreviations

SIZING
Measurements given in centimetres followed by inches in parentheses

To Fit	76–81 (30–32)	86–92 (34–36)	97–102 (38–40)	107–112 (42–44)	117–122 (46–48)	127–132 (50–52)
Finished Measurements						
Actual Bust Size	89 (35)	100 (39½)	111 (43½)	121½ (48)	131 (51½)	140 (55)
Length to underarm	30½ (12)	32 (12½)	33 (13)	34½ (13½)	35½ (14)	37 (14½)
Armhole Depth	16½ (6½)	18 (7)	19 (7½)	20 (8)	21½ (8½)	23 (9)
Finished Length	47 (18½)	50 (19½)	52 (20½)	54½ (21½)	57 (22½)	60 (23½)
Shoulder to shoulder	35½ (14)	39 (15½)	43 (17)	47 (18½)	51 (20)	54½ (21½)
Sleeve Length	11½ (4½)	13 (5)	13 (5)	13 (5)	14 (5½)	14 (5½)

Garment shown in photographs is for second size 86–92 (34–36)

BACK
Using 2.75mm needles and MC, cast on 96 (110, 124, 138, 150, 162) sts and work in rib as folls:
Next row (RS): * K1, P1, rep from * to end.
Rep this row until work measures 9cm (3½in) from cast on edge.
Change to 3.25mm needles and working in stocking stitch throughout, work in stripes as folls:
Work 2 rows A.
Work 2 rows MC.
Rep these 4 rows throughout and at same time, inc 1 st at each end of 5th and every foll 6th row until there are 116 (130, 144, 158, 170, 182) sts. Work without further shaping until work measures 30½ (32, 33, 34½, 35½, 37) cm (12, 12½, 13, 13½, 14, 14½ in), ending with a WS row using A.

Shape Armholes
Maintaining stripe patt, cast off 6 (8, 10, 12, 13, 14) sts at beg of next 2 rows (104, 114, 124, 134, 144, 154 sts), then dec 1 st at each end of next 6 rows (92, 102, 112, 122, 132, 142 sts). Work 4 more rows in stripe patt, then work 4 further rows in MC only.

Place Chart
Work rose motif in a combination of Fair Isle and intarsia techniques, carrying colours across single motifs but not from one motif to the next, using separate small balls of yarn for each motif.
Row 1 (RS): K5 (0, 5, 0, 5, 0), reading from right to left, work all sts from row 1 of chart, repeating marked section 4 (5, 5, 6, 6, 7) times, K5 (0, 5, 0, 5, 0).
Row 2 (WS): P5 (0, 5, 0, 5, 0), reading from left to right, work all sts from row 2 of chart, repeating marked section 4 (5, 5, 6, 6, 7) times, P5 (0, 5, 0, 5, 0).
Cont to work from chart as set until row 15 is complete. †
On completion of chart, work in stocking stitch using MC only, until armhole measures 10 (11½, 12½, 13½, 15, 16½) cm (4, 4½, 5, 5½, 6, 6½ in), ending with a WS row.

Divide for Back Opening
Next row (RS): K 46 (51, 56, 61, 66, 71) sts, turn, place rem sts on stitch holder and continue on these 46 (51, 56, 61, 66, 71) sts only.
Next row (WS): K1, P to end.
Next row: K.
Rep these 2 rows until armhole measures 16½ (18, 19, 20, 21½, 23) cm (6½, 7, 7½, 8, 8½, 9 in), ending with a WS row.

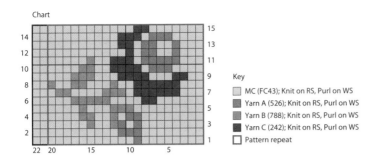

Chart

Key
- ▢ MC (FC43); Knit on RS, Purl on WS
- ◼ Yarn A (526); Knit on RS, Purl on WS
- ◼ Yarn B (788); Knit on RS, Purl on WS
- ◼ Yarn C (242); Knit on RS, Purl on WS
- ▢ Pattern repeat

Shape Shoulder

Cast off 9 (10, 11, 12, 13, 14) sts at beg of next and foll 2 alt rows. Place rem 19 (21, 23, 25, 27, 29) sts on holder.

With RS facing rejoin MC to rem 46 (51, 56, 61, 66, 71) sts. K to end of row.

Next row (WS): P to last st, K1.

Rep these 2 rows until armhole measures 16½ (18, 19, 20, 21½, 23) cm (6½, 7, 7½, 8, 8½, 9 in), ending with a RS row.

Shape Shoulder

Cast off 9 (10, 11, 12, 13, 14) sts at beg of next and foll 2 alt rows. Place rem 19 (21, 23, 25, 27, 29) sts on holder.

FRONT

Work as for back to †

On completion of chart, work in stocking stitch using MC only, until armhole measures 14 (15½, 16, 17, 18, 19) cm (5½, 6, 6½, 6¾, 7, 7½ in), ending with a WS row.

Shape Neck

Next row (RS): K31 (35, 39, 43, 47, 51), K2tog, turn and leave rem sts on stitch holder. Cont on these 32 (36, 40, 44, 48, 52) sts, dec 1 st at neck edge of every foll row until 27 (30, 33, 36, 39, 42) sts rem.

Work without further shaping until front matches back to commencement of shoulder shaping ending with a WS row.

Shape Shoulder

Cast off 9 (10, 11, 12, 13, 14) sts at beg of next and foll 2 alt rows.

With RS facing, place centre 26 (28, 30, 32, 34, 36) sts on holder and rejoin MC to remaining sts, K2tog, then K to end of row. Dec 1 st at neck edge of every foll row until 27 (30, 33, 36, 39, 42) sts rem. Work without further shaping until front matches back to commencement of shoulder shaping ending with a RS row.

Shape Shoulder

Cast off 9 (10, 11, 12, 13, 14) sts at beg of next and foll 2 alt rows.

SLEEVES

Using 2.75mm needles and MC, cast on 74 (80, 86, 94, 100, 106) sts and work in rib as folls:

Next row (RS): * K1, P1, rep from * to end.

Rep this row a further 11 times, then change to 3.25mm needles and work in stripe pattern as for back, inc at each end of 3rd and every foll 4th row until there are 90 (96, 102, 110, 116, 122) sts.

Work without further shaping until sleeve measures 11½ (13, 13, 13, 14, 14) cm (4½, 5, 5, 5, 5½, 5½ in), ending with a WS row in A.

Shape Sleeve Head

Maintaining stripe pattern, cast off 3 (4, 5, 5, 5, 7) sts at beg of next 2 rows (84, 88, 92, 100, 106, 108) then dec 1 st at beg only of next 10 rows (74, 78, 82, 90, 96, 98 sts).

1st size only

Change to MC and dec 1 st at beg only of next 2 rows (72 sts). Work 2 rows in MC without shaping.

2nd, 3rd, 4th, 5th & 6th sizes only
Change to MC and dec 1 st at beg only of next 4 rows
(74, 78, 86, 92, 94 sts).

All Sizes
Place chart as folls:

Next row (RS): K2tog, K3 (4, 6, 10, 3, 4), work all sts
from chart, repeating marked section 3 (3, 3, 3, 4, 4) times,
K3 (4, 6, 10, 3, 4), K2tog (70, 72, 76, 84, 90, 92 sts).
Work until chart is complete, continuing to dec 1 st at each
end of every knit row (56, 58, 62, 70, 76, 78 sts). Change to
MC and dec 1 st at each end of every row until 24 sts rem.
Cast off rem sts.

NECK RIBBING
Join shoulder seams.
Using 2.75mm circular needle, MC and with RS facing,
and commencing at left back neck, K across 19 (21, 23, 25,
27, 29) sts, pick up and K 19 (19, 23, 23, 27, 30) sts down
left front neck, K across 26 (28, 30, 32, 34, 36) sts at centre
front, pick up and K 19 (19, 23, 23, 27, 30) sts up right
front neck, then K across 19 (21, 23, 25, 27, 29) sts at right
back neck (102, 108, 122, 128, 142, 154 sts).
Next row (WS): * K1, P1, rep from * to end.
Rep this row a further 11 times, then cast off loosely in rib.

MAKING UP
Press pieces on WS under damp cloth, avoiding ribbing.
Sew in zip down back opening of jumper (see 'Fit and
Finish' chapter). Join side and sleeve seams, carefully
matching stripes. Insert sleeves, taking care to match centre
of sleeve head and shoulder seam, and matching side seams
and pattern. Darn in all ends.

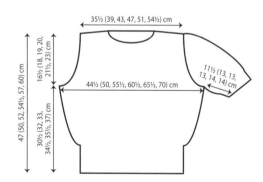

TRIMMED WITH ROSES

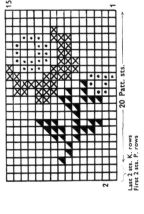

MATERIALS: Of Patons Beehive Fingering 3-ply, Patonised, 12 ozs. lime, 2 ozs. each pink and dark red, and ¼ oz. of dark green for leaves of rose motif. A pair each No. 12 and No. 10 "Beehive" needles. Seven buttons. 4-inch zip-fastener.

MEASUREMENTS: To fit 34–36-inch bust; length from top of shoulders, on jumper, 19½ inches, on cardigan, 20½ inches, sleeve seam, 5 and 18 inches.

TENSION: 7½ stitches and 9½ rows to an inch over stocking-stitch.

N.B.—L = lime; D = dark red; M = pink. (Plain square, cross and spot respectively on chart; black triangle is green).

JUMPER

BACK

With No. 12 needles and L. wool, cast on 110 sts. and work 3½ inches k. 1, p. 1 rib. Change to No. 10 needles and continue in stripes thus:—1ST ROW: Knit in L., drop L. 2ND ROW: Purl with M., drop M. 3RD ROW: Knit with D., drop D. 4TH ROW: Purl with L., drop L. 5TH ROW: Knit wool with M., drop M. 6TH ROW: Purl with D., drop D. Repeat these 6 rows, increasing at each end of 5th and every following 6th row until there are 130 sts. Work straight until side edge measures 12½ inches, ending with a purl row in D.

With right side facing, shape armholes by casting off 8 sts. at beginning of next 2 rows, then decrease at each end of next 6 rows (102 sts.). Work 4 more

rows in stripe pattern, then break D. and M. wool.

Work 4 rows straight in L. Now work rose motif from chart right across yoke, repeating the 20 pattern sts. 5 times across and last 2 sts. on knit rows and first 2 sts. on purl rows as indicated. Read knit rows from right to left and purl rows from left to right.

Now continue in L. until armhole measures 4½ inches, then divide for back opening. Work on first half of stitches only until armhole measures 7 inches. With right side facing, shape shoulder by casting off 10 sts. at beginning of next and following 2 alternate rows, armhole edge. Cast off remaining stitches.

Join wool to other half of work at neck edge, and work to correspond.

FRONT

Work exactly as for back to end of rose motif across yoke, then continue in L. until armhole measures 6 inches. With right side facing, shape neck thus:—k. 35, k. 2 tog., turn and leave remaining stitches on spare needle. Continue on these 36 sts., decreasing 1 stitch at neck edge on every row until 30 sts. remain. Work a few rows straight until front matches back, then shape shoulder by casting off 10 sts. on next 3 alternate rows, armhole edge.

Return to remaining stitches, leave centre 28 on a spare needle, and work last 37 sts. to correspond with first.

SLEEVES

With No. 12 needles and L. wool, cast on 80 sts. and work 12 rows k. 1, p. 1 rib. Change to No. 10 needles and striped pattern, increasing at each end of 3rd and every following 4th row until there are 96 sts. Work a few rows straight until sleeve measures 5 inches, ending with a purl row in D.

Shape top by casting off 4 sts. at beginning of next 2 rows, then 1 stitch at beginning of next 10 rows (78 sts.). Change to L. and work 4 rows, decreasing at beginning of each row (74 sts.). Now work the roses across sleeve thus:—k. 2 tog., k. 5, repeat 20 pattern sts. from chart 3 times, k. 5, k. 2 tog. Now finish working chart, still decreasing at each end of every row. Continue in L., but shaping sleeve top by decreasing 1 stitch at each end of every row until 24 sts. remain. Cast off.

NECK RIBBING

Join shoulder seams. With No. 12 needles, right side facing and L. wool, pick up and k. 108 sts. all round neck. Work 12 rows k. 1, p. 1 rib; cast off loosely in rib.

CARDIGAN

FRONTS

Left: With No. 12 needles and L. wool, cast on 60 sts. and work 3½ inches k. 1, p. 1 rib. Change to No. 10 needles and continue in stocking-stitch and L. wool, increasing at beginning of 5th and every following 6th row, 10 times. Now keep this edge straight.

At the same time, when side edge measures 10½ inches, start to shape front edge thus:—With right side facing, decrease 1 stitch at end of next and every following 4th row, front edge, 6 times. Work 3 rows straight.

Still decreasing at front edge, with right side facing, shape armhole by casting off 8 sts. at beginning of next row, then k. 2 tog. on every row at this edge 7 times, k. 1 row (46 sts.).

With wrong side facing and still decreasing at front edge, work 5 stripes thus:—M. D. L. M. D. Change to L. and work 4 rows in L. (44 sts.).

Now work roses across yoke thus:—1ST ROW (right side facing): Repeat 20 pattern sts. from chart twice, k. 4 L. 2ND ROW: p. 4 L., repeat 20 pattern sts. twice. 3RD ROW: Repeat 20 pattern sts. twice, k. 2 l., k. 2 tog. L. Continue thus, and when the 15 pattern rows are done continue in L., still decreasing at front edge until 33 sts. remain.

Work straight until armhole measures 7¾ inches, then with right side facing shape shoulder by casting off 11 sts. at beginning of next and following 2 alternate rows, armhole edge.

Right: Work to correspond with left front, reversing shapings. When you come to work roses your first 3 rows will read:—1ST ROW (right side facing): k. 4 L., repeat 20 pattern sts. twice. 2ND ROW: repeat 20 pattern sts. twice, p. 4 L. 3RD ROW: k. 2 tog. L., k. 2 l., repeat 20 pattern sts. twice.

BACK

With No. 12 needles and L. wool, cast on 112 sts. and work 3½ inches k. 1, p. 1 rib. Change to No. 10 needles and continue in stocking-stitch and L. wool, increasing at each end of 5th and every following 6th row until 132 sts. are on needle. Work straight until side edge matches front.

With right side facing, shape armholes by casting off 8 sts. at beginning of next 2 rows, then k. 2 tog. at each end of every row until 102 sts. remain. Now work straight until roses, join in M. and work 5 rows in stripes thus:—M. D. L. M. D.

Change to L. and work 4 rows straight, then work roses across yoke exactly as for jumper. Now continue straight in L. until back matches front. Shape shoulders by casting off 11 sts. at beginning of next 6 rows. Cast off remaining stitches.

SLEEVES

With No. 12 needles and L. wool, cast on 60 sts. and work 3 inches k. 1, p. 1 rib. Change to No. 10 needles and stocking-stitch, increasing at each end of 5th and every following 6th row until there are 98 sts. Work straight until sleeve measures 18 inches, ending with a purl row.

Shape top by casting off 4 sts. at beginning of next 2 rows, then 1 stitch at beginning of next 7 rows. Work 5 rows in stripes M., D., L., M., D., still decreasing 1 stitch at beginning of every row (78 sts.).

Now finish top exactly as given for short sleeve until 18 sts. remain; cast off.

RIBBED BORDER

Join shoulder seams. With No. 12 needles and L. wool, cast on 11 sts. and work a strip in k. 1, p. 1 rib to fit up right front, across back of neck and down left front when slightly stretched. Make 7 buttonholes in right front, the first to come ¼-inch from bottom edge, the last at beginning of front slope and remaining 5 at equal intervals. Mark position of buttons on left front with pins to ensure even spacing. To make a buttonhole:—Rib 4, cast off 3, rib to end and back, casting on 3 over those cast off. Sew in position as you go along.

TO MAKE UP

Press parts carefully on wrong side under a damp cloth, avoiding ribbing. Join all seams; insert sleeves. Sew in zip-fastener down back opening on jumper. Sew on buttons to match buttonholes on cardigan. Press all seams.

This Winter's High-Spot

MATERIALS
Excelana DK Luxury Wool 100% pure new British wool (119m/130yds per 50g ball)
18 (21, 23, 27, 31) balls shade Ruby Red
1 pair 3.25mm (US #3) needles
1 pair 3.75mm (US #5) needles
2 Stitch holders
8 buttons

TENSION
24 sts & 32 rows = 10cm (4in) using 3.75mm needles over twisted rib pattern
28 sts & 36 rows = 10cm (4in) using 3.25mm needles over stocking stitch

ABBREVIATIONS
See page 13 for standard abbreviations

SIZING
Measurements given in centimetres followed by inches in parentheses

To Fit	81–86 (32–34)	97–102 (38–40)	107–112 (42–44)	117–122 (46–48)	132–137 (52–54)
Finished Measurements					
Actual Bust Size	93½ (37)	106½ (42)	120 (47)	133½ (52½)	146½ (57½)
Length to underarm	60 (23½)	61 (24)	62 (24½)	63½ (25)	65 (25½)
Armhole Depth	25½ (10)	28 (11)	30½ (12)	33 (13)	35½ (14)
Finished Length	85½ (33½)	89 (35)	92½ (36½)	96½ (38)	100½ (39½)
Back Neck	11½ (4½)	14 (5½)	16½ (6½)	18½ (7)	19 (7½)
Sleeve Length	40½ (16)	42 (16½)	43 (17)	44½ (17½)	46 (18)

Garment shown in photographs is for first size 81–86 (32–34)

Twisted Rib Pattern
Row 1 (RS): P1, * K2, P2, repeat from * to last 3 sts, K2, P1.
Row 2: K1, * YO, K2, pass YO over K2, K2, repeat from * ending last repeat K1 instead of K2.
These 2 rows form pattern. Whilst having the appearance of a rib, please note when working WS rows (row 2) that every st should be worked as a knit stitch.

BACK
Using 3.75mm needles, cast on 148 (164, 180, 196, 212) sts and commence working as folls:
** **Row 1** (RS): P1, * K2, P2, repeat from * to last 3 sts, K2, P1.
Row 2: K1, * P2, K2, repeat from * to last 3 sts, P2, K1.
Repeat these 2 rows 5 more times.

With RS facing and commencing with row 1, work in twisted rib pattern as shown above. Continue working in patt until back measures 17¾cm (7in) from beginning of work, ending with a WS row. **
Whilst maintaining pattern, shape sides by dec 1 st at each end of the next and every foll 8th row until 118 (134, 150, 166, 182) sts rem. Work straight until back measures 60 (61, 62, 63½, 65) cm (23½, 24, 24½, 25, 25½ in) from cast on, ending with a WS row.

Shape Raglans
With RS facing cast off 4 (5, 7, 8, 11) sts at beginning of next 2 rows (110, 124, 136, 150, 160 sts), then K2tog at each end of next and every alt row until 28 (34, 40, 44, 46) sts rem. Cast off.

POCKET LININGS
Using 3.75mm needles, cast on 40 sts and commencing with row 1, work in twisted rib patt until work measures 14cm (5½in), ending with a WS row. Leave pocket on spare needle. Work a second pocket the same.

LEFT FRONT
Using 3.75mm needles, cast on 68 (76, 84, 92, 100) sts and work as for back from ** to **
With RS facing, start side shaping and attach pocket as folls:
Next row: K2tog, then maintaining pattern, work 14 sts then slip next 40 sts onto stitch holder and in their place patt across 40 sts of one pocket lining, patt to end.
Cont in patt over all sts, decreasing 1 st at side edge on every foll 8th row until 53 (61, 69, 77, 85) sts rem. Work straight until front matches back at commencement of raglan shaping, ending with a WS row.

Shape Raglan

Cast off 4 (5, 7, 8, 11) sts at beginning of next row and patt to end (49, 56, 62, 69, 74 sts).
K2tog at this edge on every alt row until 19 (22, 25, 29, 31) sts rem.

Shape Neck

With WS facing, K2tog at neck edge on next and foll 7 (10, 13, 15, 16) rows and at the same time continue to decrease 1 st at armhole edge on every alternate row as before until 1 st remains. Draw yarn through and break yarn.

RIGHT FRONT

Using 3.75mm needles, cast on 68 (76, 84, 92, 100) sts and work as for back from ** to ** but ending with a RS row.
With WS facing, start side shaping and attach pocket as folls:
Next row: K2tog, then maintaining pattern, work 14 sts then slip next 40 sts onto stitch holder and in their place patt across 40 sts of one pocket lining, patt to end.
Cont in patt over all sts, decreasing 1 st at side edge on every foll 8th row until 53 (61, 69, 77, 85) sts rem. Work straight until front matches back at commencement of raglan shaping, ending with a RS row.

Shape Raglan

Cast off 4 (5, 7, 8, 11) sts at beginning of next row and patt to end (49, 56, 62, 69, 74 sts).
K2tog at this edge on every alt row until 19 (22, 25, 29, 31) sts rem.

Shape Neck

With RS facing, K2tog at neck edge on next and foll 7 (10, 13, 15, 16) rows and at the same time continue to decrease 1 st at armhole edge on every alternate row as before until 1 st remains. Draw yarn through and break yarn.

SLEEVES

Using 3.25mm needles, cast on 52 (56, 60, 64, 68) sts and work in rib as for lower back for 5cm (2in) inc 4 sts evenly across last row (56, 60, 64, 68, 72 sts), ending with a WS row.

Change to 3.75mm needles and beg with row 1, work in twisted rib patt as for back. Inc 1 st at each end of 5th and every foll 4th (6th, 6th, 6th, 6th) row until there are 96 (100, 104, 108, 112) sts, taking extra sts into patt. Work without shaping until sleeve measures 40½ (42, 43, 44½, 46) cm (16, 16½, 17, 17½ 18 in) ending with a WS row.

Shape Raglans

Cast off 4 (5, 5, 5, 7) sts at beginning of next 2 rows, then K2tog at each end of next and 1 (4, 5, 8, 12) foll 4th rows (84, 80, 82, 80, 72 sts). Work one row.
K2tog at each end of next and every foll alt row until 10 sts rem. Work one row.
Cast off.

FRONT AND NECKBANDS

Join raglan seams very neatly taking care to match the patt on front, back and sleeves.

Left Front Band

Using 3.25mm needles cast on 17 sts and work as folls:
Row 1 (RS): K8, Sl1, K8.
Row 2: K1, P to last st, K1.
Repeat these 2 rows until piece fits up left front to start of neck shaping. Leave sts on safety pin for the time being.
Pin WS of long border edge to RS of left front. Sew in place using neat back stitch. Place pins to mark position of 8 evenly spaced buttons, with the first being 14cm (5½in) from cast on edge, and the last falling approx 4 rows below start of neck shaping.

Right Front Band

Using 3.25mm needles, cast on 17 sts and work as for left front until piece measures 14cm (5½in) ending with a WS row.

Next row (buttonhole): K3, cast off 3, K2, Sl1, K2, cast off 3, K3.

Next row: K1, P to last st, casting on 3 sts over each set cast off on previous row, K1.

Continue in patt as set working 7 further buttonholes to match positions marked on left front border, leave sts on a safety pin. Attach right front border as for left front border.

Neckband

Using 3.25mm needles and with RS facing, patt across 17 sts of right front border, pick up and knit 72 (78, 84, 88, 90) sts all round neck, patt 17 sts of left front border (106, 112, 118, 122, 124 sts). Work as folls:

Next row (WS): K1, P to last st, K1.

Next row: K8, Sl1, K to last 9 sts, Sl1, K8.

Rep these 2 rows until band measures 2½cm (1in), ending with a WS row.

Next row (RS): Patt 17, K30 (33, 36, 38, 39) [K2tog] 6 times, K30 (33, 36, 38, 39), patt 17 (100, 106, 112, 116, 118 sts).

Work in patt for a further 5 rows, maintaining slip sts as before

Next row (RS): Cast off 17 sts, patt to end.

Next row: Cast off 17 sts, P to end (66, 72, 78, 82, 84 sts).

Commencing with a K row, work in stocking stitch for a further 4cm (1½in) then cast off loosely.

MAKING UP

Fold front bands in half along column of slip stitches and pin in place over seam. Slip stitch in place.

Fold neckband in half, level with cast off sts and slip stitch loosely in place along cast on row. Join side and sleeve seams.

Pocket Tops

Using 3.25mm needles and with RS facing place 40 sts from holder on right front onto needle and work in rib as folls:

Next row (RS): P1 * K2, P2, rep from * to last 3 sts, K2, P1.

Rep this row a further 11 times. Cast off in rib.

Repeat for left pocket.

Slip stitch sides of ribbing and pocket linings into place. Over sew round double buttonholes. Sew on buttons. Darn in all ends.

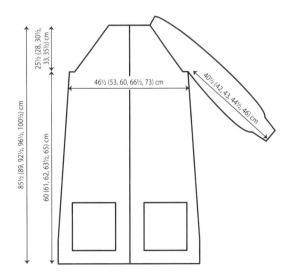

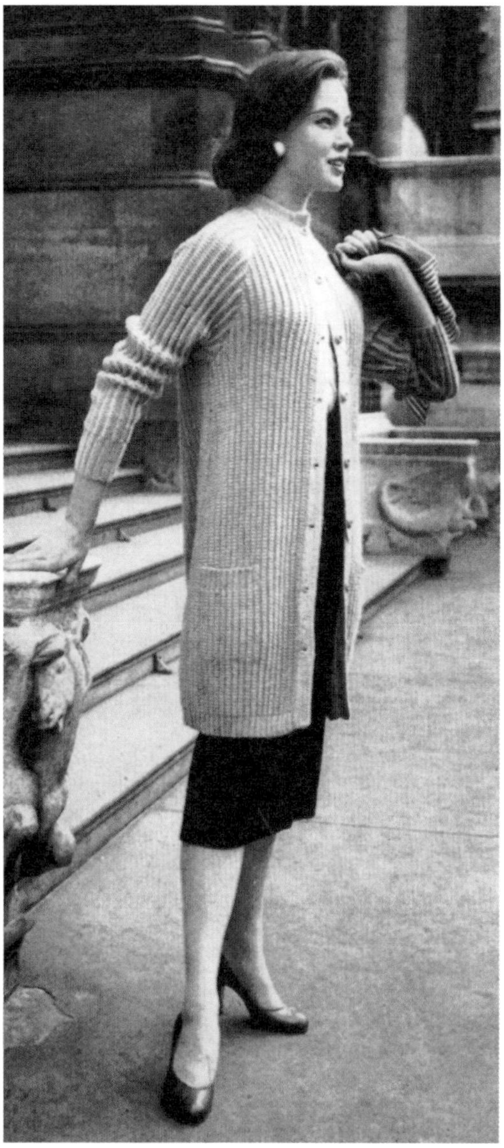

This winter's high-spot

the cardigan-coat!

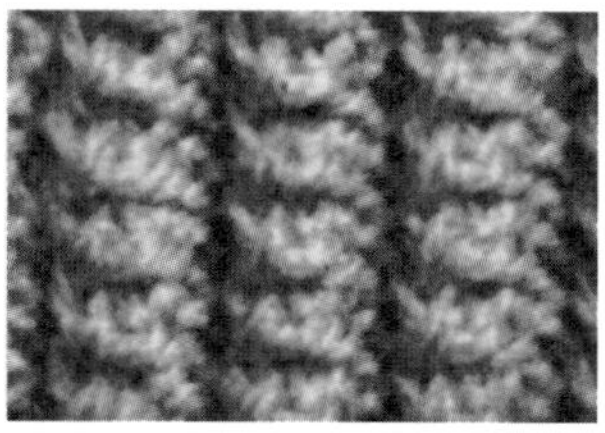

seven-eighths cardigans looked rather staggering at first, but now they've proved their worth, and make a really useful wearable garment for outdoor or indoor wear—high-fashion as well as practical!

Materials: Of Patons Quickerknit Botany, Patonised, 27 ozs. in Gay Turquoise 110. A pair each No. 10 and No. 11 "Queen Bee" needles, the 10's to be 14-inch. 8 matching buttons.

Measurements: To fit 34–35 inch bust; length from top of shoulders, 35 inches; sleeve seam, 17 inches.

Tension: 7 sts. and 9 rows to an inch over stocking-stitch on No. 10 needles.

BACK

With No. 10 needles cast on 180 sts. loosely and work in rib as follows:—

**1ST ROW: right side facing, p. 1, * k. 2, p. 2; repeat from * to last 3 sts., k. 2, p. 1. 2ND ROW: k. 1, * p. 2, k. 2; repeat from * to last 3 sts., p. 2, k. 1. Repeat these 2 rows 5 times more.

With right side facing, change to twisted rib pattern as follows:—1ST ROW: right side facing, p. 1, * k. 2, p. 2; repeat from * to last 3 sts., k. 2, p. 1. 2ND ROW: k. 1, * wool forward, k. 2, pass the wool forward over the k. 2, k. 2; repeat from * ending last repeat k. 1 instead of k. 2. These 2 rows form pattern.

Continue straight in pattern until back measures 7 inches from start.**

With right side facing, continue in pattern and shape sides by decreasing 1 stitch at each end of next and every following 8th row until 150 sts. remain. Work straight until back measures 24½ inches at centre. Here shape raglan.

With right side facing, cast off 7 sts. at beginning of next 2 rows, then k. 2 tog. at each end of next and every alternate row until 40 sts. remain. NEXT ROW: In pattern. Cast off, taking together every 9th and 10th stitch.

FRONTS

Begin by making pocket linings. With No. 10 needles, cast on 40 sts. and work 5½ inches straight in twisted rib pattern as for back, ending with a row on wrong side; leave stitches on a spare needle. Make another the same.

Left: With No. 10 needles, cast on 84 sts. and work as for back from ** to **. With right side facing, start side shaping and introduce pocket:—

NEXT ROW: k. 2 tog., pattern 14, slip next 40 sts. on to a spare needle and in their place pattern across 40 sts. of one pocket lining, pattern to end.

Continue in pattern over all stitches, decreasing 1 stitch at side edge on every following 8th row until 69 sts. remain. Work a few rows straight until front matches back at side edge.

With right side facing, shape raglan by casting off 7 sts. at beginning of next row, then k. 2 tog. at this edge on every alternate row until 21 sts. remain. Here shape neck:—

With wrong side facing, k. 2 tog. at neck edge on next and following 13 rows and *at the same time* continue to decrease 1 stitch at armhole edge on every alternate row as before until all stitches are gone; fasten off.

Right: Work to correspond with left, reversing all shapings. Your pocket row will read:—with right side facing, pattern 28, slip next 40 sts. on a spare needle and in their place pattern across 40 sts. of 2nd pocket lining, pattern to last 2 sts., k. 2 tog.

SLEEVES

With No. 11 needles, cast on 60 sts. and work 3 inches in rib as given for back, increasing 4 sts. across last row, 64 sts.

Change to No. 10 needles and twisted rib pattern and shape sides by increasing 1 stitch at each end of 5th and every following 6th row until there are 104 sts., taking extra stitches into pattern as they are made. Work a few rows straight until sleeve seam measures 17 inches.

With right side facing, shape top by casting off 5 sts. at beginning of next 2 rows, then k. 2 tog. at each end of next and every following 4th row until 80 sts. remain. Pattern back.

Now k. 2 tog. at each end of next and every following alternate row until 10 sts. remain. Pattern back. Cast off.

FRONT AND NECK BORDER

Join raglan seams very neatly, taking care to match the patterns on front, back and sleeves.

FRONTS: *Left:* With No. 11 needles, cast on 17 sts. and work as follows:—1ST ROW: right side facing, k. 8, slip 1 purlways, k. 8. 2ND ROW: k. 1, purl to last stitch, k. 1. Repeat these 2 rows until piece fits up left front to start of neck shaping. Leave stitches on a safety-pin for the time being.

Work a similar piece for right front with the addition of 8 buttonholes. First to come about 5½ inches above lower edge, 8th about ¼ inch below start of neck shaping, and remainder spaced evenly, *i.e.*, 34 rows between. Mark position of buttons with pins on left border to ensure even spacing, then work holes to correspond.

To make a buttonhole:—with right side facing, k. 3, cast off 3, k. 2, slip 1 purlways, k. 2, cast off 3, k. 3, turn; work back, casting on 3 over those cast off.

Neckband: with right side facing and No. 11 needles, pattern across 17 sts. of right front border, pick up and k. 84 sts. all round neck, pattern across 17 sts. of left front border. Work 1 inch stocking-stitch, keeping slip-stitches on each border as before. NEXT ROW: right side facing, pattern 17, k. 36, (k. 2 tog.) 6 times, k. 36, pattern 17. Work a further ½ inch stocking-stitch, keeping slip-stitches as before.

NEXT ROW: right side facing, cast off 17, purl to last 17 sts., cast off last 17 sts. Break wool. With wrong side facing, rejoin wool to remaining 78 sts. and work a further 1½ inches stocking-stitch. Cast off.

TO MAKE UP

Do not press. Join side and sleeve seams. Fold front borders in half, then join lower edges on wrong side; turn right side out, then sew borders very neatly in position to main work. Join top of borders neatly, then fold rest of neckband in half to wrong side and slip-hem in position.

With right side facing and No. 10 needles, work 12 rows k. 2, p. 2 rib on each of the pocket stitches beginning and ending with a p. 1 to keep continuity of rib; cast off.

Catch down sides of ribbing and pocket linings. Oversew round double buttonholes. Sew on buttons. Press seams and stocking-stitch borders only.

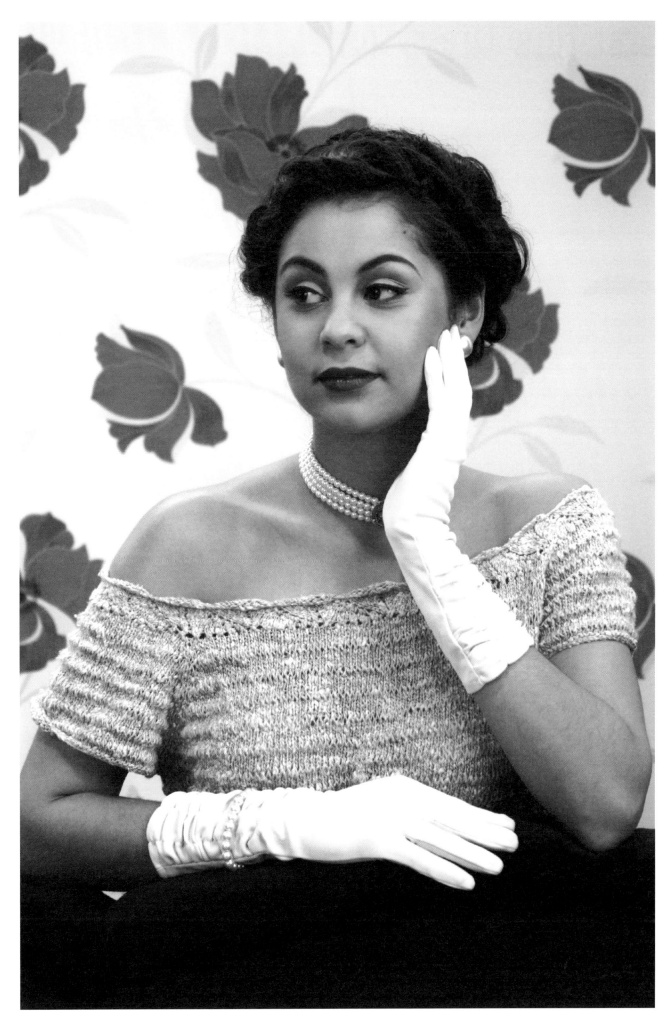

Star Time Dressy Top

MATERIALS
Texere Thai Silk 100% silk (300m per 100g cone)
2 (2, 2, 3, 3, 3, 3) cones
1 2.75mm (US #2) circular needle (length 60cm)
1 3.25mm (US #3) circular needle (length 60cm)
4 stitch markers

TENSION
22½ sts & 32 rows = 10cm (4in) using 3.25mm needle over body stitch pattern
26 sts = 10cm (4in) using 2.75mm needle over crown pattern

ABBREVIATIONS
See page 13 for standard abbreviations

SIZING
Measurements given in centimetres followed by inches in parentheses

To Fit	76 (30)	81 (32)	86 (34)	92 (36)	97 (38)	102 (40)	107 (42)
Finished Measurements							
Round Shoulder	76(30)	80½ (31½)	84½ (33)	89 (35)	93 (36½)	97½ (38½)	101½ (40)
Actual Bust Size	81 (32)	85½ (33½)	94 (37)	98½ (39)	109½ (43)	112 (44)	117½ (46)
Length to underarm	28½ (11)	30½ (12)	33 (13)	37 (14½)	39 (15½)	40½ (16)	42½ (17)
Armhole Depth	19½ (7½)	19½ (7½)	21½ (8½)	21½ (8½)	23½ (9)	24 (9½)	24 (9½)
Finished Length	48 (19)	50 (19½)	54½ (21½)	58½ (23)	62½ (24½)	64½ (25½)	66½ (26)

Garment shown in photographs is for third size 86 (34)

PATTERN NOTES
This garment is knit in the round from the top down with raglan shaping. The garment is worked with a shaped body to create a nipped in waist.

CROWN PATTERN (CP)
Round 1: * K2tog, YO, K1, YO, K6, K2tog, repeat from * to end.
Round 2 and all even rounds: K.
Round 3: * K2tog, K1, YO, K1, YO, K5, K2tog, rep from * to end.
Round 5: * K2tog, K2, YO, K1, YO, K4, K2tog, rep from * to end.
Round 7: * K2tog, K3, YO, K1, YO, K3, K2tog, rep from * to end.
Round 9: * K2tog, K4, YO, K1, YO, K2, K2tog, rep from * to end.
Round 11: * K2tog, K5, YO, K1, YO, K1, K2tog, rep from * to end.
Round 13: * K2tog, K6, YO, K1, YO, K2tog, rep from * to end.
Round 14: K.

BODY PATTERN (BP)
Rounds 1–4: K.
Round 5: * YO, K1, rep from * to end.
Round 6: K, dropping YO from LH needle.
These 6 rounds form pattern.

YOKE
Starting at neck edge and using 2.75mm needles, cast on 198 (209, 220, 231, 242, 253, 264) sts. Join into a round taking care not to twist cast on edge, placing a marker on needle to mark start of rounds.

Commencing with row 1, work 14 rounds of CP.

1st, 3rd, 5th & 7th sizes only
Next round: * K2tog, YO, rep from * to end (198, 220, 242, 264 sts).

2nd, 4th & 6th sizes only
Next round: * K2tog, YO, rep from * to last 3 sts, K1, K2tog (208, 230, 252 sts).

All sizes
Set up raglan seams by starting at beginning of round and work as folls:
K42 (42, 44, 44, 44, 46, 46) (right sleeve), PM, K57 (62, 66, 71, 77, 80, 86) for front, PM, K42 (42, 44, 44, 44, 46, 46) (left sleeve), PM, K57 (62, 66, 71, 77, 80, 86) for back, PM.
Change to 3.25mm needle and work in BP, inc 1 st each side of 4 markers every other round (8 sts inc in round) until 5 (5, 6, 6, 7, 7, 7) patt reps have been completed ending with round 6 (318, 328, 364, 374, 410, 420, 432 sts).
Work 1 more inc round (326, 336, 372, 382, 418, 428, 440 sts).

Divide Work

Cast on 1 st, work across 74 (74, 82, 82, 88, 90, 90) sts of right sleeve to next marker, place 89 (94, 104, 109, 121, 124, 130) front sts on a holder, place 74 (74, 82, 82, 88, 90, 90) sts for left sleeve on a 2nd holder, and place rem 89 (94, 104, 109, 121, 124, 130) sts for back on to another holder.

RIGHT SLEEVE

With WS facing, Kfb, K to end of row (76, 76, 84, 84, 90, 92, 92 sts). Cast off.

LEFT SLEEVE

Return sts for left sleeve to needle and with RS facing, rejoin yarn and work as folls:
Row 1 (RS): Kfb, K to end (75, 75, 83, 83, 89, 91, 91 sts)
Row 2 (WS): Kfb, K to end (76, 76, 84, 84, 90, 92, 92 sts). Cast off.

BODY (Worked in rounds)

Return sts of both front and back onto 3.25mm needle. Rejoin yarn to 1st st of front, work (round 2 of BP) across front sts, cast on 1 st, place marker on needle for underarm seam, cast on 1 st, work across back sts, cast on 1 st, put a 2nd marker on needle for other underarm seam (this will also serve as marker for start of the round), cast on 1 st (182, 192, 212, 222, 246, 252, 264 sts).
Commencing with round 3 of BP, work in rounds for a further 24 (30, 30, 30, 36, 30, 36) rounds. Adjust rows here to lengthen or shorten garment above waist.

Place Front Darts

Patt 28 (29, 33, 34, 39, 40, 42) sts, PM, patt 35 (38, 40, 43, 45, 46, 48) sts of front, PM, patt to end of round. Dec 1 st each side of underarm markers and each side of front dart markers every 6th round, 4 times (150, 160, 180, 190, 214, 220, 232 sts).

Continue to dec at underarm markers only on every 6th round 1 (1, 2, 3, 3, 4, 4) times more (146, 156, 172, 178, 202, 204, 216 sts).
Work without further shaping for 10 rounds.
Next round (Inc): Inc 1 st each side of underarm markers on every 4th round, 5 (5, 6, 7, 7, 8, 8) times (166, 176, 196, 206, 230, 236, 248 sts), working to round 6 of BP.
K 3 rounds, removing all markers other than end of round marker.
P 1 round removing final marker. Cast off knitwise.

MAKING UP

Sew up sleeves at underarm. Darn in all ends. Block lightly through a damp cloth taking care not to touch fabric with iron.

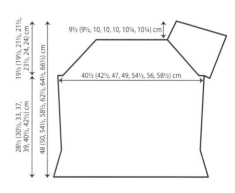

STYLE No. 3910
(Shown on right)

These directions are for size 12.
Changes for sizes 14 and 16 are in parentheses.

MATERIALS
SPINNERIN Star Time Dressy
(1 oz. pull skeins) — 8(9-10)
1 each 24-inch circular needles Nos. 3 and 4
1 steel crochet hook No. 4

GAUGE:
7 sts = 1 inch   10 rows = 1 inch on No. 3 needles
6 sts = 1 inch   8 rows = 1 inch on No. 4 needles

CROWN PATTERN STITCH: Multiple of 11 sts
Round 1: * K 2 tog, y o, K 1, y o, K 6, K 2 tog, repeat from * to end of round.
Round 2 and all even rounds: Knit.
Round 3: * K 2 tog, K 1, y o, K 1, y o, K 5, K 2 tog, repeat from * to end of round.
Round 5: * K 2 tog, K 2, y o, K 1, y o, K 4, K 2 tog, repeat from * to end of round.
Round 7: * K 2 tog, K 3, y o, K 1, y o, K 3, K 2 tog, repeat from * to end of round.
Round 9: * K 2 tog, K 4, y o, K 1, y o, K 2, K 2 tog, repeat from * to end of round.
Round 11: * K 2 tog, K 5, y o, K 1, y o, K 1, K 2 tog, repeat from * to end of round.
Round 13: * K 2 tog, K 6, y o, K 1, y o, K 2 tog, repeat from * to end of round.
Round 14: Knit.

BODY PATTERN STITCH
Rounds 1 through 4: Knit.
Round 5: * Y o, K 1, repeat from * to end of round.
Round 6: Knit, dropping off y o's of previous row.
Repeat these 6 rounds for body pattern stitch.

DIRECTIONS: Starting at neck edge with No. 3 needle, cast on 220(231-242) sts. Join, being careful not to twist sts. Put a marker on needle to mark start of rounds. Work 14 rounds of Crown Pattern Stitch. On the next round * K 2 tog, y o, repeat from * to end of round — 220(231-242) sts on needle. SET UP RAGLAN SEAMS: Starting at the beg of a round, K 44 (right sleeve), put a marker on needle, K 66(73-80) sts for front, put a marker on needle, K 44 sts (left sleeve), put a marker on needle, K 66(70-74) sts for back. Change to No. 4 needle and work in Body Pattern Stitch, inc 1 st each side of 4 markers every other round (8 sts increased in a round) until 6(6-6) y o patterns have been completed, ending with Round 6 — 364(375-386) sts on needle. Work 1 more inc round, ending at start of round. DIVIDE

WORK: Cast on 1 st, work across sts of right sleeve to next marker; put sts to next marker on another holder for front; put sts to next marker on another holder for left sleeve; put remaining sts on another holder for back. RIGHT SLEEVE: Working back and forth, at the beg of the next row cast on 1 st and K to end of row. Bind off. With right side facing you, work 1 row s c on sleeve edge. LEFT SLEEVE: Sl sts from holder onto No. 4 needle and work in same manner as right sleeve. BODY: Sl sts of front and back onto No. 4 needle. Work across front sts, cast on 1 st, put a marker on needle for underarm seam, cast on 1 st, work across back sts, cast on 1 st, put a marker on needle for underarm seam, cast on 1 st. Work round and round in Body Pattern Stitch for 2(1½-1½) inches. FRONT DARTS AND UNDERARM SHAPING: Work across front sts, putting a marker on needle each side of center 40(42-44) sts of front. DEC ROUND: Dec 1 st each side of underarm markers and each side of front dart markers every 6th round 4 times. Then discontinue dec each side of dart markers, but continue to dec 1 st each side of underarm markers every 4th round until there are 8(9-9) y o patterns below armhole, ending with Round 6. Work even for 10 rounds. Then inc 1 st each side of underarm markers every 4th round until there are 6 more y o patterns, ending with Round 6. K 3 rounds even. P the next round. Bind off. Work 1 row s c around lower edge. FINISHING: Sew sleeve seam and sew to body. With right side facing you, work 1 row s c around neck edge. Block.

Tailored Cape Stole

MATERIALS
Excelana Luxury DK wool 100% pure new British wool (119m/130yds per 50g ball)
7 balls shade French Rose
1 pair 3.25mm (US #3) needles
1 pair 4mm (US #6) needles
Stitch markers
Stitch holders

TENSION
30 sts & 25 rows = 10cm (4in) using 4mm needles over unstretched rib

Standard Yarn Tension
23 sts & 28 rows = 10cm (4in) using 3.75mm needles over stocking stitch

ABBREVIATIONS
See page 13 for standard abbreviations

SIZING
Measurements given in centimetres followed by inches in parentheses

One size to fit up to 111cm (44in)
Finished measurements
Total Width	131½ (52)
Front Length	66 (26)
Back Length	37 (14¾)

BACK
Using 3.25mm needles cast on 267 sts and work as folls:
Next row (RS): * [P1, K1] 4 times, P1, K1tbl, [P1, K1] 37 times, P1, K1tbl, rep from * to last 9 sts, [P1, K1] 4 times, P1.
Next row: * K1, [P1, K1] 4 times, P1tbl, K1, [P1, K1] 37 times, P1tbl, rep from * to last 9 sts, K1, [P1, K1] 4 times.

Row 1: [P1, K1] 4 times, P1, PM, K2togtbl, rib 73, PM, K2togtbl, [P1, K1] 4 times, P1, PM, K2togtbl, rib 73, PM, K2tog, [P1, K1] 4 times, P1, PM, K2tog, rib 73, PM, K2tog, [P1, K1] 4 times, P1 (261 sts).
Row 2: K1, [P1, K1] 4 times, * P1tbl, rib 73, P1tbl, [K1, P1] 4 times, K1, rep from * to end of row.
Row 3: [P1, K1] 4 times, P1, K2togtbl, rib 72, K1tbl, [P1, K1] 4 times, P1, K1tbl, rib 73, K1tbl, [P1, K1] 4 times, P1, K1tbl, rib 72, K2tog, [P1, K1] 4 times, P1 (259 sts).
Row 4: K1, [P1, K1] 4 times, P1tbl, rib 72, P1tbl, [K1, P1] 4 times, K1, P1tbl, rib 73, P1tbl, [K1, P1] 4 times, K1, P1tbl, rib 72, P1tbl, [K1, P1] 4 times, K1.

Continue as for last 4 rows, dec 1 st at markers at side panels on next and every foll alt row, and at centre panel markers as well on next and every foll 4th row until 69 sts rem (6 decreases worked on every row 1 repeat, 2 decreases worked on every 3rd row repeat).
Work 1 row. Cast off rem 69 sts.

POCKETS (Make two)
Using 4mm needles, cast on 33 sts, and work in rib as folls:
Row 1 (RS): * P1, K1, rep from * to last st, P1.
Row 2: * K1, P1, rep from * to last st, K1.
Rep these 2 rows until work measures 9cm (3½in) ending with a RS row.
Slip sts on to a stitch holder and leave to one side.

LEFT FRONT
Using 4mm needles, cast on 53 sts, and work in rib as folls:
Row 1 (RS): * P1, K1, rep from * to last st, P1.
Row 2: * K1, P1, rep from * to last st, K1.
Rep these 2 rows until work measures 9cm (3½in) ending with a WS row.

Place Pocket
Next row (RS): Rib 18, K next 33 sts, then placing them on to a stitch holder, rib last 2 sts (20 sts).
Next row: Rib 2, slip stitches for pocket on to LH needle, rib across 33 sts from pocket, rib 18 (53 sts).
Continue in rib as set, until work measures 26½cm (10½in) from cast on ending with a WS row. Mark row end with waste yarn.

Shape Raglan
Dec 1 st at beg of next and every foll alt row until 15 sts rem, then dec 1 st at raglan edge on every row until 1 st rems.
Draw through yarn and fasten off.

stitch as for bottom edge border, dec 1 st at each end of 2nd and every foll alt row until 305 sts rem. Cast off rem sts.

BACK BORDER

(To fit from end of bottom edge borders, around outside edge of scarf front pieces and around back) Using 3.25mm needles, cast on 405 sts and work in moss stitch as for bottom edge border, dec 1 st at each end of 2nd and every foll alt row until 391 sts rem. Cast off rem sts.

MAKING UP

Block work with WS facing, stretching out lower edges. Stitch pockets into position using a flat slip stitch. Catch pocket tops into position on RS of work. Using a flat slip stitch join back to front pieces from top edge to marked position on fronts. Using flat slip stitches attach front and back borders matching centre of each piece to centre back of garment, and border ends to bottom corners of garment pieces, stretching and easing remaining fabric into place. Stitch bottom edge borders into position, joining all mitred corners neatly. Darn in all ends.

RIGHT FRONT

Work as for left front until work measures 9cm (3½in) ending with a RS row.
Place pocket as for left front, then continue in rib until work measures same as left front to commencement of raglan shaping ending with a RS row. Work raglan shaping as for left front.

POCKET TOPS

Slip 33 sts from stitch holder onto 3.25mm needle and with RS facing, rejoin yarn. Work in moss stitch as folls:
Next row (RS): * K1, P1, rep from * to last st, K1.
Rep this row until moss stitch border measures 4cm (1½in). Cast off in moss stitch.

BOTTOM EDGE BORDERS (Make two)

Using 3.25mm needles, cast on 67 sts and work in moss stitch as folls:
Next row (RS): * K1, P1, rep from * to last st, K1.
Rep this row and at same time dec 1 st at each end of next and every foll alt row until 53 sts rem. Cast off.

FRONT EDGE BORDER

(To fit front of each side and round neck)
Using 3.25mm needles, cast on 319 sts and work in moss

136—4ᴰ

TAILORED
CAPE
STOLE

in Totem or Double Quick

P&B
WOOLS

This cape stole fits

A great deal of thought has gone into the design of this cape stole The raglan style shaping and the deep cape back combines a secure-feeling fit with all the casual comfort of an ordinary stole. It stays on and it's deliciously warm!

MATERIALS

14 oz. balls PATONS TOTEM* Double Knitting or PATONS DOUBLE QUICK Knitting.
Two No. 8 and two No. 10 BEEHIVE needles, or QUEEN BEE if stainless rigid needles preferred, measured by BEEHIVE gauge. Two BEEHIVE stitch-holders.
You must use the P & B brands recommended above to be sure of a successful result.

MEASUREMENTS

Depth at centre back approximately 15 ins. Width at ends, approximately 11½ ins. Length along Front edge approximately 58 ins.

These instructions apply to the above measurements only; adaptations to other sizes are not available.

ABBREVIATIONS

K. = knit; P. = purl; K.B. = knit into back of stitch; P.B.=purl into back of stitch; st.=stitch; tog.= together; t.b.l.=through back of loops; dec.=decrease by working 2 sts. together; beg.=beginning; alt.=alternate; rep.=repeat: ins.= inches.

HOW TO CHECK YOUR TENSION

Before you knit this design check your tension carefully. Take a pair of No. 8 needles and some Patons Totem Double Knitting, or Patons Double Quick Knitting. Cast on 11 stitches and work in stocking stitch— 1 row knit; 1 row purl—for 15 rows. Cast off; press **lightly** on wrong side. The tension should be 5½ stitches and 7½ rows to one square inch and the

---

knitted square should measure 2 inches each way. If the square is bigger your work is too loose; try a size finer needle. If it is smaller your work is too tight; try a size coarser needle.

If you knit to the correct tension in stocking stitch, you will knit naturally to the correct tension for any stitch in this booklet. If you alter the needles to obtain the correct tension in stocking stitch, corresponding alterations must be made to the needles throughout.

WASHING
DOUBLE KNITTING

As this design uses a substantial weight of double knitting wool, special care in washing and drying is essential if it is to keep its shape. Surplus water should be removed as quickly and as thoroughly as possible (a light wringer is permissible); while the garment is wet it should be continually supported and should on no account be hung up to dry.

CAPE BACK

Using No. 8 needles, cast on 267 sts.
1st row—(P.1, K.1) 4 times, P.1, K.B.1, (P.1, K.1) 37 times, P.1, K.B.1, (P.1, K.1) 4 times, P.1, K.B.1, (P.1, K.1) 37 times, P.1, K.B.1, (P.1, K.1) 4 times, P.1, K.B.1, (P.1, K.1) 37 times, P.1, K.B.1, (P.1, K.1) 4 times, P.1.

2nd row—K.1, (P.1, K.1) 4 times, P.B.1, K.1, (P.1, K.1) 37 times, P.B.1, K.1, (P.1, K.1) 4 times, P.B.1, K.1, (P.1, K.1) 37 times, P.B.1, K.1, (P.1, K.1) 4 times, P.B.1, K.1, (P.1, K.1) 37 times, P.B.1, K.1, (P.1, K.1) 4 times.

Shape as follows:—

1st row—(P.1, K.1) 4 times, P.1, K.2 tog.t.b.l., rib 73, K.2 tog.t.b.l., (P.1, K.1) 4 times, P.1, K.2 tog.t.b.l., rib 73, K.2 tog., (P.1, K.1) 4 times, P.1, K.2 tog., rib 73, K.2 tog., (P.1, K.1) 4 times, P.1.

2nd row—K.1, (P.1, K.1) 4 times, P.B.1, rib 73, P.B.1, (K.1, P.1) 4 times, K.1, P.B.1, rib 73, P.B.1, (K.1, P.1) 4 times, K.1, P.B.1, rib 73, P.B.1, (K.1, P.1) 4 times, K.1.

3rd row—(P.1, K.1) 4 times, P.1, K.2 tog.t.b.l., rib 72, K.B.1, (P.1, K.1) 4 times, P.1, K.B.1, rib 73, K.B.1, (P.1, K.1) 4 times, P.1, K.B.1, rib 72, K.2 tog., (P.1, K.1) 4 times, P.1.

4th row—K.1, (P.1, K.1) 4 times, P.B.1, rib 72, P.B.1, (K.1, P.1) 4 times, K.1, P.B.1, rib 73, P.B.1, (K.1, P.1) 4 times, K.1, P.B.1, rib 72, P.B.1, (K.1, P.1) 4 times, K.1.

Continue working in this manner, dec. on side panels on next and every alt. row as before and on centre panel on every 4th row as before until 69 sts. remain.

Work 1 row.

Cast off.

POCKET

Using No. 8 needles, cast on 33 sts.

1st row—* P.1, K.1, rep. from * to last st., P.1.

2nd row—* K.1, P.1, rep. from * to last st., K.1.

Rep. these 2 rows until work measures 3½ ins. from beg., finishing at end of a 1st row.

Slip sts. on to a stitch-holder and leave.

FIRST END PIECE

Using No. 8 needles, cast on 53 sts.

Work in rib as on Pocket for 3½ ins., finishing at end of a 2nd row.

Place pocket as follows:—

Next row—Rib 18, knit next 33 sts. on to a stitch-holder, rib 2.

Next row—Rib 2, slip sts. from Pocket on to left-hand needle, rib across these sts., rib to end.

Continue in rib until work measures 10¼ ins. from beg., finishing at end of a 2nd row.

Dec. 1 st. at beg. of next and every alt. row until all sts. are worked off.

POCKET TOP

Slip 33 sts. from stitch-holder on to No. 10 needle.

Work in moss stitch, every row "* K.1, P.1, rep. from * to last st., K.1" for 1½ ins.

Cast off.

POCKET, SECOND END PIECE AND POCKET TOP

Work as First Piece, reversing position of Pocket and shaping.

END BORDERS (TWO)

Using No. 10 needles, cast on 67 sts.

Work in moss stitch, dec. 1 st. at both ends of 2nd and every alt. row until 53 sts. remain.

Cast off.

FRONT EDGE

(neck edge of Cape)

Using No. 10 needles, cast on 255 sts.

Work in moss stitch, dec. 1 st. at both ends of 2nd and every alt. row until 241 sts. remain.

Cast off.

OUTSIDE BORDER

Using No. 10 needles, cast on 405 sts.

Work in moss stitch, dec. 1 st. at both ends of 2nd and every alt. row until 391 sts. remain.

Cast off.

Note—*In order to preserve the lovely crepe appearance of Totem Fabrics, these must be pressed very lightly as over-pressing will spoil the appearance of the finished fabric.*

TO MAKE UP

With wrong side of work facing block each piece by pinning out round edges.

Press each piece **very lightly** using a warm iron and damp cloth.

Using a flat seam, stitch Pockets into position on wrong side of work, and Pocket Tops in position on right side of work.

Using a flat seam throughout join shaped portion of End Pieces to shaped edge of Cape Back. Stretching Front Borders and easing in Back Border, stitch Borders into position joining mitred corners. **Very lightly** press seams.

An Elegant Longliner

MATERIALS
Excelana 4 Ply Luxury Wool 100% pure new British wool (159m/174yds per 50g ball)
9 (10, 10, 11, 12, 13, 14) balls shade Powdered Egg
Set of 2.75mm (US #2) DPNs
1 pair 2.75mm (US #2) needles
1 pair 3mm (US #2-3) needles
1 2.75mm (US #2) circular needle
4 stitch holders
1 7cm (2¾in) deep buckle

TENSION
28 sts and 36 rows = 10cm (4in) over stocking stitch using 3mm needles

ABBREVIATIONS
See page 13 for standard abbreviations

SIZING
Measurements given in centimetres followed by inches in parentheses

To Fit	76–81 (30–32)	81–86 (32–34)	86–92 (34–36)	92–97 (36–38)	97–102 (38–40)	102–106 (40–42)	106–112 (42–44)
Finished Measurements							
Actual Bust Size	86½ (34)	90½ (35½)	95 (37½)	99½ (39)	108 (42½)	112 (44)	116½ (46)
Length to underarm	35½ (14)	38 (15)	38 (15)	40½ (16)	40½ (16)	43 (17)	43 (17)
Armhole Depth	20½ (8)	21½ (8½)	21½ (8½)	22½ (9)	23½ (9¼)	24½ (9½)	25½ (10)
Finished Length	61 (24)	64½ (25½)	64½ (25½)	68 (27)	69 (27¼)	72½ (28½)	73½ (29)
Sleeve Length	42 (16½)	43 (17)	43 (17)	44½ (17½)	44½ (17½)	46 (18)	46 (18)

Garment in photographs is for first size 81–86 (30–32)

BACK
Using 2.75mm needles, cast on 121 (127, 133, 139, 151, 157, 163) sts and commencing with a K row, work in stocking stitch until work measures 7½cm (3in).
Change to 3mm needles and continue without further shaping until back measures 35½ (38, 38, 40½, 40½, 43, 43) cm (14, 15, 15, 16, 16, 17, 17 in) ending with a WS row.

Shape Raglans
Cast off 4 (4, 6, 6, 8, 8, 9) sts at beg of next 2 rows (113, 119, 121, 127, 135, 141, 145 sts), then dec 1 st at each end of next and every alt row until 39 (41, 43, 45, 49, 51, 53) sts rem. P one row. Place rem sts on holder.

FRONT
Using 2.75mm needles, cast on 121 (127, 133, 139, 151, 157, 163) sts and commencing with a K row, work in stocking stitch until work measures 4cm (1½in) ending with a RS row.
Next row (WS): P52 (55, 58, 61, 67, 70, 73) [Pfb, P1] 8 times, P53 (56, 59, 62, 68, 71, 74) (129, 135, 141, 147, 159, 165, 171 sts).
Next row: K50 (53, 56, 59, 65, 68, 71), P2, [K1tbl, P1] 12 times, K1tbl, P2, K50 (53, 56, 59, 65, 68, 71).
Next row: P50 (53, 56, 59, 65, 68, 71), K2, [P1tbl, K1] 12 times, P1tbl, K2, P50 (53, 56, 59, 65, 68, 71).
Repeat last 2 rows until front measures 7½cm (3in) from cast on edge.
Change to 3mm needles and cont as set by last 2 rows, working twisted rib stitch on centre panel, until front measures 35½ (38, 38, 40½, 40½, 43, 43) cm (14, 15, 15, 16, 16, 17, 17 in) ending with a WS row.

Shape Raglans
Cast off 4 (4, 6, 6, 8, 8, 9) sts at beg of next 2 rows (121, 127, 129, 135, 143, 149, 153 sts), then dec 1 st at each end of next and every alt row until 57 (59, 61, 63, 67, 69, 71) sts rem. Patt one row.

Shape Neck
Next row (RS): K2tog, K9, turn and leave rem sts on a spare needle (10 sts).
Next row: P.
Decrease 1 st at each end of every RS row until 2 sts rem, K2tog.
Fasten off.

Work without further shaping until sleeve measures 42 (43, 43, 44½, 44½, 46, 46) cm (16½, 17, 17, 17½, 17½, 18, 18 in) ending with a WS row.

Shape Raglans

Cast off 4 (4, 4, 6, 6, 8, 8) sts at beg of next 2 rows (83, 85, 85, 85, 85, 85, 85 sts).
Dec 1 st at each end of next and 9 (10, 10, 12, 14, 16, 17) foll 4th rows (63, 63, 63, 59, 55, 51, 49 sts), then dec 1 st at each end of every alt row until 27 sts rem. P 1 row. Place rem sts on holder.

COLLAR

Join raglan seams neatly. Using 2.75mm circular needle, and with RS facing, K39 (41, 43, 45, 49, 51, 53) sts across back of neck, K 27 sts across top of sleeve, 35 (37, 39, 41, 45, 47, 49) sts from front neck, and 27 sts across second sleeve (128, 132, 136, 140, 148, 152, 156 sts).
Working in rounds, K each round until collar measures 30½cm (12in). Cast off loosely.

BELT

Using 2.75mm needles, cast on 33 sts and work in twisted rib patt as folls:
Row 1: K1, * K1tbl, P1, repeat from * to last 2 sts, K1tbl, K1.
Row 2: * K1, P1tbl, repeat from * to last st, K1.
Repeat last 2 rows until belt measures 71 (76, 81, 86, 91, 96, 101) cm (28, 30, 32, 34, 36, 38, 40 in).

Shape Point

Dec 1 st at each end of every row until 1 st rems.
Fasten off.

MAKING UP

Press lightly on WS under damp cloth avoiding ribbing. Join side and sleeve seams. Turn under 4cm (1½ in) around lower edge and slip stitch loosely on WS. Fold collar in half to WS and slip stitch in position. Press lightly then fold collar in half to RS. To cover buckle, cast on 12 sts using 2.75mm needles and work in st st until piece is long enough to fit around surface of buckle when slightly stretched. Cast off. Join short ends together and stretch strip over buckle, slip stitching into place at back of buckle. Sew straight end of belt to buckle. Darn in all ends.

With RS facing, rejoin yarn to rem sts, placing centre 35 (37, 39, 41, 45, 47, 49) sts on a holder, then K to last 2 sts, K2tog.
Next row: P.
Dec 1 st at each end of every RS row until 2 sts rem, K2tog, then fasten off.

SLEEVES

Using 2.75mm needles, cast on 63 (63, 63, 67, 67, 71, 71) sts and work in twisted rib patt as folls:
Row 1: K1, * K1tbl, P1, repeat from * to last 2 sts, K1tbl, K1.
Row 2: * K1, P1tbl, repeat from * to last st, K1.
Repeat the last 2 rows until work measures 7½cm (3in).
Next row: [K3 (3, 3, 4, 4, 4, 4), inc in next st] 4 (4, 4, 2, 2, 4, 4) times, [K0 (0, 0, 3, 3, 0, 0), inc in next st] 0 (0, 0, 2, 2, 0, 0) times, K1, P2, [K1tbl, P1] 12 times, K1tbl, P2, K1, [K0 (0, 0, 3, 3, 0, 0), inc in next st] 0 (0, 0, 2, 2, 0, 0) times, [inc in next st, K3 (3, 3, 4, 4, 4, 4)] 4 (4, 4, 2, 2, 4, 4) times (71, 71, 71, 75, 75, 79, 79 sts).
Change to 3mm needles.
Next row: P21 (21, 21, 23, 23, 25, 25), K2, [P1tbl, K1] 12 times, P1tbl, K2, P21 (21, 21, 23, 23, 25, 25).
Next row: K21 (21, 21, 23, 23, 25, 25), P2, [K1tbl, P1] 12 times, K1tbl, P2, K21 (21, 21, 23, 23, 25, 25).
Cont in patt, inc 1 st at each end of 11th and every foll 8th row until there are 91 (93, 93, 97, 97, 101, 101) sts, working inc sts as stocking stitch.

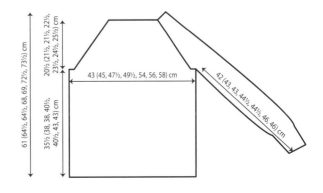

Two elegant longliners

Materials: Of Patons Beehive Fingering 4-ply, Patonised, 13 (14) 15 ozs. Spun Gold 2042. A pair each No. 11 and No. 10 "Queen Bee" needles. A set of four No. 12 "Queen Bee" needles, pointed both ends for collar. 1 yard 2½-inch wide belting; one 3-inch buckle.

Measurements: To fit 33–34 (35–36) 37–38 inch bust; length from top of shoulders, 22 (22½) 22½ ins.; sleeve seam, 16½ ins. all sizes.

Tension: 7 sts. and 9 rows to an inch over stocking-stitch on No. 10 needles.

N.B.—Instructions are given for 3 sizes. Where one set of figures is given this applies to all sizes.

BACK

With No. 11 needles, cast on 121 (127) 133 sts. and work 3 ins. stocking-stitch.

Change to No. 10 needles and continue straight in stocking-stitch until back measures 15 ins. down centre.

With right side facing, shape raglan armholes by casting off 4 (4) 6 sts. at beginning of next 2 rows, then decrease 1 stitch at each end of next and every alternate row until 39 (41) 43 sts. remain. Purl back. Cast off.

FRONT

With No. 11 needles, cast on 121 (127) 133 sts. and work 1½ ins. stocking-stitch, ending with a knit row.

NEXT ROW: p. 52 (55) 58, [p. twice in next st., p. 1] 8 times, p. 53 (56) 59: 129 (135) 141 sts. NEXT ROW: k. 50 (53) 56, p. 2, [k. 1 through back of loop, p. 1] 12 times,

k. 1 through back of loop, p. 2, k. 50 (53) 56. NEXT ROW: p. 50 (53) 56, k. 2, [p. 1 t.b.l., k. 1] 12 times, p. 1, t.b.l. k. 2, p. 50 (53) 56. Repeat the last 2 rows until front measures 3 ins. from start.

Change to No. 10 needles and continue straight in stocking-stitch and twisted rib until front measures same as back at side edge.

With right side facing, shape raglan armholes by casting off 4 (4) 6 sts. at beginning of next 2 rows, then decrease 1 stitch at each end of next and every alternate row until 57 (59) 61 sts. remain. Pattern back.

Here shape neck. NEXT ROW: right side facing, k. 2 tog., k. 9, turn and leave remaining stitches on a spare needle. NEXT ROW: Purl. Now decrease 1 stitch at each end of every knit row until 2 sts. remain; k. 2 tog. and fasten off.

Rejoin wool to remaining stitches, cast off centre 35 (37) 39 sts., k. to last 2 sts., k. 2 tog. Finish to correspond with first shoulder.

SLEEVES

With No. 11 needles, cast on 63 (63) 63 sts. and work in twisted rib as follows:—1ST ROW: k. 1, * k. 1 t.b.l., p. 1; repeat from * to last 2 sts., k. 1 t.b.l., k. 1. 2ND ROW: * k. 1, p. 1 t.b.l.; repeat from * to last stitch, k. 1. Repeat the last 2 rows for 3 ins.

NEXT ROW: [k. 3, increase in next stitch] 4 times, k. 1, p. 2, [k. 1 t.b.l., p. 1] 12 times, k. 1 t.b.l., p. 2, k. 1, [increase in next stitch, k. 3] 4 times: 71 sts.

Change to No. 10 needles. NEXT ROW: p. 21, k. 2, [p. 1 t.b.l., k. 1] 12 times, p. 1 t.b.l., k. 2, p. 21. NEXT ROW: k. 21, p. 2, [k. 1 t.b.l., p. 1] 12 times, k. 1 t.b.l., p. 2, k. 21. Continue in pattern thus and shape sides by increasing 1 stitch at each end of 11th and every following 8th row until there are 91 (93) 93 sts., taking increased stitches into stocking-stitch as they are made. Work straight until sleeve seam measures 16½ ins.

With right side facing, shape raglan top by casting off 4 sts. at beginning of next 2 rows. Now decrease 1 stitch at each end of next and every following 4th row until 65 sts. remain. Work 3 rows straight, then decrease 1 stitch at each end of next and every alternate row until 27 sts. remain. Pattern back. Cast off.

COLLAR

Join raglan seams neatly with a tailored seam. With the set of No. 12 needles and right side facing, pick up and k. 39 (41) 43 sts. across back of neck, 21 sts. across top of sleeve, 41 (43) 45 sts. all round front of neck, and 21 sts. across top of sleeve: 122 (126) 130 sts. Arrange stitches evenly on 3 needles and work straight in stocking-stitch; i.e., every round knit, until collar is 12 ins. deep. Cast off loosely using a bigger needle.

BELT

With No. 12 needles, cast on 33 sts. and work in twisted rib as follows:—1ST ROW: k. 1, * k. 1 t.b.l., p. 1; repeat from * to last 2 sts., k. 1 t.b.l., k. 1. 2ND ROW: * k. 1, p. 1 t.b.l.; repeat from * to last stitch, k. 1. Repeat the last 2 rows until belt measures 28 (28) 29 ins., or length required, then shape for point by decreasing 1 stitch at each end of every row until all stitches are gone. Fasten off.

TO MAKE UP

Press parts lightly on wrong side under a damp cloth avoiding ribbing. Join side and sleeve seams. Turn under 1½ ins. all round lower edge and slip-hem loosely on wrong side. Fold collar in half to wrong side and slip-hem in position all round. Press lightly, then fold collar in half to right side. Pin belting to ribbed belt on wrong side shaping point carefully; sew neatly in position. With No. 12 needles, cast on 12 sts. and work a strip in stocking-stitch long enough to cover outside edge of buckle when stretched. Join short ends neatly and stitch strip over buckle. Sew on buckle to straight end of belt. Press all seams.

Sports Sweater

MATERIALS
Jamieson's Spindrift 100% Shetland wool (105m per 25g ball)
8 (10, 11, 13, 14, 16) balls shade 563 (Rouge)
1 pair 2.75mm (US #2) needles
1 pair 3.25mm (US #3) needles
Waste yarn or stitch markers

TENSION
30 sts & 32 rows = 10cm (4in) using 3.25mm needles over Fancy Rib stitch

Standard Yarn Tension
30 sts & 32 rows = 10cm (4in) using 3.25mm needles over stocking stitch

ABBREVIATIONS
See page 13 for standard abbreviations

SIZING
Measurements given in centimetres followed by inches in parentheses

To Fit	81–86 (32–34)	92–97 (36–38)	102–107 (40–42)	112–117 (44–46)	122–127 (48–50)	132–137 (52–54)
Finished Measurements						
Actual Bust Size	87 (34)	97 (38)	107 (42)	117 (46)	127 (50)	137 (54)
Length to underarm	28 (11)	33 (13)	34 (13½)	35½ (14)	37 (14½)	38 (15)
Armhole Depth	20 (8)	20 (8)	21½ (8½)	23 (9)	24 (9½)	25½ (10)
Finished Length	48 (19)	53 (21)	55¾ (22)	58½ (23)	61 (24)	63½ (25)

Garment shown in photographs is for first size 81–86 (32–34)

PATTERN NOTES
This simple sports sweater is extremely easy to knit. Interest is added with a simple Fancy Rib stitch worked throughout the main body of the garment. Worked in just 2 main pieces it is also extremely quick to knit.

Fancy Rib Stitch
Row 1(RS): P2, * K2, P2, repeat from * to end.
Row 2: K2, * YO, K2, pass the YO over the K2, K2, repeat from * to end.

BACK
Using 2.75mm needles, cast on 114 (130, 146, 158, 174, 190) sts. Work in rib as folls:
Row 1 (RS): P2, * K2, P2, repeat from * to end.
Row 2: K2, * P2, K2, repeat from * to end.
Repeat these 2 rows until work measures 12½cm (5in) ending with a WS row.

Change to 3.25mm needles and commencing with row 1, work in Fancy Rib stitch for 8 rows.
*** Whilst maintaining pattern, inc 1 st at each end of next and every foll 6th row until 130 (146, 162, 174, 190, 206) sts. Take inc sts into patt as they are made. Work straight until back measures 29 (33, 34, 35½, 37, 38) cm (11½, 13, 13½, 14, 14½, 15 in). Mark each end of last row.

Cont straight in patt until back measures 48 (53, 56, 58½, 61, 63½) cm (19, 21, 22, 23, 24, 25 in), ending with a RS row.

Shape Shoulders
With RS facing cast off 10 (12, 14, 15, 16, 17) sts at the beg of next 8 rows (50, 50, 50, 54, 62, 70 sts).
Cast off rem sts.

FRONT
Work as for back until *** reached.

Divide for neck
Next row (RS): Inc in first st, patt 45 (53, 61, 67, 75, 83), turn and leave rem 68 (76, 84, 90, 98, 106) sts on a spare needle. Whilst maintaining pattern, work on these 47 (55, 63, 69, 77, 85) sts only, inc 1 st at beg of every foll 6th row 7 times, and at same time when work measures 20½cm (8in) commence neck shaping as folls:

With RS facing dec 1 st at neck edge of next and
every foll 6th (6th, 6th, 4th, 3rd, 3rd) row, until 40
(48, 56, 60, 64, 68) sts rem, remembering to mark
start of armhole with waste yarn as before when
work measures 29 (33, 34, 35½, 37, 38) cm (11½,
13, 13½, 14, 14½, 15 in). Continue in pattern
without further shaping until left front measures
same as back to start of shoulder shaping, ending
with a WS row.

Shape Shoulder
Cast off 10 (12, 14, 15, 16, 17) sts at beg of next
and foll 3 alt rows.

With RS facing rejoin wool to rem sts, cast off centre
22 sts, and patt to end, inc in last st (47, 55, 63, 69,
77, 85 sts). Work as for left front, reversing all
shapings.

NECKBAND (Knitted in two pieces)
Join shoulder seams. With RS facing and using
2.75mm needles, pick up and knit 156 (180, 192,
204, 212, 228) sts up right front from cast off edge
at centre front to centre back of neck.
Row 1 (WS): P1, * K2, P2, rep from * to last 3 sts,
K2, P1.
Row 2: K1, * P2, K2, rep from * to last 3 sts, P2, K1.
Repeat these 2 rows 4 times more, then first row
only, once more. Cast off in rib.
Work left side in the same way.

ARMHOLE BANDS
Using 2.75mm needles and with RS facing, pick up and
knit 144 (144, 152, 164, 172, 184) sts all round each
armhole. Work 11 rows in K2, P2 rib, decreasing 1 st at
each end of every alternate row (134, 134, 142, 154, 162,
174 sts). Cast off in rib.

MAKING UP
Sew up side seams and shaped edges of armhole ribbing.
Slip stitch 7½cm (3in) of ribbing at centre front together
and to cast off edge of front neck. Join seam at back of neck
using a flat slip stitch. Darn in all ends.

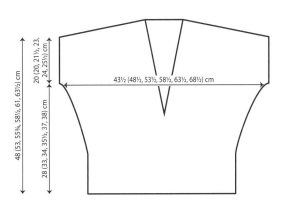

SPORTS SWEATER

No holiday is complete without some sort of sports casual, and this one is perfect—very comfortable and so smart. The extra-low neck is the latest thing in hand-knits, and the wide shoulders give a cap-sleeve effect.

MATERIALS: **5** ozs. Patons Fair Isle Fingering. A pair each No. 10 and No. 12 "Beehive" needles.

MEASUREMENTS: To fit 32–34-inch bust; length from top of shoulders, 19½ inches.

TENSION: 7½ sts. to an inch.

BACK

With No. 12 needles cast on 114 sts. and work 5 inches in rib as follows:—1ST ROW: Right side facing, p. 2, * k. 2, p. 2; repeat from * to end. 2ND ROW: k. 2, * p. 2, k. 2; repeat from * to end. Change to No. 10 needles and fancy rib pattern as follows:—

1ST ROW: Right side facing, p. 2, * k. 2, p. 2, repeat from * to end. 2ND ROW: k. 2, * wool forward, k. 2, pass wool forward over the k. 2; k. 2; repeat from * to end. These 2 rows form pattern.

Work 6 more rows in pattern, then continue in pattern, increasing 1 stitch at each end of next and every following 6th row until there are 130 sts., taking increased sts. into pattern as they are made. Work straight until back measures 11 inches. Mark each end of last row with a coloured thread, as this is start of armholes.

Continue straight in pattern until back measures 19 inches. With right side facing, shape shoulders by casting off 10 sts. at beginning of next 8 rows. Cast off.

FRONT

Work welt as for back, then change to No. 10 needles and pattern for 8 rows. NEXT ROW: Increase in 1st stitch, pattern 45, turn and leave remaining sts. on a spare needle. Continue in pattern on these sts. until work measures 8 inches, increasing 1 stitch at beginning of every following 6th row, side edge.

With right side facing, shape front edge by decreasing 1 stitch at end of next and every following 6th row; at the same time, continue increasing at side edge on every 6th row, as before, until 8 increasings have been done in all, then keep this edge straight. When work measures 11 inches, mark start of armhole as before.

Continue in pattern, still decreasing at front edge on every 6th row until 40 sts. remain. Work straight until front matches back, then with right side facing, shape shoulder by casting off 10 sts. at beginning of next and following 3 alternate rows, armhole edge.

With right side facing, rejoin wool to remaining sts., cast off centre 22, pattern to end increasing in last stitch. Work to correspond with left side.

RIBBED BANDS

Join shoulder seams. With right side facing and No. 12 needles, pick up and k. 156 sts. up right front from cast-off edge at centre, to centre back of neck. Work 11 rows k. 2, p. 2 rib; cast off in rib. Work left side in the same way.

In the same way, pick up and k. 144 sts. all round each armhole. Work 11 rows k. 2, p. 2 rib, decreasing 1 stitch at each end of every alternate row. Cast off in rib.

TO MAKE UP

Press very lightly under a damp cloth. Join side seams and shaped edges of ribbing. Join 3 inches of ribbing at centre front, and ribbing at back of neck. Press seams.

Angora Makes Pretty Separates

MATERIALS
Orkney Angora 4 ply 100% angora (400m/437yds per 50g ball)
3 (4, 4, 5, 5, 6, 6, 7) balls shade 35 (Blackberry)
1 pair 2.75mm (US #2) needles
1 pair 3.25mm (US #3) needles
Cable needle
6 buttons

TENSION
3 patt reps of 12 sts (36 sts) = 12½cm (5in) 5 patt reps of 12 rows (60 rows) = 12¾cm (5in) using 3.25mm needles

ABBREVIATIONS
See page 13 for standard abbreviations

Specific abbreviations for this pattern
cross P2tog – Slip next st off left needle onto cable needle and leave at front of work, slip next st on to right hand needle, with left needle pick up st from front of work then slip st from right needle onto left needle and purl these 2 sts together.
Alternatively, P2togtbl can be used instead.

SIZING
Measurements given in centimetres followed by inches in parentheses

To Fit	81 (32)	86 (34)	92 (36)	97 (38)	102 (40)	107 (42)	112 (44)	117 (46)
Finished Measurements								
Actual Bust Size	82 (32½)	87 (34½)	92½ (36½)	97½ (38½)	103½ (40¾)	108½(42¾)	112 (44)	117 (46)
Length to underarm	20 (8)	20½ (8¼)	22 (8½)	23 (9)	24 (9½)	25 (10)	26½ (10½)	27 (10¾)
Armhole Depth	27½ (10¾)	29½ (11½)	31½ (12½)	33¾ (13¼)	35¾ (14)	37¾ (15)	40 (15¾)	42 (16½)
Finished Length	47½ (18¾)	50 (19½)	53¾ (21)	56¾ (22¼)	59¾ (23½)	62¾ (24½)	66½ (26¼)	69 (27¼)
Sleeve Length	39 (15½)	40½ (16)	42 (16½)	43 (17)	44½ (17½)	45¾ (18)	47 (18½)	48¼ (19)

Garment shown in photographs is for first size 81 (32)

PATTERN NOTE
In its original form, the lace pattern had some decreases that were not mirrored (both sides of the pattern using P2tog for example). These have been changed in the instructions below to give smooth lines of decreases along the sides of the pattern.

BODY (Knitted in one piece from cuff to cuff)
Beginning at right cuff edge, and using 2.75mm needles, cast on 62 (74, 86, 98, 110, 122, 134, 146) sts. Work in rib patt as folls:
Next row (RS): * K1, P1, rep from * to end.
Rep this row until work measures 7½cm (3in) from cast on ending with a WS row.
Change to 3.25mm needles and work in lace patt (also shown on chart) as folls:
Row 1 (RS): Sl1, K1, * P2, K2tog, YO, K2, YO, Sl1, K1, psso, P2, K2, repeat from * to end.
Row 2: Sl1, * P1, K1, cross P2tog, YO, K1, P2, K1, YO, P2tog, K1, P1, repeat from * to last st, K1.
Row 3: Sl1, K1, * K2tog, YO, P2, K2, P2, YO, Sl1, K1, psso, K2, repeat from * to end.
Row 4: Sl1, * P2tog, YO, K3, P2, K3, YO, cross P2tog, repeat from * to last st, K1.
Row 5: Sl1, K1, * YO, Sl1, K1, psso, P2, K2, P2, K2tog, YO, K2, repeat from * to end.

Row 6: Sl1, * P1, K1, YO, P2tog, K1, P2, K1, cross P2tog, YO, K1, P1, repeat from * to last st, K1.
Row 7: Sl1, K1, * P2, YO, Sl1, K1, psso, K2, K2tog, YO, P2, K2, repeat from * to end.
Row 8: Sl1, * P1, K3, YO, cross P2tog, P2tog, YO, K3, P1, repeat from * to last st, K1.
These 8 rows form patt.

Shape Sleeves
Cont in lace patt as set, and inc 1 st at each end of next and every foll 4th (4th, 4th, 4th, 5th, 5th, 5th, 5th) row, 24 times in total (110, 122, 134, 146, 158, 170, 182, 194 sts). Work inc sts in reverse stocking stitch until there are 12 inc sts worked on each side, then take them into patt. Work 1 (7, 15, 19, 1, 7, 15, 19) rows without shaping.
Cont in patt, inc 1 st at each end of next and every foll alt row, 24 times in all, taking extra sts, into patt as before (158, 170, 182, 194, 206, 218, 230, 242 sts). Work one row.

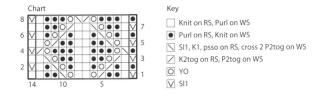

Chart

```
8  V  ● ● ● O \ / O ● ● ●      7
6  V    ● O / ● \ O ● ● V      5
4  V /  ● O ● ● ● ● O \ V      3
2  V    O ● ● ● ● ● ● O \ V    1
   14      10        5
```

Key

☐ Knit on RS, Purl on WS
● Purl on RS, Knit on WS
◺ Sl1, K1, psso on RS, cross 2 P2tog on WS
◿ K2tog on RS, P2tog on WS
O YO
V Sl1

Shape Body

With RS facing, cast on 36 (38, 42, 44, 48, 50, 54, 56) sts at beg of next 2 rows (230, 246, 266, 282, 302, 318, 338, 354 sts) working in patt as set over cast on sts, with rev st st at edges if there are not enough sts for a whole patt repeat **
Maintaining patt, work without shaping until 72 (78, 82, 88, 92, 98, 100, 106) rows worked from ** ending with a WS row.

Shape Neck

With RS facing, cast off 115 (123, 133, 141, 151, 159, 169, 177) sts at beg of next row, patt to end (115, 123, 133, 141, 151, 159, 169, 177 sts).
Work 47 (47, 51, 51, 57, 57, 61, 61) rows without shaping.
With WS facing, cast on 115 (123, 133, 141, 151, 159, 169, 177) sts at beg of next row, patt to end (230, 246, 266, 282, 302, 318, 338, 354 sts).
Maintaining patt, work without shaping for 72 (78, 82, 88, 92, 98, 100, 106) rows, ending with a WS row.

Sleeve Shaping

With RS facing, cast off 36 (38, 42, 44, 48, 50, 54, 56) sts at beg of next 2 rows (158 170, 182, 194, 206, 218, 230, 242 sts), then dec 1 st at each end of next and every alt row 24 times in all, working in reverse stocking stitch as appropriate to match first side (110, 122, 134, 146, 158, 170, 182, 194 sts).
Work 1 (7, 15, 19, 1, 7, 15, 19) rows straight.
Dec 1 st at each end of next and every foll 4th (4th, 4th, 4th, 5th, 5th, 5th, 5th) row, 24 times in all (62, 74, 86, 98, 110, 122, 134, 146 sts). Work 9 rows without shaping.
Change to 2.75mm needles and work 7½cm (3in) in rib as for first cuff. Cast off in rib.

Waistband

Join side and underarm seams. With RS facing and using 3.25mm needles, pick up and K 52 (56, 60, 64, 66, 70, 72, 76) sts across left front, 112 (120, 126, 132, 142, 148, 152, 160) across back, then 52 (56, 60, 64, 66, 70, 72, 76) sts across right front (216, 232, 246, 260, 274, 288, 296, 312 sts). Work in rib as folls:
Next row (WS): * K1, P1, rep from * to end.
Work in rib as set until rib measures 2½cm (1in).
Change to 2.75mm needles and continue in rib as set until until rib measures 7½cm (3in). Cast off in rib.

BAND

Using 2.75mm needles, cast on 11 sts and work in rib as folls:
Next row (RS): K1, * P1, K1, rep from * to end.
Next row: * P1, K1, rep from * to last st, K1.
Work as set making a buttonhole as folls when band measures 1cm.
Row 1 (RS): Rib 4, cast off 3 sts, patt to end.
Row 2: Patt to cast off sts, cast on 3, patt to end.
Cont in patt working 5 further buttonholes every 4 (4, 4, 4½, 4½, 5, 5, 5) cm (1½, 1½, 1½, 1¾, 1¾, 2, 2, 2 in).
Continue in rib until band fits up right front, around back of neck and down left front when slightly stretched. Place on safety pin.

MAKING UP

Press lightly on WS under a damp cloth. Sew band into place using, placing band slightly over edge of body and pinning in position. Adjust to fit if necessary then cast off sts. Sew through both layers from RS of work using a neat back stitch. Darn in all ends. Sew on buttons.

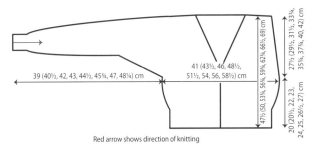

Red arrow shows direction of knitting

Angora makes pretty separates

LACE-STITCH CARDIGAN

Materials: 13 ½-oz. balls of Patons Fuzzy Wuzzy Angora in Bitter Sweet 5517. A pair each No. 12 and No. 11 "Beehive" needles. 6 buttons.

Measurements: To fit 34–36-inch bust; length from top of shoulders, 19½ inches; sleeve seam, 17½ inches.

Tension: It is difficult to measure this lacy stitch in angora but it is equivalent to a basic tension of 8 sts. and 10 rows to an inch over stocking-stitch on No. 11 needles.

BACK AND FRONT IN ONE

Begin at right cuff edge. With No. 12 needles, cast on 62 sts. and work 3 inches k. 1, p. 1 rib.

Change to No. 11 needles and pattern. 1ST ROW: right side facing, sl. 1, k. 1, * p. 2, k. 2 tog., wool forward, k. 2, wl. fwd., sl. 1, k. 1, p.s.s.o., p. 2, k. 2; repeat from * to end.

2ND ROW: sl. 1, * p. 1, k. 1, p. 2 tog., wool over needle, k. 1, p. 2, k. 1, wool round needle, p. 2 tog., k. 1, p. 1; repeat from * to last st., k. 1.

3RD ROW: sl. 1, k. 1, * k. 2 tog., w.r.n., p. 2, k. 2, p. 2, w.o.n., sl. 1, k. 1, p.s.s.o., k. 2; repeat from * to end.

4TH ROW: sl. 1, * p. 2 tog., w.o.n., k. 3, p. 2, k. 3, w.r.n., slip next stitch off left needle and leave at front of work, slip next stitch on to right-hand needle, with left needle pick up stitch from front of work, then slip stitch from right needle back on to left needle and purl these 2 sts. together; this will be called "cross p. 2 tog."; repeat from * to last stitch, k. 1.

5TH ROW: sl. 1, k. 1, * wl. fwd., sl. 1, k. 1, p.s.s.o., p. 2, k. 2, p. 2, k. 2 tog., wl. fwd., k. 2; repeat from * to end. 6TH ROW: sl. 1, * p. 1, k. 1, w.r.n., p. 2 tog., k. 1, p. 2, k. 1, p. 2 tog., w.o.n., k. 1, p. 1; repeat from * to last st., k. 1.

7TH ROW: sl. 1, k. 1, * p. 2, w.o.n., sl. 1, k. 1, p.s.s.o., k. 2, k. 2 tog., w.r.n., p. 2, k. 2; repeat from * to end. 8TH ROW: sl. 1, * p. 1, k. 3, w.r.n., "cross p. 2 tog.," p. 2 tog., w.o.n., k. 3, p. 1; repeat from * to last stitch, k. 1. These 8 rows form pattern.

Continue in lace pattern and shape sides by increasing 1 stitch at each end of next and every following 4th row, 24 times in all, keeping extra sts. in reversed stocking-stitch until you have increased 12 sts. each side, then take them into pattern. When the 24 lots of increasings have been done, pattern back. At this point you will have worked the 6th row of 13th pattern and you will have 110 sts. on needle.

Continue in pattern, increasing 1 stitch at each end of next and every following alternate row, 24 times in all, taking extra sts. into pattern as before, 158 sts. Pattern back. At this point you will have worked the 6th row of 19th pattern and increased 4 complete patterns up each side. This completes sleeve shaping.

With right side facing, cast on 36 sts. at beginning of next 2 rows for side edges, working the 7th and 8th pattern rows exactly as given over all sts.: 230 sts. Now work straight over all sts. in pattern, beginning with 1st pattern row, until 9 complete patterns have been done from cast-on sts. of side edge.

With right side facing, cast off 115 sts. at beginning of next row, then work 6 complete patterns on remaining sts. for back of neck. Now cast on 115 sts. at beginning of next row and work straight in pattern over all sts. until 9 complete patterns have been worked across left front.

With right side facing, cast off 36 sts. at beginning of next 2 rows, then decrease 1 stitch at each end of next and every alternate row, 24 times, remembering that once you have broken into a pattern to keep these sts. in reversed stocking-stitch to correspond with right sleeve. Work 1 row straight.

Now decrease 1 stitch at each end of next and every following 4th row, 24 times, 62 sts. remain. Work 9 rows straight. Change to No. 12 needles and work 3 inches k. 1, p. 1 rib. Cast off in rib.

Waistband: Join side and underarm seams. With right side facing and No. 11 needles, pick up and k. 216 sts. all round lower edge (112 on back and 52 on each front). Work 1 inch k. 1, p. 1 rib. Change to No. 12 needles and continue in rib until 4 inches have been done in all. Cast off loosely in rib.

Ribbed Border: With No. 12 needles, cast on 11 sts. and work in k. 1, p. 1 rib, rows on right side having a k. 1 at each end, until strip fits up right front, round back of neck and down left front when slightly stretched. Sew border in position as you go along and make 6 buttonholes up right front—first to come ¼-inch from lower edge and remaining 5 at 1½-inch intervals. To make a buttonhole:—With right side facing, rib 4, cast off 3, rib to end and back, casting on 3 over those cast off.

Press only very lightly on wrong side under a damp cloth. Sew on buttons. Press all seams.

Waistcoat and Cap

MATERIALS
Biggan Design 4 ply 100% merino first cross pure new wool (180m/196yds per 50g ball)
4 (5, 5, 6, 6, 7) balls shade 925 (Rose)
Cap requires 1 further ball
1 pair 3mm (US #2–3) needles
1 pair 2.75mm (US #2) needles
1 cable needle
6 buttons
3 press studs
1 2½cm (1in) buckle

TENSION
28 sts & 38 rows = 10cm (4in) using 3mm needles over stocking stitch

ABBREVIATIONS
See page 13 for standard abbreviations

Specific abbreviations for this pattern
MB (make bobble) – (K1, P1, K1, P1, K1) all into next st, turn and purl these 5 sts, turn again, K5tog.
C4F – Slip 2 sts on cable needle, leave at front of work, knit next 2 sts, knit the 2 sts from cable needle.
C4B – Slip 2 sts onto cable needle, leave at back of work, knit next 2 sts, knit 2 sts from cable needle.

SIZING
Measurements given in centimetres followed by inches in parentheses

To Fit	81 (32)	86 (34)	92 (36)	97 (38)	102 (40)	107 (42)
Finished Measurements						
Actual Bust Size	87½ (34½)	92½ (36½)	98 (38½)	103½ (40½)	108 (42½)	113 (44½)
Waist	63½ (25)	68½ (27)	75 (29)	78 (31)	85 (33)	89 (35)
Length to underarm	22 (8½)	23 (9)	24 (9½)	25 (10)	26 (10½)	27½ (11)
Armhole Depth	16½ (6½)	18 (7)	19 (7½)	19 (7½)	20 (8)	21½ (8½)
Finished Length*	38½ (15)	41 (16)	43 (17)	44 (17½)	46 (18)	49 (19½)
Shoulder to shoulder **	34½ (13½)	36 (14)	37½ (15)	39½ (15½)	41 (16)	42½ (16½)

*Finished length does not include "pointy bits" on fronts, but is based on back length
** before armband added

Garment shown in photographs is for fourth size 97 (38)

Waistcoat

BACK (Worked in stocking stitch throughout)
Using 3mm needles cast on 89 (95, 105, 109, 119, 125) sts and starting with a knit row, work in st st for 6 rows.
Next row (RS): K.
Next row (WS): K (indicates hem line).
Commencing with a K row, work in stocking stitch for 8 (12, 20, 16, 26, 32) rows, then inc 1 st at each end of next row and every foll 4th row until there are 123 (129, 137, 145, 151, 157) sts. Work 11 rows straight.

Shape Armholes
Cast off 5 (6, 6, 7, 7, 8) sts at beg of next 2 rows (113, 117, 125, 131, 137, 141 sts), dec 1 st at each end of foll 5 (5, 6, 6, 7, 7) rows (103, 107, 113, 119, 123, 127 sts), then dec 1 st at beg of foll 6 (6, 8, 8, 8, 8) rows (97, 101, 105, 111, 115, 119 sts).

Work 49 (55, 56, 56, 59, 65) rows without further shaping, ending with a WS row.

Shape Shoulders
Cast off 9 (10, 10, 11, 12, 12) sts at beg of next 2 rows (79, 81, 85, 89, 91, 95 sts).
Cast off 9 (10, 11, 11, 12, 13) sts at beg of next 2 rows (61, 61, 63, 67, 67, 69 sts).
Cast off 10 (10, 11, 12, 12, 13) sts at beg of foll 2 rows (41, 41, 41, 43, 43, 43 sts).
Cast off rem sts.

LEFT FRONT
Using 3mm needles cast on 3 (1, 1, 3, 3, 1) sts.
Row 1: K.
Row 2: Pfb, P to end.
Row 3: Cast on 3 sts, K to last st, Kfb.

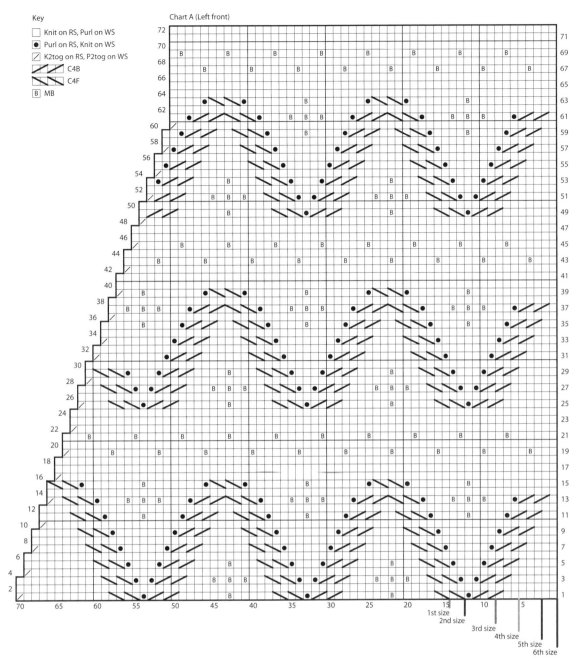

Key

☐ Knit on RS, Purl on WS
● Purl on RS, Knit on WS
╱ K2tog on RS, P2tog on WS
▨ C4B
▧ C4F
B MB

Chart A (Left front)

Repeat last 2 rows 7 (8, 9, 9, 10, 11) more times (43, 46, 51, 53, 58, 61 sts).

Next row (WS): As row 2.

Next row (RS): Kfb, K to end (45, 48, 53, 55, 60, 63 sts).

Next row: P.

Continue in st st, inc 1 st at beg of 5th and every foll 4th row until 62 (65, 69, 73, 76, 79) sts.

Work 5 rows straight.

Commence working yoke pattern as folls:

Row 1: [K5, MB] to last 2 (5, 3, 1, 4, 1) sts, K2 (5, 3, 1, 4, 1).

Row 2: P.

Row 3: K2, [MB, K5] to last 6 (3, 7, 5, 2, 5) sts, MB, K5 (2, 6, 4, 1, 4).

Row 4: P.

Row 5: K.

Row 6: P.

Shape Armhole and Front

Please note: When working shaping in pattern from chart, replace partial cables with stocking stitch. The 4th, 5th and 6th sizes all work one further front edge decrease, which is not shown on chart. On first neck front decrease please place marker or waste yarn to mark position of neck band.

Row 7: Cast off 5 (6, 6, 7, 7, 8) sts, counting the stitch now on right needle as first stitch shown on chart, work row 1 from chart A, reading from right to left, starting as indicated and working to end of row (56, 58, 62, 65, 68, 70 sts).

Row 8: Reading from left to right, starting at st 70 and ending as indicated, work from row 2 of chart A.

Row 9: K2tog, then cont to work patt from row 3 chart A, lining up sts with previous row (55, 57, 61, 64, 67, 69 sts). Cont to work in patt from chart A as set until row 31 is complete and AT THE SAME TIME, shape armhole and neck as foll:

Dec 1 st at armhole edge of foll 5 (5, 6, 6, 7, 7) rows, then dec 1 st at armhole edge of foll 2 (2, 3, 3, 3, 3) alt rows and

AT THE SAME TIME dec 1 st at neck edge on next and 9 foll 3rd rows. Neck shaping is also shown on chart for further clarification (38, 40, 42, 45, 47, 49 sts).

Maintaining continuity of patt, dec 1 st at front edge on 2nd and every foll 3rd row until 28 (30, 32, 35, 37, 39) sts rem.

4th, 5th and 6th sizes only
Dec 1 st at neck edge of 3rd row (34, 36, 38 sts). Please note, this decrease is not shown on chart.

All sizes
Work straight in stocking stitch until front matches back to start of shoulder shaping, ending with a WS row.

Shape Shoulder
Cast off 9 (10, 10, 11, 12, 12) sts at beg of next row (19, 20, 22, 23, 24, 26 sts).
Work 1 row straight.
Cast off 9 (10, 11, 11, 12, 13) sts at beg of next row (10, 10, 11, 12, 12, 13 sts).
Work 1 row straight.
Cast off rem sts.

RIGHT FRONT
Using 3mm needles, cast on 3 (1, 1, 3, 3, 1) sts.
Row 1: K.
Row 2: Cast on 3 sts, P to last st, Pfb.
Row 3: Kfb, K to end.
Repeat last 2 rows 7 (8, 9, 9, 10, 11) more times (43, 46, 51, 53, 58, 61 sts).
Next row (WS): Pfb, P to last st, Pfb (45, 48, 53, 55, 60, 63 sts).
Continue in st st, inc 1 st at beg of 7th and every foll 4th row until 62 (65, 69, 73, 76, 79) sts.
Work 5 rows straight.
Commence working yoke patt as foll:
Row 1: K2 (5, 3, 1, 4, 1), (MB, K5) to end.
Row 2: P.
Row 3: K5 (2, 6, 4, 1, 4), (MB, K5) to last 3 sts, MB, K2.
Row 4: P.
Row 5: K.

Shape Armhole and Front
When working shaping in pattern from chart, replace partial cables with stocking stitch. The 4th, 5th and 6th sizes all work one further front edge decrease, which is not shown on chart. On first neck front decrease please place marker or waste yarn to mark position of neck band.
Row 6: Cast off 5 (6, 6, 7, 7, 8), P to end (57, 59, 63, 66, 69, 71 sts).
Row 7: Reading from right to left, work from chart B row 1, starting on st 1 and ending as indicated (56, 58, 62, 65, 68, 70 sts).
Row 8: P2tog (armhole decrease), then reading from left to right, cont to work patt from row 2 of chart B, lining up sts with previous row (55, 57, 61, 64, 67, 69 sts).
Row 9: Work from row 3 of chart B to last 2 sts, K2tog (armhole dec) (54, 56, 60, 63, 66, 68 sts).

Cont to work in patt from Chart B as set until row 31 is complete and AT THE SAME TIME, shape armhole and neck as folls:
Dec 1 st at armhole edge on next 4 (4, 5, 5, 6, 6) rows and on foll 2 (2, 3, 3, 3, 3) alt rows, AT THE SAME TIME dec 1 st at neck edge on next and 9 foll 3rd rows. Neck shaping is also shown on chart for further clarification (38, 40, 42, 45, 47, 49 sts).

Keeping continuity of patt, dec 1 st at front edge on 2nd and every foll 3rd row until 28 (30, 32, 35, 37, 39) sts rem.

4th, 5th and 6th sizes only
Dec 1 st at neck edge of 3rd row (34, 36, 38 sts). Please note, this decrease is not shown on chart.

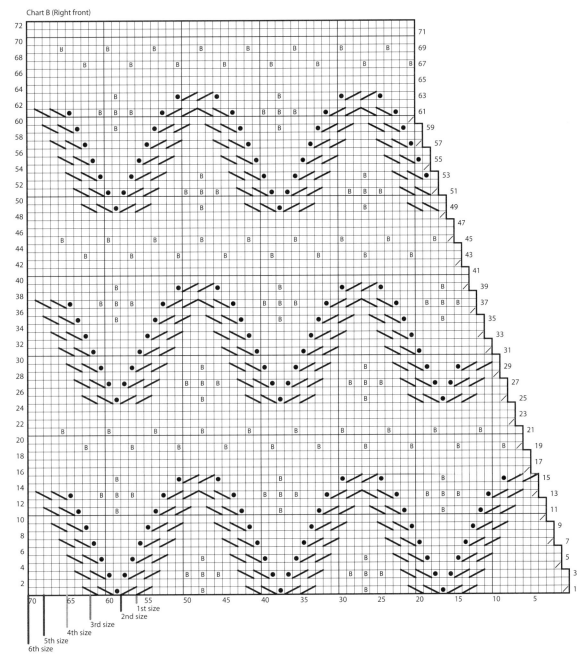

Chart B (Right front)

All sizes

Work straight in st st until front matches back to start of shoulder shaping, ending with a RS row.

Shape Shoulder

As left front.

BORDERS

Lower Edge of Left Front

Using 3mm needles, and with RS facing, rejoin yarn to cast on edge at centre front edge, and pick up and K 18 (20, 22, 22, 24, 26) sts along lower edge to point then pick up and K 27 (30, 33, 33, 36, 39) sts from here to side edge (45, 50, 55, 55, 60, 65 sts).

Row 1: P26 (29, 32, 32, 35, 38), [Pfb] twice, P17 (19, 21, 21, 23, 25) (47, 52, 57, 57, 62, 67 sts).

Row 2: K.

Row 3: P27 (30, 33, 33, 36, 39), [Pfb] twice, P18 (20, 22, 22, 24, 26) (49, 54, 59, 59, 64, 69 sts).

Row 4: K1 (3, 5, 5, 1, 3), [MB, K5] 8 (8, 8, 8, 10, 10) times, MB, K1 (3, 5, 5, 1, 3).

Row 5: P28 (31, 34, 34, 37, 40), [Pfb] twice, P19 (21, 23, 23, 25, 27) (51, 56, 61, 61, 66, 71 sts).

Row 6: K4 (0, 2, 2, 4, 0) [MB, K5] 2 (3, 3, 3, 3, 4) times, MB, K7, [MB, K5] 4 (4, 5, 5, 5, 6) times, MB, K2 (5, 2, 2, 5, 2).

Row 7: P29 (32, 35, 35, 38, 41), [Pfb] twice, P20 (22, 24, 24, 26, 28) (53, 58, 63, 63, 68, 73 sts).

Row 8: K.

Row 9: P30 (33, 36, 36, 39, 42), [Pfb] twice, P21 (23, 25, 25, 27, 29) (65 sts).

Row 10: K.

Row 11: K to indicate hem-line.

Work 6 rows straight.

Cast off.

Lower Edge of Right Front

Using 3mm needles, and with RS facing, rejoin yarn to cast on edge at side edge, and pick up and knit 27 (30, 33, 33, 36, 39) sts along lower edge to point and 18 (20, 22, 22, 24, 26) sts from here to front edge.

Work as for left front reversing pattern.

Armbands

Join shoulder seams. Using 3mm needles, and with RS facing rejoin yarn to armhole and pick up and K 114 (126, 132, 132, 138, 150) sts evenly spaced around armhole edge.

Row 1: P2tog, P to last 2 sts, P2tog (112, 124, 130, 130, 136, 148 sts).

Row 2: K.

Row 3: As row 1 (110, 122, 128, 128, 134, 146 sts).

Row 4: K4, [MB, K5] to last 4 sts, MB, K3.

Row 5: As row 1 (108, 120, 126, 126, 132, 144 sts).

Row 6: K6, [MB, K5] to end.

Row 7: As row 1 (106, 118, 124, 124, 130, 142 sts).

Row 8: K.

Row 9: P.

Row 10: K.

Row 11: K to indicate hem-line.

Work 3 rows straight.

Cast off.

Work other armhole in same way.

Neck Border

Using 3mm needles and with RS facing, rejoin yarn to 1st decrease row at right front edge indicated by marker or waste yarn, and pick up and K 138 (138, 150, 150, 162, 162) sts evenly spaced around neck edge, ending at marker on left front edge.

Work as for armbands ending with 130 (130, 142, 142, 154, 154) sts.

BACK BELT

Left Half

Using 3mm needles and yarn doubled, cast on 12 sts and work in rib as folls:

Next row (RS): * K1, P1, rep from * to end.

Rep this row until work measures 20½cm (8in). Cast off in rib.

Right Half

Using 3mm needles and yarn doubled, cast on 12 sts and work in rib as folls:

Next row (RS): * K1, P1, rep from * to end.

Rep this row until work measures 12½cm (5in).

Next row: Rib 4, work 2sts tog, wrap yarn around needle twice (making 2 sts), work 2 sts tog, rib 4.

Rib 7 rows.

Repeat last 8 rows 3 times more, then dec 1 st at beg of every row until 2 sts rem.

K2tog and fasten off.

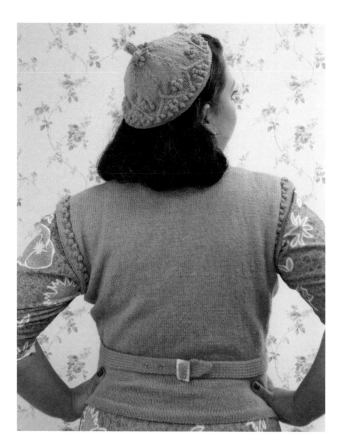

MAKING UP

Press work lightly on WS through a damp cloth. Join side seams. Fold back hem all round outer edges and loosely slip stitch in place on WS.

Using 2mm crochet hook and with RS of work facing, work a row of DC (SC) along each front edge.

Sew a buckle to one end of left half of belt as shown then sew belt to side seams about 6½cm (2½in) from lower edge. Attach press studs to fronts, placing one at top of straight edge of centre front and the others at equal intervals apart, with last press stud positioned immediately above lower border.

Scroll Trimmings (Make three)

Using 3mm needles, cast on 4 sts and work in single rib as for belt for 13cm (5in). Cast off. Curl each end into a ring and sew into position, leaving a hole in centre to take button. Knit 6 buttons (see 'Fit and Finish' chapter). Sew 3 buttons to right front, then sew 3 to left front, placing these 2½cm (1in) lower than those on right front. Button the scrolls into position on right front. Darn in all ends.

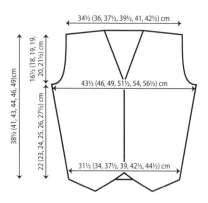

34½ (36, 37½, 39½, 41, 42½) cm

16½ (18, 19, 19, 20, 21½) cm

43½ (46, 49, 51½, 54, 56½) cm

38½ (41, 43, 44, 46, 49)cm

22 (23, 24, 25, 26, 27½) cm

31½ (34, 37½, 39, 42½, 44½) cm

Cap

Using 2.75mm needles, cast on 150 sts and starting with a knit row work 8 rows in stocking stitch.

Next row (RS): K.

Next row (WS): K to indicate hem-line.

Work 4 rows in stocking stitch.

Row 1 (RS): (K5, MB) to end.

Row 2: P.

Row 3: K2, (MB, K5) to last 4 sts, MB, K3.

Row 4: P to last 2 sts, P2tog (149 sts).

Row 5: Work from Chart C row 1, repeating marked section 7 times in each row.

Cont to work from Chart C as set until row 16 is complete.

Row 21: K.

Row 22: P.

Work extra rows of stocking stitch at this point if a slightly deeper cap is preferred.

Shape Crown

Row 1: K2, (K2tog, K16, K2tog tbl, K1) to end (135 sts).

Row 2: K2 (K2tog, K14, K2tog tbl, K1) to end (121 sts).

Row 3: K2 (K2tog, K12, K2tog tbl, K1) to end (107 sts).

Work 3 rows without shaping.

Row 7: K2 (K2tog, K10, K2tog tbl, K1) to end (93 sts).

Work 3 rows without shaping.

Row 11: K2 (K2tog, K8, K2tog tbl, K1) to end (79 sts).

Work 3 rows without shaping.

Row 15: K2 (K2tog, K6, K2tog tbl, K1) to end (65 sts).

Work 3 rows without shaping.

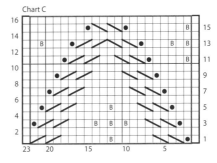

Chart C

Row 19: K2 (K2tog, K4, K2tog tbl, K1) to end (51 sts).

Work 3 rows without shaping.

Row 23: K1, (MB, K2tog, K2, K2tog tbl) to last st, K1 (37 sts).

Row 24: P.

Row 25: K2, (K2tog, MB, K2) to end (30 sts).

Row 26: P.

Row 27: (K1, K2tog) to end (20 sts).

Row 28: P.

Break off yarn, leaving a longish end, run it through rem sts, draw up and fasten off.

TOP KNOT

Using 2.75mm needles, cast on 4 sts and work in single rib as for belt until work measures 20½cm (8in). Cast off in rib. Fold the strip into 3 loops as shown and insert into top of cap before sewing up seam. Join seam. Turn up hem at lower edge and slip stitch loosely into position on WS. Press lightly.

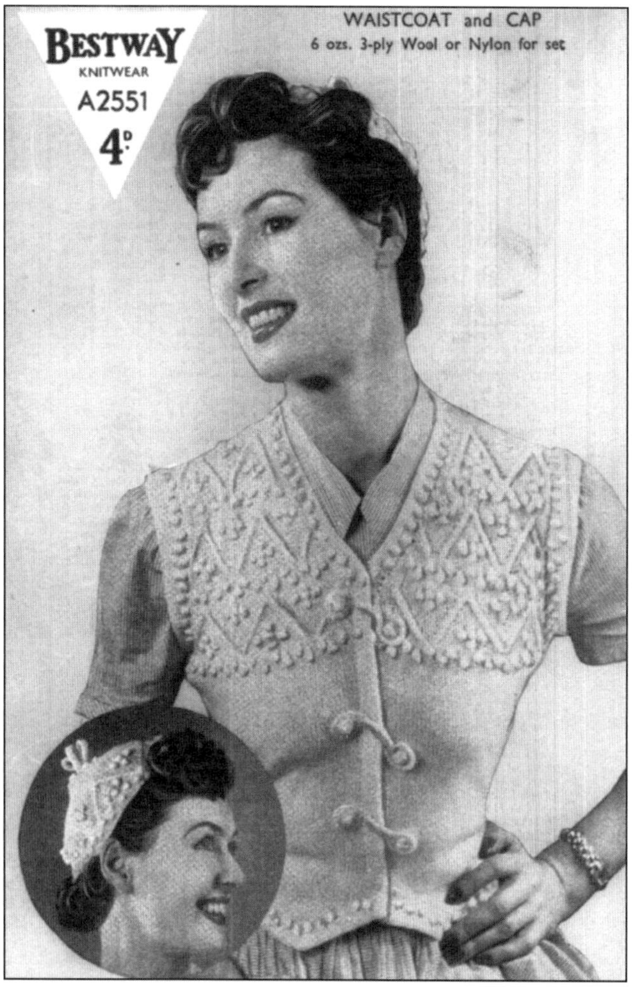
WAISTCOAT and CAP
6 ozs. 3-ply Wool or Nylon for set
BESTWAY
KNITWEAR
A2551
4D

THE SET IN WOOL

MATERIALS : *6 ozs. of Ramada Super Knitting Wool 3-ply, for the set ; 1 pair each of Nos. 11 and 12 knitting needles ; 6 buttons ; 3½ yards of binding ribbon ; 3 press studs ; 1 buckle.*

TENSION : *Over the stocking-stitch on No. 11 needles, 17 sts. to 2 inches and 11 rows to 1 inch. On No. 12 needles. 9 sts. and 12 rows to 1 inch.*

MEASUREMENTS : The Waistcoat—*To suit a 34 to 36-inch bust size ; length from shoulder at side edge, 15 inches.* The Cap—*To fit an average head size.*

ABBREVIATIONS : *K., knit ; p., purl ; st., stitch ; sts., stitches ; rep., repeat ; tog., together ; t.b.s., through back of sts. ; m.a.b., make a bobble ; inc., increase (by working twice into same st.) ; dec., decrease (by taking 2 sts. tog.) ; st.-st., stocking-stitch (1 row k. and 1 row p. alternately).*
Sts. in brackets must be worked along row to the extent stated after 2nd bracket.

NOTE ON PATTERN : *To "make a bobble," k. 1, p. 1, k. 1, p. 1 and k. 1 all into next st. ; then turn and p. these 5 sts. ; turn again and k. 5 tog., thus completing a bobble.*
To "twist A," slip next 2 sts. on to a spare double-pointed needle, and leave at front of work, k. next 2 sts., then k. the 2 sts. from spare needle. To "twist B," slip next 2 sts. on to a spare needle and leave at back of work, k. the next 2 sts., then k. the 2 sts. from spare needle.

THE WAISTCOAT

THE BACK

With No. 11 needles, cast on 109 sts. and work in st.-st. for 6 rows.

Next row : K.

Next row : K. to indicate hem-line.

Starting with a k. row, continue in st.-st. for 16 rows, then inc. 1 st. at each end of next row and every following 4th row until there are 145 sts. Work 11 rows straight.

To shape armholes, cast off 7 sts. at start of next 2 rows, then dec. 1 st. at each end of the following 6 rows, after which dec. 1 st. at start of the following 8 rows. Work 56 rows straight.

To shape shoulders, cast off 11 sts. at start of next 4 rows, and 12 sts. at start of the following 2 rows. Cast off.

THE LEFT FRONT

With No. 11 needles, cast on 3 sts.

1st row : K.

2nd row : Inc. in first st., p. to end.

3rd row : Cast on 3, k. to 1 from end. inc. in last st.

Rep. 2nd and 3rd rows 9 times.

22nd row : As 2nd.

23rd row : Inc. in first st., k. to end.

Next row : P. 55.

Continue in st.-st. but inc. 1 st. at start of 5th row and every following 4th row until there are 73 sts.

Work 5 rows straight.

1st yoke pattern row : (K. 5, m.a.b. as explained in "Note on Pattern") to last st., k. 1. **2nd row :** P.

3rd row : K. 2, (m.a.b., k. 5) to last 5 sts., m.a.b., k. 4. **4th row :** P. **5th row :** K. **6th row :** P.

Continuing in pattern, shape armhole and commence front decreases thus :

7th pattern row : Cast off 7, which leaves 1 st. on right-hand needle, k. 6, (twist A, k. 5, m.a.b., k. 6, twist B, p. 1) twice, twist A, k. 11, k. 2 tog.

8th row : P. **9th row :** K. 2 tog., k. 6, (twist A, k. 2, m.a.b., k. 1, m.a.b., k. 1, m.a.b., k. 3, twist B, p. 1, k. 1, p. 1) twice, twist A, k. 11.

10th row : P. 2 tog., p. 60, p. 2 tog.

11th row : K. 2 tog., k. 5, (twist A, k. 3, m.a.b., k. 4, twist B. p. 1, k. 3, p. 1) twice, twist A, k. 9.

12th row : P. 59, p. 2 tog.

13th row : K. 2 tog., k. 4, (twist A, k. 6, twist B, p. 1, k. 5, p. 1) twice, twist A, k. 6, k. 2 tog.

14th row : P. 56, p. 2 tog.

15th row : K. 2 tog., k. 3, (twist A, k. 4, twist B, p. 1, k. 7, p. 1) twice, twist A, k. 6. **16th row :** P. 2 tog., p. 54.

17th row : K. 2 tog., k. 3, (twist A, k. 2, twist B, p. 1, k. 4, m.a.b., k. 4, p. 1) twice, twist A, k. 4. **18th row:** P.

19th row : K. 2 tog., k. 3, (twist A, twist B, p. 1 k. 3, m.a.b., k. 1, m.a.b., k. 1, m.a.b., k. 3, p. 1) twice, twist A, k. 1, k. 2 tog. **20th row :** P.

21st row : K. 2 tog., k. 4, (twist A, p. 1, k. 7, m.a.b., k. 7, p. 1) twice, twist A. **22nd row :** P. 2 tog., p. 49.

23rd row : K. **24th row :** P.

25th row : K. 6, (m.a.b., k. 5) 7 times, k. 2 tog. **26th row :** P.

27th row : K. 3, (m.a.b., k. 5) 7 times, m.a.b., k. 3. **28th row :** P. 2 tog., p. 47.

29th row : K. **30th row :** P.

31st row : K. 6, m.a.b., k. 6, twist B, p. 1, twist A, k. 5, m.a.b., k. 6, twist B, p. 1, twist A, k. 3, k. 2 tog. **32nd row :** P.

33rd row : K. 4, (m.a.b., k. 1, m.a.b., k. 1, m.a.b., k. 3, twist B, p. 1, k. 1, p. 1, twist A, k. 2) twice, k. 1.

34th row : P. 2 tog., p. 45.

35th row : K. 6, m.a.b., k. 4, twist B, p. 1, k. 3, p. 1, twist A, k. 3, m.a.b., k. 4, twist B, p. 1, k. 3, p. 1, twist A, k. 1. **36th row :** P.

37th row : (Twist A, k. 6, twist B, p. 1, k. 5, p. 1) twice, k. 2, k. 2 tog.

38th row : P. Keeping the continuity of the pattern, dec. 1 st. at front edge on 2nd row and every following 3rd row until 34 sts. remain, then work 8 rows st.-st. To shape shoulder, cast off 11 sts. at start of next row and the following alternate row ; work 1 row ; cast off

THE RIGHT FRONT

With No. 11 needles, cast on 3 sts.

1st row : K. **2nd row :** Cast on 3, p. to 1 from end, inc. in last st.

3rd row : Inc. in first st., k. to end.

Rep. 2nd and 3rd rows 9 times.

22nd row : Inc. in first st., p. to 1 from end, inc. in last st.

Continue in st.-st. on these 55 sts., but inc. 1 st. at end of 5th row and every following 4th row until there are 73 sts. Work 5 rows straight.

1st yoke pattern row : K. 1, (m.a.b., k. 5) to end. **2nd row :** P.

3rd row : K. 4, (m.a.b., k. 5) to last 3 sts., m.a.b., k. 2.

4th row : P. **5th row :** K.

Now commence armhole shaping :

6th row : Cast off 7, p. to end.

7th row : K. 2 tog., k. 11, twist B, (p. 1, twist A, k. 6, m.a.b., k. 5, twist B) twice, k. 7. **8th row :** P. 2 tog., p. 63.

9th row : K. 11, twist B, (p. 1, k. 1, p. 1, twist A, k. 3, m.a.b., k. 1, m.a.b., k 1, m.a.b., k. 2, twist B) twice, k. 5, k. 2 tog.

10th row : P. 2 tog., p. 59, p. 2 tog.

11th row : K. 9, (twist B, p. 1, k. 3, p. 1, twist A, k. 4, m.a.b., k. 3) twice, twist B, k. 4, k. 2 tog.

12th row : P. 2 tog., p. 58.

13th row : K. 2 tog., k. 6, (twist B, p. 1, k. 5, p. 1, twist A, k. 6) twice, twist B, k. 3, k. 2 tog.

14th row : P. 2 tog., p. 55.

15th row : K. 6, (twist B, p. 1, k. 7, p. 1, twist A, k. 4) twice, twist B, k. 4.

16th row : P. 2 tog., p. 52, p. 2 tog.

17th row : K. 4, (twist B, p. 1, k. 4, m.a.b., k. 4, p. 1, twist A, k. 2) twice, twist B, k. 4. **18th row :** P. 2 tog., p. 52.

19th row : K. 2 tog., k. 1, (twist B, p. 1, k. 3, m.a.b., k. 1, m.a.b., k. 1, m.a.b., k. 3, p. 1, twist A) twice, twist B, k. 4. **20th row :** P. 2 tog., p. 50.

21st row : (Twist A, p. 1, k. 7, m.a.b., k. 7, p. 1) twice, twist A, k. 5.

22nd row : P. 49, p. 2 tog.

23rd row : K. **24th row :** P.

25th row : K. 2 tog., (k. 5, m.a.b.) 7 times, k. 6. **26th row :** P.

27th row : K. 3, (m.a.b., k. 5) 7 times, m.a.b., k. 3. **28th row :** P. 47, p. 2 tog.

29th row : K. **30th row :** P.

31st row : K. 2 tog., k. 3, (twist B, p. 1, twist A, k. 6, m.a.b., k. 5) twice, k. 1. **32nd row :** P.

33rd row : K. 3, (twist B, p. 1, k. 1, p. 1, twist A, k. 3, m.a.b., k. 1, m.a.b., k. 1, m.a.b., k. 2) twice, k. 2.

34th row : P. 45, p. 2 tog.

35th row : K. 1, (twist B, p. 1, k. 3, p. 1, twist A, k. 4, m.a.b., k. 3) twice, k. 3. **36th row :** P.

37th row : K. 2 tog., k. 2, (p. 1, k. 5, p. 1, twist A, k. 6, twist B) twice.

38th row : P.

Keeping the continuity of the pattern, dec. 1 st. at front edge on 2nd row and every following 3rd row until 34 sts. remain. Work 9 rows st.-st., then shape shoulder as for left front.

THE BORDERS

Lower edge of fronts : With right side of right front facing you, join wool to base at inner edge, and using a No. 11 needle, pick up and k. 22 sts. along lower edge to point, and 33 sts. from here to side edge.

1st row : P. 32, inc. in next st., inc. in next st., p. 21. **2nd row :** K.

3rd row : P. 33, inc. in next st., inc. in next st., p. 22.

4th row : K. 5, (m.a.b., k. 5) 9 times.

5th row : P. 34, inc. in next st., inc. in next st., p. 23.

6th row : K. 2, (m.a.b., k. 5) 3 times, m.a.b., k. 7, (m.a.b., k. 5) 5 times, m.a.b., k. 2.

7th row : P. 35, inc. in next st., inc. in next st., p. 24. **8th row :** K.

9th row : P. 36, inc. in next st., inc. in next st., p. 25. **10th row :** K.

11th row : K. to indicate hem-line. Work 6 rows st.-st. Cast off.

With right side of left front facing you, join wool to side edge at base of left front, and using a No. 11 needle, pick up and k. 33 sts. along lower edge to point, and 22 sts. from here to front edge.

Now work as given for right front border, but read each pattern and inc. row backwards.

The Armbands : Join shoulder seams. With right side of work facing you, join wool to one armhole, and using a No. 11 needle, pick up and k. 132 sts. along one armhole edge.

1st row : P. 2 tog., p. to last 2 sts., p. 2 tog.

2nd row : K. **3rd row :** As 1st.

4th row : K. 4, (m.a.b., k. 5) to last 4 sts., m.a.b., k. 3. **5th row :** As 1st.

6th row : K. 6, (m.a.b., k. 5) to end.

7th row : As 1st. **8th row :** K.

9th row : P. **10th row :** K.

11th row : K. to indicate hem-line.

Work 3 rows st.-st. Cast off.

Finish 2nd armhole in the same way.

The Neck Border : With right side of work facing you, join wool to 1st dec. row at right front edge, and using a No. 11 needle, pick up and k. 138 sts. all round neck edge, finishing at 1st dec. row of left front. Work the border as given for armbands.

The Back Belt : *Left Half*—Using double wool and No. 11 needles, cast on 12 sts. and work in k. 1, p. 1 rib for 8 inches. Cast off ribwise.

Right Half—Using double wool and No. 11 needles, cast on 12 sts. and work in k. 1, p. 1 ribs for 5 inches.

Next row : Rib 4, take 2 tog., wool twice round needle to make 2 sts., take 2 tog., rib 4. Rib 7 rows. Rep. last 8 rows 3 times more, then dec. 1 st. at start of every row until 2 sts. remain. Take 2 tog. and fasten off.

TO COMPLETE

Press work lightly on wrong side. Join side seams. Fold back hem all round outer edges and tack down on wrong side, then face in the edges, also front edges, with binding ribbon. Sew a buckle to one end of left half of belt, then sew belt to side seams about 2½ inches from lower edge. Fasten fronts with the press-studs, placing one at the top and the others at equal intervals apart.

The Scroll Trimmings (3 *alike*): With No. 11 needles, cast on 4 sts. and work in k. 1, p. 1 ribs for 8 inches. Cast off. Curl each end into a ring and sew into position, leaving a hole in centre to take the button. Sew 3 buttons to right front, then sew 3 to left front, placing these one inch lower than those on right front. Button the scrolls on to the buttons, then sew scrolls into position on right front, leaving remainder free.

THE CAP

With No. 12 needles, cast on 150 sts. and work 8 rows st.-st. **Next row :** K.

Next row : K. to indicate hem-line. Work 4 rows st.-st.

1st pattern row : (K. 5, m.a.b.) to end. **2nd row :** P.

3rd row : K. 2, (m.a.b., k. 5) to last 4 sts., m.a.b., k. 3.

4th row : P. to last 2 sts., p. 2 tog.

5th row : K. 1, (p. 1, twist A, k. 5, m.a.b., k. 6, twist B) to last st., k. 1.

6th and every following alternate row : P. **7th row :** K. 2, (p. 1, twist A, k. 2, m.a.b., k. 1, m.a.b., k. 1, m.a.b., k. 3, twist B, p. 1, k. 1) to end.

9th row : K. 3, (p. 1, twist A, k. 3, m.a.b., k. 4, twist B, p. 1, k. 3) to end, but finish last rep. with k. 2.

11th row : K. 4, (p. 1, twist A, k. 6, twist B, p. 1, k. 5) to end, but finish last rep. with k. 3.

13th row : K. 5, (p. 1, twist A, k. 4, twist B, p. 1, k. 7) to end, but finish last rep. with k. 4. **15th row :** K. 1, (m.a.b., k. 4, p. 1, twist A, k. 2, twist B, p. 1, k. 4) to last st., k. 1.

17th row : K. 1, (m.a.b., k. 1, m.a.b., k. 3, p. 1, twist A, twist B, p. 1, k. 3, m.a.b., k. 1) to last st., k. 1.

19th row : K. 1, (m.a.b., k. 7, p. 1, twist A, p. 1, k. 7) to last st., k. 1.

20th row : P. **21st row :** K.

22nd row : P.

1st dec. row : K. 2, (k. 2 tog., k. 16, k. 2 tog. t.b.s., k. 1) to end.

Work 3 rows st.-st. without shaping.

2nd dec. row : K. 2, (k. 2 tog., k. 14, k. 2 tog. t.b.s., k. 1) to end.

Work 3 rows without shaping.

3rd dec. row : K. 2, (k. 2 tog., k. 12, k. 2 tog. t.b.s., k. 1) to end.

Work 3 rows without shaping.

4th dec. row : K. 2, (k. 2 tog., k. 10, k. 2 tog. t.b.s., k. 1) to end.

Work 3 rows without shaping.

5th dec. row : K. 2, (k. 2 tog., k. 8, k. 2 tog. t.b.s., k. 1) to end.

Work 3 rows without shaping.

6th dec. row : K. 2, (k. 2 tog., k. 6, k. 2 tog. t.b.s., k. 1) to end.

Work 3 rows without shaping.

7th dec. row : K. 2, (k. 2 tog., k. 4, k. 2 tog. t.b.s., k. 1) to end.

Work 3 rows without shaping.

Next row : K. 1, (m.a.b., k. 2 tog., k. 2, k. 2 tog.t.b.s.) to last st., k. 1.

Next row : P.

Next row : K. 2, (k. 2 tog., m.a.b., k. 2) to end. **Next row :** P.

Next row : (K. 1, k. 2 tog.) to end.

Next row : P.

Break off wool, leaving a longish end, run it through remaining sts., draw up and fasten off, then join seam. Turn up hem at lower edge and slip stitch down on wrong side. Press lightly.

The Top-knot : With No. 12 needles, cast on 4 sts. and work in k. 1, p. 1 rib for 8 inches. Cast off. Fold the strip into 3 loops and sew to top of cap.

THE SET IN NYLON

MATERIALS : *Allow 6 ozs. Pearsall's Nylon Knitting 3-ply for the set; 1 pair each of Nos. 12 and 13 knitting needles ; 6 buttons ; 3½ yards of binding ribbon ; 3 press-studs and 1 buckle.*

TENSION, MEASUREMENTS, ABBREVIATIONS AND NOTE ON PATTERN : *See the set in wool.*

TO MAKE THE SET

Work exactly as given for the set in wool, but use No. 12 needles where No. 11 are mentioned, and No. 13 needles instead of No. 12.

Designed in Paris

MATERIALS
Excelana 4 Ply Luxury Wool 100% pure new British wool (159m/174yds per 50g ball)
7 (8, 9, 10, 11, 12, 12) balls shade Cornflower Blue – MC
5 (6, 7, 7, 8, 8, 9) balls shade Alabaster – CC
1 pair 3.25mm (US #3) needles
3 buttons
Stitch holders

TENSION
24 sts & 46 rows = 10cm (4in) using 3.25mm needles over slip stitch pattern

Standard Yarn Tension
28 sts and 36 rows = 10cm (4in) over stocking stitch using 3mm needles

ABBREVIATIONS
See page 13 for standard abbreviations

SIZING
Measurements given in centimetres followed by inches in parentheses

To Fit	81–86 (32–34)	86–92 (34–36)	92–97 (36–38)	97–102 (38–40)	102–106 (40–42)	106–112 (42–44)	112–117 (44–46)
Finished Measurements							
Actual Bust Size	95 (37½)	100 (39½)	105 (41½)	110 (43½)	115 (45¼)	120 (47¼)	125 (49¼)
Hip *	85 (33½)	90 (35½)	95 (37½)	100 (39½)	105 (41½)	110 (43½)	115 (45¼)
Length to underarm	39½ (15½)	40½ (16)	42 (16½)	43 (17)	44½ (17½)	46 (18)	47 (18½)
Armhole Depth	20½ (8)	21½ (8½)	23 (9)	24 (9½)	25½ (10)	26½ (10½)	28 (11)
Finished Length	60 (23½)	62 (24½)	65 (25½)	67 (26½)	70 (27½)	72½ (28½)	75 (29½)
Shoulder to Shoulder	41 (16)	42½ (16¾)	44 (17¼)	46 (18)	47½ (18¾)	49 (19½)	51 (20)
Sleeve Length	43½ (17)	44½ (17½)	47 (18½)	47 (18½)	48 (19)	48 (19)	49½ (19½)

* Please Note: This garment is cut to be narrower at the bottom edge which sits around the hips. If the intended wearer is wider at the hip than at the bust I would suggest opting for the larger of the two size ranges offered, bearing in mind this will give more ease at the bust.

Garment shown in photographs for first size 81–86 (32–34)

LOWER POCKET LININGS (Make two)
Using 3.25mm needles and MC, cast on 24 sts and commencing with a K row work in stocking stitch until work measures 6½cm (2½in) ending with a WS row. Leave sts on a spare needle or holder.

UPPER POCKET LINING (Make one)
Using 3.25mm needles and MC, cast on 20 sts and commencing with a K row work in stocking stitch until work measures 6½cm (2½in) ending with a WS row. Leave sts on spare needle or holder as before.

FRONT
** Using 3.25mm needles and MC, cast on 102 (108, 114, 120, 126, 132, 138) sts loosely and commencing with a K row, work in stocking stitch until work measures 4cm (1½in) ending with a WS row. Work in pattern as folls:
Row 1 (RS): Using CC, K2, * knit into loop only below next st dend drop st off needle, K1, repeat from * to end.
Row 2: Using CC, K to end. Do not break off yarn.
Row 3: Using MC, K2, * K1, knit into loop only below

next st and drop st off needle, repeat from * to last 2 sts, K2.
Row 4: Using MC, K to end. Do not break off yarn.
These 4 rows form patt. Continue in pattern until work measures 10cm (4in) from start of main patt, ending with a WS row **

Join Pockets
Next row (RS): Patt 6 (9, 12, 15, 18, 21, 24), slip next 24 sts onto spare needle and in their place patt across 24 sts of one of the pocket linings, patt 42, slip next 24 sts onto a spare needle and in their place patt across 24 sts of 2nd pocket lining, patt to end.

Maintaining pattern, work straight in patt over all sts until front measures 18cm (7in) from start of main patt, ending with a WS row.
Next row (RS): Patt 76 (79, 82, 85, 88, 91, 94), slip 20 sts onto spare needle and in their place patt across 20 sts of top pocket lining, patt to end.
Maintaining pattern, work straight until front measures 20½cm (8in) from start of main patt, ending with a WS row.
*** With RS facing, cont in patt, shaping sides by inc 1 st

at each end of next and every foll 12th row until there are 114 (120, 126, 132, 138, 144, 150) sts, taking inc sts into patt. Work straight until front measures 39½ (40½, 42, 43, 44½, 46, 47) cm (15½, 16, 16½, 17, 17½, 18, 18½ in) from start of main patt ending with a WS row.

Shape Armholes

Maintaining patt, cast off 4 (5, 5, 6, 7, 8, 9) sts at beg of next 2 rows (106, 110, 116, 120, 124, 128, 132 sts), then K2tog at each end of next and every foll alt row until 98 (102, 106, 110, 114, 118, 122) sts rem.
Work without further shaping until armhole measures 20½ (21½, 23, 24, 25½, 26½, 28) cm (8, 8½, 9, 9½, 10, 10½, 11 in) from start of main patt ending with a WS row ***

Shape Shoulders

Next row (RS): Cast off 10 (10, 11, 11, 12, 12, 13), patt to end.
Next row (buttonhole): Cast off 10 (10, 11, 11, 12, 12, 13), patt 4, cast off 2, patt to end.
Next row: Cast off 10 (10, 11, 11, 12, 12, 13), patt to cast off sts, cast on 2, patt to end.
Next row: Cast off 10 (10, 11, 11, 12, 12, 13), patt 4, cast off 2, patt to end.
Next row: Cast off 10 (10, 10, 11, 11, 12, 12), patt to cast off sts, cast on 2, patt to end.

Next row: Cast off 10 (10, 10, 11, 11, 12, 12), patt to end.
Leave rem 38 (42, 42, 44, 44, 46, 46) sts on stitch holder, making a note of last row worked.

BACK

Work exactly as for the front from ** to **
Maintaining patt, work straight until back measures 20½cm (8in) from start of main patt then work as for front from *** to *** (98, 102, 106, 110, 114, 118, 122 sts).

Shape Shoulders

Cast off 10 (10, 11, 11, 12, 12, 13) sts at beg of next 6 (6, 4, 6, 4, 6, 4) rows, then 0 (0, 10, 0, 11, 0, 12) at beg of next 0 (0, 2, 0, 2, 0, 2) rows then leave rem 38 (42, 42, 44, 44, 46, 46) sts on a stitch holder.

SLEEVES

Using 3.25mm needles and MC, cast on 48 (54, 60, 66, 72, 78, 84) sts loosely and commencing with a K row, work in stocking stitch until work measures 4cm (1½in) from cast on, ending with a WS row. Commencing with row 1, work in main patt as for front until main patt measures 4cm (1½in). Cont in patt, inc 1 st at each end of next and every foll 10th row until there are 80 (86, 92, 98, 104, 110, 116) sts, working inc sts into patt. Work without further shaping until sleeve measures 43½ (44½, 47, 47, 48, 48, 49½) cm (17, 17½, 18½, 18½, 19, 19, 19½ in) from start of main patt, ending with a WS row.

Shape Sleeve Head

Cast off 3 sts at beg of next 2 rows (74, 80, 86, 92, 98, 104, 110 sts), then K2tog at beg of every foll row until 20 sts rem. Cast off rem sts.

NECKBAND

Join left shoulder seam. Using 3.25mm needles, MC and with RS facing, patt 38 (42, 42, 44, 44, 46, 46) sts on holder at back of neck and patt across 38 (42, 42, 44, 44, 46, 46) sts on holder at front, continuing in patt from last row worked on front (76, 84, 84, 88, 88, 92, 92 sts).
Work 2 rows straight in patt, commencing with appropriate row of pattern.
Next row: Patt 36 (40, 40, 42, 42, 44, 44), [K2tog] twice, patt to end.
Work 3 rows straight.
Next row: Patt 35 (39, 39, 41, 41, 43, 43), [K2tog] twice, patt to end.
Next row (buttonhole): Patt to last 6 sts, cast off 2, patt to end.
Next row: Patt to cast off sts, cast on 2, patt to end.
Work 1 row straight.
Next row: Patt 34 (38, 38, 40, 40, 42, 42), [K2tog] twice, patt to end (70, 78, 78, 82, 82, 86, 86 sts).

Work 2 rows straight.

Using MC only, and commencing with a K row, work in stocking stitch for 2 rows.

Next row: K34 (38, 38, 40, 40, 42, 42), [Kfb] twice, K to end.

Work 3 rows straight.

Next row (buttonhole): K35 (39, 39, 41, 41, 43, 43), [Kfb] twice, K to last 6 sts, cast off 2, K4.

Next row: P to cast off sts, cast on 2, P to end.

Work 2 rows straight.

Next row: K36 (40, 40, 42, 42, 44, 44), [Kfb] twice, K to end (76, 84, 84, 88, 88, 92, 92 sts).

Work 1 row straight.

Cast off loosely.

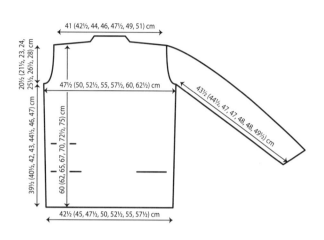

MAKING UP
Press hems only through a damp cloth.

Pocket Tops
Using 3.25mm needles and MC, K across sts on holder of each pocket. Work in stocking stitch for 2½cm (1in) ending with a WS row. Cast off. Rep for each pocket.

Join first 10 sts of right shoulder, side and sleeve seams. Inset sleeves, carefully matching centre of sleeve head and shoulder seam and matching side seams. Turn under all bar 3 rows of stocking stitch hem to WS of lower edge of body and very loosely slip stitch into place. Repeat for cuffs. Turn under stocking stitch edging round neck, again slip stitching into place very loosely. Turn over half of pocket top edging and slip stitch into place. Sew pocket linings into position.

Right Back Neckband
Using 3.25mm needles, MC and with RS facing pick up 30 (30, 32, 33, 35, 36, 38) sts across right shoulder and neck opening. Work 16 rows in garter st, inc 1 st at neck edge on next and every foll alt row until 38 (38, 40, 41, 43, 44, 46) sts. Cast off loosely.

Catch down edge of neckband at shoulder edge to underside of main body. Sew on buttons. Darn in all ends.

Materials: Of Patons Purple Heather Fingering 4-ply, 7 ozs. Mimosa 194 and 8 ozs. Marguerite Green 175. A pair No. 11 "Beehive" needles. Three buttons. One press-stud.

Measurements: To fit 35–36-inch bust; length from top of shoulders, 23½ inches; sleeve seam, 17 inches.

Tension: This slip-stitch pattern is difficult to measure, but it is equivalent to a basic tension of 7½ sts. and 9½ rows to an inch over stocking-stitch on No. 11 needles; see life-size close-up on page 20.

N.B.—M. = Mimosa. G. = Green.

high fashion trends

*designed in Paris
this elegant tweed-
stitch sweater with
shoulder fastening
and 3 smart pockets*

FRONT

Begin by making pocket linings. *Lower pockets:* With G. wool, cast on 24 sts. and work 2½ inches straight in stocking-stitch, ending with a purl row; leave stitches on a spare needle. Make another the same. *Top pocket:* In the same way, cast on 20 sts. and work 2½ inches stocking-stitch, ending with a

purl row; leave stitches as before.

** With G. wool, cast on 102 sts. fairly loosely and work 1½ inches stocking-stitch, ending with a knit row.

With right side facing, change to pattern:
1ST ROW: With M., k. 2, * knit into loop *only* below next stitch and drop stitch off needle, k. 1 in the usual way; repeat from * to end. 2ND ROW: Knit in M. Leave M. hanging.

3RD ROW: With G., k. 2, * k. 1, knit into loop only below next stitch and drop stitch off needle; repeat from * to last 2 sts., k. 2. 4TH ROW: Knit in G. Leave G. hanging. These 4 rows form pattern.

Continue straight in pattern until front measures 4 inches from start of pattern. **

With right side facing, introduce two lower pockets thus:—
NEXT ROW: Pattern 6, slip next 24 sts. on a spare needle and in their place, pattern across 24 sts. of one pocket lining, pattern 42, slip next 24 sts. on a second spare needle, and in their place pattern across 24 sts. of 2nd pocket lining, pattern 6. Work straight in pattern over all sts. until front measures 7 inches from start of pattern.

With right side facing, introduce top pocket:—NEXT ROW: Pattern 76, slip next 20 sts. on a spare needle and in their place pattern across 20 sts. of top pocket lining, pattern 6. Work straight until front measures 8 inches from start of two-colour pattern.

¶¶ With right side facing, continue in pattern, shaping sides by increasing 1 stitch at each end of next and every following 12th row until there are 114 sts., taking increased sts. into pattern. Work straight until front measures 15½ inches from start of pattern.

With right side facing, shape armholes by casting off 4 sts. at beginning of next 2 rows, then k. 2 tog. at each end of every alternate row until 98 sts. remain. Work straight until front measures 23¼ inches from start of pattern¶¶

With right side facing, shape shoulders and make buttonholes for opening in right shoulder thus:—NEXT ROW: Cast off 10, pattern to end. NEXT ROW: Cast off 10, pattern 4, cast off 2, pattern to end. NEXT ROW: Cast off 10, pattern to end, casting on 2 over those cast off in previous row. NEXT ROW: Cast off 10, pattern 4, cast off 2, pattern to end. NEXT ROW: Cast off 10, pattern to end, casting on 2 over those cast off. NEXT ROW: Cast off 10, pattern to end. Leave remaining 38 sts. on a spare needle.

BACK

Work exactly as for front from ** to **.
Continue straight in pattern until back measures 8 inches from start of pattern then work as for front from ¶¶ to ¶¶ (98 sts.).

With right side facing, shape shoulders by casting off 10 sts. at beginning of next 6 rows; leave remaining 38 sts. on a spare needle.

SLEEVES

With G. wool, cast on 48 sts. loosely and work 1½ inches stocking-stitch, ending with a knit row.
With right side facing, change to pattern as given for front and work 1½ inches straight. Continue in pattern, shaping sides by increasing 1 stitch at each end of next and every following 10th row until there are 80 sts. Work straight until sleeve measures 17 inches from start of pattern.
With right side facing, shape sleeve top by casting off 3 sts. at beginning of next 2 rows, then k. 2 tog. at beginning of every row until 20 sts. Cast off.

NECKBAND

Join left shoulder seam. With right side facing and G. wool, pattern 38 sts. across back of neck, then pattern across 38 sts. of front, (76 sts.). Work 2 rows straight in pattern.
NEXT ROW: Pattern 36, (k. 2 tog.) twice, pattern to end. Work 3 rows straight. NEXT ROW: Pattern 35, (k. 2 tog.) twice, pattern to end. NEXT 2 ROWS: Pattern to last 6 sts., cast off 2, pattern to end and back, casting on 2 over those cast off. Work 1 row straight. NEXT ROW: Pattern 34, (k. 2 tog.) twice, pattern to end. Work 2 rows straight.
Change to G. wool and stocking-stitch, starting with a knit row and work 2 rows straight. NEXT ROW: k. 34, knit twice in each of next 2 sts., k. 34. Work 3 rows straight. NEXT ROW: k. 35, knit twice in each of next 2 sts., knit to last 6 sts., cast off 2, k. 4. Work 3 rows straight. NEXT ROW: k. 36, knit twice in each of next 2 sts., knit to end. Work 1 row straight; cast off loosely.

TO MAKE UP

Press stocking-stitch parts only on wrong side under a damp cloth. *Pocket tops:* With G. wool, work 1 inch stocking-stitch on each of the 3 sets of pocket sts.; cast off.

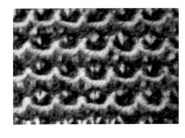

Join first 10 sts. of right shoulder, side and sleeve seams; insert sleeves. Turn under 1½ inches of reversed stocking-stitch round lower edge and cuffs, and slip-hem in position; turn under stocking-stitch rows round neck and pocket tops in the same way; catch down pocket linings. With right side facing and G. wool, pick up 30 sts. across back of right shoulder and neck opening. Work ¾ inch garter-stitch; cast off loosely. Catch down side of underlap at shoulder edge to main work. Press seams, hems and pocket tops. Sew on buttons; sew on press-stud at base of neck.

Cocktail Jumper

MATERIALS
Knitshop Mulberry Silk 100% silk (250m per 100g skein)
6 (6, 7, 8, 9) skeins shade light pink – MC
1 skein shade black – CC
1 pair 2.75mm (US #2) needles
1 pair 3.25mm (US #3) needles
3.25mm crochet hook

TENSION
32 sts & 33 rows = 10cm (4in) using 3.25mm needles over pattern

ABBREVIATIONS
See page 13 for standard abbreviations

Specific abbreviations for this pattern
cross 2: Insert point of needle into next stitch and and knit the 2nd stitch through the first stitch then knit the first stitch through the back

SIZING
Measurements given in centimetres followed by inches in parentheses

To Fit	76–81 (30–32)	86–92 (34–36)	97–102 (38–40)	107–112 (42–44)	117–122 (46–48)
Finished Measurements					
Actual Bust Size	86¼ (34)	96¼ (37¾)	106¼ (41¾)	116¼ (45¾)	126¼ (49¾)
Waist Circumference	70 (27½)	80 (31½)	90 (35½)	100 (39½)	110 (43½)
Length to underarm	20½ (8)	23 (9)	25½ (10)	26½ (10½)	28 (11)
Armhole Depth	17 (6¾)	18½ (7¼)	20½ (8)	21½ (8½)	23 (9)
Finished Length	37½ (14¾)	41½ (16¼)	46 (18)	48 (19)	51 (20)
Shoulder to shoulder	33 (13)	35½ (14)	38 (15)	40½ (16)	43 (17)
Sleeve Length	31¾ (12½)	32¾ (12¾)	33¾ (13¼)	34¾ (13½)	35¾ (14)

Garment shown in photographs is for first size 76–81 (30–32)

BACK
Using 2.75mm needles and MC, cast on 112 (128, 144, 160, 176) sts.
Row 1 (WS): K1, P to last st, K1.
Change to 3.25mm needles and work in patt as folls:.
** **Row 2**: K1, * cross 2, rep from * to last st, K1.
Row 3: K1, P to last st, K1.
Row 4: K2 * cross 2, rep from * to last 2 sts, K2.
Row 5: K1, P to last st, K1 **
Rep from ** to ** once more, then work row 2 once more.
Continue in pattern, inc one st at each end of next and every foll 4th row (increases are worked on WS) until 138 (154, 170, 186, 202) sts. Continue without further shaping until work measures 20½ (23, 25½, 26½, 28) cm (8, 9, 10, 10½, 11 in), ending with a RS row.

Shape Armholes
Cast off 6 (10, 7, 9, 11) sts at beg of next 2 (2, 4, 4, 4) rows (126, 134, 142, 150, 158 sts), then dec one st at each end of next and every foll alt row until 106 (114, 122, 130, 138) sts ***
Continue in pattern without further shaping until armhole

measures 17 (18½, 20½, 21½, 23) cm (6¾, 7¼, 8, 8½, 9 in) ending with a WS row.

Shape Shoulders
Rows 1 & 2: Work to last 12 (13, 14, 16, 16) sts, turn.
Rows 3 & 4: Work to last 23 (25, 26, 27, 30) sts, turn.
Rows 5 & 6: Work to last 35 (38, 40, 43, 46) sts, turn.
Row 7: Work to end of row. Cast off all stitches.

FRONT
Work exactly as Back to ***
Work 1 more pattern row.

Shape Neck
Next row (WS): K1, P25 (28, 30, 33, 36), cast off 54 (56, 60, 62, 64) sts, P to 25 (28, 30, 33, 36) sts on right needle after cast off, K1 (52, 58, 62, 68, 74 sts).
Turn and continue in pattern on these 26 (29, 31, 34, 37) sts only, leaving rem sts on holder. Inc 1 st at neck edge on 2nd and every foll 4th row until 35 (38, 40, 43, 46) sts on needle, then continue without shaping until work measures same as back ending at neck edge.

Shape Shoulder

Row 1 (WS): Work to last 12 (13, 14, 16, 16) sts, turn.

Row 2: Work to end of row.

Row 3: Work to last 23 (25, 26, 27, 30) sts, turn.

Row 4: Work to end of row.

Cast off all 35 (38, 40, 43, 46) sts.

With RS facing rejoin yarn at neck edge and working on remaining 26 (29, 31, 34, 37) sts, complete neck and shoulder to correspond with other side reversing all shapings.

SLEEVES

Using 2.75mm needles and MC, cast on 96 (104, 112, 120, 126) sts.

Row 1 (WS): K1, P to last st, K1.

Change to 3.25mm needles and work in patt as folls:

Row 2: K1, * cross 2, rep from * to last st, K1.

Row 3: K1, P to last st, K1.

Row 4: K2 * cross 2, rep from * to last 2 sts, K2.

Row 5: K1, P to last st, K1.

Rows 2–5 set patt. Work row 2 once more, then cont in patt and dec 1 st at each end of next and every foll 4th row until 84 (92, 100, 108, 114) sts (decs are worked on WS).

Change back to 2.75mm needles and work as folls:

Next row (RS): K2, * P1, K1, rep from * to end of row.

Repeat this row 14 times more, then change back to 3.25mm needles.

Work from row 2 to row 5 twice then work 2nd row only once more (the pattern should now be reversed for turn back cuff).

Continue in pattern, inc one st at each end of next and every foll 6th row until 112 (120, 128, 136, 142) sts.

Continue without further shaping until work measures 31¾ (32¾, 33¾, 34¾, 35¾) cm (12½, 12¾, 13¼, 13½, 14 in) from start of ribbing, ending with a RS row.

Shape Sleeve Head

Whilst maintaining patt, cast off 3 sts at beg of next 4 rows (100, 108, 116, 124, 130 sts), then cast off 2 sts at beg of every row until 28 sts rem. Work 0 (0, 0, 0, 1) row straight.

Next row: K1, [P2tog] 13 times, K1 (15 sts).

Cast off rem sts.

WAISTBAND

Using 2.75mm needles and MC, cast on 32 sts.

Row 1 (WS): K1, P to last st, K1.

Change to 3.25mm needles and work in patt as folls:

Row 2: K1, * cross 2, rep from * to last st, K1.

Row 3: K1, P to last st, K1.

Row 4: K2 * cross 2, rep from * to last 2 sts, K2.

Row 5: K1, P to last st, K1.

Rep rows 2–5 until work measures 38 (43, 48, 53, 58) cm (15, 17, 19, 21, 23 in) from cast on, ending with a RS row.

Whilst maintaining the patt, dec 1 st at each end of next and every foll alt row until 2 sts rem.

Break off yarn, pass the first st over the second st, draw end through and fasten off securely.

Work another piece in exactly the same way.

MAKING UP

Block each piece and press carefully through a damp cloth. Sew up sleeve, shoulders and right side seams, then sew up left side seam leaving 12½cm (5in) open above cast on edge. Set in in sleeves carefully matching centre of sleeve head and shoulder seam, and matching side seams. Pin then stitch zip into place in left hand seam with zip upside down (ie. when zip closed, tab of zip is at cast on edge). See 'Fit and Finish' chapter for more information.

Make a 2cm (¾in) pleat along the cast on edge (short edge) of each waistband and sew in place, then with RS together and with pleats lined up, join the the two cast on edges together. Sew waistband to jumper, easing in the bodice slightly and leaving ends to tie at left side as shown.

CROCHET EDGING

Using 3.25mm crochet hook, MC, and commencing at underarm seam on cuff, work a round of DC (SC) evenly all round the edge of the cuff, change to CC, then work 2 more rounds of DC (SC).

Looped Edge

Next Round: 1 DC (SC), * 5 ch, miss 2 DC (SC), work 1 DC (SC) into next DC (SC), rep from * all round to form a looped edge. Break off yarn and fasten off securely. Work this edging around neck edge, decreasing at front corners when working subsequent rounds of DC (SC) to keep the band flat.

CROCHET BOWS

Using 3.25mm crochet hook and CC, make 50 ch, work 1 row in DC (SC) along the chain.
Work 8 more rows of DC (SC), dec 1 st at each end of every row. Fasten off.

Press the bows, tying a knot in the centre and attach to each side of neck as shown. Darn in all ends.

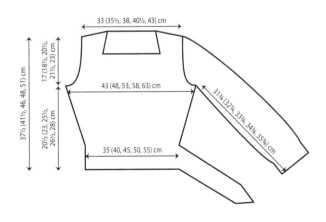

COCKTAIL JUMPER

MATERIALS.—8 ozs. **Penelope's W.B. Melody 3-ply Wool** in Main colour and about ½ oz. in a Contrasting shade. A pair of No. 9 and a pair of No. 12 knitting needles. A 5 in. Lightning zip fastener. Contrasting sequins (about 150). A No. 14 steel crochet hook.

MEASUREMENTS.—To fit 32/33 ins. Bust Length to waist 15 ins. Sleeve seam (with cuff turned up) 12½ ins.

TENSION.—8½ sts. to 1 inch.

ABBREVIATIONS.—K.—knit, P.—purl, st.—stitch, tog.—together, inc.—increase, dec.—decrease, rep.—repeat, patt.—pattern, cont.—continue, beg.—beginning, foll.—following, alt.—alternate, st. st.—stocking stitch, cross 2—insert point of needle into next stitch and knit the 2nd stitch through the first stitch then knit the first stitch through the back, ch.—chain, dc.—double crochet.

N.B.—This trimming should be worked AFTER PRESSING as the sequins will shrivel if subjected to the heat of an iron.

THE FRONT.—Work exactly as Back as far as ***.
Work 1 more pattern row.

Shape Neck.—K. 1, P. 25, cast off 54 sts. P. 25, K. 1.
Cont. in patt. on last 26 sts. inc. one st. at neck edge in 2nd and every foll. 4th row until there are 35 sts. on needle, then cont. without shaping until work measures same as back ending at neck edge.

Shape Shoulder.
1st row.—Work to last 12 sts. turn.
2nd row.—Work to end of row.
3rd row.—Work to last 23 sts. turn.
4th row.—Work to end of row.
Cast off.
Join in wool at neck edge and work on remaining 26 sts., complete neck and shoulder to correspond with other side reversing all shapings.

THE SLEEVES (Both alike).—Cast on 96 sts. with No. 12 needles and Main colour and work from 1st to 5th row of Back (changing to No. 9 needles after 1st row), then work 2nd row once.
Cont. in patt. dec. one st. at each end of needle in the next and every foll. 4th row until 84 sts. remain.
Change to No. 12 needles.
Next row.—K. 2, * P. 1, K. 1 ; rep. from * to end of row.
Rep. this row 14 times.
Change to No. 9 needles.
Work from 2nd to 5th row of Back twice then work 2nd row, **(the work should now be reversed for turn back cuff).**
Cont. in patt. inc. one st. at each end of needle in the next and every foll. 6th row until there are 112 sts. Cont. without shaping until the work measures 12½ ins. from **bottom of ribbing** measured at side and ending with a cross 2 row.

To Shape Top.—Work in patt. cast off 3 sts. at beg. of each of next 4 rows then cast off 2 sts. at beg. of foll. 36 rows (28 sts. remain).
Next row.—K. 1, (P. 2 tog.) 13 times, K. 1.
Cast off.

WAISTBAND.—Cast on 32 sts. with No. 12 needles and Main colour and work as Back as far as the second **.
Cont. in patt. until the work measures 15 ins. from beg. ending with a patt. row.
Keeping the patt., dec. one st. at each end of needle in the next and every alternate row until 2 sts. remain.
Break off wool, pass the first st. over the second st., draw end through and fasten off securely.
Work another piece in exactly the same way.

TO MAKE UP.—Pin out each piece and press carefully with a hot iron over a damp cloth. Sew up sleeve, shoulder and right side seams, then sew up left side seam leaving, 5 ins. open from hem. Sew in sleeves and sew slide fastener (upside down) to left side opening. Make a ¾ in. pleat along the cast on edge (short edge) of each waistband and sew down lightly, then join the two cast on edges together. Sew waistband to Jumper, easing in the bodice slightly and leaving ends to tie at left side as illustrated.

Crochet Edging.—With the crochet hook and Main colour, commence at underarm seam on sleeve and work a round of dc. evenly all round the edge of the cuff, then work 2 more rounds, using contrasting wool.
Next round.—1 dc., * 5 ch., miss 2 dc., 1 dc. in next dc. ; rep. from * all round to form the looped edge.
Break off wool and fasten off securely.
Work this edging round neck, **decreasing at front corners to keep the band flat.**
To make the crochet bows, make 50 ch. with the Contrasting wool and work 1 row dc. along this chain.
Work 8 more rows dc., dec. one st. at each end of every row ; fasten off. Press the bows, make a knot in the centre and attach to each side of neck as illustrated.
Press all seams and edging.
Sew sequins in alternate rows on front and cuffs as illustrated, working diagonally to allow for stretching.

About the Authors

Susan Crawford is a knitwear and clothing designer and the author of two previous books, A Stitch in Time, Vintage Knitting & Crochet Patterns 1920-1949: Vol. 1 and Vintage Gifts to Knit. Susan's vintage aesthetic can also be seen in her designs which have been featured in online publications such as Knitty and knitonthenet and in magazines such as Knitting and The Knitter and also in her photography, artistic direction and styling. Susan also re-writes the knitting patterns from her and Jane's vast vintage collection for others to enjoy in the A Stitch In Time books. You can see more of Susan's work at: www.susancrawfordvintage.com

Jane Waller has published many books on a range of subjects in a writing career spanning 40 years, covering topics as diverse as Sculpture and Children's Fiction. These books also include several knitting pattern collections, and in particular the original A Stitch in Time, published in 1972. Jane is an enthusiastic social historian as well as an artist and sculptor. Her vintage magazine collection formed the basis of A Stitch in Time Vintage Knitting & Crochet Patterns 1920-1949: Vol. 1 published in 2008.

You can see more of Jane's work at: www.janewaller.co.uk

Other titles from Arbour House

A Stitch in Time, Vol. 1
Vintage knitting & Crochet Patterns 1920-1949
Jane Waller & Susan Crawford

Vintage Gifts to Knit
Susan Crawford

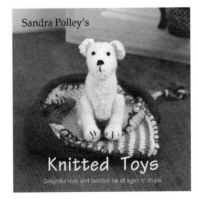

Sandra Polley's Knitted Toys
Delightful toys and teddies for all ages to share
Sandra Polley

Available from shop.knitonthenet.com
and good yarn stores and bookshops everywhere

For wholesale enquiries please contact info@arbourhousepublishing.com

Made in Excelana

Page 40

Page 45

Page 68

Page 84

Page 89

Page 106

Page 112

Page 121

Page 131

Page 136

Page 163

Page 182

Page 197

Page 201 & 206

Page 235

Page 261

Page 279

Page 319

Page 329

Page 349

Page 358

Page 362

Page 382

Excelana
═ *vintage yarns for fashion lovers* ═

395

Personal Measurement Chart

	Measurement required	Centimetres	Inches
A	Back at widest point		
B	Front Bust across widest point		
C	Round Chest (A + B = C)		
D	Armhole Depth		
E	Round Arm		
F	Underarm to Waist		
G	Total length to Waist (D + F = G)		
H	Round Waist		
I	Round Hip (optional)		
J	Shoulder to Shoulder		
K	Single Shoulder length		

Date measurements recorded: ....

If possible wear a close fitting vest top with side seams. This will help you take the correct measurements.

A. Using side seams as starting and ending points, measure across your back at its widest point below your armhole.
B. Again using side seams as a guide, measure across your 'front' bust only, at its widest point. It is important to wear the same bra or other undergarments that you most regularly wear, when you take this measurement.
C. This measurement provides you with your 'to fit' bust measurement to compare to sizing charts.
D. Starting with the tape measure at the underarm, take it over the shoulder and back to the underarm, so that the tape measure encircles your armhole joint. Keep one finger under the tape measure to prevent the tape from pulling too tight round the arm. Divide the resulting measurement in half for your armhole depth.
E. Take the tape round your upper arm at its widest point, again placing a finger under the tape.
F. Measure from just under your armpit to your natural waistline (if wearing a regular fitting vest, measure from the top of the armhole seam to your natural waistline).
G. This is your total upper body measurement to the waist.
H. Measure round your natural waist.
I. Measure round your hips at their widest point.
J. Measure from where your shoulder meets the arm socket across the upper back – not pulling too tightly, but letting the tape follow the very upper curve of the shoulders. If wearing a regular fit vest, measure from outer armhole seam to outer armhole seam following the same shoulder curve.
K. Measure from the same point as J, to the start of neck slope, across the top of the shoulder.

Yarn Resources

Biggan Design (Worldwide)
P.O. Box 798
Kenmore Qld 4069
Australia
+61 (0)7 3378 4453
www.biggandesign.com

Excelana (Worldwide)
Fibre Harvest
John Arbon Textiles
P.O. Box 8 Lynton
North Devon EX35 6WY
Tel: 01598 752490
juliet@jarbon.com
www.jarbon.com

Fyberspates (Worldwide)
Unit 6 Oxleaze Farm Workshops
Broughton Poggs Filkins
Lechlade Gloucester GL7 3RB
Tel: 07540 656660
fyberspates@btinternet.com
www.fyberspates.co.uk

Jamieson's (UK and Europe)
Sandness Industrial Estate
Sandness
Shetland Islands UK
Tel: 01595 693114
lerwick@jamiesonsofshetland.co.uk

Jamieson's (USA and Canada)
Simply Shetland
18375 Olympic Avenue South
Seattle WA98188
info@simplyshetland.net
www.simplyshetland.net

Jamieson & Smith (Worldwide)
Shetland Wool Brokers
90 North Road, Lerwick
Shetland Islands, UK
Tel: 01598 693579
sales@shetlandwoolbrokers.co.uk
www.shetlandwoolbrokers.co.uk

J C Rennie (Worldwide)
Knit Rennie Ltd – c/o JC Rennie & Co Ltd
Milladen Mintlaw
Peterhead, Aberdeenshire AB42 5DF
Scotland UK
Tel: 01771 622422
www.knitrennie.com

Knitshop (Worldwide)
326 Lee High Road Lee Green
London SE13 5PJ
Tel: 0208 144 4523
www.knitshop.co.uk

Orkney Angora (Worldwide)
www.orkneyangora.co.uk

Posh Yarn (Worldwide)
www.poshyarn.co.uk

Rooster (Worldwide)
www.laughinghens.com

Rowan (UK)
Green Lane Mill
Holmfirth West Yorkshire
HD9 2DX
Tel: 01484 681881
mail@knitrowan.com
www.knitrowan.com

Rowan (USA)
Westminster Fibres
4 Townsend West Unit 8
Nashua NH 03063
Tel: 800 445 9276
wfibers@aol.com

Shilasdair (Worldwide)
The Shilasdair Shop
10 Carnach Waternish
Isle of Skye IV55 8GL
Tel: 01470 592297
www.theskyeshilasdairshop.co.uk

Skein Queen (Worldwide)
www.skeinqueenshop.co.uk

Texere Yarns (Worldwide)
College Mill
Barkerend Road
Bradford BD1 4AU
Tel: 01274 722191
www.texere-yarns.co.uk